Sorry – You've Been Duped

For Mo – the Incomparable !

Melvin Harris

Sorry – You've Been Duped

Weidenfeld and Nicolson . London

Illustration Acknowledgments

The photographs in this book are reproduced by kind permission of the following:

BBC Hulton Picture Library 11, 14 above left: *Al Campbell Photography Ltd* 16 below; *Colchester and Essex Museum* 15 above; *Mary Evans Picture Library* 3, 13, 14 below; *National Film Archive* 4 below; *The Photo Source* 15 below; *Syndication International* 2.

Copyright © 1986 Melvin Harris

Published in Great Britain by
George Weidenfeld & Nicolson Limited
91 Clapham High Street
London SW4 7TA

All rights reserved. No part of this publication may be reproduced, stored in a retrieval system, or transmitted, in any form or by any means, electronic, mechanical, photocopying, recording or otherwise, without the prior permission of the copyright owner.

ISBN 0 297 78964 3

Printed in Great Britain at The Bath Press, Avon

Contents

	Acknowledgments	vi
	Introduction	vii
1	The Amityville Horror-Mongers	1
2	The Celestial Bus-Conductors	10
3	The Dark Fiddler	21
4	The Clueless Crime-Busters	27
5	The Yorkshire Ripper and the Psychic Circus	36
6	The Murderer and the Medium	43
7	I Captured Jack the Ripper	53
8	The Unquiet Grave of Prince Louis	61
9	Regiment of the Damned ?	69
10	The Angels with Newspaper Wings	80
11	The Wraith with Wet Wellies	94
12	Death Beckons Lord Dufferin	102
13	Once More unto the Lift Dear Friends	110
14	Cry 'Halt !' to Hitler	116
15	Dr. Soal's Mr. Hyde	134
16	The World Shall Hear from me Again	143
17	The Dark Vaults of the Mind	148
18	Solving the Bloxham Mystery	153
19	Meet me at Midnight	163
20	*Notes.*	175

NOTE: Chapters 16, 17 and 18 are best read in that order. Likewise with chapters 12 and 13, and chapters 2 and 3.

Acknowledgments

My thanks to the helpful people who dragged out books and files for me to delve into. In particular, thanks to Alan Wesencraft, Guardian of The Harry Price Library (University of London); Nick Clarke and Eleanor O'Keeffe of The Society for Psychical Research; Tony Ortzen, Editor of *Psychic News*, and Mike Hutchinson, Secretary of The British Committee for the Scientific Investigation of Claims of the Paranormal.

Special thanks to Simon Welfare who was repeatedly bludgeoned with the full weight of my enthusiasms!

Introduction

This book was not conceived as part of a crusade against the paranormal. It grew out of the natural exercise of my dual occupations as a professional broadcaster and a professional researcher. The two occupations inevitably interpenetrate. As a result many of my investigations arose out of the search for programme material. Sometimes I initiated this search myself. Often television companies asked me to look at various stories and check them out.

In all cases I began investigating with a cautious but open mind. I just did not know if the accounts in front of me were true or not. So I went back to primary sources. I checked and checked – and in the end I was able to say over and over again and with authority : 'Sorry – you've been duped !'

Chapter One

THE AMITYVILLE HORROR-MONGERS

The Exorcist started the trend. Unbelievable, horror-filled books and films featuring possession began to slime on to the market. Unbelievable, that is, to the alert, informed and rational mind. Unfortunately, far too many people have never had a fair chance to develop the questioning and reasoning part of their minds. They stand crippled by the fears, phantasms, cruel superstitions and distorted values picked up during their vulnerable childhoods. Cash-hungry authors batten on to their credulity. Possession is real. Demons stalk the suburbs. Supernormal horror *can* visit uninvited – unexpected. That is the dollar-earning, irresponsible claptrap in essence.

But does *The Amityville Horror* fall into this category? After all, it is unambiguously presented as a real-life documentary 'more hideously frightening than *The Exorcist* because it actually happened!' Real life? Let us see . . .

Was there ever real horror at Amityville? Yes, and it erupted on the early morning of 13 November 1974. It began when twenty-four-year-old New Yorker Ronald DeFoe ran screaming into a bar near his home. Someone, he sobbed, had broken into the DeFoe house and slaughtered his family. The police discovered his mother, father, two sisters and two brothers shot dead as they lay in their beds. But they refused to take the idea of an intruder seriously and Ronald DeFoe was brought to trial charged with the crimes.

The prosecution saw the motive as a wild attempt to lay

hands on $200,000 worth of life insurance plus the sizeable funds in the family cash-box. The defence attorney, William Weber, countered by bringing on a parade of psychiatrists to back up his pleas of insanity. But the jury rejected those pleas and Ronald DeFoe was sentenced to six consecutive life-terms.

With the trial over, the tarnished DeFoe house was put up for sale. It was an imposing three-storey Dutch Colonial building sited at 112 Ocean Avenue, Amityville, Long Island. An expensive piece of property by normal market standards, but its history led the agents to offer it at the bargain price of $80,000. Even so, it stood empty for almost a year until, on 18 December 1975, the Lutz family moved in.

At 28, George Lutz was the owner of a land-surveying company. His wife Kathy had a full-time job looking after her two young sons and her five-year-old daughter. And the rambling house seemed an ideal place for a lively family to flourish in. Yet the Lutzes fled from the place after only twenty-eight days. Victims, so they said later, of a relentless, nameless terror.

The full story of their ordeal appeared in *The Amityville Horror*, written by Jay Anson but based on many interviews with the Lutzes themselves. The book became a best-seller and was hailed as 'one of the most terrifying true cases ever of haunting and possession by demons ... breathless ... heart-stopping ... chilling.'

According to this account, it all began when the house became filled with overpoweringly foul stenches. Simultaneously, the bathroom porcelain became stained with a black slime that resisted household cleaners. Then came the flies – hundreds of them swarming into a second-floor bedroom.

Following this the massive front door was discovered wrenched wide open and hanging from its one remaining hinge. And George found that his whole body seemed chilled to the bone, despite the huge blazing fire that roared in the living room. To complicate things further, a four-foot high ceramic lion began moving around the house without any human help!

Within days cloven-hoof tracks were spotted in the snow

around the house. When followed they led directly to the garage and stopped dead in front of the door. The door itself hung almost torn off its metal frame – a feat which would 'require a strength far beyond that of any human being.' At last it began to dawn on the Lutzes that their dream-house was a place of nightmares, haunted by malignant presences.

Kathy Lutz was the first to be truly terrorised by the entities. Invisible arms embraced her and tried to gain possession of her body. 'Escape was impossible and she felt she was going to die.'

Meanwhile, others were being hit by 'the horror'. A priest who had befriended the Lutzes was stricken with an enervating, unknown infection, while the Rectory where he lived was smothered by a horrible odour that drove all the priests out of their rooms into the open air!

At Ocean Avenue, George now began to experience his own private horror – the sound of a marching band parading around the house, boots thumping, horns blaring. 'There must be at least fifty musicians,' he thought. Yet not a single one was ever seen, though the chairs, couch and tables were found pushed back against the walls, as if to make room for the many marching feet.

When the loathsome green slime started appearing it proved harmless enough, but the red weals that shortly erupted on Kathy's body were hideously painful. She looked as if she had been slashed with a red-hot poker. But it was simply 'the entity' indulging in its sadistic play. And then, of course, there were the personality changes, the levitations and the demons . . .

By rights it should all have ended after the Lutzes made their dramatic exit from the house on 14 January. But according to the sequel, *The Amityville Horror – Part II*, the evil followed them on to their new homes. It stayed 'coiled malevolently around them. Holding them with its unstoppable power.'

An incredible grim story if true, but so like fiction that it prompts the question: was there ever an authentic horror in the first place? Competent investigators unite in their answer – emphatically they say No!

Doctor Stephan Kaplan, Director of the Parapsychology

Institute of America, has written: 'After several months of extensive research and interviews with those who were involved in "The Amityville Horror" ... we found no evidence to support any claim of a "haunted house". What we did find is a couple who had purchased a house that they economically could not afford. It is our professional opinion that the story of its haunting is mostly fiction.' (*Theta No. 4, 1977.*)

Jerry Solfvin of the Psychical Research Foundation visited the house and wrote: 'The case wasn't interesting to us because the reports were confined to subjective responses from the Lutzes, and these were not at all impressive or even characteristic of these cases.' (*Skeptical Inquirer*, Summer 1978.)

But the most damning report of all originates with investigators Rick Moran and Peter Jordan. They went to Amityville and interviewed people mentioned in the book. The results were startling. The police rejected the book's claim that they had investigated the house. In particular, Sgt Cammorato denied that he had ever entered the place while the Lutzes were in residence. Yet the book has Cammorato touring through the house and even inspecting a 'secret room' in the basement. Tales that turn out to be so much eyewash.

Then Father Mancuso (real name Pecorara), who is featured throughout the book, also flatly denied that he had ever entered the Lutzes' home. So that tale about him blessing the building and about the phantom voice that ordered him out is quite bogus. As well as that, the Pastor of the Sacred Heart Rectory dismissed as 'pure and utter nonsense' the Lutzes' yarn about 'an unrelenting, disgusting odour that permeated the Rectory' – the alleged 'Scent of the Devil' which was supposed to have driven the priests out of their building.

In fact, little in the book stood up to close scrutiny. Local repairmen and locksmiths knew nothing of the paranormal damages they were supposed to have rectified. Not even the story that the Lutzes were driven out of the house by hauntings stood up. The real reasons for their exit were much more prosaic – a cash crisis and a near-breakdown.

Naturally the Lutzes have responded to these revelations by staging a pantomime of bluff and bluster, but significantly they have repeatedly avoided meeting informed critics on radio or TV. They have good reason for these evasions, for the first accounts put out by them spoke only of things felt and sensed – never anything about objective phenomena.

Indeed little notice would have been taken of the couple if they had not been pushed into the limelight by Ronald DeFoe's attorney, William Weber. Weber's motives were unconnected with psychical research. He was simply aiming to win a new trial for his client. DeFoe had spoken of a voice that urged him to kill and Weber hoped to establish that the Ocean Avenue house contained some force able to influence the behaviour of anyone who lived there. So he began to pin his hopes on the Lutzes and won them time on New York Channel Five's *Ten O'Clock News* programme.

At first Weber's involvement seemed to be on a purely professional basis. It was only much later that he admitted helping to sensationalise the Lutzes' story. In an Associated Press release of 27 July 1979, he said: 'We created this horror story over many bottles of wine that George was drinking. We were really playing with each other.'

Yet the case against the Lutzes does not rest wholly on these statements by outsiders. The Lutzes themselves have provided ample proof of their unreliability. The proof is contained in the interviews they gave before the book came into being.

For a start, there is the account published in the *Long Island Press* on 17 January 1976. In this article George Lutz sets out his experiences at 112 Ocean Avenue. But his story centres on things that were 'sensed' and not seen. In fact, he contradicts earlier stories about 'flying objects', 'moving couches' and 'wailing noises.' The only physical phenomenon mentioned concerns a window which opened of its own accord. Later investigations were to show that the counterweights in the window were simply too heavy! So at that date the Amityville happenings were tame, purely subjective and hardly worth noting.

Just over a year later, though, George Lutz came out with a new version of events. He related it to journalist Paul Hoffman and it appeared in the April 1977 issue of *Good Housekeeping (USA)*. This is a vital text worth studying in detail, for it shows just how the whole tale was progressively embroidered.

What is more, it contradicts George Lutz's earlier account and is in conflict with the Anson book as well!

In *Good Housekeeping* the story begins with a Roman Catholic priest blessing the house. On leaving, he warns the Lutzes about one of their bedrooms, saying: 'Don't let anyone sleep there. Keep the door closed. Spend as little time as possible in there.' But in the book the priest does nothing of the sort. His alleged advice about not using the room is given one week after the blessing – and then only following a whole series of nasty events.

After the priest, the next person to be affected by the house is said to be Kathy Lutz's aunt, described in *Good Housekeeping* as 'a normally placid ex-nun.' When she came to visit, she behaved quite out of character. She became hostile towards George, who said she 'sat there and cut me down for three hours.' In the book, though, this event is reshaped to make it more dramatic, for the aunt can only stand the house for a very short while. There is no three-hour harangue. She simply inspects the house, refuses to enter certain rooms, and leaves. In fact, she 'hadn't been in the house for more than half an hour when she decided it was time to go' – and go she did!

This same re-vamping technique is used with the 'old crone' incident. In *Good Housekeeping*, George states that on Saturday 10 January 1976 he woke up at night 'with a compulsion to flee the house.' He yelled at his wife and shook her, but just could not wake her up. Then, as he watched, his sleeping wife 'turned into a ninety-year-old woman.' Her hair became 'old and dirty', she dribbled, and creases and crow's feet formed on her face. 'It took several hours before she returned to her normal self.'

When this story appears in the book, however, it contains major differences. To begin with, it is placed three days earlier, on Wednesday 7 January. And George does not wake up wanting to flee the house. On the contrary, he is unable to get to sleep – and in this wide-awake state, he has the urge to go out to the local tavern for a beer. He does not shake or yell at his wife, for when he turns to speak to her, he finds her levitating 'almost a foot above him.' He pulls her down to the bed, where she wakes. And it is then, while awake, that she turns into a ninety-year-old woman. But this state only lasts for a minute or so – not several hours.

Now, in the book this levitation of 7 January is the second that is alleged to have happened. The first had taken place on 4 January and then Kathy floated 'two feet above the bed.' A further levitation happens on 15 January, only this time both Kathy and George float around at the same time. Yet nothing was ever said about these remarkable levitations in the *Good Housekeeping* account. The only claim there is that on Sunday 11 January George 'awoke to find Kathy sliding across the bed, as if by levitation', which is very different from the 'floating in the air' claims, and also involves a different date.

The ultimate horrors of all are the visitations by the 'gigantic hooded figure in white' who is also described as a 'demon with horns' with half its face shot away. In *Good Housekeeping*, there is not even a hint of his visits. There is mention, though, of Kathy turning white and stating: 'I just saw some eyes at the window.' But these are described as 'red, beady eyes' – and that is the end of the incident. Yet when this story reaches the book it becomes a point of high drama.

This drama is set in a second-storey bedroom at night. The Lutzes' young daughter points to a window and both George and Kathy see 'two fiery red eyes! No face, just the mean little eyes of a pig' looking in. Then Kathy rushes at the window 'screaming in an unearthly voice.' She smashes the glass with a chair and then they hear an 'animal cry of pain, a loud squealing – and the eyes were gone!' This squealing goes on for a while, out in the grounds of the house. But George does not go looking for the flying pig. Instead he comforts his wife, who sobs out: 'It's been here all the time! I wanted to kill it! I wanted to kill it!'

Plainly the story has undergone a most remarkable transformation. And it is the same with event after event in the book. These findings, then, coupled with the investigator's reports, make it certain that the whole bizarre tale is beyond belief.

So what sparked the whole thing off? Well, without a confession from the Lutzes we will never have a complete answer. But we do know that George Lutz was a man with problems.

When his first marriage broke up he tried group therapy, then turned to Transcendental Meditation. His second marriage seemed to help for a while, but even that brought along its own problems. And *before* he moved into Amityville he was already facing a crisis. The two boys tried to run away. His business was in difficulties. And the Internal Revenue people were acting tough. Then to crown it all he became completely irresponsible. Instead of cutting back on expenditure he decided to buy a house that was way above his means.

Once in the new house, matters came to a head fast. He grew so apathetic that for a while he did not wash or shave and he stopped going to the office. He even lists his problems in the book.

They were 'a second marriage with three children, a new house with a big mortgage ... taxes in Amityville three times higher than in Deer Park. Did he really need that new speedboat? How the hell was he going to pay for all this? The construction business was lousy on Long Island ... so who the hell needs a land-surveyor?' Before long 'he was beginning to choke with the pressure of mounting bills for the house ... and for the office where he would shortly have a very serious payroll deficit.'

All this turmoil soon took its toll. He began to blame his inertia, his bad temper and his worries on the house. When he was short with his employees, or when he hit the children, it became the fault of the house and not his lack of control. And in that frame of mind George Lutz began to identify with the murderer Ronald DeFoe. He even became convinced that he was the physical double of DeFoe. When he first saw DeFoe's picture he recorded that 'the bearded twenty-four-year-old face staring back ... could have been his own!' And if a physical double, why not a mental double? There is little doubt that George Lutz felt murderous black thoughts in that house. But they came from his own plight and deep frustrations, not from any paranormal agencies. That house and its ghastly reputation served initially as nothing more than a catalyst for morbid ideas. Later they were to serve as a catalyst for cash-register ideas!

After his exit from Amityville, his imaginings started to grow out of control. The meeting with Anson finalised this process and the many fantasies were crystallised and put into a sensational and saleable form.

And sell they did! *The Amityville Horror* spent eight months in the best-seller lists. By the end of 1979, some three and a half million copies had been sold and a film version was well under way. Such was its impact that during the production of the film American International Pictures received over 13,000 enquiries from members of the public eager for progress reports.

The Lutzes had discovered that gullibility equals gold, especially when the fiction masqueraded as truth. As fiction pure and simple it would probably have ended up in the ever-yawning waste paper basket. And rightly so!

Chapter Two

THE CELESTIAL BUS-CONDUCTORS

'PARROT CRY PROVES SURVIVAL. "DEAD" ONE-LEGGED FATHER IS SPEEDILY RECOGNISED'

Honestly, I promise I have not invented that headline. It comes from *Psychic News*, 10 June 1978. It leads into a story about famous medium Doris Stokes, who has recently completed volume three of her life story. Hordes of people believe or want to believe in mediumship. Yet strong beliefs are not enough. Is there any firm proof that mediums are a link with another world on another plane? A world peopled by the spirits of those who are nominally dead?

If you search for the answers on the lengthy shelves of spiritualist writings, prepare to feel dispirited. The pomposity and sheer dreariness of much of what you will find there can try one's patience to the limit. Consider this gem from Wordsworth penned in spiritland:

> You walked upon the earth in darkness
> You walked out of the earth in light
> And now you know that angels
> Are round you ever bright
> When you yourself do right
> Their gentle wings unfurl
> Not feathers, but pearl after pearl
> A blessing falling down upon the earth
> Peace, beauty and gentle mirth.

Does this Christmas cracker doggerel lift your heart? Do you really believe that the poet has lost all touch with his genius? Still, if you grit your teeth hard enough it becomes possible to wade through the incredible literature.

You will find that since 1848 the world has been offered a changing variety of mediumistic experiences. Slate-writing was once a high point of spiritualistic fashion. Henry Slade and William Eglington, the top Victorian mediums, were noted for this phenomenon. Apparently the spirits would inscribe blank slates with messages and drawings, completely unaided by the medium. He was there simply to help them concentrate their powers.

But the slate craze passed out of fashion when magicians like Maskelyne and Davey and researchers like David Abbott and Hereward Carrington showed how the baffling stunts were engineered. Carrington forcefully concluded: 'If we were to read carefully through the historical evidence for the phenomenon of slate-writing, we should find it to consist in one long and practically unbroken series of exposés of fraud and trickery, with no real evidence worth mentioning for the genuine manifestations of any supernormal power, nor any indication of any force or agency whatever at work beyond the muscles of the medium.

'In short, there is no good evidence, in the whole history of spiritualism, for the occurrence of writing on slates by other means than such as might have been produced fraudulently by the medium; and I have gone carefully through a vast bulk of spiritualistic literature before making this statement.' (*The Physical Phenomena of Spiritualism*)

Longer lasting than the slate-writing phase was the era of materialisations. Spirits would apparently take on a temporary solid form and cavort around the dimly-lit seance rooms. The most famous of these was Katie King who was conjured up by Florence Cook, and actually posed for the photographer. Others of her kind posed as well but with gloomy results – the fakery was shown up by the camera.

As early as 1892, spiritualist W.T. Stead regretfully owned up that: 'I have made great efforts to obtain the services of a trustworthy materialising medium who has not at any time been detected in fraud .... The net result of my enquiries came to this: that, in the whole of the United Kingdom, so far as was known to the spiritualist community, there was only one person of the undoubted materialising faculty and undoubted character who could almost always secure the presence of phenomena, and who had never been detected in a trick of any kind ... I refer to Mrs Mellon, late of Newcastle-upon-Tyne, whose success as a materialising medium is undoubted.'

Unfortunately even his Mrs Mellon was caught out at last in a circle staged in Sydney, Australia, on 12 October 1894. A Mr T.S. Henry grabbed the figure of the alleged spirit and found that he 'held the form of Mrs Mellon, and that she was on her knees, and had a white material like muslin round her head and shoulders.'

In the following years similar exposures became commonplace. The mediums who were not caught out were the ones who took special care that the curious and the informed investigators were kept at a distance. Among those ranking as 'unexposed' are Estelle Roberts and Isa Northage.

Estelle Roberts used to materialise her guide, a Red Indian known as Red Cloud. People saw him and were even allowed to feel his hair and his short, soft silky beard. Apart from being the only bearded redskin I know of, I was enthralled to see a photograph of spirit Red Cloud. For some strange reason every time I look at it I see a very western face wearing a feathered war-bonnet. Equally strange, I find the face looks just like that of Estelle Roberts at her most grim and earnest. Of the beard, there is no trace. Very strange.

Equally strange is the case of Isa Northage. In 1939, I find that she materialised a lady who kissed her grieving husband, then allowed the sitters to handle her spirit drapery. Following that, an Egyptian gentleman materialised and spoke in his own tongue. Good measure, you would think – but there was more. Along came a monk who left a crucifix behind, and a Chinese lady who brought a valuable incense-burner and a bangle from her own tomb.

In later years, she qualified – if you believe the reports – as the most astounding materialisation medium ever. Under the glare of a 150 watt electric light bulb, she materialised a dead Irish surgeon called Dr Reynolds. This surgeon then carried out spirit operations on assorted patients in full light. Cancers, ulcers and malignant growths were said to have been removed. At one time more than one hundred people witnessed the operations.

All that was startling, but consider this: at one point the doctor decided that he would have to fetch something from the spirit world, so he disappeared through the floor and in a few moments reappeared with a special liquid which he used to control a haemorrhage.

You may well ask where the world's press was when all this was going on. And why was it that the medical profession did not turn up in bus loads? Your guess is as good as mine. But I have noticed this, that when I look at a painting of Dr Reynolds – yes, he posed for one – I am reminded of the experience with Estelle Roberts. For strangely enough, Dr Reynolds looks remarkably like Isa Northage with her hair scraped back and an unbelievable stage beard glued in position.

Am I being unfair? Hardly! The claims these people make violate all logic and are at loggerheads with everyday experiences. If they are true then it is up to them to demonstrate that truth. Yet none of these claimants ever submitted themselves to informed and impartial examination. They reserve their antics for the believers. And, tragically, believers have a terrible tendency to go on believing, come what may.

This compulsive need to believe was shown in the months following the Paul McElhoney affair of March 1983. McElhoney first made news in 1978 as a spiritual healer. By 1981 he had graduated to a more exalted level.

The delighted editor of *Psychic News* wrote: 'The age of physical psychic phenomena is not over. Last week a young materialisation medium gave his first ever sitting for a newspaper. All told, several feet of brilliant white ectoplasm gushed from his mouth. Two roses were apported into the room.'

From then on, McElhoney's ectoplasm and flower factories seemed to be working on an overtime basis. And there were sizeable metal apports as well, ranging from a model of Cologne Cathedral to a copper and bronze statue and an ornate nine-inch brass bowl decorated with dolphins. It was all so breath-taking.

Unfortunately, McElhoney's guide Ceros began mouthing a series of philosophical teachings. The Ceros teachings were a worn-out, embarrassing collection of mock-simple homilies and platitudes. Each paragraph had the buoyancy of a lead balloon.

Take this as a sample: 'I say to all people in friendship it must always be remembered that the flowers and fruits of your earth are always growing even if at times you may not be able to see them.'

Unbelievably, these trite sayings were solemnly printed issue by issue in the spiritualist *Two Worlds*. They were then collected into book form and recorded on cassette!

Despite the handicap of Ceros, McElhoney became Medium Of The Year in 1982. But his triumph was short-lived. The intense rivalries and envies among the psychics led to his downfall. Spiritualist minister Ronald Baker and the President of the Spiritualist National Union, Gordon Higginson, joined forces in a bid to see if McElhoney could pass a crucial test.

It was a weird set-up, for Higginson himself had earlier been accused of fraud by fellow-spiritualist Mrs Phyllis Simpson of Bristol. However, in March 1983 it was McElhoney who was under judgment and the Sunday newspaper *News Of The World* agreed to cooperate in setting up a test seance. Without, of course, the knowledge of the medium.

The fatal seance took place at a house in Osset, Yorkshire. This house was owned by a sixty-nine-year-old widow, Mrs Joan Stubley. She believed implicitly in McElhoney. She had donated generously to his brainchild, the United World organisation. And she was now on the point of signing over the deeds of her house to the medium. By that gesture, her property would 'benefit world harmony'.

Mrs Stubley was warned in advance and gave her consent. If McElhoney was genuine, he had nothing to fear from the test.

The medium walked into the seance room, he put his tape recorder down and prepared to mentally limber up. At that point, he was informed that Mrs Stubley wished to speak to him up in her third floor flat. He nervously left the room and immediately the sitters entered and began searching. Spiritualist David Edgar took charge of the tape recorder and noticed a heavy black tape bound around the battery compartment. He slowly unpeeled it and opened up the back of the machine. Inside he found a row of carnations taped to a plastic strip, a key-ring torch, small enough to place in the mouth and other objects.

The finds were quickly witnessed and photographed. The recorder was reassembled. By the time McElhoney returned everything seemed normal.

Before the seance began, McElhoney was stripped and searched. Then the lights were switched off and Ceros took possession of the medium. The Ceros messages began to pour out and then a hymn was asked for. David Edgar was on full alert and heard the back of the tape recorder being opened. Ceros next ordered the lights to be put on and sitters watched as a carnation dropped out of McElhoney's lips. Off went the lights, and then back on again so that another carnation could jump into view. Now was the time for decisive action.

Edgar was close to the recorder. He looked behind it and saw that the back was off and only one carnation was still left taped inside. That was enough. He walked over to the light switch and told McElhoney to leave the lights on.

'The game's up, Paul,' he said.

The medium froze on the spot, recovered and asked what was going on. Edgar explained and asked McElhoney to submit to another search. Then everyone could see what lay behind the suspicious bulge in one of his pockets. Paul tremblingly denied that he had cheated but refused a search. He would only allow the police to search him. So someone phoned the police. At that point McElhoney ran out of the house into the street, leaving his recorder behind.

The affair made a front page story for the *News Of The World*, complete with photographs of the rigged tape recorder. McElhoney of course had lost everything, including the house! He tried tears and protests and a promise that once he had got his strength back he would stage an unquestionable test seance. But his big August United World Festival – his crowning glory – had to be cancelled. It was farewell to McElhoney and silence for his garrulous Ceros. Even so, the spiritualists broke up into feuding camps and incredibly McElhoney still found quite a following among those prepared to believe at any cost.

Materialisation mediumship, then, seems akin to tight-rope walking. But other forms have been just as precarious – like spirit photography. This branch of mediumship excited the spiritualist camp well up until the 1930s. It all started, so it is claimed, as early as 1861 when a Boston photographer, William H. Mumler, is said to have captured a spirit face on a photographic plate. How did he know it was a spirit? Easily – he recognised it as a cousin who had died twelve years earlier.

Mumler gave up his exacting job as an engraver and opened up a psychic photography studio. He was never short of clients, who flocked in hoping to see their loved ones once more. Many of them left, fully satisfied that some sort of photographic evidence had been given to them. Even President Lincoln's widow dropped in and was photographed. Days later she received a print which seemed to show a shadowy Abraham Lincoln standing behind her touching her shoulders.

The practice spread rapidly to Europe. In London, Frederick Hudson was the pioneer, followed by the roguish Richard Boursnell of Shepherd's Bush. In France, the supreme practitioner became Edouard Buguet, who accumulated quite a bevy of aristocratic and influential sitters.

And what did they get for their money? Well, most of the time, simple double exposures. At other times, quite elaborate fake set-pieces. But don't take my word for it. Photographs are meant to be looked at, not described in words and I have provided some gems from the master fakers, leaving you to make your own judgments.

If nothing else, many of these photographs are amusing but they were not intended to amuse. Their aim was to dupe the gullible, and milk those in need of comfort. But they did not have it all their own way. One after the other most of these photographers were caught either cheating or preparing to cheat. Then, when plate cameras went out of fashion, the practice became much more difficult, and in the 1930s it dwindled almost to the point of extinction.

But while they reigned, these people were skilled and cunning. So much so that Dr d'Aute Hooper, a medium who was never caught out, has only just recently been proven to be a cheat. One of his famous pictures, of a small spirit girl, was taken back in 1905. The event involved a patient who was staying with him in order to receive spiritual healing. Dr Hooper reveals the story behind the picture in these words:

'One day he (the patient) had been out for a walk, and when he came back, he said: "Doctor, I feel so queer, I feel as if there is someone with me; will you get your camera and take a snapshot of me?" I got the camera and before I exposed the plate I told him I saw a beautiful child with him. I put a dark tablecloth over the door in the drawing room to form a background and then exposed the plate. The gentleman himself took the plate to the darkroom and developed it; and there appeared the beautiful spirit form of a little girl with a bouquet of flowers in one hand and a roll of paper in the other. The exclamation of the gentleman was "Good heavens! It's my daughter, who died thirty years ago."'

This picture, together with its touching story, first appeared in print in 1919 and has been celebrated ever since.

In 1978, this well-loved story and photograph was included in Fred Getting's book *Ghosts In Photographs* and a new generation was introduced to the tale. But nemesis was at hand. A year later, Camden Graphics of London decided to reprint some Victorian poster designs in the form of greetings cards. Among their charming selection was a painting by Charles Trevor Garland called *For You*. It depicts a young girl with a letter in her right hand and a bunch of roses in the other.

As the greetings cards circulated, sharp-eyed investigators, including Dr. C.M.Cherry of the Society for Psychical Research, felt a tingle of recognition. Comparisons were made and all became clear. Dr Hooper had conned his patient and his admirers by printing in a degraded photo of the original Garland poster!

That story well illustrates the problems researchers have in showing up deception. Evidence is all too easily concealed, or is difficult to locate. In this case, the deception reigned for over sixty years.

Not all mediumistic deception is intentional, though. Often self-deception is at work. The medium allows chains of thought, or images to run through the head and interprets them as if they were messages from outside the brain. It is easily done, especially if you start off expecting messages.

When I draw on my own experience, I have to conclude that most mediumship shows signs of a mixture of deliberate deception and naive self-deception.

Take the case of voice mediums, like British champion Leslie Flint and USA contender Keith Milton Rhinehart. Flint has tape-recorded a host of his spirit visitors. He claims that these voices do not emerge from his mouth but from a spot near him. Apparently an ectoplasmic larynx is created by the spirits for this special purpose. Now I have listened attentively to his tapes of these voices. Regretfully, I have to conclude that his spirits are awfully mixed up. His Valentino speaks with a stage French accent – shades of Charles Boyer – while his George Bernard Shaw sounds like an irascible English colonel, with no trace of his precise and memorable soft Irish brogue.

Apart from that, his visitors have unaccountably lost all the wisdom and charm they exhibited on earth. So is plain and inadequate mimicry at work? Is Mr Flint deceiving himself? He says not. He points to tests where his mouth has been filled with liquid, his lips have been sealed with adhesive tape and still the voices have rung out. In the USA, Mr Rhinehart has also undergone such a test.

Yet are these tests stringent enough? Are there loopholes? The career of medium William Roy may provide some answers. But before considering him, what briefly can we say about mediums who shun gimmicks and rely on the plain transfer of messages?

Perhaps Doris Stokes is a good example. She packs huge theatres and exudes an air of complete control and conviction. Her audiences seem convinced as well. But only a handful at each gathering ever receive messages. And of those messages, some show signs of being gained by guesswork or fishing. Yet, Mrs Stokes triumphs because even though a few are blessed, the rest take comfort from that. They think one day it will happen to them, in turn.

That is part of the key to the lure of spiritualism. It can score over other religions because of its offer of direct comfort. 'Your daughter is here at your side.' 'Your father watches over you and sends his love.' This style of comfort wins hands down over the abstractions, the remoteness, and the almost antiseptic utterances of the orthodox clergy.

But even top-of-the-league Doris Stokes goes too far at times. She started developing a hot-line to dead show-business figures back in 1983. Her most impressive visitor at that time was John Lennon, who came through to say that he bore his killer no bitterness. By 1985, Doris had seemingly cornered a sector of spiritland Hollywood. Mae West had been through, so had Peter Sellers, Elvis Presley, James Dean, Jimi Hendrix, Diana Dors, and even megastar Marilyn Monroe.

The *Daily Mirror* newspaper wanted a piece of the action. It contracted her and ran a double-spread interview on 2 October 1985. She proved true to form. She got through to Marilyn Monroe and found that Robert Kennedy was there as well! She listened intently to Robert's protests. 'You were just good friends with Marilyn? Nothing more? I see.'

Then it was through to Marilyn herself, to observe: 'You didn't mean to kill yourself? You tried to phone Robert that night, but he was out at a dinner party? Yes, I see ... You tried to get help, but you were too proud to phone the police or hospital? And there was nothing between you and Robert? He just liked to be seen with beautiful women, but he always loved his wife? I understand, lovey.'

It was incredible gush like this that led the Editor of *Psychic News* to make a front-page protest headed End 'Kiss And Tell' Seances. In his article (25 October 1985) he wrote: 'It does spiritualism no good to give the impression that at the drop of an astral hat mediums can tune in to anyone at will and receive meaningful messages ... to be candid, whenever famous personalities return they rarely impart information of much import.

'They drone on about the mistakes they made on earth and, like someone picking at an angry spot, would seem endlessly to examine their earthly lives, their failures, their disasters and, according to some mediums, their love lives ... I am concerned by her messages said to come from the famed and acclaimed.

'I am not saying Doris Stokes is a liar. She is not. I am not saying she is making it up. I am sure she is not. I am not hinting it is all wishful thinking, that Doris is deluding herself.

'But – and this applies to all mediums – once again the acid test, the only test, that one can apply is this: what is the evidence, the supporting testimony, that James Dean, for example, truly is communicating?'

But Editor Tony Ortzen's protest raises a further question. Just what *is* happening in the medium's mind? If she is not able to separate the suspect messages from the others, then what reliance can be placed on anything she says? Tony Ortzen might argue that in the valid cases people recognise the information passed on to them. But again what does this mean? Think of Dr Hooper's patient who recognised a poster image as his long-dead daughter. People with strong yearnings will *force* information into the shape of their heart's desire. The evidence for this, from psychic photography alone, is overwhelming.

Then again, even if some seemingly exact information is offered, how can we be certain that it is paranormal in origin? Mediums are like sponges when it comes to soaking up details and storing them. And can we be sure that their information has not been deliberately gathered?

We have a right to be on guard, to be doubtful, even suspicious. The history of spiritualism is not a pretty or uplifting one. But does it offer useful lessons for today? Does it show us what to anticipate? Here the William Roy case should be of some help. Some of the answers are there for certain. Remember, he was top-rank. He produced materialisations, apports, spirit voices – and shoals of evidential messages. He even went one better than show business: he ushered from spiritland to the seance parlour none other than Queen Victoria herself!

Chapter Three

THE DARK FIDDLER

When William Roy died in August 1977, *Psychic News* said of him: 'In spiritualism's long history there has never been a greater villain. He is now in a world where he cannot cheat.'

There were many who would not accept that verdict, for over the years Roy had so raised false hopes among his dupes that a good percentage of them could never face the fact that he was phoney. And the people he took in were not always simple, ill-educated types – far from it. They included prominent Society figures, among them the late Mackenzie King.

Mackenzie King's involvement began during the Second World War when he was Prime Minister of Canada. It was a post that he had held before, but wartime brought with it extra responsibilities. These included top-secret visits to London to confer with the War Cabinet. And it was on one of these hush-hush visits that he went to consult William Roy, then famed as Britain's outstanding medium.

Since King's visit to Britain was so secret he did not give his true name in advance. So, on the surface, it looked as if Roy had no clue to the real identity of his client. And yet Roy was able to give the Canadian P.M. some pretty convincing messages, and all from top people – those who in real life would naturally and easily talk to a head of government. The grandest of all these was Queen Victoria herself! And dear, deluded Mackenzie thrilled as he chatted away to 'Her Majesty'.

More thrills came when Mr Gladstone came through and gave a message of hope – just the sort of thing to cheer one up in the dark days of war. It was all very satisfying and comforting. So much so, that the Prime Minister went back for further sessions and was overwhelmed when his dead brother and sister spoke to him.

Mackenzie King returned to Canada overjoyed and without any suspicions whatsoever, completely unaware that he had been most thoroughly deceived by a scheming rogue. For Roy's 'gifts' were non-existent. His sessions involved nothing more than play-acting, phoney voices and stage-effects, while his revelations were all due to elaborate cunning and trickery. So how did he do it?

Well, his tricks were usually based on techniques that had been used way back in the last century. He had added a few of his own, of course, but in the main he had stuck with stunts that had been well tried by other tricksters before him.

He had found most of his tricks carefully explained in a book called *Behind The Scenes With The Mediums*. This enlightening book was written by David Abbott in 1907 and only published in the USA. A few copies, though, were sold in England by the Magical And Unique Novelty Company in London. Roy had the good fortune to find one of these copies and it set his mind reeling. Here were all the details he needed to set up a lucrative business. From then on, that book was like a portable treasure chest.

By the time Roy set himself up as a medium he had mastered most of the tricks in the book. He even worked out a few refinements, so his clients innocently walked into a trap every time they visited his home. They were expected to leave all coats and bags in a special cloakroom, and this gave Roy's accomplice a chance to search through their belongings for bits of useful information. What is more, they were kept waiting before each seance began. And as they chattered to pass the time away, hidden microphones picked up their words.

By these means Roy always knew more about them than they dreamed possible. Sometimes he would even overhear them list the dead relatives they hoped to contact. In this way, every sitting was neatly rigged beforehand. And when Roy ran out of authentic tit-bits, he was adroit enough to bluff his way through the rest of the time.

Part of his bluff was worked by calling on colourful 'spirit guides'. There was one called Joey, another called Dr Wilson, and – best of the lot – a Red Indian called Tinka. Tinka was not only fashionable, he was invaluable, for if the questions became awkward he would just sulk and grunt: 'No can answer ... me just simple Indian.' And that would quickly smooth over any rough parts of the evening.

The microphones and searches were not the only preparations made. Once Roy knew the names of his clients he would check on their families at the Registry in London's Somerset House. He would look up death notices and entries in *Who's Who*. He would even contact other fake mediums for extra information.

His most masterly research, though, involved his initial session with Mackenzie King. For in that case he had no opportunity to go through the Premier's pockets and no chance to listen in to his conversation. And all he knew about the booking was that it was made by a member of the Duke of Connaught's staff. That clearly was not much to go on, but he had to start somewhere. So he read up on everything he could find on the Duke of Connaught, and discovered that the Duke had been Governor-General of Canada from 1911 to 1916. As soon as he read that, Roy made a brilliant deduction – this mysterious visitor could easily be a distinguished Canadian friend of the Duke's. And the most distinguished Canadian known to embrace spiritualism was their Prime Minister, Mackenzie King.

Roy was so convinced that his deduction was right that he began practising passages in the voices of Gladstone and Queen Victoria. The Queen's high-pitched voice was a bit of a strain, but by the time Mackenzie King turned up it was good enough to fool him and make him want to know more.

But Roy was not just famed for the messages he gave – it was the way he gave them that brought him renown. He could make a luminous trumpet float through the air in the darkened seance room and induce 'spirit voices' to speak through the mouth of that trumpet. Sometimes there would even be two voices at once. And remarkably enough, he could even produce extra voices in full light.

When he appeared at public meetings he worked even more baffling stunts. In 1947, at Kingway Hall, London, his hands were tied to the arms of a chair, his mouth was filled with coloured water and his lips were sealed with sticking plaster – yet he still produced spirit voices. And after the plaster was removed his mouth was found still full of the coloured water. So fakery seemed ruled out.

That of course, is what his audience believed. For they knew nothing about his careful research and they never realised that Roy was adept at picking their brains. He had a considerable skill in picking up small hints from his clients. He would delicately pump them for information then feed it back to them in a new way – and they never realised just what was happening.

As for those voices – well, at the public meetings Roy was responsible for all of them. Even when his mouth was filled and sealed up. For him that was just a minor problem. In the darkness he found it easy to bend his head down and loosen the plaster with one tied hand. Then the water was ejected through a rubber tube into a small container in his breast pocket. At the end of the event the water was sucked back up again, the plaster was smoothed back into place and everyone was over-awed.

The private seances were somewhat different. Although most of the voices were Roy's, some were provided by his assistant while others were tape recordings. In that way he was able to produce more than one voice at a time. And the methods he used apart from the tape recordings were all drawn from that invaluable handbook by Abbott.

First of all, the trumpet flew through the air on the end of a telescopic rod, just as Abbott described. And the assistant next door passed information through to Roy by telephone – again exactly as in the book. Of course, that telephone connection was made without cords, for that would have given the game away. Instead, Roy wore copper plates on the soles of his shoes and these were soldered to thin wires which ran up his trouser legs and through his jacket to a small earphone on his wrist. To link up with his assistant, he only had to put his feet onto metal carpet tacks and he was connected – for the tacks were wired up to cables running through the wall.

That cunning system worked beautifully, especially when voices were produced in the light, for the earphones would double as a tiny loudspeaker. But it had its limits, so a second connection to the other room was called for and this was provided by a dummy power socket on the wall. It was not wired to the mains but to an amplifier. So Roy could plug a cable into it and energise a miniature loudspeaker fixed on the tip of his telescopic rod. While his assistant's voice came through this speaker Roy imitated one of his 'guides' and threw occasional comments in his own voice. Small wonder that he was famed for his spell-binding sessions.

We know all about Roy's trickery because in 1952 he fell out with his assistant, who promptly paid a visit to the offices of *Psychic News*. There he opened up a large suitcase and took out the apparatus used to fake the seances. It was all there, from the telescopic rod to the shoes fitted with copper plates and it looked like the end for Roy. His exposure seemed inevitable.

But later on there was a problem, for the assistant did not want the matter to go any further. Following this Roy promised to give up mediumship and leave the country saying that he wanted to make a new start in South Africa. In fact, he did leave England and the whole sorry affair was silently laid to rest – or so it seemed.

Yet the old habits were hard to kill and within a few years Roy was organising seances in South Africa. Then he had the supreme cheek to return to Britain and start up again. This proved too much for the rest of the spiritualist fraternity and one of their papers, *Two Worlds*, named Roy as a fraudulent medium.

Dramatic results followed this newspaper report. Roy's wife attacked the paper's editor with a riding crop and Roy himself started a lawsuit against the editor. Roy's wife was fined three pounds for the assault and Roy paid the fine with a smile for he knew that his lawsuit meant that he could go on milking his clients. His action had prevented any further newspaper comment on the case until after the court hearing. Court actions can sometimes take years before they get to be heard, and that is just what happened in Roy's case.

He carried on his fakery until February 1958. Then he dropped a lawsuit he knew he could not win and agreed to pay costs to the editor of *Two Worlds*. Following that he brazenly sold his story to the *Sunday Pictorial*. It was published in five instalments and the *Pictorial* readers marvelled at the way in which he had cheated his way to fame and fortune. At the end of his articles Roy wrote: 'I know that even after this confession I could fill the seance rooms again with people who find it a comfort to believe I am genuine.'

At the time that sounded like hot air or bravado but Roy went on to make his boast come true. He set up shop under the name Bill Silver and for years he ran his old racket without challenge. And believe it or not, among his clients he numbered people who knew his real identity and who were fully aware of his sordid confessions!

Chapter Four

THE CLUELESS CRIME-BUSTERS

Six grim-faced detectives grouped around the woman in the armchair. The guarded cellar was darkened and lit only by a single dim red bulb. The silence was death-like. The men held their breath.

'Then their hair almost stood on end as they watched the handsome face of the old lady transform slowly into a visage of dreadful evil. The kindly mouth was drawn back into a bestial snarl; eyes burned like living coals . . .'

It was 1929. The place – the German city of Dusseldorf. Three sadistic murders had brought a mounting fear to its streets. In desperation, the police were seeking help from a 'psychic detective'.

'Her lips moved, saliva dripped from the corners of the mouth, and weird and awful sounds filled the room. It was not the gentle old lady speaking; it was the spirit voice of some horrible creature who in his earthly days had butchered and tortured like a maniac. No sane creature could have mouthed the awful oaths and blasphemies which came from between the snarling lips . . . the senior officer pulled himself together, and asked in steady tones: "We want to know who is killing our people here in Dusseldorf. We shall not harm him. Will you tell us?"

'The awful voice shrieked: "No! No! Let him kill them – it is good. I like blood – blood – blood" . . . The medium licked her twisting lips at the mention of the word, squirming in her chair like some fearful vampire ... "I know him. I control him. He does what I command. When I want blood he drinks it for me," the maniacal tones shrilled. "But you shall not find him. You shall not take him from me."

'Suddenly the medium sprang to her feet and leapt like a tigress upon the detective ... hands like steel claws gripped his shoulders ... it took four strong men, used to rough-and-tumble fighting, to shake off those clawlike hands.'

Over fifty years ago, such melodrama introduced the public to psychic sleuthery. It is from 'The first book to be written on the relationship of crime to the supernatural.' This volume was appropriately ghost-written for ex-Detective Sergeant Edwin T. Woodhall, late of Special Branch of the CID and Scotland Yard.

In *Crime And The Supernatural*, the wily Woodhall (we will meet him again!) gave false authority to a string of dubious yarns. Since then, 'psychic detective' tales have proliferated. But are they to be taken seriously?

Unfortunately, while a lie can be coined in minutes, months may be taken up in exposing that lie. And that is where you have the difficulty in grappling with accounts of psychic detection.

Let us accept these difficulties. Let us set legitimate doubts to one side and take some recent, well-reported cases as examples. Given adequate documentation, we may be able to judge fairly and firmly.

The case of the Dartmoor Air Cadets provides a good starting point. In April 1981, this odd affair took up many columns of the national and local newspapers.

Each year hundreds of children and teenagers descend on Dartmoor in Devon, in the last week of April. They come in organised groups to practise for the Ten Tor Expedition held in May. The groups have to cover some fifty-five miles of inhospitable moorland following predetermined routes. It is a test of skill and endurance under the best of conditions. But in late April 1981 freak blizzards hit Dartmoor.

Rescue teams set out and brought the most isolated groups back to safety. Other groups made their own way off the moors. But one group of five air cadets from Cornwall went missing, lost somewhere in the raging snow. The police organised search parties. A systematic sweep of the moors began and after about fifty hours the cadets were located at Brat Tor, near the north west edge of Dartmoor.

Then the story broke: 'Medium's message leads to lost boys,' wrote the *Daily Telegraph* of 28 April. 'Medium's "Psychic Guide" leads the Dartmoor boys to safety' proclaimed the *Daily Express* next day. It went on to ask 'Can we explain these amazing powers?' Most of the other papers chimed in on a similar theme.

Apparently Mrs Frances Dymond, a fifty-five-year-old mother of seven and a medium, had directed the baffled search party to the right place and just in the nick of time!

A radio news-flash had reported that the boys were missing. Minutes later Mrs Dymond was on full mental alert: 'My guide kept telling me that I had to save the boys,' she said. 'It made me so upset. I did not really know what I could do. I just had to give up cooking the Sunday lunch. My mind was in a turmoil.'

She telephoned the police. They took no notice. Sunday night proved sleepless: 'The messages kept coming from my guide. I could see an old man and he was living in a tumbledown cottage on the moor and he kept pointing to a monument with spikes on the top.'

She went to the police station near her home at Perranporth. There she pored over their Ordnance Survey map and put two fingers on the place where the boys could be found.

Her information, so she claims, was passed at once to the rescue team in this area. The team followed her lead, headed for the spirit-inspired location and the boys were found. Their equipment and tent had kept them alive and reasonably fit.

Press statements by William Ames, Secretary of the Dartmoor Rescue Group, seemed to back up Mrs Dymond's story: 'There was only one place that matched that description, Widgery Tor, and we were clutching at straws because we had searched over a hundred square miles ... But this lady's description of the monument was too clear to ignore.'

Police statements on the other hand presented a very different picture. They pointed out that when the boys were found they were walking towards the edge of the moor. In ten or so minutes they would have reached the main Okehampton–Tavistock road. Even if the boys had not reached that road they would have been discovered by one or other of the search parties working in that section. For the moors were not being combed haphazardly but systematically, square by square. And this all-embracing sweep was nearing completion.

So our medium had every natural factor in her favour. For all such late forecasts draw on the 'drought factor'. In other words, the longer a drought goes on, the closer we are to rain. And it is just so with a systematic search of the type mounted at Dartmoor.

Now Mrs Dymond lived over fifty miles west of Dartmoor. Despite this, the main landmarks of the moor are extremely well known to people in her area. They have frequently featured in newsreels and documentaries shown on the local south west of England television channels.

The lady did live, though, just seven miles from Truro, where four of the cadets came from. From the beginning of the drama details of the search were the talk of Truro town. And the radio and television coverage kept the matter to the fore. Any information the medium needed about the boys themselves or about the stages of the search was freely available.

The police have summed up her contribution in this way: 'During the operation, Mrs Dymond did contact the search headquarters by telephone and described certain landmarks on Dartmoor. Her information fitted about forty locations on the moor and was of no practical use whatsoever. The problem arose in that when the boys were finally located by a team from the Dartmoor Rescue Group an enthusiastic volunteer informed the press that they had been guided to the spot by Mrs Dymond's vision, thus establishing her credibility. She then sold various stories to national newspapers including a £400 feature for the *Sunday Mirror* . . .' (Roger Busby, Devon & Cornwall Constabulary, Public Relations Officer.)

But could this just be pique on the part of the police? Not a bit of it. Mrs Dymond, of course, may well have genuinely believed that she had used her gifts to assist the police, but it is surprising that she appears to have no track record as a medium. At the time checks were made on her at the offices of *Psychic News*. This paper carries files on all mediums great and small, but Mrs Dymond was not listed. In fact, when *Psychic News* rang one of their Cornish contacts with an extensive knowledge of the spiritualist movement in that area, they found that Mrs Dymond's name meant nothing.

Yet this lady who was so little known – who had presumably done nothing newsworthy in her life before – was within days announcing that the first volume of her autobiography was going to be published that summer! Further statements showed that five papers were competing with each other for exclusive interviews.

But the lady overreached herself. She gained further press and radio publicity when she announced that she knew strange things about other murders. She claimed to have 'psychic insights' into the killings of black youths in Atlanta, Georgia. And she claimed that she knew about the true fate of the missing Devon schoolgirl Genette Tate.

Genette had disappeared in August 1978. Mrs Dymond now announced that Genette had been strangled and her body had been walled up in a house in the Exeter area. The house belonged to the killer. It had bay windows and the upstairs window had been repaired.

The police called her bluff. There was little they could do about the Atlanta killings, but the Genette Tate case was within their province. So an officer called at Mrs Dymond's house in Perranporth to take a statement. After all her boasts she backed down and refused to expand on her public claims. Her excuse? She said that: 'her spirit guide had told her not to cooperate.' From now on she had to 'stick to faith-healing.' All the hopes she had raised were dashed.

So ended the meteoric career of Mrs Dymond. Yet few people know of this outcome. The newspapers which had yelled long and loudly on her entrance took care only to whisper about her exit!

Lone Ranger Dymond was not the first 'psychic detective' to dabble in the Genette Tate case. There were many others, right from the start in August 1978.

On the early afternoon of Saturday 19 August, Genette

cycled off on her newspaper round, a round that took her along the quiet country lanes, circling the village of Aylesbeary in Devon. Hours later her abandoned bicycle was found at the side of Within Lane. Of Genette there was not the slightest trace or sign. The alarm was raised. The hunt began.

A police helicopter slowly scanned the fields, farmlands and woods for miles around the area. Seven thousand gum-booted searchers trudged across the ground, probing in every ditch, hedge and copse. But even 'Genette's Welly Army' (as the press dubbed them) failed to find a single worthwhile clue.

The crass materialists with their sole reliance on physical methods were clearly at a loss. But the psychics were more than confident that their extra-special knowledge could crack the case. There were phone calls, letters, to the police and to the Tate family. Then came the visits. As Genette's father John Tate affirms: 'A dowser turned up ... and took away with him personal items belonging to Genette. He then locked himself away at the police incident centre to study the items and area maps ... He came up with a number of suggestions which were duly followed up. They all proved false hopes ... Many people came to us offering threads of hope. We clutched at them desperately in the early days ... But the promises of the psychics were all lies. They raised false hopes in us. At times we really believed we were onto something. The suggestions and ideas preyed on our minds ... But always, when it came to the crunch, the so-called leads and ideas led absolutely nowhere but into a pit of despair.'

One of the callers at the Tates' house stated that he was the reincarnation of a five-thousand-year-old eastern god. He prophesied that Genette would be beamed down from Venus into a nearby field at 2.30 the following Thursday.

Another caller was a woman who arrived clutching a bamboo table. As credentials, she affirmed that she was the slave of a masterful Indian spirit. 'She bounced this table up and down for three hours calling up her master and going through the alphabet each time to spell out the words.'

In all, almost five hundred psychic theories and suggestions were put forward and the police have stated that they had a schedule of more than two thousand items of information from such sources in their case index. So the possibility for inspired guesswork was certainly great. And yet all the 'insights' led nowhere.

Some of the police comments are worth noting. Roger Busby, Public Relations Officer for the Devon Force had this to say: 'One of the first psychics on the scene, a medium from Cornwall, shook like a leaf when he visited the scene, much to the amazement of the DCI who was accompanying him, and then predicted that Genette's body would be found within two days and the offender arrested the following day ... when his predictions failed to come to pass he was not seen again (although at a much later stage he did claim in a newspaper interview to have been called in by the police).

'Another psychic, awakened by a vivid dream at his home in Leicester, jumped into his car in the early hours of the morning and drove over two hundred miles to the incident room where he told an officer: "I've solved it. Genette's in the boot of a car ..."

"Can you tell me what make of car?"

"I'm sorry I can't."

"Registration number?"

"Afraid not ..."

He was given a cup of tea and then drove home.

'There were many such instances in which psychic information was offered (and I must add that much of it was certainly in good faith) which was just too vague to follow up. "She's in a country cottage with honeysuckle near the door," was a typical example. Plenty to choose from in Devon. "She's been devoured by a wild animal which escaped from a zoo. You won't know the animal has escaped because it ate its keeper first" – that was one of my favourites.

'At one stage, dowsers (they're the ones who dangle objects over maps) were queueing up to have a crack at the case.

'We decided in view of the psychic interest in the case that we would approach ... Dr Croiset of Utrecht, through an intermediary, i.e. the *Daily Express* ... He duly came across but after an inconclusive day during which he provided some quite startling observations on the case, even down to describing the offender and the sequence of events surrounding

Genette's disappearance, he finally confessed that he had no way of knowing whether the information he received through his extrasensory powers related to the past, present or future. Again, a problem for accepted police procedure.

'Needless to say the Genette Tate case is still unresolved and if the Ufologists (flying saucer experts) are to be believed, it will stay that way. They maintain she was kidnapped by a Venusian space craft evidenced by a crescent-shaped scorch mark from its exhaust in a field adjacent to the lane. A somewhat more mundane explanation of this came from a local farmer who said he had inadvertently spilled a little too much lime in that corner of the field.'

Don Crabb, now Police Superintendent at Newton Abbott, writes: 'We never invited psychics in, but when we said we would listen to anyone who might help we opened the floodgates. We had nearly 1,200 letters from people claiming to be mediums or possessing ESP and many more of them turned up ... some suggested she was bricked up in chimneys; some said she was in roadworks; some said she was in water. One thought she was under a bridge. We listened to them all, but they didn't do anything to help our enquiry.'

There was even a highly respectable psychic search party set up in December 1978. It was headed by television scriptwriter Andrew Wilson and had the cooperation of an ex-Detective Chief Inspector, Dick Lee. They tried to take some of the crankiness out of the atmosphere, but for all their scientific pretensions, they simply wasted much time and money on wild-goose chasing. Nothing of value was contributed by this group.

As far as Genette is concerned, perhaps her father should have the last word. He said: 'We soon found that the psychics who came up our garden path were foot-in-the-door types who, once they had wormed their way in, were very reluctant to leave again. They were strong characters who were not afraid to assert themselves. They rode roughshod over our feelings, which were in a desperate state already. In one week our emotions and normal grip on life had gone through a wrenching upheaval, and the influence of psychics started to have an unpleasant effect. Even when we didn't want them they were there on our doorstep, always expecting to be met with an open door.'

And he bitterly added later: 'We discovered that the work of the psychics was not just ludicrous and laughable. It was sinister and evil. Once we got into that web of deceit – and that was what it was – we found it very hard to struggle free. None of it ever led anywhere except to despair and disappointment, misery and confusion. We had become enslaved to the suggestions of the psychics.'

Talk of the sinister and evil naturally brings us back to our starting point – to the melodrama enacted in Dusseldorf in 1929. How did it end? Well, despite all those mediumistic writhings and mouthings the killer went on killing. Six more victims at least were slaughtered. In the end the Dusseldorf Ripper was delivered to the police – by his wife!

He was an outwardly calm, stuffily respectable, middle class citizen. A secret admirer of London's Jack the Ripper. His name was Peter Keurten. Remember it. It will resonate. It ties in strangely with the psychic flim-flam surrounding the Yorkshire Ripper murders.

Now *there* was a real challenge to the psychic detectives of the world. They had a full five years to focus their powers. So, just how did they face up to that challenge? And what was their final score?

Chapter Five

THE YORKSHIRE RIPPER AND THE PSYCHIC CIRCUS

The trail of terror began on the morning of 30 October 1975. On that bleak wet day Wilma McCann was found murdered on a deserted playing field in the Chapeltown area of Leeds. Her skull had been smashed by two vicious blows. Her body was marred by fifteen stab wounds. The Yorkshire Ripper had chalked up his first killing.

He was to kill twelve more women before he was caught, over five years later. And for the greater part of those five years the air was thick with rumours and theories about his identity. The police were constantly baffled and at loggerheads with each other. The pressmen were eternally speculating. And the gaudy psychic circus brought out its clowns great and small!

The police have never released the number of psychics who approached them with examples of their 'special insights', but in the less spectacular Genette Tate case more than 450 mediums of one sort or another were known to have been in touch with the detectives. In the Ripper case it would be fair to guess that the number was equally great, and possibly greater.

The most prominent among this group have fortunately gone on record, sometimes more than once. That allows us to make a fair judgment of their forecasts when compared with the real events as they unfolded.

One of the most dramatic forecasts of this type was printed

in the *Sunday People* of 1 July 1979. It was the lead on the front page and its startling headline set in large type read: FACE OF THE RIPPER. Alongside the headline was a large sketch of the Ripper drawn by artist Bob Williams. The account went on to say that 'famous clairvoyant Doris Stokes has "seen" the face of the Ripper.' The remarkable sketch was based on her description as given to the newspaper's artist.

According to this description, the Ripper had a 'scar below his left eye which twitches when he gets agitated.' He was five foot eight inches tall. He was called Robbie or Johnnie with a surname beginning with the letter 'M'. He lived in a street named Berwick or Bewick.

In detail, the sketch shows the Ripper as clean shaven with long, straight hair – 'mousey hair which covers his ears.' The hair is parted on the right, where 'there is a small bald patch which he tries to cover up.'

In filling in the Ripper's background, Doris Stokes claimed that she had got through to his mother, Molly or Polly, who told her that the killer was married but his wife had left him. Doris was also able to add that she believed the Ripper had received treatment at a hospital, 'possibly Cherry Knowle Hospital at Ryhope, near Sunderland, which specialises in mental cases'.

It should be noted that Mrs Stokes terms herself a clairaudient, rather than a clairvoyant. In other words her information comes in the form of voices instead of visions or pictures. Nevertheless, this did not stop her from being certain that the artist's impression really matched the face of the Ripper. Her certainty led her to repeat this information on Tyne Tees Television.

Her description led to considerable anger on the part of a Mr Ronnie Metcalf. The poor man unfortunately lived at Berwick Avenue, Downhill, Sunderland. He had a Wearside accent and was a long-distance lorry driver, working for an engineering firm. These were some of the features the police were looking for in their hunt. And to top it all, his travels took him regularly to Yorkshire and Lancashire where all the victims had died.

In a statement to the press, he said: 'It's not me, so just

lay off. I seem to fit the bill almost exactly. At first I didn't mind having my leg pulled but this really is no laughing matter. There are bound to be people who take this clairvoyant stuff seriously and who will be pointing their finger at me. I haven't been seen by the police, but I have no doubt that I could quickly convince them that the Ripper and I are two completely different people.'

Doris Stokes' conviction that the Ripper lived on Tyneside or Wearside came after she had heard a broadcast of a tape recording said to have been made by the killer. We now know that the tape was nothing but a cruel hoax. At the time, though, even the police gave the tape full credence. As a result the police took Mrs Stokes seriously or so it seems, for Brian Johnston, Northumbria's Chief Constable, was quoted as saying that the police would be checking on all places with the names Berwick and Bewick in their region.

Five months later the Dutch 'psychic detective' Gerard Croiset made his solemn pronouncement. Remarkably, he seemed to agree broadly with Mrs Stokes. In *The Sun* on 28 November 1979 he said that the Ripper had 'long hair cut straight across the neck.' He limped due to a damaged right knee, and he lived in the heart of Sunderland in a large block of service flats over a garage. Croiset added that when about six years old the Ripper had been in 'a kind of institution for psychologically disturbed children.'

Quite different conclusions were reached by clairvoyant Flora MacKenzie. She forecast the killer would live in the Barnsley/Sheffield area. This brought her into direct conflict with a Mr Patrick Barnard who seemed to have seen more than anyone else and in much more detail.

Mr Barnard's story took over the front page of the Southend *Evening Echo* of 24 November 1980. 'I HAVE SEEN THE RIPPER' yelled the headline. Then Mr Barnard went on to describe how he had looked down on the Ripper 'as if from my bedroom window.' The killer was a man of average build with dark hair, either wavy or curly.

'I could only see his back,' he said. 'But on the shoulders of his black duffel coat were the white letters R.N. It seemed that he was walking out of a submarine dockyard. I felt that it was in Scotland and I got the impression he was working on a nuclear submarine.

'Wouldn't that explain everything? A crewman on a sub, at sea for months at a time, while the police are chasing their own tails looking for him ashore?'

In his visions Mr Barnard saw an old and abandoned green railway coach in an overgrown and disused siding. This was the place where the Ripper came after each murder to change his clothes. He even saw the Ripper's home. A place also close to a railway – a top flat in fact, in a dilapidated grey house sited over a railway tunnel. And one more place was visible to him. An old wartime air raid shelter. In this shelter was a cardboard box and he sensed that inside it were parts of his victims!

Mr Barnard had no doubts whatever about the accuracy of his visions. 'I have seen these things as plainly as slides projected on a screen,' he insisted. 'I am not a nutter.'

Despite his certainty, the Leeds police were not impressed. They first reacted by saying: 'We get thousands of people like this, all ringing us up and telling us something different.' And they added: 'Railway coaches in these parts don't have green livery.'

Yet two days later an *Evening Echo* reader reported that he had seen green railway coaches on a disused line close to 'a remote coastal road near Hull.' Since Hull is close enough to Leeds to make the information exciting, the *Echo* rang Hull police. Inspector Terry Lamb, at Hull, took the tip-off seriously enough to send out officers to trace these coaches. But later reports show that the searches led nowhere.

In the days following Patrick Barnard's disclosures there came a crop of forecasts. The *Daily Star* ran a front page lead story and devoted a double page spread to what it termed an 'amazing dossier.' This dossier was supplied by an anonymous medium who claimed that the Ripper was aged between forty and forty five years. He was of stocky build with blue eyes, moles on his face, and fair hair that could have recently been dyed. He was born in London but moved north when six years old. By trade he was possibly a plumber, but he had once worked as a miner. He was unmarried, partly owing to the influence of his mother – a domineering and religious woman 'probably in her eighties.'

A list of twelve 'psychically supplied' names of acquaintances was included, together with other fine details, one being the remarkable fact that the Ripper perhaps owned a parrot!

This 'amazing dossier that comes from beyond the grave' was illustrated by seven drawings supplied by a 'famous psychic artist.' An eighth drawing, of the Ripper himself, was held back in case it hindered police investigations.

The next development came when the medium David Walton went into print in *Psychic News* on 6 December 1980. His information included the tit-bit that the Ripper 'sometimes disguises himself as a woman.' Walton also believed that he had contacted the Ripper's dead father and had homed in on a terraced house where the killer occupied a small back room.

Following that, Joan Gricks called at the *Psychic News* offices and revealed information which she had passed on to the police. In her view, the killer 'disguises himself and has, on occasion, dressed as a woman.'

In reporting these things *Psychic News* wisely made no attempt to list all the other confident claims made up to that date. Had the paper done so, then it would have recorded statements by Alfred Cartwright, Simon Alexander, Reginald du Marius and others. So, in the interests of fairness, let us consider those people as well.

Starting with Alfred Cartwright we find he told the police: 'As soon as I saw a picture of this girl (Jayne MacDonald) I began to see pictures of the man who killed her. He is an ordinary working man, aged about twenty eight or thirty, who lives in Bradford. In four weeks time he will strike again in the Chapeltown area but he will then be caught.

In reality, the Ripper struck ten days after Mr Cartwright's statement and went on to kill eight more women.

Seventeen days after Mr Cartwright's intervention, clairvoyant Simon Alexander was taken to five of the murder sites – one in Bradford and four in Leeds. He then said: 'I think the first death was probably an accident after the man was taunted, and it has built up from there. Obviously there is something very wrong with the man, but I don't think he will murder another woman.'

But there was obviously something very wrong with Mr Alexander for the murders continued for three more years!

Reginald du Marius, by contrast, was refreshingly precise. He was a Manchester astrologer who sent his deductions to the police on 26 July 1979. He announced that the Ripper strikes 'when the moon is positioned in an orbital course of 22 degrees.' This allowed him to know that the Ripper would 'strike tomorrow, Friday night' – that is on the 27th. He was also able to add 'I've also deduced that the Ripper was born at 9.30 p.m. on 15 September 1946, making him thirty two years of age.' For the record there was no attack on Friday 27 July 1979 – and the Ripper was born some time after eight o'clock on 2 June 1946.

Not all the psychic detectives, however, were British. In August 1979 Dutch engineer Wim Virbeek said that the Ripper was a twenty-seven-year-old washing machine mechanic living in Aberdeen. At the same time another Dutchman, the clairvoyant Dono Meijling, actually came to England and spent his Christmas and New Year prowling around Chapeltown in search of clues. He was finally able to supply fairly specific leads – none of which were of any use. The most controversial of these was the suggestion that the Yorkshire Ripper was in some way related to Detective Chief Superintendent Jim Hobson!

They all seemed to be at it, with pendulums and maps, crystal balls, trances and seances and group meditations, to list just some of the strange methods employed. Even the self-styled King of the Witches, Alex Sanders, felt impelled to chip in with a pearl of wisdom. One of his trances had brought him into contact with the spirit of the killer, so with authority he announced: 'He lives alone in a flat in South Shields, overlooking railway arches.' Regrettably, he forgot to list the street name and house number.

So many words, so many theories and so much conviction – yet it was all nothing but pretentious blather. The arrest and conviction in 1981 of Peter Sutcliffe showed every published psychic forecast had been hopelessly wrong. The 'clean-shaven' man who was alleged to have posed as a woman had sported a dense black beard and moustache all along. His 'dead' father was very much alive; his 'living' dominant mother was two years dead. Far from being a bachelor skulking away in a small back room he turned out to be a married man owning a large detached house. He was thirty five, with a thick mop of black curly hair, and no scars or moles on his face. Born a Northerner, he was living at Bradford in his native Yorkshire!

Now the sincerity of these forecasters is not in doubt. But the inescapable conclusion is that five years of psychic probings failed to bring to light one single useful clue as to the Ripper's identity or whereabouts. On the contrary, the psychic information was wholly misleading. If taken seriously it would have led to the waste of thousands of hours of police time. As such it ranks as arrogant and mischievous nonsense.

Chapter Six

THE MURDERER AND
THE MEDIUM

'Eighteen months before the police arrested Peter Sutcliffe, the Yorkshire Ripper, Kent medium Nella Jones drew a picture of him, described where he lived and worked and accurately predicted two more murders before he was caught ... Eventually Nella went to Yorkshire and accompanied police to help them locate clues and places. Her mental pictures were always accurate. Nella could exactly describe details of a location before they ever arrived on the spot. Police were amazed that the psychic could direct them to places she had never seen.' (*Psychic News*, 5 June 1982.)

Note the words of that report. The exaggerations are already creeping in. A new myth is already being minted. The real truth is only to be found in Mrs Jones' writing – the logical starting point.

On the surface, her Ripper forecasts seem to score an inexplicable number of significant hits. Unlike the other psychics we have looked at, her major predictions were never published in advance. But she insists that they were witnessed. So in her case every detail warrants the closest possible scrutiny.

We begin, though, with a handicap. I have written to Nella Jones and asked her to deposit copies of all her original forecasts involving these murders with the Society for Psychical Research. In that way they could be analysed at leisure by believers and sceptics alike – a very fair proposition.

To date no documents have been deposited and Mrs Jones

has chosen not to reply to my polite letter. You may draw your own conclusions from this. So, in proceeding, we are forced to rely on the twenty one pages in her book *Ghost Of A Chance* and the various newspaper reports of her sayings. Fortunately, even this incomplete record shows up the fatal flaws. And there is enough left to demonstrate that her apparent hits are ultimately, albeit unconsciously, derived from analogies with similar crimes and from published information. Now I do not make those statements lightly. Consider the proofs.

Dark-haired Jacqueline Hill was murdered in Leeds on the rainy night of Monday 17 November 1980. Mrs Jones' book claims that the death had been previsioned fourteen months previously, early in September 1979. Then she had said: 'The next victim will be found on a small patch of waste ground.'

Nearer to the date she had added: 'I suddenly saw with tremendous clarity the scene of the Ripper's next attack. It was a small piece of waste land ... The girl, I knew without seeing, had dark hair ...'

Amazing foresight? Let us see. Prior to Jacqueline's death only one woman had died in a bedroom. Of the others, one was found on a rubbish pile, one in the grounds of a wood yard, two on sites described as grassland and six on waste land. Of the Ripper's twelve victims, ten had dark hair. Clairvoyance was hardly needed to infer that the same pattern would recur!

Of the Ripper himself, she said: 'I believe he lives in Bradford and that he is a long-distance lorry-driver ... I had the strongest feeling that the police had already spoken to him.' In the end all these things turned out to be true. But where is the psychic element?

As early as October 1975 the police had announced that they were looking for a lorry driver in connection with the murder of Wilma McCann.

On 26 October 1977, after the murder of Jean Royle, a team of Manchester detectives swept into the Bradford area. They announced that together with detectives from West Yorkshire 'we will be visiting factories in the Bingley, Shipley and Bradford areas and are interviewing all male employees.'

On the following day the police gave their reasons. A near-mint five pound note had been found in Jean Royle's handbag. The note had been traced to its bank of issue, the Shipley and Bingley branch of the Midland Bank on the edge of Bradford.

Following this announcement, the police launched a massive appeal to all workers in Bradford, Shipley and Bingley to check their wage packets for five pound notes within a short range of serial numbers. They searched for a full three months. Over five thousand people were interviewed. In the end Detective Chief Superintendent Jack Ridgeway was able to say (17 January 1978): 'It is more than likely that we have interviewed the person who received the fiver.'

So everything she had spoken about had been given national publicity ages before. Anyone interested in the Ripper killings could have toyed with those ideas. For example take author David Yallop. By looking at the published material, and without any psychic indulgences, he was able to deduce that the clues 'pointed unquestioningly to the Baildon/Bingley/Shipley areas near Bradford as the killer's place of work and almost certainly residence.'

He was so sure of this that on Wednesday 25 June 1979 he met with Assistant Chief Constable George Oldfield at the police offices in Wakefield. As Yallop in his *Deliver Us From Evil* testifies: 'I put it to George Oldfield that in my view the five pound note had come from the killer, that he most certainly worked in the Baildon/Bingley/Shipley area and equally certainly lived there, and that he was probably a lorry driver.'

Yallop has a tape recording of the interview. His deductions refute the view that Mrs Jones' visions gave her extraordinary and valuable information.

She had another try in 1979 when she declared: 'He's older than the police think – about thirty six.' At that time the Ripper had just turned thirty three. But it is easy to see how she arrives at her figure. A year earlier, Dr Stephen Shaw had developed a possible profile of the Ripper. This profile appeared in the *Yorkshire Post*, the newspaper Mrs Jones was cooperating with. The significant age mentioned by Shaw was thirty five. At the same time as Mrs Jones' guess, and without clairvoyance, writer Michael Nicholson guessed the Ripper's age as thirty two.

Was she any better at revealing his killing and mutilation techniques – or even his height? She seems to think she was. She says: 'The murders, it was disclosed during the trial, *did* involve the use of a hammer, among other weapons ...' She put his height at somewhere between five foot seven and five foot eight.

The hammer reference presumably refers to her horror dreams of August 1979. Yet these plagued her after newspaper articles had already made the information public. First, consider the prominent article in the *Daily Express* of 30 June 1979. It said the killer 'uses workbench equipment to mutilate his victims.'

Twelve days later the *Bradford Telegraph & Argus* revealed the truth for the first time. It stated: 'Kills with an engineers' ball-pein hammer. Wears size seven boots ...' So from July onwards the hammer-weapon and his small size became national knowledge.

Her 'foreknowledge' concerning the Ripper's house is presented as spot-on. She pictured ' ... a grey house with a wrought iron gate in front ... the impression of a small garage nearby.' The house number was six.

When it was revealed that Sutcliffe lived at number six Garden Lane, Heaton, Bradford, an exact correspondence was chalked up. Yet the Garden Lane house had exterior walls of a *light pinkish* hue. And the 'psychically revealed' address was *not* one in Garden Lane; it was number six Chapel Street, Bradford.

There are four Chapel Streets in Bradford, as well as Chapel Walk, Chapel Lane, Chapel Place, Chapel Fold, and the Chapel Road. None of those places had the slightest connection with the Ripper!

That leaves us with just a few items that seem to be different in quality. At one point the name Ainsworth had leapt into her mind. It turned out that the last-but-one murder actually occurred in the grounds of a Leeds magistrate named Hainsworth. Then she had had the name Peter in mind. And long before the murder of Jacqueline Hill she had recorded the initials J.H. Finally, weeks before Jacqueline's death, she predicted that the Ripper would strike in November, possibly on the 17th or the 27th. Jacqueline was murdered on Monday 17 November.

So how does anyone pluck such information out of thin air? They don't. This is past knowledge recycled as future knowledge. It becomes extra-convincing by sheer coincidence, as we shall see.

Consider the mind of the psychic. He or she constantly looks for cycles, patterns or portents linked with their current interests. When these things are discovered they are projected forward and used as a framework for picturing future events. Sometimes this is a conscious search. Sometimes subconscious. At other times it will be a mixture on both levels.

Next consider the special interest factor. In short, we all take extra notice of anything that reflects or impinges on our special interests. So naturally the psychics will register anything that falls within their field, even marginally. Books and articles dealing with the spiritualist or occult worlds are inevitably taken notice of. Whether the interest is deep or superficial matters little, for even a superficial glance at a text can be enough to register ideas and images in the subconscious. Hold this well in mind. It is often the key to psychic revelations.

Since the revealer is essential to the revelation, what sort of person is Mrs Jones? Her own statements show that she has been levitated by invisible hands; been transported twice to a phantom village; has seen the ghost of a cowled monk; has practised faith healing and psychometry; and has initiated exorcisms.

In a less enlightened age she would have been accused of witchcraft. Indeed as a schoolgirl she was ostracised by her schoolmates. When she asked why they would not talk to her any more, one yelled: 'Because you're a witch. You said that old lady would die ... and she did. Witch! Witch! Witch! Witch!'

So much for her psychic background. But has she a good memory for detail? Certainly. Her book records: 'I was just beginning to discover what a good memory I had. Our school teacher had read *Hiawatha* to us twice in class and just from those two readings I had memorised the whole poem.' And that poem involved twenty two sections spread over seventy pages, broken down into one hundred and forty columns and involving roughly five thousand three hundred and twenty lines. These lines in turn embody one hundred and thirty unfamiliar Indian names!

So she brought a phenomenal memory to bear on the Yorkshire Ripper case. And there was no lack of material around to fire her imagination. At the time psychics and non-psychics alike were looking back at earlier Ripper-style murders in a search for some sort of guidance, for significant patterns.

They looked far back to the original Jack the Ripper murders. Then forward to Jack's notorious imitator, the Dusseldorf Ripper of the 1920s, Peter Keurten. Peter Keurten's name and record was mulled over repeatedly.

In 1979, in the very first book on the Yorkshire murders, Michael Nicholson devoted four pages to Peter Keurten's crimes, emphasising: '... it is possible to draw several lessons from his pattern of behaviour which may be helpful in an interpretation of the Yorkshire killer's psychology and motives.'

We see then that in truth the only Christian name constantly associated with the Ripper murders was the name Peter. That it popped up in Mrs Jones' mind is hardly electrifying.

The name of Ainsworth, though, looks quite baffling. Does it present an insoluble problem? To begin with, we find that only one person with the name Ainsworth has achieved national and popular fame in Britain in the last two centuries. That was novelist W. H. Ainsworth. At one time his books were bestsellers. Now they are out of favour, which is why they often turn up for the next to nothing in street markets, junk shops and thrift shops.

We already know that Mrs Jones is deeply involved in all things occult. Consciously or subconsciously she will take note of anything she meets with in this field. It is her special mental circle of interest.

Now one of Ainsworth's frequently seen titles is *The Lancashire Witches*. To Mrs Jones its significance may not be great. But it is strong enough for the title to register. The subconscious is a marvellous magpie.

Once this connection has been made the name Ainsworth gains extra significance. Any future titles by him will be noted and mentally filed. Later on a completely unconnected set of events sets up a resonance. The mental files are shuffled and the mind brings up the author's name, seemingly out of nowhere.

In this particular case, the vital resonating factor is provided by the only Christian name shown on the covers of Ainsworth's novels. That name is Harrison. A name in common with the Ripper's second victim – Joan Harrison, killed in 1975.

But why should this victim's name be specially significant for Mrs Jones? Well, incredible as it may seem, the published picture of Joan Harrison shows a woman whose face resembles that of Nella Jones. This is no fleeting resemblance. It is one so close that the picture could be passed off as a snap of a younger sister. The ultra-significant killing of Harrison took place in Lancashire in the town of Preston.

We now have in front of us all the evidence we need to show the essential interconnections.

The Lancashire connection brings to mind the novel *The Lancashire Witches*. And Preston as a place of violence resonates with another of Ainsworth's titles, *Preston Fight*. Then the three factors – the name of the county, the name of the town, and the name of the victim – couple inexorably with the name of the author. In Mrs Jones' mind the name Ainsworth is erected as a mysterious mental signboard.

It does not stop there. The Harrison murder is behind other mental leaps. Mrs Jones conceived the idea of a November killing involving the initials J.H. Those, of course, were Joan Harrison's initials. And she, in fact, *was* killed in November.

This is a splendid example of the past being refurbished as a glimpse of the future. It was only the coincidences surrounding Jacqueline Hill's death that gave this forecast a spurious splendour. But note this: earlier on, the Christian name produced in connection with the initials was not Jacqueline but Jean – which is simply another form of Joan!

All that is left are the dates, the 17th and 27th. How were they arrived at? Firstly, a murder prediction involving the 27th of the month had been advanced by Mr du Marius in

July 1979. His forecast appeared in the press and on page 114 of Michael Nicholson's book. On the *same page*, Nicholson reports Nella Jones' forecasts. There is one possible sparking point.

Next, in the whole range of attack dates considered by her, the bulk of them fell in the last fortnight of the month. There were missing days but the only ones of significance to her were the 27th, for which she had already been primed by du Marius, and its logical associate, its ten interval partner, the 17th.

This is not far-fetched reasoning. On the contrary, such elementary numerical pattern associations are common. In more elaborate forms they are freely employed by stage magicians.

Having noted all this, we now need a realistic perspective. What in total did she claim? By that I mean including all the things that had been left out.

In July 1979 she claimed she had 'been inside the mind of the Ripper.' More than once she had a view of his face. Time and again she had seen the Ripper walking, trailing a woman through rain-drenched streets, 'drinking tea out of a thick white china cup' in a cafe, 'eating a chocolate eclair.'

She witnessed him having trouble with the axle of his lorry, even saw 'his lips moving as he spoke to another man' at a depot. Finally she 'saw' him murder Jacqueline Hill and mentally followed him for some hundreds of yards as he walked away.

The result of all these clairvoyant viewings led her to make a drawing of the Ripper's face. The drawing shows that all along she had seen a long-nosed, straight-haired, completely clean-shaven man. A man able to dress as a woman and get away with it. And she alleged he did dress as a woman.

It needs to be emphasised that there is no resemblance whatsoever between this psychically observed man and the real murderer, Peter Sutcliffe. He was bearded, and had been throughout all the killings.

In July 1979 she dramatically forecast that his next victim could be a young boy of fifteen or sixteen. It turned out to be a young woman aged twenty. Her unwarranted confidence

The Murderer And The Medium

led her on to say: 'I don't think he has ever married, but I believe his mother is dead and that his father was a cripple ... I have the feeling that he was taken away from his mother when he was ten or eleven years old.'

Yes, Sutcliffe's mother was dead. But the rest was rubbish. Equally false is the statement that she had 'accurately forecast two more murders before he was caught.' There were three more murders before he was arrested, to be accurate. Those of Barbara Leach, Marguerite Walls and Jacqueline Hill.

As for the killing of Jacqueline Hill, her complete psychic picture was as follows. She said that on the night of the murder the Ripper had left his car in the city centre of Leeds, then travelled out to Headingley. There he killed Jacqueline, walked along Chapel Street and along an unmade road leading to the railway station at Headingley. He then boarded a pay-train to Leeds city centre where he collected his car and made his getaway.

Mrs Jones insisted that this is what had happened. She even convinced a newspaper that there was something in it. They took her north to retrace the Ripper's path from the attack point along the dirt road to Headingley station.

It was an absurd scenario from start to finish. Sutcliffe would never have risked having to travel on public transport. He could never be sure just how dishevelled or blood-stained he would be. When the full story emerged it turned out that at 9.30 on 17 November he was sitting in his car in Headingley outside the Arndale Centre. There was a bus stop opposite and he spotted Jacqueline as she left the bus. He watched her cross the street and turn into Alma Road. He followed her in his car, overtook her and sat waiting until she walked by. When she was a short distance in front he got out of his car, trailed her, chose the right moment, leapt forward and struck her across the head. He dragged his unconscious victim onto a piece of waste ground where he stabbed her repeatedly with a sharpened screwdriver.

Those are the facts. Everything set down by Nella Jones was sheer fiction.

The fiction does not end there. In her book she records her 'final' forecast: 'He is killing indiscriminately now. But he is coming to the end of the road. He will try to do another, but it will go wrong and he won't finish the job. He will be caught before he gets the chance.'

That was made in early October 1980, and after the murder of 17 November Sutcliffe did come to the end of the road. But the account in the book clashes with the real statements she made to the press after the murder of Jacqueline. Mrs Jones said: '... he will strike again almost immediately. I see him coming back to claim another victim within the week.'

This statement was made to the *Daily Mirror* (21 November 1980). The *Mirror* then went on to summarise: 'She said the next victim would be a youngish woman, but refused to give further details. "I do not want to frighten the life out of some poor young girl with a similar description."'

There was no murder within the week. It was, in fact, the last of Sutcliffe's killings. So Nella Jones was wide of the mark to the very last. Unfortunately, few people take the trouble to examine all her statements in detail. And I forecast that her legend and myth will grow despite all the absurdities that can be brought to light.

It can be said with certainty that at no time did she supply a single name, location, address, or description connected with any of the murders that was of any use to the police. The impression that she in some way cooperated usefully with them and supplied valuable information is false. If they had gone chasing around trying to tie real people and places to her nebulous descriptions they would still be on the search. And if they had taken her psychically inspired drawing as evidence they would still be hunting for that imaginary long-nosed, straight-haired, clean-shaven culprit.

Fortunately for us all, the police are wiser than that! Their blue lamp needs no astral light.

Chapter Seven

I Captured Jack The Ripper

Both Jack the Ripper and the Yorkshire Ripper excited the avid interest of mediums and clairvoyants. It is even claimed that the Victorian case was eventually solved by the timely intervention of a gifted medium, the late Robert James Lees.

This claim rests on a document 'dictated by the medium' and released after his death in 1931. Its validity is strengthened by the further claim that his story has never been contradicted by the police.

According to the spiritualist movement, Robert Lees developed his amazing powers during boyhood, and they were so outstanding that Queen Victoria consulted him when he was a mere thirteen years old. Other Royal consultations are said to have followed. By the time of the Ripper murders his sensitivity was at its peak and this led unexpectedly to a 'loathsome clairvoyant experience.'

His posthumous statement records that shortly after the third Whitechapel murder, while writing in his study, Lees became convinced that the Ripper was about to strike again. He had a vision of an East End location – a narrow court with a gin-palace nearby. He could see the name of the court clearly, he could even see that the bar clock stood at 12.40 a.m. – pub closing time.

A man and a woman entered a dark corner of the court. The man was cold sober, the woman the worse for drink. In her drunken state she leaned against the wall for support and the man quickly closed her mouth with his hand, drew a knife and slit her throat. Then he let her drop to the ground, stabbed her repeatedly, coolly wiped his blade on her dress and walked off into the night.

All this was seen in full harrowing detail. Shaken, Robert Lees hurried to Scotland Yard to warn them, but he was treated as a harmless lunatic, though to humour him the duty officer wrote down the time and place of 'the forthcoming murder.'

The following night, the Ripper slew a prostitute in the very manner, at the very time, and in the very court named by Lees.

The news of this murder disturbed Lees so much that he found himself unable to sleep at night. His health suffered badly and his doctor advised a holiday abroad, so Lees moved for a while to the Continent. During this vacation the Ripper murdered four more women, but Lees was untroubled by visions and he returned to London renewed in health.

About a year later he came face to face with the man seen in his vision. At the time he was riding with his wife on an omnibus bound east from Shepherd's Bush. At Notting Hill a medium-sized man boarded and sat near them. Lees took no notice at first and then he experienced the strange sensations that heralded his vision. He looked hard at the man, turned to his wife and said: 'That is Jack the Ripper.'

At first she took his words lightly, as a foolish fancy, but his sincerity finally convinced her. They kept watch surreptitiously until the man alighted at Marble Arch; then Lees leapt off the bus and followed his suspect down Park Lane. About halfway down the Lane he spotted a policeman and told him that the Ripper was just yards away from them and should be arrested. The policeman simply laughed and threatened to run Lees in as a nuisance. And then it was too late to take any other action, for the Ripper took fright at Apsley House and jumped into a passing cab which sped off rapidly along Piccadilly.

A minute or so later Lees met a police sergeant and poured out his suspicions to him. The sergeant reacted with dismay and anger. 'Show me the constable who refused to arrest him,' he cried. 'Why, only this morning we received news at Bow

Street Station that the Ripper was coming in this direction.'

That night Lees had another premonition. This time the vision was far less clear than his first, but he was able to see the murdered woman's face. He also noted the peculiarity of the mutilations – one ear completely severed, the other left clinging to the face by a mere strand of flesh.

On recovering from the trauma of his trance, Lees visited Scotland Yard again. There he insisted on seeing the Head Inspector of Police and in great anguish told his story. This time his tale was received with awe and from his desk the inspector drew out a shabby postcard and handed it to Lees.

The card was written in red ink and adorned with two bloody fingerprints. It read: 'Tomorrow night I shall again take my revenge, claiming, from a class of women who have made themselves most obnoxious to me, my ninth victim. JACK THE RIPPER. P.S. To prove that I am really Jack the Ripper I will cut off the ears of this ninth victim.'

The inspector now looked on Lees' story as a warning sent from heaven, since no one but himself knew of the postcard message. Extra police were drafted into Whitechapel and by the next day the alleys and courts of the area were swarming with plain-clothes men. But despite these precautions the Ripper struck. As in the vision, he left his victim with one ear severed and the other hanging from her face.

Robert Lees suffered a further breakdown in health and left for a rest on the Continent once more. While he was abroad the Ripper killed his sixteenth prostitute and informed the Yard that he was to go on until he reached twenty, then cease.

Shortly afterwards Lees returned to London and dined at the Criterion with two Americans. Halfway through the meal Lees cried out 'Great God! Jack the Ripper has committed another murder.' They checked the time at 7.49 p.m. Then all went post-haste to the Yard.

The police there knew of no such murder, but before Lees could finish dictating his statement a telegram arrived stating that a body had been found in Crown Court. The time of discovery was given as ten minutes to eight!

An inspector at once drove to Crown Court with the medium. On reaching the Court, Lees pointed across to a dark corner and said: 'Look in the angle of the wall. There is something written there.' The inspector ran forward, struck a match and for the first time saw that chalked on the wall were the words 'Seventeen, Jack the Ripper.'

The inspector needed no more convincing. He now seemed to see Lees as an instrument of Providence and he became determined to make use of the medium's 'marvellous though incomprehensible powers.' To fully appreciate the policeman's attitude it must be borne in mind that the madman had for years baffled all the resources of the greatest police force in the world.

After an earnest appeal from the inspector, Lees 'consented to try to track the Ripper much in the same way as a bloodhound pursues a criminal. There seemed to be some magnetic wave connecting him ... with the fugitive.'

All that night Lees allowed that strange magnetic influence to guide him. He moved swiftly through the London streets, guiding the inspector and his detectives. At last, at four in the morning, Lees stopped. He pointed to the gates of a West End mansion and gasped: 'There is your murderer – the man you are looking for.'

Yet the inspector simply stood there dumbfounded, for he recognised the house as the residence of one of the most celebrated society physicians. It was unthinkable to link such a distinguished man with the East End slaughter. But the medium vehemently insisted the Ripper was inside.

Lees' insistence made the inspector waver and he set the medium a new task. 'Describe to me the interior of the doctor's hall and I will arrest him, but I shall do so at the risk of losing my position.' Without hesitation Lees said: 'The hall has a high porter's chair of black oak on the right hand as you enter it, a stained glass window at the extreme end, and a large mastiff is at this moment asleep at the foot of the stairs.'

The police waited until the servants rose at seven o'clock, then they rang the door bell. The door opened to disclose a hall exactly as described by Lees, except for one thing – there was no dog in sight. But, as the servants explained, there *was* a mastiff in the house and it did sleep at the foot of the stairs, but every morning it was let out into the garden as

How the public were fed the Amityville Horror . . . from the film released in 1980.

William Roy demonstrates how to cheat the throat microphone.

The Prince Imperial died in Zululand. But did he signal from his African grave?

Lord Dufferin – a miraculous deliverance?

A Dufferin saga off-shoot even reached the screen, in *Dead of Night*'s 'Room for One More' episode.

'Spirit Photography' began in the 1860s in Boston, Massachusetts. The innovator was William H. Mumler, who specialised in offerings like this gem!

French 'spirit photographer' Buguet began sessions with theatricals. An intense assistant mesmerised him into a dynamic state of mind!

Buguet's clients came away with 'convincing' proof.

In Britain the champion 'spirit forms' were recorded by the roguish Boursnell.

This client of Boursnell's was visited by 'Beauty'...

... but this poor chap got the 'Beast'.

But with all good fairy tales, there's a happy ending!

soon as they rose.

'This is the hand of God,' whispered the inspector and he asked for the doctor's wife to be called.

Under examination the wife sobbed out an incredible story. Her husband was a dual personality. To the outside world he was always a kindly and sympathetic man. Only she knew that at times he became a brutal and uncontrollable sadist. His favourite sadistic pastime involved the systematic torture of helpless animals. He would often cut the eyelids from captive rabbits and then expose them to the blinding sun, revelling all the time in their agonised contortions. One night she had even found him slowly burning a cat to death.

There had even been times when she had locked herself and the children into a bedroom to escape his vicious side. Then came the most horrible part of all. The Ripper murders began and she '... noticed with heart-breaking dread that whenever a Whitechapel murder had occurred her husband was absent from home.'

After hearing the wife's account the inspector called in two experts on insanity and the doctor was sent for. When confronted, the doctor admitted that his mind had been unbalanced for some years and there were times when he had complete lapses of memory. Once he had found his shirt-front soaked with blood, but he attributed this to a nosebleed during one of his stupors.

A search of his house brought proof that the Ripper had been found at last and the doctor was overcome by horror and remorse. He begged to be killed at once, since he 'could not live under the same roof as a monster.' But this was never seriously considered. Instead, twelve doctors were summoned to constitute a Commission in Lunacy. The Ripper was declared insane and all parties to the proceedings were sworn to secrecy.

The mad doctor was promptly removed to a private asylum for the insane in Islington, where he was lodged under an assumed name. But in order to account for the doctor's disappearance a sham death and burial were arranged, and the public was convincingly duped. Even the asylum keepers and inspectors never dreamed that they had custody of the infamous Jack the Ripper. To them he was simply inmate 124 – until the day he died!

This detailed and elaborate account gained a massive circulation when it was published in the *Daily Express* in March 1931. From then on it was repeated in newspapers, magazines and books throughout the world. Its very wealth of detail made it look authentic. It was treated seriously by investigators of standing such as Hereward Carrington and Dr Nandor Fodor. And leading spiritualist editor Maurice Barbanell often retold it and never had any doubts about its accuracy. Yet, for all that, his story is completely untenable. There is no possible way of matching it up with the real facts of the murders and their investigation!

To begin with, there were not seventeen murders but five. It is true that some earlier and later murders were at times muddled in with the Ripper's but that was solely due to a circulation-hungry Press and a sensation-hungry public. Sir Melville Macnaghten of Scotland Yard was adamant that 'the Whitechapel murderer had five victims and five victims only.'

Again, the murders were not spread over a period of years, as in the document, but took place over a short period of a mere ten weeks – beginning on 31 August 1888 and ending on 9 November.

Police records show that none of the murders took place at the times quoted and no murder took place at Crown Court. And no postcard was ever received bearing the quoted message. There *was* a postcard written in red ink with red smudges, but this was posted in London on 1 October after the double murders of 29 September, and after details of these murders had become public knowledge. The writer of this card and of a previous letter was in fact the first to use the name Jack the Ripper. It was believed to have been the work of some seamy journalist out for some extra copy.

Finally, the police have denied that Lees was involved with the Ripper hunt. In fact Robert Lees' own diary entries contradict this part of the tale. They show that he did not approach the police until 2 October 1888, three days after the murders on the 29th.

His diary records: 'Tuesday 2 Oct. Offered services to police to follow up East End murders – called a fool and a lunatic. Got trace of man from the spot in Berner Street.

'Wednesday 3 Oct. Went to City police again – called a madman and fool.

'Thursday 4 Oct. Went to Scotland Yard – same result but promised to write me.'

Now these are not the words of someone already involved with the police. Neither are they the words of someone who has already forecast two murders. His reception confirms this. With two correct predictions to his credit he would have been received with respect and welcomed. But he was simply treated like any of the other psychics and clairvoyants who were clamouring to have their 'special knowledge' taken seriously.

In that case, what prompted Lees to dictate this grossly absurd statement? The answer is amazing – there never was such a statement! That claim can now be shown up as a deplorable journalistic device used to sell the story.

The truth is that the *Daily Express* story of 1931 turns out to be nothing more than a slightly modified reprint of a hoax article dating back to the end of the last century. The original article first ran in *The Sunday Times–Herald* of Chicago – as long ago as 28 April 1895.

Superficially, this Chicago piece posed as sound information. Its small opening section was said to be based on the revelations of 'Dr Howard, a well-known London physician . . . who sat on the Commission in Lunacy', while the greater part was supposed to have been supplied by 'a London clubman living in Chicago' who knew the inside story and was willing to unseal his lips. Despite these credentials the whole piece was reckless, pseudo-dramatic fiction. In truth, not a single event in the whole story corresponds with any of the real-life events of the Whitechapel murders!

What remains true, however, is that Lees did independently state that he had cornered the murderer. But others made similar claims. Robert Clifford Spicer, for one, claimed that he had arrested the Ripper, while Dr Lyttleton Stewart Forbes asserted that it was his actions alone that had brought the murders to a halt.

Those killings certainly bred a good many illusions and

Sorry – You've Been Duped

delusions. And in the case of Robert Lees there is not a scrap of proof to show that his firm belief was anything more than just one of his many cherished and carefully nurtured delusions.

Chapter Eight

THE UNQUIET GRAVE OF PRINCE LOUIS

It was a cruel callous murder! ... Political assassination cunningly engineered by Freemasonry! ... Perhaps even Queen Victoria had a hand in the affair!

Outlandish rumours along these lines percolated through French society in the summer of 1879. Louis Napoleon, the Prince Imperial, had been slain in British Africa. The last fond hope of a French monarchist revival had perished in the service of the British Army.

But what was a French Prince doing on British soil? Well, his family were domiciled in England. As they viewed it, they were there marking time until the day came when the French people would once more clamour for a monarchy.

The Napoleons had fallen into disgrace after the Franco–Prussian War. Napoleon III had striven to imitate his famous uncle. He was desperate to cover himself in military glories, but he had none of his uncle's brilliance and in 1871 his campaign against the Prussians was feeble and pathetically ill-planned. As a result he suffered a humiliating defeat and lost his throne. France reverted to a Republic and the ex-Emperor and family scuttled across the Channel into exile.

In Britain they dreamed of their glorious return. And this dream came to be of paramount importance to Napoleon's son, Prince Louis. Indeed, after his father's death, the Prince's dream was encouraged by the French Royalists. In their eyes the Prince was now Napoleon IV.

In order to win more support in France, Louis began to polish up his misty image. He knew that the French adored military prowess, so he looked around for ways to gain experience in battle. This was far from easy, and for six years he had to content himself with military studies. His only fights were the occasional mock battles staged during the army manoeuvres. It was during this period that the hostile French Press dubbed him Napoleon III$\frac{1}{2}$!

Then, in 1879, came the chance to prove himself. Now he was grimly determined to end the Republican sneers. For in South Africa the British were locked in a war against the Zulus. And Louis won permission to join up with the British troops. It was made clear, though, that he was to keep out of danger. He was there to observe and make a map or two, but not to ride into the fighting line.

Before he left for Africa, he made a moving appeal to his mother: 'Owing to the accident of my birth I am not my own master. God has willed it so ... Whether I like it or not, I happen to be the nominal and eventually the effective head of a great party which believes itself to be ... truly representative of France ... but I can say that in France, although my name may be an emblem, my personality and my moral value, such as they are, are unknown ... At the age of twenty three I am still a child to them ...

'I am continually having it thrown at my head that the Orleans Princes have seen fighting, and that I have not seen any. My enemies have even gone so far as to call me a coward, simply because I have never had the opportunity of proving the contrary ... In Africa I shall be able to show that I am no coward, and that when I have proved that I am willing to risk my life for a country which is not my own, but to which I owe a debt of gratitude, I shall *a fortiori* have proven that I am equally ready to risk it in the service of my own country when she has need of me.'

Once in South Africa, the guide lines issued for Louis' safety were ignored. In practice he was allowed to join a number of forward patrols in Zululand. And each one of these placed him in potential danger. Indeed, the patrol he joined on Sunday 1 June led to his tragic death.

The Unquiet Grave Of Prince Louis

On that day he and his companions had dismounted and dallied for half-an-hour in a deserted kraal. They brewed coffee, smoked and corrected their maps. But they stupidly neglected to post a lookout. So they were easy prey for a small band of Zulus. The British troops tried to make a hasty getaway but in doing so they left behind the Prince. He desperately tried to mount his charger which had panicked and was galloping off. He kept pace with the horse and grabbed at the holster strap on the saddle. He swung upwards to the saddle but the strain was too much for the strap. It broke and the Prince rolled under the hooves of his horse.

When he reached his feet he knew he was doomed. His sword had been lost, his revolver held only a few cartridges and he was alone, facing seven fearsome Zulus. Seventeen spear thrusts left the Prince dead and mutilated.

The thorough investigation and army hearings that followed his death were reported in every detail in England. But even so, this did not stop the rumour-mongers. The wildest stories persistently circulated – including the claim that the Prince was still alive. Most persistent were the allegations that he was the victim of a plot. In France the atmosphere was so hostile that for a while Englishmen found it wise to stay out of sight.

With time, though, the fantastic tales submerged. Yet as they submerged an even more fantastic tale surfaced. It featured the Empress Eugenie in the incredible role of a psychic detective!

It seems that Eugenie yearned to bring her son's body back from Africa, to rest beside his father in the family vault. The problem was to find his body. The exact spot where he had fallen and been hurriedly buried was not known.

The Empress turned to Field Marshal Sir Evelyn Wood for help. A year after Prince Louis' death, Eugenie and Sir Evelyn landed in South Africa and the search began.

At first they tried offering a reward for information that would lead them to the grave. A number of natives came forward, eager to help and enrich themselves. But in each case the information they offered was either worthless or badly invented. One claimant even took them on a week-long trek to the 'burial site.' He knew the place well – but the trip ended when he completely lost himself in the tangled bush!

Eugenie was exhausted by the journey and deeply frustrated by the lack of dependable help. Sir Evelyn grew concerned enough to beg her to give up the quest. She stayed determined. She would carry on until she found the grave. 'In the end we shall find it,' she insisted. 'I know it.'

Then it seemed to her that her faith was to be rewarded. A giant Zulu approached Sir Evelyn and offered his help. He claimed to have been one of the party involved in the attack on the British in which Prince Louis had died. This made him certain that he could guide them to the site of the skirmish.

It meant a three-day journey into the bush, but the safari set out in high spirits. When they finally reached the place where the Zulu said the action had been fought, they grew dispirited. The whole area was covered in dense undergrowth.

Under those conditions finding an unmarked grave seemed an impossible task. The Zulu guide himself had lost all sense of certainty. He was sure that they were in the right area, but unsure as to the direction of the final search.

The stalemate was ended by Eugenie. 'My son lies somewhere in that direction,' she said, and she moved off stumbling through the bush. The search party followed her wonderingly.

Once she halted and asked if they could detect an unusual scent. But her followers could only detect the normal scents of the bush. Eugenie, however, insisted that she was picking up the strong scent of violets – her son's favourite perfume.

'He always said he loved it because he remembered me wearing it when he came to kiss me good night as a little boy,' she said.

At that point people in the search party began to have doubts about her sanity. Indeed, the public at large had been entertaining such doubts for some time. For the persistent quest of the Empress for her son's grave had been making news headlines. And it was feared that the triple tragedy she had suffered – the loss of throne, husband and son – had unbalanced her mind.

Despite their doubts they faithfully trudged behind her. For two hours she led them on, guided, she claimed, by the mysterious perfume. The scent that only she could detect. Finally, completely exhausted she stopped and pointed at a patch of scrub. There was nothing to distinguish it from the rest of the bush that they had passed through. But the Empress was unshakable.

'Under there,' she said, 'we shall find the body of my son.'

The men drew their cutlasses and slashed through the undergrowth and soon the markings of a grave became visible. The picks and spades went to work and a body was uncovered. There was no possible doubt about its identity. It was Prince Louis!

So there we are. The quest was one that made headlines. The search was proclaimed by public appeals. And in later years the Empress confirmed that a paranormal perfume had led her to her son's corpse.

In other words, it is a story that can be researched and verified in every fine detail. Let us turn to the Press then. Let us see what it has to say.

The date and manner of Louis' death are confirmed. The Press gave the tragedy the fullest possible coverage. It also reported the events of 2 June, the day after the tragedy.

But rather than quote one newspaper, let us look at the official report sent by Captain Molyneux to Lord Chelmsford. He wrote: 'In accordance with your instructions, I this morning accompanied the cavalry commanded by Major-General Marshall to find the body of His Highness the Prince Imperial. Surgeon-Major Scott, Lieutenant Bartle Frere, and the servants of His Imperial Highness were with me ... We went first to the kraal where the attack took place ... and speedily came upon the bodies of the two soldiers of the Natal Horse. At nine o'clock Captain Cochrane drew my attention to another body at the bottom of a donga, which on examination was recognised as that of His Imperial Highness.

'He was about two hundred yards north-east of the kraal ... the body stripped bare except for a gold chain with medallions which was about his neck. His sabre, his revolver, his helmet and his other clothes had disappeared, but we found in the grass his spurs with their straps, and a sock marked N ...

'The body had seventeen wounds, all in front, and the marks on the ground as on the spurs indicated a desperate resistance. At ten o'clock a bier was made of lances and blankets, and the body was brought out of the donga....'

Louis' corpse was carried in front of the mounted procession for an hour. Then an ambulance wagon from the camp at Itelezei met up with them and the Prince Imperial was transferred to its interior.

On 2 June at twilight the Prince's body was laid on top of a fieldgun at the camp. The whole camp took part in a memorial procession to honour the dead Prince. At the end of this ceremony the body was taken to the field hospital and handed over to the camp surgeons. The surgeons undertook the task of embalming the corpse using whatever materials they had on hand – it was crude but they hoped effective. Meanwhile the sappers using saws, cold chisels and hammers crafted a metal coffin out of empty zinc tea chests.

Early in the morning an ambulance wagon loaded with the zinc coffin set out for the coast, escorted by a body of the 17th Lancers. The ambulance reached Pietermaritzburg on Sunday night 8 June, and there the body was transferred to a lead-lined wooden coffin. The next day the sad procession moved under escort to Durban.

By the 15th the coffin was on board HMS *Orontes* bound for England. She reached Plymouth on 10 July. There the Royal coffin was unloaded onto the deck of the Admiralty yacht *Enchantress*, which steamed out of the breakwater bound for Woolwich.

At Woolwich the remains of the Prince Imperial were placed on board a gun carriage and taken to the Great Hall of Woolwich Arsenal, where a group of doctors examined the body.

The funeral of the Prince took place the next day. Queen Victoria was present. Four Royal Dukes, including the Prince of Wales, were among the pall-bearers. Three batteries of the Royal Artillery fired minute-guns. Other regiments lined the route. And some forty thousand mourners and onlookers crowded into the tiny village of Chislehurst in Kent, where the Napoleons lived.

After a short Mass in the local Roman Catholic church, the Prince was taken to the private memorial chapel erected by Eugenie in 1873. There he was laid to rest beside his father – just three weeks after his death.

So there never was a missing grave in Zululand! No grave means no quest. No public appeals. No rewards. No time-wasting applicants. No giant Zulu guide. No exhausting trek. And no paranormal perfume!

'Here are the stories, here is the evidence – collected, examined, verified ...' So claims the *Reader's Digest Book of Strange Stories, Amazing Facts*, and then goes on to offer the paranormal perfume baloney! Brad Steiger presents it as 'a dramatic case study of a ghostly scent.' And Fred Archer, one time editor of *Psychic News*, vouches for the story, saying of it: 'Sight, hearing, touch, even smell can operate as a psychic sense.'

I won't bore you by listing all the other appearances of this asinine yarn. But I can imagine someone asking: 'Isn't there just a teeny weeny bit of truth in this lovely legend?' Well, there is. It is true that Eugenie made the trip to South Africa a year after her son's death. And that's all the truth there is.

The Empress yielded to an irresistible urge. She wrote: 'I feel myself drawn towards this pilgrimage as strongly as the disciples of Christ must have felt drawn towards the Holy Places. The thought of retracing the stages of my beloved son's last journey, of seeing with my own eyes the scene upon which his dying gaze had rested, of passing the anniversary of the night of 1 June watching and praying alone with his memory, is for me a spiritual necessity and an aim in life. Since the end of the war has allowed me to regard this possibility more hopefully, it has become my dominant thought ... This thought sustains me and gives me fresh courage; without it I should never have sufficient strength to endure my life, and I should allow myself to become submerged in my sorrow ...'

Eugenie arrived in Cape Town on 18 April 1880. By the evening of 25 May she had reached the kraal where her son fell. There was not the slightest uncertainty about the location. The kraal was less than two hundred yards from the east bank of the River Ityotyosi. In fact, nothing was uncertain about the Prince's end. The fatal spot where he had fallen had been marked by a cairn of stone the day after his death. And shortly before her arrival Queen Victoria had a stone cross erected at the spot.

So when Eugenie left her tent that evening and walked towards the place of Louis' death she was saddened and disappointed. She felt that her own sorrowful intuition would guide her irresistibly to the exact spot, but she was thwarted. The Queen's Cross stood there; all trace of the grass watered by her son's blood had disappeared beneath a layer of white cement. And surrounding the area was an iron railing. The place had all the peaceful and orderly appearance of an English cemetery.

This authentic mission of hers was extensively covered by the world's Press. In fact, few lives are as well documented as that of this Empress. It is dramatic, tragic, even doom-laden. It can well do without the tawdry inventions of psychic penmen.

Chapter Nine

REGIMENT OF THE DAMNED?

'In the course of the fight . . . there happened a very mysterious thing . . .' Those were the opening words of a curious dispatch sent to Lord Kitchener in 1915. The dispatch came from the Dardanelles and was written by General Ian Hamilton. He had the soul of a novelist, and the tone of his dramatic dispatch set off a long train of unwarranted speculation. For he was concerned with the complete 'disappearance' of a body of British troops. And for some here was a golden chance for a spot of 'out of this world' tomfoolery.

In 1965, the tomfoolery reached its peak and the Dardanelles became the setting for an awe-inspiring paranormal mass-kidnapping!

The Dardanelles venture itself began with a hare-brained scheme to knock Turkey, then Germany's ally, out of the War. The plan involved seizing Turkey's long sea channel that stretches from the Mediterranean to the Black Sea. If the Allies had been successful the direct links between Germany and Turkey would have been severed. The Russian grain ships could have steamed freely to and from the Black Sea. And the Turks would have been so weakened and demoralised, they might even have sued for peace.

It was all a grand dream that turned into a ghastly nightmare. The planning was hasty, improvised and totally unrealistic. General Hamilton had this to say about his marching orders:

'Within twenty four hours I must hand over a command

three times larger than the British Expeditionary Force; receive my instructions; select a staff; get the hang of the Dardanelles and of the nature and whereabouts of my new force and bundle off. Equally serious was the fact that there was no time to get my staff together. I had to start without any of my administrative officers, whether for supply, medicine or discipline. They were not destined to join me for more than three weeks. Until they came I and my small group of General Staff officers had to undertake their work, including matters so remote from our experience as unloading and reloading ships and making arrangements for the wounded.'

Throughout March and April heavy naval guns hammered the Turkish forts and defence lines. And on 25 April the first landings were made. The conditions were appalling. The beaches were yawning death-traps. By the time the troops were able to secure a foothold they were too exhausted to move forward. Then while they rested and regrouped to build up their strength, enemy reinforcements were free to move up to counter them. Almost everything favoured the enemy. They knew the area and they had ample water supplies. So they simply dug in and held the Allies at bay.

For over three months the Allied forces remained pinned down, suffering in the furnace-like heat. Then in an attempt to break the deadlock fresh landings were made in August. One of these took place at Suvla Bay. And among the troops landed there were officers and men of the Norfolk Regiment. This is the Regiment that is alleged to have suffered the paranormal kidnapping.

John Keel says of it: 'the one Fourth Norfolk Regiment marched into a "peculiar brown cloud that hugged the ground in their path." The cloud rose up, joined a group of similar clouds and sailed off against the wind! And the regiment had vanished – eight hundred men gone – or taken – from the face of the earth!' (*Our Haunted Planet*)

Robin Collyns tells a similar story and suggests that the abduction could have been the work of a giant spaceship, while Otto O. Binder 'the renowned UFO and space expert', puts forward the view that the regiment was kidnapped by a long cigar-shaped UFO surrounded by mysterious mists.

REGIMENT OF THE DAMNED?

The story crops up in books by many other writers. There are discrepancies in the numbers of troops involved. The numbers vary from eight hundred down to two hundred and fifty. But all the writers agree on one thing, that the event was witnessed by twenty two soldiers of the New Zealand forces. Few of them take the trouble to quote the exact statements made by these New Zealanders. One writer who does quote the eye-witnesses is Charles Berlitz, one of the *Bermuda Triangle* merchants. The first thing to take note of is that twenty two men did not make statements or even agree to a single statement. The whole story rests on one statement only, drafted by one man, ex-sapper F. Reichardt, and countersigned by two of his former comrades who claimed that they were witnesses as well.

As quoted by Berlitz, Reichardt's document reads: 'The following is an account of a strange incident that happened ... in the morning, during the severest and final days of the fighting which took place at Hill 60, Suvla Bay ...

'The day broke clear, without a cloud in sight, as any beautiful Mediterranean day could be expected to be. The exception, however, was a number of perhaps six or eight "loaf of bread" shaped clouds – all shaped exactly alike – which were hovering over Hill 60. It was noticed that in spite of a four- or five-mile-an-hour breeze from the south, these clouds did not alter their position in any shape or form, nor did they drift away under the influence of the breeze. They were hovering at an elevation of about sixty degrees as seen from our observation point five hundred feet up. Also stationary and resting on the ground right underneath this group of clouds was a similar cloud in shape, measuring about eight hundred feet in length, two hundred feet in height and two hundred feet in width. This cloud was absolutely dense, almost solid-looking in structure, and positioned about fourteen to eighteen chains from the fighting in British-held territory. All this was observed by twenty two men of No. 3 Section of No. 1 Field Company, N.Z.E., including myself, from our trenches on Rhododendron Spur, approximately two thousand five hundred yards south west of the cloud on the ground. Our vantage point was overlooking Hill 60 by about three hundred feet. As it turned out later, this singular cloud was straddling a dry creek bed or sunken road (Kaiajik Dere) and we had a perfect view of the cloud's sides and ends as it rested on the ground. Its colour was a light grey, as was the colour of the other clouds.

'A British Regiment, the First Fourth Norfolk, of several hundred men, was then noticed marching up this sunken road or creek towards Hill 60. It appeared as though they were going to reinforce the troops at Hill 60. However, when they arrived at this cloud, they marched straight into it, with no hesitation, but no one ever came out to deploy and fight at Hill 60. About an hour later, after the last of the file had disappeared into it, this cloud very unobtrusively lifted off the ground and, like any fog or cloud would, rose slowly until it joined the other similar clouds ... On viewing them again, they all looked alike as peas in a pod. All this time, the groups of clouds had been hovering in the same place, but as soon as the singular ground cloud had risen to their level, they all moved away northwards, i.e. towards Thrace (Bulgaria). In a matter of about three quarters of an hour they had all disappeared from view.

'The Regiment mentioned is posted as missing or wiped out, and on Turkey surrendering in 1918 the first thing Britain demanded of Turkey was the return of this regiment. Turkey replied that she had neither captured this Regiment, nor made contact with it, and did not know that it existed. A British Regiment in 1914–18 consisted of any number between eight hundred and four thousand men. Those who observed this incident vouch for the fact that Turkey never captured that Regiment, nor made contact with it.'

That, then, is the only first-hand testimony to an event which is said to have happened on 21 August 1915. What you should know about it, though, is that this testimony is suspicious from the start. This statement as quoted by Charles Berlitz in his *Without Trace* is incomplete. A vital sentence has been left out. That missing sentence shows that this so-called evidence was not written down until 1965 – fifty years after the paranormal exit!

But could it still be true despite that suspicious fifty-year gap? Writer Brad Steiger certainly thinks so. He labels it 'one of the most horrifying incidents ever recorded' and cites 'official records' to support his view.

He writes: 'The official record books on the Dardanelles campaign state: "They (the First Fourth Norfolk Regiment) were swallowed up by an unseasonable fog. This fog reflected the sun's rays in such a manner that artillery observers were dazzled by its brilliance and were unable to fire in support. The two hundred and fifty men were never seen or heard of again."'

Having produced his evidence Steiger then sarcastically comments: 'An "unseasonable fog" capable of snatching up two hundred and fifty British soldiers certainly makes the most noxious of our industrialised smog clouds seem extremely feeble in comparison. How do the authorities explain such a disappearance with any degree of satisfaction to the survivors of those who vanish into fog clouds?'

Yet all this talk about official confirmation is nothing but bluster. There is not the remotest possibility of the testimony being true. In the first place, the First Fourth Norfolks was not a regiment, it was simply one battalion within the Norfolk regiment itself. What is more, it did not disappear on Turkish soil, or anywhere else, but went on fighting right up until the end of the Great War.

It is true, though, that a minor disaster did hit part of the Fifth Battalion of the Norfolks. The Fifth Norfolks were included in the 163rd Brigade which set out to occupy the strategically important heights of Kavak Tepe and Tekke Tepe. These were commanding heights to the east of Suvla Bay. And the original plan was to seize them before the Turkish reinforcements could arrive and entrench on their summits.

The action began on 12 August and the Fifth Norfolks were ordered forward at 4.45 p.m. together with the rest of the 163rd. Optimistically, they intended to clear the way through the jungly tree-covered ground at the foot of the mountains. But they met with tenacious opposition and the enemy fire grew heavier and more deadly.

When the Brigade reached the farm called Anafarta Ova, the Fifth Norfolks found themselves ahead of the rest of the force. Then occurred a galling setback that prompted the famous dispatch from General Hamilton.

In full it reads: 'In the course of the fight, creditable in all respects to the 163rd Brigade, there happened to be a very mysterious thing. The 1/5 Norfolks were on the right of the line, and found themselves for a moment less strongly opposed than the rest of the brigade. Against the yielding forces of the enemy Colonel Sir H. Beauchamp, a bold, self-confident officer, eagerly pressed forward, followed by the best part of the battalion. The fighting grew hotter and the ground became wooded and broken. At this stage many men were wounded or grew exhausted with thirst. They found their way back to camp during the night. But the Colonel, with sixteen officers and two hundred and fifty men, still kept pushing on, driving the enemy before him. Among these ardent souls was part of a fine company enlisted from the King's Sandringham estates. Nothing more was ever seen or heard of any of them. They charged into the forest and were lost to sight or sound. Not one of them ever came back.'

General Hamilton's somewhat mystical streak led him to colour his words a little too garishly. Others at the time were much more realistic. War correspondent H. W. Nevinson wrote of the Norfolks: 'One cannot doubt that their bones lie among the trees and bushes at the foot of that dark and ominous hill and the last real hope of Suvla Bay faded with their tragic disappearance.'

Nevinson gave his opinion in 1918 and sure enough, a year later, corpses of the missing Norfolks were uncovered. They had been tossed into a ravine by a local farmer who had found the bodies scattered on various parts of his land. It is true that only one hundred and twenty two bodies were those of the Norfolks. But one hundred and twenty two is still a large enough number to demolish the idea of a mass disappearance. And there is little mystery about the bodies that were not located. Under the atrocious conditions of that campaign it was more than easy for bodies to vanish without trace. One only has to think of the prowling animals, the natural crevasses, the countless shell-holes and the dense forests of the battle area to realise how. Apart from that, any Norfolks captured and imprisoned stood little chance of surviving, especially if

Regiment Of The Damned?

they were wounded. The Turkish prison camps were hellish. The Turkish regard for prisoners was non-existent. The treatment of the prisoners taken at Kut proves this. Nearly five thousand prisoners captured at Kut died in Turkish hands, since the dull brutality of the Turks, who treated their own soldiers like dogs, had no mercy for sick or starving prisoners.

So the undisputed real-life disaster that overtook the Norfolks had no supernormal or extra-terrestrial features. In that case, what on earth prompted the strange tale that surfaced in 1965? Well, the date given for this claimed event provides the essential clue. For on 21 August 1915 another set of odd circumstances surrounded a further large-scale action by the Allied Forces.

On that day the scheme of attack involved a series of advances aimed at securing control of Scimitar Hill and Hill 60. The master plan was wrecked by a perfectly normal but dense out-of-season mist. As Sir Ian Hamilton reported: 'By some freak of nature Suvla Bay and the plain were wrapped in a strange mist on the afternoon of 21 August. This was sheer bad luck, as we had reckoned on the enemy's gunners being blinded by the declining sun and upon the Turkish trenches being shown up by the evening light with singular clearness, as would have been the case on ninety nine days out of a hundred. Actually we could hardly see the enemy's line this afternoon, whereas out to the westward targets stood out in strong relief against the luminous mist. I wished to postpone the attack, but for various reasons this was not possible . . .'

Tragically, the attack went ahead with the basic strategy unaltered. And the brigades of the 29th Division, supported by the Yeomanry, drove forward against the Turkish defences. Shell fire threw up plumes of smoke and dust that thickened the mist. Then raging bush fires added thick, acrid black clouds of smoke and smut. The Allied troops found themselves half-blinded and when they attacked Scimitar Hill they were easy targets for the Turks, who were in elevated strongholds to the north and south west. As a result the British were cut to pieces by sustained and vicious cross-fire from the enemy's rifles and field guns.

When I first researched this story I drew the provisional

conclusion that the three New Zealanders had talked over old times and quite innocently confused two different military actions. The thick, unexpected mist that hit the 87th Brigade on 21 August was remembered as if it was the cause of the Norfolks' disaster nine days earlier. In combining the two separate events their final tale became shaped along the lines of the flying saucer mysteries that were becoming popular in the 1960s.

In short, I believed it to be a comparatively recent confusion. Then in 1982, Frederick Reichardt's son wrote a letter to *The Unexplained* which said: 'The statement, I can assure you, was made by him throughout his life, from the earliest days I can remember (I was born in 1932).

'Because of this the story was not written down until the reunion on the fiftieth anniversary of the landing, when he came in contact with the other witnesses – for the first time, I believe, since the First World War ... I have written this for the sake of an old man who, when he died at the age of 84 years, still firmly believed in what he saw.

Signed, W. A. Reichardt.'

This nullified the idea (put forward by Paul Begg) that Reichardt had possibly picked up information from the *Final Report of the Dardanelles Commission* (edition of 1965). As a supposition it was, in any case, unnecessary and unlikely as we shall see.

For all the pleading by Reichardt's son, the odour of fakery and manipulation hangs thickly around his father's story. In the first instance, the quote from official documents advanced by Steiger and others is a forgery. It will not be found in any legitimate government document. When it is analysed it can be shown to be a parody of some of the words used by General Hamilton on two distinctly separate occasions. The opening sentence – 'They (the First Fourth Norfolk) were swallowed up by an unseasonable fog' – is based on Hamilton's report of 21 August, with the regiment name filled in. The second sentence again refers to 21 August, but the final sentence – 'The two hundred and fifty men were never seen or heard of again' – is based on the dispatch of 12 August.

Secondly, Mr I. C. McGibbon, former historian at the New

Zealand Ministry of Defence, has taken a special interest in this matter and made his own investigation of the people involved. In 1982, he wrote: 'Information that has recently come to light in New Zealand throws further doubt on the "sighting." Newnes, one of the alleged witnesses, turns out to have been a trooper in the Auckland Mounted Rifles rather than a sapper in the New Zealand Field Engineers. A person who forgets which unit and arm of service he was in can hardly be regarded as a reliable witness. Neither Newnes nor Newman ... was on Gallipoli at the time given in the original statement – "in the morning" of 28 August 1915. (The date originally published in the New Zealand UFO magazine *Spaceview*.) Both were evacuated because of illness – Newman on 5 August and Newnes on 21 August. These facts, drawn from their service records at the New Zealand Ministry of Defence, immediately throws serious doubts on the authority of the statement.'

The intrusion of an extra date of 28 August can be dismissed without much problem, since Reichardt's story refers unmistakably in its substance to 21 August. This view holds good even though McGibbon's research shows that Reichardt was not present on Rhododendron Spur on the 21st. But McGibbon throws extra light on my original idea that the story had been influenced by the UFO craze. He writes: 'Reichardt had attended a public meeting in Rotorua to discuss UFOs early in 1965. Following the meeting he approached Gordon Tuckey and "intimated that he had a story of his own to tell." A meeting was subsequently arranged at a private house and Reichardt recounted his story. He refused to allow a tape recording to be made, but some weeks afterwards provided a written statement. "It was in his own handwriting," recalled Tuckey, "and was signed by himself and the two other alleged witnesses." Tuckey never met the latter. Reichardt had obviously seen them at the fiftieth jubilee of the ANZAC landing, which took place at Rotorua between 24 and 26 April 1965. (Signing the statement would have been one of Newman's last acts, for he died on the 26th!)'

McGibbon then gives his own view of the birth of Reichardt's story. It is a view that corresponds so closely with the view I had reached in 1978 that it is worth quoting:

'It seems most unlikely that such a visually striking cloud formation could have been present all day – Reichardt implies that it was visible at daybreak – without attracting widespread attention from the thousands of men in the vicinity. The fact that a mere three "witnesses" have so far belatedly come forward suggests that few saw the clouds.

'My own conclusion is that Reichardt's memory had become confused. I believe that he may have seen a unit march into a patch of ground mist at some stage of his service at Gallipoli and that the men of the unit may have taken cover – perhaps, viewed from a distance, given the illusion of having disappeared.

'Probably he heard accounts subsequently of the battle on 21 August, in which several battalions in the Suvla Bay area lost their direction and inclined too far to the north. He may have heard rumours of the disappearance of the Norfolks and later read accounts of the "lost battalion." As time passed he may have convinced himself that he had witnessed the mysterious event described in the dispatch sent by Sir Ian Hamilton . . .

'This explanation is given added weight by the importance Reichardt attached to the account of the incident, along with two earlier "disappearances", that he claimed to have seen "in one of the official histories of the Gallipolli campaign." No official history recounting such events can be located.

'More probably, Reichardt saw accounts of them in some popular book dealing with unidentified flying objects or military mysteries and mistakenly decided that they were authoritative accounts. He was not a well-read man . . . and possibly fell a victim to one of the more sensational descriptions of the loss of the First Fifth Norfolks . . .'

There were indeed plenty of chances for Reichardt to pick up sensational treatments of the Fifth Norfolks' disappearance. It was one of the events that constantly cropped up in the many popular histories of the Great War that were churned off the presses between 1918 and 1940. For example the story occurs in *Deeds That Thrill The Empire*, the popular series published by Hutchinson; and *Twenty Years After*, another immensely popular series. An extract from *Twenty Years After* will give a good idea of the graphic and sensational treatment employed.

Of the action of the 21st, it says: 'No one knew exactly what the position was, where the enemy were, or how far their own comrades had got. Nevertheless they plunged into the din of battle and the clouds of mist and smoke and fire that veiled the field. Stumbling blindly forward, they too reached Scimitar Hill, and a gallant handful pushed on beyond and were never heard of more.'

In the end it all boils down to a synthetic mystery created by the muddled mind of one old Anzac veteran. A man charismatic enough to have successfully carried two other old-timers along with him in his fantasy. I do not think we should blame these old soldiers too much, though. Memories can play exceedingly strange tricks. Just try thinking back over the years and you will be surprised how hazy and muddled the past can seem. And these men, remember, were thinking back over half a century to a time of enormous stress, anguish and confusion. So they can be excused. But how can we excuse the many writers who have made capital out of this tale?

Chapter Ten

THE ANGELS WITH NEWSPAPER WINGS

Did God take sides in the Great War of 1914? Did flights of angels wing their way over the Belgian landscape? Were miracles wrought among the blood-drenched battlefields of Flanders?

It was in Flanders that the first major battle of the war was fought. And there, at Mons, the British troops held back a numerically superior German force and fought with an amazing ferocity. But in the end the pressure of numbers became too great and in order to avoid being trapped the British were instructed to make an orderly withdrawal. And they did this successfully, even though they suffered heavy losses.

Now there were two main reasons for their success. In the first place there was the devastating marksmanship of the riflemen. In fact their rapid-fire techniques were so spectacular that at times the Germans imagined they were facing machine-gunners! Secondly, every soldier carried a special entrenching tool in his haversack. With this tool, protective ramparts of earth could be thrown up in minutes. Thus even in exposed places the troops could shield themselves and then fight back. So there was nothing in any way uncanny about the whole episode. The uncanny explanation only crept in later.

It began with a short story by Arthur Machen called *The Bowmen*. This was printed in the afternoon and evening editions of the London *Evening News* on 29 September 1914, and it proved to be the most influential piece that Machen ever wrote. Here is a brief outline of it.

It opens with the description of a large-scale retreat of the British Expeditionary Force. Then in the heat of battle one of the soldiers remembers a restaurant he used to visit. He recalls the blue and white plates with their pictures of St George. And he shouts out the motto that ran round the edge of the plates: 'Adsit Anglis Sanctus Georgius' – St George Help the English.

Suddenly the battlefield is shaken as thousands of voices call out the name of St George. And there facing the Germans stands a long shining line of Agincourt archers. Then the air is dark with arrows which cut down the advancing enemy troops ... the day is saved! Ten thousand dead Germans lie scattered on the battlefield, but not one of them bears a single wound!

Now that tale wasn't one of Machen's best. And he, for one, thought it would soon be forgotten. But within a few days Machen received letters from the editors of *The Occult Review* and the magazine *Light*. And they asked whether the tale had any foundation in fact. They were naturally told that it was just a piece of imaginative writing.

Then in the following months various parish magazines wrote in for permission to reprint the story. And the editor of the *Evening News* said yes to every one of them. He had no idea that the story was already being misused.

But one of these magazines ran out of copies, so the vicar wrote direct to Machen and said that he would like to re-issue *The Bowmen* as a pamphlet. And he asked Machen to write a short introduction, giving the exact authorities for the story. Machen wrote back to say that there were no authorities, since the story was pure invention. But the vicar refused to believe him and insisted that the story must be true. It was then that Machen realised that he had 'succeeded unwittingly in the art of deceit.'

Very soon variations of the tale were being told as established fact. But all the stories were clearly traceable back to Machen's flight of fancy.

Take the version published by the Roman Catholic paper *The Universe* in its issue of 30 April 1915. This was a second-hand account said to be based on a letter from 'a Catholic officer from the Front.' This letter claimed that: 'A party of about thirty men and an officer was cut off in a trench when the officer said to his men: "Look here – we must either stay here and be caught like rats in a trap, or make a sortie against the enemy" ... The men all agreed with him, and with a yell of "St George for England!" they dashed out in the open. The officer tells how as they ran on he became aware of a large company of men with bows and arrows going along with them, and even leading them on against the enemy's trenches ... Afterwards when he was talking to a German prisoner, the man asked him who was the officer on the great white horse who led them? For although he was such a conspicuous figure, they had none of them been able to hit him. I must also add that the German dead appeared to have no wounds on them ...'

The Protestant version was just as colourful. As told by the Rev. Fielding Ould of St Albans, it ran: 'A sergeant in our army had frequented a house of the Young Men's Christian Association and had seen there a picture of St George slaying the dragon. He had been deeply impressed by it, and when at the front he found himself in an advanced and rather isolated trench, he told the story of St George to his men ... When shortly afterwards a sudden charge of the grey-coated Germans in greatly superior numbers threatened the sergeant's trench, he cried: "Remember St George for England!" to his men as they advanced to meet the foe. A few moments afterward the enemy hesitated, stopped and finally fled, leaving some prisoners in our hands. One of the latter seemed dazed and astonished and demanded to be told who were the horsemen in armour who led the charge. Surely they could not have been Belgians dressed in such a way!'

Even the spiritualists had their own variation! Miss Callow, Secretary of the Higher Thought Centre in Kensington, wrote to *The Weekly Despatch* to say: 'An officer has sent ... a detailed account of a vision that appeared to himself and others when fighting against fearful odds at Mons.

'He plainly saw an apparition representing St George the patron saint of England, the exact counterpart of a picture that hangs today in a London restaurant. So terrible was their plight at the time that the officer could not refrain from appealing to the vision to help them. Then, as if the enemy had also seen the apparition, the Germans abandoned their positions in precipitate terror.'

After a while, though, some people grew unhappy with the bowmen. Perhaps they were too militant and too secular for comfort. So a transmutation began, and the shining archers were turned into shining angels. Winged creatures who intervened not aggressively, but in an awe-inspiring fashion! A poem, After Mons, published in *Light* (15 May 1915) seems to mark this shift of emphasis. Its second verse read:

> 'You saw, O friend, the forms, the light, the sheen?
> Our foes, their horses, saw; they turned and fled,
> As troops of silent angels filed between
> Our broken ranks and theirs, and stilled our dread.'

And so the bowmen were pushed into the background. The angels proved much more reassuring and acceptable. Even so, people were reluctant to give up all the glamour of Machen's tale and St George managed to survive in many of the yarns that untiringly circulated.

From July 1915, angels were in season with a vengeance. Sheaves of articles appeared in the Press. So did a mass of heated correspondence. Many clergymen preached sermons using the angels as the central theme. Even Machen was swept up in the fervour. He was pressed to issue *The Bowmen* in book form, tying it in with some extra stories of 'Legends of the War' – and he obliged.

He delivered three more fantastic pieces, one of which was again taken as true. But the best part of his slim book was the twenty four pages he used to explain how and why the legend had become confused with fact.

The Bowmen And Other Legends became a best-seller – three thousand copies a day were snapped up and it was translated into six languages. But this did little to dampen people's ardour for the angelic myth. For suddenly the public was overwhelmed by 'testimony and evidence' in favour of the angels. Late in the day certainly, but there it was, in glorious believable print!

First in the field was Ralph Shirley, Editor of *The Occult Review*. His pamphlet *The Angel Warriors at Mons* claimed to be 'an authentic record' including 'numerous confirmatory testimonies'. Then the Rev Herbert Wood of Liverpool issued his *Wonderful Works of God* which recounted visions of angels. Other reverend gentlemen followed suit.

After that, Harold Begbie intervened. He was an extremely popular writer of the time. He was also an ardent patriot. And he felt the story was inspiring and had to be defended. So he waded in with a book entitled *On The Side Of The Angels*, the weightiest defence of all.

Begbie was furious with Machen's attempt to set the record straight. He even suggested that Machen may have picked up information about the angels direct from the battlefields by telepathy! But telepathy apart, both *The Occult Review* and Harold Begbie relied heavily on the statements of a young girl, Nurse Phyllis Campbell.

This Miss Campbell was an extraordinary figure with an extraordinary batch of tales to tell. But they can wait for a while. First let us consider the fate of the other impressive testifiers.

One of the widely quoted testimonies was that of Miss Marrable, daughter of the well-known Canon Marrable. The copy distributed by the Rev M.P. Gillson read: 'Last Sunday I met Miss Marrable and she told me she knew two officers both of whom had seen the angels who saved their left wing from the Germans when they came right upon them during our retreat from Mons. They expected annihilation ... when to their amazement the Germans stood like dazed men, never so much as touched their guns nor stirred until we had turned round and escaped ...

'The other man she met in London and asked him if he had heard the wonderful story of the angels. He answered that he had seen them himself while he and his company were retreating. They heard the German cavalry tearing after them. They had made for a place ... of safety, but before they could reach it the German cavalry were upon them. So they turned round to face the enemy expecting instant death when, to their wonder, they saw between them and the enemy a whole troop of angels, and the horses of the Germans turned round terrified out of their senses and regularly stampeded, and tore away in all directions from our men ... this gave them time to save themselves.'

This testimony convinced thousands. For here were the considered words of a lady of quality from a committed Christian family. Small wonder then that her statements were used by the Rev. R.F. Horton in a famous sermon, often reprinted, and understandable that her claims were embodied in parish magazines, religious pamphlets and Harold Begbie's book.

Just as convincing was the testimony of Private 10515 Cleaver of the 1st Cheshire Regiment. He asserted that supernatural intervention had indeed saved the British troops from annihilation. And there was no questioning this, for he had been at Mons himself and seen the vision of angels. What is more, he swore out an affidavit to this effect before George S. Hazelhurst, a Justice of the Peace, of the County of Flint.

This sworn and confident statement was seized on by the Press – 'striking confirmation', *Light* called it. And Begbie agreed and triumphantly flourished it in his book. But his triumph was to prove short-lived.

Unfortunately for all concerned Magistrate George Hazelhurst picked up some rumours concerning Private Cleaver. This led to enquiries at the headquarters of the Cheshires. And there the Major in charge of records turned up details showing that Cleaver had in fact been in England during the Battle of Mons and the subsequent retreat! Hazelhurst broke the news in a crestfallen letter to the *Daily Mail*. And he ended with the sad plea: 'Will none of the officers who were at Mons and saw the angels of whom Miss Marrable speaks come forward and confess it?'

His plea was never to be answered, and Miss Marrable herself explained why. In a letter to the *Evening News* she revealed that she knew nothing at all about any supernatural episodes during the retreat from Mons. Those stories, using her good name, were nothing but fabrications!

Despite these exposures 'Miss Marrable's Testimony' continued to circulate, often with her name left out. And Private Cleaver's lying affidavit was still being reprinted eight months after it was discredited. But in September 1915 such exposures made Begbie's 'powerful defence' look somewhat dubious.

It is true that he still had other testimonies, but most were third, fourth and even sixth-hand statements. A number of them were patently absurd. And most led back to witnesses who were untraceable. In truth, he was left with only one body of evidence worth considering – those impressive statements of Nurse Phyllis Campbell as featured in *The Occult Review*.

Now Miss Campbell was no ordinary nurse. She was highly articulate. Her mother was a novelist while her aunt was Lady Archibald Campbell, also a writer. So she came from an imaginative family.

When the slaughter began Miss Campbell was living in France. She immediately volunteered as a nurse, took a crash course, then worked at a dressing station at one of the railway halts in the forest of Marley. And there she met the men who had 'met the angels.'

There was the Lancashire Fusilier who had seen St George on horseback leading the British. There was the Royal Field Artilleryman who declared: 'It's true, Sister ... we all saw it ... a tall man in golden armour on a white horse, holding his sword up ... Then before you could say "knife" the Germans had turned and we were after them ... We had a few scores to settle and we fairly settled them.'

Then there were the two officers and three men of the Irish Guards who told her roughly the same story.

So Phyllis Campbell presented testimony that differed markedly from that offered by everyone else. In truth, she seemed to know more about the angels than anyone else anywhere! She even added to her claims by asserting that the French soldiers had seen Joan of Arc. Said one: 'I know her well, for I am of Domremy. I saw her brandishing her sword and crying, "Turn! Turn! Advance!" ... No wonder the Boche fled down the hill.'

And remarkably other Frenchmen had seen St Michael on horseback flourishing his sword and shouting 'Victory!'

Her remarkable knowledge did not end there. To crown it all she further stated that St Michael had also appeared frequently during the battles on the Russian front. Her Russian knowledge naturally came from the very best of sources – from a letter 'received by her friends in France before 14 September 1914' and written by, of all people, a Russian princess!

Clearly this Miss Campbell is the key figure in this whole affair and deserves very close scrutiny. Such a scrutiny shows that she was no stranger to occult fancies. Her influential aunt, Lady Archibald Campbell, turns out to have been a noted clairvoyant and medium who believed in fairies, while young Phyllis herself had written two articles on French ghost stories (under the name Phil Campbell) for *The Occult Review* just before the war. So she had a lively imagination fired by psychic teachings.

She also had a very strange view of evidence. When challenged by Arthur Machen to produce first-hand confirmations she countered by saying that the troops were forbidden to talk about the events, which was an outright lie. Then she fielded the following quote as proof. It was part of a young officer's letter: 'I had the most amazing hallucinations marching at night so I was fast asleep, I think. Everyone was reeling about the road and seeing things too, they said ... marched on for the rest of the night ... most tiring; I again saw all sorts of things, enormous men walking towards me, and lights and chairs and things in the road.'

And that passage from Mabel Collins' *The Crucible* was, in Miss Campbell's view, one in the eye for Machen! Yet if anything it showed the real weakness of her case. When put to the test she offered nothing but a letter which describes the hallucinations suffered by battle-fatigued soldiers. Such visions were common on forced marches on many fronts.

Simply contrast that letter with the following. It is a report from the South West Africa Campaign of 1915: 'The fatigue became awful. I began to get lightheaded. The sky seemed to become a straight wall in front of us, and the effect of the moonlight through the dust made me imagine I saw great palaces and churches, with the stars as little windows. Then I would pull myself together and look at the men riding in front, and they would turn into funny old giantesses dancing in the moonlight. I learnt afterwards that everyone suffered from these hallucinations.' (*A Great Soldier of the Empire* by Keith Morris, 1915, page 52.)

In clashing with Machen, Miss Campbell escaped the drubbing she had invited. For Machen was hampered by his chivalrous outlook and he held back. So she continued to shine as the leading light among the 'Divine Interventionists'. Indeed she promised that 'evidence exists ... and when the war is over and when the embargo of silence is removed, Mr Machen will be overwhelmed with corroborative evidence.' Having said that, Miss Campbell apparently changed her mind. For there was talk of a book written by her, one which would provide all the answers.

That particular book never appeared, not even after the war. But another book of hers came out called *Back of the Front* and it proves to be a revelation. It gives dramatic insight into her mind. It shows that she was driven by a fanatical type of patriotism. And this led her to accept and repeat every atrocity story that came her way. At no time did she bother to check the truth or otherwise of these tales. What is more, for every atrocity tale that circulated Miss Campbell had one better. She actually claimed to have seen these atrocities for herself!

The atrocity-mongers had shrieked that Belgian women were having their breasts cut off by the Huns. Miss Campbell confirmed this by writing: 'In one wagon, sitting on the floor, was a naked girl of about twenty three. One of her suffering sisters, more fortunate than the rest in possessing an undergarment, had torn it in half and covered the front of her poor body. It was saturated with blood from her cut-off breasts. On her knees lay a little baby, dead.'

Then it was said that the Huns cut off the hands and feet of children, tortured women, burned people alive and impaled and crucified civilians, including priests. Phyllis Campbell 'knew all this to be true.'

In one railway wagon she saw 'women covered with sabre cuts, women who had been whipped, women burned alive escaping from their blazing homes, little boys maimed in the hands and feet ...'

And she further catalogued the horrors of 'priests impaled,

of little children done to death in such ways that they cannot be spoken of ... of crucified sons and fathers.'

Her warped patriotism even led her to write of 'the utter depravity of the German soul ... It seemed to me that all the wickedness, all the fear and filthiness imaginable that exists can be summed up in one word: GERMAN.'

She was so certain of this that she was drawn to an inevitable conclusion: 'When I saw the German prisoners ... when they stood blinking in the sun with their square heads and putty-coloured faces, their colourless eyes and lashes, it suggested to me a creation of some monstrous spirit of evil. Is it strange that saints and angels should fight against this dreadful foe? I have seen no vision, but in my heart I believe that the Captains of God are leading the Allies to victory.'

And there you have a glimpse of Miss Campbell's secret. The Hun was so loathsome that anything could be used as a weapon against him, even lies. Used in a good cause – perhaps the greatest of all good causes – lies, rumours, half-truths and myths could stiffen people's resolve, could make them that much more determined to stamp out the 'monstrous spirit of evil.'

At the time, of course, no one dared openly call her a liar. The lady was too well-placed. In addition, she was a disarming, beguiling creature. She was described as 'extremely pretty, child-like and sensitive.' But it was also noted that 'she seems to possess extraordinary powers of self control and endurance.'

Another factor that stilled people's tongues was her record of devotion in the military hospitals. Yet, logically considered, her conduct as a nurse is wholly irrelevant. It may have helped confuse the issues at the time but it has no bearing on the accuracy of her statements.

On the other hand, we have firm evidence from the First World War that some sweet young ladies and nurses were guilty of inventing the most incredible tales. Just consider two examples.

On 16 September 1914, *The Star* reported the murder of Nurse Grace Hume from Dumfries, Scotland. Her hospital at Vilvorde in Belgium had been overrun by the Germans. She had been mutilated by two soldiers who had sadistically cut off her breasts. Before dying she had scrawled a last note to her sister Kate and slipped it to a friend, Nurse Mullard. Luckily the Allies then liberated the remaining nurses and faithful Nurse Mullard made a pilgrimage to Dumfries to break the news.

Seven leading newspapers took up this grim story and the public was rightly enraged – but not for long. Within a few days it was found that Nurse Hume was living happily and in one piece in Huddersfield! She had certainly volunteered for service at the front but had never been called on. She had never even set foot in Belgium!

Following this her sister Kate stood trial and it was proved that she had fabricated the whole story. The published letters from her sister and from 'Nurse Mullard' were nothing but forgeries from her own fair hand.

Later on ex-Nurse Catto came up with another batch of horrors. She claimed to have actually nursed mutilated Belgians – children with their hands cut off, women with their breasts cut off. She even named the hospital as Ramsgate General. But an investigation at that hospital showed there was not a word of truth in her story.

Now those cases merely serve to restore a correct perspective. For the proof of Miss Campbell's duplicity cannot be established by analogy. To prove this we need to contrast competent accounts by people who lived through the retreat from Mons. Fortunately there is no shortage of these.

Just two accounts, though, will be sufficient. Accounts by men who were ministers of religion working as army chaplains. Men who would have welcomed news of angelic aid had it been forthcoming.

The first writings to consider are those of Abbé Felix Klein, a French Army Chaplain attached to the Ambulance Division of the American Hospital at Neuilly north-east of Paris. He writes that he: 'was privileged to go forth to gather in the wounded from the very front ... We went forth to it in the morning and came back from it in the evening ... The wounded, brought back from them (the battlefields) after twenty four or forty eight hours, retain an only too lively impression of them.'

The Angels With Newspaper Wings

From 3 August to 28 December 1914 Abbé Klein kept a lengthy diary. In it he recorded the views and 'lively impressions' of the troops and details of the campaigns as they came in, including significant rumours. He even notes the famous rumour about Russian troops coming to the aid of the British Expeditionary Force. But nowhere does he mention any talk or rumours of divine intervention in the battles.

This is telling since Nurse Campbell endorsed *The Occult Review*'s claim that: 'no French paper would have made itself ridiculous by disputing the authenticity of what was vouched for by many thousands of independent eye-witnesses... Whole battalions of French soldiers had seen apparitions of Joan of Arc... and St Michael.'

Yet Abbé Klein, in daily touch with the troops during and after the retreat, had clearly never heard of any such talk from any quarter. And his diary, *La Guerre Vue d'Une Ambulance* (published January 1915), recorded events as they happened. *The Occult Review*, by contrast, spoke of events over a year after they were alleged to have happened. And it failed to produce a single verifiable statement from any of the 'many thousands.'

The second significant record was kept by the British Chaplain Owen Spencer Watkins. He was attached to the 14th Field Ambulance with the British Expeditionary Force. He was at Mons, took part in the retreat and his account was published in March 1915 (*With Field Marshall French in France and Flanders*). It is a book rich in detail but without any mention whatsoever of the angels, either as realities or even rumours.

So was it all imagination run riot? A great mythical tapestry woven from threads of hope, anguish and blind patriotism? No – there was much more to it than that! More even than Machen's crucial story. For behind the angels myth lay an even greater myth. One created by the Government itself in the interests of recruiting.

This Government myth went into print on Sunday 30 August 1914 in a special Sunday edition of *The Times*. Basically it was a heart-rending despatch from Arthur Moore in France. It was headlined Fiercest Fight in History. It opened with the poignant words 'This is a pitiful story I have to write.

Would to God it did not fall to me to write it.' The body of the story spoke of 'very great losses' – of 'a retreating broken army' – of German troops so numerous 'that they could no more be stopped than the waves of the sea.' These were words that shocked the nation.

Now normally such a despairing piece would have been slashed to pieces by the official censor. But this despatch was passed with the full approval of officialdom. You see, the Director of the Press Bureau recognised that Arthur Moore had been swept away by fierce emotions. His piece was a misinterpretation based on muddled, incomplete information, exaggerations and misunderstandings. The Government itself knew far better. Things were nowhere near as bad as the despatch made out. And losses were by no means as great as imagined. Yet there was an awareness that fresh recruits were urgently needed. And the public deserved to be sharply shaken out of its complacency. So this sincere but misleading despatch was waved through with blessings!

More than that, it was furnished with a new ending written by F. E. Smith, Director of the Government Press Bureau. This read: 'England should realise, and should realise at once, that she must send reinforcements, and still send them. Is an army of exhaustless valour to be borne down by sheer weight of numbers, while young Englishmen at home play golf and cricket? We want men and we want them now.'

The ploy worked. Britain stiffened its backbone and the recruits poured in. But from then on the myth of the Battle of Mons as the clash that saved civilization grew in stature, while the contributions of the French and Belgians were overshadowed and under-valued.

This dramatic despatch inspired two trains of thought that led directly to the angels legend. For Machen's *Bowmen* was written after he was moved by the anguished words of Arthur Moore. And people at large began to reason that if the British had escaped from such an enormous force, then it was nothing short of a miraculous event. From then on nothing could stop the gradual growth of speculation and fantasy.

In short, there was a desperate need to believe in the rightness of the Allied cause. And divine intervention was surely the ultimate proof of such rightness. As the *Christian Commonwealth* observed, proof of angelic aid 'would strengthen religious faith, which has been greatly weakened by the war, and would reinforce belief in the justice of the cause for which so many men fell during that magnificent retreat and almost miraculous recovery on the banks of the Marne.'

In the years after the war, as the real events at Mons became forgotten, people grew even more reckless. It became easy to find 'witnesses' who had claimed to have seen those angels. And many inventive yarns were spun about their doings. But it was very different in 1915, at a time when these events were supposed to have been 'vouched for by many thousands.'

As Machen pointed out in August of that year: 'It has been claimed that "everybody" who fought from Mons to Ypres saw the apparitions. If that be so, it is odd that nobody has come forward to testify at first hand to the most amazing event of his life. Many men have been back from the front, we have many wounded in hospital, many soldiers have written home. And they have all combined, this great host, to keep silence about the most wonderful of occurrences, the aspiring assurance, the surest omen of victory.'

Twenty five years later Machen was not so kind. He had grown weary of the contradictions, become fed-up completely with the failure to grasp the requirements of worthwhile evidence. And when he looked back on the assorted angels stories he said: 'There was not one word of truth in them, those stories were lies. Everyone of them lies, sir!'

For myself, though, I prefer a more charitable verdict. I would call it tragic self-deception and leave it at that!

Chapter Eleven

THE WRAITH WITH WET WELLIES

The two giant battleships were designed like immense can openers. They were everything that ranked as up-to-date in 1893 – armour-clad in parts, bristling with formidable guns in revolving turrets and even sporting torpedo tubes. Yet their bows harked back to Roman times, for each one carried an enormous steel ram!

The larger ship of the two was the HMS *Victoria*, flagship of Vice-Admiral Sir George Tryon. The slightly smaller ship was HMS *Camperdown*, commanded by Rear Admiral Markham. They were the pride of the Mediterranean Squadron of the Royal Navy.

On the afternoon of 22 June 1893 Sir George led his squadron northwards following the line of the Syrian coast. He intended to turn about on reaching Tripoli and enter the anchorage there.

The fleet steamed along in two parallel columns, five ships in one, six in the other. The five were led by HMS *Camperdown*, while the other column was headed by Tryon's *Victoria*. The distance separating them was a mere six cables – a trifle over 1,200 yards. At that distance many manoeuvres were possible, even intricate ones, but not the strange one dreamed up by Sir George. He ordered the two columns to turn inwards simultaneously and reverse direction before anchoring. A monstrously inept order by any standards, for the turning circles of the ironclads were huge – 800 yards easily. This meant that the warships would be set on an inevitable collision course.

This danger was at once apparent to Admiral Markham. He knew that even eight cables would have been scarcely sufficient separation to guarantee complete safety. So he queried the signalled orders, but they were immediately repeated. After that no one argued – indeed, few people ever dared argue with the arrogant Sir George. Instead Markham acquiesced, blindly trusting that Tryon had some elaborate master-plan hidden up his gold-braided sleeve – and the *Camperdown* swung inwards.

HMS *Victoria* began its turn at the same time, and the two giants steamed towards each other as if they were foes bent on using the vicious steel rams on their bows. No one took evasive action. Markham still hoped that his chief would prove to be a tactical genius.

But aboard the *Victoria* Captain Bourke grew apprehensive. He spoke to the Vice-Admiral and warned of the danger. Yet Tryon remained dumb – almost as if he were locked in a trance. And the ship relentlessly turned on its collision course.

The Captain then urgently asked for permission to go astern at full speed. But Tryon still remained transfixed and silent. The question was repeated again and again until finally the Admiral answered with one word: 'Yes!'

By then it was far too late to save the flagship. For even though the *Camperdown* had reversed her screws she still drove forward and inexorably smashed into the *Victoria*'s bows with her ram. Behind that ram was the weight of the ship's 10,600 tons. So the flagship's armour plate was pathetically weak protection. It was caved in and split open by sheer brute force, and the sea poured in.

The end was horrific. The *Victoria* began to turn turtle and the engine-men were trapped at their posts. Many leapt from the sloping decks. Then came a fresh horror. As an eye-witness put it: 'The powerful engines, deep down in the heart of the ship and enclosed in the water-tight compartments, kept throbbing and working, and the formidable steel flanges of the twin screws whirled round and round, at first high up in space, and then gradually nearer and nearer to the surface of the water, until the ship descended in the midst of the mass of human beings struggling for life. The propeller blades struck the calm sea and sent an enormous cloud of spray into the air. Then as the ship disappeared the suction increased until it became a perfect maelstrom, at the bottom of which these deadly screws were moving like circular saws, gashing and killing the poor creatures who had battled vainly for life.

'Then came the scene that caused the officers on the decks of the remaining vessels of the fleet to turn sick. Shrieks were heard, and then the waves and the foam were reddened by the blood of the hundreds of victims. Arms, legs wrenched from bodies, headless trunks, were tossed out of the vortex to linger on the surface for a few moments and then disappear.'

Three hundred and fifty eight lives were lost and among the dead was Tryon. Indeed, Sir George made no attempt whatsoever to save himself. With his death went all chance of knowing what he really had in mind in ordering the fatal manoeuvre. There are some, though, who claim that he was supernaturally doomed. They say his mind was unhinged by the remorseless working out of a curse. Prominent amongst the 'curse' advocates is Mr Richard Winer, one of the *Bermuda Triangle* jokers.

In his *From The Devil's Triangle To The Devil's Jaw*, Winer takes ten dreary pages to tell the story and spices it with the claim that 'there is a "mummy's curse," and it originated, or began to unfold, on the shores of the Mediterranean.' According to Winer, hundreds of Syrian Arabs had waited and watched for the British Fleet to be hit by this curse. Apparently, they had been alerted a week before by a local fakir. And he had 'prophesied that Allah was determined to visit the vessels of the infidels.'

To add strength to his supernatural view, Winer then relates the amazing tale of Sir George Tryon's last London appearance. It took place at a late morning tea party organised by Lady Tryon at her Eaton Square home.

'The majority of the guests were wives of the Royal Navy's leading commanders. About noon, Admiral Tryon was seen walking down the stairs and across the drawing room. The Admiral was attired in his full dress uniform but appeared to be oblivious to the guests in his home.'

We then learn that this party was held on that sorrowful

22 June, so that the solid-looking Admiral was nothing but a spectre. The real Sir George was, at the time, some thousands of miles away on the bridge of the doomed *Victoria*.

There is no doubt that the author imagines that he is on safe ground in recounting this story. In various forms it has been cited for years by many other authors. People like Peter Underwood, Christina Hole, Ray Lamont Brown to name a few. They have all presented it without any doubts – indeed, James Wentworth Day has even described it as 'one of the best authenticated ghost stories in living London history.'

But for all that, I am afraid Mr Winer's confidence is misplaced. Like many of the other tales he vends, it has no validity. None whatsoever. A careful comparison of the different versions shows that the story has the same mythical quality as the Lord Dufferin saga. And there is the usual conflict over the most basic things.

One account has it that he walked through the reception room at Eaton Square then disappeared. Another states that he walked through the 'crowded ballroom' and was seen by some three hundred guests. Yet another claims that he appeared at a party in the drawing room at the exact time of his death – that is, at 3.40 in the afternoon. But the most detailed account of all gives the time of his appearance at 11.30 in the evening. That is, some eight hours after his death.

According to this last and lengthy account (by Ian Fellowes-Gordon), Sir George made his entry through the east door of the ballroom, walked across the ballroom floor and made his exit through the west door. Some fifty or so guests are said to have recognised the Admiral and some even spoke to him. But he did not reply – just walked in, walked through and walked out!

So here we have discord over the time, the exact place and the number of witnesses. There is one point of close harmony though, for they all agree that Lady Tryon saw nothing of the apparition. The claim that she did is Richard Winer's own special variation.

Now these disagreements are significant enough. But even more significant is the total absence of contemporary references or witnesses. When I questioned James Wentworth Day he was amiable enough to admit that he really had no material which would authenticate this story! I looked around for anything and everything that could throw light on this mystery. And for a short while there were two leads that looked very promising.

The first was in an account by Ian Fellowes-Gordon where he quotes from and elaborates on the testimony of an alleged eye-witness. He writes: 'Months later Sir Jasper Hoad was to explain what had happened. And his account, verified by every other guest present in the ballroom at 11.25 that evening, would go down in history. "I had to summon up a bit of courage to ask Clementina if she'd seen what I'd seen. But I did. And she let me have it."

"I don't know what you saw, Jasper. I only had the sensation of watching as all my guests ridiculously moved heads like mechanical toys from one side to the other. I saw nothing else, not a thing. Yet it seems that they imagined they were seeing something..."

"But Clementina," I said to her, "It was George." That's what I said to her, and she said: "Don't be ridiculous, Jasper, George is at the far end of the Mediterranean. If he'd got back on some sudden leave, well then obviously I'd have seen him too."

"Clementina, my dear. I only hope and pray that this means nothing sad and supernatural. But I assure you that every man and woman in that ballroom saw your husband walk in the east door and out the west. He turned and smiled at everyone – including you, my dear – but he didn't stop. And when he got to the west door, well, he just vanished."'

Naturally, something as meaty as that looks mighty impressive. Unfortunately, when I spoke to Ian Fellowes-Gordon, he had not the remotest idea where the information came from! He was cheerfully helpful but, as he explained, his story had been written while he was working for the BBC World Service. Because of pressure of work he was unable to carry out his own research and simply sent a note down to the librarians at the BBC library. They obliged by sending up collections of press cuttings, magazine articles and books and he delved into them to create the story. Somewhere or other he had come across a mention of Sir Jasper Hoad who had talked to Lady Tryon about the sighting. From the same source he had gleaned the statement that there were at least fifty people to back up Sir Jasper's story.

My own search for the elusive Hoad source proved futile. But in the event this was unimportant. On checking the peerage lists for 1893 and afterwards, I discovered that there never was a Sir Jasper Hoad. So the testimony of a man who never existed counts as nothing but the rankest fiction.

The second promising lead had a very different feel about it. It was found in the most bizarre account of the Tryon case in print. It is included in Will Eisner's *Spirit Casebook Of True Haunted Houses And Ghosts*. This is a book with comic-style illustrations, but nevertheless a serious intent.

This time dear Sir George appears in the library of his London house in 'Bristol Square' where guests found him standing behind his desk. His eyes were rivetted on 'his globe, his finger pointing to Tripoli ... on the Mediterranean. They greeted him. He nodded absently ... trance-like in his movements.'

The guests excused themselves and rushed off to tell the glad news to Lady Tryon and was she astounded! What was Sir George doing back home? He was supposed to be at sea. She ran to the library – it was empty! But on the globe of the world was a still-moist fingerprint exactly at the point where the two ships had collided. The ship's clock on Tryon's desk had stopped at 3.44 – the exact time of the collision. And, most startling of all, there was a damp footprint the Admiral's size on the floor behind the desk!

Bizarre as it is, this version does have the merit of giving a checkable source. It says: 'Two months after the incident this account appeared in the August 1893 issue of the *Review of Reviews*.'

Two months after the event makes the account fresh enough to be exciting. Sorry to have to tell you, though, that the reference turned out to be quite bogus. The account in that issue of the *Review of Reviews* contains nothing but a straightforward report of the collision at sea. There is no mention of the ghostly portent in London. What is more, there is no mention of the event in any issue of the *Review of Reviews* from 1893 to 1895.

That, in itself, is most revealing. For the *Review*'s editor was W.T. Stead, an ardent spiritualist. A man who went out of his way to collect and print any good story which had a supernatural slant. In fact his Christmas 1892 issues were crammed full of 'true ghost stories'.

Among these ghost stories is one which, oddly enough, turns out to be the welcome genesis of the Tryon legend! It is entitled *A Ghost In A Ballroom*.

The account tells how a Mr W. walked through, and out of, a ballroom without speaking to any of the people present, including the lady he was due to partner. Then on the following morning the witnesses learned that Mr W. had been found drowned. Remarkably his watch had stopped at 10.15, the exact time at which he had been seen in the ballroom.

So the tale of the drowned ballroom ghost was circulating at least six months before the *Victoria*'s end. But that end was so spectacular and puzzling that it simply invited rumour, speculation and fantasy. It also gave a new slant to an old story and the shadowy Mr W. became the beefy and arrogant Sir George, complete with wet boots.

But how about that curse? Does that stand up to scrutiny? Not for one moment! As Admiral Colomb has testified, Sir George acted 'with a strong and frequently expressed impatience of all mathematical calculations and mechanical certainties.' And he indeed had a mathematical blind spot. For he occasionally confused the radius of a ship's turning circle with its diameter. This confusion had almost led to a disaster some three years earlier. Then he had signalled precisely the same fatal manoeuvre during the 1890 naval exercises off Plymouth. But at that time Rear Admiral Tracey had refused to comply and Tryon eventually cancelled the orders.

As for Tryon's 'trance state', well, he had been ill for some time, plagued by a painful ulcer on the leg which refused to heal. And the medication and pain-killers he was using were more than probably laced with laudanum and opium derivatives. Enough to slow anyone's reflexes and double-glaze the eyeballs!

So I am afraid that the Tyron tales have to be filed along with all the many other bright stars of the 'factual-fictional' firmament.

The Wraith With Wet Wellies

Inevitably, this will not please Richard Winer, who has been impetuous enough to write: 'Could an Arab fakir have caused one of the greatest peacetime tragedies in the annals of the Royal Navy? Could the Admiral of one of the ships involved have been removed spiritually from the bridge of his ship until seconds before the tragic event occurred, by which time it was already too late? ... the answer is yes.'

But the real and politely restrained answer is surely 'hogwash!'

Chapter Twelve

DEATH BECKONS LORD DUFFERIN

Fate was exceptionally kind to the first Marquis of Dufferin and Ava. He died peacefully on 12 February 1902, nine years after a dramatic escape from violent death. An escape made possible only by supernormal intervention – or so some of his chroniclers tell us.

His career had been one of sustained brilliance. After a short Parliamentary period, Lord Dufferin became in turn Governor-General of Canada, Ambassador to Russia, Ambassador to Constantinople, Viceroy of India, Ambassador to Rome and finally Ambassador to France. In all, a bustling active life punctuated by spells of leave in his beloved Ireland.

The awesome part of his saga begins in the 1880s at the country house of Tullamore in County Wexford, Ireland. He was there enjoying a welcome break from the incessant whirl of diplomatic life. And the great house seemed to provide an ideal refuge for anyone seeking tranquillity. But one night the whole atmosphere of the place changed and Lord Dufferin woke up sick with terror.

His sleep had been cruelly broken into by strange sounds from the grounds outside – terrifying sounds. But terrifying as they were, he was no coward. So he climbed out of bed to investigate. With racing heart and trembling body he reached the french windows and peered out.

From there he overlooked the trim lawns bathed in moonlight. Almost every section was in plain view except for a spot where tall trees cast long black shadows. And from these shadows came the sounds that had awakened him. Heartfelt sobs, more animal than human.

He fumbled with the window latches, but as he did a man staggered out of the shadows into the moonlight. He was agonisingly bent over with the weight of a load on his back. At first sight it looked like a long linen-chest. Yet as he drew closer it suddenly became clear that his burden was a crudely-made coffin.

At that Lord Dufferin threw open the windows, ran across the lawn and shouted at the man to halt. Until then the man's face had been held down and hidden, but on hearing the shout the man lifted his head and turned it towards Lord Dufferin. And the moonlight fell on a face loathsome and unforgettable, so contorted with hate that Lord Dufferin stopped dead in his tracks. Then he drew on his reserves of courage, advanced on the man – and walked right through him!

Simultaneously the man disappeared, coffin and all. And with his disappearance the gloom lifted and the house and grounds became as calm and restful as ever.

Lord Dufferin returned to his bedroom shaking and puzzled. Then, after writing a complete account of the event in his diary, he managed to snatch some sleep.

At the breakfast table he read out his account and appealed to his host and fellow guests for an explanation. But no one could help. The description of the man matched no one in the area past or present. There was not even a local ghost to blame, so the event remained an inexplicable mystery.

Over the years, the memory of that night stayed with Lord Dufferin. But it no longer puzzled him. He grew to believe that it really might have been nothing more than an extra vivid nightmare. And that is how things stood for the next ten years. Then, in 1893, the vision took on a new significance.

By that time Lord Dufferin was the British Ambassador to France and was obliged to attend a diplomatic reception at the Grand Hotel in Paris. When he entered the hotel foyer he found it jam-packed with impatient guests, for the lift was taking ages to make its trips to the reception area on the top floor. So with his secretary he joined the queue for the lift.

After an age he reached the head of the queue, the lift arrived, its door squealed open and the lift attendant waved the guests in.

Lord Dufferin blanched, stood fast and refused to enter. He mumbled an excuse to the officials with him, then stepped backwards, pulling his secretary after him. Nothing would persuade him to use that lift, for the lift attendant was, in every feature, the double of that hideous man he had seen years before in Ireland!

The other officials ignored the eccentric Englishman. They crowded into the lift and it began its laborious climb. Lord Dufferin meanwhile went hunting for the manager's office. He had to know who the lift attendant was and where he had come from. But before his Lordship reached the office, disaster struck. The lift cable snapped and it plunged down the shaft to destruction. The passengers were killed outright, as was the ghastly lift attendant, so he could never be questioned. The hotel manager could answer no questions either, for the attendant was a casual worker taken on for the day. A man without documents or records.

To add to the eeriness, no one ever came forward to claim or identify the lift man's body. Lord Dufferin was baffled. Not even his money and influence could turn up a single fact about the man. The one certainty was that the hideous creature had saved Dufferin's life. But why only his life? Why not the others?

That, in its essentials, is the remarkable story that has been told many times before. These published accounts often vary in detail, but no one ever questions the basic truth of the tale. On the contrary, it is always asserted that the facts have been fully researched and investigated.

One writer, for example, states: 'The evidence is incontrovertible ... the details of this story have been carefully investigated ... by the well-known French psychologist de Maratray, who brought them to the attention of the British Society for Psychical Research.'

Another writer adds: 'The accident was reported in the Press ... but neither the management of the hotel nor the accident investigators could find any record of the man's name or background.'

So here we seem to have a case that cannot be challenged. In truth, though, the whole account is nothing more than a grotesque pastiche of myths.

To begin with, this case was never investigated by the Society for Psychical Research. The Society was certainly in existence at the time of the alleged event, but its files prove that it heard and knew nothing about it. And no newspaper carried reports of the accident – for very good reasons. In fact, the first written account of the Dufferin case did not emerge until 1920. That is eighteen years after the death of Lord Dufferin and twenty six years after the alleged lift crash.

The primary account was written by the French psychologist Monsieur R. de Maratray on 18 July 1920. He gave it to the French astronomer Flammarion who then included it in his book *Death And Its Mystery*. De Maratray added force to his account by claiming that his wife was related to Lord Dufferin and his family had been kept informed of the events at the time. 'The accident is historic,' he wrote, 'and its precise date could be easily verified.'

Flammarion made no attempt to check the story for himself. He even neglected to ask why de Maratray had kept quiet for so long. He enthused that 'this fantastic adventure was an actual happening.' Then he went on to conclude: 'Warnings of this sort are certainly most strange! They prove to us the existence of the unknown world, the mysteries of which we hope to penetrate.' Thus he took de Maratray's word for everything and published a document that is both false and ludicrous.

You see, the fatal accident in the lift of the Grand Hotel took place in 1878 – some five years before the vision in Ireland and fifteen years before the date of Lord Dufferin's 'miraculous escape.' At the time of that genuine accident there was no diplomatic reception at the hotel. In any case, Lord Dufferin was not even in Paris but was serving in Canada as the Governor-General! On top of that, in the real accident only a young lady died, not a lift full of people, and certainly no unknown lift attendant!

Now all these facts were firmly established shortly after Flammarion's book appeared. The intrepid investigator who nailed the story as a lie was Paul Heuze, a journalist with the Paris magazine *L'Opinion*. Heuze proved that when it came to psychical research Flammarion jettisoned all the logic and care that went into his astronomical work. As a result his books were crammed full of unsubstantiated stories and hearsay. To his discredit, Flammarion made no attempt to revise these books and the Dufferin story was given wide circulation and picked up by author after author. In fact, of all the tales vended by him, tall or otherwise, this is the only one which has achieved international fame.

But how did such a tale become linked with Lord Dufferin? The files of the Society for Psychical Research provide part of the answer. They show that in November 1949 a Mr Louis Wolfe of New York wrote to the S.P.R. and asked for details of the Society's Dufferin investigation. The S.P.R. replied that it had never been asked to check the case. But prompted by this enquiry the Society's Secretary then wrote to Lady Dufferin and asked for her help.

Lady Dufferin replied that the tale did not apply to the first Lord Dufferin himself. It was simply a new version of an old story her grandfather used to tell about someone else! In the original version an un-named man had taken his holiday in Scotland, at Glamis Castle. And the vision had involved a hearse driven by a man with an ugly and hateful face.

In that case, where did Lord Dufferin find the story in its original form? And was it in any way based on facts? These proved to be tricky questions, but a search through scores of books yielded up a passage that seemed to clinch things. It appears in Marc Alexander's *Haunted Castles*, and it explains that the Glamis coach story originated with the writer Augustus Hare. Marc Alexander also states that Hare was actually staying at Glamis when a fellow guest saw the coach and driver. Unfortunately, a check with Hare's journal showed that Alexander is quite mistaken.

The crucial testimony by Hare is printed as an appendix to *My Solitary Life*. It proves that though he had stayed at Glamis he knew nothing about its frightful coachman until many years after his stay. Until 29 July 1902, to be exact. And on that day he was told the full story by Eustace Cecil, but Cecil made it clear it was not based on his experience. He was simply repeating an account once given him by Lady F. Trevanion.

In Lady Trevanion's account, a guest at the castle saw a carriage (not a hearse) whose driver had a 'marked and terrible face.' Shortly afterwards this un-named guest stayed on the third floor of an un-named hotel in Paris. He rang for the lift, but refused to take it when he saw the attendant's face. Seconds later the lift cable snapped and the cage hurtled down the shaft to destruction.

Hare had already heard this story before, often in fact, but never before linked with Glamis. And it is plain that neither he nor Cecil nor Lady Trevanion had ever associated the tale with Lord Dufferin, nor with any other named individual.

But this is not surprising since further research showed that the yarn first appeared as an anonymous secondhand account in the spiritualist paper *Light* of 16 April 1892.

The Editor of *Light* at the time was the Reverend Stainton Moses and his behaviour paralleled that of Flammarion's, since he took the tale completely on trust. He wrote this about it: 'It has been communicated to me by a personal friend, and is both authentic and trustworthy.'

The anonymous lady wrote: 'I have just heard from a friend of a remarkable dream. She thought she heard a loud knock on the door, and on looking out she saw that a hearse had stopped at the house. Being greatly surprised, she rushed downstairs and herself opened the hall door. A strange-looking man was on top of the hearse; on seeing her, he said: "Are you not ready yet?" She said: "Oh, no; certainly not," and slammed the door. The sound seemed to have caused her to wake.

'She was much puzzled to know what could be the significance of such a very unusual dream. The face of the man haunted her, and for weeks she could not get the remembrance out of her head. All her family and friends were told about the dream, and all the circumstances of it had been discussed.

'Some weeks had passed when one day the young lady happened to be in a large warehouse in the City, and was just going to step into the lift when she looked at the man who had charge of it and immediately drew back, having recognised the face of the man she had seen in her dream. When she drew back her consternation was added to by the exclamation from the man of the very words she had heard in her dream: "What, are you not ready yet, Miss?" Her determination not to ascend in the lift was confirmed, and she declined to go into it. It only reached to the next floor when the machinery gave way, the lift being smashed to pieces and the man killed.'

From then on the lift tale travelled to the United States and Europe, becoming constantly transmuted in its passage. Sixteen years later it returned to England in a new guise, now posing as an authentic American happening! Ironically enough it was promptly picked up and reprinted in the pages of *Light*. It seems the new editor and his staff had completely forgotten their earlier account furnished by a 'personal friend' of the Rev Moses. And on 9 February 1907 it ran this story under the heading *Saved By A Vision*: '*The Progressive Thinker* gives an instance of a warning dream, as related by Miss Gray, a young woman prominent in educational work in Washington State. While staying in Chicago, where she had planned to visit a new department store which had just been opened, whose elevators were death-traps, she woke up in the middle of the night and saw an unknown face at the window, twenty feet above the ground. On going to the window she saw a hearse standing in the street below, with her nocturnal visitant occupying the driver's box; he looked her squarely in the face and beckoned to her. The next day she visited the store and on going to one of the crowded elevators the man in charge beckoned to her and said that there was room for one more. His features were those of the man on the hearse in her dream or vision of the night before. She refused to enter the elevator, which 'started down, stuck, and dropped four storeys, killing two of its passengers and injuring everyone else in the car.'

In the meantime, another variation of the story had been incorporated in Lord Dufferin's bag of after-dinner yarns. One day he related it to a young impressionable nephew and gave it special treatment. Adult wiles were not fully appreciated. The twinkle in Dufferin's eye was missed. And when he spun out the tale as his very own real-life adventure, the boy was awestruck and convinced. The boy grew up to become a diplomat and writer. Out of conviction he retold this 'true story' frequently – possibly to the de Maratrays. The innocent culprit, the unwitting father of one branch of this tenacious myth, was none other than the late Harold Nicolson!

But his version still faithfully retained the coach and horses. The one featuring the coffin-bearer was Monsieur de Maratray's very own embellished handiwork!

Chapter Thirteen

ONCE MORE UNTO THE LIFT DEAR FRIENDS

As we have seen, the Dufferin version eclipsed all the other lift myths for over half a century. But since 1950 two new interlopers have elbowed their way into the mythology. And what bounders they are!

The first story opens in Atlanta, Georgia, in the 1950s. Elise Barnhardt from New York was making a visit. She had accepted an invitation from Ruthanne Reeves, a girl she had met that summer in Greece. At the airport she was greeted by Ruthanne and her brother John. All three squeezed into John's tiny sports car and they sped off into the country.

It was dusk and the drive took on a dream-like quality as they swept past the deserted cottonfields and countless little tin-roofed shacks. At last they reached the Reeves' plantation, motored down its private entry road and pulled up outside an immense, sprawling mansion. For Elise the mansion was the very essence of everything romantic. Tall columns supported the front and east and west wings, while its rear piazza overlooked a sleepy river that gleamed silver in the light of the full moon.

That evening friends arrived from the nearby towns and plantations for a dinner party and dance on the piazza. The lively party ended soon after midnight and by 1.30 a.m. the girls settled down to sleep. But Elise was so excited by the unexpected romance of the evening that she tossed from side to side in her four-poster bed, unable to sleep.

When she heard the grandfather clock in the hall strike two, she swung out of bed and opened the curtains to let in some cool air. At that very moment she heard the strange clatter of horses' hooves. She looked out with unbelieving eyes and saw a gold and black stagecoach drawn by four gleaming black stallions. It stood motionless on the circular drive beneath her window. Beside it stood a coachman dressed in a black coat and breeches. He held the door of the coach open, gestured towards the house with his free hand and called out: 'Room for one more!'

Elise stared down at his swarthy face. A long scar staggered irregularly across the man's left cheek, running from the corner of his eye to the top of his full lips. It was the sort of face that was hard to forget.

Before she could recover from her surprise the coach and coachman seemed to literally dissolve into the darkness and disappear.

She was so frightened by this grotesque episode that she stayed awake for hours. At daybreak she managed to snatch a short bout of sleep.

Next day, despite her fears, she was far too embarrassed to tell her friend about the eerie coach and its driver. But the memory haunted her all day. By evening Elise began to feel depressed and uneasy. Yet as soon as she eased herself into bed she fell asleep at once. An hour later she woke to the sound of horses' hooves. She hastened to the window and there, below, stood the coach and coachman.

'Room for one more!' she heard him shout and he looked up towards her window and smiled evilly. With that the coach vanished again and Elise sat back on her bed trembling with terror.

By the following morning she was so exhausted that it proved easy to convince Ruthanne that she was not well and needed to return home to New York. Unfortunately she was not able to book a reservation on the flight she wanted so she insisted on going on standby.

On arriving at the airport she bought a ticket and was told that even though the plane was full, there was always the chance of a last minute vacancy and she was head of the standby queue.

Sorry – You've Been Duped

John and Ruthanne waited with her at the entrance gate, and she chatted with them cheerfully now that she knew she was leaving the haunted plantation house behind. Then her cheerfulness evaporated in an instant as she heard the cry: 'There is room for one more.'

It came from the gate attendant who was walking towards them. Elise quivered with shock. She moved forward to inspect the attendant's face and as she did, so he looked directly at her and called: 'Room for one more.' She stared at him in terror. There was the swarthy face with its prominent scar. This was the ghastly coachman who had twice summoned her in the night!

Almost hysterical, she begged her friends to take her back to the waiting room. Nothing would induce her to board that plane. But now she had to unburden herself to her friends. They listened with growing bewilderment as her story unravelled. They had never seen or even heard of a phantom coach and driver in the whole of their area. They agreed, though, that Elise would be wise to wait for a later plane. By then she might be more relaxed and fit to travel.

When the later plane was due to depart the Reeves escorted Elise back to the departure gate. In attendance was a thin, blond young man – very different from the villainous creature all three had seen earlier.

'Where's the man with the scarred face?' Elise asked. 'The one who was here at 12.30.' The young attendant looked baffled.

'You surely must be mistaken?' he said. 'I've been in attendance since early morning ... and no one who looks like that even works here.'

The young man was so convincing that argument was out of the question. So Elise said farewell to her friends and boarded her plane. A smooth take-off led to a pleasant uneventful flight. Once back in New York, Elise felt too exhausted to ponder over the strange events of the past few days. Her sleep was deep and untroubled. But the headlines of the morning paper sent a shock through her. PLANE CRASHES ON THE WAY TO NEW YORK, it read. She shivered as she checked the details. The plane had set off from Atlanta. Its take-off time – 12.30. It was the very plane she had meant to take – the one that had 'room for one more.'

The second 'true' story is much more precise. Now we encounter exact times, dates and locations – all the helpful features we need for a sound investigation.

It opens in Philadelphia in mid-June 1968, two weeks before schoolteacher Janice Metz was due to fly to Europe. She intended to take a vacation with 25-year-old fellow teacher Laura Shepherd. Their plans involved a ten-day stay in London before exploring Paris for a few days.

It should have been a time of growing excitement, but all Janice felt was a growing anxiety. Night after night she was disturbed by an odd, inexplicable dream. The dream involved a man's face. He had dark piercing eyes, thin bloodless lips and a long bony nose. On his head was a military-style cap with a badge – the letters H.F. encircled by braid. The man was quite unknown to her and the initials on the cap held no significance whatsoever.

Eventually she told her friend Laura about the dream. Laura probed for the complete story but Janice explained that precious little happened in the dream. The man said nothing – simply stared at her, though at times it seemed that he wished to speak to her. But at that point iron bars moved in front of his face, then he swiftly disappeared.

Following this talk Janice tried to concentrate her mind on the coming pleasures of the holiday, but the strange dream still visited her every night.

Two days before the start of her vacation she felt impelled to consult a psychiatrist. He questioned her at length and asked if she had flown before.

'Only once,' she answered.

The psychiatrist now felt that he understood her problem. He diagnosed her repeated dreams as a symptom of a subconscious anxiety about flying. The strange face was that of an airline pilot! Her worries about flying could be subdued by a mild sedative taken half an hour before boarding her plane.

On 30 June she and Laura flew by BOAC to England. They spent ten enjoyable days in and around London and for this period the unwelcome dream was absent.

While in London they bumped into several friends from back home and among them was Mary Childress who had been Janice's room-mate at college.

Mary was due in Paris ahead of them. 'Be sure to look me up when you arrive,' she insisted. 'I'm staying at the Hotel Fauborg. It's in the Second Arrondissement, near the Bourse-Opera.'

On the night Janice and Laura arrived in Paris the dream returned with a difference. She told Laura about it at breakfast. Now the iron bars in front of the stranger were seen to be connected with wire mesh, like a cage. In this cage were several people, one of whom Janice recognised as Laura herself!

Laura was greatly amused by this. 'It's probably a prison cell. I'll have to watch my step,' she joked.

The dream came again the next night. This time it came with a growing terror and Janice remembered crying out to Laura, imploring her to escape from the cage before it was too late. Janice woke up feeling that something terrible was about to happen. But what?

Later that morning they phoned Mary Childress at the Hotel Fauborg. She was excited to hear from them and suggested that they meet her that afternoon at two in her room.

The two girls arrived at the hotel shortly after two. Laura went ahead into the lobby while Janice paid off the taxi. By the time Janice reached the lobby Laura was already in the lift together with several other people. But as Janice walked toward this old-fashioned lift she felt a growing disquiet. There was something vaguely familiar about the scene. Then she caught sight of the lift operator. He gazed at her with penetrating eyes. His nose was long and bony, his lips thin and bloodless.

This was the face that had haunted her dreams. And on his head was a peaked cap with the initials H.F. – the insignia of the Hotel Fauborg.

Janice screamed: 'Laura! Come back before it's too late!'

But it *was* too late. The door clanged shut and the crowded lift creaked upwards. Although two people got off at the third floor and one more left on the fourth, the ancient cables had already been weakened by the severe strain, as the police pointed out later.

The cable snapped before the lift reached the fifth floor and it plunged downwards. The exact words of the original account tell us that: 'At 2.25 p.m. on 13 July 1968, all eight passengers crashed to their death at the bottom of the pit. Among them was Janice's friend Laura Shepherd. The ninth victim was Paul Routier, 47, the elevator operator.'

Janice Metz never saw him in her dreams again. 'Nor has any psychic investigator been able to explain the supernormal phenomena of his repeated warnings' – so concludes Emile Schurmacher in his book *More Strange Unsolved Mysteries*.

But are we really considering mysteries?

In the Atlanta, Georgia, tale, written by Nancy Roberts, the dates are too vague to make a newspaper check worthwhile. Tracing the Reeves would be equally difficult, since their plantation is located imprecisely, some miles out in the country from the airport at Atlanta. Still, these are no real problems. The account is unmistakably bogus. It is a modern update of the original coach and coachman legend of 1892.

The precise Philadelphia/Paris story is equally bogus. All its exactness is just pure bluff designed to give it the air of authentic reporting.

There is no Hotel Fauborg in the Second Arrondissement in Paris and there never was. Enquiries with the police of the Second Arrondissement show that there was no lift crash in their area on 13 July 1968. Neither was there such a lift crash in the whole of Paris on that day. Hardly surprising, though. Here is the Dufferin story once again juggled around with and modernised.

But stories do not write themselves. The choice of names, dates, locations and events result from deliberations. So perhaps the inventors of these stories would like to stand up and receive a well-deserved brickbat or two? After all, some people rightly resent being taken for a ride!

Chapter Fourteen

CRY 'HALT!' TO HITLER

'The European War, which the Mars in Hitler's horoscope tells us so much about, will not break out ... An invisible power has written strange signs in the skies. Not everyone can decipher their meaning, but in flaming letters they cry "HALT!" to Hitler.'

With such enormously confident phrases, Leonardo Blake launched his book *Hitler's Last Year Of Power*. Unfortunately for Mr Blake it rolled off the presses in August 1939. It was reviewed in the spiritualist weekly *Two Worlds* on 8 September. And the paper gave his views independent support. Its front-page reported that the amazing trumpet-medium, Mrs McCallum, had relayed spirit messages from a former editor, Ernest Marklew. Over in spirit land he was very much concerned with the international situation. He actually said that he had been in touch with General Foch, Earl Haig, Lord Roberts and several others. These military gentlemen were doing all in their power to secure peace and overcome the war scare. So he was of the opinion, even then, that 'there would be no war.'

Alas, the eighth page of the paper had to be reset at the last moment to announce: 'WAR! A TEMPORARY SETBACK TO OUR IDEALS.'

It was much more than that, because for months, even years, the psychics had been reassuring the public that Hitler was overrated and misjudged. In *Prediction* of 1936, leading astrologer and mystic R. H. Naylor took up three pages to analyse Hitler's horoscope. He pronounced: 'He personally would never be a willing party to war ... this gloomy and idealistic careerist is at heart a kindly soul and a lover of little children.'

The December issue of the same magazine revealed that Josef Ranald, the well-known palmist, had read Mussolini's hand and forecast that his career as a ruler would end at the age of fifty four, giving him only two more years to throw his weight around.

Throughout the earlier part of 1939 spirit guides galore were lisping, whispering and even bawling that there would be an age of peace. War was not on the cards, or in the stars, or in the offing.

There was such unanimity that Maurice Barbanell, editor of *Psychic News*, was able to write: 'I am confident there is no possibility of error when the prophecy is so unanimous. From every well-known guide and from home circles all over the world there has come the assurance that never again will England be involved in war. While individual spirits are fallible when dealing with lesser issues I refuse to believe in the possibility of a mistake in this particular instance. (22 July)

A cautionary tale certainly, and it poses the direct question: Can we really foretell the future? Can we do more than just guess at what might be possible? Many people are obviously convinced that we can. That is why every day millions of them read horoscopes or consult fortune tellers of one type or another. But are they justified in their beliefs? Just what does the record show?

Consider those questions and you run up against difficulties. The claims are many and you could possibly fill shelf after shelf with the great number of books which set out to provide the answers. Yet, for all that, the reliable evidence is, in my view, completely lacking. Let me give you some examples. Examples chosen not because they are easy to demolish, but because they have been widely believed in. Examples that at first sight seem most convincing.

First of all we simply have to look at the French sage Nostradamus. He is rated as the greatest prophet of the past, and how can you ignore someone who is placed top of the bill?

Surprisingly, though his books were written in 1555, they are still earnestly and painstakingly combed through in the search for clues to today's and tomorrow's events.

I first heard about this 'seer' at school. The article I then read was breathtaking. It said that Nostradamus had correctly forecast the rise of Hitler and Napoleon and mentioned them by name. Now that was certainly staggering. But when I finally came to read the original I found that this was just untrue. The Hitler references are to a river called the Hister, not to a man. And the Napoleon forecasts are cleverly wangled by jumbling up the names of three French villages: Pau, Nay and Loron.

In other cases the striking forecasts have been deliberately faked or biased by adding words which are not found in the original French version. Here is a glaring example. It is supposed to forecast Napoleon's end.

> 'The captive prince, conquered, is sent to Elba;
> He will sail across the Gulf of Genoa to Marseilles;
> By a great effort of the foreign forces he is overcome,
> Though he escapes the fire, his bees yield blood by the barrel.'

This translation of Quatrain, or Verse, 24 of his Century 10, appears in *Prediction and Prophecy* by Keith Ellis. Similar translations can be found in other books. And the verses do seem to contain an amazing hit. For Napoleon *was* conquered, captured and sent in exile to the isle of Elba. Thus at first sight we are presented with something that looks like a real glimpse of the future.

There is a catch, though. The words 'sent to Elba' were never written by Nostradamus. He simply mentioned a 'captive prince conquered in Italy' which is very different and could mean anyone!

For the record, Nostradamus interpreter Henry C. Roberts summarises the authentic verse thus: 'A prince, captured in Italy, shall be brought back to France for trial in Marseilles. His friend shall obtain his release by bribing the city officials.'

The truth is that playing around with the verses of Nostradamus is simply an engrossing game. That is why one interpeter can find Verse 40, Century 10, to be a forecast of the abdication of Edward VIII in 1936, while others mark it down as a prophecy relating to James I, first King of Scotland and England! This game is without rigid rules. That is why comparisons of the many interpreters show that in scores of cases the same verse has been attributed to the far past, the recent past, the present, the near future and the far distant future.

But what of our present-day prophets? Is it the same for them? I would say yes. Perhaps an examination of the legend surrounding Jeane Dixon might underline why I feel that way. For Mrs Dixon not only wears the mantle of the prophet, but has been described as 'one of the most remarkable women who ever lived.'

When Mrs Dixon visited Britain every paper that mentioned her emphasised that she had forecast the assassination of President Kennedy years before it had happened. This was repeated on radio programmes and even told me by a lapel-grabbing and thoroughly convinced newspaper reporter – who was sober.

I decided to look into the claim. There was no shortage of references backing up the view that she had foreseen Kennedy's end. Many magazines and a stack of books said so. As well as that, it turned out that it was this particular prediction that won Mrs Dixon her real fame.

Jeane Dixon's biography gives this account: 'reporters from *Parade* magazine were interviewing her ... she declared: "A blue-eyed Democratic President elected in 1960 will be assassinated" ... Her prediction appeared in the *Parade* issue of 13 May 1956.'

But did it? Well, when I looked into the text of the article in *Parade* I found a new twist to the story. It became clear that none of the commentators, writers and reporters who enthuse over this story have ever taken the trouble to check it out. For the report itself says something quite different. It reads: 'As to the 1960 election, Mrs Dixon thinks it will be ... won by a Democrat. But he will be assassinated or die in office, though not necessarily in his first term.'

So the man is not identified in any way. There is no mention of blue eyes. And the assassination is only one of two possibilities – the other a mere death in office. Then, since the

Presidential term is four years, this death might occur any time during a span of eight years. So this 'remarkably accurate' prophecy was nothing of the sort.

Yet even if Jeane Dixon had not been so vague and woolly, even if she had firmly mentioned the assassination of the man elected in 1960, this would still have proved nothing at all.

At the time she made her prophecy, every President of the United States for almost a century had been sought after by assassins. One slaughtered President Lincoln. Another killed President McKinley. Yet another shot President Garfield. And Theodore Roosevelt was only saved from death by a wad of papers which deflected an assassin's bullet. His nephew, President Franklin Roosevelt, escaped death by an inch or two when the bullet meant for him killed the Mayor of Chicago, while President Harry Truman narrowly escaped assassination at the White House itself!

Unpleasant as it is, we have to face it that it is only the tight security around the President that keeps him alive. Take that security away and I doubt if any President would last for six months. That high and powerful office acts as a veritable magnet for cranks, fanatics and the mentally disturbed. And the United States has more than its fair share of these. These misfits come to see the President as the cause of all their problems. They dream that all will come right if only that evil man at the top is eliminated. Their dreams often lead to action, even if the ultimate deed is thwarted by the vigilance of the police or intelligence services.

So, put into context, Mrs Dixon's famous forecast becomes transfigured. It is little more than a piece of lax reporting based on some quite unremarkable guesswork. Guesswork part-prompted by her awareness of the then approaching centenary of Lincoln's assassination.

Other even more impressive predictions wilt when placed in proper context. Like the famous dream-prediction of Bishop de Lanyi. Brian Inglis features this 'strikingly prophetic dream' in his *Science and Parascience*. He introduces it by saying: 'Before the First World War broke out there had been countless portents of a coming Armageddon from mediums in trances, in automatic writing, in dreams and in visions ... Most were

'For you', Charles Trevor Garland's Victorian painting used as an advertising poster. Its reissue in 1978 exposed a famous 'spirit photograph' as a sixty-year-old hoax.

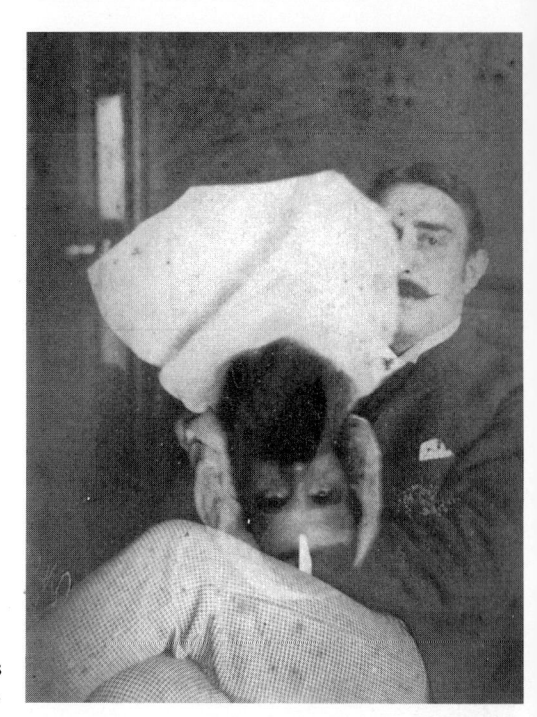

Not all spirit photographers were nimble fingered.

More devastating than pictures were seance-room 'materialisations'. Medium Eglinton obliges.

The preliminaries are not at all unpleasant

Just going to begin

SPIRITUAL GARMENTS

AWFUL!!

Be thou a spirit of health or goblin damn'd

Materialisations sometimes came amiss.

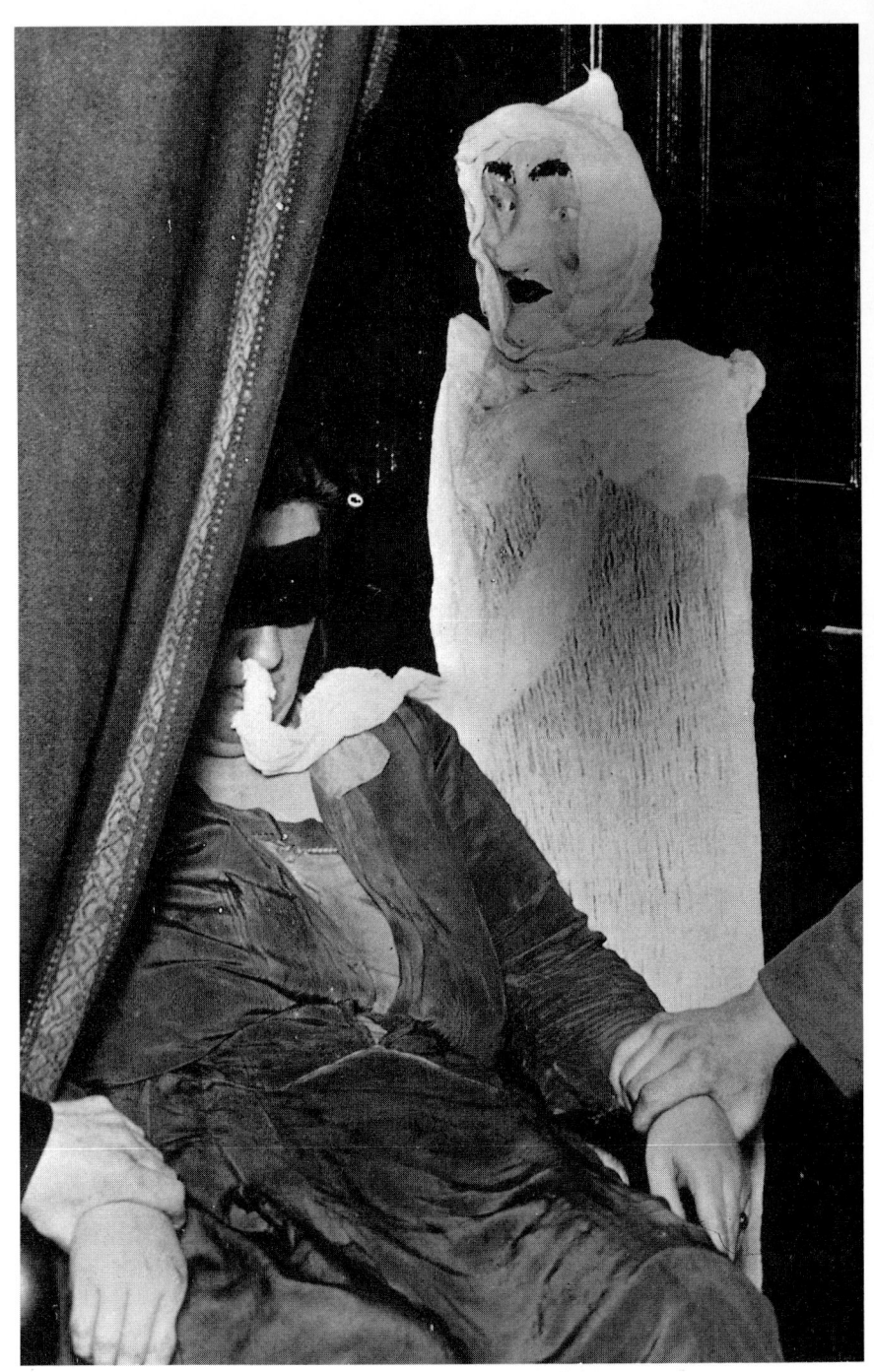

Helen Duncan and friend from Spirit Land.

Did this catastrophy beget a ghost?

Sir George Tryon – wraith with wet wellies?

Above left: Arthur Machen: Wing Commander of the Newspaper Angels.

Above right: The legendary Angels became stock figures in popular war art.

Right: Secretive, sly and slightly sinister, Samuel Soal – Faker Extraordinary.

Marcus Favonius Facilis: first-century Roman centurion, used in a third-century novel by Louis De Wohl, and later in a past-life fantasy.

Louis De Wohl, whose novel *The Living Wood* was re-vamped as a reincarnation memory by Jane Evans.

Arnall Bloxham: the face that launched a thousand slips.

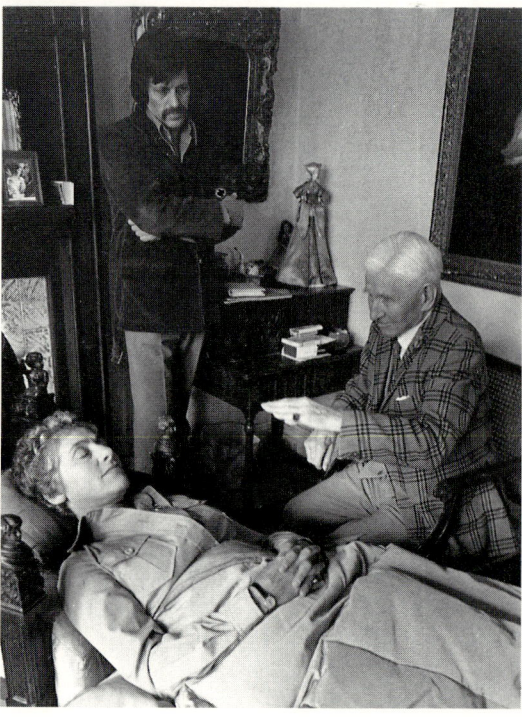

(*Below*) Geoffrey Iverson hovers tentatively in the background.

in similarly vague general terms; but a few contained more specific prophetic glimpses ... most striking of all was the nightmare which Richet was to recount in his thirty years of psychical research, from the story which had appeared in *Psychische Studien* in 1918. The facts, it was claimed, had been checked.'

The account used by Brian Inglis reads as follows: 'Monsieur Joseph de Lanyi, Bishop of Grosswardin, dreamed on the morning of 28 June at 4 a.m. that he saw on his study table a black-edged letter bearing the arms of the Archduke. M. de Lanyi had been professor of the Hungarian language to the Archduke. In his dream he opened the letter and at its head saw a street into which an alley opened. The Archduke was seated in a motorcar with his wife; facing him was a general, and another officer by the side of the chauffeur. There was a crowd about the car and from the crowd two young men stepped forward and fired on the royal couple. The text of the letter ran: "Your Eminence, dear Dr Lanyi, my wife and I have been victims of a political crime at Sarajevo. We commend ourselves to your prayers. Sarajevo, 28 June 1914, 4 a.m."

'"Then," says Mgr de Lanyi, "I woke up trembling; I saw that the time was 4.30 a.m. and I wrote down my dream, reproducing the characters that had appeared to me in the Archduke's letter. At six, when my servant came, he found me seated at my table, much shaken and telling my rosary. I said at once to him: "Call my mother and my host, that I may tell them the dreadful dream I have had."'

In commenting on this dream Brian Inglis assures us that 'during the day a telegram arrived with the news of the assassination. It was not quite as the dream had forecast: the assassins threw bombs. But otherwise the dream had been accurate.'

A correction is in order here. The Archduke and his wife were in fact shot. So in that respect the dream was more accurate than Mr Inglis realised. But he seems blissfully unaware of the real problems surrounding this dream. In the first place there are a number of conflicting versions. In the version quoted by Keith Ellis (*Prediction and Prophecy*) the dream telegram ends: 'Cordial greetings from your Archduke Franz,

Sarajevo, 28 June, 3.15 a.m.' And when de Lanyi springs out of bed his clock shows 3.15.

The version printed in the December 1967 *Journal of the Society for Psychical Research* has the same telegram ending: 'Cordial greetings from your Archduke Franz. Sarajevo, 1914, half past 3 a.m.'

These differences in times (there are others as well) cannot be dismissed as mere trivialities. If there is a master statement made at the time by the Bishop there should be no divergences. Let us presume, though, that de Lanyi did have a dream broadly along the lines of the various versions. Is there anything in this dream that entitles us to regard it as paranormal, as a genuine glimpse into the future?

We can only do justice to ourselves and to the Bishop by now introducing the necessary context – the historical background that is so often and so conveniently missing from prediction accounts.

In 1914 Sarajevo was included in the province of the Austro–Hungarian Empire known as Bosnia–Hercegovina. It had been annexed in 1908 but the Bosnian people were still mentally wedded to their brothers over the border in Serbia. The day chosen for the Archduke's visit was the worst possible day in the eyes of the Serbians. Sunday 28 June, was the sacred anniversary of Vidovan, or St Vitus' day. It was a commemoration of the Serbian defeat at the battle of Cosovo in 1389.

Around this defeat at Cosovo the South Slavs had woven a starkly tragic tradition. The Sultan of the arrogant conquering Turks had been assassinated by a Serbian nobleman, Milos Obilic. From then on the practice of tyrannicide was looked on as a sacred and patriotic act.

Patriotic anger and a desire to unite with Serbia led to the founding of the Young Bosnian Movement. On 15 June 1910 Bogdan Zerajic, one of the founders of this movement, trailed the Austrian Emperor through the streets of Sarajevo. He was bent on an assassination attempt but in the end he fired five shots at General Marijan Varesanin, the Governor of the two provinces. This attempt was made on the same street in Sarajevo that witnessed the shootings in June 1914.

On 8 June 1912 the Obilic cult led student Luka Jukic to attempt to assassinate the Governor of Croatia, Count Slavko Cuvaj. Cuvaj was again shot at by Ivan Planinscak four months later.

The unrest among Serbian patriots led to mass arrests. Then in the first four months of 1913 some two hundred high-treason trials were held. Yet these trials did nothing to curb the assassins' zeal, for on 18 August 1913 the Governor of Croatia, Baron Ivo Skerletz, was attacked by Stjepan Dojcic. Two months later the Trieste police informed Vienna that a wide-ranging conspiracy was being hatched and the dissidents were planning to kill Archduke Ferdinand.

The fatal visit of the Archduke to Sarajevo was announced in the press as early as mid-March 1914. As soon as the announcement was made, fears for his safety grew. It was recalled that an earlier journey planned for 1911 had been postponed because of the fear of assassination. And it was recalled that in 1911 Father Galen had been sent in confidence to Sarajevo to sound out the city's possible reaction to a visit from the Heir Apparent. On his return Galen had produced an unfavourable report. Josip Sunaric had even told him: 'I know the Serbs. I know that they will wait for him in ambush as murderers.'

Now in 1914 Sunaric was still adamantly opposed to a visit. He despatched a telegram to Bilinski, Joint Minister of Finance, warning him that the Archduke and his wife would face great danger in Sarajevo. He was not alone.

Toso Zurunic, Chief of the Department of the Interior of the Bosnian Government, received many warnings that the Archduke was in danger. Similar warnings came from many sources in contact with Serbian nationalists. They came in from Vienna, from Budapest, from Berlin and even from the USA. Berchtold, the Minister of Foreign Affairs, even had a detailed dossier on the suspicious movements of Serbian students in Croatia. One of these students was quoted as saying: 'The time for empty boasting is over and now we must start working in earnest. Bombs and not merely loose tongues must go into action.'

Despite all these warnings and the dread fears amongst the people closest to him – people like Prince Montenuovo, his son Maximilian and his doctor Eisenmenger – the plans went ahead. On 23 June 1914, against the advice of the Chief of Police at Sarajevo, the exact route of the official procession was disclosed. Then, as 28 June approached, Chief of Police Gerde tried to warn General Potiorek and the Military Committee in charge of the visit about the menacing and dangerous atmosphere in the town. He was ignored but he covered himself by having the warnings entered into the official minutes.

When the Archduke and his wife set out for Sarajevo they were both weighed down by morbid thoughts. They knew all too well that the Serbs were seething with resentment – that they regarded the visit as a calculated insult. The many warnings they had received had had their effect. Presentiments of disaster coloured their outlook. So much so that on the 23rd the Archduke himself said after his special railway coach had been damaged by fire: 'Our journey starts with an extremely promising omen. Here our car burns and down there they will throw bombs at us.'

In the event they escaped death by bombs only to fall victims to the bullets of a lone gunman, Gavrilio Prinsip. His shots were the opening shots of the First World War.

Now, Bishop de Lanyi had been close to the Archduke and was still an intimate member of the courtly circle surrounding the Austrian Royal Family. As such, he was acutely aware of the doubts and anxieties raised by the mistimed, provocative and crassly foolish visit. Like scores of the others in that privileged circle, and like many others outside it, he dreaded the outcome of the visit. The mood of the Serbs was known. Their violent traditions had been openly demonstrated, repeatedly. Their dark plots were all aimed at the hated monarchy and its administrators.

The Bishop's fears were, therefore, hardly surprising. He shared the same agonies of mind as many others. His agony culminated in a realistic dream that was right in parts. But only in parts – for example only one gunman was involved, not a pair as featured in his dream. Still, my point is not to fault the gentleman's subconscious but to show there was nothing of mystery in his mental tableau.

The Sarajevo visit was suicidal. As Tudor Edwards has put

it: 'Even a schoolboy would have foreseen the ambush, the rain of bombs and bullets.'

Yet if de Lanyi's one-off forecast fails our tests, how do the many predictions of Cheiro measure up? As I write, Cheiro's name is being brought to the fore. The fiftieth anniversary of the Abdication of King Edward VIII in 1936 has reminded journalists of Cheiro's amazing prevision of that emotional constitutional crisis. Cheiro, or Count Louis Hamon as he styled himself, wrote: '... the Prince who may be fond of a light flirtation with the fair sex ... is determined not to settle down until he feels a *grande passion*, but it is well within the range of possibility, owing to the peculiar planetary influences to which he is subjected, that he will in the end fall a victim of a devastating love affair. If he does, I predict that the Prince will give up everything, even the chance of being crowned, rather than lose the object of his affection.'

I quote from *Cheiro's World Predictions* (1931 edition). But that text was actually in the hands of his publishers as early as 1925 – years before Mrs Wallis Simpson came on the scene, won Edward's heart, and precipitated the crisis. It is a direct hit by any standards, but does it really display a paranormal content?

Decidedly not! I have talked with people who were deeply involved in the abdication turmoil. People who were intimates of the King, like Lord Carnarvon. What they disclosed showed me that Edward's aversion to the throne had been well observed long before 1936. He had emotional problems that made it pretty certain that the right, dominant, masterful woman would place him under her spell to the exclusion of all other things. Even to the point of abdication.

When you come to read everything that Cheiro says on this topic, you will find that despite his astrological flourishes he actually reveals the real source of his knowledge. First of all he draws parallels with the lives of earlier Princes of Wales. Then he records that: 'The present Prince of Wales has piqued curiosity many times by rumours of marriages that have faded away into the air ... Princesses from Italy, Russia, Sweden, Norway, Bulgaria and Greece have been confidently spoken of as future Princesses of Wales. Rumour says that Queen

Mary, and in a lesser degree King George, have worried themselves seriously over this problem of the Prince . . .'

Cheiro further observes: 'At the present time the widespread impression gaining ground that the present Prince of Wales has no taste for the wearing of a crown has fixed increasing interest upon the studious attention of his brother, the Duke of York, to the exacting duties of the life ceremonial.'

Cheiro's society contacts were many and close. He was party to all the tittle-tattle, rumours and informed gossip that swirled around in those circles. Because of this he knew more about the real problems faced by the Prince than many of the Members of Parliament who were later to discuss Edward's fate in the Commons.

A nil score so far! How does it stand, though, with his predictions about the Second World War? These are often being quoted, and they are found again in the 1931 edition of *World Predictions*. In Charles Neilson Gattey's book *They Saw Tomorrow* they are presented in this fashion: 'England will be attacked in all her Mohammedan possessions. She will give India her freedom, but religious warfare will rend that country from end to end until it becomes equally divided between the Mohammedan and the followers of Buddha. Italy and Germany will at the same period be at war with France . . . The United States will be engaged in war with Japan and will not take part until later in the European carnage . . . In Ireland there will be civil war between the North and South.'

A remarkably accurate set of forecasts, most people feel. But this quotation has been doctored in a deplorable way. Its 'accuracy' rests on chicanery. The proof lies in the real, unedited text in Cheiro's book. It reads: 'England will be attacked in all her Mohammedan possessions. She will give India her freedom, but religious warfare will rend that country from end to end until it becomes equally divided between the Mohammedan and the followers of Buddha. All her colonies will again send large numbers of men to help the Mother Country. Italy and Germany will at the same period be at war with France, and Spain under a Dictator will be engaged in a life and death struggle in North Africa. Germany and England will become allies and pour immense numbers of troops into Palestine and Egypt.

'Russia will draw enormous masses of Chinese and Tartars with her and all Mohammedan races will be brought into the conflict. The United States will be engaged in war with both Mexico and Japan and will not take part until later in the European carnage.

'Great Britain will suffer terribly in the prolonged warfare, the most of London and towns on the east coast will be destroyed by fleets of aeroplanes from Russia.

'In Ireland there will be Civil War between the North and South, and a new Irish Republic will inflict considerable damage by aeroplanes on such cities as Liverpool, Manchester, Birmingham and the west of England.'

Historians in particular will be puzzled to learn that in the Second World War Germany and England were allies and that most of London and the east coast towns were destroyed by Russian aircraft. It will also be news to them that the Irish Republic used its miniscule air force to bomb Britain so dramatically. They will at once spot, though, that the section involving war between the United States and Mexico and Japan is simply based on the text of the notorious Zimmerman telegram of February 1917! At that time the German Government did its best to persuade Japan and Mexico to enter the war on their side and attack the USA.

Cheiro's original forecast was simply a meaningless mishmash drawing on past history and a few current trends. Nothing can excuse the later falsification of his words in an attempt to make sense of them.

Having rescued Cheiro from the hands of his manipulators, let us look at the man himself. He has made many claims to spectacular successes. One of his most famous successes dates back to the early part of his career in 1893. At the time he had had a breakdown in health and after recovering he decided to have a change of scene and visit the United States. On arrival in New York he rented a fine apartment on Fifth Avenue and set up business as a palmist. For a while business was bleak, and then a woman journalist from the *New York World* called in and proposed a test. If he accepted and proved successful, the paper's Sunday edition would give him tremendous publicity.

The newspaper would collect a number of handprints on paper and keep the identities secret. Cheiro would then examine each one in turn and give a reading. His comments would be recorded and matched up against the lives behind the handprints.

Cheiro took up the challenge. The lady reporter bustled around collecting handprints, then returned to carry out the test. As each palm impression was handed to him he studied it, pondering at length, and then gave his verdict. Everything was taken down in shorthand.

When the test ended the exhausted palmist was told that he would have to wait for the following Sunday's edition of the *World* in order to know the results. Cheiro himself says: 'It was then Tuesday. I lived under a very anxious strain for the following days. Saturday night I scarcely slept till near morning. About nine o'clock my black servant knocked at the door and woke me. In the most matter-of-fact way he said: "Get up, sir, there are over a hundred people sitting on the stairs waiting to see you."

'I did not ask the reason; in his hand was the *New York World* with its entire front page devoted to the interview. I can still see the heading in big type: "Cheiro reads successfully the Lives of the Mayor, the District Attorney, Nicoll Ward McAllister, Dr Meyer," etc.'

According to Cheiro the most astonishing reading of all was the one which had involved the handprint of a murderer. The man was a Dr Meyer from Chicago, aged forty four, who at the time was actually in prison awaiting trial. Cheiro's reading brought all that to light. His account in his memoirs says: 'Then came the climax – it was about the fourth or fifth impression she put before me.

'"There is something in this hand so abnormal," I said, "that I shall refuse to read it unless you can bring me the consent of the owner to tell what I see."

'"We have the consent of all these people," was the reply, and she showed me a letter from the *New York World* stating that the consent had been obtained from the various persons who had given these impressions.

CRY 'HALT!' TO HITLER

'Under these conditions I agreed to proceed. The hand before me was that of a murderer, of that I was certain. I could make no mistake. There was clear evidence that such a man had used his intelligence to obtain money by crime, and that a little over the middle of his life his very self-confidence would betray him into the hands of the law.

'"Whether this man has committed one murder or twenty," I remarked, "is not the question; at about his forty fourth year he will be tried for murder and condemned. It will be found that for years he has used his intelligence, and whatever profession he has followed, to obtain money by crime, and that he has stopped at nothing to obtain his ends. He will be condemned, will go under the greatest strain and anxiety, will live under the very shadow of death; but his life will not end in this manner, for he will pass the remainder of his life in prison."'

A wealth of detail like that has to be impressive. But was it correct? Cheiro insisted it was. Once he knew the identity of the murderer he was able to check. Then he wrote: 'What really did happen was this. This man, Dr Meyer, was convicted of insuring people's lives in Chicago – he was either their doctor or managed later to attend them – and in exercising his profession it was believed he poisoned his patients and later collected the insurance money . . .

'When Dr Meyer's case came on, my prediction was fulfilled to the letter; after a long, sensational trial in which he fought every inch of the ground, he was condemned to death, but within a few days of the electrocution chair, on a technical point, the sentence was altered to imprisonment for life.'

Little wonder, then, that enthusiastic writers and broadcasters have jumped on this story to retell and expand on. Frank Edwards, for one, used the tale in his radio programmes, in his books, and in his syndicated articles. Neilson Gattey features it as well. A great pity that not one of them opened the files of the *New York World*!

A copy of the *New York World* for Sunday 26 November 1893 is in front of me. 'I can still see the heading in big type,' said Cheiro. So much for his memory. The heading, in quite small type, at the top of only one column reads: 'Character

Read In The Hands.' And the entire front page is not devoted to the interview – just two columns. However, the rest of the interview does take up a further three columns on page eighteen.

Let us allow him a little licence – the really important things are all there in those five columns. Each palm print is shown in facsimile and each reading is printed in full. The alleged forecast claimed by Cheiro in his *Memoirs* and elsewhere, is not there. On the contrary, we find that he did not even attempt to read the palm print of Dr Meyer but passed over it as the newspaper reporter testifies – in these words : 'A sudden change passed over the face of Cheiro as he fixed his gaze upon the next imprint that I handed him. After a moment of apparent indecision he handed it back, saying quietly as he did so: "I refuse to read that hand to any one but the owner."

'I was speechless with astonishment. It was the hand of Dr Henry W. Meyer, the man accused of wife poisoning, and who is at present in the Tombs awaiting trial.'

Cheiro was streets ahead of the people who set out to test him. The security around the test was ultra-sloppy. The young journalist even took a palm print from someone who had already consulted Cheiro.

When the prints were handed to him, his experience gave him the edge over the trusting pressmen. He was able to gauge their moods, notice all their exchanged glances and subtle reactions.

The moment the Meyer print was extracted and handed over, he was able to spot the change in atmosphere. The extra air of anticipation and solemnity was enough to alert him that this was an extraordinary print. So he took no chance, refused to comment on it and handed it back.

He was able to fake his account because he knew all too well that his gullible readers would be unlikely to bother with anything as exacting as real truth. He was to continue faking stories for the rest of his life.

Yet one of his most grotesque stories still circulates without effective challenge. If it is true, then we have to reverse our verdict on the man. For even a liar sometimes tells the truth.

His story involves predictions made to a man named Douglas

Murray. Murray called on Cheiro some time in 1887. He was a stranger and was in light-hearted mood. 'Which of my hands are you going to take?' he laughed. Cheiro took the right hand, and as he did an inexplicable feeling of horror and dread seemed to ooze from the palm.

Cheiro dropped the hand back onto the cushion and Murray, still amused, asked what was wrong. Cheiro found himself unable to explain but in his later account he said: 'The hand seemed to speak to me. It was not that I attempted to read it. There was no need for me to make such an effort. It was as if I was taken possession of by some occult force of which I cannot give any explanation. Without any regard to the effect my words might have, and with the feeling of listening to myself speaking without the power of preventing the words coming, I blurted out rapidly: "I feel this right hand of yours will not be yours for long. A picture forms in my mind of a gun of some kind bursting and shattering it to pieces. This is followed by terrible suffering and finally the entire arm will have to be amputated," and I added quickly: "Your hand, sir, seems to be calling to me to try and save it from this impending disaster."'

At this point Murray burst into laughter, completely unconvinced, then Cheiro continued: 'Your hand shows me another picture. It draws a number out of a lottery, the number gives you a prize that you do not want to have. Out of obstinacy and fatalism you take it, and from that moment on commences a series of misfortunes, beginning with the loss of your right arm.'

His client still stayed amused and said that he had never won a thing in a lottery ever. What is more he did not believe he ever would. Still, he asked: 'Does this wonderful hand of mine tell you what this extraordinary prize is likely to be?'

A picture began to form in Cheiro's mind. First the shape of an oblong object. Then strange hieroglyphics appeared and the shape became revealed as an Egyptian sarcophagus with a carved figure on the lid. He described what he saw to Murray and begged him not to touch it. If Murray did, it would bring misfortune to him and anyone else involved with it.

But his warnings failed to overturn Murray's cheerfulness.

He left smiling, handing his card to the palmist.

A year later Douglas Murray went to Egypt on a shooting expedition with two friends. They planned a trip up the Nile but before leaving Cairo they learnt of a mummy case of rare beauty that was up for sale. In those days Egyptology was all the rage, so Murray went along to see the case and found that it had once housed a priestess of the Temple of Amen-Ra.

Her image was depicted in superb colours on the case. It was vivid and impressive. Even though it dated from 1,600 BC time had been kind to it. His two friends admired the mummy case as much as he did, and the all-round admiration was so great that in the end they decided to draw lots to see which one of them should end up owning it. The lots were drawn and Murray won the case.

He arranged for the precious antique to be crated and despatched to London. Then he set off on his shooting expedition. Tragically, a few days later the gun Murray was carrying exploded in his right hand. Immediately his boat headed back for Cairo but unusually strong head-winds made their progress gruellingly slow. It took ten days to reach the hospital. By this time gangrene had set in and despite the efforts of the doctors he was in danger of losing his life. They saved him by amputating the right arm above the elbow.

Misfortune followed Murray on his voyage back to England. Both his companions were taken ill, died and were buried at sea. On arrival at Tilbury two trunks containing valuable scarabs and curiosities were stolen. From then on misfortune after misfortune hit Murray, his family, and anyone who came into close contact with the mummy case. Finally Douglas Murray gave the case to the British Museum, hoping that in some way this would negate its malign influence.

The mummy case story does not end there, though it does for us, because we now have to look at the evidence for Cheiro's reading. When Cheiro told this story he believed, like most people, that Douglas Murray had bought the mummy case in 1888 and lost his arm in the same year. What he did not know, however, was that Douglas-Murray (correct form) had given a complete account of his expedition and his diaries to Mrs H. Spoer. Another account had also been provided by the sister of A.F. Wheeler, the man who had actually brought the mummy case to England.

Both accounts show that the history of the mummy case had become garbled. But more importantly, they prove that the 1888 date is absurd. The visit to Egypt, the purchase of the mummy case and the loss of the arm took place twenty years earlier, in 1868.

Though Cheiro was a charming fellow and a honey-tongued raconteur, he was beautifully bogus. He was not a count, his name was not Hamon. He was plain William John Warner, born at Bray, County Wicklow, Ireland. His birthdate? 1 November 1866. Which means that at the time of Douglas-Murray's tragic Egyptian excursion, Cheiro was a tiny tot aged two!

If anything, this proves that the surest way of predicting the future lies in cultivating the faculty of one hundred per cent hindsight. By comparison all other approaches are dismal non-starters!

Chapter Fifteen

Dr Soal's Mr Hyde

A musical box tinkled away in the background while a dead man spoke freely about his past. The university lecturer sat enthralled as he listened. The voice was that of an old school acquaintance. He had died a soldier's death. And yet here were his familiar tones issuing from the end of a fibre megaphone held to a woman's lips.

The woman was the British 'direct voice' medium, Blanche Cooper. The message that came through her lips that night marked the first stage in the unfolding of a strange case that has baffled psychical researchers ever since 1925. It became known as the Gordon Davis Case and Muriel Hankey has said it 'posed a problem to which there has been no conclusive explanation ... it is the classic of its kind. So far as I know it has never been repeated.' Many other commentators agree with her. Conan Shaw has devoted a sixteen-page study to it and Gracia-Fay Ellwood has published an eighteen-page analysis. So what made this case so special?

At the start we have to consider the lecturer, Mr (later Doctor) S.G. Soal. His speciality was mathematics, but during the First World War he began to consider the question of survival. In April 1919 he joined the London Spiritualist Alliance and a month later received his first puzzling message. At one of their meetings, medium Annie Brittain had turned to him and asked if he knew of 'Canuter' or 'Canuder' – she wasn't sure if it was a place or person.

Soal was highly impressed. She was aiming at Canewdon, a tiny village just two miles away from his one-time home. At the age of six he had walked to Canewdon every day to attend classes held at the rectory. Later other mediums offered him the name of this obscure village from his past. Mr Soal became hooked. This was surely an exhibition of supernormal faculty.

But on me this incident had a very different effect. As soon as I read of it I developed a wariness where Soal was concerned. Did he want to believe so much that he could blot out so many significant memories? You see, tiny Canewdon is the one village in all Essex that is justly famous in occult circles. It is in the very heart of an area still known as Witch Country. Within recent memory children of Canewdon danced seven times around its church to ward off witchcraft. Its history is full of legends of ghosts and uncanny events. And when Soal was a boy in the 1900s, Master of Witches George Pickingale still skulked around its lanes browbeating the superstitious villagers.

Now the mediums knew Soal's address in south east Essex. It was on their register. So the Canewdon connection, conscious or otherwise, was an obvious one to them. And it should have been to Soal – yet he blocked out the thought. Very odd indeed. But then Soal was a very odd fish, as I went on to discover!

On 1 September 1921 he embarked on a series of sittings with Mrs Blanche Cooper. They were to last until June 1922 but were not published until late 1925 in the *Proceedings of the Society for Psychical Research* (Vol. XXXV). Following publication the furore began.

All the reports raised many interesting questions, but the Gordon Davis report was unique. For Soal had recently discovered that the dead man was very much alive. The recorded messages had been checked and verified. And a strange new set of problems had emerged.

These problems centred on the description of Davis' house. At the sitting of 9 January 1922 the 'dead' Davis had not spoken directly but had passed these details through the medium: '... about his house. He says something about a funny dark tunnel ... there's five or six steps and a half ... Think it's the front.'

When asked to describe the inside, the medium replied: 'He says there's a very large mirror and lots of pictures ... these pictures are all scenes ... glorious mountains and the sea – there's one picture where a road or something seems to go between two hills ... some vases – very big ones with such funny tops and saucers, but not to drink out of ... Oh, downstairs there's two funny brass candlesticks ... think they are on a shelf ... there's something right in front of his house – not a verandah – something that's not in front of the other houses.'

Soal asked if the house was in a street. If so, what was the street name? The medium described the house as: 'joined up to others – don't think it's a proper street – like half a street ... Get the letter Es.' The Gordon Davis message ended at that point.

Soal had earlier found that he was impressed by the 'lifelike reproduction of Davis' mannerisms of speech, tone of voice and accent.' This helped give the messages an extra-convincing air, even if he did not understand why Davis was bothering to make contact.

That the details matched so well was astounding. More arresting still were some dates provided by Gordon Davis. In 1922, at the time of the sitting, he did not live in that house, but in a London flat. His move to 54 Eastern Esplanade only took place on 13 December 1922. He had certainly inspected that house as early as 6 January 1922, but it was then already tenanted, needing repairs, in a dirty condition, and with quite different pictures – mainly cheap prints – on its walls.

In 1925 researchers noted these anomalies and debated their implications. Rivalries in the bustling world of the spiritualists led to an attack on the report by H. Dennis Bradley, a writer who imagined that he had a near-monopoly on correct intepretations of messages from spirit land.

Bradley derided the Gordon Davis case. Merely a number of commonplace coincidences, in his eyes. Soal challenged Bradley to find another house in the whole of England which corresponded to every item of the description given by the supposed spirit of Davis. Bradley ignored the challenge and Soal triumphantly said: 'I was able to demonstrate that the odds were of the order of millions to one against such a group of correct items being the result of chance coincidence.'

Soal's reasoning won the day. It became accepted that for some unaccountable reason the spirit of a living man had posed as dead, and had spoken about events that had not even happened. Psychical researchers have pondered and stayed perplexed ever since. And yet the answers have been there in front of their eyes all along. Regrettably the vital primary sources were neglected.

Let us rectify that now. But first, a closer look at Soal's personality. Was he naive? Did he understand the necessity for accuracy? Did he understand the importance of witnessed accounts and the need for a full revelation of his working conditions? In his *My Thirty Years Of Psychical Research* he says: 'As a mathematician I've always disliked vagueness of every kind.' Then in his review of Dunne's *An Experiment With Time* he wrote: 'Mr Dunne is very chary throughout his narrative of giving us the exact dates and times of the various occurrences described ... it is a matter for regret that Mr Dunne, who has such a keen sense of experimentation, and who seems fully alive to the psychological possibilities of his subject, should have omitted to take the simple precaution of getting his dream records witnessed and posted immediately to some responsible scientific man. Cases of prevision, in which the evidence is unimpeachable, are at present as rare as lunar rainbows, and it is a pity that such good cases as Mr Dunne presents may possibly have to be discounted on the grounds of insufficient corroboration.'

So he does know how to act responsibly. But in practice Soal violated all the rules.

In mid-February 1922 he is told Gordon Davis is alive. His records now assume a new importance. Yet no 'responsible scientific man' is allowed to examine and witness them. No copies are sent post-haste to the SPR or any other body. Instead, he sits on these potentially exciting documents for over six weeks – until *after* his visit to see Gordon Davis.

And why this extraordinary delay in visiting Davis? He could have been with him in under ten minutes any time he chose. For the nebulous, vaguely located Prittlewell is, in fact, part of Southend! Soal's house was a mere mile down a straight main road from Gordon Davis' offices. You would never guess this, though, from reading Soal's account. He is free and exact with distances that do not matter – but Prittlewell...?

But as we shall see, Mr Soal was a devious character. And it is clear that in the six weeks at his disposal he had plenty of chance to find out things about number 54. I have visited the house myself and noted that all Soal had to do was walk past the place, then ride past on the double-decker bus and record everything that could be spotted through the plain glass windows.

Let us not mince words. I am asserting that the house forecasts were faked. The original exercise books he used to record his sittings were easily falsified. The metal staples only had to be sprung and the pages would lift out, allowing newly written accounts to be inserted. In that manner he was able to create a cunning enigma.

Here I should emphasise that there were genuine 'messages' in the accounts that needed no doctoring, but these were the parts dealing with schooldays and other trivia. These did not exhibit precognition or anything vaguely startling and Soal could have learned of all the bits and pieces involved by quite normal means. Only the house forecasts were destined to make this affair noteworthy and extraordinary. So only those passages needed to be rejigged or invented.

Is this just a wild, spiteful theory? Or is there any proof to back it up? Yes, there is proof. Even though Soal carefully covered his tracks, he blundered.

Initially, he was clever. When he called on Gordon Davis he took with him a typed copy of the handwritten accounts of the relevant sessions. The typed and written accounts naturally had to be identical, since Soal wanted Davis to comment on each item and sign a statement of either dissent or agreement. Up to that point everything looked foolproof.

His blunder came after leaving number 54 on the night of his visit. He walked with Gordon Davis up to the Davis & Hollins Agency offices, some five minutes away. At the offices Soal became too elated by his success and overreached himself. He suddenly 'remembered' something that fell outside the scope of the typed records. He called it a 'curious oversight.'

As he later put it: 'I entirely overlooked the statement concerning "black dicky bird on piano" ... I remembered to mention it. Mr Davis then informed me that he had in his possession a small ornament in the form of a kingfisher which stood on a black china pedestal. At the time of my visit it was actually standing in a plant-pot on the piano, and owing to its being almost hidden inside the plant-pot, had escaped my notice.'

A nice little extra touch, so it seemed. And Soal made the most of it, devoting almost three columns of comment on it in his published paper. Naturally he had to locate this new information somewhere. So he claimed that this delightful dicky bird had popped up in a passage found towards the middle of the sitting of Monday 30 January 1922.

But this is pure fiction. His knowledge of the bird came from his observation of Davis' kingfisher ornament, not from any seance. When he spontaneously invented this morsel, he had forgotten one vital factor. He had forgotten that a complete record of the essential sitting had been in private hands for the past three years.

In January and February 1922 the Reverend A. T. Fryer of Bath had helped Soal investigate some Cooper messages concerning James Miles, a young boy who had drowned. In the end it was accepted that the messages were based on newspaper reports. But as an aid to his investigations, Reverend Fryer had been sent copies of all the sittings involved. Luckily for truth, one of these copies was of the sitting of 30 January 1922. It survives.

This copy is in Soal's own handwriting. It lists, stage by stage, every statement made that day and it even lists every pause during the sitting. Nothing is omitted, even when the message is as slight as a single letter. Yet there is no mention of Gordon Davis on any page of this record. The dickybird message simply does not exist.

So, fittingly the faker stands betrayed by his own heady enthusiasm.

But why should a gifted academic want to deceive and bemuse people in this way? There we really have a problem. The search for motives can often prove unrewarding and highly frustrating. In Soal's case we can only make inspired guesses – and stay frustrated.

We know that Soal was first attracted to spiritualism following the death of his brother Frank, who was killed on the Somme in September 1918. He recalls: 'I argued that if Sir Oliver Lodge could get in touch with the surviving spirit of his son Raymond through the intermediary of (medium) Mrs Leonard, then surely I ought to be able to make contact with my brother Frank through the powers of this same Mrs Leonard or some other medium.'

Initially, then, he was sincere. He proved this by diligently sitting week after week with Blanche Cooper, recording everything that he heard. Or rather thought he heard. In the end he admitted: 'The net result of my thirty-odd sittings with Mrs Cooper was to weaken seriously any belief I had in the spiritistic interpretation of these phenomena.' As he saw it, the messages were either telepathic or just scraps of knowledge obtained from normal sources.

By 1925 he had developed strong suspicions that he himself may have played an active part in creating the seance messages, though he did not make these doubts public until years later. So at a time of semi-disillusionment he was suddenly presented with new possibilities in the Gordon Davis case.

On learning that Davis lived, he understandably wished to make contact. His nearby library had (and still has) a shelf of local street directories going back many years. In the then current directory for 1924 he found the home and office addresses for Davis. At the same time he would naturally wonder why he had missed seeing Davis around for all these years. Perhaps he had not been in Southend long? A glance at the earlier directories would show him that Davis' home address had only come in with the 1924 edition.

Now the original unaltered Cooper records may have contained references to a house. Out of excited curiosity, Soal would be drawn to take a quick look at Eastern Esplanade to see if they coincided. A 1922 glimpse of a 1924 home would set the psychic world reeling. But the details did not coincide – after all, why should they? This discovery must have been specially galling for Soal. The one case that promised to be so very different was now drastically diminished in interest.

Back home he may have had a battle with his conscience, but in the end his bizarre side conquered. And he faked the records. The Davis case became the locomotive that hauled all his other cases into public view. It brought him his first brush with national fame. And it created a long-lasting puzzle.

The results were more than gratifying for him. He wrote: 'The Blanche Cooper report received very favourable notice in the better newspapers. The *Observer* devoted a column and a half to it and I had the distinction of being one of the few persons who have been accorded a leading article in the *Morning Post*.'

Soal was cast in the strangest of moulds. As Betty Markwick observes, he was '... obsessive, absorbed, secretive and subject to bouts of dissociation.'

Under certain conditions, with one hand held by a woman, he would write automatically and fluently at the reported rate of 3,000 words an hour. In this fashion he delivered whole chapters ostensibly from Oscar Wilde. Soal later discovered that many of the Wildean descriptions came from the assorted literature he had read, while other people discovered that a secret, well-hidden, poetic side of Soal was involved, for some of the Wildean flourishes were actually 'borrowed' from letters Soal had earlier written while in the Army.

Then he was dogged by involuntary whispering. Here the implications for his Blanche Cooper sittings are enormous. Blanche used to hold one of Soal's hands and she hummed incessantly when she was not struggling with hardly audible words. Under those conditions Soal most likely went on to semi-automatic pilot, vocalised away, and with the lady's humming acting like a carrier-wave, ended up by listening to his own voice!

Years after his first triumph the doctorer was doctored. Weighty ESP experiments brought Dr Soal fame once more. A fame that teetered unsteadily along until 1978, when statistician Betty Markwick revealed that his marvellous, significant results rested on 'data manipulation.' In other words, fakery. Dr Soal's Mr Hyde had struck once more.

So it was goodbye to one of the most impressive series in

experimental parapsychology. But a few questions still remained – perhaps some always will. However, the most important of all these is now answered, allowing us to wave goodbye to Gordon Davis – whose time is truly up!

Chapter Sixteen

THE WORLD SHALL HEAR FROM ME AGAIN

'WHO WERE YOU IN 1432?... Joan of Arc had just been burnt at the stake, the Hundred Years War dragged on and an infant was King of England. You may have had a hand in those events that shaped history. Now you can see for yourself. You can explore your own past lives, see who you have been and learn who you can become...'

That is an advert for a Past Life and Future Freedom Hypnotic Regression Seminar. It may seem funny to some, but for many thousands in the western world hypnotic regressions are alluring. For them, these sessions are able to lift heavy veils from their memories. And now the domestic tape recorder has become the invaluable ally of truth as it captures the 'authentic' accounts of long-hidden life cycles.

It all began with the Bridey Murphy case of 1952. 'Ruth Simmons,' an American housewife apparently regressed back to an earlier life in nineteenth-century Ireland. The book of the case topped the US best-seller list and was translated into five other languages. The book spawned a motion picture; a disc from one of the recorded sessions sold tens of thousands of copies; and all over the United States tape recorders began purring away at innumerable regression sessions.

Twenty years after the Bridey Murphy sensation a much more impressive group of 'past lives' startled the public. The Bloxham Tapes were first presented as a BBC Television documentary produced by Jeffrey Iverson. Then they were included and enlarged on in Iverson's book *More Lives Than One?* They were regarded as 'the most staggering evidence for reincarnation ever recorded ... amazingly detailed accounts of past lives – accounts so authentic that they can only be explained by the certainty of reincarnation.' Inevitably they achieved international renown.

The tapes themselves had been accumulated for years by an elderly Cardiff-based hypnotherapist, Arnall Bloxham. He was a lifelong believer in reincarnation, but his 'past life' regressions only emerged quite late in his career. Despite that, he managed to collect a cupboard full of 'past life' tapes drawn from his experiments with over four hundred people.

Jeffrey Iverson first heard about this collection casually at a party. As a producer with the BBC in Cardiff he was constantly on the lookout for programme ideas, so in October 1974 he called at Bloxham's house. After listening to the calm old man's claims, Iverson concluded that if these claims were true then the recordings were possibly the largest investigation ever undertaken into this type of regression. If true, Iverson thought, 'then that single famous case ... the search for Bridey Murphy, was just a tune on an Irish fiddle compared to his symphony of voices.'

Iverson began with a weeding-out process, discarding those tapes which he felt could not be researched and proven. Gradually he came to concentrate on a limited number of the tapes where it seemed to him that the details 'coincided remarkably with known but quite obscure periods of history ... in which people talked about cities and countries they had apparently never visited in their present lives.'

Two outstanding cases resulted from all this weeding. In one, Graham Huxtable, a Swansea man, regressed to a squalid life aboard a Royal Navy frigate engaged in action against the French some two hundred years ago. But the most important case involved a Welsh housewife, Jane Evans.

Mrs Evans produced a remarkable set of six 'past lives'. They were remarkable not so much for their number and diversity as for the sheer, almost overwhelming, amount of detail packed into three of them. In her minor 'lives' she was first a London sewing girl named Anne Tasker living about 1702;

then a lady-in-waiting to Catherine of Aragon two centuries earlier; and finally Sister Grace, an American nun living in Des Moines, Iowa, up until the 1920s.

Of the three major 'lives' two centre on the town of York. The earliest was set in the third century at the time of the rebellion of Carausius, the Roman Admiral who seized power in Britain and declared himself Emperor. Jane Evans was then Livonia, the wife of Titus, tutor to the young son of Constantius (Governor of Britain) and his wife Helena.

As Livonia, she describes how Constantius had to return to Rome and how the rebellion is engineered in his absence. As a consequence she and her husband and the rest of Constantius' household flee from Eboracum (York) to Verulam (St Albans) where they live apprehensively until the rebel regime is overthrown by an army led by Constantius. Yet her husband's triumphant return only brings sadness for the Lady Helena. Roman power struggles have dictated that her husband has had to divorce her and contract a new marriage with Theodora, daughter of the Emperor Maximianus.

Helena, therefore, decides to stay in Verulam. There they are influenced by a Christian woodcarver, Albanus, and Titus becomes so zealous that he volunteers for the priesthood. On the eve of Titus' induction as a priest, Roman troops swoop on Christian houses and burn them. Titus dies in the melée and Livonia apparently dies in some terror a short while afterwards.

Her next life in York also ended tragically. It unfolded at the year 1189 in the north of the city where 'most of the wealthy Jews live.' Then, she was Rebecca, wife of Joseph, a rich Jewish moneylender. For her and the rest of the Jews, the times were troubled. Anti-Jewish risings had occurred in Lincoln, London, and Chester. In York they were subject to abuse and threats. One of their community, Isaac of Coney Street, was even murdered by a mob.

By the spring of the next year it was obvious that violence was inevitable. So Rebecca and her family prepared their flight from the city, but they left their move too late. An armed band broke into the next-door house, killed their inhabitants, looted the place, then set fire to it. Joseph, Rebecca and her two children were able to run only as far as the castle of York. But even there they were unable to reach safe shelter. They finally found refuge of a sort when they entered a church, took the priest and his clerk captive and hid down in the cellars.

Later, from the safety of the church roof, they could see flames and hear distant mobs screaming 'burn the Jews, burn the Jews!'

Their respite turned out to be short-lived. Their captives escaped and alerted the mob and the soldiers came into the church to deal with the family. At this high point in the story Jane Evans became 'almost incoherent with terror' as the soldiers took her daughter. Then, whispering 'dark ... dark' she presumably died.

Her other major 'life' was lived in medieval France about 1450. At that time she was apparently a young Egyptian servant named Alison in the household of Jacques Coeur, the outstanding merchant prince of that period. She was able to talk at length and knowledgeably about Coeur's intrigues, about the king's mistress, Agnes Sorel, and about the clash between the Dauphin Louis and King Charles VII. She knew a great deal about Coeur's possessions and his extraordinary house at Bourges. Her knowledge of the clothes worn by her master is accurate: 'tunic edged with miniver, red hose ... shoes of red Cordovan leather ... a jewelled belt around his waist and a chain around his neck.'

She is again accurate when she tells of Jacques Coeur's fall from favour. He was once close to the King, but after the death of Agnes Sorel rumours spread at the Court hinting that Coeur had poisoned Agnes. Coeur was arrested, tried on a number of charges and imprisoned. But Alison knew only of the arrest. According to her, when the soldiers came for her master he gave her a poisoned draught to drink and she ended her life by accepting it.

When television viewers saw Jane Evans under hypnosis and heard the astonishing stories come naturally from her, they were rightly impressed. Her narratives seemed completely free from any attempts at acting a part. When fear and anguish came into her voice, it was clear that she was racked with real emotions. And her easy grasp of often difficult names of people and places made it seem that she was indeed remembering things that she had once known about intimately. But Jane Evans in her unhypnotised state was adamant that she knew nothing of Jacques Coeur, nothing of Carausius and his times and nothing of the massacre of the Jews at York.

Iverson's conclusion was that 'the Bloxham Tapes have been researched and there is no evidence that they are fantasies. In our present state of knowledge about them, they appear to convey exactly what they claim: a genuine knowledge and experience of the past.' But were these tapes ever researched as painstakingly as they should have been? And was the search for Bridey Murphy ever thorough enough? And is it possible that quite another phenomenon, rather than reincarnation, can account for these rich narratives?

Chapter Seventeen

THE DARK VAULTS OF THE MIND

Are 'past life' regressions really evidence for reincarnation? Or could they be glimpses of ancestral memories? Both theories have their followers. Yet rigorous research provides a distinctly different answer. These regressions are identified as fascinating examples of cryptomnesia.

To understand what cryptomnesia is, we have to think of the subconscious mind as a vast, muddled storehouse of information. This information comes from books, newspapers and magazines; from lectures, films, television and radio; from direct observation and even from overheard scraps of conversation.

Under everyday circumstances much of this knowledge is not subject to normal recall, but there are times when some of these deeply buried memories are spontaneously revived. Some of these revived memories re-emerge in a baffling form, since their origins are completely forgotten. This is cryptomnesia proper.

Because the origins are forgotten, the information can seem to have no ancestry and can be mistaken for something newly created. The late Helen Keller was tragically deceived by such a cryptomnesic caprice. In 1892 she wrote a charming tale called *The Frost King*. It was published and applauded, but within a few months it was revealed that Helen's piece was simply a modified version of Margaret Canby's story *The Frost Fairies*, published twenty nine years earlier.

Helen Keller had no conscious memory of ever having been told the story. She was blind and deaf, completely dependent on others for her knowledge. But enquiries revealed that a friend had in fact read a batch of Miss Canby's stories to her by touch in 1888. *The Frost Fairies* was among them.

When this was made plain, Helen was devastated. She wrote: 'Joy deserted my heart ... I had disgraced myself ... yet how could it possibly have happened? I racked my brain until I was weary to recall anything about the frost that I had read before I wrote *The Frost King*; but I could remember nothing.'

Other authors have been trapped in the same way, as Samuel Rosenberg has testified. Rosenberg worked for Warner Brothers pictures as a literary consultant on plagiarism cases. He records the valuable advice given him by his legal supervisor, who said: 'Don't be fooled by the sometimes astonishing resemblances you will find when you compare any two films, plays, stories, books, or film scripts. During the past twenty five years we have made hundreds of such comparisons in preparation for court trials, and in a great many cases we have found that both of the quarrelling authors – each convinced that he was honest and that the other writer was an idea-thief – had copied their plots, ideas, sequences from an earlier literary classic or from the Bible or some forgotten childhood story.'

In a similar fashion a number of cases of automatic writings, supposed to be from discarnate spirits, have been traced to published works. For example, the famous 'Oscar Wilde' scripts of the 1920s were gradually shown to be derived from many printed sources, including Wilde's own *De Profundis* and *The Decay of Lying*.

Dr S.G. Soal, one of the writers of these automatic scripts, was led to remark: 'The variety of sources from which the script is drawn is as amazing as the adroitness with which the knowledge is worked up into sentences conveying impressions of the different mannerisms of Wilde's literary style.'

This is a significant verdict, but even so, could such unconscious plagiarism account for Bridey Murphy and her offspring? Were the 'past existences' nothing but subconscious fantasies yielded up in order to please the hypnotists? Were they simply a pastiche of buried memories made gripping by the sincerity that accompanies cryptomnesia? In 1956 Dr Edwin Zolik of Marquette University set out to answer these questions.

Once he had hypnotised his subjects he instructed them to 'remember previous existences' and his subjects obliged by providing convincing accounts of 'past lives'. Everything was tape-recorded, preserving every subtlety and nuance in the voice as the tales unfolded. The recordings were listened to by the subjects in their waking states. Their verdicts were clear – they knew nothing about these 'past lifetimes.'

Their disclaimers were obviously sincere. But when he rehypnotised and re-examined his subjects they were able to remember the fictitious sources they had used in constructing their 'past life' adventures. In brief, Zolik's detailed analysis showed that 'past life' memories could easily be nothing but a mixture of remembered tales and strong symbolically coloured emotions.

Zolik's method of probing for the real-life origins of reincarnationist material was something he recommended to anyone seriously interested in the truth. Unfortunately few, if any, of the enthusiastic hypno-regressionists took any notice of his advice, and session after session was committed to tape and marvelled over without any effort being made to verify the origins or meaning of this material. Hypnotherapist Arnall Bloxham, for one, recorded over four hundred 'past life' regressions without ever once digging for the possibly mundane origins of these alleged 'lives'. On the other hand, the Finnish psychiatrist Dr Reima Kampman devoted years to the systematic investigation of the cryptomnesic origins of 'past life' accounts.

Dr Kampman of the Department of Psychiatry at the University of Oulu, Finland, began his work in the 1960s. He found his subjects among large groups of volunteers drawn from the three highest grades of the secondary schools of Oulu. All those who could enter a deep hypnotic state were selected for closer study. Kampman found it relatively easy to induce 'past life' recall as a response to his instruction: 'Go back to an age before your birth, when you are somebody else, somewhere else.'

His most amazing subject proved to be a girl who conjured up eight 'past lives'. In one 'life' she lived in ancient Babylonia, her next 'life' began in Nanking, then followed a 'life' in Paris, another in England and a final existence in revolutionary Russia.

One of her 'past lives' was as Karin Bergstrom, a seven-year-old girl who had died in an air raid back in 1939. She was able to supply an address for her old home and she knew the names and occupations of her former parents. Enquiries showed that indeed there had been an air raid on the exact date she had given. What is more, the addresses she had given had been hit. But the population records showed that neither a real Karin Bergstrom nor her relatives had died in the raid.

So the girl was asked to age-regress to the time when she had first heard of the Bergstroms or the bombing, and she soon remembered herself as a little girl turning over the pages of a patriotic book. In that book were photographs of the streets and houses hit by the bombs; and something about the people made homeless. The exact date of the raid was given and one picture showed two of the victims killed that day – significantly a mother and her seven-year-old daughter. So the complete regression was assembled from nothing more than the disjointed material found in this one book.

But the really exciting adventure involved her thirteenth-century 'English life' as Dorothy, an inn-keeper's daughter. This brought to light a very explicit account of contemporary happenings. And she astonished everyone by singing a song that none of the listeners was familiar with. She called it the summer song.

The unusual language used in the song was later studied by a student with high honours in the English language. He had no difficulty in identifying the words as examples of an old-style English – possibly Middle English. But this meant nothing to the girl, who had no memory of ever having heard the words or music of the song before.

The solution to this riddle came during a later experiment. She was asked to go back to a time when she might have seen the words and music of the song, or even heard it sung. She then regressed to the age of thirteen and remembered taking a book from the shelves of a library.

This was a casual choice. She made no attempt to read and absorb its contents. She merely flicked through its pages. Yet she not only remembered its title, but was able to state just where in the book her 'summer song' could be found.

The crucial book was *Musiikin Vaiheet*, a Finnish translation of *The History of Music* written by Benjamin Britten and Imogen Holst. And the mystery music was, of all things, the famous round *Sumer is Icumen In* with words rendered in a simplified medieval English.

A spate of similar successes led Kampman to conclude that he had demonstrated 'that the experiences of the present personality were reflected in the secondary personalities, both in the form of realistic details and as emotional experiences. The recording of a song from a book simply by turning over the leaves of a book at the age of 13 is an outstanding example of how very detailed information can be stored in our brain without any idea whatever of it in the conscious mind, and how it can be retrieved in deep hypnosis.'

These findings allow us to look at the Bridey Murphy and Bloxham cases with extra understanding.

Chapter Eighteen

SOLVING THE BLOXHAM MYSTERY

When the Bridey Murphy case first surfaced it was greeted with naive enthusiasm and this inevitably provoked a sour reaction. The *Chicago American* published a stinging 'exposure' claiming that Ruth Simmons' Bridey-knowledge came from her relatives and acquaintances in Chicago. The *Denver Post* countered by sending their man, William J. Barker, to Ireland in search of supporting material. The rival papers fought fiercely for their totally opposed viewpoints. Yet neither side produced a conclusive answer.

But in the end the onus of proof must always lie with the side which makes the positive claims. Regrettably, Bernstein and his friends were far too quick to make claims on the basis of slender research. And even this slender research is marred by flaws.

Let us note how they marvelled over Ruth's knowledge of the old custom of kissing the Blarney Stone, yet failed to spot a complete work on the custom, written by John Hewlett and called *The Blarney Stone*. It was published in New York, of all places, in 1951. They were equally over-awed by her knowing about the Irish Uillean pipes, about Irish jigs and about Irish customs and geography. She had never set foot in Ireland, they reasoned, and yet she knew all this fine detail concerning last century Erin. But their skimpy research failed to uncover the fact that Americans had twice had the chance of delving deeply into Irish life and customs without moving a single inch out of the USA.

Sorry – You've Been Duped

In 1893 The World's Columbian Exposition was staged in Chicago. Among the exhibits at this giant fair was an Irish village, the brain-child of Lady Aberdeen. Her original idea was modest – just a single Irish cabin. Yet by the opening day this had grown into a complete village of fifteen cottages. They were grouped around a green facing a full-sized replica of the tower of Blarney Castle.

To give the exhibit life, Ishbel Aberdeen travelled to the farthest corners of Kerry, Connemara and Donegal and chose girls who could spin, sing, make butter and dance jigs. The rose-cheeked colleens were then shipped, suitably chaperoned, over to the States to live and work in the Chicago village.

Every day for the six months of the fair visitors could hear the burbling Uillean pipes, listen to the songs of old Ireland and see the traditional jigs danced on the green. A huge relief-map of Ireland could be viewed from on high; books and souvenirs could be bought; and to crown it all, a replica Blarney Stone could be kissed in the traditional manner at the summit of the massive Blarney Castle tower.

On opening day some twenty thousand visitors paid their twenty five cents to enter the Irish village. After that the crowd grew, the sales mounted and the village became one of the three shows that made money. So by the end of the fair over three and a half million people had been brought into contact with all things Irish. And it did not end there! The whole venture was so wildly successful that an Irish village, complete with the full-size tower of Blarney Castle, was erected once more for the St Louis Fair of 1904.

Now Ruth Simmons (or rather Virginia Tighe) was born in 1923, so during her formative years there was still a veritable army of people around who had first-hand experiences of these Irish villages. The possibilities for gaining knowledge of Ireland in her home town of Chicago were obviously enormous.

Just as the possible sources were neglected, so was the tried and proven method of probing, under hypnosis, for the real-life origins of the Bridey saga. Perhaps it is still not too late. An independent hypnotist could still put the crucial questions to Virginia. Until she consents to this the case can only reasonably qualify as a famous curiosity – and no more.

It is very different, though, with the Bloxham Tapes. The extravagant claims made for these tapes impelled me to investigate them, even with the limited amount of time and funds at my disposal. The snags were great. Graham Huxtable proved unable to help in any constructive way, while Jane Evans flatly refused to co-operate. As a result the only course left open lay in a scrutiny of the texts and a laborious search for the probable origins of the previous 'lives.'

In the event the Huxtable naval regression proved empty. Its verifiable content was nil. Even its period flavour was grossly overrated. I carefully listed every archaic and little-used word in this regression and found that there were only two of them that were not known to me as a schoolboy. And my own schoolboy memories reminded me that there were large numbers of historical novels and boys' adventures based on the Royal Navy of the relevant period. A check with publishers' lists showed that there were, indeed, scores of books falling into this category. Apart from that, there were innumerable magazine stories along the same lines.

The ship that the 'seaman' Huxtable sailed in is clearly fictional. He calls it the *Aggie*. It has thirty two guns. No ship of that description served in the Royal Navy at that period. Remember, we are not talking about an obscure period in British history, but one which is extremely well documented. For example, Captain Manning and Commander C. F. Walker's book *British Warship Names* (Putnam, 1959) lists the name of every warship of importance for centuries. A thirty-two gun frigate is automatically in this category. But you will not find an *Aggie*, or any name resembling this, in their listings.

Some people, as a last-ditch attempt to salvage this story, have nominated the *Agamemnon* as a possibility. But this is out of the question. The *Agamemnon* was a sixty-four gun giant.

Little need be said about Huxtable's voice transformation. It has been described as having 'a much deeper tone and a strong South of England accent.' In other words, a real-life character from the past has emerged. In reality, however, what we encounter is simply the easily assumed pantomime-style *Treasure Island* accent, with all its unsubtlety. As such it has no evidential value.

Sorry – You've Been Duped

The six 'past lives' of Jane Evans were obviously the real challenge. Iverson himself considers this to be 'the most consistently astonishing case in Bloxham's collection.' I agreed – hers was the case to concentrate on.

My reinvestigation soon showed that the claims made for the tapes were false and the result of misdirected and inadequate research. For example, one of Jane Evans's minor 'lives' as a hand-maiden to Catherine of Aragon could easily have been based, sequence for sequence, on Jean Plaidy's historical novel *Katherine, The Virgin Widow*.

But the three major 'lives' proved to have the most illuminating ancestries. Her recital as Alison, a teenage servant to Jacques Coeur the 15th century French merchant prince was said to prove that she 'knew a remarkable amount about medieval French history.' Yet in her waking state she said: 'I have never read about Jacques Coeur. I have never heard the name.'

Jeffrey Iverson even concluded that she could not have picked up her many facts through the standard sources. After all, she knew so much, including inside knowledge of the intrigues surrounding the King's mistress, Agnes Sorel. Among other things, she was able to describe fully the exteriors and interiors of Coeur's magnificent house even giving details of the carvings over the fireplace in his main banqueting hall. More surprisingly, she spoke of the carved tomb of Agnes Sorel that was housed in a church. According to Iverson, this tomb 'had been cast away by French revolutionaries and spent a hundred and sixty five years, until its rediscovery in 1970, out of sight in a cellar.' But like a number of observations in the book *More Lives Than One?* this does not stand up to scrutiny.

The truth is that the Sorel tomb was placed in its present setting in 1809. It has been a tourist attraction for the whole of this century and it is described in detail in H.D. Sedgwick's *A Short History Of France* published in 1930, a book popular for decades and often found in public and school libraries. Apart from that, the tomb has been referred to in many other books and photographed frequently.

It is very much the same with Jacques Coeur's house. In fact, this is one of the most photographed and filmed houses in all France. Fine, explicit photographs are included in Dame Joan Evans' book *Life in Medieval France*. There one can see the stone carvings over the fireplace and gain a sound idea of how the place looked, both inside and out. There is now little doubt that Jane Evans has seen these or similar pictures.

There is overwhelmingly strong evidence that the rest of Jane's material was drawn from a source not known to Iverson – a 1948 novel, *The Moneyman* by C.B. Costain. This is based on Coeur's life and provides almost all of the flourishes and authentic-sounding touches included in her 'past life' memory.

In particular, the novel very neatly answers an important question raised by Iverson and other commentators, a question prompted by the curious fact that Alison does not know that her master is married! As Iverson puts it: 'How is it that this girl can know Coeur had an Egyptian bodyslave and not be aware that he was married with five children – a fact published in every historical account of Coeur's life? If the explanation for the entire regression is a reading of history books in the twentieth century, then I cannot explain how Bloxham's subject would not know of the marriage.'

Thomas Costain's short introduction to his novel clears up the mystery. He writes: 'I have made no mention of Jacques Coeur's family for the reason that they played no real part in the events which brought his career to its climax ... When I attempted to introduce them into the story they got so much in the way that I decided finally it would be better to do without them.'

Yet the view that her tapes were simply the result of cryptomnesia could still be contested, if it were not for the confirmation provided by the vetting of her remaining two major 'lives.'

As Rebecca, the Jewess of York, she was supposed to have met her death during the massacre of 1190. At that time most of the Jewish community died in the York Castle Keep, but Rebecca's death came in the cellar of a church where she had taken refuge. Around this cellar episode a formidable legend has grown up. It is now asserted that the church was positively identified as St Mary's Castlegate, and that a crypt was actually discovered there after Jane's regression. The truth is that the original TV programme script stated that there were three possible churches that could qualify as the place of refuge.

St Mary's was chosen to film in simply because it was the most convenient, since it was being converted into a museum. And it was this conversion which led to the uncovering of an aperture under the chancel. For believers, this was naturally a medieval crypt and proof of Rebecca's story.

For many of them it was joyfully received, almost as if it were some sign from heaven! It gave a fillip to their beliefs or yearnings, so it had to be true.

Writer after writer gloried in unravelling the tale of the wonderful evidential crypt. 'This really makes the sceptics' doubts stick in their throats,' wrote one, while Brian Inglis wrote: 'It is little touches of this kind which rule out cryptomnesia ... It is no longer possible, therefore, to maintain that cryptomnesia (or, for that matter, deliberate fraud – the pretence of remembering a past life) is an adequate explanation.'

To add strength to their assertions the believers constantly cited Professor Barrie Dobson of the Department of History, University of York, as if he were a supporter and ally. In doing so they drew on phrases found in Iverson's book. But the point needs to be made, and made as strongly as possible, that some of the references to Professor Dobson in that book are misleading. They are based on informal correspondence never intended for publication. As such they are easily open to misinterpretation.

It is significant, though, and predictable that not one of the believers ever took the trouble to check things out with Professor Dobson. Had they done so, they would have found that his views on the crypt are as follows (I quote with his full permission from his helpful letter to me dated 15 January 1986): 'There remains the issue of whether the "cellars under the church" in which Rebecca alleges she is sheltering at the time of the massacre of the Jews at the castle of York can be proved to have existed in 1190. The answer to this can only be a definite negative, for it now seems overwhelmingly most likely that the chamber which workmen reported encountering when renovating St Mary's Castlegate in 1975 was not an early medieval crypt at all but a post-medieval charnel vault.

The Royal Commission on Historical Monuments' *Survey of York, Vol. V (The Central Area)* 1981 says of it on page 31: "Beneath the east end of the chancel is a charnel vault with a barrel vault of stone rubble, probably a later insertion and now inaccessible."

'The fact that this vault or chamber remains inaccessible in January 1986 must not, in my opinion, persuade anyone into believing that Rebecca's reference to cellars under a church adds any authenticity to her story. The evidence available is now revealed as so weak in this instance that it fails to support any thesis which suggests that Rebecca's regression contains within it genuine and direct memories of late twelfth-century York.'

For all that, the furore over the crypt is meaningless, since the Rebecca regression is clearly a fantasy. It is an amalgamation of at least two different stories of persecution taken from widely separated centuries.

The proof that we are dealing with a fantasy lies in the historical absurdities found in the tale. Rebecca repeats four times that the Jewish community in York was forced to wear yellow badges '. . . circles over our hearts.' But the Jewish badge was not introduced until the following century and even then the English pattern consisted of two oblong white strips of cloth, representing the tablets of Moses. The yellow circle was, in fact, the badge worn in France and Germany after 1215. This is one aspect of Jewish history over which there are no legitimate doubts whatsoever.

A group of further absurdities was discovered in passages from the tapes that were excluded from both the book and the film. In these revealing passages Rebecca repeatedly speaks of living in the ghetto in the north of York. This ghetto was a quarter without street names where only the rich Jews lived, and she pointedly mentioned a poor Jew who could only afford to live in '. . . the middle of York in a street called Coney Street.'

There never was a special Jewish quarter in York. The Jews lived scattered among the Christians in places like Micklegate, Fosgate, Bretgate, Feltergayle and near the centre in Jewbury. And the idea that a Jew would live in Coney Street because of his poverty is ludicrous. Coney Street was in truth the choice place for many of the rich Jews to settle, including Josce the wealthy head of the Jewish community!

As for the notion of the ghetto itself, this involved a leap in time of over three hundred years, since the first ghetto was not set up until 1516 in Venice. It was established on an old foundry site and the very name is derived from the Italian *geto* or foundry.

This means, inevitably, that Jane Evans has the ability to subconsciously store vivid accounts and combine and edit these creatively to the point where she becomes one of the characters involved. The clinching proof that this is so is provided by the Roman wife, or Livonia regression, for this is the purest of all, based on one source only.

This particular life involves a turbulent period in Britain's history, a time of rebellion and instability. At the opening of this period the name of the Roman Governor in Britain is unrecorded in existing historical records. The 'past life' memories seem to fill this gap for us by stating that Constantius, father of Constantine the Great, was in charge. After consulting his reference books Iverson was happy to conclude: 'Nor can the regression be dismissed as a fiction built around a blank area of history. Livonia knows a considerable number of verifiable historical facts that fit perfectly into her vision of the missing years. No modern student of history could contradict the names and events she describes . . .'

After hearing the tape Professor Brian Hartley, an authority on Roman Britian, seemed to agree since he commented: 'She knew some quite remarkable historical facts, and numerous published works would have to be consulted if anyone tried to prepare the outline of such a story.'

Professor Hartley was right. Much painstaking research went into the making of Jane's story, but the research was undertaken by the late Louis De Wohl. In 1947 he wrote a best-selling novel *The Living Wood* and Jane's life as Livonia is taken directly from that novel. Brief comparisons will show just how.

Livonia's tale opens in Britain during 286 AD. She describes the garden of a house owned by the Legate Constantius. His wife is named as Lady Helena, his son as Constantine. The son is pictured being taught the use of shield, sword and armour by his military tutor Marcus Favonius Facilis. This entire sequence is taken from Chapter II, Book II of the novel, where Constantine trains in the use of arms and armour under his military tutor Marcus Favonius, called 'Facilis ... because everything was easy to him.' De Wohl based this character on a real-life centurion whose tombstone is now in Colchester Castle Museum. But his account of this centurion's life is pure fiction, since Facilis died in the first century AD.

Livonia then describes a visit by the historical character Allectus. He brings Constantius an urgent message from Rome, but despite the urgency he had 'stopped at Gessoriacum to see Carausius who is in charge of the fleet.' This section is drawn from the same section of the novel, where the visit leads up to the take-over of rule in Britain by the rebellious Carausius aided by Allectus. Iverson writes: 'Livonia gives a basically accurate picture of this quite obscure historical event.' Quite so, but only because the whole of the material rests on De Wohl's research.

In the same way every single piece of information given out by Jane Evans can be traced to De Wohl's fictional account. She uses his fictional sequences in exactly the same order and even speaks of his fictional characters, such as Curio and Valerius, as if they were real people.

There are two minor differences worth noticing, since these involve her editing faculty. In the first instance, she takes the slight character Titus Albus, a Christian soldier willing to die for his faith, and recasts him as a tutor to Constantine. But only the name itself is taken, for all of Titus' feelings and actions are those of De Wohl's character, Hilary. Hilary is converted to Christianity by Albanus, ordained as a priest by Osius and killed during a violent campaign against his faith. All these things happen in turn to Jane Evan's Titus!

In the second instance, she takes another insignificant character, Livonia, described as 'a charming creature with pouting lips and smouldering eyes,' and amalgamates her with Helena. A composite character recast as the wife of Titus emerges. This new character is able to act as both an observer and as someone who voices Helena's sentiments, thus making the story that much fuller and far easier to relate.

This feat of editing reveals a little of the psychology behind these fantasies. For Hilary is the eminently desirable male in the novel, described as having 'a beautiful honest face with eyes of a dreamer.' He is also secretly in love with Helena. As Titus, he becomes the lover of Livonia of the pouting lips and smouldering eyes – in other words of Jane Evans herself. And there we have all the combustible material that warmed a young girl's day-dreams. And all inspired by an exciting historical novel.

Now if the subconscious can engineer all that, why bother to drag in the extravagant notion of reincarnation? By all means let us study the mind's strange abilities through regressions – but in the direction that cryptomnesia points. The other way leads to chasing antique moonbeams. And that is a sport best left to nimble, grass-green leprechauns.

Chapter Nineteen

MEET ME AT MIDNIGHT

Could a coffin develop a homing instinct? That is a problem worth considering. For strangely enough, there is such a case in the supernormal archives. It rests alongside a group of allied tales. They are all about the drive of the dead to return to a loved one, a close friend, or even a precious place.

One of the best known is that of Lord Brougham. It involves a youthful friendship that defied death, time and place. In 1799, when he was twenty one, Brougham was travelling through Sweden. He reached an inn on the road to Gothenburg, hired a room and, tired and cold, sank into a hot bath. By then, it was about one in the morning. As he soaked and relaxed he idly glanced at the chair where he had dumped his clothes. He was then severely shocked to see an old school and college friend sitting silently on the chair, calmly looking at him.

Brougham next found himself out of the bath sprawled on the floor, as if he had fallen into a faint. The apparition, or whatever it was, had vanished. Later Brougham reflected on the unnerving event. At college his friend and he had often discussed the immortality of the soul. What did the future state have in store? Could the dead appear to the living? At one time they had gone beyond speculation and drawn up an agreement written in their own blood. In this pact they vowed that whoever died first should appear to the other. In that way the problem of survival would be resolved.

After leaving college their two paths diverged. His friend joined the Indian Civil Service while Brougham stayed put in Europe.

This unique vision seemed to mark the fulfilment of the blood-pact. His friend must have died far off in India, and his sudden appearance had to be seen as a proof of an after-life. All this happened, according to Brougham's *Memoirs*, on 19 December 1799.

When drafting his memoirs in October 1862 Brougham added this: 'I have just been copying out from my journal the account of this strange event ... And now to finish the story begun about sixty years since. Soon after my return to Edinburgh there arrived a letter from India announcing G–'s death, and stating that he died on 19 December.'

This story has often been repeated. It seems a clear case of an apparition appearing at the exact time of death. An apparition motivated to fulfil a solemn promise. And yet there is not the slightest reason for accepting it as truthful.

The journal Brougham quotes from is always taken to refer to a record made at the time of the event. But careful examination shows that it was written some time afterwards. Its wording is in the past tense, for example: 'One day I had taken a hot bath ... I had no inclination to talk about it, or to speak about it ...'

Then, since the story was 'begun about sixty years since,' that would put the journal account at roughly three years after the event. Still, is there any independent proof of any sort?

Well, Brougham did not tell his companion Stewart at the time, neither did he tell anyone else. Then he constantly referred to his friend as G–, even as late as 1862. There was no possible reason for keeping this cloak of anonymity. But by concealing the name Brougham prevented any accurate check on his story taking place.

But then Brougham was that kind of man. Lord John Russell observed that Brougham had an obstinate disregard for the truth. Chambers' biography went further, speaking of his 'arrogance, self-confidence and eccentricities which sometimes verged on insanity.' As for his memoirs, those were 'written in extreme old age and are very untrustworthy.' His untrustworthiness is never disputed by modern historians.

A rather different problem surrounds the celebrated story of John Donne and the vision of his dead child. It is related by his biographer Walton, who says that he was told it by a close friend of Donne's. Oddly enough, it does not appear until the fourth edition of his *Lives* in 1675. It has been surmised that the delay was the result of time taken to check that the details were correct.

The account involves Donne's reluctant visit to France in 1612. He had been asked to accompany the new Ambassador, Lord Hay, on his visit of appointment to the French Court. Sir Robert Drury strongly urged him to agree. But Donne's wife was in bad health and heavily pregnant, so at first he refused to consider the idea. Sir Robert continued to press his point and Donne eventually agreed, providing the visit was limited to two months.

It took twelve days to reach Paris from London. Two days later Sir Robert found Donne in a completely altered state of mind. He sat silently in his room, his face changed, seemingly in a state of shock. Sir Robert was understandably anxious. Yet at first Donne appeared unable to speak. He stayed like that for some time, then said: 'I have seen a dreadful vision since I saw you: I have seen my dear wife pass twice by me through this room, with her hair hanging about her shoulders, and a dead child in her arms.'

Sir Robert hastened to comfort him by suggesting that this had been nothing but a melancholy dream. But Donne remained firm. He had not slept and he was sure that at his wife's second appearance she had stopped and looked him in the face before vanishing.

His stout confidence troubled Sir Robert, who sent a servant over to England to visit Mrs Donne and report on her health. Twelve days later the servant returned. He brought sad news. Mrs Donne was in low spirits and confined to bed. After a dangerous labour her child had been born dead. This death had occurred on the very day and at the very time of the vision witnessed in Paris.

This poignant story was a favourite of W. T. Stead's. It

appears in Brian Inglis' *Natural And Supernatural* and in June 1962 it featured in a piece sent by Professor Ian Stevenson to the *Journal* of the SPR.

I am grateful to Professor Stevenson for saving me the time and trouble of checking out this story. For in the June 1984 *Journal* of the SPR he provided a sequel to his earlier piece. He wrote: 'It is almost certain that Donne never had any such vision, and on the grounds that it should never be too late to correct a mistake, I should like to have this noted in the Society's record.

'Walton wrote incorrectly about several of the background facts pertinent to Donne's visit to France in 1612. For example, he described the English embassy as being sent to King Henry IV of France; but Henry IV was assassinated in 1610. He said that the English Ambassador was Lord Hay; but Hay was not in fact sent on an embassy to France until 1616.

'These errors weaken confidence in Walton's account of Donne's vision. It receives, however, a more decisive blow from letters that Donne actually wrote from France in April 1612, more than two months after the expected (and actual) date of his wife's delivery. He complained in these of having no news of his wife's delivery, specifically "whether I be increased by childe or diminished by the loss of a wife." These letters are incompatible with Walton's claim that Donne's vision had been verified almost immediately after it occurred by a messenger sent back to England . . .'

Perhaps we shall have more luck with the wonderful wandering coffin. Its history seems to be well backed up by research. Frank Edwards even describes it as 'one of the best documented'.

Its astounding history first reached international fame about 1928, after Robert Ripley included it in his syndicated *Believe It Or Not!* series. Headed by the drawing of a coffin, his brief text read: 'Charles Coghlan Comes Home! He died in 1899 and was buried in Galveston. When the tragic flood came his coffin was washed out to sea and the Gulf Stream carried him around Florida and up the coast to Prince Edward Island – 2,000 miles distant – where he lived.'

The tragic flood he mentions followed the great hurricane which struck Galveston Island on 8 September 1900. Over six thousand people died in the disaster and thousands of buildings were reduced to rubble. The flood waters hammered into the cemeteries, shattered vaults and wrenched coffins out of the earth. Some of the coffins sank, others floated out into the Gulf of Mexico and were scattered in all directions by the waves.

According to the story given to Ripley, actor Charles Coghlan's coffin was one of these. It was caught up by the West Indian currents, carried into the Gulf Stream, drifted around the tip of Florida and began moving northwards. It was presumably buffeted about for years, but its northward progress never ceased. Finally, in October 1908, following a series of gales, it came to rest on the shores of Prince Edward Island. There it was spotted by fishermen who dragged it on to the beach and scraped away the thick crust of barnacles. Under the barnacles they discovered a silver plate screwed to the casket. It was engraved with the words 'Charles Francis Coghlan – born 1841, Prince Edward Island, Canada. Died 1899, Galveston Texas.' Charles Coghlan had come home to rest, and with full honours he was buried near the church where he had been baptised.

When Ripley's potted version appeared in the *Evening Post* (USA), it was read by Charles Coghlan's daughter, wife of Augustus Pitou, who was once Coghlan's manager. She was more than intrigued. She had hired men for long periods and spent thousands of dollars on a twenty-seven-year-long search for her father's body.

The Pitous made contact with Robert Ripley and asked him where his information came from. He supplied them with references in books published by Sir Johnston Forbes-Robertson and Lily Langtry.

In Forbes-Robertson's book *A Play Under Three Reigns* he relates how he took Coghlan from his home on Prince Edward Island to play Mercutio in *Romeo and Juliet* in London. He later adds: 'In about a year, I think he died at Galveston. Shortly after his burial there was a great storm came up from the Gulf which swept his coffin, with others, into the sea. The Gulf Stream bore him around Florida, up the coast, about 1,500 miles to Prince Edward Island and he came ashore not far from his home.'

Having read the accounts, the Pitous asked Sir Johnston Forbes-Robertson for more clarification. Who gave him the story? Forbes-Robertson then grew rather vague but suggested that they ask George Tyler, who had been Coghlan's manager at one time. When Tyler was approached he said: 'I've heard that story ... not once but many times ... close friends of his have told me since of his coffin having been found on Prince Edward Island. It was washed ashore, as I heard it, at Fortune Bridge ...'

And there the Pitous' involvement seems to melt away, though logically it should have led to a grand finale.

The story retreated into limbo for a while. Then it was resurrected by the notoriously inaccurate American broadcaster, the late Frank Edwards. He made it into a piece for radio, and a chapter of a book. It was picked up and enlarged on by Vincent Gaddis. It then became embraced by the strange breed of *Bermuda Triangle* word-spinners.

Richard Winer uses it in his *The Devil's Triangle 2*, and wangles it into the strait-jacket of *Triangle* theory. Then in 1979 Alan Vaughan wove the story into his book *Incredible Coincidence*. From there it crept into the *Daily Express* columns.

It all looks so good and wholesome. Yet something is missing. Where are the newspaper columns reporting the coffin's recovery in October 1908? Where are the records of the re-burial? Where are the photographs of the church where he was re-interred? And what does his new tombstone say?

Amazingly, none of these things exist. It is the same pattern all over again. None of the believers, Ripley included, have ever searched the newspaper files and public records of Prince Edward Island.

Had they done so they would have found that the whole story is a fantasy. The fate of Coghlan's coffin is unknown to this very day!

Our last case is in some ways the strangest of all. It was recounted in 1892 by freelance journalist Mr R. D'Onston. He had supplied articles to the spiritualist and editor W.T. Stead, and when he knew that Stead was looking for true ghost stories he gave him, free of charge, the following convincing account:

'To those instances of ghosts who have kept promises made in life to appear to those dear to them, may I add my own experience? The incident occurred to me some years ago, and all the details can be substantiated. The date was 26 August 1867, at midnight. I was then residing in the neighbourhood of Hull, and held an appointment under the Crown which necessitated my repairing thither every day for a few hours duty. My berth was almost a sinecure.

'I had a love affair with a girl in Hull. I will call her Louise. She was young, beautiful and devoted to me. On the night of 26 August we took our last walk together and a few minutes before midnight paused on a wooden bridge running across a kind of canal, locally termed a "drain."

'We paused on the bridge, listening to the swirling of the current against the wooden piles, and waiting for the stroke of midnight to part for ever. In the few minutes interval she repeated *sotto voce* Longfellow's Bridge, the words of which, "I stood on the bridge at midnight," seemed terribly appropriate. After nearly twenty-five years I can never hear that piece recited without feeling a deathly chill and the whole scene of two souls in agony again arising before me.

'Well! midnight struck, and we parted; but Louise said: "Grant me one favour, the only one that I shall ever ask you on this earth: promise to meet me here twelve months tonight at this same hour." I demurred at first, thinking it would be bad for both of us, and only reopen partially-healed wounds. At last, however, I consented, saying: "Well, I will come if I am alive!" but she said: "Say alive or dead!" I said: "Very well then, we will meet dead or alive."

'The next year I was on the spot a few minutes before the time, and punctual to the stroke of midnight Louise arrived. By this time I had begun to regret the arrangement I had made; but it was of too solemn a nature to be put aside. I therefore kept the appointment, but said that I did not care to renew the compact. Louise, however, persuaded me to renew it for one more year, and I consented, much against my will; and we again left each other, repeating the same formula: "Dead or alive."

'The next year after that passed rapidly for me until the

first week in July, when I was shot dangerously in the thigh . . .

'As soon as I was able to be removed (two or three weeks) I was taken home, where Dr Kelburne King of Hull attended me. The day – and *the* night – (26 August) came. I was then unable to walk without crutches, and that for only a short distance, so had to be wheeled about in a Bath chair. The distance to the trysting place being rather long, and the time and circumstances being very peculiar, I did not avail myself of the services of my usual attendant, but specially retained an old servant of the family who frequently did confidential commissions for me, and who knew Miss Louise well.

'We set forth "without beat of drum," and arrived at the bridge about a few minutes to midnight. I remember it was a brilliant starlight night, but I do not think that there was any moon . . "Old Bob," as he was always affectionately called, wheeled me to the bridge, helped me out of the Bath chair and gave me my crutch. I walked on to the bridge and leaned my back against the white painted top rail, then lighted my briar-root and had a comfortable smoke.

'I was very much annoyed that I had allowed myself to be persuaded to come a second time, and determined to tell Louise positively that this should be the last meeting. So, if anything, it was in rather a sulky frame of mind that I awaited Louise. Just as the quarters before the hour began to chime I distinctly heard the clink, clink of the little brass heels which she always wore sounding on the long flagged causeway, leading for two hundred yards up to the bridge. As she got nearer I could see her pass lamp after lamp in rapid succession, while the strokes of the large clock at Hull resounded through the stilly night.

'At last the patter-patter of the tiny feet sounded on the woodwork of the bridge – and I saw her distinctly pass under the lamp at the farther end – it was only twenty yards wide and I stood under the lamp at my side. When she got close to me I saw that she had neither hat nor cape on, and concluded that she had taken a cab to the farther end of the flagged causeway and (it being a very warm night) had left her wraps in the cab, and for purposes of effect had come the short distance in evening dress.

'Clink, clink, went the brass heels, and she seemed about passing me when I, suddenly urged by an impulse of affection, stretched out my arms to receive her. She passed through them, intangible, impalpable, and as she looked at me I distinctly saw her lips move and form the words "dead or alive." I even heard the words, but not with my outward ears, with something else, some other sense – what, I know not. I felt startled, but not afraid, until a moment afterwards. Then my blood seemed turned to ice.

'Recovering myself with an effort, I shouted out to Old Bob, who was safely ensconced with the Bath chair in a nook out of sight round the corner: "Bob, who passed you just now?" In an instant the old Yorkshireman was by my side. "Ne'er a one passed me, sir!" "Nonsense, Bob," I replied. "I told you that I was coming to meet Miss Louise, and she just passed me on the bridge, and must have passed you, because there's nowhere else she could go! You don't mean to tell me you didn't see her?" The old man replied solemnly: "Maister Ros, there's something uncanny aboot it. I heerd her come on the bridge, and off it, I'd knaw them clickety heels onywhere; but I'm henged, sir, if she passed me. I'm thinking we'd better gang." And "gang" we did; and it was the small hours of the morning (getting daylight) before we left off talking over the affair and went to bed.

'The next day I made inquiries from Louise's family about her and ascertained that she had died in Liverpool three months previously, being apparently delirious for a few hours before her death, and our parting compact evidently weighing on her mind, as she kept repeating: "Dead or alive! Shall I be there?" to the utter bewilderment of her friends, who could not divine her meaning, being of course entirely unaware of our agreement.'

As it stands, this is a story of considerable charm. Probably the best of its kind. But true? Well, Stead and his daughter believed it to be. Indeed, Estelle Stead gave a copy of this narrative to the Reverend C. L. Tweedale for inclusion in his book *Man's Survival After Death*. Its publication by Tweedale ensured a wide readership for the tale. And over the past ninety or so years not a breath of suspicion has surrounded it. And then I started probing!

There was something vaguely familiar about D'Onston's story and about D'Onston himself. Yet I knew this familiarity had nothing to do with my research into the paranormal. My files were raked through systematically and two distinctly different paths interlocked.

In 1930 Fleet Street crime reporter Bernard O'Donnell began looking back at the crimes of Jack the Ripper. He had been given a tip that an old lady in Balham had something new to add to the saga. The lady was a Baroness Vittoria Cremers, a theosophist and a former friend and companion of writer Mabel Collins.

O'Donnell called on her and wrote down her revelations. They centred on a man who had once written for the *Pall Mall Gazette* – Stead's paper. This journalist's name was Stephenson, but he wrote under the name Tautriadelta, a name which had links with black magic cults. Stephenson lived in a lively swirl of fantasy. He claimed he had studied magic with Sir Edward Bulwer Lytton, studied chemistry at the University of Giessen, then carried out successful Doppelganger experiments! After that, he had joined Garibaldi's army as a medical officer and visited India to observe the methods of the fakirs.

In 1888 he became so obsessed by the Jack the Ripper murders that he became an object of suspicion. When he roomed with Cremers and Collins he talked about the murders so often and in such detail that they became convinced that he *was* the Ripper. Oddly, even W.T. Stead thought so for a while. It was this suspicion that made the two ladies acutely conscious of everything he said and did. In his dealings with them, though, he dropped the commonplace name Stevenson and used a more exotic aristocratic-looking name. He called himself Dr Roslyn D'Onston!

One of the curious tales that stayed in their memory involved his shattered romance with a young lady called Ada. In 1930 Vittoria Cremers revealed that story: 'As a young man D'Onston held a commission in the army. He came from a fairly well-off yeoman family, and it was generally understood that he would marry the daughter of a wealthy neighbouring family who was very much in love with him. However, on one of his jaunts to town with some of his brother officers he met a woman of the streets named Ada. He began to visit her regularly, fell in love with her and, Gissing-like, determined to marry her and take her away from her miserable life.

'Understandably, his family was appalled. His father cut off his allowance. Always a gambler, D'Onston lost a lot of money at the tables one night and, unable to pay his debts, was forced to seek his father's help. His father agreed to discharge those debts, on one condition – that he undertook to end his association with Ada and marry the heiress. Reluctantly, D'Onston agreed.

'And so D'Onston and Ada parted, but not before they had made a solemn pledge that whatever happened, dead or alive, they would meet at midnight on the anniversary of their parting at the place where they had first met – the middle of Westminster Bridge.

'Then – tragedy. Within half an hour of D'Onston's departure, Ada walked to Westminster Bridge and threw herself into the river.

'True to his vow, D'Onston kept his tryst with the dead woman on Westminster Bridge. He leant over the parapet where Ada had flung herself to her death twelve months before. As the chimes of Big Ben sounded, he heard the click-clack of heels coming towards him. He saw nothing, no one, but he knew that Ada, too, had kept her promise.'

And there we have it. The touching tryst at midnight resolves itself into a tear-jerking fantasy dreamed up by a man whose whole life was make-believe. His background was a humble one, not the well-off one he had boasted about. His medical qualifications were bogus. Even his claims to know the identity of Jack the Ripper were derisively rejected by the police.

To the Steads he offered the gentle version of his tryst tale, while Cremers and Collins were entertained by the more earthy version.

And as those imaginary heels click off into fairyland, I will

Sorry – You've Been Duped

bet that someone, somewhere, is at this very moment cooking up a brand new hoax to keep the spines a-tingling. In the meantime, have you heard the one about the man who got stuck in a treacle-mine?

Notes

The Amityville Horror-Mongers

1. I first exposed *The Amityville Horror* in the former magazine *Alpha*. When the film of the book was launched in Britain, Fleet Street journalist Dan Slater learned of my work and invited me to meet the publicity people boosting the film. We met at lunch. The Lutzes' publicity agent considered what I had to say and declared that the Lutzes would be quite happy to meet me when they reached Britain. As it turned out, this was a rather naive view, for I had made it clear that I wished to meet the Lutzes face-to-face on radio and TV programmes and present them with the accumulated evidence of their complete unreliability. In the meantime Dan Slater considered the case I had presented against the Lutzes and in the *Sunday People* of 6 January 1980 he wrote an article debunking the film.

When the Lutzes reached London, they declined to meet me. My invitation to attend the movie premiere was withdrawn. My phone call to the publicity agents received no reply. And the Lutzes hopped around from place to place making sure that they spoke to no one who was well informed! In this shabby way they escaped – but only for a while.

In 1982, the sequel *Amityville II* was published and I received a review copy. Here again was the same old tiresome nonsense and the same old cynical disregard for impressionable readers. But they went too far. Their twenty-fifth chapter gave a distorted account of their appearance on the *Tonight* programme of the BBC. On that programme they were interviewed by my friend the late Dr Anita Gregory. The account of the interview in this chapter was an arrogant and gross libel on Anita. It bore no relationship whatsoever to the real interview, which fortunately was preserved on videotape. Everything in the chapter was rigged to make George Lutz look like some sort of saintly hero confronted by a vicious, back-biting creature, described as a vulture.

They even dragged in the representative of Pan Books as an alleged witness to the interview, writing of her: 'Bravo, she thought. George and I may have some friction of our own, but he does know how to handle these vultures in close combat.'

Dr Gregory brought an action against the Lutzes. Pan Books backed her up by repudiating the alleged role played by their representative. The BBC ran the tapes of the interview and provided a transcript. As a result the Lutzes apologised for the libel, paid damages to Dr Gregory, and the book was withdrawn.

Since then this flagrantly dishonest book has been reissued with a new chapter twenty five minus the invented interview. For no matter what happens, the pursuit of cash is more important than any pangs of conscience. But then I doubt if the Lutzes worry too much about anything as trivial as that.

2. In the United States the Lutzes have also run into trouble. They have tried their best to avoid exposure by refusing to meet intelligent investigators. Peter Jordan and Rick Moran who actually made revealing on-the-spot checks have repeatedly tried to interview the Lutzes. But their letters were never answered, neither were their phone calls. However, the Lutzes were not able to avoid the legal action brought against them by Jim and Barbara Cromarty, present owners of the Ocean Avenue house. Their action charged that the book was a hoax which had damaged their lives because of the sensation-hungry creatures who had been drawn to the place by the Lutzes' fiction. The suits were settled in the Cromartys' favour. According to Clarence Peterson (*Chicago Tribune*, 23 September 1982) they received a six-figure sum in settlement.

Peterson goes on to say: 'The Cromartys are happy at home; the imaginary demons are long gone; and as Ed Lowe puts it, the Wackos, the card-carrying certifiable organised lunatics who descended upon Amityville in 1976, finally have dwindled to a precious few – at least until *Amityville II* comes out.'

And Ed Lowe, *Newsday* columnist adds this: 'It had to have been a setup since Day One. The day after the Lutzes fled, supposedly in terror, they returned to hold a garage sale – just lots of junk. It was obvious they hadn't moved in there with anything worth anything. And during the entire 28-day 'siege' that drove them from the house, they never once called the police.'

THE CLUELESS CRIME-BUSTERS

1. A cool appraisal of psychic detectives shows that they often make use of an artful dodge. They make claims about events that have happened in far-off places. This makes it extra-difficult to check on newspaper and other reports. Interviewing people is often out of the question. For example Doris Stokes, in Britain, has claimed that she was able to help the Baltimore County Police in a case involving the disappearance of teenager Jamie Griffin. But a statement by Joseph A. Shaw, Colonel, Chief of Field Operations, of the Baltimore County Police Department in Towson, Maryland, USA, refutes her claims. It reads: 'Ms Stokes was making an appearance in Baltimore and attracted the attention of Mrs Griffin, whose seventeen-year-old son Jamie has been missing under suspicious circumstances since 2 April 1982. Mrs Griffin made contact with Ms Stokes and discussed her son's disappearance. The next day we made contact with Ms Stokes in company with and at the request of Mrs Griffin. Ms Stokes did not go to the Gunpowder State Park. We had earlier dug up twenty four acres of the park in search of the missing person's body. Ms Stokes was aware of this. She was never at the park. She visualised the empty grave. We dug numerous acres with negative results. Ms Stokes was given maps by our Department. Ms Stokes did not contribute any useful or informative information nor did she supply any new information which could not have

been given her by the Griffin family or by newspaper articles printed prior to her visit. Everything she told us was after she had extensive conversations with Griffin relatives and had access to newspaper files collected by the Griffin family.'

In Britain itself, her claims are just as suspect. In her book *Voices In My Ear*, chapter eleven, she describes at length how she was involved usefully in the police investigation of the murder of a girl at Kirkham in Lancashire, and the murders of three children found dead in the children's ward of Blackpool's Victoria Hospital. If you believe her, she actually told the detectives who the ward murderer was and told them that if they acted fast they would find him in the hospital's operating theatre. The murderer in fact was a surgeon at the hospital. But was he identified by Mrs Stokes?

This is what Detective Chief Superintendent Brian Woods of the Lancashire Constabulary Headquarters at Preston has to say: 'I can confirm that Mrs Stokes made no contribution whatever to the detection of either the murderer of the children at Blackpool or the girl at Kirkham.'

2. In Australia psychic detective Zandra-Marie is circulating newspapers with claims of her marvellous successes with crime cases in Britain. Among her absurd claims is one which involves the Yorkshire Ripper. She says that eleven days before the police arrested Peter Sutcliffe she had visited the graves of his victims and drawn an exact sketch of the murderer. She gave this sketch to the police and as a result they were able to make their arrest. The facts are that no portrait, whether artist's impression, psychically-inspired or photo-fit, played the slightest part in the arrest of Peter Sutcliffe. His arrest came after police had been monitoring motorists who took on board prostitutes. His parked car was spotted. The police observers checked his licence plates with their national computer records and discovered that he was using false licence plates. He was taken to the police station for questioning and later the grounds near his parked car were searched and his murder weapons came to light. Following that Sutcliffe confessed.

3. An illuminating 'successful' psychic detective story appeared in the May 1983 issue of *Fate* magazine. An eighty-two-year-old psychic Ann Hunt led searchers along the banks

of the San Joaquin river looking for missing nine-year-old Steven Brown. He had disappeared over six weeks before on 23 August 1982. The body was found on the river bank but strangely enough the psychic messages that led to the discovery were not picked up by Ann Hunt. They were intercepted, so it seems, by Jackie Skeels, the girlfriend of the boy's father.

The search party had dug in several spots unsuccessfully and searched through bushes in vain. Jackie in the meantime went along the bank making her own search. In about fifteen minutes she returned crying hysterically. She said that she had heard Steven's voice crying: 'Daddy, find me. Daddy, I'm here.' She then led the party along the river and every now and again stopped as if listening. Eventually Steven's body was found partly hidden under vines. And that, it seemed, was a successful conclusion to a tragic hunt.

It turned out, though, that there was much more to it. The November issue of *Fate* published a letter from Helen McCay, of Fresno, California. She pointed out that Jackie Skeels hardly had a psychic experience. She knew exactly where the dead boy's body would be located. That was why she had been found guilty of first-degree murder. Steven had been drowned by her.

The Murderer And The Medium

1. Some readers might feel that my unravelling of Nella Jones's thought processes is far-fetched. After all, I can't see into her mind. Agreed. But we do know enough of the workings and vagaries of the mind to make worthwhile judgments.

In considering her claims I started by asking just what was available to her in the form of books, photographs, newspaper, television and radio reports. Having located this material I then examined it just as she had. Some of her pronouncements were traced to their common-knowledge sources at once. The more obscure pieces – things like the 'Ainsworth' name – became clear after a second slower examination.

It is indisputable that mediums do find 'future forecasts' by examining the patterns of the past and present. Cheiro did it often – I've given some examples.

If anything, I have understated my case. The tortured wanglings they indulge in are even more convoluted and grotesque than I have shown. Consider this excellent example of the way that psychic Alan Vaughan has tried to hijack the past in the interests of soothsaying.

After the assassination of Robert Kennedy in June 1968, Vaughan began thinking about the assassin Sirhan Sirhan. He sets down his chain of reasoning in his *Patterns Of Prophecy*. He begins: 'What will be Sirhan's fate? Could it be foretold by synchronistic links with another assassin? Those were questions I asked myself as Sirhan's trial for the assassination of Robert Kennedy began. I looked through the records of assassination: Charles Guiteau, assassin of President Garfield ... no; Leon Czolgosz, assassin of President McKinley ... no; but then, there he was – John Schrank, who attempted to assassinate another presidential candidate of another famous family, Theodore Roosevelt ...'

The attempted assassination of Theodore Roosevelt took place on 14 October 1912. Roosevelt was saved by the bulky folded speech in his breast pocket, together with the cover of his metal spectacle case. These absorbed the energy of the bullet leaving him shaken, with a fractured rib. For Vaughan, time is swept to one side. The radical differences between this event and the Kennedy shooting are ignored and he goes on to say: 'Synchronistic parallels seem to link Schrank and Sirhan in an archetypal pattern of assassination:

* Both shootings took place at night at a hotel during campaigning for the presidency.
* In both shootings the weapon was a revolver.
* Both victims made a speech the night of their shooting.
* Both assailants were immigrants, Schrank from Germany, Sirhan from Jordan.
* Both Schrank and Sirhan were unusually short, and both were bachelors.
* Both Schrank and Sirhan were loners. Schrank said: "I never had a friend in my life." Sirhan said: "Sirhan means wolf, and I became more and more of a lone wolf."
* Both Schrank and Sirhan were tackled by football players immediately after the shooting, narrowly escaping being

lynched. Provocatively, one of Sirhan's tacklers was Roosevelt Grier.

'Even the very names of Schrank and Sirhan are similar, having five common letters. But already credulity is strained by the search for synchronicities – if indeed these coincidental parallels are. The test for that lies in the future, in the final fate of Sirhan Sirhan. If this pattern of assassination is prophetic, then his fate should correspond to Schrank's ... If the parallel goes further, it may even be shown that like Schrank, whose bullets were non-fatal, Sirhan's bullets too were non-fatal – that is, the fatal bullet fired from behind Kennedy's head was fired by someone else.'

All this is enough to leave one speechless. So I rest my case!

2. Another factor needs to be underlined. Two or more unrelated events, words, or pictures may be perceived on different occasions and yet all of them will lead to just one resting point in the brain. In the case of the odd name from nowhere – 'Ainsworth' – I have shown the strongest leads to that name. There might well have been others that helped reinforce the name. For example, at the time when Nella Jones was involved with the Genette Tate case, there was a book on sale and display called *The Phantom Cyclist*. It was a book of ghost stories and its eerie cover depicts a wraith-like figure in shorts on a bicycle. The cyclist could be either a young boy or a tomboy.

In the story a young boy cycles along a country lane, passes two other boys, then disappears completely. Later on, his abandoned wrecked bicycle is found. In the Tate case something very similar happened. Genette cycled past two of her friends, then disappeared completely, leaving her bike sprawled in the hedge of a country lane.

This eye-catching book with its prompting title was written by RUTH AINSWORTH!

Mrs Jones could also have picked up a link from her very involvement with the *Yorkshire Post*. For strangely enough (something that is not even hinted at in her book) one of the *Yorkshire Post* Group reporters was named Richard Hainsworth. Believe it or not, he is the son of Magistrate Peter Hainsworth, in whose grounds Sutcliffe strangled Marguerite Walls!

3. Though a great deal of mediumship involves conscious planning I accept that often mediums are deceived by the caprices of their own subconscious minds. At those times they honestly do not know where their visions, words or forebodings come from. This happens to Nella Jones. She records that at one point she saw a sneering face hovering in front of her eyes and the word 'Dudley' written underneath. 'Even now,' she says, 'I am unable to explain the significance of that one word.'

Yet there is an obvious significance. She starts off with Bradford in mind. In 1976 enormous publicity surrounded the trial of another Bradford murderer. This was Donald Neilson, who had been dubbed the 'Black Panther'. For almost a year before Neilson's arrest his murderous exploits were common knowledge. In that year he shot Gerald Smith at the Freightliner Terminal at Dudley, and kidnapped Lesley Whittle. Later the kidnap car was found abandoned in Dudley. Dudley then became the centre for the police search headquarters. The bizarre kidnapping, imprisonment and tragic death of Lesley Whittle kept the name Dudley constantly before the public eye.

4. After hearing the tape sent by the hoax 'Ripper', Nella phoned Shirley Davenport of the *Yorkshire Post*. Nella had woken up with a strong sense of foreboding. She felt the Ripper had travelled south of Manchester and something was about to happen. Nothing did happen. Nella had failed to realise that her subconscious had fed her false clues. For on the tape she had listened to, the hoaxer had boasted: 'I will strike again ... I am not sure where, maybe Manchester.'

A similar thing happened when she was thinking over the Genette Tate case. She records that she heard a voice 'saying clearly over and over: "Find Genette."' This psychic message, however, was simply a repetition of the exact wording of the car stickers issued in their thousands by the police force.

These examples show again how already existing knowledge can be imagined as psychically inspired and a forewarning.

5. I have asserted that pure coincidence, in the case of Jacqueline Hill, has helped make Mrs Jones' predictions look sensational. It could be thought that my introduction of the element of coincidence is simply an easy solution to a vexing problem.

On the contrary, coincidences can be found in so many cases of crime that this is just one of the many factors one has to be on guard against. Some examples from the Ripper case will make this clear.

For those who see significance in everything, note that the same Ripper story appears on page 115 of Nella Jones's book and page 115 of Michael Nicholson's book. Meaningless? Of course. Next note that Ripper victim Yvonne Pearson had shared a flat just a few hundred yards away from Sutcliffe's house in Heaton, Bradford.

His next victim, Helen Rytka, was murdered in Huddersfield, over ten miles south of Bradford. Yet once she had not only lived in Bradford, but had frequently visited Tanton Crescent at the time when Ripper Sutcliffe was living there. Even stranger, she had actually been a guest at the house next door to the Sutcliffes. This incredible state of affairs all came about because she had made friends with a girl who happened to be related to Ronnie Barker, Sutcliffe's neighbour.

Coincidences abound but have no meaning or significance. This can be demonstrated by the Victorian Jack the Ripper murders, where strings of such coincidences have led to some dozen or more people being branded as the culprit.

I CAPTURED JACK THE RIPPER

1. Many spiritualists will undoubtedly protest that Lees was a saintly creature who never indulged in fantasies or lies. So it is worth noting that he never publicly repudiated the false claims made in the Chicago article. In that way he gained himself a false renown and gave respectability to blatant untruths. And it must be recorded that he made false claims himself about his involvement in police investigations.

He told his daughter Eva that in 1883, when 'acting as a guide for some American visitors, taking them around places of interest in London, he heard a voice telling him to report them to the Yard. He did so several times before the police would listen. Then he was seen by Sir John (sic) Anderson who knew him. He told Sir John they were staying in Villiers Street. They were arrested. One of them was the notorious

Irish revolutionary Dr Gallagher.' (Interview with Dr D.J.West of SPR, 10 November 1948.) In checking out this claim we find that Dr Gallagher arrived in London on Easter Monday, 26 March 1883 and booked into Room 312 of the Charing Cross Hotel under the alias 'Fletcher'. He toured Westminster – on his own – on the 27th to finalise plans for a Fenian bombing campaign. Prior to his arrival a member of his team, James Murphy, had opened a paint shop at 128 Ledsam Street, Ladywood, Birmingham on 6 February. He used the alias 'Alfred George Whitehead.'

A third member of the team calling himself Wilson rented a room at 17 Nelson Square, Blackfriars. From there he wrote to Whitehead in Birmingham on 2 April.

Whitehead busied himself buying large quantities of chemically pure glycerine, a necessary basis for the nitroglycerine bombs he had in mind. These uncommon purchases aroused the suspicions of George Pritchard, a storeman with the suppliers. He shrewdly guessed that the glycerine was not being used to make hair oil, Whitehead's bluff. He began checking up on Whitehead and found enough incongruities to go to the police.

The police used skeleton keys to enter and search the shop at 2 a.m. on 2 April. They left knowing that they had found a bomb factory, but since they wanted to capture the whole gang they simply posted men to watch the place.

The gang began to move the nitro on 4 April. For a while the police lost track of the member who was carting two hundred pounds of the stuff. So they swooped on Whitehead and found Wilson's letter with its address in Blackfriars.

The London police were informed and they waited at Nelson Square for Wilson to return. When he turned up Dr Gallagher was with him and both were arrested. Finally, the complete team was brought to trial and imprisoned.

So the arrests were due to the alertness of storeman George Pritchard and owed nothing to Lees's 'supernormal insights.' And the assertion that Lees had assisted Anderson five years prior to the Whitechapel murders was exposed as sheer bunkum. If it had been true, then Lees would have had an impeccable reputation among the police and would have had no trouble in winning a hearing in 1888.

2. In June 1981 I gave the late Maurice Barbanell a sporting chance to repudiate this story if he wished, but he was quite happy to stick with it. When I asked him if he had ever seen the famous 'document' he replied: 'I do not know what happened to the document dictated by R. J. Lees. It was in the possession of his daughter for some time, but she has now passed on. I never saw it, but one of my colleagues, Arthur Findlay, did so. He said it confirmed all we had written in *Psychic News*.' (Letter 1 July 1981.)

Yet as I have shown, there never was such a document. (Even Eva Lees herself said so.) That explains why Maurice Barbanell's most lengthy account (in *Cavalcade*) was little more than a reworded version of the *Express* articles.

So Findlay and Barbanell, two of the outstanding leaders in British spiritualism, both endorsed this spurious history without making any precautionary checks. They then used it to add lustre to their movement.

3. The Lees story was inevitably resurrected in *Psychic News* and tied in with 'psychic information' about the Yorkshire Ripper. And it has been given a further boost by being incorporated in the 1979 film *Murder By Decree* – a Sherlock Holmes adventure in which Lees is a vital character!

The Angels With Newspaper Wings

1. Among supplementary 'evidence' brought forward in 1915 was a tale which plainly had no connection with Machen's fiction. This spoke of a 'Comrade in White' who roamed the Front bringing succour to the dying and wounded. The Comrade was immune to shell and bullet alike – clearly a supernatural being.

Two different versions of this tale were included in *On The Side Of The Angels*, one alleged by Begbie to have been sent home 'by a distinguished British officer who took it down from the soldier's own lips, a man named Casey.' The basic story was a moving one, which ended with George Casey saying to the Comrade: '"You are wounded too" ... he answered gently: "This is an old wound, but it has troubled me of late." And then I noticed sorrowfully that the same cruel mark was on his feet. You will wonder that I did not know sooner. I wonder myself. But it was only when I saw His feet that I knew Him.' So Christ himself had been there on the pitiless battlefields. The testimony was inescapable.

But the full truth was revealed in October 1915 when the British publishers H. R. Allenson brought out a volume of stories by W. H. Leathem. It was called *The Comrade In White*, and included the full text of 'George Casey's statement.' This was the origin of all the subsequent versions and once again it was simply dramatic fiction – a short story which had first appeared in the June number of *Life and Work*. In his book's preface, Leathem showed how the story was being misrepresented and wrote: 'It is essential, therefore, to say that the contents of this little book are of no evidential value whatsoever.'

Regrettably, the American public never had the chance to know of this warning. When Leathem's book was published in the USA in 1916 by the Fleming H. Revell Co. his disclaimer was not included in the text.

2. There is one seamy aspect of this affair which it would be dishonest to conceal. The fact is that the legend was often forced on wounded soldiers by sensation-seeking women. These haunted the hospital wards in search of strange thrills and satisfactions. They were a peculiar breed whose deep, hidden frustrations had been brought out by the tensions of war.

Vera Brittain, for one, observed their behaviour at close quarters: 'Sister J. came in and told us about some very bad cases of wounded from Neuve Chapelle ... After that the ladies seemed to try to outdo one another in telling of war horrors ... In those days I knew, of course, nothing of psychology ... I was still too young to realise how much vicarious excitement the war provided for frustrated women cut off from vision and opportunity in small provincial towns, or to understand that the deliberate contemplation of horror and agony might strangely compensate a thwarted nature for the very real grief of having no one at the Front for whom to grieve.' (*Testament of Youth*, page 103)

Such women were quick to press the wounded for tales of

supernatural signs and portents. All too often semi-literate men from rough backgrounds found that they could become the focus of posh female interest simply by confirming or repeating the yarns that these ladies eagerly thrust at them.

3. Twelve years after the end of the war the inventive were still churning out fresh legends about Mons. In February 1930 Colonel Friedrich Herzenwirth, described as an ex-officer of the Imperial German Intelligence Service, wrote a newspaper article which claimed that the Angels had definitely appeared at Mons. But they had been nothing but motion-picture images beamed onto the cloudbanks by German aircraft equipped with enormously powerful Zeiss projectors. The initial idea was to create panic among the British, but it had misfired and brought hope instead. However, this scheme had worked well against the Allies on the Russian Front. There 'entire regiments who had beheld the vision fell on their knees and flung away their rifles.' Within days of this claim, a spokesman from the German War Ministry declared that the story was a hoax. What is more, there was no such person as ex-Colonel Herzenwirth of Army Intelligence either!

4. One remarkable statement, published in the *Evening News* on 14 September 1915 was taken by some as providing oblique proof of supernatural activities during the Retreat. This account from a Lieutenant-Colonel at the Front read: 'On 26 August 1914 was fought the battle of Le Cateau. We came into action at dawn and fought till dusk. We were heavily shelled by the German artillery during the day, and in common with the rest of our division had a bad time of it.

'Our division, however, retired in good order. We were on the march all night of the 26th and on the 27th, with only about two hours rest.

'The brigade to which I belong was rearguard to the division, and during the 27th we took up a great many different positions to cover the retirement of the rest of the division so that we had very hard work, and by the night of the 27th we were all absolutely worn out with fatigue – both bodily and mental fatigue.

'No doubt we also suffered to a certain extent from shock; but the retirement still continued in excellent order, and I feel sure that our mental faculties were still . . . in good working condition.

'On the night of the 27th I was riding along in the column with two other officers. We had been talking and doing our best to keep from falling asleep on our horses.

'As we rode along I became conscious of the fact that in the fields on both sides of the road along which we were marching I could see a very large body of horsemen.

'These horsemen had the appearance of squadrons of cavalry, and they seemed to be riding across the fields and going in the same direction as we were going, and keeping level with us . . .

'I did not say a word about it at first, but I watched them for about twenty minutes. The other two officers had stopped talking.

'At last one of them asked me if I saw anything in the fields. I then told him what I had seen. The third officer then confessed that he too had been watching these horsemen for the past twenty minutes.

'So convinced were we that they were real cavalry that at the next halt one of the officers took a party of men out to reconnoitre, and found no one there. The night then grew darker and we saw no more.

'The same phenomenon was seen by many men in our column. Of course we were all dog-tired and overtaxed, but it is an extraordinary thing that the same phenomenon should be witnessed by so many different people.

'I myself am absolutely convinced that I saw these horsemen, and I feel sure that they did not exist only in my imagination . . .'

Yet you only have to compare that account with the one that follows to see that such phantom horsemen were part of the hallucinatory experiences arising from extreme stress and grinding fatigue. It was provided by Lance-Corporal A. Johnstone, Royal Engineers, and appeared in the *Evening News* on 11 August 1915.

'We had almost reached the end of the retreat, and after marching a whole day and night with but one half-hour's rest in between, we found ourselves on the outskirts of Langy, near Paris, just at dawn, and as the day broke we saw in front of us large bodies of cavalry, all formed up into squadrons – fine, big men on massive chargers.

'I remember turning to my chums in the ranks and saying: "Thank God! We are not far off Paris now. Look at the French cavalry."

'They too saw them quite plainly, but on getting closer, to our surprise the horsemen vanished and gave place to banks of white mist with clumps of trees and bushes dimly showing through them . . .

'When I tell you that hardened soldiers who had been through many a campaign were marching quite mechanically along the road and babbling all sorts of nonsense in sheer delirium, you can well believe we were in a fit state to take a row of beanstalks for all the saints in the calendar.'

5. It is impossible to ignore the maverick account of the Angel of Mons related by author Arch Whitehouse. Whitehouse fought in the First World War and authored a number of books based on his experiences. In *Epics And Legends Of The First World War* he tells of a single Angel that appeared to the Coldstream Guards during the retreat. At Mormal Forest the Guards were the last to be withdrawn and in the half-light of a false dawn they became lost and wandered about trying to join up with their main body. Finding they were completely out of touch, they dug in ready to make a stand at daylight. Then the men saw a bright light approaching them. As it grew closer the Coldstreamers saw the dim outline of a female figure. Then it became more distinct and they realised they were looking at an Angel – the sort of angel seen in regimental chapels: tall, slim and wearing a white flowing gown. Around her hair was a gold band, there were eastern sandals on her feet and against her slim back were folded a pair of white wings.

The Angel beckoned to them, and after puzzled indecision the guardsmen began to crawl out of their shallow trenches. They followed the glowing figure across an open field and eventually she led them to the end of a sunken road. She then floated up the bank and pointed towards a covering copse a few dozen yards away. Then with a smile she vanished, leaving the guardsmen overjoyed to find the escape route. Yet having made their escape, no one was ever to find the sunken road again. The Coldstreamers pored over every available map, but not one of them showed the slightest trace of any track that could be identified as the angelic path!

6. There was a childish eagerness during the war to locate omens pointing to victory. Mis-shapen clouds were sometimes interpreted as patriotic emblems or even supernatural figures. For example, here is a story sent 'by a Russian General who is with the army operating in East Prussia.' (To Ralph Shirley in October 1914.)

'While our troops were in the region of Suwalki, the captain of one of my regiments witnessed a marvellous revelation.

'It was eleven o'clock at night and the troops were in bivouac. Suddenly a soldier from one of our outposts, wearing a startled look, rushed in and called the captain. The latter went with the soldier to the outskirts of the camp and witnessed an amazing apparition in the sky. It was that of the Virgin Mary, with the Infant Christ on one hand, the other hand pointing to the west.

'Our soldiers knelt on the ground and gazed fervently at the vision. After a time the apparition faded, and in its place came a great image of the Cross, shining against the dark night sky. Slowly it faded away.

'On the following day our army advanced westward to the victorious battle of Augustovo.'

The French and English troops were a little more cautious though, as the following newspaper story shows:

'THE STAR OF VICTORY

'*Angers, 30 September* 1914.

'Tonight as the soldiers of England and France lay sleeping in the trenches, sentries noticed what seemed to be a new star in the heavens. Its colour appeared strange and novel. They looked again, and to their wonder discovered that it twinkled and shone with the national colours of the Allies – red, white and blue.

'Field-glasses were taken out and groups of officers and men looked up at the wonderful heavenly light. It was an optical illusion, of course, but amongst those who saw it there were men who believed it to be an omen of victory and success. (Central News.)'

7. The public was, in a sense, visually primed in favour of Angels by a set of illustrations in the immensely popular *King Albert's Book* published at Christmas 1914. Chandler Christy's wash drawing shows an Angel holding a laurel wreath over the head of an exhausted soldier; Briton Riviere shows St George and the dragon; Frank Dicksee's picture shows a mailed figure carrying a crucifix and a French standard striding across the battlefield, while J. J. Shannon's pastel shows the mailed and winged figure of St Michael of Belgium supporting a Belgian soldier clutching his country's flag. This last illustration served as the basis for a crudely drawn postcard published by the Church Army. The card showed Christ on the Cross in the background, a sky full of Angels and a mailed, winged figure encouraging an infantryman and a sailor, both of them gripping rifles with fixed bayonets. The slogan on the card read: 'ENLISTED UNDER THE CROSS! AM I?'

DEATH BECKONS LORD DUFFERIN and ONCE MORE UNTO THE LIFT DEAR FRIENDS

1. Many myths have their origins in strange but explicable real-life experiences. And the chances are strong that the lift-crash saga derived from an incident reported in *The Boston Budget* on 31 August 1890.

'A strange incident occurred one night last week at one of the Boston Back Bay hotels. It was just before the gas was lighted, and was already growing dusky in the corridors, when a resident guest stepped out of her room to go to the elevator. She touched the electric bell and then went down to the end of another corridor to look out of the window for a moment while the elevator was coming up. Returning to it, she was about to advance precipitately to the side of it that the door was on, when the sight of a man standing exactly in front of the elevator door caused her to stop short, that she might not be so rude or awkward as to run into him, so to speak, as she was in danger of doing in her rather heedless haste. The hall was dim, but a window opposite the elevator showed the form of the man plainly enough, and the lady waited at a decorous distance. But what was her amazement when the elevator came up, brightly lighted inside, to see, first, that the upper door was wide open, and that thus the entire well of the elevator was exposed. The lady had been a guest for many years in the house, and had never known such a thing as an elevator door left open to happen before. But the second fact was far more startling, *there was no man there*! The appearance of this man, or her impression of his appearance there, undoubtedly saved her from plunging head first down the elevator well . . .

'Now, here is a fact for Dr Richard Hodgson and his Psychical Society. It may be added that the lady in question immediately went to the hotel desk to report the terrible carelessness of the boy who had left this door open, but not ambitious to acquire the reputation of a lunatic, or even a seer of visions or a dreamer of dreams, she took very good care not to relate the other half of the occurrence, although it was just as palpable a fact as the material fact that the door was open. Was this the apparition of a spiritual presence which had materialised to save her from a terrible fate? Who shall say?'

Dr Richard Hodgson of the American SPR knew the lady well and wrote to her. She answered: 'My dear Mr Hodgson, No, I did not recognise the form at all. I simply didn't notice – didn't think anything about it, as it is rather the rule than the exception to meet people at the elevator in a hotel. Then, too, I am very near-sighted, and I did not have my eye-glasses on, so I shouldn't have recognised even my most intimate friend in the dusky light and at the little distance.

It occurred on Tuesday night, 26 August.

Faithfully yours,

(Signed) A.B.'

There is plenty of evidence that the unconscious self can often spot problems and difficulties way ahead of the conscious. And there is ample evidence that subconscious anxieties and expectations can generate hallucinations.

F.W.H.Myers (British SPR) admirably analysed this case by saying: 'Assuming this . . . incident to be correctly reported, the least marvellous way of explaining it will perhaps be to suppose that Miss A.B.'s subliminal self perceived the open doorway at a distance somewhat beyond the eyesight of her supraliminal self, and then generated the hallucinatory figure in order to avert the fall.'

2. Indiana University Folklore Institute at Bloomington, USA, has a small folder entitled *Urban Belief Tales – Room For One More*. This contains five stories along the lines of the lift crash disaster. All of them except one feature a coach and horses. They are all located in different parts of the United States and one of them is said to have happened to the cousin of a visitor to a Mrs Carrols of East Lansing, Michigan. It is, of course, fiction.

Dr Soal's Mr Hyde

1. Soal presents his invented dickie bird forecast on page 566 of his Blanche Cooper paper. It reads: 'In the record of my sittings I have found one and only one more slight reference to Gordon Davis. It was during sitting number twenty three, held on Monday 30 January 1922, 3.40 p.m. This reference occurred during a pause in the middle of the sitting. James Miles had been communicating and was apparently resting. I asked Nada if Gordon Miles could come again.

Nada: Is not coming any more.
S: Can't he come and talk to you? He need not use the voice directly.
Nada: He can't because he's too far away now.
S: Try to get him.
Nada: Only see his house, but it's not clear – can't get anything. There's something about black dickie bird – think it's on piano – not sure about it.
S: Would this be in Gordon Davis's house?
Nada: Think it would be his house – it's very uncertain because he isn't here.
(Frank then speaks and tries to give a book test, which is unsuccessful. Afterwards James Miles is mentioned again and sitting concludes).'

2. I have accepted the difficulty of fully understanding Soal's motives, but other cases drawn from completely different fields can sometimes offer clues. For example the strange case of

Georges Fouré, a language teacher of Berlin. In the 1880s he was one of the top-ranking German philatelists and editor of the *Berliner Illustrierte Briefmarkenzeitung*. He waged, through his paper, an unrelenting war against forgers. At the same time he used his skill and understanding of the collector's mentality to create completely bogus early stamps. As Gustav Schenk observes in *Romance of the Postage Stamp*:

'This dangerous game became a vice and he played out his curious forger's existence like a virtuoso. He took no one into his confidence, so there were no witnesses to his truly magnificent art; he kept his counsel and possessed so little vanity that he was able to live as a lone craftsman without praise or admiration ... He must have had a strange streak in his character to derive pleasure in making a mockery of his colleagues and fellow experts ... His silent laughter over the serious gentlemen of the profession whom he had fooled with his creations was confined to his own room ... He was an artist, a tight-rope dancer on the adventurous wire of the unreal and the irrational.'

THE COST OF COURAGE

By the same author
Dark Talisman
Consequences

THE COST OF COURAGE

CAROL THOMAS

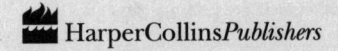

HarperCollinsPublishers

A special thank you to Bill Watts of Black's Point, who trekked up to the site of the Energetic Mine with me and explained the history of the area; to Peter Lawn, curator of Black's Point Museum, for helpfully providing me with old school registers and lists of inhabitants; and to Tony Fortune of Reefton for turning out on a bitterly cold night to show me his excellent collection of historical photographs of the district. And last but not least, thank you to my husband, Bryan, who helped me in all sorts of ways.

National Library of New Zealand Cataloguing-in-Publication Data

Thomas, Carol (Carol Ann)
The cost of courage / Carol Thomas.
ISBN 1-86950-458-5
I. Title.
NZ823.2—dc 21

First published 2003
HarperCollins*Publishers (New Zealand) Limited*
P.O. Box 1, Auckland

Copyright © Carol Thomas 2003

Carol Thomas asserts the moral right to be identified as the author of this work.

This novel is a work of fiction. Any references to historical events; to real people, living or dead; or to real locales are intended only to give the fiction a sense of reality and authenticity. Other names, places, characters and incidents are either the product of the author's imagination or are used fictitiously, and their resemblance, if any, to real-life counterparts is entirely coincidental.

All rights reserved. No part of this publication may be reproduced, stored in a retrieval system or transmitted in any form or by any means, electronic, mechanical, photocopying, recording or otherwise, without the prior written permission of the publishers.

ISBN 1 86950 458 5

Set in New Baskerville
Designed and typeset by Pages Literary Pursuits
Printed by Griffin Press, Australia, on 50 gsm Bulky News

For my family, with love.

Chapter 1

An icy draught licked the back of Alice's neck, sending a wave of gooseflesh down her spine, as the kitchen door swung open to admit, along with her father and a flurry of swirling snowflakes, a brown, sodden mass with a vigorously wagging tail.

'Oh, send him outside! Look at the mess he's making — he's filthy! Out! Out! Go on, get out, Peer!' Dropping her ladle on the bench, Alice lunged forward and grabbed hold of the dog's thick ruff as he bounded past her with a view to making a second muddy circuit of the kitchen.

'Michael!' She cocked her head crossly at the dog's young owner, who was presently sprawled across the rug in front of the fire, and making no attempt to deal with the wretched animal. 'Get this dog of yours outside where it belongs!'

Pulling one of his faces, nine-year-old Michael pushed himself to his feet and walked over to her. 'Why can't he stay inside? It's too cold for him in the shed. It's draughty and it leaks. Why can't he lie by the fire?' he demanded, rallying to the dog's defence. He reached down to pat its wet flank, causing Peer, in his usual exuberant fashion, to reciprocate by rearing up and planting two large, muddy paws on his chest.

Alice rolled her eyes in exasperation. In addition to

a filthy floor, there was now a dirty shirt to deal with.

'Because he's wet, filthy and he stinks,' advised Matthew Thorpe firmly. 'Now do as your sister tells you — send him outside and bar the door before we have a kitchen full of snow as well as mud.'

'He wouldn't be wet if he could stay by the fire,' Michael grumbled, reluctantly taking hold of the dog's ruff.

'He's full of lice and so will you be if he lies on the rug next to you. Do you want to finish up having your hair washed with vinegar every night?' Alice asked.

Michael glanced up, lips firmly compressed, but self-preservation evidently outweighed compassion in this instance and he shoved Peer outside.

With the dog finally out of the kitchen and the door bolted once more against the wintry blast, and orderliness if not cleanliness restored, Alice turned her attention to her father. He was still standing in the middle of the kitchen, looking as if he hadn't even the energy to take off his wet clothes. He looked frozen to the bone. His lips were blue, the flesh of his cheeks grey and pinched, and melting snow was dripping from his moustache. Stepping behind him she helped him out of his oiled cape then hung it on the hook on the back of the door to drip. 'You look very cold, Father,' she said. 'Sit by the hearth and warm yourself. Have your dinner by the fire tonight.'

With slow, stiff steps he walked towards the fire and lowered himself deliberately into the old armchair where he spent most of his evenings in the winter months. Eyes closed, he leaned forward and held out his hands to warm them. They were white-knuckled with cold and the veins stood out thick and blue against the pale flesh. Tall and lithely built, his black hair showing barely a trace of grey, he normally looked far younger than his years, but tonight as he sat hunched before the flames with the shifting shadows of the firelight playing on his face, he looked all of his fifty years and more.

Alice watched him, frowning. 'Have you had a hard day, Father?' she asked. He certainly looked as if he had.

He nodded, reluctantly opening his eyes again. 'I have, Alice. Mr Hardaker's bull broke through the fence during the night — took fright with all the thunder and lightning, I suppose. We found it at the bottom of a gully, half a mile up the valley. It wasn't harmed, although it would have been easier if it had been. It's taken us all day to haul it out. We were short-handed too. Bill Groves is sick in bed with a fever so there was only John Barnes and myself to do the work.'

'How did you manage to rescue it?' she asked. Not easily, she suspected. Mr Hardaker's bull was not only very large, it was a cross-tempered beast.

He shrugged as he leaned forward to undo the laces of his boots. 'With ropes, horses, and a good deal of sweating and swearing.' Easing the boots off his feet, he placed them on the hearth to dry, then peeled off his sodden socks.

'Here. Give those to me.' Alice walked across the room and took them from his hand. 'I'll squeeze some of the water out before you hang them up to dry or they'll still be damp in the morning.' Her gaze flicked down to the misty plumes of steam curling from his knees. 'Your trousers are soaked too, Father.'

He reached out to pat her arm and settled wearily back into his chair. 'They'll dry as well on my legs as off, Alice.'

She lingered by his chair for a moment, debating

whether to press the point, then turned away and went to ladle some hot broth into a bowl for him, watching him out of the corner of her eye. It had been a long hard winter — most were — but this one seemed to have taken its toll on her father. For the last month or two he'd returned home from his day's work looking exhausted. He was rubbing his chest again too, she noticed. Indigestion — and too stubborn to take medicine for it.

'Have you done all your school lessons, lad?' Matthew enquired as Michael stretched out on the rug at his feet to resume battle with his lines of toy soldiers.

Michael glanced up, nodded, then bent his head back to the more important business of the warring combatants on the rug.

'Ah, bless you, Alice.' Matthew gave a tired smile as Alice held out a brimming bowl of vegetable broth for him to take. Cradling it in his hands he lifted it to his face, closed his eyes as the steam drifted into his nostrils and inhaled deeply. 'You're a good cook, Alice. Just like your mother was.' On the edge of her vision Alice saw Michael's head shift slightly as he pricked up his ears. Barely eighteen months old when Mother had died, he had no memory at all of her and whilst he seldom enquired about her outright, he always listened intently to any passing conversation about her.

Leaving her father to his broth and Michael to his soldiers, Alice settled down at the table to do some mending. She felt quite exhausted herself — it had been a long, hard day at the milking shed. Mr Hardaker's cows had all been wickedly unsettled after last night's storm and hadn't been at all cooperative. It had taken Ellen Pryde and herself two hours longer than normal to milk them. The rat trap, she thought absently. She must remember to set the rat trap in the pantry before she went to bed. With a sigh she reached for the reel of white thread. She wasn't in the mood for mending at all, but needs must.

By eight o'clock soft snores were coming from her father's chair. Michael's eyelids were drooping too, she noticed. It didn't surprise her; he'd been awake half the previous night, coughing.

'Michael.' She nudged his leg with her toe. 'Put your soldiers away now. It's time you were off to your bed.' As she expected, she was treated to another of his looks. Michael had quite a selection of them. In this instance it was the crooked pout.

'Bed!' she said, treating him to one of her own looks. Ten minutes later the regimental ranks were in their wooden box and the general had reluctantly retired for the night, which was what she would be doing as soon as she'd finished her mending. Yawning, she reached into her sewing tin for another pin. Not watching what she was doing, she misjudged and the tin landed with a clatter on the floor, spilling pins everywhere. The noise was loud enough to rouse her father. Blinking like an owl in the firelight, he let out a deep sigh then slowly lifted his hands and rubbed his eyes with his knuckles as if to scrub the sleep out of them.

'Sorry, Father,' she apologised, crouching beside the table as she picked up the scattered pins.

He shook his head dismissively, smiling as he turned towards her. 'No. It was high time I woke up.' His gaze drifted to the crumpled fabric on the table. 'What is it that you're sewing, Alice?'

'It's just mending. One of Michael's shirts,' she said, casting her eye further afield around the floorboards to see if she had missed any pins. They could jump for miles. Hoping she'd retrieved them all, she rose to her feet again.

'When is it that Ellen Pryde marries George Withers?' he asked.

'Two months this coming Saturday,' she said.

He nodded absently. 'I thought it must be not far hence. Her mother and father will be pleased to see her well settled.'

'They will,' she agreed, reaching for Michael's shirt as she sat down again. Ellen had made quite a good match in George Withers. He was presently employed in Mr Dick's butchery, but George Withers was not without ambition and Alice had no doubt that eventually George would have his own shop.

'I hope to see you well settled one day, Alice.'

Studiously ignoring the comment she continued to pin together the ruptured shoulder seam.

'John Barnes asked me today whether I thought you might consider accompanying him to the dance next Saturday evening.' There was a short pause. 'I told him I thought you'd be very glad to accompany him.'

She looked up sharply, thinking she must have misheard him, but one glance at the firm set of her father's mouth as he anticipated her response was sufficient to tell her she hadn't misheard at all.

'Then I would be grateful,' she replied, 'if you would tell Mr Barnes tomorrow when you see him that I thank him for his offer but I'm not intending to go to the dance.'

'I've told him you *will* go, Alice.' Pushing himself to his feet, Matthew turned to face the fire, gazing down at the orange flames leaping from the logs. In tones so soft she had to strain to hear above the soughing of the wind down the chimney he said, 'It happened a long time ago, Alice. You must put it behind you.'

A wave of anger rose in her throat, sharpening her voice. 'Do you think I've not tried?'

He turned to face her and nodded. 'I do think you've tried. And I'm proud of you for it,' he said gently. 'But you must try harder still.'

She drew in a deep breath. 'Father, I —'

'No, Alice — hear me out,' he said, lifting a silencing hand. 'You can say your piece when I'm done speaking. I've something to say to you and I wish to say it without interruption.' He lowered his gaze to the floor and fell silent, as if considering carefully his next words. 'I'm fifty, Alice,' he said at length. 'And by the time Michael is a man I shall be close on sixty, should God see fit to grant me so many years. But He may not see fit. More men die before they reach sixty than after, as any cemetery will bear witness. I know you've said often enough that you'll never marry, but for young Michael's sake, if not for your own, I think you must make up your mind to do so.' He paused and his gaze drifted towards the small bedroom which she and Michael shared. In the silence she could hear Michael's soft, even breathing.

'He's a strong lad, Alice,' he said quietly. 'He's strong-willed even now at nine and he needs a strong arm to rear him. A man's arm. I'd like to think that if anything were to happen to me there'd be another man there to see he grows up as he ought.'

A cold finger of fear ran down her spine. 'What do you mean . . . if anything were to happen to you?'

'We none of us know our day of reckoning,' he stated gravely. 'Had the ropes slipped around that bull today I would've been crushed to death. Death doesn't always announce itself before it steps through the door.

And if I *had* died, what would have become of you and Michael?' One dark eyebrow lifted fractionally, inviting her response.

The truth was she didn't know — she'd never considered it before. 'I'd manage somehow,' she said dismissively.

He shook his head. 'No, Alice, you wouldn't. Not on your wages.' Stepping forward, he laid a hand gently on her shoulder. 'I can't force you to marry. Nor will I try. But will you give me your word that you will set your mind to consider it?'

She shook her head, as much in disbelief as anything. 'No, I won't consider it!' she said loudly.

'Alice, I'll thank you not to raise your voice to me like that!' he admonished sharply. He stood for a moment looking down into her anger-flushed face, then slowly removed his hand from her shoulder. 'You're twenty-five, Alice. The only twenty-five-year-old woman in Reefton who isn't either married or being courted. And you're becoming the butt of jokes and ridicule,' he said quietly. 'I learned today that one of the publicans has offered to pay five pounds to the first man you give some encouragement to, "who manages to get both his feet over your doorstep" is the wording of the challenge, I believe. He'd heard, you see, from one or two of the single miners how they'd tried to court you and were given short shrift, and how you kept Arthur Black standing outside in the pouring rain for an hour and wouldn't ask him inside into the dry while he talked.'

Alice's blue eyes widened into scandalised incredulity. 'Which publican?' she demanded.

'Mr McGaffin.'

'Well, Mr McGaffin,' she retorted angrily, 'had no business to go offering a five-pound note on my account and Arthur Black had no business to go telling that tale! It wasn't my fault he got wet — he should have picked a fine day to call, not the wettest Sunday afternoon we'd had for weeks. It was his fault he stood in the rain for so long too. It took him half an hour to pluck up the courage to tell me what he'd come for. I told him straightaway I wasn't willing to walk out with him, but he still stood there for a further half-hour, giving me an account of himself.' She sucked in a calming breath, slapped Michael's shirt angrily on the table, and narrowly missed sending the tin of pins sailing through the air a second time. 'It's a wonder I've not had every single man in Reefton knocking on the door,' she said in outraged tones.

'Well, it's not the five pounds that John Barnes is interested in,' advised Matthew evenly. 'I doubt he even knows of it. He doesn't frequent public houses and he's very sober in his ways. He's a good man, is John.'

'I know he's a good man,' Alice agreed shortly, aware where the commendations were leading. 'But I still don't wish to accompany him to the dance.'

There was a small silence, then her father said in quiet but nonetheless definite tones, 'I've told him you *will* accompany him, Alice. It won't be as hard as you think. John's a very gentle lad.'

She looked down at her hands, folded tightly in her lap, and compressed her lips.

'And make sure you're civil to him, Alice,' he added. Matthew Thorpe was very good at reading his daughter's mind.

Alice couldn't sleep. She'd been awake for hours, tossing and turning. John Barnes, Arthur Black, Mr McGaffin . . . they were buzzing through her mind like mad bees. But principally John Barnes. The dance — it would only be the beginning if her father had anything to do with it. She had nothing against John Barnes, nothing at all, but she didn't want to marry him. Or Arthur Black. Or anyone. She flung her arm out of bed and pushed back the blankets. Despite the coldness of the night she was lathered in sweat. Twisting out of bed, she pushed herself to her feet. She needed a drink of water. Her throat always went as dry as paper when she was worried or upset.

Disturbed by the creak of the floorboards as she padded across the room, Michael roused slightly, murmuring in his sleep. She stopped by the foot of his bed, watching him. The curtains were parted a little way and a shaft of moonlight was falling across his head, flecking the bright copper of his hair with silver. Her own hair, which by day she wore twisted and pinned into a neat coil at the back of her head, was hanging loose about her shoulders for the night. 'A crowning glory for a woman and a crown of thorns for a lad.' She smiled as her father's words drifted back into her mind. They'd proved true on many an occasion. Her own bright coppery locks drew nothing but compliments; for Michael though, inclined as he was to mischief, his locks were more of a curse than a blessing. The only red-headed lad in Reefton, it was quite impossible for him to deny his guilt when his telltale hair was glimpsed at the scene of a petty misdemeanour. She tilted her head, studying his face, relaxed in sleep, the long, thick lashes, freckle-sprinkled nose and full, soft mouth. How could a lad look so angelic in sleep yet in his waking hours get up to such devilment, she wondered. A dead mouse — that had been the latest incident. And not a very fresh one either. It had been a bit aromatic by all accounts. God knows how he'd managed to get it into young Hannah Anderson's food tin, right under the nose of a schoolmaster and a classroom full of pupils. But he had. While the actual placement of the dead rodent had gone unnoticed, Mr Chattock, the schoolmaster, had had no doubts as to the culprit. It was to be hoped Michael never considered taking up poker, she thought. He certainly didn't lack in imagination but as for keeping a blank, guileless face . . . Mr Chattock had known for a full hour before the mouse was discovered, to the accompaniment of piercing screams, that Michael had been up to something. The twinkle of expectant glee in his eyes had apparently shone out like a beacon fire on a moonless night, and he'd cast more than one ill-advised glance at Hannah's leather school satchel. The incident had cost him his lunch, which he'd been made to give to Hannah — the girl having understandably not much appetite for her own — and a very sore hand after six strokes of the cane. It had been three days before he could curl his swollen fingers round far enough to touch his palm again. When it came to punishment though, Michael had a very short memory, and she could guarantee that within a month or two he would be up to fresh mischief.

The floorboards creaked as she gave a sudden shiver. Her damp skin was starting to feel cold and clammy beneath her nightgown in the chill air. Glancing dubiously at her bare feet she pulled open the bedroom door and stepped into the kitchen. Now would be the test of whether she'd found all the pins she'd dropped on the floor.

Compared with the bedroom the kitchen was pitch-black, the curtains a better fit at the windows and a thicker fabric. She waited for a moment until her eyes began to adjust and she could make out vague, shadowy shapes — the table and chairs on the left, her father's big armchair on the right — then steered a course between them, placing each foot gingerly on the floorboards, feeling for the telltale prick of a pin before putting her full weight down. She was concentrating so much on her feet that it was only as she began to make her way back to the bedroom that she noticed the legs protruding from her father's chair. He quite often sat in front of the fire in the dark before he retired to bed; tonight he had fallen asleep there. Clad only in his shirt and trousers he would be frozen, the fire was long dead. Pins forgotten, she hurried over to him.

'Father,' she whispered. She reached out and shook him gently by the shoulder. His head had lolled to the side in sleep and shifted slightly with the movement. Getting no response, she shook him again. 'Father. Father, wake up.'

Her fingers slipped from his shoulder and she slowly straightened. 'Father?' In the silence she could hear her voice quaver. A wave of panic rose from the pit of her stomach and as she stepped sharply back she sent the poker clattering across the hearth, making enough noise to wake the dead. It woke Michael, who called out from the bedroom, but it didn't wake Matthew Thorpe.

Chapter 2

'Come away, Alice. Go back to the house now.' Ellen Pryde's fingers tightened around her arm in a small squeeze.

Alice nodded numbly but her feet remained rooted to the ground. 'Why didn't he say, Ellen? Why didn't he tell me? He knew he was ill.' She dug her hand into her pocket, groping for a handkerchief as a fresh wave of tears threatened to spill from her eyes. She had wept so much over the last two days her eyes pricked beneath swollen lids and her whole body ached with grief.

Fumbling for her own handkerchief, Ellen gave her nose a loud blow. 'I don't know. I truly don't, Alice.'

'I imagine he wished not to worry you, Miss Thorpe.' Moving across to stand beside the two women, Reverend Sedgwick laid a sympathetic hand on Alice's shoulder. 'Dr Martin had told him that there was little he could do for him. There's no cure for a weak heart, other than lying abed all the while, and a man cannot do that I fear, not when he has a family to provide for.'

'If there's anything I can do, Miss Thorpe...' Walter Grey murmured in concerned tones over her left shoulder. She turned her head slightly and nodded in acknowledgement. Walter Grey — a cousin of George Withers, Ellen's fiancé — along with about twenty other neighbours and acquaintances, had solemnly processed behind the hearse bearing her father's coffin to its final resting place. Mr Hardaker, her father's employer, being lame had followed on horseback. He had stayed only briefly at the graveside, offered his condolences then departed, explaining that his wife was unwell. It was an excuse, but Alice couldn't in honesty blame him. The situation was as difficult for him as it was for her.

She glanced across at Michael. He was standing alone, his grey woollen cap clutched in both hands, staring with unblinking eyes at the freshly carved inscription on the headstone. *Also Matthew Thorpe . . . departed from this life 20th September 1881 . . . aged 50 years . . . At peace.* Above it, partly obscured by lichen, were etched the few brief words which had marked the end of her mother's life eight years ago. Michael had walked alone following the coffin to the cemetery and had stood alone throughout the committal service, refusing to take her hand. His hair, wet from the fine grey drizzle that had shrouded Reefton all morning, looked darker than usual against his pale face. He had slept little since her father's death two nights ago. She'd heard him tossing and turning and occasionally caught the sound of his muffled sobs beneath the blankets, but throughout the day he'd remained manfully dry-eyed. Her father would have been proud of him. In life he seldom was.

Drawing in a weary breath she turned to Reverend Sedgwick and mustered a small smile. 'Would you care to come back to the house, Reverend Sedgwick? There's tea and some beef sandwiches for anyone who wants to come for a short while.' The cold beef had generously been supplied by Mrs Hardaker and the sandwiches made with Ellen's help. Over the last two days Ellen had spent every free moment at the cottage with Alice, doing her best to lift her spirits and when that failed, weeping with her.

Reverend Sedgwick nodded, his solemn young features etched with concern. 'I should like nothing better. I shall follow you directly. I see Sam Kenyon is at his wife's graveside. If you'll excuse me I shall enquire how he's faring.' Turning to leave, he glanced up at the billowy thunderclouds massing in the sky. 'Don't linger too long, Miss Thorpe,' he advised quietly. Lifting the collar of his black cloak against the chill wind he strode briskly through the long wet grass towards the solitary figure holding a small child in his arms.

'Are you ready to leave now, Alice? George has offered . . .' The rest of Ellen's words drifted away in the grey mist as Ellen's mother's voice caught Alice's hearing. She glanced across to see who she was talking to. It was John Barnes' mother, as tall and spindly as Mrs Pryde was short and stout. The topic — the late wife of Sam Kenyon, the bootmaker.

'Such a pity, she was such a handsome-looking woman. Hair as black as coal and skin like ivory. He's taken her death very badly, poor man. I took a pair of shoes into his shop for him to sole yesterday and he looked so weary. It's hard on a man being left with a child so young to care for . . . barely twelve months old, poor mite. She was in his workshop with him when I went in, crying at the top of her lungs while he was hammering away at his last, mending a boot. I asked him how he was managing but . . .' She paused and sighed deeply. 'He was plainly not inclined to talk about it. He thanked me for enquiring and just said he was managing as well as could be expected.'

Mrs Barnes' wide-brimmed black bonnet rocked

slowly from side to side as she shook her head in sympathy. 'The child is weaned, I've heard, so that's a mercy.'

'It is indeed,' agreed Mrs Pryde. Her voice dropped confidentially, but Ellen's mother, being slightly deaf, had a tendency to talk quite loudly even when she was supposedly whispering. 'He'll fare better than poor Alice though. Mr Hardaker has told her she must be out of the cottage by the end of October, barely six weeks hence.'

'Tch — how could he be so unfeeling?' came Mrs Barnes' scandalised retort.

'Well, he said he was very sorry but, with her father dead, he would have to find a new labourer and he would need the cottage for the new man and his family — so Alice told Ellen. He said the best he could manage was to let her stay for six weeks to give her time to find lodgings somewhere. I called on her yesterday and told her there was a . . .'

'Alice?' Ellen's voice, accompanied by a small shake of Alice's arm, tugged her distracted attention back.

'I'm sorry, what did you say?' she murmured.

'I was asking if you're ready to leave.' Ellen's gaze drifted upwards and her brow furrowed in a worried frown beneath her black bonnet as she scanned the dark clouds.

'Yes, I'm ready,' Alice said quietly. She glanced round, frowning, wondering where Michael had gone, then saw him in the distance walking beside Ellen's father.

Taking a deep breath, she stepped forward to take a parting look at the wooden coffin in which her father's body lay, to take her last farewell of him. The lid was strewn with the handful of earth she'd thrown onto it during the committal service. Soon it would be buried deep beneath the pile of earth presently mounded beside the headstone. Pushing back tears, she turned away. Ellen took her arm and together they slowly made their way across the cemetery to the road. In the silence she could hear the scrape of the sexton's shovel and the hollow thuds as spadefuls of earth landed on top of the coffin. Though the noise faded as they made their way back to the cottage, it reverberated in her mind far longer, echoing in the emptiness created by her father's death.

Given the choice she would have preferred to have no funeral wake at all, but it would have seemed a poor thank you to the mourners who'd braved the cold and rain to pay their last respects at the cemetery. She was expecting the gathering to be something of an ordeal and it was.

'You will consider our offer, Alice, won't you?' Mrs Pryde urged. 'As I mentioned to you before, when Ellen marries in two months time there will be a spare bed in the house. You'll be most welcome to it. And we can find a corner for Michael as well. We can come to an arrangement about board, I'm quite sure.'

Alice mustered a smile and made no comment. The arrangement, she had no doubt, would involve Bert Pryde, Ellen's elder brother. And whilst there would indeed be a vacant bed when Ellen married George Withers, it wasn't that bed which Mrs Pryde was keen for Alice to eventually occupy. John Barnes' mother had yesterday made her a similar offer of board. There was certainly no shortage of spare beds in Reefton for a young single woman recently bereaved of her father, but they appeared to have as many strings attached to them as a hammock.

'It must have been such a dreadful shock for you to

find your father like that,' continued Mrs Pryde; her fat cheeks wobbled sympathetically as she shook her head.

'And such a blessing that we live quite close by,' added Mrs Barnes. 'John will be only too glad to help if there's anything you need a man's arm for. John was such a help to me when my husband died six years ago, God rest his soul. I swear I don't know how I'd have managed without him. He's so practical, and so very considerate. He was only saying this morning that we should invite you to share a meal with us one evening, Miss Thorpe. Would you care to come for dinner on Sunday, you and your brother?'

Oh dear God, Alice thought wearily — dinner and several hours of polite, strained conversation with John Barnes and his mother — no, she simply couldn't. It was rude but there was no help for it. 'I hope you won't think me ungrateful,' she replied, 'but I'd prefer not to, Mrs Barnes.'

It wasn't the reply Mrs Barnes had been anticipating, that much was obvious by the way her brows momentarily disappeared beneath the black silken folds of her bonnet.

'I was intending to ask you to dinner myself on Sunday.' Mrs Pryde laid a consoling hand on Alice's arm. 'But Ellen said she thought you'd prefer to be quiet for a bit. Such a dreadful shock for you to find your father like that. Many a young woman would have fainted in such circumstances. Do you recall the time young Grace Muir—'

'Er, would you excuse me?' Alice cut in, sensing the onset of another lengthy morbid account. 'I want to speak to Reverend Sedgwick.' Stepping behind the two women, she walked across the room to join him. He was standing alone by the window, hands clasped behind his back, silently observing the proceedings. He was quite a thin, wiry man, not much taller than Alice, and not much older, but stature and age notwithstanding he had a quiet strength about him and a wisdom far beyond his years.

'A difficult time,' he remarked quietly. 'You will be glad no doubt when you can bar the door behind the last mourner and enjoy some peace of sorts again.'

Her deep sigh answered for her.

'You have some difficult decisions to make in the weeks that lie ahead, Miss Thorpe. And no shortage of advisers it would seem.' His gaze travelled casually around the room. Not everyone had braved the rain and mud to return to the cottage, but the dozen who had were sufficient to make the small room appear crowded. Eventually his eyes came to rest on Alice again. 'I cannot nor would I presume to advise you as to your best course, but if you have need of an impartial ear you may be assured that I am always at your disposal.'

She smiled appreciatively. 'Thank you. But I'm sure Michael and I will manage well enough.'

'I too believe you will manage,' he returned. 'You and your brother both. For a lad of his tender years Michael has made a brave show today.'

She nodded, casting a sidelong glance in Michael's direction. He was standing tall and straight, his pale, solemn face upturned to Ellen as she did her best to engage him in conversation. Reverend Sedgwick was right — Michael had made a brave show today. His bravery, however, was inclined to outrun wisdom on occasions. He'd announced before breakfast that he was intending to seek work the next morning at the brewery. Alice had advised him gently but firmly that the Reefton brewery made it a rule not to employ lads till they were at least eleven, so he would consequently be going to the schoolroom as usual. Michael had stated with some volume that he was nonetheless resolved to try. A loud, cross exchange had resulted, which had left them both red-faced and Michael with a stinging left ear. It had been a poor start to the day and hadn't made the rest of it any easier.

She could tell by the way Reverend Sedgwick's eyes shifted over her shoulder that someone was approaching and hear by the footsteps that the approacher was male. She knew before she turned who it was — the small cough of introduction was as easy to recognise as Walter Grey's lean face.

'Miss Thorpe. Reverend Sedgwick.' Walter Grey politely dipped his head. 'I regret to say I must leave now,' he apologised. 'I would like to stay longer, but I've some business to attend to which won't wait, I fear. I wished to say to you before I leave however, Miss Thorpe, should you require assistance in any way all you need do is ask and I shall do my utmost to help you.'

'Thank you. That's very generous of you, Mr Grey,' she returned, though she had no intention of asking Walter Grey for anything. He too was looking for a wife.

He smiled and inclined his head again. 'Well . . .' He glanced towards the door, plainly expecting her to accompany him there, but in the event of Alice's feet remaining firmly where they were, he eventually murmured, 'My condolences once again, Miss Thorpe.' And left. She watched him through the window as he mounted his horse, a dappled grey mare which he'd left tethered to the fence, then with a sigh turned her attention back to Reverend Sedgwick.

Alice had thought the morning long, but the afternoon proved even longer. The conversation, though well intentioned, was tedious and the prolonged standing was making her back ache. She'd have given every penny she had to shut herself in the bedroom, fling herself on the bed, and leave her guests to the devil. Instead she was obliged to spend a gruelling three hours listening to Mrs Pryde's rambling accounts of every other bereavement she could call to mind; Mrs Barnes, with little regard for subtlety, praising her son's various virtues; George Withers' lengthy explanation as to why mutton was currently the exorbitant price it was; while Ellen's brother, Bert, and John Barnes plied her with tea and cold beef sandwiches, neither of which she had any appetite for.

It was well into the afternoon when the last mourner finally left, with the exception of Ellen, who had insisted on staying for a while.

'I don't understand why my father didn't try to find another position — something less strenuous. He must have known that labouring on a farm, with the hard toil that he did every day, would be the death of him. Dr Martin told me he'd made it quite plain to him he believed it was his heart and not indigestion that was causing him the pain in his chest.' Alice glanced across at Ellen, her brow creased in a deep frown. The two of them were seated at the table, alone in the house at last. She'd sent Michael outside to chop some kindling, not that there was any shortage of it, but simply to give him something to do.

'What would he have done instead, Alice? Farm labouring was all your father knew. My father and brothers are the same — mining is all they know. If the gold mines were to close I don't know what they'd turn their hand to.' Ellen lifted her cup of tea and took a small sip. 'Have you decided what you'll do, Alice?'

Alice reached for her own cup, clasping it between her hands, and shook her head. She desperately wanted to believe she could manage on her meagre wages to support Michael and herself, but the truth was it wasn't nearly enough to pay for board and lodgings for the two of them, along with all the other incidentals. Whilst she could manage for several years if need be with the clothes she had, Michael's sprouting young limbs would be rather more costly to keep decently clothed.

'Did your father have any savings put aside?' Ellen asked.

'Twelve pounds, six shillings and four pence.' Alice inclined her head in the direction of the tin box on the wooden mantel. It wasn't much, but she was surprised it was as much as it was. Mr Hardaker, like many landowners, provided rent-free cottages for his workers; the weekly wages he paid were consequently very modest, making it hard to put much aside. 'Some of it is spoken for though,' she added. 'I owe Mr Sheppard two guineas for the coffin and the mason eight shillings and thrupence for carving the lettering on the headstone.'

'Eight shillings and thrupence for that bit of work!' Ellen gave a sharp click with her tongue. 'It couldn't have taken him more than half a day to do. Tell him you'll give him seven shillings and thrupence. The man seems to think he can charge whatever he likes, being the only mason for fifty miles. Mother told me he asked the Edwards family for nine shillings for carving the inscription for their youngest lad and Mr Edwards told him he'd pay not a penny more than eight. The mason argued a bit but he took it at the finish.'

Alice nodded and took a sip of tea. She couldn't see herself arguing with the stonemason though — she barely had the strength to lift her cup let alone argue with the mason about his bill. In any case, a shilling was going to make little difference to their future.

'Er, did Mother mention to you about boarding with them when I marry George?' Ellen asked tentatively.

'You know very well she mentioned it. You were standing beside her at the time,' Alice said.

Ellen nodded, flushing. 'Have you given it any thought? You could do worse than —'

'Marry your brother, Bert,' Alice finished for her, though she doubted Ellen had intended to state so bluntly what lay at the bottom of her parents' offer.

'They didn't make the offer for that reason!' Ellen stated in offended tones.

'Ellen — they did,' she said.

Ellen stared at her for a long moment, brows raised, then gave a small, defeated shrug. 'Well, maybe they did in part. I can't deny that my mother and father would like to see you settled with Bert. It isn't the only reason they made the offer though. It will still stand whether you take Bert or not.'

Alice didn't doubt the offer would stand, but she couldn't accept it, knowing that Bert Pryde would interpret it as tacit encouragement. 'You heard, I daresay, Mrs Barnes saying that we could board with them if we wished,' she said.

'I heard,' Ellen returned sourly. 'She's hoping you'll accept her son, John.' She seemed to hesitate then said, 'Do you have some feeling for him?'

Alice shook her head and met Ellen's eyes squarely. 'No.'

Ellen lifted her cup again, took another sip, then replaced it with a small clink on its saucer. 'You'll not be accepting Mrs Barnes' offer either?'

'No.'

'What will you do then?'

She lowered her eyes and stared into her empty cup at the stranded tea leaves in the bottom. 'I don't know yet.'

There was a small silence then Ellen said gently, 'You can't always do what you wish, Alice. Sometimes you have no choice but to do what you must.'

They turned in unison as the door swung open and Michael, buckling under the weight of a pile of freshly split logs, staggered across the kitchen and dropped them with a loud thud in the wood box beside the hearth.

Alice's blue eyes widened with ice-cold horror. 'Michael! I told you to chop kindling, not split logs! What did you use to split them? Father's big axe?' He had, she knew very well that he had, he could never have split logs that size with the light kindling axe. It was a miracle he hadn't chopped his foot off.

Straightening, Michael turned towards her. Judging by the sour look on his face, he'd expected a rather better response to his efforts. 'There's plenty of kindling. We had no logs for the fire though. Father didn't split any last Sunday. The weather was too wet.'

She drew in a calming breath. It was a foolhardy act, but . . . well, he'd meant well. Nevertheless, she didn't want him wielding that lethal axe again. 'You're too young to be splitting logs,' she said. 'Willing as you are to do it.'

'I'm not too young!' He raised a grubby sleeve and wiped it across his nose. His face, shirt and trousers were splattered with mud and his forehead was glistening with sweat from his exertions. 'And I'm as strong as you are!'

'No, you aren't,' she said. 'You aren't as careful as I am either. You could have split your leg open.' Still immature in muscle, Michael was no match for her in strength; he was her match in willpower though. His eyes were presently stubbornly meshed with hers like steel traps and to Alice's vexation it was her eyelids which blinked first.

She waved a dismissive hand, too tired to argue further. The easiest remedy was to hide the axe. And in the meantime let the matter drop. 'You'd better go and wash yourself in the sink. You're filthy,' she said.

He stood, making no show of moving, then in a sullen voice asked, 'Can I take Peer down to the river?'

She hesitated then nodded. 'Yes, all right, Michael. But make sure you're back before dark.'

Ellen, who'd been sitting with diplomatically downcast eyes throughout the exchange, lifted them slightly as Michael strode to the back door and began to don his jacket. She smiled then mouthed, 'He's a good lad.'

Alice nodded. Michael was a good lad — mostly. He had a good heart and good intentions, but he could also be deceitful and wilful and on occasions downright dishonest.

'Will you be milking tomorrow, Alice?' Ellen enquired. 'If you think you can't manage it I'll see if my mother can lend a hand again.'

She shook her head. 'No, don't ask your mother. I shall be all right tomorrow. There's nothing more to be done now, with the funeral finished. If I stay here I shall only brood and weep.'

Rising to her feet, Ellen reached across the table and began to stack the dirty plates and cups and saucers. 'Come along. I'll help you wash these dishes,' she said quietly.

Chapter 3

'Mi-chael! Mi-chael!' Alice tilted her head, listening in the doorway of the cottage, eyes narrowed against the wind. Cupping her hands to her mouth she shouted again. 'Mi-chael!'

Where in God's name was he? She wound her arms tightly around her middle, trying to stay calm, but the truth was she was worried. It was over four hours since Michael had left to go down to the Inangahua River with Peer. She had told him to be home by dark and it had been dark for a good two hours now. She cupped her hands and shouted again, hoping to hear Peer's answering barks somewhere in the distance, but the only sounds were the dying echo of her voice in the hills, the wind rustling the trees and rattling the tin chimney, and the creak of the door as it swung to and fro. Michael had stayed out late a few times before — and felt her father's belt on his backside when he'd eventually returned home — but today, the day of father's funeral, surely he wouldn't deliberately worry her like this. She pushed her hair back impatiently. Long strands of it had come loose in the wind and were whipping into her eyes.

'What shall I do?' she said aloud. She glanced over her shoulder at the wooden clock on the mantel above the fire, trying to reassure herself. Eight o'clock. Not late. But the fact remained, Michael should have been home long ago. Reaching a decision, she turned back into the house and strode into the bedroom to get her coat.

It was the first time she had ventured into Reefton alone after dark, and she didn't like it. She hurried along the main street, picking her way between the puddles and the ever-present litter of horse dung. The shops were all shuttered, long closed for the day, but the public houses were doing a brisk trade judging by the laughter and voices coming from within and the reek of ale and spirits drifting through their doorways. It was a bad night for a woman to be abroad in town alone. It was payday, the day the miners from the golden hills came to wash the quartz dust from their throats. Mr McGaffin's bar was doing a very healthy trade, she noted sourly as she strode past.

Once off the main street, her feet plunged into sudden darkness. There was little moon tonight, the sky blanketed with thick, drifting grey cloud. She made her way carefully down to the river, more by feel than sight, then walked along the pebbly banks to the horseshoe bend where Michael liked to play, a short distance up-river from the township. He wasn't here tonight though. The riverbank was deserted. She walked on further, peering across the water and into the shifting shadows of the trees edging the bank, calling his name. She listened intently after each call, but there was no answering call, no bark from Peer, only the surge and gurgle of the river and the thin keening of the wind. Eventually she drew to a halt. She had walked quite some distance. What now? Should she continue further, or turn back?

Alice bit her lip, trying to decide what to do. What would her father have done, she wondered. Her eyes blurred with tears as she stared out across the dark surface of the water. She did miss him, and never more than right now.

'Have you mislaid your husband?'

Alice spun round so fast she nearly lost her footing. She stepped back instinctively, away from the advancing bulk of the shadowy figure emerging from the trees. 'Who's there? Who are you?' she demanded, her voice high and shrill with fear. She stepped back again, feeling the soft slop of water around her ankles, and glanced in the direction of the town, now hidden from view by the bend in the river. Whatever had she been thinking to walk so far along the riverbank to this remote spot? She could scream her head off here, and felt as if she might at any moment, but no one would hear her.

'It's all right, I mean you no harm.' He stopped and lifted his hand in what she assumed was meant to be a gesture of reassurance. It didn't reassure her at all. He was drunk. She could hear it in the slur of his speech, see it in the way he moved.

'I, I'm searching for my brother,' she stammered. She swallowed; her throat was so tight she could barely push the words out. 'He, he has red hair. Have you seen him?'

'Red hair?' He gave a soft laugh. 'Can't say I've seen a lad with red hair. Not easy to see red hair in the dark.' He laughed again, swaying slightly, clearly pleased with his small joke. 'So tell me, what colour is your hair?' She caught the slight shift of his shadowy silhouette as he tilted his head, studying her, then he began to move towards her again.

She didn't wait to see what he intended. She bolted, splashing through the shallows in order to avoid the outstretched hand that made a lazy grab for her as she hurtled past him. Within twenty yards it was obvious that he wasn't quite as intoxicated as she'd thought. At any rate, he could still run; she could hear the crunch of his boots on the pebbles as he pounded after her, just yards behind. She screamed and tried to run faster. But if she had the advantage of a clear head, her pursuer had another major advantage. A heavy woollen coat, a thick cotton skirt and two winter-weight petticoats weren't flapping around *his* legs. She stooped, clawing blindly at her skirt as she ran, trying to gather the layers of fabric up above her knees to give her legs more freedom. Stooping was a bad mistake. She stumbled, landed full length on the pebbles and before she could scramble to her feet again, a panting male body was kneeling astride her, roughly rolling her over onto her back. She screamed again, flailing desperately with her arms at his face, kicking her feet, twisting, writhing, in short doing anything she could think of. But within seconds both her wrists had been pinned to the riverbank, held in a pinching grasp, and his mouth was grinding her lips against her teeth as he kissed her. He was crushing her nose with his cheek; she was having trouble breathing and for a panic-stricken moment thought she was going to faint, then just as she felt her lungs were going to burst he pulled away. She coughed, gulping air like a beached fish.

He was talking to her again, or rather the whisky was talking, she could smell the fumes of it on his breath. 'Just a kiss, a few kisses, lovey, that's all. I'll not harm you.' His head started to come forward again. She twisted away, wrenching at her wrists in a vain effort to free them. 'Come on, just a few kisses,' he coaxed. His lips were trailing hers — it was a game — whichever way she twisted her head, his head followed, chuckling all the while. It was no game to her. She was terrified. Terrified of what he would do next. And she had no doubt as to what that was. Her skirts had somehow been pushed up her legs, and through his trousers she could feel the hardened ridge of his penis pressing against her thigh. She twisted her head yet again to avoid his lips, glimpsed an ear and, on a sudden desperate impulse, screamed into it.

The effect was instantaneous. Alice had never had anyone scream into her own ear so she could only surmise what it felt like, but one thing was certain — it was painful. The faceless bulk which had moments before been straddling her body was now lurching around on the pebbles, both hands clasped to his head, groaning very loudly. Scrambling to her feet, Alice hitched up her skirts and ran for her life.

She didn't stop running till she reached the main street of Reefton. She was shaking like a leaf, her breath was coming in gasping sobs and there was a razor-edged pain biting into her side. She glanced up and down the street. It was by no means deserted. There was a group of four or five men standing outside the City Hotel and several others walking along the street. She didn't recognise any of them though and, God knows, she would be a fool to blurt out what had happened. She didn't want it known all over Reefton that she'd been assaulted on the riverbank, especially knowing how tales could grow. There was enough humiliating gossip about her as it was, thanks to Arthur Black and Mr McGaffin. The last thing she wanted was to give the town more to talk about. In any case, what was there to be gained by telling what had happened? She had no idea who her assailant was and he'd be long gone now. She wiped her hand hastily across her eyes, suddenly realising she was crying, then turned down the street and set off for Ellen's house to enlist some help. She was far too shaken to continue searching on her own.

It was what she ought to have done in the first place — enlist help. What had held her back was knowing how Michael's disappearance would be interpreted — people would say that she couldn't manage him, that she needed a man. On the two other occasions when Michael had gone missing only she and her father had known about it. This time the whole town would know, for Ellen's mother, though a kindly soul, was a gossip. Telling her anything was akin to telling the town crier.

'Alice.' Mr Pryde's grey eyes widened in surprise as he pulled open the door. 'Whatever brings you into Reefton at this hour?'

'It's Michael,' she said in a shaky voice. 'He's not come home. He went down to the river and —'

'Come inside, Alice,' he interrupted. 'You're as white as a sheet.' Taking her arm, he chivvied her into the hall.

Two minutes later she was sitting on the sofa in the parlour in front of a crackling fire. Having briefly recounted Michael's disappearance she was now firmly and repeatedly refusing the offer of a cup of hot tea that Mrs Pryde was insisting she should drink. She didn't want tea, she didn't want to be fussed over, she wanted to find Michael.

'Oh, your lip's cut, Alice,' Ellen said, bending over to peer at it in concern.

'Yes, I know,' she said. She lifted a shaky finger to touch it. 'I, I must have scratched it on something.' She turned back to Mr Pryde. 'I don't know where Michael could be. I don't know where to start looking, Mr Pryde,' she said. She lowered her eyes and stared into the flames of the fire. He could be anywhere. Anywhere.

'He has his dog with him, you say?' Mr Pryde scratched his chin thoughtfully.

She looked up and nodded, following his train of thought. If Michael was hurt — she gave an involuntary swallow — and was incapable of alerting them to his whereabouts, Peer was more than capable. The dog barked at the slightest incitement and he would certainly bark when he heard voices calling. Moreover, wherever Michael was, Peer would be. The dog was devoted to him.

'Well, I think the best place to start looking is your cottage,' Mr Pryde stated practically. 'There's no point in scouring the riverbank and the town until we establish that he's still not returned home. I'll hitch up the wagon.'

'I'm sure you'll find your brother well and unharmed, my dear,' Mrs Pryde reassured, reaching across to pat Alice's arm as her husband disappeared through the parlour door. 'He can't be far afield. What a pity Bert is out. He would have been only too glad to help search for him. Now, you're sure that I can't persuade you to take a cup of tea? You really do look very pale.'

'No, thank you,' she said yet again.

'Oh, what a dreadful day you've had, Alice,' Ellen said, chewing on her lip as she sat down beside her on the couch.

Yes, Alice thought, dreadful fairly well summed it up.

It was a good quarter of an hour before she and Mr Pryde finally left in the light wagon and a further quarter-hour before the cottage came into view.

'Well, it looks as if your brother has found his way home,' Mr Pryde said in matter-of-fact tones. Shining out against the solid blackness of the hill was a small square of light, a pale gold glow coming from her kitchen window. She stared at it, relief washing over her in great waves. Oh, thank God! she breathed.

Alice almost fell off the wagon in her haste to get down as it slowed to a halt in front of the cottage. Leaving Mr Pryde to clamber down at a more sedate pace she ran across to the door. Michael was home, yes, but was he intact?

It took no more than a two-second head-to-toe appraisal to establish that Michael was entirely intact. She stood in the doorway, her hand still on the latch, staring at him. He was sitting on the couch, reading. Reading. Michael *never* read voluntarily. Which meant only one thing. The book was there to mollify her.

'Where have you been?' she demanded in a loud, shaky voice. Dropping her hand from the latch she strode across the room and stood in front of him.

He looked up at her guiltily. 'I lost my way.'

'Lost your way?' She stared at Michael, feeling an almost insuppressible urge to grab his shoulders and shake him till his teeth clattered. Had Mr Pryde not just arrived in the doorway she would have done. 'How could you lose your way? You only went to the river!' she said sharply.

His right shoulder lifted in an awkward shrug, his eyes following the progress of Ellen's father across the kitchen. 'I went up into the hills,' he mumbled.

'You've worried your sister half out of her wits,' Mr Pryde stated sternly. Having raised four sons of his own, now all grown to adults, Mr Pryde was quite familiar with guilty faces and lame excuses. So was Alice.

'Which hills?' She compressed her lips further, the bruised throb of her bottom lip bringing an unwelcome reminder of what Michael's actions had almost cost her. Not that she'd forgotten; she was still shaking like a leaf.

He shrugged again, eyes lowered to his book, avoiding her eyes. 'The hills round the gold mines. You didn't need to go out searching for me.'

She wound her arms tightly across her middle then turned away and went to stand in the open doorway, staring out into the darkness. Her head was so full of fiercely conflicting emotions — relief, anger, hurt — she really could find no more words to say to Michael at present. Mr Pryde seemingly had no shortage of them though. He was giving Michael a thorough telling-off.

Michael had returned home late deliberately, she was quite sure of that. She knew why too. He was angry with her — firstly for telling him this morning he wasn't old enough to seek employment at the brewery, and secondly for rebuking him for using the big axe. Michael liked to think he was considerably older than his years. He'd been trying to be the man of the house, take her father's place, and she hadn't let him. *He's strong-willed even now at nine and he needs a strong arm to rear him. A man's arm* . . . Tears filled her eyes as her father's words drifted back into her mind. Belligerence aside, Michael was upset too; he was struggling to come to terms with his father's sudden death just as much as she was. Brushing away her tears with her fingers, she turned back into the kitchen.

Hearing her footsteps Mr Pryde brought his reproaches to a close and turned towards her. 'Well, your brother's safe enough, it would seem,' he said, tossing Michael a pointed look over his shoulder. 'I'll let you get him to his bed. You'll no doubt want to have a few more words with him first.'

She gave a tight-lipped nod and followed him to the door.

'That lad was no more lost than my right foot!' Mr Pryde said in hushed, vexed tones, once outside the cottage. 'What the devil was he thinking of, worrying you like that? And on the day of your father's funeral too! As if you haven't enough worries at present.'

'I'll speak to him before he goes to bed,' she said. 'And I'm sorry for wasting your evening, Mr Pryde.'

He shook his head and waved a dismissive hand. 'No call for you to apologise, Alice. We're only too glad to help you in any way we can.' He paused, frowning slightly, then added in quieter tones, 'Have you given any more thought to what you'll do?'

She shook her head. He was referring to when she left the cottage.

'You'll be most welcome to board with us, you know that.' He reached out to pat her arm then glanced back through the open doorway, eyes narrowing to reproachful slits as they alighted on Michael. 'Anyway, I'd best be on my way,' he said, turning to leave. 'It's late and you'll doubtless be ready for your bed. It's been a long day for you.'

A very long day, and not over yet, she thought. Turning on her heel she went back into the cottage, closed the door firmly behind her and strode across to Michael.

'You weren't lost at all!' she said, fixing an accusing blue eye on him. 'You know those hills like the back of your hand.'

'It was dark,' Michael murmured, looking rather more subdued after his chastisement by Mr Pryde.

She made a sharp noise in the back of her throat. 'You were supposed to be home before dark! If you'd done as I told you there would have been no question of you losing your way.' She curled her fingers, gathering up handfuls of the coarse woollen fabric of her coat in frustration. She had more chance of getting the truth out of the dog than out of Michael. When he was in one of these moods there was only one way to deal with him — with a belt. That was how her father would have dealt with him.

'Well, I can promise you one thing, you'll not be getting yourself lost tomorrow or Sunday,' she said, 'because you'll not be venturing further than the privy and the church.' She cocked her head towards the bedroom. 'Go on, off with you to your bed!'

He went, leaving her alone in the kitchen. She sat for an hour by the fire, staring at the dying embers, shaking uncontrollably, then went to bed and did something she hadn't done for many years — she stared into the shifting darkness, seeing the shape of a man in every shadow, hearing a footfall in every creak.

The demons were back.

Chapter 4

Alice ran her fingers over the coarse woollen fabric of her father's work jacket. It was hanging where it always hung when he wasn't wearing it, on the brass hook on the kitchen door. It still brought tears to her eyes whenever she glimpsed it, yet she hadn't been able to bring herself to remove it. Removing it would only take away a bit more of the little she had left of him, so though it upset her to see it she'd let it stay. She slid her hand down the sleeve to the frayed cuff and pulled gently at the loose threads. She'd been meaning to mend it for some weeks but never had.

With a sigh she turned away and stood silently, surveying the empty room. In the two weeks since her father's death she had rarely been alone in the cottage. Aside from Ellen's regular visits in the evening she had also received several calls from John Barnes and two visits from Walter Grey. Today, though, she was alone. Michael, after attending church with her, had been invited to spend the rest of the day at the Camerons' home, pray God not wreaking too much mischief with their youngest son, Alfred. She had consequently returned alone to the house where she had been brooding ever since.

Alice had still not reached a decision as to where they would live. She changed her mind like the wind, but with little more than a month now remaining till they had to leave the cottage she was finding herself awake at all hours of the night worrying about what best to do. Thinking that she might be able to find better paid work and cheap 'uncomplicated' board in Reefton, she had made numerous enquiries in the town, but whilst board was readily available it wasn't as cheap as she had hoped and as for work . . . well, there was none to be had. Mr Hardaker had assured her she was more than welcome to stay on milking for him, but the reality was the wages he paid her were very poor. Which in a nutshell meant she had three options — accept the offer of cheap board with the Prydes or with Mrs Barnes, or give Walter Grey some encouragement then accept the offer of marriage he was clearly keen to make. Walter Grey was without a doubt in the best financial position to provide for her and Michael, but the very thought of marrying him made her feel ill.

She sighed again and walked slowly across the kitchen and into her father's bedroom to tackle another task she'd been putting off — sorting through his clothing. A few items she could cut down and resew for Michael, and the rest she would give to Reverend Sedgwick to send to the needy.

She had barely made a start when three raps sounded on the kitchen door, making her jump like a flea. She had been jumpy ever since the terrifying business on the riverbank. She hadn't been sleeping well either. Too loud for Ellen's knock, she thought, and if it were Ellen she would follow it by a cheery call then let herself in. No, this was a man's knock. Too loud for John Barnes too, she thought, frowning. Which meant it was more than likely Walter Grey again. It was unlikely to be Bert Pryde — he seemed content to leave the handling of both her and his future in his mother's capable hands.

Remaining perfectly still, she waited. If she made no sound the caller would eventually go away, thinking her out.

Three more raps sounded.

Well, she thought, as a noisy pattering on the shingled roof announced the arrival of another heavy shower, Walter Grey wouldn't linger for long, particularly if he had donned his good black suit as he had on his last visit. Then to her surprise came another sound, carrying quite clearly above the clatter of the rain. A child, crying.

Pushing herself up from her knees she went to open the door. She opened it so suddenly her visitor very nearly fell inside. With the sudden onset of rain he'd pressed himself against the door, taking advantage of what little shelter the lintel offered to protect the small bundle in his arms. A wide-brimmed hat was pulled well down over his face to shield him from the weather so that all she could make out was the tip of his nose, his moustache, and dark bushy beard. She had no doubt who he was though. Only one man would be abroad, alone, carrying a small child in his arms. Sam Kenyon, the bootmaker. Whatever did he want? It seemed a bit tardy to be calling to offer condolences. Her father had been dead for two weeks now. The only thing she could think of was that he was owed some money — an outstanding bill for his cobbling services.

He lifted his hand to remove his hat, at the same time shifting his child into a more manageable position, rocking her gently in an attempt to soothe her fretful whimpers. A chubby hand appeared, wriggling free from the blanket, then an arm, pushing back the grey woollen folds to reveal a small, tearful face.

'Miss Thorpe?' he asked tentatively.

She nodded and waited.

'I'm Samuel Kenyon,' he said in the same quiet tones. 'I have a bootmaking business just outside of Reefton. I know you're in mourning, but might I speak with you for a few minutes?'

Yes, an outstanding debt, she thought, wondering how much it might be. Not too much, she hoped. 'Yes, of course. Come inside out of the wet,' she said, moving aside for him to pass.

He paused to stamp his boots on the doorstep to rid them of loose dirt then stepped inside.

'Would you care to sit down, Mr Kenyon?' she invited, waving her hand in the general direction of the wooden table and chairs which, apart from her father's old armchair and a wooden-armed sofa, was more or less all the furniture the room boasted.

With a nod of thanks he went to seat himself at the table.

She closed the door then walked across to join him. His daughter, still wriggling to free herself from the last folds of the blanket, was sitting astride his knee. Sam Kenyon's late wife had been a woman of rare beauty by all accounts. Her daughter was certainly very pretty. She had the fairest skin and blackest hair Alice had ever seen in a child and quite unusual pale-green eyes. Instinctively she glanced up at the father, wondering if the child's eye colouring came from him or from her mother. From him, she decided, but that was all she'd inherited from her father. Sam Kenyon's hair was a nondescript brown, as was his beard. And his skin . . . the little that was visible between his hair, moustache and beard was just an ordinary wind-reddened flesh colour.

Folding her hands in her lap, she waited for him to state his business. A very awkward silence had settled. Only Sam Kenyon's daughter seemed oblivious to it. Eyes bright and wide, she had ceased her crying and was inspecting the unfamiliar surroundings and the unfamiliar woman seated at the opposite side of the table with great curiosity. Sam Kenyon seemed for the moment intent on keeping his gaze firmly fixed on the floorboards.

She cleared her throat, and taking the hint he looked up.

'You'll be wondering why I'm calling on you, Miss Thorpe,' he said. 'It's presumptuous of me, I know, knocking on your door when I've never spoken to you before, and with your father so lately deceased.' She had in fact exchanged a few words with him in his workshop about a year ago when she'd taken her father's boots to be mended, but he evidently did not remember. Not that she expected him to — she was but one customer of many who walked briefly in and out of his workshop.

'I quite understand. There's no need for apologies, Mr Kenyon,' she said. 'If you'd care to tell me how much is outstanding I'll settle with you directly.'

He stared at her for a moment then said in clipped tones, 'I'm not abroad collecting debts, Miss Thorpe.'

That she had offended him was very plain and in hindsight her assumption had been a bit foolish — Sunday afternoon was not generally regarded as the appropriate time for collecting debts. But if he wasn't here collecting a debt then why was he here?

'Then might I ask why you are calling on me?' she enquired.

He lowered his eyes briefly to his daughter, who was

wriggling around in his lap and doing her best to get off it. 'Reverend Sedgwick put it in my mind to do so,' he said, looking up again.

Her eyes widened in surprise.

'I was at the cemetery when you were burying your father,' he continued. 'Reverend Sedgwick came over to speak with me. I asked him who it was that was being buried, and he told me about . . .' He paused as if carefully selecting his next words. 'Your situation.' There was another pause then he said, 'You've heard that my wife passed away recently?'

'Yes, I did hear,' she said quietly. 'I'm very sorry for your loss, Mr Kenyon.'

'I'm sorry for your loss too, Miss Thorpe,' he returned. Unconsciously, he reached for his daughter's hand, stroking her small fingers with his large ones. 'That's why Reverend Sedgwick suggested I should come to speak with you, because we're each placed the way we are through loss.' He cleared his throat and straightened. 'I've come to make you an offer. I doubt you'll accept it but I shall make it nonetheless and if you say no then that will be the end of the matter. It's my way to speak my mind plainly, Miss Thorpe, so I shall be plain with you now. I'm recently widowed, I have a daughter to rear, and I can't care for her on my own. I'm here to ask if you'll consider marrying me. I need a mother for my daughter and Reverend Sedgwick told me you're in need of a home and someone to provide for you and your brother. I can't offer you a great deal, I'm not a wealthy man, but I earn enough to promise you that you'll never go hungry or cold.'

Alice stared at him in astonishment. Suddenly aware that she was gaping, she snapped her mouth shut.

'I don't expect you to give me an answer at once,'

he said in the same quiet, even tones. 'I shall call on you again in a week's time, with your permission, to hear your answer.' One eyebrow lifted very slightly, inviting her response.

She was too stunned to speak. All she could do was stare at him. She evidently did something which gave the impression she was agreeable though, or maybe he simply took her lack of dissent to be assent — at any rate Sam Kenyon rose to his feet, gathering his daughter up into the blanket again. 'In a week then,' he said, and with a small nod strode over to the door and let himself out.

She was still staring at the closed door half an hour later. Then on impulse she donned her coat and set off down the hill for the manse. It's my way to speak my mind plainly, Sam Kenyon had informed her — she intended to be equally plain in her discourse with Reverend Sedgwick.

'Reverend Sedgwick, did you suggest to Mr Kenyon that he should call on me?' she demanded. He was seated behind his desk, his own neat appearance seeming quite at odds with the clutter of books and documents that littered it. The rest of his study was no better. The floor was so strewn with papers she'd been hard pressed to pick a path between them to get to the chair. Even the chair had had to be cleared of books before she could sit upon it. He'd been having a sort-out.

'Yes, I did suggest it,' he replied.

The unapologetic blunt admission was not what she had expected. She hadn't expected an admission at all in fact, rather a surprised denial.

'You did?'

'I did,' he repeated. 'It seemed a solution to your

present difficulties, and to Sam Kenyon's also. I saw no harm in suggesting it. It was, after all, merely a suggestion. Sam Kenyon was at liberty to decide whether he acted upon it or not, just as you are at liberty to either accept or refuse his offer, as you choose. I presume your presence here means that he has called upon you?'

'Yes, he has. Today. Just a short while ago,' she said sharply. She could scarcely believe it — a man of God meddling in such matters! She narrowed her eyes at him. 'Why did you not warn me that he might call? Why did you not tell me that you'd suggested what you did?'

He was still wearing the black surplice which he customarily wore on Sundays to lead worship; the stark black made his slight frame seem even leaner. 'I didn't know for certain Mr Kenyon would call, Miss Thorpe. I was inclined to think he would not. He was very fond of his late wife and is grieving sorely for her loss. He will find it hard to contemplate marrying again so soon after her death.'

Alice stared at him, unable to make any sense of his irrational explanation. 'You know he doesn't wish to marry again, so you suggested that he should.'

He nodded with a calmness she found quite irritating, given the difficult situation his action had created for her. 'I made the suggestion largely for his daughter's sake. Whilst I was speaking with him in the cemetery, he told me he'd made up his mind to pay someone to care for her during the day — a mother with children of her own, if he could find one willing to do so. He was clearly not at ease about the prospect of her being raised in another household though, nor do I blame him. Most mothers have little enough time to spare for their own children. He said he would much prefer to keep her by him, raise her in his home, but he saw little prospect of that eventuating. Good housekeepers are not easy to come by, nor do they come cheap. Added to which there's no knowing how long or short a time they will stay.' He gave a small wry smile, the unspoken implication being that a wife was a cheaper option, being an unwaged housekeeper; moreover she was bound to stay. He reached across the desk and picked up a discarded pen and began absently twisting it between his thumb and forefinger then in quiet tones said, 'When your own mother died, Miss Thorpe, your brother Michael was much the same age as Sam Kenyon's child. You have cared for him more like a mother than a sister and managed your father's home better than many a woman of twice your years. I recommended you to Sam Kenyon because I believe you would care for his daughter as he wishes her to be cared for. I also believe that Mr Kenyon would care for you and your brother . . .' He paused and his thin lips curved into a kindly smile. 'As I wish you to be cared for.'

Alice lowered her eyes and bit hard into her lip. She wasn't normally given to weeping, but since her father's death she could weep at the smallest provocation. Two kind words was all it took and Reverend Sedgwick had said rather more than two.

'Sam Kenyon is a good man, Miss Thorpe. You could do worse than marry him.' In the silence of the small study the statement rang out with the solid conviction he normally reserved for the pulpit.

Solid conviction of that nature was not what she'd come to seek from the rector, however. Her immediate reaction was to find something which would put a crack or two in it, a flaw or failing which would render Sam Kenyon less *good*. Knowing practically nothing about the man, she could think of only one thing. She looked up and said in disapproving tones, 'He doesn't attend church.'

The chair creaked as he leaned back and tossed the pen back onto the paper-strewn desk. Steepling his fingers thoughtfully, he regarded her over the top of them. 'Good men are found in all manner of places, not only in a church pew on a Sunday morning. I have discovered saints and good Samaritans in the most godless places imaginable, and by the same token I have seen most uncharitable acts committed by some who regularly attend worship. I would dearly love to see Mr Kenyon worshipping inside my church, but he presently chooses not to attend. His lack of attendance, however, whilst it doubtless diminishes the weekly offertory, in no way diminishes my opinion of his good character.'

A wave of heat flooded Alice's cheeks. Her comment had been both uncharitable and unfounded. 'I'm sorry. I had no cause to say that. What Mr Kenyon does on a Sunday morning is no one's business but his own,' she said. She'd been guilty over the last two weeks of a number of uncalled for and unkind comments. They were largely a reaction to Ellen's well-meaning but wearying commendations about her brother's good character, or if it wasn't Bert, then George Withers' cousin, Walter Grey. Irrationally and quite perversely, each time Ellen set about commending them, she felt an immediate urge to demean them in return. God alone knew why she was doing it — she might well end up the wife of one of them.

She looked back to find, to her surprise, a small smile lodged on the rector's face. 'Many years ago,' he said, 'when I was just a boy, I sensed that the Almighty was calling me into his service. But I had dreams, as lads do, of making my fortune and owning a fine house and . . . oh, many things. So for some years I ignored the call. It was difficult though and not as easily dismissed as I would have liked — a thorn which pricked my soul. So I set about finding fault with the scriptures and . . .' He paused and his smile widened slightly. 'I am ashamed to say even with God himself. I thought that by making Him less almighty, less good, less godly, I could better justify my decision not to serve Him. I thought that distancing myself from Him might help also, so I found excuses not to attend worship. I'd omitted to consider one small matter, though.' A soft silence fell on the room then he said quietly, 'My own need. I discovered that I had a need of God in my life. He needs me to do His work in this place, but I need Him also. And so I became a priest.'

Alice straightened on the hard seat and waited for him to continue. Presumably he was going to offer her some explanation of why he had volunteered an account of his decision to take the cloth. It seemed to have precious little relevance to why she had come here.

'I have observed,' he continued in the same quiet, unhurried fashion, 'that a number of admiring glances drift in your direction from certain parties during worship. I have observed also that you do not return their glances. Forgive my bluntness, Miss Thorpe, but the reason, I imagine, is that you do not wish to offer false hope.'

The statement was more in the nature of a question and the pause which followed suggested Reverend Sedgwick was expecting an answer.

With equal frankness she replied, 'I have no wish to marry, Reverend Sedgwick, but my circumstances are now such that I shall in all likelihood be forced to do so.'

He nodded, his features etched with sympathy and understanding. 'In the absence of a shared love,' he said gently, 'perhaps a shared need is almost as good a reason for marrying.'

'Reverend Sedgwick, if you'll forgive *my* bluntness,' she returned, 'need falls a long way short of love.'

'Miss Thorpe,' he said quietly, 'love and need are not as great a distance apart as you may think.'

Chapter 5

He was standing a few yards back from the door when she opened it, his hands clasped behind his back. Alice glanced past him, wondering where his daughter was. Not with him. He was alone, dressed much the same as on his previous visit in a dark brown jacket and black trousers and a fine pair of black leather boots — his own handiwork no doubt.

'Mr Kenyon.' She dipped her head and wiped her hand nervously on her skirt. 'Will you come inside?'

He nodded and removed his hat. 'Thank you, I will.' The floorboards creaked noisily as he entered. He was quite a tall man, about the same height as her father had been, but more solidly built.

'Er . . . please . . . sit down,' she said, closing the door behind him.

He glanced over his shoulder, briefly meeting her eyes. 'I'll stand if you've no objection.'

Alice clasped her hands tightly together in the hope it might somehow stop her legs from shaking. They'd been shaking ever since she'd returned from church, in anticipation of his visit. 'No, I've no objection.' She walked past him and stationed herself by her father's armchair. He followed her as far as the table then halted.

'You know why I've come, Miss Thorpe,' he stated quietly.

She did. Of course she did. But she hadn't expected him to raise the issue quite this promptly. She had expected some polite preliminary conversation first, about the weather or . . . well, about anything really. Breaking loose her clasped hands she gestured towards the two teacups and plate of biscuits set out on the kitchen bench in readiness for his arrival. Sam Kenyon might not feel the need for polite preliminaries, but she certainly felt as if she would benefit from a few. 'Would you like some tea, Mr Kenyon?' she offered.

He glanced briefly in the direction of her extended hand then his gaze returned to her face again and he shook his head. 'No, thank you. I think I'd prefer to simply hear your answer to the proposal I made you a week ago. If your answer is no I shall leave directly and not trouble you further.'

Alice clasped her hands again and licked her lips. She'd rehearsed what she was going to say to Sam Kenyon more times than she cared to remember over the last two days after finally making up her mind. You've nothing to lose, Alice, just say it, she told herself. She cleared her throat.

'Before I can give you a definite answer as to whether I accept your offer of marriage, I have two conditions which I shall require you to accept, Mr Kenyon. The first is to do with my brother. I wish you to give me your assurance that you will raise Michael as your own son, and in return I shall give you my assurance that I shall care for your daughter as if she were my own. And the second condition . . .' she continued, lowering her eyes. The second condition was rather more delicate. She took a breath and fixed her gaze firmly on Sam Kenyon's shiny black boots. '. . . is to do with the practicalities of the arrangement. I'm in mourning, Mr Kenyon, as you know, and while I'm prepared to marry while I'm in mourning I'm not prepared to, well, to formalise the marriage . . . immediately.'

She looked up again, uncomfortably aware that her cheeks were burning, wondering if he had understood what she meant by *formalise*, but one glance at Sam Kenyon's face was sufficient to tell her he'd understood perfectly. And if she was reading his expression correctly the conditions, one or both, weren't to his liking.

'Miss Thorpe.' His voice, though still quiet, had a fine edge running through it. 'I have a reputation for being fair in this town and I shouldn't have to give you assurances that I'll do right by your brother. As for your other condition . . .' He straightened, squaring his shoulders, and lifted his bearded chin, regarding her down the bridge of his nose. 'I'm not long bereaved of my wife, Miss Thorpe.'

He didn't expand on the statement but the look he gave her was crystal clear. He had no more burning desire to *formalise* their proposed wedding than she. Had she not raised the topic though, he might well have felt obliged to, that being the expected thing after all.

A statement and a look. It was not enough. She wanted a clear verbal assurance — a binding promise from Sam Kenyon, in fact. There was nothing for it but to take the bull by the horns. Stepping past him she walked across to her father's bedroom and reappeared a few moments later cradling a large Bible in her arms. She held it out in front of him.

'I would like you to swear on this. It's something we're in the habit of doing in my family — swearing on the Bible when the matter is of some significance,' she said. It wasn't, but it was the only explanation she could think of which wouldn't cause further insult. She held the Bible doggedly in front of his chest. He made no move to take it from her though and to make the point that he had no intention of doing so, he clasped his hands behind his back.

'Well, I'm afraid it's not the custom in my family,' he returned. 'I'm not a religious man. I don't attend church, as I'm sure you're aware.'

'Do you believe in God?'

He stared at her, looking thoroughly taken aback by the question. 'I don't know,' he said stiffly. 'Some days I think I do and some days I don't.'

'Well, I do,' she said. She held out the Bible another inch.

A tight and uncomfortably long silence settled. She was just about to put the Bible down and inform him that she would have to decline his offer of marriage when to her surprise he unclasped his hands and took it from her. 'While it's not of great significance to me, I can see that it is to you,' he said, giving a small nod at the Bible. 'It was important to my late wife too,' he added quietly. Placing his right palm on the black leather cover, he fixed his eyes on hers. 'I give you my word that I shall raise your brother as my own son and that I shall . . .' He paused, evidently searching for suitable words to describe the activity in question. '. . . make no demands of you until such time as is agreeable to us both.'

He handed her back the Bible. 'May I have your answer now?'

She swallowed and nodded. 'Yes. I shall be very pleased to accept your offer now, Mr Kenyon.' She placed the Bible carefully on the table, feeling as if a millstone had just slipped from her shoulders, along with one or two large bones from her legs. They were wobbling like custards. Catching sight of the teacups and plate of biscuits she turned back to him and mustered a smile of sorts. 'Would you, er, like some tea now, Mr Kenyon?'

He nodded and mustered a smile of sorts in return. 'Thank you. I would.'

She busied herself in the kitchen, uncomfortably aware of his eyes on her. It was something she would have to get used to — his eyes following her around. One of many things she would have to get used to. It was a small enough price to pay, though, for a roof over their heads and for the promises he had made.

'Your brother — where is he today?' he asked after a minute or two.

She glanced back at him. 'He's at Mr and Mrs Cameron's home. They have a son of Michael's age.'

'Is he away from home often?'

'No. Not often,' she returned. She could understand why he was asking. Sam Kenyon had visited her home only twice and on both occasions Michael had been absent. She had in fact engineered Michael's absence today. She had asked the Camerons if Michael could spend the afternoon there again, as he had the previous Sunday, being of the firm opinion that conversation with Sam Kenyon would be a great deal easier if Michael was not around. As yet she'd said nothing to him about the possibility of her marrying; there'd seemed no point in mentioning something which might very well not happen.

She reached for the kettle and began to fill the teapot. The shaking in her legs had unhelpfully spread to her hands and, even two-handed, she was having difficulty directing the water into the pot. Was he shaking too, she wondered. He looked quite calm, but then she probably looked quite calm too.

'Michael is nine, I believe.'

She turned in surprise. 'Yes, he is.'

'Reverend Sedgwick told me,' he said, answering the unspoken question in her eyes.

'Oh,' she said. Reverend Sedgwick seemed to have told Sam Kenyon quite a number of things. 'And your daughter? Where is she today, Mr Kenyon?' she asked, turning her attention back to the task of making tea.

'Sleeping. Charlotte usually sleeps for two or three hours in the afternoons. Joel Miller, my neighbour, is watching over her till I get back.'

With her back to him she couldn't see his face but she could tell by the tone of his voice that he wasn't altogether happy about the arrangement. She was inclined to share his unease. Joel Miller was in his seventies and she doubted he would have the faintest notion how to deal with a twelve-month-old child if she woke.

'Charlotte may be a bit difficult until she becomes acquainted with you.' There was no apology in Sam Kenyon's voice. It was merely a statement of fact, as was Alice's reply.

'My brother may be a little difficult too, Mr Kenyon.' And rather more than a little, she suspected.

She walked across to the table, a cup and saucer in each hand, hoping she could get them there with most of the tea still in the cups. Not waiting to be invited, Sam Kenyon pulled out a chair and seated himself at the table. 'Reverend Sedgwick told me you must leave here by the end of the month.' His brow furrowed slightly. 'The last day of the month is a Monday, I believe. If you're agreeable I'll set the wedding date for then. That will give sufficient time for the banns to be read.' His frown deepened. 'Unless you've a strong preference to be married on a Sunday.'

'No, I've no objections to marrying on a Monday,' Alice returned, sitting down opposite him. 'But if you've no objections I'd like to be married in the church rather than at home.'

'No, I've no objections,' he said. 'I married Eliza in a church.' Eliza was his first wife.

She lifted her cup and took a small sip. 'I presume the wedding will be conducted very quietly.'

'As quietly as is possible in a town where everyone knows everything within five minutes of its happening,' he said drily. He seemed to hesitate then said, 'People will wonder no doubt why you've chosen to marry me, freshly widowed as I am, a man you barely know, and with a young child.'

'And you are wondering too,' she said. It seemed pointless to avoid the issue. He was bound to raise the question at some stage.

He nodded. 'I am, Miss Thorpe.'

Alice lowered her eyes to her cup of tea. 'I do have my reasons, Mr Kenyon. But as you rightly said, I barely know you, and my reasons are . . .' She lifted her eyes to meet his. 'Personal.'

To her relief he gave a small, unconcerned shrug. 'Well, whatever your reasons I count myself fortunate you've accepted my offer. I hope you'll not have cause to regret it.'

'I hope neither of us will,' she said.

'Have you some relatives who should be asked to the ceremony?' he enquired, turning his mind to the more practical issues of the forthcoming event.

She shook her head. 'No. I've no one. Michael is my only living relative now.'

'You have no other brothers and sisters?' he said in surprise. He was clearly thinking, as everyone else did, that there was a very large age gap between Michael and herself. Nearly sixteen years.

'I did have two younger sisters, but they died some years ago,' she said. 'They're buried in Akaroa. That's where I come from originally. We shifted here eight years ago. And you, Mr Kenyon — do you have relatives in the district?'

He shook his head. 'Not in these parts. I have two brothers in Nelson and a sister in Christchurch.'

'Your parents are dead then?'

He nodded.

'Well, since you have no relatives and since mine are all distant from here,' he said, returning to the earlier topic, 'it would seem there's no necessity to invite family guests. We shall need two witnesses though to sign the marriage papers . . .'

If Sam Kenyon mended boots with even half the speed and economy with which he had made the wedding arrangements there was no doubt in Alice's mind that they'd never starve. Less than an hour after he stepped inside the cottage he was riding back down the hill again, brown coat tails flapping in the wind.

All was agreed. They were to be married on Monday, 31 October, at noon. All Hallows Eve. It was just as well she wasn't superstitious.

Drawing his mare to a halt further down the track, out of sight of Alice Thorpe's cottage, Sam Kenyon pulled off his hat and flapped it in front of his face. He felt hot and sweaty and he desperately needed to pee. Swinging down from the saddle he stepped into the bushes and relieved himself.

He stared in a somewhat bemused fashion at a dry leaf floating on the muddy puddle he was creating and shook his head. She had accepted — Alice Thorpe had accepted his proposal of marriage. 'God knows why,' he said aloud. He'd been fully expecting to get no further than her doorstep, to be given a polite but very definite refusal. He'd been so sure of it in fact he'd been berating himself all week for approaching her.

Doing up the buttons of his trousers, he walked back to the waiting horse then swung up into the saddle again, frowning. She seemed pleasant enough, she kept a clean and tidy house, and she could cook by the look of it. If she had a fault — and she did — it was that she was more than a little outspoken. Laying conditions upon the marriage, insisting that he swear on the Bible. He shook his head. As for the conditions themselves . . . He gave a small shrug. The first one, pertaining to her brother — he would have done his best to raise the lad as his own whether she'd asked him to promise it or not. And as for the second — well, he was only too pleased to delay that side of the business. Eliza was barely cold in her grave.

Joel Miller was sitting on the back doorstep, scraping the dirt out of his nails with a twig, when Sam arrived back at his home.

'Back already?' Joel squinted at him, interrupting his manicuring to shield his eyes from the sun.

'I am.' Dismounting, Sam tossed the reins over the mare's back and walked across to his neighbour.

'She's sound asleep. Not heard so much as a chirrup from her,' Joel reported, tipping back his head towards the silent interior of the house.

Sam nodded and smiled. 'Thank you, Joel. I didn't think she'd wake. She usually sleeps for two hours or more in the afternoon.'

'Well, did Miss Thorpe give you an answer?'

Setting a log of wood end down on the ground, Sam sat on the makeshift seat opposite his neighbour. He had known Joel for over two years now and had grown so accustomed to the old man's blunt manner of speaking he barely noticed it any more.

'She did.' He drew his brows together in a puzzled frown. For the life of him he still couldn't fathom why she'd accepted him. But she had, and for Charlotte's sake he was damned glad of it.

Joel nodded sympathetically. 'Well, it was worth asking her, I suppose. Nothing ventured, nothing gained, as they say. I did warn you that you'd probably come home disappointed. 'Tis my experience that women don't like to be hurried in matters of marriage. They like to be courted. They like to be . . . what's the word?' He lifted a bony hand and scratched the side of his nose with the stick. 'Coy. Women like to be coy when they sense a man is interested in them, they like to let him worry whether they'll have him or not, keep him waiting. They don't like to be rushed in such matters, Sam.'

'You seem to know a lot about women, Joel, for a man who's never married,' commented Sam in some amusement.

Joel laughed, then began to cough — the one invariably followed the other. 'I've never married, no, that's true enough . . .' He paused to suck in a wheezy breath. 'But you don't reach my years without learning a thing or two about women, and you don't have to marry one to learn it. I've seen the way women behave when they sense there's a man sniffing the air, and heard the miners' tales. Oh, I know a thing or two about women, I do. Anyway, as for this woman . . . I'm sorry she wouldn't have you, Sam, but I can't say I'm surprised. And you did say yourself you thought she'd refuse your offer.'

'As a matter of fact, Joel,' Sam said quietly, 'Miss Thorpe has agreed to marry me.'

Joel's white brows floated up like surprised clouds. 'She agreed?'

He nodded. 'She did.'

'You're quite sure she agreed, Sam?' Joel leaned forward, frowning. 'Women — they sometimes have a way of saying a thing so that it means neither the one thing nor the other, but a man can sometimes mistakenly think they mean the one or the other when they don't. If you understand my meaning.'

Sam's mouth twisted in a wry smile. 'I think I do, Joel. But I don't believe I've misunderstood Miss Thorpe's answer. She's agreed to marry me on the last day of October.'

'Well, bless my soul!' Joel murmured. The stick broke with a crack between his fingers.

'Will you witness for us, Joel?'

Joel nodded absently. 'The last day of October . . .' He blinked, breaking his glassy stare, and fixed a curious eye on Sam. 'What's she like?'

Sam scratched his beard. To be truthful he hadn't paid a great deal of attention to her looks. He'd not have cared had she the looks of a cow. All he wanted was a good mother for his daughter and someone to manage his household affairs, and Reverend Sedgwick had assured him that Alice Thorpe would more than adequately fill both of those roles. What was she like? Quite a tall woman, perhaps five feet five or six. Tall and slender. As for her face . . . well, she certainly didn't possess Eliza's striking beauty. All those freckles across her nose and cheeks . . . Eliza's skin hadn't a blemish on it. She wasn't what he would call plain though. No, quite pretty in fact. And she had lovely hair — a rich deep cinnamon colour. 'She's . . .' He paused, shrugged and said in bland tones, 'Oh, she's quite a pretty woman, I suppose. Though not particularly so.' The less so in black. The colour didn't suit her at all — that black mourning dress she'd worn today and the previous Sunday suited neither her complexion nor her hair. 'In her middle twenties, I should say,' he added. He hadn't enquired about her age.

Joel raised his brows again. 'Pretty, and in her middle twenties — how is it she's not married before this?'

'I don't know,' Sam replied. 'No doubt she has her reasons.' Just as she had her reasons for accepting his proposal of marriage. *Personal* reasons she had said — what the devil had she meant by that? Weren't all reasons personal? Joel was right — sometimes women did have a way of saying things that meant neither the one thing nor the other.

It took a full week for Alice to muster the courage to tell Ellen of her forthcoming marriage to Sam Kenyon. Her friend, to put it mildly, would be shocked. Added to which, with Ellen's own wedding only weeks away, Ellen spent most days exuberantly talking about all the arrangements. Alice's own wedding arrangements, by comparison, were so completely lacking in anything even distantly festive she felt almost embarrassed to voice them. It was the following Saturday, at the finish of milking for the day as they were both donning their coats that she eventually raised the topic. She had little choice — the banns would be read for the first time in church tomorrow.

'Ellen,' she said hesitantly, 'I've something to tell you. Some news.' She could tell by the way Ellen's eyes lit up like small bonfires that she was anticipating some tittle-tattle. And tittle-tattle is what it would shortly be.

'It's about me,' she said, doing her best to smile. 'I'm to be married in a fortnight. To Sam Kenyon.'

Ellen's mouth fell open so wide Alice could have dropped a goose egg into it. 'Sam Kenyon? Sam Kenyon, the bootmaker?' she said, staring in shock.

Alice nodded. 'He made me a proposal of marriage two weeks ago and I've accepted him.'

'But, but . . . he's freshly widowed . . . it's little more than a month since he buried his wife . . . she's scarcely cold in her grave! Oh, you surely cannot be serious, Alice! And for him to ask you so soon after her passing, and after your own father's death. Alice, whatever are you thinking of!' she exclaimed in scandalised tones.

'I'm thinking of Michael,' Alice said firmly.

Ellen folded her arms across her middle and her ample breasts swelled beneath her grey dress as she sucked in a sharp breath. 'If it's Michael you're thinking of then accept my mother's offer of board. The offer is for the two of you. Or marry Walter Grey — he's willing to take Michael, he said as much to George only last week.'

'I've accepted Mr Kenyon,' she repeated.

'Well, if you have any sense at all you'll tell him you've changed your mind!' Ellen stated. 'Can you not imagine the talk it will cause in the town if you marry him so soon after his wife's death, with not a decent time of mourning passed!'

'Yes,' she said, 'I can imagine.' She was presently witnessing a small sample of it.

Ellen unfolded her arms, dropped them to her sides, then promptly refolded them. Her feet seemed to be having similar difficulty deciding what to do — her skirt was swirling in all directions. 'You barely know him,

Alice! How can you think of marrying him?'

'I can think of it for Michael's sake!' Alice returned sharply. 'And Mr Kenyon can think of it for the sake of his daughter! It's all very well for you to talk of a decent time of mourning — you don't have a child for whom you're responsible. I do! And Sam Kenyon does! He needs a mother for his daughter and I need someone to provide for Michael!'

A very solid silence settled on the milking shed. If the angry outburst had achieved nothing else it had certainly left Ellen very subdued. It was a good minute before she found her tongue again and when she did speak her voice was so soft it was almost a whisper. 'I'm sorry, Alice. I didn't mean what I said. I was vexed with you. I'd set my heart on your marrying my brother. I've nothing against Sam Kenyon. He's well thought of in the town, I know. I'm just . . . shocked, that's all.'

Alice nodded and gave a deep sigh. 'I daresay the whole of Reefton will be shocked.'

'They indeed will,' Ellen agreed with conviction, then seeing the worry in her friend's face she added more gently, 'But they'll understand, I dare say, circumstanced as you both are.' Unfolding her arms she dropped them to her side and, as if on a sudden impulse, she reached for Alice's hand and towed her over to the wooden bench where they customarily sat to eat their midday meal. 'You'd better tell me all about it.'

She told her what little there was to tell. Ellen listened in silence, but Alice could see from the alternating frowns of dismay and disapproval that her reaction was going to be less than encouraging.

'Oh Alice, you're making a bad mistake,' she said, shaking her head. Loops of fair hair flapped against her cheek. It was looking quite dishevelled from the recent assaults of her fretful fingers. 'I know you need someone to provide for you and Michael and I know Sam Kenyon is placed in bad circumstances with the loss of his wife. But to marry him . . .' She shook her head more vigorously. 'Compassion is one thing, Alice, but . . . oh no, to marry him, scarcely knowing him . . . no, it's a bad mistake, it truly is.'

'If I had the choice do you think I would be marrying at all?' she asked sharply.

'I know you must marry, but must you marry Sam Kenyon?' Ellen's brows rose in exasperation. 'You could have your choice of any single man in Reefton — God knows there are enough of them looking for a good wife. There are three to my knowledge who would marry you tomorrow if you'd have them. Yet you accept Sam Kenyon's offer! Why? It makes no sense. You can't have any strong feelings for him, for you don't know him well enough to have any feelings at all. Nor can he have any for you. And from the tales I've heard he had a deep fondness for his late wife, which won't make it easy for you to step into her shoes. And on top of it all he has a child! For pity's sake, Alice, take a man who at least has some feeling for you even if you have none for him.'

'Ellen, that's why I've agreed to marry him,' Alice replied. 'Because he has no feelings for me. The reason I don't wish to marry your brother or Walter Grey or John Barnes is because they do.'

Ellen stared at her, lips tightly pursed. 'Alice, if you'll pardon me for saying so, that is the most foolish thing I've ever heard!'

'Foolish it may be,' she said, 'but I won't take what I can't return.'

Ellen clucked her tongue. 'The more you say the less sense you make!'

'Ellen.' She drew in a steadying breath and reached across to place her hand over her friend's. She paused, searching for the right words. 'George has a deep fondness for you and you return that fondness. But if you didn't, if the fondness were only on George's part, and if you knew you could never return it with your heart and with your body, would it be right to marry him knowing that you could only cause him hurt?'

Ellen looked away, staring across the barn at the line of empty milk churns.

'Ellen, do you understand what I'm trying to say?'

Her head dipped in a small nod. 'I suppose I do understand,' she said resignedly. 'But I don't know about my mother.'

If Alice could possibly have put off telling Michael her news she would have. But having told Ellen, and with the banns due to be read the next day, she had no choice. She was fully expecting Michael's reaction to the announcement to make Ellen's seem mild by comparison. They had not been getting on well of late — a combined result of a lack of sleep and patience on her part and an abundance of insolence on Michael's. They'd had at least one loud argument every day since her father's death. To his credit, though, Michael had done his chores without being asked and, unprompted, done some of the tasks which had previously been her father's. He was missing his father — that was very clear. They both were.

Michael, however, surprised her. He took the news of her coming marriage and the subsequent shift into Sam Kenyon's home with an acceptance which completely took her aback. His only concern was the dog.

'Can I take Peer?' he asked. He was sitting beside

her on the couch in front of the fire and turned to fix a worried eye on her.

To be honest she had completely forgotten about the dog, but one look at Michael's face was sufficient to tell her that it would have to come.

'Yes, of course,' she assured. 'I'm sure Mr Kenyon will be agreeable to it.' She hoped he would. Well, he would have to be.

'Oh, there's one more thing — Mr Kenyon has a small daughter. She's just turned a year old,' she added casually.

'Does he have a dog?' Michael asked, frowning.

'I really don't know, Michael,' she replied. 'But he does have a daughter and you must be very gentle with her. She's little more than a baby. And you'd better make sure that Peer is gentle with her too.'

'He's never bitten anyone!' Michael exclaimed, leaping to the dog's defence.

'He's big. And inclined to be boisterous,' she said. 'So mind you watch him if Mr Kenyon's daughter is nearby.'

'Oh, she'll like Peer.' Michael flapped a hand, as if dismissing his sister's concerns as mere nonsense. 'She'll be able to ride on his back.'

Along with all the fleas and lice, Alice thought. Peer's thick pelt was full of them, though Michael absolutely refused to acknowledge that the animal's energetic scratching was anything other than exercising its back legs.

'I'm sure she'll enjoy that very much, when she's a little older,' she returned, mentally adding to the list of things to be done: dealing with the dog's small, lively companions.

'I'm glad you're not going to marry Mr Grey, Alice.'

Alice started so much her spine cracked and the legs of the couch gave a loud creak. 'Michael — Mr Grey hasn't asked me to marry him,' she said. 'Who told you that?'

Michael shrugged. 'Nobody. It's just that Alfred Cameron said he thought Mr Grey had a liking for you. He looks at you in church when he's supposed to have his eyes closed while Reverend Sedgwick is praying. He turns his head a bit and squints through one eye at you.'

It was all she could do not to laugh. 'I'm sure he does not,' she said. 'Anyway, why are you glad that I'm not going to marry him?'

'He lives a long way from school. My feet would be frozen if I had to walk that far every morning in the frost.'

The answer was so ridiculously practical it sent a broad smile to her mouth. 'And do you think your feet will survive the walk from Mr Kenyon's house?'

Michael laughed, something he hadn't done within the walls of the cottage since her father's death. 'Of course they will. And I'll be able to walk partway with Alfred.' A pensive frown crinkled his brow as he tilted his head back and stared at the ceiling. In the firelight his hair was a blaze of bright copper. 'It will be a long way for you to walk to do the milking, Alice.'

'I won't be milking after I marry Mr Kenyon. I shall have to stay at the house and look after his daughter, Charlotte.'

Michael's head swivelled towards her and a delighted smile spread across his face. 'Peer will like that, Alice. He gets lonely when he sees nobody all day.'

Alice was still pondering Michael's unexpectedly calm reaction at midnight, long after he had gone to his bed. In hindsight she could perhaps see why the new arrangements bothered him so little. He knew they couldn't stay in the cottage beyond the end of October — she had told him that soon after her father's death — so he had been expecting to move somewhere. As for her marriage, she had a feeling that Michael regarded that as entirely her affair and therefore of no concern to him. She strongly suspected, however, that what he didn't realise was, once under Sam Kenyon's roof he would be subject to Sam Kenyon's authority and discipline. He would realise soon enough, and then the trouble would start. But in the meantime Michael appeared to be quite happy with her marital plans. He was possibly the only living creature in Reefton who *was* happy about them — and Peer, of course.

Chapter 6

'Therefore, if any man can shew any just cause why they may not be lawfully joined together, let him now speak, or else hereafter for ever hold his peace.'

A profound silence settled over the empty pews. The pause was a required part of the marriage proceedings, a time during which objections could be voiced. They seldom were and it was most unlikely that any would be voiced today, since the only persons present of objecting age were the bride and groom, the two witnesses and the minister. Alice drew in a low breath. As she quietly let it out, specks of dust floated and swirled like miniscule silver birds, illuminated by the pale shaft of sunlight drifting through the sanctuary window.

'Samuel Kenyon,' continued Reverend Sedgwick solemnly, 'wilt thou have this woman to thy wedded wife, to live together after God's ordinance in the holy estate of matrimony? Wilt thou love her, comfort her, honour and keep her, in sickness and in health, and, forsaking all other, keep thee only unto her, so long as ye both shall live?'

'I will,' Sam replied in a clear, steady voice.

Alice's own 'I will' was equally clear and steady, as were the rest of her responses and vows. She felt oddly calm in fact. It was only when Sam took her hand and slipped the ring on her finger that her legs started to shake.

'Those whom God hath joined together, let no man put asunder,' proclaimed Reverend Sedgwick in ringing tones. 'Forasmuch as Samuel Kenyon and Alice Thorpe have consented together in holy wedlock, and have witnessed the same before God and this company, and thereto have given and pledged their troth to each other, and have declared the same by giving and receiving of a ring and by joining of hands — I pronounce that they be man and wife together. In the name of the Father, and of the Son, and of the Holy Ghost. Amen.'

The deed was done. All that remained was the signing and witnessing of the marriage papers.

'Where do you wish me to make my mark, Reverend?' enquired Joel Miller, carefully dipping the pen into the glass inkpot. He leaned over the table, squinting shortsightedly at the document which would soon legally ratify the marriage.

'Just here, next to where I've written your name.' Reverend Sedgwick tapped a thin finger on the paper.

Stooping, Joel penned a large X below Ellen's neatly scribed signature. He was seventy-one apparently and looked every day of it. Alice had never seen a face more deeply lined and weathered. His eyes too were showing the ravages of time. The lids drooped permanently at the corners and the whites of his eyes were an opaque yellowish colour. His hair, what little was left of it, was pure white. In the light of the window it framed his thin old face in a wispy halo. He had plainly been of a sturdier build at one time, as the loose fit of his collar testified, but as often happened in age the flesh had slowly dropped off his bones.

'That's the finish of it then, is it? That's all I have to

do?' he enquired, handing the pen back.

Reverend Sedgwick nodded. 'It is, thank you, Mr Miller.'

'That being the case, this will be the time when I should wish the pair of them well,' he said. Turning towards Alice, he extended a bony hand. 'I wish you well, Mrs Kenyon,' he said.

Alice smiled and shook his hand.

While Joel turned to offer his congratulations to Sam, Ellen stepped forward and gave her a watery-eyed hug. 'I wish you well too, Alice,' she said hoarsely. She was smiling, but with her forehead creased in a deep frown and her eyes brimming with tears, it looked more like a smile of commiseration than congratulation.

'Thank you, Ellen,' she returned. 'Thank you for coming and witnessing for me too. I know it can't have been easy for you.'

Ellen shook her head dismissively and hastily wiped a tear from her cheek. 'There are no ill feelings against you, Alice. Mother is still a bit upset but Father told her you'd made no promises so you'd broken none and therefore there was no cause to blame you. I came with their blessing. They told me to tell you they wish you joy in your marriage.'

Joy. If there was to be any, there was little evidence of it this morning. A more joyless assembly it was hard to imagine. She had seen gayer funerals.

'You have a busy day ahead of you by the look of your husband's wagon, Mrs Kenyon,' commented Reverend Sedgwick, walking around the table to join them.

'I have,' Alice agreed, returning his warm smile. Sam Kenyon had brought his wagon up to the cottage earlier in the morning in order to collect the last of her furniture, but he'd arrived late and the loading had taken much longer than he'd anticipated so they'd ended up bringing the laden wagon to the church with them.

'Ah well, the Almighty has blessed you with a fine day,' Reverend Sedgwick said positively.

She nodded and smiled again but she couldn't help thinking that it rather poignantly reflected the very practical nature of their marriage when the only comments the minister could find to make were to do with furniture and the weather.

'When are we leaving, Alice?' Michael's bored whine came from behind her.

'Soon,' she said.

It turned out to be much sooner than she expected. Charlotte, hungry and cross at the disruption to her afternoon sleep, had also decided she'd had enough of the proceedings and began to scream, making conversation impossible. Five minutes later they were heading homewards. A very odd wedding party they must have looked too — the bride dressed in black with a screaming child thrashing about on her lap, wedged between her new husband and old Joel Miller, while Michael perched on the back of the wagon, surrounded by dismantled beds, flock mattresses, chairs, assorted boxes and the tin bath. They looked more like tinkers than newlyweds.

Sam Kenyon's house was situated a short distance out of Reefton, about half a mile along the road to Black's Point. Alice's father had jested about its relative remoteness, saying that Sam Kenyon had chosen the spot deliberately so his customers would have to walk further, thereby further wearing down the leather of their shoes. It was a solidly built house with a shingled roof and a small fenced garden at the front. What had originally been the parlour had been converted into a workshop. The slab hut on the opposite side of the road belonged to Joel Miller. It had stood there for years, though *stood* implied that it was in a considerably better state than it was. The timbers were cracked and riddled with worm and it looked as if a strong wind would be the finish of it. Tucked in a small clearing in the bush, it was protected from the worst of the weather, which was possibly the only reason it had survived as long as it had.

Once inside the house Sam wasted no time in settling his fractious daughter in her cot in the bedroom. Alice waited in the kitchen, casting her eye over her new home. Michael, too, was dubiously appraising it. It was the first time they had set foot inside Sam Kenyon's house, although to be fair he had invited them to dinner the previous Sunday. She had declined, making an excuse. If she'd been seen visiting him before their marriage it would only have made tongues wag all the more, and they were wagging quite enough as it was. Their marriage was the talk of Reefton.

'It smells like a privy in here,' Michael muttered, crinkling up his nose.

'Michael!' she whispered sharply, casting a quick sideways glance at the door that led to the bedrooms. 'Keep your voice down. Mr Kenyon will hear you.'

Michael was right though. The room did smell like a privy. A metal pail in the corner of the kitchen — the source of the unpleasant aroma — was piled high with soiled napkins. The pail wasn't the only item in the room showing the lack of a woman's hands. The carpet looked as if it hadn't felt the bristles of a broom for weeks.

'Why hasn't he drawn back the curtains? It's dark in here,' Michael grumbled.

'I expect Mr Kenyon has forgotten,' she said, giving a sudden shiver. The room was not only dark, it was cold. It was possible that the curtains had been left closed deliberately, of course — some people kept curtains drawn for weeks as a sign they were in mourning. The curtains in question, a thick, dark brown velvet, kept out the light almost as well as a wall. She walked across to them and drew them back a little, blinking as bright warming sunlight flooded the room.

Wearing an expression of mingled curiosity and dislike which seemed to have curdled in the mixing, Michael continued to scrutinise his new home, clearly not enamoured of it. He had been difficult all week, ever since Alice had started to pack up their belongings. It was as if the act of packing had suddenly brought home to him that his life was about to change dramatically. Alice had undergone a similar reaction herself. Like Michael, she had initially felt quite easy in her mind about the coming change to her circumstances. While the event was still weeks away it was easy to feel relaxed, but when the weeks had diminished to days she'd begun to worry and question whether she was doing the right thing. Right or wrong, she had done it and there was no undoing it now.

She turned as footsteps sounded in the hallway. The door swung open and Sam Kenyon reappeared. 'Has Joel finished unhitching the horses?' he asked, shrugging off his jacket.

'I don't know,' she replied. 'He's not been in the house.'

His eyes met hers briefly as he stepped past her towards the back door, then flicked to Michael, who was standing beside her. 'Come on, lad,' he said, tapping him on the shoulder. 'You can help to unload the wagon and store the furniture in the shed. You look as if you have a few muscles underneath that jacket.'

At an age where an inch of flattery was worth a yard of cooperation, Michael eagerly followed Sam outside, leaving Alice standing alone in the middle of the kitchen like a stranded fish.

She had felt a bit piqued when Sam had informed her that her furniture would have to be stored in his shed but she could see now there was no space for it in the house, and to be truthful Sam's furniture was in much better condition than hers. She glanced down at the table with four spindle-backed chairs tucked beneath it and ran her fingertip over the lace edge of the white linen tablecloth, wondering if Sam's late wife had had a hand in its making, then turned her attention to the rest of the room. A large bulbous couch, upholstered in a dark-green flocked velvet, and two matching armchairs were arranged in a semicircle around the fireplace, in the area which now served as the parlour. The fabric was showing signs of wear here and there, but there was no evidence of sagging in the seats, which suggested that the springs were still sound. Turning, she ran her eye over the sideboard — oak by the look of the pale gold wood. On it stood two brass candlesticks, several pretty china figurines and a gilt-framed likeness of Sam's late wife, Eliza. She walked across to it, feeling a prick of resentment at its presence. She and Sam hadn't married for love, nevertheless she did think he might have had the sensitivity to shift his late wife's portrait somewhere less blatant, at least for today. She picked it up and moved to the window where the light was better. Eliza Kenyon had been a beautiful woman — the likeness had captured her in profile. Her hair, black as coal and sleek as a seal's pelt, was swept loosely back then pinned in a neatly plaited coil at the nape of her neck. Whereas Alice's nose tilted at the end and to her mind was rather too long, Eliza's was as straight as a needle and in perfect proportion to the rest of her lovely face. She looked up sharply as a thud sounded close to the back door and hastily returned Eliza to the sideboard.

She was standing in the kitchen again when Sam appeared, backing through the door, to her surprise dragging in her father's large armchair, with Michael pushing furiously on the other end. Sam glanced up as they manoeuvred it past her. 'I think this will fit in the alcove by the fireplace if we shift the sideboard along the wall a foot or two. Michael said it used to be your father's.'

'Yes, it was,' she said, feeling quite touched by his thoughtfulness. 'Thank you.'

'Where's this to go, Sam?' Joel Miller appeared in the doorway, hauling in the flock mattress from Michael's bed.

Sam looked up from his labours with the armchair, frowning. 'In the bedroom where Charlotte is sleeping, but don't go in or you'll wake her. Put it in the other bedroom for now.' His gaze shifted to Michael and he added in matter-of-fact tones, 'You'll be sharing a room with my daughter.'

Michael nodded, looking quite at ease with the arrangement. He'd been used to sharing a bedroom with his elder sister. This new arrangement, in which he would now be the senior occupant, would be far more to his liking. Considerably less at ease with the proposed sleeping arrangements was the new Mrs Kenyon. Naively perhaps she had assumed that, in view of the promise Sam had made her, she would have her own bed and share a room with Michael as she had in the past. It was possible, of course, that she was jumping to conclusions and she'd share a room with Charlotte and Michael, if the bedroom was a large one. Following close on Joel's heels she went to investigate.

One quick peep inside the room where Charlotte slept was sufficient to show her she wouldn't be sleeping in that bedroom. There was barely room for Michael's bed and certainly no room for hers as well. She walked across the narrow hall into the second bedroom, almost colliding with Joel on his way out.

'I've put the mattress on your bed for now,' he said, smiling affably.

Her bed, as she suspected, was a double one. She would have to have a small discussion with her husband at a suitable moment.

'I used to be a miner,' Joel informed her conversationally, preceding her into the kitchen. 'Started work in a coal mine in Lancashire in England when I was nine, and finished up here in Reefton in a gold mine. Of the two, I think I'd sooner mine gold than coal. Coal's dirty stuff to work with. It gets into your eyes and makes them prick something fierce. It has a way of getting into your tongue somehow too — makes all your food taste of it. I was a miner for fifty-five years — spent more time below ground than atop it.' He paused and gave a wheezy laugh. 'Still, I suppose we all spend more time below ground than above it at the finish.'

Alice gave a small smile, but given the recent bereavements which Sam and she had suffered, she couldn't help thinking Joel's small joke was not in the best taste. Blithely unaware of his faux pas Joel continued to reminisce about his mining days, occasionally stopping in his rambling account as a coughing bout took him in its grip. 'I blame mining for this damned cough.' He slapped his chest with the palm of his hand as he struggled for breath. 'It's the cold that's to blame — cold and damp as a grave in a mine — it settles in the chest and once it's settled there nothing seems to shift it.'

'I have a bottle of syrup that might help relieve it,' Alice volunteered. She surveyed the clutter of boxes which had recently appeared in the kitchen and frowned. 'Somewhere . . .'

Joel waved a hand dismissively. 'Don't trouble yourself on my account, Mrs Kenyon. But if you happen across it I'll try a spoonful.'

Two hours later she had found the bottle of cough remedy and the house was starting to show some semblance of orderliness again. While Sam, with the help of Joel and Michael, had been busy outside stacking furniture in the shed, she'd been busy inside storing away linen and clothing. Stowing her pots and pans into the already cluttered kitchen cupboards was proving rather more difficult though. Difficult or not, she would have to fit them in somehow, having insisted she didn't want them stored in the shed. It was all very well for Sam Kenyon to glibly say there were already plenty of pots and pans in his cupboards — they were his late wife's pots and pans. She blew out an exasperated sigh. There was simply not enough room — it was like trying to pour a quart of milk into a pint jug. Nor were matters helped by Charlotte's curious hands and head. As fast as Alice put things into the cupboard Charlotte pulled them out again. But frustrating as her small stepdaughter was, she couldn't help but smile at her antics. She could remember Michael having a similar fascination for pots and pans when he was little. He'd also been entranced by wooden clothes pegs. Lifting the peg box down from the shelf, Alice placed it on the floor some distance from the cupboard then seated her step-daughter next to it. Within half a minute Charlotte was busily transferring pegs from the box to her lap then transferring them back again, the repetitious nature of the game not appearing to detract from its appeal in the least. Making the most of it, Alice set about stowing away the last of her pots and pans. Her thoughts, however, were more atuned to what lay on the other side of the cupboard — namely, the double bed in Sam Kenyon's bedroom. She would have to speak to him about it soon, while there was still time to rearrange things. Joel had gone home, which left just Michael to somehow dispatch out of hearing. He was presently watching Sam reassemble his dismantled bed.

Leaving Charlotte to play with the pegs she walked down the narrow passageway and stood in the doorway of the small bedroom which, under the present arrangements, was destined to be the two children's. Sam was in the process of tightening up a bolt on the bed frame with a large spanner.

'Michael, I think you should take Peer for a walk around Mr Kenyon's property before it goes dark. He needs to realise this is his home now,' she said.

'Fetch a couple of pails of water from the creek and fill the horse trough while you're about it,' added Sam.

She waited till she heard the sound of the back door opening and closing, then said in a quiet but firm voice, 'Mr Kenyon, I'm afraid I'm not comfortable with the arrangements you've made regarding the night-time. I'd prefer to sleep alone please, until . . . well, until it is agreeable to us both to have a different arrangement.'

Sam slowly straightened. For several seconds he

stared at her in silence then, tossing the spanner onto the bed he folded his arms across his chest. 'Mrs Kenyon,' he said, mimicking the formal tones she had used to address him. 'We are man and wife now, albeit in name only at the present time, and as my wife you will be sharing my bed.' Unfolding his arms he picked up the spanner again and resumed tightening the bolts on the bed frame. He was evidently assuming the matter was now closed. It wasn't.

'You gave me your word you'd not press me,' she reminded from the doorway.

Twisting, he regarded her above the crook of his elbow. 'Are you saying you don't trust me to keep my word?'

'No!' she said in surprise. She hadn't been implying that at all; she had simply been trying to make the point that she wished to sleep alone.

'Well, I can't think why else you'd be asking to have your own bed,' he said bluntly. He held her eyes for a moment then his gaze travelled slowly down the length of her, his features assuming the kind of expression one might wear when examining a very inferior piece of merchandise. 'Rest assured, I'll not be pressing my attentions on you for quite some time,' he said definitely, and turned back to his bolts again.

Alice compressed her lips, her cheeks burning hot. She hadn't intended to insult Sam Kenyon, but insulted he was. And he had just returned insult for insult — with interest. She stood watching him for a moment or two as he continued to wrench at nuts, then spun on her heel and strode back to the kitchen where Charlotte, judging by the din, was rootling through the pots and pans again.

Their first meal together as a family proved a strained affair. Michael, not excelling in tact and unused to dining with a young child and a bearded male, alternated his stares between Charlotte's gravy-coated chin and a small piece of potato which had lodged itself on Sam Kenyon's whiskers. Added to which, Michael was plainly wondering why Charlotte was being allowed to use her fingers as forks. Afraid that he might make an inappropriate comment, Alice glowered warningly at him, while Sam confined his glowers to his plate. He appeared to be not particularly fond of liver. Charlotte too had spat out more than she had swallowed; small brown mounds resembling wormcasts were dotted around her plate. Her table manners were dreadful. She had clearly been allowed to shovel food into her mouth with her fingers and to spit out anything that didn't take her fancy. Reaching across the table, Alice placed a teaspoon in her hand, gently curling her small fingers around the handle, then helped her to scoop some potato onto it. Out of the corner of her eye she could see that Sam had stopped eating and was watching her. Lifting Charlotte's hand, she guided the spoon into her mouth.

'I've not taught her how to use cutlery,' he said matter-of-factly.

She glanced across at him. She was still smarting from the altercation in the bedroom earlier and felt very tempted to furnish a reply that would make him smart a bit. Several sprang to mind. *So I see*, spoken in a suitable tone would more than do. Repaying sting for sting was hardly going to pave the way for a peaceful marital relationship though. It would be unkind too — table manners would have been a long way from Sam's thoughts while he was tending his dying wife. She settled therefore for a bland, 'I'll teach her.'

At the finish of what had been a largely silent meal, Sam ran his hand down his beard, mercifully dislodging the snarled morsel of potato. Rising to her feet she began to clear the table.

'It's past Charlotte's bedtime. See to her before you do the dishes,' he said quietly.

Setting the stack of dirty plates on the bench by the sink, she returned to the table with a damp cloth to wipe her stepdaughter's face and hands. Satisfied she was clean, Alice lifted her down from the chair, smiling as the pretty little face grinned up at her. At least his daughter wasn't being objectionable, she thought. Charlotte had a lovely disposition and she was being remarkably accepting of the strange faces that had suddenly appeared in her home. 'Say good night to your papa, Charlotte,' she said, leading her across to Sam.

Smiling, Sam stroked his daughter under the chin with his finger. 'Time for your bed now, Charlotte. I'll come to see you when you're tucked into your cot.'

Sam was seated in an armchair reading a book when Alice returned from putting Charlotte to bed. Michael was seated at the table swinging his legs back and forth like scissors, wearing his bored expression. 'Get your school books and practise your handwriting, Michael,' she said, stretching past him to collect the rest of the dirty crockery.

'I don't need to practise. I can write very well,' he retorted.

'Get them.' Dropping his book onto the arm of the chair Sam rose to his feet and fixed a narrow eye on Michael. 'When I return I want to see you sitting at the table with your books in front of you, practising your writing.'

Quiet as the order had been, it was effective. When

Sam returned a few minutes later Michael's coppery head was bowed low over his school book.

Alice busied herself in the kitchen. After dealing with the dirty dishes, she protractedly and not particularly quietly sorted through the contents of the cupboards and pantry. She had never quite seen the point in making a silent protest; to her mind if you were going to protest you might as well do it to the tune of noisy bugles or whatever was to hand — in this instance the clatter of pots and pans. Sam had tossed her more than one disapproving frown, but had thus far suffered the din in silence. She wasn't normally given to peevish bloodymindedness but she had to admit it did have its attributes. That aside, rattling around in the pantry was also providing her with an excuse for not joining her husband in the parlour. Evidently sharing her lack of enthusiasm for Sam's company, as eight o'clock chimed on the mantel clock Michael did the unthinkable and announced he was going to bed.

Having thoroughly clattered everything clatterable, a little before nine she sat down on the sofa with her sewing. As she pricked the point of the needle through the fabric she glanced across at her husband. He was buried in his book, as he had been all evening. He was still annoyed with her, she could tell. Well, that makes two of us, she thought. Never in her whole life had she had anyone look at her in the belittling, cheapening, humiliating way he had. But then he'd probably never had his word called into question before either. It certainly hadn't been her intention to question it but . . . well, she had to admit it might have sounded that way. Sam Kenyon placed quite a high value on his good name and it wasn't the first time she had accidentally dented it. She seemed to be making something of a habit of it.

She'd offended him the very first time he'd called on her, when she had erroneously concluded he was collecting debts. If Sam had his pride, she had hers too. Added to which he had *deliberately* insulted her; there'd been nothing accidental about that look. He certainly didn't deserve an apology from her, nor was she going to get one. In the interests of ongoing harmony, however, she thought she might condescend to offer a small olive branch. A twig at least.

'Have you any clothes that need repairing?' she enquired coolly.

He looked up from his book, frowning slightly. 'No. I can't think that there's anything. Thank you,' he added.

Silence settled again, broken only by the soft riffle of paper as Sam turned a page or the snip of scissors as Alice cut a fresh length of thread. Well, Alice, you knew it wouldn't be easy, she told herself.

A quarter-hour later he looked up again. 'You'll be needing some money to buy provisions — groceries and the like. You'll find some in the tin box on the top shelf in the pantry. My wife . . . my late wife, that is . . . she used to tell me when it needed replenishing.'

She nodded, murmured, 'Thank you,' and continued with her hemming, pricking the needle in, out, in, out, in, out, in, out . . . She had never known an evening to pass so slowly. Every few minutes she found her eyes drifting to the clock on the mantelpiece, expecting at least half an hour to have passed. She squinted sideways at the door leading to the two bedrooms. When would be an acceptable time to retire? Would it look very rude if she decamped at half-past nine after gracing him with just a half-hour of her company? Well, rude or not, she was going to. Better to risk rudeness than risk retiring at the same time as her husband and be faced with having to undress in front of him.

'I think I shall go to bed now,' she said, replacing her bobbins, scissors and tin of assorted needles in her mending basket. To her relief Sam made no move to leave his armchair but merely looked up and nodded.

'What time do you normally rise in the morning?' she asked. Whatever time it was she would be rising later, in private.

'When Charlotte wakes,' he said drily. 'About six o'clock, sometimes earlier.'

'Do you like porridge for breakfast?'

'I do.'

'And Charlotte?'

'I usually give her warm milksops for her breakfast. She's never eaten porridge.'

Picking up her sewing basket, she rose to her feet. 'Good night then,' she said.

'Good night,' he returned.

As she walked down the passageway she could hear the faint sound of Michael's soft snores coming from the other bedroom. She doubted she would sleep so soundly tonight.

Sam closed his eyes and leaned back against the armchair, pushing back his shoulders. He had been tense all day, still was, and his neck ached; it always ached when he was tense. Thank God she'd gone to bed early so he could relax for a while! Setting down his book on the arm of the chair, he reached up with both hands and tried to massage the back of his neck to loosen the muscles, the way Eliza used to do for him. God, he missed her. He had missed her all the more today, seeing Alice Thorpe — no, *Kenyon* — the woman was his wife now . . . seeing her walking about the house, cooking dinner in Eliza's kitchen, sitting on the sofa where Eliza used to sit . . . And tonight she would be lying in his bed with that fiery hair of hers spread across the pillow. Eliza's pillow. Why in God's name had he not agreed to let her sleep alone when she'd asked him? He shook his head, eyes still closed, and dug his fingers deeper into his neck. To make a point, that was why. To show her who was head of the household. Start a marriage as you mean to go on. He couldn't remember who'd told him that, but it was damned sound advice.

With a sigh he let his hands fall loose into his lap. He stared at the calloused palms then with another sigh dug his elbows into his knees and rested his forehead in his hands. He felt bone weary. He wanted to go to bed, but he couldn't, not yet, not till he was sure Alice was safely in bed. That was why she had retired so early, so she could undress in private. Well, he had no wish to see her undressing. *You promised you'd not press me,* she'd said. He shook his head wearily in his hands. She need have no fear on that score. He felt no desire for her whatsoever.

Letting out another deep sigh he lifted his head and looked over to the sideboard where Eliza's likeness stood. Pushing himself stiffly to his feet he walked across and picked it up. He gazed at the picture for a moment then ran his fingertip across the cold glass, tracing the familiar features that lay beneath. 'I do miss you, Eliza,' he whispered.

Swallowing, he pressed the portrait against his cheek, and giving in to the aching tightness in his throat, wept.

Chapter 7

Sam glanced sideways to the doorway of his workshop where Michael was standing. The lad had been hovering there for some time like a lost moth, watching him. He wasn't used to being watched and he didn't like it. It interfered with his concentration.

'Have you nothing to occupy yourself with, lad?' he enquired brusquely.

Michael shook his head. 'No, sir.'

'Have you done your school lessons?'

'Yes, sir.'

'And your chores?'

'Yes, sir.'

'You've filled the wood box for your sister?'

'Yes sir.' A pause, then, 'Is that a riding boot you're making, Mr Kenyon?'

Through the open doorway Sam caught a brief glimpse of Alice walking across the kitchen with Charlotte in her arms, singing quietly to her. She was more than keeping her part of the bargain they had made. And *you* promised, he reminded himself, to show a similar interest in her brother, to raise him as your son. *Promised*, yes, but he'd made little effort so far during the ten days they'd been married. Feeling a stab of guilt he nodded at Michael and smiled. 'It is a riding boot. Are you interested in becoming a bootmaker?'

Michael shook his head. 'No. I want to be a seaman.'

'A seaman?' Sam set down his hammer. 'In the merchant navy?'

Hesitantly, Michael walked over to the workbench. 'No. I want to be a cabin boy aboard a trading vessel so I can visit all the different countries in the world. Mr Chattock has a big globe in the schoolroom and he turns it round and points out all the different countries and tells us about them. He says that though they look near on the globe they're all a great distance away and the only way to see them is to sail to them.'

Sam's mouth tilted in a wry smile. He could remember having similar enthusiastic aspirations himself as a lad. Like most youthful aspirations though, they'd come to nought. 'Well, you could do worse than become a seaman,' he said. 'It's a good healthy life. If you don't drown.'

Not realising he was being teased, Michael's face remained a mask of seriousness. 'Mr Cameron says that drowning is a very pleasant way to die. He says that when you're drowning you see all your life floating before your eyes in the waves, everything you've ever done, and then it just fades away and you're dead. He says it doesn't hurt at all.'

'He speaks from experience, does he, this Mr Cameron?' Sam enquired drily.

Michael shrugged. 'I don't know how he knows about it — he didn't say. I suppose somebody told him.'

Sam's gaze rested on him for a moment. The lad had altogether failed to see the point. Michael was a likable lad but not blessed with a particularly quick wit. Still, he was only nine, he reminded himself. He forgot sometimes how young the lad was; he was tall for his years and sturdily built. Not like Alice, she was as slender as a reed. Michael was like her in the face though, the same blue eyes and bright coppery hair, except Alice's had a nice wave to it whereas Michael's was straight and had a tendency to stick out in all directions, as it was doing now. He had the same sprinkling of brown freckles across his nose and cheeks too. In some families it was difficult to see likenesses among siblings, but not in the Thorpe family.

'Well, don't believe everything you're told,' Sam advised, picking up his hammer again. He reached into the tin box on the bench for a tack. 'So, you want to be a seaman, do you? My father was a seaman.'

Michael's eyes sparked with interest. 'On a trading vessel?'

Sam shook his head. 'No. He was a fisherman.'

'Oh,' Michael said, not troubling to hide his disappointment. He stood watching while Sam continued to hammer small tacks into the leather sole, then after a minute or two asked, 'Did he like the sea?'

'I think so,' Sam said. 'He never complained about it. It was Greymouth that he sailed from — that's where I lived before I . . . married.' His voice thickened slightly on the word and he cleared his throat. 'Your sister told me your family came from a fishing port. From Akaroa. I expect your father spoke to you about it, did he?'

'No, sir.' Michael lowered his eyes, kicking the toe of his boot against the head of a nail that was standing proud of the floorboards. 'He never talked about where we lived before we moved here.'

Sam cleared his throat again. What was he thinking of to mention the lad's father to him so soon after he'd passed away? 'Well . . . there's not much to tell about it, I expect,' he mumbled. 'It's not a large port by all accounts.' The stool creaked as he stretched over the bench for his pincers. He glanced across at the bowed coppery head and pursed his lips. Should he talk a bit longer to the lad? Or send him off now? He wrestled with his conscience for a few seconds then decided to send him off. He found it almost as difficult to converse with Michael as he did with Alice. And young Michael was of an age where given an inch he would take a mile, and he didn't want the lad thinking he could come into his workshop whenever it took his fancy. 'Off you go now, Michael,' he ordered quietly, dipping his head towards the door. 'I need to get on with my work. See if your sister can find you something to do.'

'Alice is busy,' Michael said sullenly.

Sam fixed a narrow eye on him. 'All the more reason for you to lend her a hand.'

Alone again, Sam bowed his head over the last and continued to hammer in tacks. The workshop was the only place he could relax these days; it had become a sanctuary into which he could escape, sink himself into his work, not have to think or make conversation, save to his customers. Speak o' the devil, he thought, as footsteps and voices sounded outside the house. The shop door swung open to admit Mrs Bray and her young daughter, Beatrice, from Black's Point. He had quite a bit of trade from Black's Point, the mining community a mile or two down the road.

'Good afternoon to you, Mrs Bray,' he said cheerfully, halting his hammering as she walked over to his bench.

'Good afternoon, Mr Kenyon,' she returned.

'You've some boots needing mending, I see,' he said, eyeing the pair of black work boots she'd produced from her basket.

She nodded. 'My husband's. They're requiring new

soles. And he says will you put some hob-nails in to make them last longer?'

'I will,' Sam said. He turned them over in his hands, examining them.

'I see you've a lot of repairs on hand at present,' she commented, running a frowning eye over the shelf of waiting boots, each neatly tagged with a label to denote the owner, date of arrival, and the date he had promised to have them repaired by. 'How long will it be before you can mend them? If it's going to be a long while I'll maybe see if Mr Collings in Reefton can mend them quicker.'

'The day after tomorrow,' Sam said.

Her left brow rose a fraction. 'Oh, I thought it might have been closer to a week. Two days — that will be quite satisfactory. Friday morning, will that be?'

'I'll have them ready for you by ten o'clock on Friday,' he said.

'And those are your prices, are they?' she asked, pointing to the sheet of paper pinned to the wall.

'They are.'

She nodded approvingly. 'You're a halfpenny cheaper than Mr Collings.' Her eyes drifted to the doorway that led into the house. It was slightly ajar and Alice's voice could be plainly heard as she spoke to Michael. Charlotte was crying and Michael, it seemed, was to blame for it. Rising to his feet Sam walked across and closed the door, the boots still in his hands.

'I believe you married again recently, Mr Kenyon,' Mrs Bray said tentatively.

'I did,' Sam said, seating himself at his workbench again. 'Do you want the heels on these boots levelled too, Mrs Bray? They're well worn down. I can piece them — they'll not need a full heel.'

She peered over the top of her daughter's head as Sam held up the boots so that she could see the angle of the worn heels. 'No, just sole them for now,' she said. She looked across to the shut door again. 'And how is your daughter adjusting to all the changes?' She smiled sympathetically as Charlotte's distressed cries continued on the far side of the door.

'She's well, thank you,' Sam replied evenly. 'You'll call for the boots on Friday then, Mrs Bray?' he asked, reaching up to place them on the shelf.

'I shall,' she said.

He picked up his hammer and adjusted the position of the boot on the last. 'I'll make sure they're ready for you.'

Taking the hint she ushered her daughter out of the shop.

Alone again, Sam turned his head to listen to the continuing dialogue between Alice and Michael, able to hear it better now that Mrs Bray had gone. Alice was accusing her brother of deliberately tripping Charlotte up by the sound of it. The lad more than likely had. He wasn't used to being pestered by a small child and Charlotte had taken a strong liking to him. She followed him round like a little lamb, bleating his name — 'My' — the nearest rendition of Michael she could manage. If the lad lost patience with her occasionally — well, he could maybe understand why. It was a trying time for them all.

Chapter 8

Marry in haste and repent at leisure. The words of the old adage drifted into Alice's mind. She had married in haste and had now had six months to repent, but so far she hadn't. Well, not very often anyway. Mostly she was quite content. She lifted the tray of biscuits from the oven and placed it on the bench to cool. Whether Sam was as content it was hard to say. His features gave little away, added to which he was quite a silent, solitary man and often spent his evenings as well as his days hammering away at his last in his workshop. Still, the small exchanges of conversation which they had were amicable enough.

The six months had seen large adjustments for all four of them; it hadn't been an easy time. For her, by far the largest had been coming to terms with sharing her husband's bed. True to his promise, Sam had made no move to touch her, but she still tensed whenever he shifted or turned over in his sleep. For Michael, the biggest adjustment had without doubt been accepting the fact that he was now subject to Sam Kenyon's authority and when the situation warranted it, his discipline. He hadn't felt Sam's leather belt on his backside yet, but it was only a matter of time before he did. Charlotte, to Alice's relief and surprise, had adjusted very quickly to the changes in her young life. It had taken her only two weeks to accept her new mama, and she'd adored Michael from the start and delighted in Peer's silly antics. Her biggest adjustment had been in adapting to the new noises that their joining the household had brought. Peer was the problem. He had a tendency to bark, very loudly, at all hours of the day and night, and if his barking coincided with Charlotte's sleeping, which it did quite regularly, she didn't remain asleep for long. The household had consequently enjoyed some very unsettled nights.

As for Sam — whilst he gave the impression of taking everything quietly in his stride she knew for a fact he was a regular visitor to Eliza's grave. Mrs Barnes had taken great satisfaction in informing her that she'd seen him turning up the road to the cemetery twice during the last month. Sam missed his late wife, Alice had no doubt of that. Often when she held Charlotte in her arms or rocked her on her knee she would glance up to find his eyes on her, glazed and distant, and she knew it was Eliza he was seeing, not her, holding his daughter. It was in the bedroom, though, that she most felt Eliza's lingering presence and she wondered many a night how Sam felt, seeing her bright coppery hair spread across the pillow where Eliza's coal-black locks had once lain.

In addition to marking six months of marriage, 30 April 1882 also marked Alice's twenty-sixth birthday. Michael had forgotten — he always did — and had gone off to school without making any mention of it. And Sam, as far as she was aware, didn't know when her birthday fell, nor she his for that matter. Her father would have remembered. She turned to look at his old armchair. It was several weeks since she'd had a tearful bout, but the sight of her father's empty chair and the knowledge that the one person who would have remembered her birthday was dead brought a sudden flood. She missed him dreadfully. Missed his smile, his quiet conversation in the evening. She missed Ellen too. She had seen her only three or four times since she'd married.

Alice wiped her eyes, sniffing loudly. The truth was, she was not as contented as she tried to make herself believe. She was lonely. Determined not to spend her birthday feeling sorry for herself she blew her nose, scooped Charlotte up from the rug along with the wooden spoon she was playing with, tossed half a dozen biscuits onto a plate and headed for Joel Miller's. She'd been a regular visitor to Joel's home and he to hers over the last six months. Like her, Joel was lonely. He was also a very bad cook and, since she was a very good cook, she suspected his visits to her were as much on account of her baking as her company.

She knocked on his door and waited. To her disappointment there was no answer. He was probably down at the river, panning for gold. Most fine days he spent an hour or two panning, and most days he came home with a few specks, or 'colours' as he called them, in his bottle. It was as much to pass the time as anything — the accumulated results of a year's panning would be worth only a shilling or two. She was on the point of leaving when Joel's voice drifted from round the back of the house. He was in the privy.

'Who is it?' he called.

'Alice Kenyon,' she called back.

'I'll be along in a minute,' he shouted.

She went inside to wait for him. His hut was in its usual muddle. His bedding lay in an untidy heap on his bed, dirty pots and pans were stacked in a large tin bowl on the table and the floor was littered with leaves, as it invariably was when the wind was blowing in the wrong direction. She cast her eye over his furniture — what little there was of it. A table, a three-legged stool, a wooden settle and a bed were the sum total of Joel's homely comforts. It was a wonder he managed to live as well as he did, having been out of regular work for the last few years. She'd quizzed him about it once, but all he'd said was he had a few savings put aside and managed well enough off them.

Frowning dubiously, she rubbed the back of her calf with the toe of her boot, not sure if she'd felt the nip of a flea. There was no shortage of them lurking among the dust and litter. She always made a point of holding Charlotte in her arms or on her knee whenever she visited Joel, in the hope that she would be less vulnerable to their attentions there.

'I've brought you a few biscuits, Mr Miller,' she said, when he eventually appeared.

'Ah, that's kind of you. Fresh from your oven by the smell of it.' Joel's wrinkled old mouth spread in an appreciative smile. 'Will you join me for a mug of tea? I've just boiled a pan of water.'

'I will, thank you,' she returned warmly.

'I saw your man abroad this morning, striding towards the town,' he commented. Joel always referred to Sam as her *man*.

'He's gone to the barber's,' she said.

Peering into the clutter of dirty dishes Joel extracted two tin mugs. 'Can you not clip his hair for him? His late wife used to. She made a neat job of it too. Used a small pair of scissors to do it.'

Alice's eyes sparked with interest. It was the first time Joel had ever mentioned Eliza Kenyon. Sam never talked about her, not that he talked about anything much. 'I think Sam misses her,' she said, hoping to draw out a few more comments.

Joel nodded as he reached for the pan of hot water. 'I dare say he does. He thought well of her.'

She lowered her eyes and fiddled with Charlotte's hair then said casually, 'What was she like?'

He paused to fill the two mugs with hot water then spooned some tea leaves into each of them. 'Well, I didn't have a great deal to do with her. She was ill more often than she wasn't. Spent most of the time lying on the couch.'

'Had they been married long before she died?' she probed.

Joel shook his head. 'No. A bit over two years. They married shortly before they arrived in Reefton. She haled from Greymouth, same as Sam. She was of Irish stock, I recall her telling me. Her family came from . . . hmm, blessed if I can remember now.' He scratched his chin thoughtfully with the teaspoon. 'Cork, I believe it was. That's where her black hair and pale skin came from — Irish blood. There was a miner at the Brunner coal mine who had an Irish wife and she was the same — black hair and white skin — not so handsome in the face as Eliza Kenyon though. She died young too, left her man with five children. He found himself a fresh wife soon after she died — same as Sam had to. No choice really. A man can't work and tend a family at the same time.'

Alice pursed her lips. Joel Miller was without a doubt more lacking in tact than anyone she'd ever met, but his tactlessness was so completely innocent and unintentional it was impossible to feel cross with him.

'She started being ill soon after she arrived in

Reefton,' Joel continued. He nodded in Charlotte's direction and said matter-of-factly, 'On account of her.' Picking up a steaming mug of tea, he held it out to her. Whether in the interests of economy or taste Joel never purchased milk — the tea was therefore black and hot. Worried that she might upset it over Charlotte, Alice set her down on the floor. Better Charlotte should risk a few flea bites as she poked about in Joel's dusty corners than be scalded.

'Do you know what she died from?' Alice asked.

Joel shook his head. 'No, but she was in a lot of pain towards the end. I could hear her calling out at night. Screamed sometimes, she did. Screamed like a woman in labour. I didn't ask Sam the cause of it — none of my business. I thought that if he wanted to tell me he would, but he never did and I never asked.'

'Had she no family who could help to care for her when she was ill?'

Joel shrugged, frowning. 'I don't know. Her mother died not long before she married Sam, and I think her father is long dead, but as to whether she had any sisters or brothers . . . no, that I don't know. She never spoke of any. Still, that doesn't mean she had none. I've five brothers but I don't speak much of them either. Not much I can say about them. I've not seen any of them for over twenty years. They may well be dead and buried for all I know. Four of them were miners like myself, but my eldest brother, Reuben, he was a seaman. Last I heard he was in Kaikoura. That was . . . oh, ten or twelve years ago.'

'Sam works very hard at his bootmaking,' she commented. Sam's working habits were another area of curiosity.

'He does. I hear him sometimes on a still night,

tapping away in his workshop,' Joel said, settling himself on the stool. He waved a hand towards the wooden settle, inviting her to sit.

Pushing aside Joel's old jacket, she sat down. 'Has he always worked late?'

Joel frowned, alternately blowing and sipping his tea. 'I can't say I recall him working in the evenings when his late wife was alive. No, I think it's only been since he married you. Still, he'll be needing some extra money, with you fetching the lad along with you. There are four mouths to feed at his table now.'

'Yes, there are,' she murmured thoughtfully. It was an explanation she hadn't considered. She had quietly drawn the conclusion that Sam's nocturnal cobbling was his way of avoiding her.

'I used to work a twelve-hour shift down the mine when I was a young lad . . .'

Sipping her tea, Alice prepared to listen to another of Joel's rambling accounts of his mining days. They were interesting tales, but on this occasion she would have preferred him to ramble on a bit longer about Eliza Kenyon or Sam.

An hour later she was back in her own kitchen again, feeling in much brighter spirits. She was sitting on the sofa brushing Charlotte's hair when she heard the key turn in the shop door — Sam, returning from the barber's. She didn't normally see him during the day, except for meal times, so she was quite surprised to see him enter the kitchen a few minutes later carrying a pair of new leather boots.

He held them out to her. 'To mark your birthday, Alice. I hope they fit. I made them the same size as your black boots.'

She was so taken aback it took her a while to find

her tongue and it wasn't only on account of the boots. Sam's visit to the barber's had rid him of considerably more hair than usual. He was completely clean-shaven, with not a single whisker left on his face. Beard, moustache — all had disappeared, and in their place was a face she scarcely recognised. Realising she was staring, she blinked and hastily turned her attention to the boots. 'Oh, I, I didn't think you knew,' she said in confusion. She wasn't the only one feeling confused. Charlotte was looking very puzzled by the changes to her father's appearance.

Sam lifted his shoulder in a relaxed shrug. 'I found out by accident a week or two ago when Michael was helping me in the workshop. We were discussing birthdays and he mentioned that yours was the last day of April.'

Laying the hairbrush aside, she reached out and took the boots from him. They certainly were a very handsome pair. She ran the tips of her fingers across the soft brown leather, admiring the workmanship. Charlotte, leaning across her knee, ran her small fingers across the toes, mimicking her. Alice smiled, watching her, then looked up at Sam. 'You really shouldn't have gone to such trouble, but thank you,' she said warmly. 'I've never had such a fine pair of boots. They're almost too fine to wear.'

He shrugged again, more awkwardly this time. 'Well, they're not only a gift to mark your birthday — they're to thank you for caring for Charlotte so well these last six months, and to thank you for your patience too. They've not been an easy six months and I've given you little of my time or attention, yet you've not once complained.' He dipped his head in the direction of the boots and smiled. 'So put on your new boots and fill a basket with some food and I'll take you and Charlotte out for a picnic.'

Alice stared at him. 'But it's Tuesday. What about your shop?'

'I'll tack a note to the door advising the shop is shut for the rest of the day,' he replied, already heading for the kitchen door. 'I'll hitch the horse up to the cart while you're gathering together some food.'

Two hours later they were sitting on the grass beneath the dappled shade of a black beech with only a few crumbs remaining from the cold beef sandwiches she'd hurriedly put together. Peer, who had wheedled his way into accompanying them, had also wheedled several chunks of bread out of Sam and was presently whimpering and thumping his tail on the ground in the hopes of getting some more.

'Go away, Peer.' Alice waved her hand in front of the dog's nose. 'There's no food left.'

Rearranging his legs into a more comfortable position, Sam looked across at her, frowning slightly. 'It's a curious name — Peer. Why was he named that? Was he poor-sighted as a whelp?'

She stared at him blankly, then the penny dropped. 'Oh — *peer*!' she said, laughing. 'No, his name has nothing at all to do with peering. It's to do with a bad habit he had as a pup. He used to come into the house and . . .' She cleared her throat and said delicately, 'Pee against the table leg. My father caught him in the act one day and took him by the scruff of the neck and shouted '*Outside, pee-er!*' Michael was watching him — he was only three — and he must have thought it was the dog's name. So he started calling him Pee-er, which was shortened to Peer, and he's been Peer ever since.'

A wide grin slowly split Sam's face. 'Well, I suppose

we must be grateful he was only peeing when your father caught him.'

She ought not to have laughed, but she did. She laughed so much, in fact, that her eyes watered. It was the first time she'd laughed, really laughed, since her father's death and she'd forgotten how good it felt. Charlotte, delighting in the unaccustomed jollity all around her, clapped her hands, giggling happily.

At length the laughter subsided to smiles and as the smiles faded too Sam reached for a pebble, turning it thoughtfully in his hand. 'When Eliza died I thought I'd never laugh again. I've been poor company these last six months, I'm afraid.' He looked up and smiled again. 'I mean to do better by you in future, Alice.' Flicking his wrist, he tossed the pebble over Peer's head and in a split-second reflex action Peer soared upwards and caught it neatly in his jaws. With vigorous, satisfied wags of his tail and excited barks he deposited it at Sam's feet.

Struggling to free her shoes from the folds of her petticoats, Charlotte scrambled to her feet. Knowing what she was about to do, Alice put out a hand to stay her.

'Leave her be, Alice,' Sam ordered quietly. 'The dog won't harm her.'

Reluctantly Alice loosed her fingers from Charlotte's skirt. Free to move again Charlotte ran forward, took the stone in her small hand and hurled it haphazardly into the air. Peer obligingly caught it and to Charlotte's delight dropped it at her feet, barking loudly.

Sam laughed, watching the game with obvious pleasure. Alice, however, still harboured a few reservations about it. 'That stone is dripping with saliva,' she said, eyeing the mucousy white froth coating the pebble. 'I hope Charlotte doesn't put it in her mouth.'

Sam made a dismissive noise in the back of his throat. 'Charlotte will take no harm from a bit of dog spittle. You worry too much, Alice. You worry over much about Michael, too. Every time he sets his foot outside the door you warn him not to make mischief. He's not a bad lad — no worse than any other lad of his age — and he doesn't need to be cautioned every day of his life. He'll make some mischief, I've no doubt of that, but in the long term his conscience and common sense must caution him, not you.'

'Conscience, common sense, and the threat of your belt,' she corrected, tossing him a cynical smile.

'Well, that too,' he conceded, grinning. 'He does nothing I didn't do as a lad though. I stole fruit many a time. I could lift an apple from a tree without making a leaf quiver.' A shaft of sunlight arrowed through the branches as they shifted gently in the breeze, making him squint. In the spangled light his pale green eyes looked almost catlike. Alice was still having to consciously stop herself from staring at him, but it wasn't easy; he looked so different. It was the first time she had seen his features properly — his moustache and beard had effectively covered the whole of the bottom half of his face. She ran a discreet, critical eye over the half hitherto hidden from view. He had quite a square chin with a small cleft in the middle, and rather a nice mouth. Rather a nice face all round, in fact. He was quite a good-looking man without all the bristles. He looked ten years younger too. He was twenty-eight, according to their marriage papers.

'I wonder why girls don't seem to be tempted to steal apples from trees,' he added. His eyes drifted to his daughter, still tirelessly tossing the stone for Peer.

'Well, it's not very easy to climb a tree in a dress,' Alice commented practically.

He laughed. 'I suppose it isn't. I've no doubt my sons will climb trees though, and steal apples, the same as I did.'

My sons. She looked away, wondering if this was a none-too-subtle way of introducing the small matter of begetting them. After six months their marriage was still unconsummated. But the new boots, this picnic — they were signalling a very clear change in Sam's attitude to her. He had plainly reached the point where he was ready to put his marriage to Eliza and the grief at her loss behind him, and move on. Was she ready to move on too? The truth was, she wasn't sure and she definitely didn't want to discuss it now and risk spoiling the nicest day she'd had in months.

'When's your birthday?' she enquired casually.

'August second.' A blade of grass squeaked in protest as he pulled it from its sheath. 'There was a terrible storm the day I was born. My father was at sea and the boat couldn't get back to port so I was three days old when he first laid eyes on me. To be truthful I can't recall seeing him much at all when I was very young. My first real recollection of him is when I was about five and I was lying across his knee with my trousers dangling round my ankles having my backside soundly slapped. I can't remember what I'd done to warrant it.' He gave a soft chuckle then said, 'I can remember one thing though — my father had a damned hard hand!'

She laughed. 'And your mother? What was she like?' It was the first time he'd talked about himself and she was curious to hear more.

He lifted the blade of grass to his mouth and chewed absently on the end of it and his eyes took on a distant expression. 'I can't remember much about her. She died when I was seven. I can remember she was tall and thin and she was always coughing, but I can't call up her face. My sister, Maud, took on the caring of me after she died, the same as you did for your brother. Maud must have had a hard time of it with my father away so much, rearing Dan and William and myself. It probably stood her in good stead though. She has seven children of her own now — seven in her last letter, that is. She's married to a parson.'

Alice's mouth curled wryly. 'I assume, since she married a parson, that she believes in God a bit more consistently than you do.'

He laughed and turned back to face her, taking the jibe in good part. 'Well, if she doesn't she wisely never admits to it.' He tilted his head slightly, lifting his hand to shield his eyes so he could see her better. 'You've not attended church once since we married. Might I ask why?'

'It's a long way for Charlotte to walk,' she replied. She hesitated, then added with rather more honesty, 'And I'm married now and I feel awkward about going to church without my husband.'

There was a small silence then he said, 'Well, I suppose I can manage to believe in God one day a week even if I have doubts on the other six. And I ought to go, I daresay.' He gave a short laugh. 'As insurance, as my father used to say. I'll accompany you on Sunday. We'll all go.' He ducked suddenly as a large bee buzzed lazily past his ear, watched it for a moment as it flew low over the grass, zigzagging back and forth in search of flowers, then turned his attention back to Alice. 'Will you tell me about yourself? I know very little except that you lived in Akaroa before you came to Reefton.'

Alice lowered her eyes and absently brushed a few stray crumbs from her lap. 'There's not much to tell. My father worked on a farm there. He was a farm labourer, doing much the same as he did on Mr Hardaker's property. I worked on the farm too when I was old enough, in the dairy shed. My sister, Mary, did too. She died though, and my sister Grace as well. They died of scarlet fever within four days of each other.' She lifted a hand unconsciously to her hair. 'They had red hair like me.'

'Do you get your hair colour from your mother?' he asked quietly.

She looked up, conscious of his eyes on her. 'Yes, but her hair was a much softer red than mine.'

'It's not red,' he said. 'I don't know why people call that colour red. It's more the colour of oiled leather. A rich leathery brown.' He paused then said, 'Your mother died some years ago, didn't she? I read the inscription on the gravestone when I was at the cemetery a week or two ago.'

'You go there quite often, don't you?' she asked bluntly.

He nodded without apology. 'Do you mind?'

She shook her head. 'No. Not at all.' What she did mind was being informed by Mrs Barnes of his frequent visits there.

'What made your father decide to leave Akaroa and come to Reefton?' he asked, turning back to the earlier topic.

'He thought we would do better here, I suppose. What made you decide to come?'

'It seemed a town with good prospects,' he replied simply. 'New mine shafts were being sunk in the hills. And miners wear boots.'

'Eliza . . .' It was the first time she'd said his late wife's name aloud and it felt awkward on her lips. 'She was from Greymouth, I believe.'

'She was,' he said. And that was all. Whatever else he had intended volunteering was destined to remain unsaid as Charlotte's sudden screams took precedence over all else. She had tripped and was sprawled full length on the grass, and her attempts to get up were not being helped by Peer's sympathetic efforts to lick her face from chin to brow.

'It's not much. Just a scratch,' Alice pronounced, examining Charlotte's damaged hand whilst Sam held her on his lap. 'She's very tired though.'

'I suppose we should go back,' he said. 'The wind's turned cool too.' Lifting Charlotte into his arms, he pushed himself to his feet then stooped to offer Alice his hand. It was the first time he'd touched her since their wedding day, when he had briefly taken hold of her hand to slip the ring on her finger.

'Come along, we'll go home,' he said, and offered her his arm.

Sam looked up from his accounts book, frowning. Wearing a similar frown, Alice looked up from the kitchen sink where she was peeling potatoes for the evening meal. Whoever was knocking on the back door had a very loud knock.

'I wonder who that could be,' murmured Sam, rising to his feet.

She glanced across at Michael, whose expression left her in no doubt at all that *he* knew who the visitor was. What mischief had he been up to this time? On her birthday too.

Their visitor was Robert Oxley. Sam, for whatever

reason, didn't invite him inside, but even with the door closed she could hear every word the two men exchanged very clearly. Michael had been stealing — plums, from a box outside Robert Oxley's store. Not surprisingly, since it was broad daylight at the time, Mr Oxley had seen him and was now loudly complaining to Sam.

Eventually the door opened again and Sam stepped back inside. He plainly hadn't enjoyed his conversation with the grocer. His face was flushed, his lips clamped tightly together, and he was breathing heavily through his nose. 'On your feet!' he said tersely, fixing a narrow eye on Michael. Coming to an abrupt halt in the middle of the room he pointed a long straight finger to the floor, directly in front of him.

Sliding from his chair, Michael walked slowly over.

'Did you steal plums from Mr Oxley's shop?' Sam enquired sternly. 'And I warn you, if you lie to me I shall make you rue it, so I'd advise you to give me the truth.'

Michael hesitated then gave a small nod.

'Have you lost your tongue?' Sam asked sharply.

'No, sir,' Michael murmured.

'Then answer me. Did you steal the plums?'

He nodded again. 'Yes, sir.'

'Why? Look at me when I'm talking to you, lad. Why?'

Michael made reluctant eye contact. 'To eat them.'

'Does your sister not feed you enough?'

'Yes, sir.'

'Then why did you steal the plums? Does stolen food taste better than food honestly come by?'

There was a long silence.

'Well?' Sam prompted.

'I don't know.' Michael threw a sheepish glance in

Alice's direction. 'Alice doesn't buy plums.'

'So that gives you the right to steal them, does it?'

Silence settled again.

Sam straightened, shifting his stance, making the floorboards creak and Michael jump.

'I dare say,' he continued, 'that you regard this as a harmless prank. But it isn't. It's theft. Theft is theft, whether it be a plum or a pound note that you take, and it's high time you understood that. You cannot blithely help yourself to whatever takes your fancy. You wouldn't take kindly to it if one of your friends helped themselves to your box of soldiers and Mr Oxley doesn't take kindly to the likes of young lads like you helping themselves to his fruit, any more than I'd welcome someone stealing boots from my shop. I've been obliged to pay Mr Oxley out of my own pocket for the plums you stole, but if you ever steal again, lad, you will be doing the repaying. And since you've no money, your soldiers will be the first things that you forfeit. Do you understand what I'm saying?'

'Yes, sir.'

'Good.' Sam gave a curt nod. 'Turn round then and bend over and clasp hold of your knees.'

Sam bowed his head and began to undo the buckle of his belt. In the silence Alice heard Michael swallow. In the past Michael had always been beaten in private, outside in the shed, and he was looking thoroughly mortified at the prospect of being thrashed in the middle of the kitchen in front of witnesses. He looked for a moment tempted to run then evidently thought better of it and reluctantly turned, bent over, and braced himself for retribution. Alice picked Charlotte up and held her close against her chest. Michael wasn't a quiet sufferer and she didn't want his yells to frighten her.

Eyes lowered to his task, Sam wound the buckle end of the belt around his hand two or three times, took a firm grip on the leather, then in a single fluid movement brought it down hard on the rounded curve of Michael's backside. The thwack it made was loud enough to make Alice jump and Charlotte's green eyes fly wide in surprise. Michael, rather closer to the site of impact, let out a high-pitched yell of pain and took an involuntary step forward. To his credit though he clasped hold of his knees again, squeezed his eyes shut and braced himself for the next blow. Alice threw Sam an anxious glance, wondering how many blows he intended to mete out. He'd hit Michael hard, using the full force of his arm. She closed her eyes as the belt swung down a second time and Michael let out another pained howl, and resolved to intercede when the count reached six. When she peeled her eyes open again it was to find, to her surprise, Sam threading his belt back through his trousers. Michael, who had also noted it, was cautiously straightening.

'You can count yourself fortunate that it's your sister's birthday,' Sam told him tersely. 'It's only because I'm loath to have you blubbering all evening that you're being let off so lightly. And make no mistake, lad, if I'd given you your full dues you'd have been blubbering very loudly by the time I'd finished. Now.' He cocked his head towards the door. 'Go and knock on Mr Oxley's back door and volunteer to do two hours' work in recompense for the trouble you caused him. And I shall be asking Mr Oxley if you've been, so make sure you go there and nowhere else.'

Moving rather painfully Michael headed for the door.

As it clicked shut behind him Sam glanced across at

Alice. 'I know I was lenient with him. If it hadn't been your birthday I would have meted out a round dozen.'

It took her a moment or two to realise he was apologising to her — for not disciplining Michael as strongly as he considered he ought.

'I hope he won't give you cause to take your belt to him again,' she said with feeling. She paused then added, 'Did you mean what you said about Michael's soldiers?'

'Indeed I did. There's no point in making threats you don't mean to carry out,' he replied.

'My father bought those soldiers for Michael,' she said.

'Then let's hope he values them,' he said, refastening his buckle. 'Because if he does steal again I mean to carry out my threat. Michael must learn that when I say something I mean it. I sincerely hope I won't have to take them from him, but if I do I shall expect you not to intercede on his behalf, Alice.'

'I hope you won't have to take them from him too,' she said. 'His soldiers are the only things Michael has by way of a remembrance of my father and I'd be very sorry to see him lose them.'

'If he values them sufficiently, he'll stay honest,' Sam stated in uncompromising tones. 'And a sound beating isn't always the best remedy. You've seen the knife with the ivory handle that I sometimes use for carving leather?' She nodded. 'It was my grandfather's. He gave it to me when I was eight. When I was ten my father took it away from me. I didn't see it again till six months later. It was my punishment for stealing. I'd taken some apples from a neighbour's tree and my sister, Maud, told him about it. In the normal way of things he would have given me a good thrashing, but for some reason on this occasion he chose to take a fresh approach. I can still remember his words to me. "How much do you value this knife, Samuel? Enough to stay honest from now on?" He didn't need to explain what he meant. His meaning was plain enough. Either I mended my ways or I'd not see the knife again.'

There was a short silence then she gave a reluctant nod. Much as she would hate to see Michael forfeit his soldiers she could see the reason in what Sam said. And if he was to have any respect and credibility in Michael's eyes, he would have to hold to his threat. The best she could do was to make sure Michael understood the threat was no idle one. 'Sam, I'm very sorry for the embarrassment he caused you with Mr Oxley,' she said quietly.

'Alice, it's Michael who ought to be saying he's sorry. Not you.' His tone was mildly impatient.

'Yes, I know,' she said. It hadn't escaped her notice either that Michael had failed to apologise. 'I feel responsible for him though. He's my flesh and blood,' she said.

'Mine too in a manner of speaking,' he said drily. 'I gave you my word that I'd raise him as my son.'

Promises cost nothing to give but they are often very costly to keep. Sam had promised to raise Michael as his own son and his promise had earlier that evening cost him a small amount of money and a considerable amount of embarrassment. Alice had made a similar promise to raise Charlotte as her own, and that too was not without cost.

Pushing back the blankets, she reluctantly swung her legs out of bed and sat for a moment, letting her eyes adjust to the darkness. The floorboards felt cold and damp against her bare feet. She turned her head towards the bedroom door, listening. Silence had settled on the house again. She sighed gratefully. Charlotte had gone back to sleep. She'd risen to her twice already during the night but couldn't fathom what had woken her and made her cry. She didn't seem too hot or too cold, her napkin wasn't soiled or overly wet, and Peer hadn't been barking. Bad dreams perhaps. Alice sat for a few moments longer, shivering in the chill air, then slipped back into bed. She was just dozing off when the wails started again.

The mattress lurched as Sam turned over, mumbling in his sleep, disturbed by his daughter's cries. With a sigh she slid out of bed and padded quietly across the floor. As she stepped into the small bedroom which Charlotte and Michael occupied she glanced across to Michael's bed. He hadn't woken, but he would if Charlotte's cries became any louder.

'What's the matter?' she whispered, leaning into the cot to pick her up. She lifted her out along with a blanket and held her snugly against her chest. 'Hush. Hush now. What is it?' she soothed, rubbing her back. She walked back and forth beside her crib, hushing and rubbing until her sobs gradually began to subside. What kept rousing her? — she wondered. Unfortunately the child was too young to tell her. She laid her fingers gently on Charlotte's forehead, checking again for signs of illness. She wasn't feverish. She seemed simply restless tonight. Alice rocked gently from side to side, murmuring softly to her. She had no idea how late it was. Three, four o'clock?

'Alice?' Sam's voice came softly from behind her, making her start. She hadn't heard him get out of bed. 'Is she ill?' he whispered.

She shook her head, turning towards him. 'No. Just restless. She's settling now.'

'She's not messed herself?' He sniffed the air speculatively.

'No.' Her voice quivered as she gave a sudden shiver.

'You're cold. Shall I fetch your shawl?' His eyes met hers in the darkness, shimmering circles of light.

'No. I'm all right,' she whispered. She glanced down at the limp, warm bundle in her arms. Charlotte was almost asleep again. 'Go back to bed, Sam. I'll see to her,' she said, looking up at him again.

He nodded, leaned forward to kiss her forehead, and went.

A small kiss on the forehead, that was all. But it wasn't all, it wasn't by any means all. It was the beginning of placing their marriage on a new footing.

Chapter 9

Alice screwed up her eyes as a sudden yell of pain erupted from the workshop.

'Well, I'm not surprised you hit your thumb,' came Sam's unsympathetic voice through the open doorway. 'How many times must I tell you? Hold the handle lightly, you don't need to throttle it. The harder you grip it the less control you have. And don't bring it down so hard. You're not driving six-inch nails into a plank of wood.' A short pause followed. 'Watch. Like this. Let the weight of the head do the work for you.' She heard a small thud as the hammer came down, presumably demonstrating the proper method. 'Now, tap the last two nails into the sole then you'd better take yourself off to bed.'

Several tentative taps followed.

'That's better,' Sam said in approving tones. 'Much better.'

Smiling to herself, Alice continued with her sewing.

Half a minute later Michael appeared, gingerly inspecting his left thumb. 'When will you teach me how to use the knife, Mr Kenyon?' He glanced back at Sam, who was following him into the room.

'When you've mastered the correct use of the hammer, I'll show you how to do the cutting and carving,' Sam replied.

'When will that be?'

'When you can hold up your left hand and show me you don't have any blackened fingernails.'

Taking the jibe in good part, Michael's mouth stretched in a cheeky smile. 'Good night, Mr Kenyon. Good night Alice,' he said, and dutifully headed for his bedroom.

'How's he faring?' she asked, setting her sewing down on her lap.

Sam tossed her a wry smile. 'Oh, not too badly. He has a good steady hand and he's not lacking in concentration — it's just patience he's short of. He's like all lads of his age — he wants to run before he's learned to walk.'

'Well, it seems to be keeping him out of mischief,' she commented. Michael, after an initial six months of relatively good behaviour, had started to slip into his old ways again. In an attempt to find a more productive use for his hands, Sam had begun teaching him the rudiments of his trade, allowing him into his workshop after school and occasionally in the evening, as he had tonight. Michael had brimmed with enthusiasm from the first day. Alice was quietly sceptical about how long his enthusiasm would last, but for the time being it was ensuring he came home promptly after school instead of getting into trouble. It was also providing a means for Sam to get to know him better, which she suspected was in part why he'd suggested it.

Sam gave a soft chuckle. His eyes met hers, twinkling with humour. 'I don't condone his mischief, but you must concede he's an inventive lad.'

She knew what he was referring to and laughed. She too could see the humour in the incident now, but it hadn't been very amusing at the time. Michael, in collaboration with young Alfred Cameron, had been responsible for the presence of two unusual additional worshippers in church the previous Sunday. They had pushed two fat frogs through a hole in one of the church windows on their way home from school on the Friday afternoon. One frog had announced its presence during the first hymn by suddenly leaping off the pew onto Mrs Ramsay's hymn book, at which point her strains had soared considerably higher than those of the rest of the congregation. Pandemonium had followed, not helped by the discovery soon afterwards that a second frog was on the loose. Had Alfred not turned round and grinned conspiratorially in Michael's direction at the beginning of the service the two would never have been suspected. Michael's backside had consequently renewed its acquaintance with Sam's leather belt on returning home. Still smiling, she turned her attention back to the shirt she was making.

'You're a fine seamstress, Alice,' Sam complimented. He stooped to examine the garment as it lay on her lap then, tilting his head to the side, he leaned forward and kissed her cheek. She lowered her eyes, wondering if he would broach the subject of 'formalising their marriage' this time. He'd kissed her a number of times since that first kiss a week ago, and each time she had expected him to say something. As yet he hadn't, but sooner or later he would, and her expectation was that it would be sooner.

Settling himself in the armchair opposite her, he picked up his book, riffled the pages several times, then dropped it back onto the arm of the chair.

'Alice.' He paused, evidently wanting her full attention. 'I wish to discuss our marriage.'

She straightened and waited.

'I think it's time we set about making our marriage

what a marriage should be between a man and his wife. I'd like more children, Alice. I want a son.'

She waited, expecting him to carry on. He didn't, and as the seconds slid past she realised that he was waiting too — for her response presumably. It's my way to speak my mind plainly, Sam had once informed her. He was speaking his mind plainly tonight. Very plainly. So this was the reason for his change in attitude towards her, she thought. She'd stupidly believed he was growing fond of her. More stupidly, she had even resolved to face the demons of the past and allow him to consummate the marriage. The boots he had made for her — she scrunched her toes up in them — the sudden flurry of complimentary remarks, the smiles, the little kisses . . . they had nothing whatever to do with fondness. They had to do with progeny. The continuation of the Kenyon line! She hadn't expected profuse professions of love, but she had expected at least some passing mention of affection.

'I'm afraid I'm not ready yet,' she said offhandedly. 'And you promised that you wouldn't press me.'

'Press you?' Sam arched his brows and gave a breathy laugh. 'We've been married for over six months! I hardly think I can be accused of pressing you.'

'For most of those six months you scarcely noticed I existed,' she returned crisply. 'And it seems the only reason you've conceded to notice me now is because you've decided you'd like a son.'

Sam compressed his lips. 'You've maybe forgotten, but I lost my wife barely a month before I married you. I was grieving badly for her during those first months of our marriage.'

'And now it seems you've stopped grieving,' she said. 'In the interests of getting yourself a son.'

'I've stopped,' he returned sharply, 'because I'm mindful of the fact I'm now *your* husband and am likely to be so for a long while to come. I'm damned if I'm going to have this kind of a marriage for the next twenty or thirty years!'

'You married me to provide a mother for your daughter — you made that quite plain. I hardly think you can complain if that's what you've got.' She picked up her sewing again, making a show of ignoring him. Reaching forward Sam plucked it from her fingers and flung it to the floor.

'I trust that last remark doesn't mean you intend never to consummate our marriage!'

'It does.' She tilted her chin defiantly. Be damned if she would be served like a brood mare whenever Sam Kenyon felt inclined to increase his family.

'You mean to hold me to my promise indefinitely?'

'Yes, I do. I trust you intend to keep it?'

'And what of your promise to me? Do you intend to keep that?'

'I have kept my promise,' she said. 'I promised you I'd raise Charlotte —'

'No, not that promise,' he cut in. 'I mean the promise you made me before the altar. You promised to obey, serve, love and honour me. If you wish me to hold me to my promise — so be it. But I shall hold you to yours also, Alice.'

She narrowed her eyes and her fingers curled involuntarily around the fabric of her dress. 'And how do you mean to do that? Are you going to *order* me to allow you to have the freedom of my body?'

Sam slammed his hand down hard on the arm of the chair and rose abruptly to his feet, so abruptly the armchair lurched back, jarring the table and making the lamp wobble precariously, filling the room with leaping shadows. 'Freedom of your body! Freedom of your body!' he repeated in incredulous tones. 'You make it sound as if I want to use you like a whore! You're my *wife*! I want to . . . to . . .' He spluttered to a halt and glared at the closed door as a fretful wail sounded from beyond it.

'She's teething,' Alice said matter-of-factly.

He waved an impatient hand then turned away, breathing heavily. 'Go and attend to her then. I suppose we'll have no peace till you do.'

She was still comforting Charlotte when she heard the back door open and slam shut again, followed by the crunch of Sam's boots as he strode past the house. Where he was going she had no idea, but wherever it was he stayed there all night.

'Where's Mr Kenyon, Alice?' Michael's smooth, wide brow crinkled into a puzzled frown as he regarded Sam's empty chair at the breakfast table.

'Out,' she said.

'Out where?'

'Michael — wherever Mr Kenyon is, it's none of your concern,' she snapped. 'Now sit down and eat your breakfast or you'll be late for school.'

Michael eyed her sullenly as he pulled out his chair. 'Why are you so cross this morning?'

'I'm not cross!' she said. She glanced across at Charlotte, who was sitting patiently on her chair, waiting for her bowl of porridge to appear. Her bottom lip had started to quiver, as it invariably did whenever Alice raised her voice. A moment later the kitchen was ringing with her loud wails. Lifting her into her arms, she paced back and forth, patting her back.

'Hush, hush,' she soothed. Charlotte, however, clearly had no intention of hushing. Her cries grew louder.

'Why's she crying,' Michael demanded, grimacing.

'I don't know,' Alice said. Probably because she was hungry, among other things. She walked across to the pan of porridge on the bench and spooned some into a bowl then sat down at the table and tried to coax Charlotte into eating. Charlotte was a very lovable child but, like all small children, she was capable of fierce little tantrums. She was apparently in the mood for one this morning. No sooner was the first spoonful of porridge in her mouth than she spat it out all over the table, slapped the spoon out of Alice's hand, and did her best to squirm off her lap, all the while maintaining a deafening wail.

'Smack her legs. Mr Kenyon does when she screams like that. I've seen him,' Michael advised helpfully.

She was sorely tempted. The next screech tipped the balance — Alice flipped her onto her stomach and gave her a sharp slap on the back of her legs. Setting Charlotte down from her knee, she fixed a stern eye on her. 'One more scream and I shall shut you in your bedroom for the rest of the morning!'

Though Charlotte had only half a dozen words of speech, she could nevertheless understand large amounts of what was said to her. She plainly understood what Alice had just said. She stared at her for a moment with huge green eyes then screwed up her face and burst into floods of tears. With a sigh Alice lifted her back onto her knee and hugged her, feeling not very far from tears herself.

'What's in my food tin today, Alice?' Slipping down from the table Michael walked across to the sink and deposited his empty bowl in it. One thing Michael never loitered over was his food.

'Bread, cheese, biscuits and apples,' she said shortly.
'What sort of biscuits?'

She closed her eyes, praying for patience. She hadn't slept a wink last night and patience was in very short supply this morning. 'Oat biscuits. Now off you go, Michael. You're late, so don't dawdle or you'll be feeling Mr Chattock's cane across your hand.'

A cool breeze floated into the kitchen, lifting Charlotte's fine dark curls as Michael opened the back door. His appearance in the doorway was as usual greeted by loud excited barks. 'Come on, Peer, we're late,' he called. He closed the door with a slam, making the pots in the sink rattle.

As Charlotte's sobs and sniffles gradually subsided and Peer's barks faded away, silence slowly settled on the house. With a sigh Alice seated Charlotte on the chair beside her, reached into the cutlery drawer for a fresh spoon and began to feed her. As the first spoonful of porridge landed in her mouth, Charlotte pulled a wry face. It was probably stone cold, but Alice really didn't care.

By mid-morning Sam was still not back and she was starting to worry. Not that he deserved it, but he had been gone for a very long time — over twelve hours. The one thing she felt certain of was that he hadn't abandoned them. No matter what Sam thought of her, he would never turn his back on his daughter, which left only two explanations. Either he had suffered an accident or else he was still in a rage.

It was in the early afternoon, not long after Charlotte had at last gone to sleep, that he finally returned and from Alice's point of view he couldn't have arrived at a worse time. She was sitting at the table nursing a throbbing head and a throbbing hand. Relief to see he was unharmed rapidly gave way to less charitable emotions. She had spent the last four or five hours intermittently considering the possibility that he might be lying badly injured somewhere, or possibly even dead. Consequently, if somewhat irrationally, she felt quite peeved to see that he was neither.

Looking away, she turned her attention back to the difficult business of binding up her hand, a task not helped by the fact that it was the right one.

The floorboards creaked as he walked across the room. He stood for a moment beside her chair, watching her, then drew out another chair and sank down heavily onto it. Whatever he had done last night, it hadn't included much sleep.

'Here — let me do it,' he said. He held out his hand, waiting. She hesitated, then extended her partly bandaged hand.

'Is it a burn or a cut?' he asked, uncoiling the long linen strip which had become tightly twisted with her clumsy left-handed efforts.

'A cut,' she returned, tossing him a brief sideways glance. She'd cut it on the carving knife while she was washing the dishes. It wasn't deep, but it had bled a lot.

They sat in silence while he bound it up properly, but as he pulled the knot tight to secure it he looked up into her face. 'I owe you an apology,' he said stiffly. He leaned back against his chair, his eyes locked on hers. 'Last night, I expressed myself very poorly. I'll not make excuses for myself, except to say that I didn't find it easy to have to ask my own wife if she would allow me to take my marital dues. I was vexed with you too, because you'd placed me in the position of having to ask.'

Alice stared at him. An apology was the last thing

she'd expected from him, even if it did hint she was in part to blame, and she didn't quite know how to respond to it.

'I . . .' she began.

'No, let me finish,' he interrupted. 'I've spent the best part of the night and all morning sorting out what I want to say. Let me say it while it's still clear in my mind.' He paused then said, 'I've something to show you.' He stood and walked across to the sideboard. Pulling open the drawer, he rummaged through the contents, pushing aside sheets of paper and rustling through envelopes. At length he found what he was looking for. Perusing the contents of a letter, he walked back to the table.

'Read this.' He held it out to her.

She took it from him and read it. It didn't take long. There were only five words to read.

Mr Kenyon. Congratulations. Charles McGaffin.

'It was accompanied by a five-pound note,' Sam continued. 'A young lad delivered it a few days after the banns were read in church for the first time. I went to see Mr McGaffin about it the next day. I couldn't fathom why he should wish to send me a gift of five pounds since I've never set foot inside his hotel, and I also thought it was in very poor taste to be congratulating me, given the circumstances of my marriage. I told him so too. He said he was very sorry to have caused me offence then explained to me that it wasn't meant to be a wedding gift. He said he'd sent the money to honour a wager. He'd apparently stated on his premises one night that he'd give five pounds to the first man you gave some positive encouragement to.' He tilted his head to the side, watching her. 'Did you know about the wager?'

She gave an awkward nod. 'Yes. My father told me about it.'

He sat down again, a deep frown wedged between his brows. 'I've always been puzzled why you chose to marry me, Alice. You're not plain and there's no shortage of eligible bachelors in the district, yet you chose to accept me when all I had to offer you was another woman's child. I was all the more puzzled after speaking with Mr McGaffin. He told me he'd only put up the wager because he believed his money was safe. He was of the opinion you'd never marry, his reasoning being that so many had tried to court you and failed.

'When you accepted my proposal of marriage you placed conditions upon it — one being that I'd not press you to fulfil your marital obligations at once. You made me swear an oath on the Bible. I thought at the time that it wasn't an altogether unreasonable request, given our circumstances, but I've wondered since whether there was more to that promise.' He seemed to hesitate then said, 'I'm not blind, Alice, I can see the way you stiffen when I kiss you. I attributed it to shyness at first, but after what you said last night I'm wondering if the truth of it is, you can't bear the thought of my touch and my attentions. If that is so then I can't understand why the hell you married me for it seems there were plenty of other men you could have taken your choice from.' He pursed his lips, then said in a firm voice, 'The day you accepted me, you told me that your reasons for accepting were personal. I want to know those reasons, Alice. I think I'm owed that much.'

Many years ago, as a child, she had seen a man flogged. Quite a young man, in his twenties. He had walked alone to the whipping post, undoing his shirt buttons as he went. Knowing the pain that he was about to be subjected to he must surely have felt like taking to his heels, yet he had walked forward with a semblance of outward calm and bared his back for the lash. As she turned back to face her husband and opened her mouth to speak she felt very much like that man.

'I was raped when I was a young woman.' The words hung in the silence like a hangman's noose. She licked her lips and forced herself to continue. 'That's why I stiffen when you kiss me — because I'm afraid. I married you because you were looking only for a mother for your child, not a wife. I couldn't marry a man who had some feeling for me, knowing that I might not be able to bring myself to . . . to . . .' She swallowed and turned away, unable to look at Sam's shocked expression a moment longer. He looked like a man who had cast his eyes upon Medusa's dreadful visage and turned utterly to stone.

Chapter 10

It had happened on a Sunday.

It was strange the things she remembered. A pair of gulls pecking a dead fish that had been washed up on the beach. A woman wearing a red-plaid shawl gathering driftwood. A barefooted Maori girl fossicking among the tangled straps of seaweed. An old man sitting on a rock reading his Bible. Alice had passed them as she walked along the shore, making her way home from church. From the beach she'd taken her usual route up the dray track that led to her parents' cottage, perched high on the hillside overlooking Akaroa Harbour. She'd walked the track hundreds of times, and knew every twist, every rut and gully, every bush and tree.

It is curious how the body sometimes senses when something is wrong. On the face of things everything is as it ought to be, yet there is something, an invisible, intangible something, which is not right. She'd had such a sense that day, about half a mile up the track to her home — the sensation that someone was watching her — real enough to make the hairs rise on the back of her neck and the flesh on her arms crawl. She'd kept turning as she walked, every dozen steps or so, turning a full circle so she could scan the bushes edging the track. After the telltale crack of twigs and the swish of foliage, he'd stepped out just ahead of her.

'Don't scream.' Those were the only words spoken. A knife was swinging casually from his hand, a bone-handled knife with a short, curved blade.

She didn't scream. She had simply stood, rooted to the spot, shaking uncontrollably, watching through wide, terrified eyes as he approached. Don't scream, don't scream, don't scream . . . the words had drummed inside her head like a desperate heartbeat. She *had* screamed though, just once — an involuntary cry of pain as he had made the first vicious lunge inside her body. She had cringed in terror afterwards, expecting him to reach for his knife and slit her throat. Instead he'd slapped her hard across the face then continued to buck and plunge into her, grunting and sweating with the effort. His face had haunted her for months. Now the memory had faded and she could remember hardly anything about him, except that he had dark hair, was filthy, and smelled of the sea.

She turned back to look at Sam. He was sitting in stony silence, his head bowed low, staring sightlessly at the floor. She watched him, trying to read his thoughts, wondering whether she dared tell him the rest. That Michael was her son, not her brother.

'Sam?' she said in a hoarse voice.

Her voice seemed to startle him. He looked up sharply, rose stiffly to his feet and walked across to the fireplace. The knuckles of his hands stood out white and stark as he gripped the edge of the wooden mantel. She sat watching him in silence until at last he turned and walked back towards the table, breathing heavily.

'Do you not think you should have told me this before we married?' he accused loudly. 'I think I had a right to know, given the effect it's had on you!'

She stared at him, taken aback — she had expected him to be shocked, but not angry like this. She compressed her lips and said coldly, 'It's not an easy thing to tell.'

'Nonetheless you should have told me!'

'Don't tell me what I should and should not have done!' she retorted loudly. 'Tell that animal who raped me!'

On the edge of her vision she caught the slight movement as Sam's hands balled into fists at his sides. He looked even angrier than last night. His face was livid. He wasn't alone in his anger though. She too was angry. Angry that through no fault of her own her life had been spoiled. Angry with Sam for not showing some compassion, some pity. She had expected better of him.

'I can see now why you made me swear an oath on the Bible that I'd not touch you!' He ran a hand roughly through his hair and shook his head. 'How could you? How could you marry me, knowing full well that you could never be a proper wife to me? You deliberately deceived me, used me, made use of my circumstances to provide for you and your brother, when all the while . . . all the while you knew you'd never consent to . . . to . . .' He shook his head again, looking lost for words.

'You didn't marry me for love. You married me because you wanted a mother for your daughter,' she defended.

He stood for a long five seconds glaring at her, his jaw working with tension, then strode out of the kitchen, leaving the back door open like a gaping mouth.

She was fully expecting him to be gone a long while again, but a quarter hour later she heard the sound of his returning footsteps along the path beside the house. She wiped her eyes and quickly blew her nose, not wanting him to see she'd been weeping. She had wept for most of the time he'd been gone, partly through the flood of memories it had brought back and partly because she knew deep down that she *had* used Sam. She had married him, knowing she might never be able to bring herself to a physical relationship. She'd made him swear on the Bible so that, if necessary, she could forever hold his promise in his face. Small wonder he had been bitterly angry with her. As for his lack of compassion . . . well, she could maybe understand that too in hindsight. She had been raped — brutally raped — and she had naively expected that pity would outstrip all other emotions. It hadn't, and it had been stupid of her to think that it would. Tantamount in Sam's mind was the knowledge she'd deliberately deceived him and that he was now doomed to spend the rest of his life with a woman who was not prepared to be a true wife to him. It was hardly surprising that anger had overridden any feelings of compassion that he might otherwise have felt.

As the latch lifted and the door swung open Alice braced herself, then let out a shallow breath of relief. He looked slightly calmer. His face was still a mask of tension, but the deep flush of anger in his cheeks had drained away. He stood in the doorway for a moment, as if assessing her mood, then closed the door behind him and walked across to the table.

'I'm sorry,' she said quietly.

He stared at her, or rather through her to some distant place, then pulled out a chair and sank down onto it. He sat quite still for a minute or more, his gaze fixed on a crimson spot of blood on the tablecloth, then at last looked up and said in a thick voice, 'Rape. God, Alice, that was the last thing I expected you to say.' He shook his head and looked away again. 'I thought you'd been disappointed in love, or that a man you'd loved had died . . . I thought that was the reason you'd never shown any interest in the men who'd tried to court you. I thought you'd married me out of pity on account of Charlotte, because you felt sorry for her, being left without a mother so young. When you said you'd been raped, I was so stunned . . .' He swallowed heavily then turned back to face her. 'I felt as if you'd hit me with a mallet. I couldn't seem to think straight. All I could think was that you should have told me before I married you, that you'd deliberately deceived me.'

'I'm sorry,' she said again. The words sounded feeble and hollow, completely inadequate. Judging by his expression, Sam was of a similar opinion.

'Sorry?' he hissed between his teeth. His eyes locked on hers, narrow with anger, confusion, and a whole host of other warring emotions. Resting his elbows on the table he covered his face with his hands, breathing heavily, as if struggling to bring his internal battle under some measure of control. It was two or three long minutes before he lowered his hands to his lap, but the turmoil in his eyes did seem to have lessened a little. 'Tell me what happened,' he said in a strained low voice.

It was a very scant account she gave him. She told him she was seventeen. It had happened in Akaroa. A seaman had done it. As for how . . . rape was rape, there was no need to describe it and she doubted he wanted to hear the finer details. Her age was a lie — she'd been fifteen. Whether Sam was ever likely to do some simple additions and subtractions regarding birthdays she really didn't know, but for Michael's sake she would sooner not risk the truth coming out. Had Sam reacted better she would have perhaps told him all.

Perhaps. But his reaction had not been good, and as things stood Sam treated Michael very well — like a son, she thought with some irony — and she wasn't willing to risk the truth about his parentage changing that. Nor was the truth likely to improve her own relationship with Sam.

She looked across the table to find his eyes were staring distantly through her again. He blinked suddenly, coming back from wherever he'd been, then slowly shook his head. 'I feel ashamed to call myself a man — the depths we sink to, to satisfy our carnal urges. We're worse than animals!' He lowered his eyes, staring at the spot of blood again. 'Did they find him — the man who did it to you?'

'No,' she said simply.

He murmured something beneath his breath too soft for her to catch then glanced up, a deep frown scoring out two long lines above his nose. 'That's why your father uprooted you from Akaroa and shifted to Reefton, is it?'

She nodded, aware that her eyes were blurring with tears. 'There was a lot of talk. I found it very difficult. People have long memories and . . . I couldn't bear the way they looked at me.' She swallowed, trying to clear the thickening in her throat. 'I should never have married you, Sam. It was wrong of me and I'm truly sorry.'

There was a long silence then he said quietly, 'Sorry you married me? Or sorry that you didn't tell me this till now?'

'That I didn't tell you, that I deceived you. I do want to be a proper wife —' The word choked in her throat and she turned away, weeping. Yesterday, before all this, she'd been so sure that she could be the wife Sam wanted to make her. Now though, the memories of that dreadful day had flooded back again, unleashed by the simple act of speaking about them, and with them had come the fear — as huge, irrational, and real as a small child's fear of the shadow somehow stuck to his feet.

The chair legs scraped against the wooden floorboards as Sam stood up. 'Alice,' he said hoarsely. Taking hold of her hands, he drew her to her feet and wrapped her in his arms.

The next week was, not surprisingly, a strained one. Sam spent his days in the workshop and in the evenings he read quietly, or made a semblance of it. He hadn't mentioned the rape again — possibly he never would. It had happened and nothing, no amount of discussion, could undo it. There was still some unfinished business to be dealt with though, namely the future of their marriage. Sam was probably mulling it over at that very moment, Alice thought as she reached for the rolling pin — he was soaking in a hot bath in the privacy of the bedroom.

'Somebody's coming,' Michael announced, looking up from his school books. 'Peer always barks like that when there's someone outside.'

'I can't imagine who would be calling on us at five o'clock,' Alice said, frowning. 'Unless it's Joel Miller.'

'No, Peer wouldn't bark like that at Mr Miller. This is how he barks at strangers,' Michael said in knowledgable tones.

Four loud knocks sounded on the back door. Alice laid her rolling pin on the bench, wiped her floury hands on her apron, and went to open it.

She took a small involuntary step back and stared in surprise at their strange visitors. 'Er, good evening,' she murmured.

Michael, who had come to stand beside her, along with Charlotte, was also staring, rather rudely. She discreetly nudged his leg with her toe. Not hard enough evidently. He continued to stare.

The visitors were Maori. A man and a woman. The man, who looked to be in his middle thirties, lifted a hand and flapped it in the direction of the kitchen, then proceeded to gabble a string of completely unintelligible sentences. One word — cannon — seemed to occur quite regularly, always accompanied by increased gesticulation towards the interior of the house. Cannon, Alice assumed, was a reference to her husband. She gathered the man wished to be invited indoors.

'I'm afraid Mr Kenyon is taking a bath.' She rubbed her face and arms and flapped her hands about, doing her best to simulate the act of bathing. Michael stifled a laugh, evidently finding the spectacle extremely amusing, whilst Charlotte unhelpfully tugged at Alice's skirt, wanting to be picked up. She lifted her up, then leaned to the side and tried to catch the Maori woman's eye. She was standing some distance beyond her husband, cradling a baby in her arms.

'Mr Kenyon. Bath,' Alice said loudly. She rolled her eyes. Neither of them had the faintest notion what she was saying.

'They don't understand you,' Michael stated, shaking his head.

'I'm aware of that,' she said. She glanced down at him. 'Knock on the bedroom door and tell Sam that we have visitors. Ask him if I should let them in.'

He went. A minute or two later he was back. 'He says you're to let them in or they'll be offended. He says he's not going to let his hot bath go cold though, so you're to give them a cup of tea while they're waiting.'

'Well, I hope he isn't going to be long in that case,' Alice muttered.

She stepped aside and beckoned them in. The man, who was clearly annoyed at being made to wait outside for so long, barged rudely past her. He was a tall, well-built man with a very broad chest which strained at the buttons of his grey shirt. His wife was tall too — a good two inches taller than Alice. Once inside, the two of them stood looking curiously round the room. Alice closed the door, walked across to the table, pulled out two chairs and gestured to them to sit down. They sat.

Leaving them to talk between themselves at the table, she made two cups of tea, whilst Michael continued to hover by the back door like a sentry.

'Michael.' Alice jerked her head, beckoning him over. He ambled across to her. 'Don't stare at them! It's rude,' she said through gritted teeth.

'Mr Kenyon told me to keep an eye on them,' he defended.

She gave a small sigh. 'Well, do it a little less obviously.' She handed him two cups of tea. 'Here. Give these to them.'

Ten minutes later there was still no sign of Sam. She could hear water swishing and slopping around, which probably meant he was soaping himself. She glanced across the room at their visitors. The man was in conversation with his wife, apparently discussing the baby. It seemed to be unwell. The poor mite had a dreadful cough.

More minutes slid past. She decided to offer them biscuits. She walked over to the pantry and took out the tin of freshly made cinnamon biscuits. Taking off the lid, she walked back to the table with it and held it out to the man. 'Biscuits?' She smiled pleasantly and pointed at the tin. He peered into it, grinned very widely, nodded and took the tin from her, then turned towards his wife. Animated unintelligible dialogue followed. Alice frowned and waited for him to take a biscuit and pass the tin back. More wide grins, nods and patting of the tin ensued, but the tin remained on his lap. Their visitors, it seemed, were under the impression that she had gifted a full tin of biscuits to them. She breathed out a small sigh and decided it was perhaps not worth making a fuss about. If the unintentional gift of the biscuits had done nothing else it did at least appear to have improved the atmosphere. The man, in an attempt to converse with her, pointed at various things in the room, gabbling all the while. She nodded and smiled politely and wished that Sam would hurry up.

Her eyes drifted back to the baby. The child really did have a dreadful cough. It was about six months old by the look of it. A pretty dark-skinned child with fine black hair. Whether it was a boy or a girl it was impossible to tell — it was swathed in a grey woollen blanket with only its face visible. The honey and eucalyptus mixture in the cupboard would probably help relieve the poor mite's cough, she thought. It would certainly do it no harm. She went to the kitchen to find it.

Holding the bottle in one hand and a teaspoon in the other she pointed at the bottle and made coughing noises. They clearly understood what she meant, but the green bottle was being eyed with great suspicion. Reassurance was evidently needed. She called Charlotte to her and dribbled a spoonful of the medicine into her mouth. The man leaned forward, watching with narrowed eyes as Charlotte toddled around the room, presumably looking for signs of imminent death. None being forthcoming, Alice pointed to the baby again, then the bottle. The man appeared still unconvinced of its safety though. Frowning, he reached for the bottle and, before she could protest, tipped back his head and took a large swig. He licked his lips several times then handed back the bottle and nodded. The woman looked wary but made no move to stop Alice as she carefully administered half a teaspoonful to her baby.

She had just put away the bottle of medicine when the door opened and to her relief Sam strode into the kitchen. She could see from the expression on his face that he recognised their visitors. He walked across to the table, smiling, but there was a definite reserve to the smile.

'Hone,' he said in formal tones.

Hone rose to his feet.

Considerable conversation followed between the two men, if dialogue in two different languages, accompanied by liberal explanatory hand and arm waving, could be called conversation. It was to be hoped Sam was gleaning the gist of it all, Alice thought — she certainly wasn't. Eventually curiosity got the better of her and she went to stand beside him. 'What's he saying? What does he want?' she whispered.

Sam glanced down at her. 'From what I can make out he's interested in that boulder in the creek, the one Michael likes to sit on. He keeps saying *pounamu* — he seems to think it's greenstone, if I've understood him rightly, that is. I think he wants to purchase it from me.'

Alice raised her brows in surprise. 'Whatever for? There must be scores of greenstone boulders lying around free for the taking? Why does he want this particular one?'

Sam's mouth twitched wryly. 'Because it's mine, I imagine. Hone is very shrewd — I've had dealings with him before. He sometimes comes to barter for shoes and he drives a hard bargain. He'll not pay me much for the boulder. The only reason he wants to purchase it is because it will give it more value. People will think it must be especially fine stone if Hone was prepared to pay for it.'

Her eyes swivelled back to the prospective purchaser. How they were going to agree on a price was hard to imagine, given the communication difficulties. She was about to see.

'Two sacks of flour,' Sam stated firmly. He strode into the kitchen and returned cradling a bag of flour in his arm then stuck up two fingers.

Hone shook his head and stuck up one finger.

'Take it,' Alice whispered. A bag of flour for a boulder which was nothing but a nuisance anyway. Her only regret was that they didn't have several dozen to sell him.

Ignoring her, Sam held up two fingers again.

Hone shook his head more vigorously and held up one finger.

Sam scratched his chin thoughtfully, frowning. At length he put up two fingers then curled one partly over.

Alice leaned across to him. 'Do you not think you should settle for the single bag? He may change his mind altogether if you—'

'Alice,' he cut in firmly. 'Go and busy yourself in the kitchen if you can't stay quiet.'

She stayed quiet.

Five minutes later all was agreed. One and a half bags of flour, and Sam would lend his assistance with hauling out the boulder from the creek. The bargain struck, Hone and his wife departed. Looking rather smug, Sam closed the door and went to settle himself on the sofa.

'Does Hone carve the greenstone himself?' Alice asked curiously.

Sam nodded. 'He's quite a skilled artisan. He wanted to barter a greenstone carving for a pair of boots once. I refused it, but I have to admit it was a handsome piece.'

'I wouldn't have thought there was much demand for that sort of thing in these parts,' she said. 'I wonder where he hopes to sell his carvings.'

'He takes them to the coast — so Joel says — and sells them to the captains of trading vessels. Greenstone trinkets fetch a good price in England by all accounts. Hone will no doubt want a bill of sale from me for the purchase of the boulder so that he can wave it in front of his prospective buyers and demand a good price from them.'

'You drive quite a hard bargain yourself,' she commented. 'Considering the boulder was of no value to you.'

'Mmm,' he said thoughtfully. 'Did you intend Hone to have that tin of biscuits he left with?'

She gave a small shrug, not wanting to make too much of it. 'I offered him a biscuit and he misunderstood and thought I was offering him the whole tin. I didn't like to ask him to give it back. I thought it might cause offence.'

Sam made a sharp scoffing noise in his throat then leaned forward to lift Charlotte onto his knee. 'Hone understood perfectly well what you were offering him. That's the second tin of biscuits he's managed to purloin from my pantry. That's why I was determined to get the other half bag of flour from him.'

'Did he take the tin deliberately, Mr Kenyon?' Michael asked, eyes widening to huge blue circles.

'I'm sure he did,' Sam said.

'You think he took the biscuits on purpose?' Alice echoed in disbelief.

'I'm certain of it,' he said.

Alice expelled a vexed breath through her nose. 'Well, I'll not offer him biscuits next time he comes!'

'Once bitten, twice shy.' Sam's eyes met hers, a smile twinkling in them.

She laughed, the strain of the last few days for the moment swept away. 'Rather more than one bite too,' she said, tossing him a wry smile. 'There were a lot of biscuits in that tin. I filled it only yesterday.'

Sam's eyes lingered on her face for a moment or two longer then with a small sigh he turned his attention to Michael, who was questioning him again.

'When will he be coming to haul out the boulder, Mr Kenyon?' he enquired, sitting down beside him on the sofa.

'Soon, I expect,' Sam returned.

'Can I help with the hauling?'

'If you aren't at your lessons you can.'

'How will you haul it out? With the horse?'

Leaving Sam to explain to Michael the tactics best employed for hauling heavy boulders from wet creeks, Alice returned to the interrupted task of making a pastry crust for the mutton pie destined for dinner.

Hone was back sooner than they expected. He arrived with the agreed one and a half bags of flour late the following afternoon.

'Can I help, Mr Kenyon?' Michael asked eagerly.

Sam nodded, stripping off his shirt in preparation for what promised to be a very arduous, wet operation.

Intrigued to see how Sam and Hone planned to get the boulder out of the creek and onto the back of the Hone's wagon, Alice went out to watch.

'What shall I do?' Bared to the waist, Michael stood on the edge of the creek, shivering in the cool easterly wind. His arms and belly were a sea of gooseflesh.

'Fetch two shovels and that stout iron bar that I keep in the shed,' Sam said, wading into the creek. It had rained heavily during the night and the creek was two or three inches deeper for it; the water was flowing quite swiftly. Hone, also bare to the waist, was crouched in the water, scooping out dirt and small stones from around the base of the boulder.

'He surely doesn't think he can dig it out with his bare hands, does he?' Alice asked.

Sam shook his head. 'No. He's trying to assess how deep it's embedded in the creek. I'd say it's buried about a foot. No deeper, I hope, or we'll be here till dark getting it out.'

'How will you get it onto the back of his wagon?'

'Ropes and a block and tackle. It shouldn't be too difficult.' His gaze shifted down to Hone, who was speaking to him in Maori; he was holding up his hands a short distance apart.

Sam grunted and nodded. 'About eight inches deep, he thinks. Well, let's hope he's right.'

He turned as Michael appeared on the bank with the implements. 'Ah good, you found them,' he said. Taking the larger of the spades he passed it to Hone, then relieved Michael of the heavy iron bar.

'Have you used a shovel before, Michael?' he asked.

To illustrate his competence, Michael grasped the

long handle in both hands.

Sam nodded approvingly. 'Right, start shovelling. Dig away the earth from the bank, just where you're standing. Make a channel about a yard wide and three yards long. Dig it so it slopes up from the creek bed to make an incline so that we can roll the boulder up it.'

As work commenced, Alice retreated from the bank into the shelter of the trees, out of the wind and out of range of the clods of muddy earth which Michael was tossing with great gusto onto the grass. In the middle of the creek Hone's spade grated against the boulder as he began to dig out the shingle from around its base. Sam's task was to ram the metal rod down into the creek bed with as much force as he could muster, then pivot it from side to side to loosen the gravel and speed the progress of Hone's shovel.

An hour later the shovelling had ceased, Michael was sitting crosslegged on the bank, Charlotte was wriggling impatiently in Alice's arms, determined to get down, and Sam and Hone were both heaving on the iron bar, trying to free the boulder from the tenacious hold of the creek bed.

'It must move soon,' Sam gritted. The veins of his neck stood out like vines, pulsing with blood, the muscles of his arms and chest bunched taut, slick with sweat.

'Aaaah!' With a loud splash Hone landed flat on his back in the water as the boulder suddenly rolled free. Sam deftly twisted and ended up on his knees. Laughing, Hone struggled to his feet and shook his head, spraying water from his long black hair. He pointed to the boulder, grinning widely. Sam nodded and grinned back at him.

With a satisfied sigh he looked over to Michael. 'Fetch the ropes, lad.'

It took a further hour to get the boulder up the bank and onto the back of the wagon. Two hours of hard toil altogether. Still, there was a bag and a half of flour in the pantry Alice thought, as she watched Hone's wagon lumber off, creaking under the weight of its heavy load. Good flour too.

Chapter 11

'What are they saying? Can you understand them?' Alice looked up at Sam, frowning. Hone, accompanied by his wife, had arrived midway through the morning and they were extremely angry about something. 'Is it to do with the boulder? Is he dissatisfied with it, do you think?'

'No, I don't think so,' Sam said, raising his voice to make himself heard above the din. 'If he was unhappy with the boulder he'd not make this fuss. The most he'd do is demand some flour back. No, it seems to be to do with you,' he said in a puzzled voice. 'Do you see how they keep looking at you?'

Her gaze swivelled to Hone, then to his wife. Her frown deepened. Sam was right. They did seem to be directing the majority of their angry looks in her direction. 'But why should they be angry with me? I've done nothing to offend them,' she protested indignantly.

Sam folded his arms across his chest, frowning in concentration as he tried to make sense of the ongoing tirade. His efforts to pick out intelligible words from Hone's angry monologue were not being helped by Hone's wife, who was shrieking like a maddened goose. Hone was plainly getting frustrated too, as was becoming obvious by the way he kept stamping his foot. He also had a very unsettling way of flaring his nostrils and protruding his eyeballs so that the whites showed. In the wake of a particularly loud stamp, he stepped forward and extended a balled fist.

Alice let out a sharp gasp as Sam's right hand whipped out to haul her safely behind him, while his left hand settled firmly on Hone's chest. Fingers splayed wide, he gave a hard push, hard enough to send Hone reeling back several steps. 'Stay away from my wife,' he gritted. 'If you lay a hand on her I shall kill you.'

It was unlikely Hone understood a word of what Sam had said, but the grim look on Sam's face left no doubt as to his meaning.

'Stay behind me, Alice,' he ordered, keeping his eyes fixed intently on Hone. 'I don't think he'll try to harm you, but if he does and I have to fight him, run into the workshop and bar the door from the inside.'

She glanced nervously from Hone to his wife and unconsciously straightened her spine. She had never fought in her life but she was prepared to try if need be. She couldn't leave Sam to fight the two of them alone. Pray God it wouldn't come to that though. She threw an anxious glance in the kitchen to see if there was a saucepan within easy reach. Swung with sufficient force a pan could probably render someone unconscious. Michael ought to be back soon too. He'd gone to Reefton to . . .

Sam's voice interrupted her reeling thoughts. 'I think it's to do with their child.'

'Their child?' she echoed. The baby wasn't with them today. With all the turmoil she hadn't even noticed.

'I think it's died,' Sam said. He glanced over his shoulder at her, frowning. 'They seem to be blaming you for its death, Alice. Can you think why?'

'Me?' she said in horror. 'But . . . why should they think that? Their child was alive when they left here three days ago — you saw yourself that it was. It was ill though — it was coughing all the time they were here.' The infant's illness had plainly been far more serious than she had realised.

'Damned if I know why they think you're responsible!' Sam said in exasperation. 'Did you give the baby any milk or food, Alice?'

She opened her mouth to say 'No', then stopped short and drew in a sharp breath. Oh God, she thought, the medicine. 'I gave their child a spoonful of honey and eucalyptus syrup to ease its cough,' she said hoarsely.

'You did what?' Sam's head spun back to face her. 'Alice, whatever possessed you? They think you've poisoned their child!'

She stared at him in shock. 'But they can't possibly believe that! I gave a spoonful to Charlotte to show them it was safe. And she's not dead. And he drank some as well,' she added, pointing at Hone.

'Go and fetch Charlotte,' Sam ordered. 'If they see she's alive and well it will perhaps convince them there was nothing amiss with it.'

Keeping a wary eye on Hone's wife she edged past Sam and hurried off to get Charlotte who, despite all the noise, was still sleeping peacefully in her cot in the bedroom. The child blinked sleepily in her arms as she carried her back to the kitchen. Far from having the desired calming effect on the proceedings though, Charlotte's appearance only seemed to make matters worse. Hone's wife began to shriek even more shrilly, which in turn caused Charlotte to start wailing and Hone to shout all the more loudly to make himself heard above the general din.

Sam, in a burst of either inspiration or desperation, pulled out a chair and officiously motioned to Hone to sit. To Alice's surprise he did. Not only that, he turned towards his wife and barked out a sharp order, presumably instructing her to shut up, since her shrieks came to an abrupt halt. Her cheeks were soaked with tears. Alice grimaced slightly — she was sorry the woman had lost her child but it was very hard to feel compassionate when she'd made such wicked, groundless accusations against her. The woman knew very well her child was ill. She must surely have known it was the cough that had caused its death.

Turning, Sam lifted Charlotte from Alice's arms. She too had ceased her noisy wailing and a very uncomfortable silence now filled the kitchen. 'Go and see if Joel is home,' he ordered quietly. 'If he is, ask him to come back with you. He speaks a bit of their language. Hone will be expecting some recompense for the loss of his child and —'

'Recompense?' Alice cut in. 'I've done nothing to harm his child! Why should you recompense him?'

'Alice!' Sam said sharply. 'Let me deal with this. Now go and fetch Joel!'

She went.

Joel was in. She wasn't surprised — he seldom went out this early in the morning. She gave him a brief account of the goings on of the last ten minutes then they set off back to the house together.

'Hone is as crafty as a weasel.' Joel turned aside to spit out some phlegm as he followed her to the back door. 'He knows very well it was the cough that killed his child. He's seen he has a chance to get some recompense out of your man.'

'Has he, indeed!' she said. 'Well, we'll see about that!'

'Your man would be best advised to give him some,'

advised Joel gravely. 'It will be the finish of it if he does and he may regret it if he doesn't.'

She glanced back at Joel, a worried frown creasing her brow. 'Do you think Hone may seek revenge if he isn't satisfied?'

Joel's bony shoulder lifted in a stiff shrug. 'I can't say. But 'tis best to settle matters, in my opinion. It'll be the finish of it then.'

Thankfully tempers appeared to have cooled somewhat by the time she rejoined Sam in the kitchen, with Joel following close on her heels. Stepping forward to meet her, Sam passed Charlotte back to her.

'Joel, I need you to speak to Hone for me,' he said, turning his attention to his elderly neighbour. 'Has Alice told you why he's here?'

The corner of Joel's mouth twitched in a cynical smile. 'To make your pocket a bit lighter, by the sound of things.'

Sam's face remained grim. 'That is why he's here and though it goes against the grain I shall have to give him something, but I want him to understand that I'm not recompensing him for his child's death. I want you to make that clear to him, Joel. Tell him I'm very sorry for his loss and that as a gesture of sympathy I shall give him a pair of leather boots. I want you to state his child died from a cough — a sickness in the chest — describe it in whatever way you will. Tell him that my wife and the medicine she gave the child had no part in the child's death. Say to him that if he accepts the boots then he accepts that.' He paused then said, 'Are you clear on what I want you to say to him? I want there to be no misunderstanding as to why I'm offering him the boots.'

Joel nodded, scratching the sparse white stubble on

his chin as his gaze alternated between Hone and Hone's wife. 'You giving anything to the woman?'

Sam's eyes hardened as his gaze settled on the Maori woman. She was seated at the table beside her husband, radiating animosity from every pore. 'I wasn't intending to.'

Joel nodded again. 'Perhaps it's wise not to. I think she probably does believe your wife has killed her child so if you give her anything it will only be wasted. Hone is the only one you need to settle with, to my mind.'

'Well, get settling with him then,' Sam said shortly. 'The sooner I settle this the sooner I can get them out of my damned house.'

Alice stood watching, keeping a tight hold on Charlotte whilst Joel, with a great deal of hand-waving and repetition of words, proceeded to explain Sam's offer. She had no knowledge of their language at all and the slow, halting way that Joel spoke suggested his grasp of it was limited. It was difficult to know how well he was managing, but Hone's frequent puzzled frowns were not altogether encouraging. Eventually, though, Joel must have felt that the message had been received because he walked over to Alice, laid a hand on her shoulder then turned back to Hone and said two or three words in Maori. At which Hone nodded solemnly.

'I'm saying that you are innocent of the child's death,' Joel explained. 'He agrees that you are.'

Joel walked across to Sam and in the same manner placed a hand on Sam's shoulder. More unintelligible words followed. They were evidently intelligible to Hone though, because he nodded again, quite vigorously this time.

'Hone accepts your gesture of sympathy,' Joel said, and added drily, 'and the boots.'

Two minutes later Hone, his wife, and a brand new pair of black leather boots walked out through the back door. Alice for one hoped never to see any of them again. She wasn't easily angered, but at the present moment she was simmering. She was upset too, more upset than she cared to admit. The Maori woman blamed her for her baby's death, thought she'd poisoned the child, and it upset her to think that she had no way to disprove it and convince her otherwise.

'Thank you, Joel,' Sam said over his shoulder as he latched the door. 'I'm indebted to you.'

Joel gave a dismissive shrug. 'I've been in your debt often enough these last two years.'

Sam gave a stiff smile as he walked across to stand in front of the mantel. 'All the same, I'm grateful to you for your help. God knows how I would have settled the matter had you not been able to converse with Hone on my behalf. Let's hope this will be the finish of it.'

'Hone won't trouble you further now you've settled with him,' Joel said in dismissive tones. 'I doubt he was much concerned by the loss of the child. It was sickly by the sound of things. He has five more children so he'll not grieve the loss of this one for long.'

'I think Hone's wife may grieve her child's loss rather longer,' Alice inserted gravely.

Joel made a sharp noise in the back of his throat. 'She's of no consequence. You needn't concern yourself about her. Anyway, I dare say Hone will get her with child again before the winter is out. She'll soon forget about the child she's lost when she feels a new one stirring in her belly.'

Alice glanced over to Sam — he looked no more reassured by Joel's flippant words than she was. Joel had never married, never had a wife or children of his own, and his simplistic comments reflected that.

'All the same, I think it would be wise for you to keep a close watch on Charlotte, Alice,' Sam said. 'I trust Hone, but I'm not sure that I trust that wife of his.'

Despite the warmth of the room, Alice shivered. Nor did Joel's next words do much to reassure her.

'Well, it will do no harm, Sam. You can't be too careful with a vexed woman,' he said, nodding thoughtfully. 'There was a woman at the Brunner mine — she did the cooking for the single miners like myself in return for a share of the food. I remember how one night one of the miners accused her of taking more than her due of meat out of the stew. Well, there was little meat in the stew to be honest, but whether she'd been eating it or whether it had shrunk in the cooking it was hard to say. Anyway, she didn't take kindly to his comments, that was plain. She didn't say anything, not a word, but two nights later Dan — Dan Shanklin, that was his name — he started with terrible pains in his belly. He was doubled up all night. It was the food that had caused it, we were all quite sure of that, but the funny thing was none of the rest of us had the pains. I think she must have mixed something into his food when she was serving it out into his dish. To the best of my knowledge nobody complained about the woman's cooking again.' He raised a hand to scratch the side of his nose. 'Aye, they can be very vengeful, women can.'

With his memory pricked, Joel proceeded to narrate several other tales about the years he had spent working in various mines. Normally Alice found them quite interesting, but today she found herself waiting impatiently for him to leave, and judging by the way Sam was tapping his fingers on the edge of the table he too was keen for Joel to be gone. Eventually he did go, leaving them alone to discuss what was uppermost in both their minds.

'This is all my fault,' Alice said, not waiting for Sam to tell her so himself.

'It is,' he agreed, fixing a reproachful eye on her. 'You should have known better than to give that child medicine, Alice. You're not an apothecary.'

'I know I'm not,' she said. 'But it was just a harmless cough remedy. I was thinking of the child. It was sick. I only did what any other Christian woman would do — I showed it compassion.'

Sam gave an impatient click with his tongue. 'I'm not criticising your compassion. I'm criticising your lack of common sense. You've maybe not had much to do with Maori before but I've had a few dealings with them and their ways are different from ours. Their ways of dealing with illnesses are different too,' he added. 'You'd do well to remember that, should the occasion ever arise again.'

She drew in a steadying breath. Much as she would have liked to defend herself, what Sam had said was perfectly true. Maori ways and healing traditions were different. She was not, however, about to apologise for trying to relieve the suffering of a sick child. In any case there was something else she wanted to discuss. 'You said I should keep a close watch on Charlotte — why did you say that? Do you think Hone's wife may try to harm her?'

Sam's gaze flicked across to his daughter, who was now sitting cross-legged on the sofa playing with a feather she had found. 'I don't know,' he replied softly. 'But she believes you murdered her child. She'll more than likely do nothing at all, but on the other hand . . .

in hindsight I'm not sure I should have told you to fetch Charlotte out of the bedroom to show them that the medicine had had no ill effects on her. Hone's wife didn't understand what we were saying and it might well have seemed that we were taunting her with the fact that Charlotte was alive and well, while her child is dead. It's probably false fears, but nevertheless don't let Charlotte play outside alone, not for the next few weeks anyway.'

She glanced at the kitchen door, frowning. Keeping Charlotte indoors was easier said than done these days. Standing on tiptoe she could now reach the latch and it was impossible to watch her every second of the day.

She spent the rest of the day feeling worried, angry and upset. She was still lying awake at midnight, alternately brooding, boiling and battling tears. Eventually the tears started to win and she buried her face in the pillow, doing her best to muffle her sobs.

'Alice?' The bed lurched in a rolling wave as Sam turned over. 'What is it? Why are you weeping?' he whispered. He eased himself up onto his elbow then gently swept aside her hair and leaned over her shoulder so that he could see her face. 'Are you upset because I scolded you for giving that child the medicine?'

She wiped her eyes with the back of her hand and shook her head. 'No. I'm upset because that woman thinks I murdered her baby and there's no way I can prove my innocence. And I'm worried about Charlotte. She may go outside while I'm not looking. She can reach the latch and I can't watch her every minute of the day and if anything should happen to her it will be my fault.' She started to sob again.

'Alice, don't weep.' Sam's hand settled on her shoulder. Exerting a gentle pressure he rolled her onto her back then slipped his arm around her waist and drew her into his arms. 'Don't weep,' he whispered again. His arms tightened around her, drawing her closer. Beneath her cheek she could hear the steady drumbeat of his heart, slow, strong beats, and smell the faint musk of his skin. She pulled away, as much as his arms would allow, and sucked in a deep breath. 'I'm sorry — I'm being very foolish. I shall be all right now,' she said.

She looked up and met his eyes awkwardly. The bedroom was bathed in the pale light of a full moon. It seemed to cast odd shadows across his face, accentuating the bone structure and making his eyes seem like pools of silver. 'You're not being foolish,' he said quietly. 'And what happened today, it wasn't your fault. I know I said it was, but it wasn't. You had no way of knowing their child was so ill and I shouldn't have chided you for giving it the medicine. You meant well and you didn't deserve to be scolded for it. As for Hone's wife . . . well, I can't do much about her, but the problem of the latch is easily remedied. I'll shift it higher up the door, out of Charlotte's reach. I'll attend to it in the morning.'

The solution, at least for the latch, was so simple it made all the hours she'd fretted about it seem quite ridiculous. It had never occurred to her to look for a practical remedy — the sole focus of her thoughts had centred on how she would manage to keep a constant watch over Charlotte. Worry was evidently not very conducive to clarity of thought.

She let out a deep sigh of relief then smiled up at him gratefully.

With an answering smile he leaned forward and kissed her lips. As he pulled away his eyes locked with hers. 'Alice . . .' he whispered.

Her heart started to pound. She knew what he was going to say — she could see it in his eyes.

'Alice,' he said again. 'I want us to have a proper marriage. I want to be a proper husband to you. I said to you before that I want more children and I do, but it isn't the only reason I want to . . .' He paused, looking as if he was struggling to find the right words, then said softly, 'Alice, I'm sure you know what I'm trying to say.'

She knew. He had given his word that he would demand nothing from her till she was willing to give it. He was asking her if she was willing. She wanted to be, oh God, she wanted to be. She wanted to be a proper wife to Sam, she wanted more children too, Sam's children, but the thought of what it entailed had already brought her out in a cold sweat. She couldn't think of it without thinking of that day. Even now images were flooding her mind.

'I, I'm not sure,' she said uncertainly. 'I don't know if I can, Sam.'

'Well, you'll not know whether you can or you can't unless you try, Alice,' he said.

She licked her lips and swallowed. 'If I find I can't, will you stop?'

He nodded, and kissed her gently on the lips. 'I will. I promise.'

Chapter 12

'That was a fine sermon, Reverend Sedgwick, but I must say I'm inclined to question the Almighty's handling of King David after he committed adultery with Bathsheba.'

Reverend Sedgwick gave a wry smile. 'You think he should have killed King David rather than the innocent child who was the issue of his adultery?'

'I do,' Sam said. 'It was the king who had sinned — he was the one who should have paid for it to my mind, not the child. The child had committed no sin, save that of being conceived adulterously and I hardly think it could be held responsible for that.'

Alice tilted her head to the side, trying to see beyond the blue frills of Ellen's hat to where Sam was discussing the morning's sermon, a topic she found far more interesting than the latest gossip about Amelia Plover which Mrs Pryde was taking great relish in narrating — at length, as usual. She was particularly interested in Sam's comments on the child which had been born to King David and Bathsheba, the king having conveniently disposed of Bathsheba's husband in order to take her as his wife. The child had committed no sin, save that of being conceived adulterously, Sam had commented. Michael had committed no sin, save that of being conceived by violence. Would Sam view that in the same sympathetic light?

'I'm inclined to agree with you,' Reverend Sedgwick replied. 'But God's ways are not our ways and His wisdom is not our wisdom.'

'So I've noted,' commented Sam drily.

'One could argue,' continued Reverend Sedgwick, 'that God showed King David great mercy in sparing his life. One could also argue He showed great wisdom in not jeopardising the lives of the people of David's kingdom by killing their king and leaving them leaderless.' He paused, then added with a lopsided smile, 'One could also argue, of course, that it was very hard on the child.'

Sam laughed. 'That's the trouble with arguments — there are always at least two sides to them.'

'There are indeed,' agreed George Withers, adding his own hearty laugh. 'It would be a dull world without the occasional argument though.' George's twinkling eyes flicked down the aisle to Ellen, who beamed happily back at him. She was pregnant and blooming like a spring flower.

'I hear there was some trouble at the Energetic mine earlier in the week,' George commented, shifting the conversation on to fresh ground.

Not particularly interested in the Energetic's troubles, Alice turned her attention back to Ellen's mother.

'She's lost so much weight. She's as thin as a reed.' Mrs Pryde shook her head, making her plump cheeks wobble like a custard. 'Amelia's mother told Mrs Anderson that Amelia hadn't eaten for days, not since she received that letter from him. Shocking, that's what I say it is, toying with the girl's affections like that!'

'I've heard that his father put him up to it. I was told that he felt his son could do a good deal better than Amelia Plover,' inserted Ellen confidentially.

Mrs Pryde's brows arched with interest. 'Oh? Who told you that, Ellen?'

'I overheard Mrs Straven talking to old Miss Dawson. Mrs Straven said she'd heard that . . .'

Alice rolled her eyes and prayed for patience. Prayers are sometimes answered in unexpected ways. Hers was, in the shape of a woody thud followed by a loud howl. Charlotte had tripped and was sprawled in the aisle. Excusing herself, she went to pick her up and quieten her.

Seating herself on the rear pew, she lifted her onto her knee and wrapped her arms around her for warmth. Charlotte's small hands felt like ice. With no heating in the church, in the winter months toes and fingers tended to be very chilly by the end of the service. She glanced across at Sam, wondering how much longer he intended to stay. It had been a scant congregation this morning — only twenty or so people had turned up and most of them had hurried away after the final amen. Walter Grey was still there. She could hear his nasal tones very clearly, conversing with Mr Cameron and Mr Pryde in the porch. Walter Grey had been cordial but cool in his brief discourses with her and Sam after church, as had Mrs Barnes and her son, John. The Prydes seemed to have forgiven her though.

She turned, smiling, as Ellen shuffled into the pew and sat down beside her. 'You're beginning to stretch the seams of your bodice, Ellen,' she teased.

'I am,' Ellen said proudly, eyeing the straining blue fabric. Alice . . .' she said, lowering her voice as she looked up again. She glanced round as if to make sure that she wouldn't be overheard, then leaned towards Alice and whispered, 'I've been meaning to say this to you for a while. When you first told me you'd accepted Sam Kenyon's offer of marriage, I said I thought you were making a bad mistake. Well, I was wrong and I'm sorry I said it. He's a good man and it's plain for all to see that he cares deeply for you.'

Plain to see, was it? Alice glanced across at her husband, wondering exactly what Ellen could see that she couldn't. Oh, Sam cared for her — but not in a way she would describe as *deeply*, not in the way he'd cared for Eliza. She didn't know if he would ever care for her in that way. She didn't know if she would ever care for him in that way either. But perhaps with time . . . Seeing a blur of movement out of the corner of her eye she deftly caught hold of Charlotte's hand as her small fingers made a sudden grab for her hat. The pearl-headed hatpins fascinated her.

Watching her, Ellen's mouth stretched in a wistful smile. 'She's a sweet child. I hope I shall have a daughter. George is hoping for a son of course. Men always want a son. I suppose your husband will when the time comes.'

'Er, yes. I expect so.' Craning her neck, Alice peered around the church.

'You're distracted, Alice. Have you misplaced something?' Ellen asked, frowning.

'Yes. Michael,' she said.

'He went outside with Alfred Cameron,' Ellen supplied. 'Mr Cameron is in the porch, talking with my father and Walter Grey. No doubt he'll be keeping an eye on them.'

'I hope so,' Alice said dubiously. She still had vivid memories of two fat brown frogs leaping between the pews.

'Ah, here comes George. He must be ready to leave,'

Ellen said brightly. As George walked over, with Sam following in his wake, Ellen's face lit up like a candle.

'Are you ready to return home, Mrs Withers?' George enquired jovially.

'Indeed I am,' she said, reaching for his arm as she shuffled out from the pew. 'We shall see you next Sunday, I hope?' she asked, looking from Alice to Sam.

'I expect we shall be here, unless the weather is too inclement,' Sam replied.

As George made for the door with Ellen on his arm, Sam reached over to lift Charlotte from Alice's lap. 'It's time we were on our way too,' he said, smiling.

Alice wrinkled her nose as she stepped into the welcome warmth of the kitchen. Sam had recently taken delivery of a consignment of freshly tanned hides and every room in the house smelled of leather.

'Can I take Charlotte outside to play, Alice?' Michael asked.

'No, Michael, I'd rather she played indoors. She's wearing her good clothes,' she said as she reached up to pull the hatpins from her hat.

'I won't let her get dirty. It's not muddy, it hasn't rained for days,' Michael persisted. 'I only want to take her for a walk with Peer. She likes to throw stones for him.'

'Let them go outside, Alice,' instructed Sam, stepping past her. 'It will do the two of them good to get some air and stretch their legs. They surely can't get too dirty walking along tossing stones.'

Evidently assuming that Sam's word would be the last on the subject, which it usually was, Michael took hold of Charlotte's hand. 'Come, Charlotte,' he said. 'We're going to throw stones for Peer.'

'Peee! Peee!' Charlotte tilted her head to fix two wide green eyes on her father. She could say only a handful of words but the ones she could say she was very proud of.

Sam's lip curled with stifled amusement. 'Peer,' he corrected.

'Peee!' Charlotte repeated and trotted off with Michael.

The door opened and closed with a slam, which seemed to be the only way Michael was capable of closing a door, and silence settled on the house.

Turning towards the sofa Sam shrugged off his jacket and tossed it onto the seat. 'Speaking of clothes, Alice, I think it's time you stopped wearing black. You've mourned your father for a decent length of time now. I'd like to see you dressed in something brighter. The blue dress hanging in the wardrobe — wear that tomorrow.' His gaze travelled slowly down the length of her, as if he was mentally picturing her in it.

She placed her hat on the table, smoothed out the black silk bow, then began to undo the buttons of her jacket. Sam hadn't moved; he was still standing by the sofa, watching her. She turned away, uncomfortably aware that she was blushing again. She'd been blushing all morning; every time Sam looked at her with anything more than a passing glance she went the colour of a ripe cherry.

The floorboards creaked as he walked over to her then his hands settled on her waist; he leaned over her shoulder to kiss her cheek then turned her round to face him, circling her waist with his arms.

'I know you feel shy today, Alice,' he said quietly. 'It's not uncommon. Eliza blushed every time she set eyes on me the first week after we married.' His mouth curled at one corner. 'The first time she did it I thought I'd left my fly buttons undone.'

Despite her shyness, she couldn't help but laugh. 'And had you?'

He tilted his head to the side and grinned. 'No. Though I did check a time or two just to be sure.' His eyes lingered on hers, the smile slowly faded, and he said softly, 'Do you mind my talking about Eliza?'

'No, of course not. She was your wife,' she replied. Her gaze shifted unconsciously to the sideboard. Normally Eliza's portrait stood there, but it had suddenly disappeared about a week ago.

'I removed it,' he said, following her gaze.

She looked up and smiled. 'You didn't need to. I don't mind if you want to put it back.'

He cocked one eyebrow at her. 'Do you not? Most wives would.'

'Well, I don't,' she said, then added with rather more honesty. 'I'd prefer it to stand somewhere a bit less obvious than on the sideboard though.' Provided it didn't take up residence in the bedroom, that was.

The bedroom was obviously somewhat central to Sam's thoughts too. 'Alice — last night — was it as bad as you feared?' he asked quietly.

The blush on her cheeks, which was just starting to recede, fired up again with a fresh, furious burst of crimson. Doing her best to ignore it she shook her head and, seeing the concern in his eyes, mustered a reassuring smile. 'No, it wasn't as bad,' she said truthfully.

He smiled, looking visibly relieved. He had been tense last night too — it hadn't been an easy night for either of them. In all honesty though, the consummation of their marriage hadn't been the awful ordeal she had imagined and dreaded. Sam had been the essence of gentleness and patience; he had spent a long time just holding her in his arms, kissing her, stroking her hair, talking quietly to her, until she had at last begun to relax, safe in the knowledge he would stop if she asked him to. But when the moment had come, her fragile composure had splintered like broken glass, her heart had hammered wildly in her chest and she'd clutched his arms in panic. 'Do you want me to stop?' Sam had asked. For a split second she had been tempted to say yes. But what would that have achieved? A postponement, that was all. And then she would have to face it all over again some other night. So she had dug her fingers into his arms a bit deeper and said hoarsely, 'No, don't stop.'

'When I was lying beside you afterwards,' Sam said quietly, 'I started thinking about when I was a young lad.'

She blinked at him in surprise. What a husband had thought about afterwards was not something a wife expected to be told. Moreover, boyhood seemed a rather odd thing for a man to think about after engaging in what was an extremely adult activity.

'I used to be fearful of the dark,' he continued. 'I wouldn't sleep with the curtains drawn and I refused to go to the privy without a candle. It wasn't surprising, given the fearful stories my brother Dan told me about ghosts and goblins. Anyway, eventually my father tumbled to what was the cause of my fears about the dark and decided to do something about it. He started by taking Dan out to the shed and gave him a thorough thrashing for filling my head with such foolish nonsense. Then he took me out to the shed. I can remember I was shivering, expecting him to thrash me for being so cowardly, but he did something much worse. He closed the door on me and locked me in the shed in the pitch dark.' Alice tilted her head, curiosity aroused, despite the oddness of the tale. 'I thumped on the door and screamed and shouted till I'd no voice left,' he said, shaking his head ruefully. 'Then I huddled in the corner staring into the darkness, shivering so hard my teeth rattled. Then I heard my father's voice outside the door. He'd been there all the time, listening to me. "Are there any goblins or ghosts in there with you, lad?" he asked me. I didn't answer at first because I thought he was mocking me. But he asked me again and so I said there didn't seem to be. Then he asked me to describe what I could see. I was a bit mystified when he asked me that because it was pitch black and I couldn't see anything at all, so I didn't know what to describe. In the end I told him that all I could see was blackness. My father spent all night sitting outside the shed, sleeping a bit I suppose, and talking to me whenever he heard me whimpering or when I called out to him. Then as dawn broke he unbarred the door. I can still see him framed there in the shed doorway, with the sun behind him, holding his hand out to me. I can remember what he said to me too. "The only ghosts and goblins are those you conjure up in your head, Samuel. So let's be having no more of this nonsense of taking candles to the privy."' He paused, and when he spoke again his voice sounded faintly apologetic. 'Alice, I'm not meaning to suggest that being afraid of the dark as a young lad can compare with the terrifying experience you had. That's not why I told you the story. I told you because I learned something that night. I learned that fears are much easier to face if you don't have to face them alone someone will stand by you and face them with you, my father did. You're my wife, Alice. Whatever there to face — we'll face it together from now on.'

Silence settled, broken only by the sound of their breathing and the scritch-scratch of a twig against the window as it shifted in the wind. Close to tears, she slipped her arms around his neck and kissed him.

Muffled swearing issued from Sam's pillow, followed by a sudden pitch of the bed as he sat up. 'Damned dog! What ails it this time?' he muttered, tossing back the blankets.

The damned dog in question was presently barking as loudly as it was possible for a large dog to bark, granted it seemed twice as loud at two or three in the morning. It was by no means the first time that Peer had roused the household in the middle of the night, usually for nothing more important than to announce that a hedgehog was trespassing on the property. Tonight, though, Peer sounded quite agitated. Perhaps the trespasser on this occasion was something larger, like a stray dog. There were always a number of them roaming the district, searching for scraps. Whatever the reason for Peer's barks, one thing was certain — they wouldn't stop till someone went outside and personally acknowledged them.

More muttered oaths followed as Sam fumbled in the darkness to find his trousers and boots. As he opened the bedroom door, Charlotte's whimpers reached Alice's ears. 'Alice — Charlotte has woken,' he said over his shoulder. He paused in the doorway, sniffing. 'Can you smell smoke?'

Before she could answer he was gone. 'Oh, God!' Alice whispered, throwing back the blankets.

'Get Charlotte and wake Michael,' Sam shouted, already running down the hall. She knew where he was heading. She too had recognised the pungent smell in the smoke. Burning leather. His workshop was alight.

She threw a cursory glance at her black dress lying across the back of the chair. No, there wasn't time to dress, she decided. Nightgown flapping around her bare ankles, she ran to the other bedroom and flung open the door. In the darkness she could see Charlotte, rubbing her eyes and crying sleepily in her cot. Michael, disturbed by the noise of Sam's shouts, was muttering in his sleep, while outside Peer's barks were still echoing eerily through the night.

'Michael — wake up!' She shook the hunched form beneath the blankets. 'Wake up, wake up!'

'Mmh? Is it morning?' he mumbled. His head emerged, and two drowsy eyes peered confusedly at the darkened room.

'Get out of bed and find your clothes and your boots and be quick about it,' she said in as calm a voice as she could muster. Bending over the cot, she scooped up Charlotte along with her blankets and, sensing that the fire might be serious, stooped to grab the handle of the wicker basket containing Charlotte's freshly ironed clothes and clean napkins and dragged it towards the door.

'Why? What's the matter?' Michael asked in a sleepy, puzzled voice.

'Something is ablaze,' she said, glancing up from her struggle with the basket. It was stuck in the doorway and in the darkness she couldn't see what she needed to do to free it. 'The workshop, I think. Hurry, Michael. Sam says we're to go outside. Gather up your clothes and anything else you can manage to carry.' She gave a massive heave and the next second was lying sprawled on her back in the hall with the basket on top of her. Charlotte, judging by the thud, had banged her head on something hard and began to scream.

'I can smell smoke,' came Michael's worried voice from the bedroom, now fully awake. The acrid smell, getting rapidly stronger, pricked Michael into action. Seconds later he was following the wicker basket down the hall, his arms laden with clothes and blankets.

Once in the kitchen the seriousness of the blaze was instantly evident. Alice stood rooted to the spot, staring wide-eyed at the blue-tipped flames bursting through the wooden slats of the wall. The workshop door was wide open. Sam stood framed in it, silhouetted against a wall of leaping orange fire. Emitting loud grunts he was thrashing about with a wet blanket in a desperate effort to beat out the flames.

'Go and rouse Joel, Alice!' he yelled, catching sight of them. 'Michael, run into Reefton and ring the fire bell. Tell the brigade we need the tender urgently!' A sudden loud boom sounded behind him, making the wooden floorboards vibrate beneath Alice's bare feet and a soaring tongue of blue fire leapt high into the air a few feet beyond Sam. He turned towards the noise, instinctively lifting the blanket to shield his face, and stepped back, coughing. Thin ribbons of bluish grey smoke began to curl into the kitchen. A second explosion sounded, followed by more blue flame and smoke. Sam's tins of leather oil were exploding.

For once Michael didn't need to be told twice. Hastily stuffing his feet into his boots, he raced across the kitchen to the back door and vanished into the night.

Clutching Charlotte, who was now screaming in terror at the top of her lungs, Alice hurried after him, still hauling the wicker basket in her wake. Behind her, she could hear Sam coughing and retching as he continued to battle against the fire. As she stumbled outside into the crisp, clear air of the night she narrowly missed colliding with Joel.

'Oh, God in heaven!' he exclaimed, gaping past her at the flames. 'Shall I go and summon help?' he shouted to Sam.

Sam shook his head but didn't turn or let up his wild beating. 'Michael's gone to summon the tender. Save what you can from the house, Joel.' He doubled over suddenly as a fierce bout of coughing took him in its grip. 'I'll keep the fire at bay as long as . . .' He began to cough again and gave up on the rest, concentrating all his energies on fighting back the crackling blaze.

'This way, Mrs Kenyon. Take the little one to safety over yonder,' Joel urged, pushing Alice away from the house.

Forced to hold on to Charlotte, she stood watching helplessly from a distance while clothes and mattresses and miscellaneous household items soared through the back door, landing with flops and crashes on the ground. From what she could see through the clouds of smoke, the blaze seemed to be still confined to the workshop, but it was gaining strength if not ground. The glass panes in the window had shattered in the heat and flames were bursting through, their blood red tongues greedily licking the night air.

She glanced towards Reefton, wondering if Michael had reached the town yet. He could run like the wind, but it would be some time before the fire tender arrived. Unable to stand still, she paced back and forth as the minutes slid past, watching as the flames soared still higher and the fierce crackle of burning timbers filled the night air. Surely Sam must give up soon, she thought, biting on her lip. Their bedroom was ablaze now. She could see flames bursting through the shingles on the roof. Joel was still inside somewhere too. She bit her lip harder, tasting blood. She was on the point of running to the house and screaming to them to come out when to her relief Joel appeared in the doorway. Even above the roar and crackle of the flames, she could hear his racking cough.

'We can maybe manage to save a bit more,' he shouted over his shoulder in a hoarse voice.

Appearing suddenly at Joel's back, Sam helped the old man outside. 'No. I'll not risk lives for the sake of a few sticks of furniture. Let the rest burn,' he yelled. Catching sight of Alice in the shadow of the trees, he ran over to her.

'Are you all right?' Grasping hold of her shoulders, he scanned her face anxiously then turned his attention to Charlotte. She had ceased her screaming and was staring at the flames with huge black eyes. 'Is she all right?' he asked in concern.

'She's frightened,' Alice said in a shaky voice. So was she.

She looked up suddenly as a new sound reached her ears, carrying quite clearly through the night. Her eyes locked on Sam's as the sound came again, still some distance away. It was Michael, yelling at the top of his voice as he ran along the road.

'It's coming!' he shouted as he hurtled into view a minute or two later. He skidded to a halt on the grass, wet with night dew, gasping for breath. 'The tender's coming!' he panted.

Sam laid a hand on his shoulder and gave it a squeeze. 'Good lad. How long, do you think?'

Michael shook his head, drawing in hoarse breaths. 'I don't know. Mr Bell said they'll be as quick as they can.'

Sam's eyes flicked resignedly back to his blazing home. All they could do now was wait.

'Did you save my soldiers, Mr Miller?' Michael asked anxiously, scanning the piles of salvaged belongings littering the grass.

'Your soldiers?' Joel echoed in a hoarse voice.

'They were in my bedroom in a wooden box beneath my bed.'

'Aye, well, they're still there then,' Joel said. 'Along with your bed. I saved your mattress though and your clothes out of the chest.'

'But they'll melt!' Michael wailed, looking in panic at the flames, and rushed headlong for the house.

'Michael! Michael!' Alice shrieked. Thrusting Charlotte into Sam's arms, she ran after him. Her run was a short one. She hadn't gone more than a dozen steps when strong fingers grasped her arm, jerking her to a sudden halt.

'No! Let me go!' She wrenched her arm frantically, desperately trying to free herself from Sam's grip.

'Joel!' Sam yelled over his shoulder. 'Come and hold her!' She landed heavily on the grass as Sam pushed her suddenly backwards, and with a soft whumph Charlotte landed in her lap.

Following instructions, Joel crouched down beside her and took a firm hold of her shoulders. 'Best leave it to your man,' he said gravely.

Sick with fear she watched Sam run back towards the blazing house.

Chapter 13

'What were you thinking of, you bloody young fool?' Sam shook Michael's shoulders, hard enough to make his teeth clatter. 'You could have been burnt alive in there!'

'I wanted to get my box of soldiers!' Michael retorted. His eyes were glistening with tears.

Sam's fingers tightened on his shoulders, making the knuckles stand out white as the bone beneath. 'You risked your life for a box of tin soldiers?' He spun him round to face Alice. 'Were they worth the anguish you caused your sister, fearing you'd died in the flames?' He shook him again. 'Were they?'

Alice was huddled on the ground clutching Charlotte to her, weeping uncontrollably, while Joel patted her back in a touching attempt to comfort her. For an agonising two minutes she had feared that both Michael and Sam had perished, trapped in the flames, then Joel had lifted a hand, pointing to the side of the house, and said hoarsely, 'Here he is.' She'd turned in time to see Michael land like a winged goose in an ungainly heap on the ground. Sam had followed seconds later, leaping from the bedroom window through which he'd just thrown Michael.

Whether for the loss of his soldiers or for the distress he had caused his sister, Michael broke down in hiccupping sobs.

'Aye, well might you sob, lad!' Sam said without sympathy. 'You —' He turned sharply as, above the crackle of burning wood and the roar of flame, new sounds reached his ears. The rumble of wheels and the thud of hooves.

'That'll be the fire tender coming,' Joel said in flat tones.

Sam gave a faint grunt. Like Joel, he knew it would be of little use now. His house was beyond saving.

The volunteer fire brigade, six hastily dressed, sleep-tousled Reefton men, knew it too. They exchanged dismal glances then briskly set about manning the tender and within minutes were dousing the flames. The blaze hissed and spat in noisy protest and clouds of steam billowed up into the night, accompanied by swirling smoke that stank of burning leather.

'Keep an eye on the bushes,' someone shouted. 'There are bits of burning char floating towards them.'

Sam glanced up, watching the progress of three glowing orange specks, drifting slowly towards the bushes that edged the road. His hair lifted in the light breeze — it was fitful and changeable, coming in small gusts, sometimes from the north, sometimes from the east. Pray God it would get no stronger, he thought. If the stringy, peeling bark of the manuka bushes caught fire, as it easily could, they would have a fight on their hands. A bushfire could take days to put out. A sudden loud crack sounded, followed by a straining creak. He looked back in time to see a large section of the shingled roof crash down as a support timber gave way. Showers of sparks flew into the air like swarms of angry bees, crackling and hissing.

Two or three of the brigade, well acquainted with the threat which fire posed to dry bushes, were already tossing pailfuls of water over the vegetation closest to the house. Snatching up a spare bucket, Sam went to help.

John Bell, the Reefton barber and a member of the brigade, frowned worriedly at Sam as they filled their pails at the creek. 'We'd better toss some water onto your neighbour's hut across the road. I don't like the way these sparks are drifting.'

The sparks, hundreds of them, were floating upwards, caught on the breeze, and were being carried over the road towards Joel's hut. It was unlikely they would set alight the wooden slabs, but they could easily ignite the straw and strips of hessian which Joel stuffed into the cracks to keep out draughts.

Another crash sounded and more sparks flew into the air, swirling in all directions. One drifted down in front of Sam's face and landed on the grass at his feet. He stamped it out with his foot and rushed across the road with a pailful of water. God, still this wind, still this bloody wind, he prayed.

The wind did not still; even as the final pailful of water was tipped onto a smouldering timber it still blew fitful and gusty. But the danger was past, the fire was out and Joel's hut was still standing, unharmed. Sam closed his eyes, swaying wearily. 'Thank God,' he murmured aloud. Thank God his family were unharmed too. He rubbed his stinging eyes with his knuckles then looked over to where Alice was standing, a pale, shadowy figure holding his daughter in her arms, her brother standing by her side.

'Do you know how it started, Sam?' enquired Oliver Johnston, wiping the sweat from his face with a grubby handkerchief. 'Did an ember fall out of the fire onto the hearth rug, do you think?' It was the most common cause of house fires.

Sam shook his head. 'No, the fire started in my workshop. Michael's dog woke us with his barking and when I got up to see what was disturbing him I found it ablaze.'

'Had you left a candle or a lamp burning?' The question came from Ted Laing, a young single miner.

Sam shook his head again, frowning as he tried to clear his mind and remember exactly what he'd done the previous evening. 'No. So far as I recall I didn't go into the workshop at all last night.' Had Michael been into the workshop though? He glanced across at him. No, the lad had been bored and fidgety last night and had gone to bed early. He'd not set foot in the workshop at all yesterday.

'You didn't hear an explosion?'

He looked back, not sure who had asked the question. His head was spinning like a top.

'You all right, Sam?' A hand gripped his arm, steadying him.

He nodded and forced a stiff smile. 'I'm all right. My head's full of smoke, that's all.'

'You've some painful-looking blisters on your face and your chest.'

'I can feel them,' he said. Every one of them. His face was burning with a vengeance and the skin of his chest felt as tight as a drum, stretched taut with water-filled blisters, some of them the size of a crown piece. Alice would have something to ease them. She had quite a store of ointments. Used to have, he corrected himself. They'd probably lost every ointment and bandage they possessed, along with a lot of other things they were going to sorely miss. He stared at the smouldering pyre which had been his home, mentally picturing what had been in each room. The iron bed that had been his parents', the oak wardrobe, table, chairs, sofa, sideboard, ornaments, rugs, the chiming mantel clock that his sister Maud had given him as a wedding present when he and Eliza had married . . . Eliza's portrait . . . He could hardly bear to think of all the things that had burned in the blaze. Alice's belongings too — her father's old armchair that she treasured so much. And Michael's soldiers — bloody little fool, he'd nearly lost his life trying to save them. He sucked in a deep breath, wincing as the fabric of his shirt slid painfully across his blistered chest. They're of no consequence, he told himself. What were furniture and keepsakes compared with what he could have lost? His gaze drifted back to Alice. She was in her nightgown, with a grey woollen blanket draped around her and Charlotte, talking to one of the brigade, pale but dry-eyed. He drew in another deep breath. How in God's name was he to provide for them? He had no home, no workshop, no tools, no leather, and damned little money. He had spent a considerable amount of his savings on the consignment of leather he'd recently purchased — the largest consignment he had ever bought. All gone.

'If you're needing somewhere to stay for a while, you're welcome to stay with us. We've no spare beds, but you can sleep on the rug in front of the fire,' offered Oliver Johnston. His hand settled on Sam's shoulder in a gesture of sympathy.

Sam turned and nodded in acknowledgement.

'You're welcome to stay with me too, Sam,' Joel echoed. He thumped his chest as a series of racking coughs shook his frail frame. His face was as black as coal from the smoke. Even his hair, normally a pure white, had taken on a sooty grey colour.

'Thank you, Joel,' Sam said quietly.

'Sam — do you know how the fire started?' The voice was Jerry Crail's this time, his lilting Irish accent recognisable anywhere. He walked over to join the group of men surrounding Sam.

'No, he doesn't,' replied Oliver Johnston, perhaps wishing to spare Sam the trouble of repeating the details a second time. 'It started in his workshop. As to how . . . he's no idea how it could have begun.'

'You don't think someone could have started it deliberately?'

Sam stared, as did the rest of the men. 'Arson, you mean?'

Crail nodded, scratching his beard pensively. 'I'm only askin' because I think I saw someone. Over yonder in the bushes.' He turned to point.

'Who was it?' Sam's expression was serious.

'Ah, that I cannot tell you. It was no more than a glimpse that I caught. I couldn't see her face. It was too dark.'

'Her?' Sam's eyes narrowed. 'Did you say *her*?'

Crail nodded. 'Aye, twas a woman I saw, I think.'

'What was she doing?' someone asked.

'Just standin' there. I only glimpsed her the once. I turned aside to toss water onto some grass that was alight and when I turned back there was no one there. She'd gone.'

'What makes you think it was a woman?' Sam asked.

'Well, I don't exactly know. It was no more than a glimpse, but I just had the impression that it was a woman.' He gave a small shrug. 'In a dress.'

'You're sure it wasn't a trick of the light, Jerry?' Oliver Johnston raised his brows sceptically. 'It seems an odd time for a woman to be wandering about on her own.'

Crail shrugged. 'Well, I can't be absolutely sure, it all happened so quickly.'

'Light can play weird tricks, make things seem to be what they aren't.' Oliver Johnston looked decidedly unconvinced.

John Bell tugged at his moustache, frowning. 'Why would a woman want to set Sam Kenyon's house alight?'

As the conversation continued among the small assembly of men, Sam glanced over to Joel and caught his eye. He could see from the old man's expression he was thinking the same thing. He shifted his head fractionally from side to side, cautioning him not to say anything. It was possible, but unless there was firm proof . . .

'It makes no sense. I'm inclined to agree with you, Oliver, that it was a trick of the light. Jerry says himself he's not sure of what he saw, and when he looked again there was no one there,' said Ted Laing.

'Can you think of any reason why a woman should wish to burn your house down, Sam?' Oliver Johnston asked.

'No,' Sam said definitely. And unless he could find firm proof he would keep his suspicions to himself. He glanced up at the sky, which was lightening by the minute as the rosy glow of dawn crept over the hills. 'Let's take a look at the ground round the bushes,' he suggested. 'If someone was standing there we may be able to see some sign of it.'

A few minutes' searching produced nothing. Sam hadn't really expected to find anything. Had the ground been soft there might conceivably have been a footprint, but even if there had, what use would it have been? Anyway, there wasn't a footprint. There was nothing at all — save leaves.

With nothing more to be done, the brigade headed homewards to wash and snatch a quick bite of breakfast before going off to work, leaving Sam to survey the smouldering remains of his home. Wisps of smoke were still curling into the air and the charred timbers were making small popping noises. He circled it twice then halted and thrust his hands into his pockets, surveying the mangled debris with a gathering sense of despair. The only thing standing was the tin chimney, buckled and grotesquely twisted with the heat. His eyes alighted on a corner of the cast-iron cooking range, buried beneath burnt beams and shingles. He stepped gingerly onto the charred floorboards, testing their strength. In the workshop, which had taken the full fury of the blaze, they had burnt through completely, but the floorboards in the kitchen seemed to have fared rather better and would still bear his weight. He spent the next two or three minutes clearing the range of debris so that he could examine it. Crouching down in front of it he ran his palms over the top and sides, feeling for cracks. There were no obvious ones. With luck it might be salvageable. He stood up again, feeling heartened by the discovery, then looked over to what until a few hours ago had been his workshop. There was a possibility some of his tools might have survived too. Iron could withstand a fair bit of heat. He glanced over to Joel's house. Alice was there, with the children — he'd seen Joel take them over some time ago. He should go to her first, to see how she was. Then he would come back to see if he could salvage any of his tools.

'Oh, Alice!' Ellen bit her lip, her eyes wide with shock. 'Oh dear, I can scarce believe it! Your poor home!' she said in a distressed voice.

'Yes, there's not much left of it, is there,' Alice said in flat tones. She lifted her hand to push her hair back over her shoulder as the wind fluttered long wisps of it across her face. With her hairpins all gone she'd had to leave it loose. Hairpins, hairbrush, comb — they'd all burnt, along with a great many other possessions.

'Not much left at all,' agreed Mrs Pryde in heartfelt tones, shaking her head. 'Fires are so dreadfully destructive. You've managed to salvage a bit though — that's a mercy,' she added, casting her eye over the haphazard heaps that lay on the grass.

Alice surveyed the piles with an incongruous mix of gratitude and grief. Most of their clothing had escaped, although it reeked of smoke, as did the bedding and linen that Joel had managed to toss out. The pile of salvaged pots and pans and unbroken crockery was heartbreakingly small — two blackened saucepans, a lid which fitted neither, a cast-iron cooking cauldron, a dented jam pan, about twenty pieces of sooty china, and miscellaneous pieces of cutlery. As for furniture . . . every last stick of Sam's furniture had been destroyed. The rescued food provisions from the pantry presented an equally depressing picture. Two bags of flour, a bag of sugar, salt, tea, a leg of bacon and very little else.

Sam, catching sight of them as he tossed aside a charred length of timber, walked over to join them.

'Ellen. Mrs Pryde,' he said hoarsely. 'It's good of you to come to see Alice — she's had a very distressing night, as you can see.' He turned to drop the iron head of a hammer into a wooden box to join the other bits and pieces he had salvaged — four cast-iron shoe lasts, hammer heads of assorted sizes, two sets of pincers, some badly pitted shears whose repair was doubtful, and an assortment of shoe and boot moulds.

'Oh what a terrible thing to have happened!' Mrs Pryde said, shaking her head again. 'Still, you're all alive and that's the main thing.'

'Yes. We've Michael's dog to thank for that.' His eyes flicked across to Peer who was lying by the shed with his head between his paws, watching them. 'Had he not woken us none of us might have lived to see the dawn.'

'Well, thank the good Lord he did wake you,' Ellen said. 'However did the fire start?' It was the question everyone had asked, and the question which was no doubt being discussed the length and breadth of Reefton.

'I don't know,' Sam replied. 'The dog was making a lot of noise — he might have been trying to warn us of an intruder, but since dogs can't talk we shall never know for sure if that was the case.'

'Sam. Sam.' It was Joel, beckoning to him from the far side of the smouldering remains of the house.

'If you'll excuse me . . .' Sam said in apologetic tones, and walked over to see what the old man wanted.

'Where are Michael and Charlotte, Alice?' Ellen asked, looking around for signs of them.

'Sleeping in Joel's house,' she said. 'They're both exhausted.'

'You look as if you are too.' Ellen cast a worried eye over her friend's face. 'You're the colour of pastry.'

Mrs Pryde reached out and patted her arm, making small clucking noises like a broody hen. 'There have been such a spate of fires this last two years. Yours will be the fourth. Last year, I believe it was about this time, the Friar family lost their barn to fire.'

'Mother, I'm sure Alice doesn't want to listen to tales of fires,' Ellen interrupted. 'And that's not why we're here.' She glanced back at the spring cart, which she'd been obliged to leave on the road. The track beside the house was too littered with debris to drive along. 'I've brought some tea chests, Alice. Mr Johnston called in early this morning to tell us your house had set on fire and he said you'd managed to salvage a fair amount. George thought the tea chests might be useful to store things in. George feels so badly because he did hear the fire bell clanging but he never dreamed your house was the cause of it or he would have got up at once.' She paused to draw in a quick breath. 'Anyway, Mother and I have brought our aprons. What would you have us do?' She glanced up, frowning at the sky. 'It's looking as if it might rain before the morning is out.'

Alice followed her gaze, eyeing the gathering black clouds with an odd lack of concern. Rain seemed a minor matter after the trauma of fire.

During the course of the morning, as word spread around Reefton more women arrived, bringing gifts of food and anything else they deemed might be useful in such a disaster. Reverend Sedgwick also stopped by briefly midway through the morning, to sympathise, encourage, and leave a basket of provisions which his housekeeper had put together. All asked the same question — how had the fire started? How indeed? How could a fire start in a workshop where nothing was alight? Alice had been pondering that question all morning.

In some ways she would have preferred to sort through the pile of salvaged items alone, but when it did start to rain around midday she was very glad that Ellen and her mother had lent a hand. Despite Mrs Pryde's wearying incessant chatter her fingers were nimble and efficient and by the time the rain set in with a vengeance all the items which would suffer from the wet were safely stowed. With nothing more to be done, Ellen and her mother set off back for Reefton.

Leaving Sam to cover the tea chests with a tarpaulin, Alice walked wearily across the road to Joel's hut. She wasn't unduly surprised to see that Michael and Charlotte were both still sound asleep. They were curled up together on Joel's narrow bed, Charlotte next to the wall to prevent her from tumbling out. Michael's arm lay across her. His face was filthy, smudged with sooty streaks, and his hair, dulled by smoke, had for once lost its bright lustre and looked a murky brown. Blinking back tears, she walked over and stood by the bed, looking down at him. 'You young fool,' she whispered. 'You could have been killed.' Her gaze shifted to his bandaged feet, miraculously the only damage he had suffered — and the damage to them wasn't from the fire. He had run to Reefton and back in his boots but with no stockings on his feet and he had some huge blisters to show for it. The ones on his toes and heels had burst and the skin had completely rubbed off; the exposed flesh was red raw. Hearing footsteps, Joel's by the sound of them, she brushed the tears from her eyelashes and turned towards the door.

'Your man is finishing tying down the tarpaulins,' he said, stepping inside the hut. He lifted a grimy hand and flapped it about in a gesture which more or less encompassed the ramshackle totality of his home. 'It's not much, but you're welcome to stay for as long as you wish.'

She smiled gratefully. Joel wasn't the only person who had generously offered them accommodation. They had had offers from Ellen, Mrs Pryde, and even from Oliver Johnston, whom they barely knew. It was Joel's offer which Sam had accepted though. It didn't surprise her. If they stayed in Reefton it would mean leaving his property unguarded, including the shed which presently housed the only furniture they now possessed. They hadn't yet had a chance to discuss the fire, but Sam was no doubt as aware as she that fires didn't start up on a whim of their own accord, and since it wasn't caused by a careless accident, there seemed a strong possibility it might be arson. Peer had been barking very loudly last night at something — or someone. Who though? Who would set fire to a house in the middle of the night? A drunkard seemed the most likely explanation, save that it was a Sunday night when the public houses were closed. But there were ways of getting ale and spirits on any day of the week for those who knew where to go.

'Finished, Sam?' Joel asked as the door creaked open again. Alice glanced down as Charlotte stirred at the sound of Joel's voice. Unused to sleeping children, it didn't occur to Joel to talk quietly. Michael was stirring too. She looked up again, watching Sam as he came inside. His face was filthy, his jacket was soaked, and he looked fit to drop.

'God, what a night! I feel exhausted,' he said hoarsely. Halting just inside the doorway, he swallowed painfully.

Frowning, Alice walked across to him. Sam had complained earlier that his throat was very sore and if the fiery red scorched skin on his neck was any indication of the state of the inside of his throat then she could well believe it. His eyes were very bloodshot too. As for the blisters on his chest . . .

'How are they?' she asked, carefully pulling aside his shirt. They had filled with more fluid since the last time she had looked at them earlier in the morning;

the skin was so taut it looked almost transparent and the surrounding area was very enflamed.

'Sore,' he said.

She nodded. They looked very sore. 'Try not to burst them,' she said.

'Well, it won't be deliberate if I do,' he returned. 'Have you anything to ease them, Alice?'

'A cloth soaked in cold tea may help,' she said, eyeing them dubiously.

He nodded and let out a deep sigh. 'I'll try it later. Right now I just want to sit down.' Removing her hands from his shirt, he walked across to the nearest chair and slumped down onto it. Joel was sitting in a similar exhausted state, with his elbows on the table, eyes closed, his chin resting in his upturned palms.

'How are you feeling, Joel?' Sam asked.

'Weary,' Joel said, eyes still closed.

'I'm very grateful to you. I'll never be able to repay you for your help, Joel. We'd have precious few possessions had it not been for you.'

One wrinkled eyelid peeled open, then the other. 'You'd have done the same for me.'

'Ow! Be careful! Mind my feet!' Michael's plaintive voice came from the bed. He hoisted both legs into the air, trying to keep his bandaged feet out of Charlotte's way as she clambered off the bed. Her black woollen stockings had slid down her legs and were hanging like long tongues off her feet beneath her cotton nightgown. She stood for a moment or two staring in surprise at the unexpected surroundings then padded over to Alice, who picked her up, stroking her hair back from her sleep-flushed face, and kissed her forehead. Her napkin was soaked and reeked of urine, which was hardly surprising given the length of time she'd been wearing it. Carrying her over to the corner of the room, Alice kneeled down to change her.

'My feet hurt, Alice,' Michael complained from the bed.

'I can't do any more for them, Michael,' she said over her shoulder. 'They'll feel better in a day or two.'

'They hurt,' he said again.

'Yes, I'm sure they do,' she said. But sore feet were presently the very least of their worries.

'What will you do to keep your wife and family fed now?' Joel enquired.

Alice looked up, keen to hear Sam's reply. She'd been wondering that herself. Michael, too, seemed to have temporarily forgotten his sore feet and was sitting quite still on the bed, his gaze fixed intently on Sam.

He didn't answer at once, but at length he said quietly, 'I shall have to find work — whatever I can get. I've not much in the way of savings, not enough to build a new house anyway.' He lowered his eyes, toying with a crumb of bread on the table. 'There will be even less after I've recompensed people for the boots and shoes that were in the shop awaiting mending.' He shook his head, frowning, and let out a deep sigh. 'It couldn't have happened at a worse time. I bought twelve good hides of leather only a fortnight ago. I had about a dozen pairs of boots waiting to be mended too, which is twice what I'd normally have on the shelf. I shall be hard pressed to remember whose they were.'

'I dare say folk will be quick to remind you, should one or two slip your memory,' commented Joel in cynical tones.

Sam gave a dry, humourless laugh and nodded. 'I dare say. It will be hard to know what sort of a price to put on the boots and shoes — some of them were in quite good condition as I recall, while others were barely worth mending.'

'I'm sure most people won't expect too much, Sam,' Alice said positively, helping Charlotte to her feet. Dry and happy again, she toddled over to Michael, grinning happily at him. Looking rather less pleased to see her, Michael tucked his feet under the bed and glowered warningly at her.

'I intend to give full recompense, Alice,' Sam returned definitely. 'I don't want others to suffer hardship on account of what's happened.'

A loud thud sounded. Turning towards it, Alice pursed her lips. Charlotte had tumbled backwards over a box and was now lying flat on her back, wedged between the box and the wall with her legs waving helplessly in the air like a cast ladybird. Alice hadn't seen exactly what had happened but she could guess. Michael had shoved Charlotte over, and in this instance she couldn't altogether blame him. Fascinated by the bandages on his feet, Charlotte had been determinedly trying to reach underneath the bed to poke them.

'Michael — help Charlotte up. She seems to have fallen over,' she said pointedly.

Sam looked over his shoulder, grimacing as the movement caused the fabric of his shirt to rub against his blisters again. Michael's features assumed a similar pained expression as he gingerly put his weight on his feet in order to haul Charlotte up.

'Are they painful, lad?' Sam enquired.

Michael met Sam's eyes sheepishly and he gave a small nod.

'Can you get your boots on if you leave the laces undone?'

'I think so,' Michael murmured uncertainly.

Sam pushed himself stiffly to his feet. 'Come along then. That dog of yours needs to be fed. He can have a few strips of that beef that Mr Dick sent round. I think he deserves some reward for saving our lives.'

A slow smile spread across Michael's face and, sore feet forgotten, he reached under the bed for his boots.

When the two of them returned ten minutes later Michael was talking to Sam in something approaching normality. He had barely spoken a word since the fire, or to be more exact, since Sam had angrily rebuked him for foolishly racing into the blazing house to search for his soldiers. Assigned the task of running to Reefton to summon help, Michael had probably felt something of a hero. There had been nothing heroic, however, about being hurled through a bedroom window like a sack of potatoes, shaken till his teeth rattled, then loudly berated. In the space of a few minutes he had plummeted from the heady heights of heroism to the depths of disgrace. He'd not surprisingly been very subdued since. Sam had noted it too and she suspected that, in addition to rewarding Peer, he had taken the opportunity to have a somewhat quieter talk with Michael.

Her own chance to talk quietly with Sam didn't come till dark when Joel's snuffly snores at last announced that he was asleep. Charlotte and Michael had been asleep for several hours, snugly curled together on a mattress in the corner of the room, whilst she and Sam were lying on a blanket on the hard floorboards. Sam, by necessity sleeping on his back, reached across to her in the darkness, groping for her hand.

'We'll manage, Alice,' he whispered. His fingers tightened on hers.

'Yes,' she said. They would manage — they would

have to — but it wouldn't be easy. 'What will you do?' she asked. 'You've lost all your leather and some of your tools.'

'Nothing at all for a day or two,' he said as he gingerly shifted position. 'Not till these blisters ease up. I think Michael's feet are paining him too.' His thumb moved gently across the palm of her hand. 'He's a brave lad, Alice. Albeit a bit foolhardy.'

'What did you say to him when you went outside to feed Peer?' she asked quietly.

'That — more or less. That he was foolish but brave. I told him it had been very courageous of him to go into the house to search for his soldiers but that in doing so he'd risked his life and mine too. Then I asked him if he thought the value of the soldiers was worth the cost of two lives.'

'And what did he say?'

'No.'

A sudden rasping cough from Joel's bed made them turn their heads in unison, fetching their faces close together, and on impulse Alice leaned in to kiss Sam. He lifted his left hand to cup the back of her head and with a sigh pulled her closer.

'Sam,' she whispered, as their lips parted. 'Do you have any inkling as to how the fire started?'

He didn't answer immediately. Then in a low voice he said, 'It may have been Hone's wife.'

'Hone's wife?' She pulled away from him in shock.

'Jerry Crail thought he saw a woman standing among the bushes on the roadside,' he expanded quietly. 'We searched the ground in the hopes of finding footprints but there was nothing there.'

'Oh God,' she murmured. 'She did it for retribution for the death of her child.'

'Alice — I only said it *may* have been Hone's wife,' he said in cautioning tones. 'Jerry Crail may just have seen shifting shadows.' He paused then added, 'But just to be on the safe side, keep a close eye on Charlotte.'

Chapter 14

'Did you have any luck?' Alice asked, pressing her hands against the small of her back as she tried to persuade it to straighten. She had been bent double over the creek for the last three hours — for the last three days in fact, on and off — soaping and scrubbing blankets, linen and clothes in an effort to rid them of the smell of smoke. Mercifully the weather had held fine. A strong easterly was blowing today which, though crisp, was a good drying wind. Sam had spent the last two days riding around the local farms trying to find work — so far with no success. Today he'd been enquiring at the gold mines.

'I did,' he said, smiling as he crouched down beside her. 'I start tomorrow at the Energetic. They're shorthanded. George Withers mentioned last Sunday that there had been a bit of dissatisfaction at the Energetic. Apparently a couple of the miners had been complaining about the wages — they'd heard that one of the other mines paid a shilling a day more. The foreman told them if they thought they could do better then they should move on, and they took him at his word it seems. Anyway, he's keen for me to start at once.'

She reached up to push a strand of loose hair behind her ear, dripping icy water down her cheek. 'The Energetic — that's one of the mines beyond Black's

Point, isn't it?' It was quite some distance away.

Sam nodded. 'It is. I think it best if we move there, and anyway it's time we left Joel in peace.' His mouth twisted. 'We're already coming close to outstaying our welcome.'

'We are,' she agreed, smiling wryly back at him. Charlotte had woken five times during their first night's stay with Joel and three during the second. Used to sound, quiet sleeps, Joel had of late been demonstrating a noticeable lack of patience with the source of the noisy disturbances.

A frown settled on Sam's brow and his features took on a more serious appearance. 'I was thinking while I was riding back from the Energetic, and doing some sums. We're not entirely penniless, Alice. I'll still have some savings left after I've reimbursed people for the loss of their shoes and boots, but not enough to rebuild the house by any means. But if I work in the mine for twelve months and if we're very frugal, I think I'll maybe have enough money to put a roof over our heads again, albeit a very modest one. I'll re-shaft the hammers I salvaged and when I can come by the rest of the tools I need I'll buy a hide or two and repair shoes in the evenings and on Sundays. That will bring in some extra money and at the same time ensure I don't lose my customers.' He paused then said, 'There is one problem — accommodation. There are no vacant cottages to be rented at Black's Point at present. The two men who moved out were both single miners and lived in huts.'

'I see,' she said. 'So where will we live?'

'Well, I thought that since the weather is still not too bad we could live under canvas for a few weeks. Once the winter sets in, if the worst comes to the worst and no cottage comes vacant we'll have to move into a hut and make do as best we can. If you've strong objections to living in a tent we can take a room at the Albion Hotel.'

'No, I've no objections,' she said dismissively. 'And as you said, the weather is still quite mild.' Though how long it would stay mild was questionable. She glanced down at the basket of wet washing, frowning. 'Do you want to move to Black's Point today? Shall I start packing?'

Sam gave a dry laugh. 'You're a very efficient wife, Alice, but I doubt even your efficiency will run to packing everything together in the space of two or three hours, not to mention getting your washing dry. No, I'll ask Joel if we can stay till Sunday morning. In the meantime I'll rise early and walk to the mine. The day shift starts at eight.'

His gaze drifted to Charlotte, who was tossing sticks into the creek a short distance away, so engrossed in her play she hadn't noticed her father's arrival.

'I'll see Mr Green and enroll Michael in the school at Black's Point,' he said, evidently considering the implications for the two children in his care. One eyebrow lifted slightly, seeking her response.

She nodded in agreement. She doubted Michael would be pleased with the new arrangements and the prospect of having to settle into a fresh school, but he would have to get used to the idea. It would be too far for him to walk to Reefton every day and no point in it either when there was a good school at Black's Point.

'How much are the wages?' she enquired, wondering exactly how frugal she was expected to be over the coming months.

'Nine shillings a day for the first three months, then

it will go up to ten shillings.'

It was more than she had expected him to say. 'We'll eat more potatoes and less meat. That will save a bit of money,' she said. She'd already been planning how she could cut back the food bill.

'Well, there are ways of getting meat without paying for it,' Sam commented, pushing himself to his feet. 'I believe pigeons are quite plentiful in the hills around Black's Point. I'll teach Michael how to use a catapult. He can maybe kill a bird or two when he gets a bit of skill with it.'

'A catapult? I'm not sure about letting Michael loose with a catapult,' she said, raising her brows. A catapult was a very tempting weapon to place in the hands of a ten-year-old lad, and knowing Michael it wouldn't be only pigeons he pelted with stones.

'Why is it that women always see a possible disaster in everything a lad turns his hand to?' Sam said, shaking his head.

'Perhaps it's because women have better eyesight than men,' she suggested.

He gave a soft chuckle then turned to look towards the road. 'Well, I suppose I'd better go into Reefton and settle the rest of what I owe for the boots and shoes that burned.' He glanced back to smile at her. 'I'll see you in an hour or two.'

She watched him as he walked slowly back to Joel's hut. Sam was putting on a very brave face, just as she was. But she suspected that deep down he was no more looking forward to taking a labouring job in a gold mine than she was looking forward to living under canvas.

It was just after six-thirty when Sam left for the Energetic the next morning and it was almost six in the evening when he returned. He was filthy, stank of sweat and looked as if he could barely drag one leg in front of the other.

'How was it?' Alice asked, helping him out of his jacket.

'Harder work than mending boots,' he said.

'It gets easier,' Joel said, grinning up from his stool. Charlotte had thankfully had a better sleep last night, as a consequence Joel had been considerably more cheerful today.

'I hope it does,' Sam said with feeling. 'I can feel every damned muscle in my body, including several I didn't know I had. God, my chest muscles are sore!' Shrugging his right arm out of the jacket sleeve he raised his hand to touch a point midway between his shoulder and the base of his throat. 'Just here.'

'It gets easier,' Joel repeated.

'How are your blisters?' Alice asked.

'Sore,' he said.

'I'll get your dinner. I've kept it hot,' she said. Food and sympathy were about all she could offer him, neither of which would make his blisters any the less painful.

'I'll wash first,' he said, glancing round for the pail. 'Is there some water, Alice?'

'I've already filled the washbowl for you,' she said, pointing to the tin bowl on the bench, beside which lay a cake of soap and a towel.

'What did you do, Mr Kenyon?' Michael asked. 'How far below the ground did you go?'

'I don't know. It seemed a very long way when we were going down the shaft though,' Sam replied.

'Did you go down in a cage?'

A burbly 'yes' emerged as Sam sluiced water over

his face then proceeded to work up a lather with the soap. 'The dirt gets everywhere,' he muttered, working a soapy finger into his right ear.

'Is it dark, Mr Kenyon? How do you see to work?' Michael, stationed at Sam's left elbow, peered up at him.

'Candles,' Sam said as he reached for the towel.

'How do they do the blasting?' Michael tossed an impatient glance over his left shoulder as Alice's fingers curled around his upper arm. 'I'm only asking Mr Kenyon if —'

'Not now,' Alice cut in firmly, and dragged him away.

'You'd be best to strip off to the waist so you can wash yourself properly,' Joel advised from his chair.

Halting his soaping, Sam squinted across at him. 'I'll settle for a clean face and neck tonight, Joel, if it's all the same to you.'

'It's all the same to me,' Joel said cheerfully. 'Though your wife may raise a few objections if you blacken her clean sheets with your dirty chest.'

'I'll put your dinner on the table,' Alice said. Sam looked so bone weary she wouldn't object if he slept in his dirty boots tonight. It was just as well there was only one more working day in the week left to go. Not that Sunday would be much of a day of rest — they would be shifting their possessions to Black's Point then. Pray God the fine weather would continue.

They woke on Sunday morning to the sound of heavy rain drumming on the shingled roof of Joel's hut. Sam muttered a few phrases not very suited to the Sabbath and pulled the blankets over his head. By the time they had breakfasted, however, the rain had subsided and a watery sun was breaking through the thin grey cloud which veiled the sky. The wind had turned southerly and it was bitterly cold. Alice cast a dubious eye over the folds of brown canvas as Sam loaded the tent onto the back of the wagon, wondering how much wind the thin fabric would keep out. She had spent the whole of yesterday morning painstakingly rubbing the outer side of the canvas with a wax candle — something Joel had recommended to make it more proof against rain.

It was the middle of the afternoon before they left for Black's Point. Sam had planned to leave considerably earlier but, whilst wriggling beneath the wagon to secure ropes, he had discovered a small crack in the back axle and had decided to strengthen it rather than risk it breaking on the journey. There was a surprisingly large load on the wagon, mainly Alice's furniture. At the time she had resented its being stored in the shed, but it had turned out to be a blessing in disguise. As for the rest of their possessions — well, they had enough to manage.

She twisted round to give a final wave to Joel as the wagon negotiated a bend in the road to take them out of sight, then turned back and settled Charlotte more comfortably on her knee. Michael had walked on ahead with Peer, his newly acquired catapult swinging at the ready from his hand. Joel had given it to him. Overhearing Sam mentioning the topic again last night, Joel had rummaged around in one of his dusty boxes and produced a cobweb-festooned catapult fashioned from an antler. Goodness knows where he'd come by it. Privately, she still held quite a few misgivings about letting Michael loose with it, but there was very little she could do about it now, other than pray that he didn't kill someone.

It was about two miles from Reefton to Black's Point. The road wormed its way around the base of the hills, following the course of the Inangahua River. The steep hills, densely covered in bush and trees — mostly black beech — seemed to be perpetually veiled in cloud at this time of year. White bands of mist floated between the trunks of the trees like delicate silk ribbons, giving the place an eerie feel. The leafy ferns and native vegetation that flourished in the shady canopy of the trees kept the ground beneath permanently moist, and the sweet, loamy smell of rotting leaves drifted on the wind. There was a lot of dead wood among the live, covered in moss and lichens, and the aptly named old man's beard trailed in profusion from branches and creepers. Occasionally the sweet, clear chimes of a bellbird or the throaty trill of a pigeon broke the silence of the forested slopes, while unseen, hidden by bush to the right of the road, came the muted sound of rushing water as the Inangahua surged past.

It was late afternoon when they reached Black's Point. Alice had been there only once before, two or three years ago. It had been a damp, murky day and her only recollection was of some fifty or so houses clustered beneath the hills, swathed in mist and smoke. It looked much the same today.

Sam let out a long sigh as he hauled on the reins, drawing the wagon to a halt. With the rumble of wheels and the creak of furniture and the clatter of pans now stilled, a silence of sorts settled. Being a Sunday and dinner time, few people were stirring in the streets. A woman was standing at the door of a nearby house talking with a neighbour, three men were conversing outside the Methodist chapel, and some girls were playing a skipping game in the middle of the street, singing a song that Alice had sung as a child. One for a butcher, two for a baker, three for a rich man, four for a thief . . .

Less tuneful than the singing, the fretful cry of a baby drifted on the wind and somewhere on the far side of the town a dog was barking its lungs out. Peer, whether in anticipation of conflict or camaraderie, pricked back his ears, wagged his tail and barked loudly back.

'Quiet, Peer!' Michael ordered, and slapped the dog's rump. 'Sit! Sit! Good dog.'

'Aye, keep him quiet,' Sam said. 'We don't want to rouse the whole neighbourhood before we've even set foot on the ground.'

'Whereabouts is Mr Wrigley's tent?' Alice asked, glancing around. Fred Wrigley and his family, she'd been informed last night, were to be her new neighbours. He also worked at the Energetic, and seemed to have struck up something of a friendship with Sam. Like themselves, the Wrigleys had decided to live under canvas until a cottage came vacant for renting; their wait would be a short one though — they had the promise of a cottage on Lucas Street in a month's time.

Sam lifted a hand to point. 'Over there. On the street that leads down to the river.'

'Is there a fee for pitching a tent?' she asked, as the issue of their finances once again drifted to the forefront of her mind.

He shrugged. 'I didn't enquire. If there is, I doubt it will amount to much.' The leather reins swept in a smooth arc across the horse's rump as Sam gave them a gentle flick.

As the wagon began to rumble along again Alice cast her eye along the cottages in the streets. It would be the first time she'd ever lived in a town, the first time she'd ever lived in a tent too. Most of her life she'd lived in a farm cottage, miles from anywhere, and Sam's house had been half a mile from the town. It would be a big change in quite a number of ways to live in Black's Point. She turned her head back as Sam pulled on the reins to steer the wagon off the road into a clearing among the trees. Three tents were already pitched there. Two of them were placed quite close together and judging by their size belonged to single miners, though there was no sign of their occupants at present. On the other side of the clearing was a tent of more substantial proportions, in front of which a family was standing around a cheery fire.

'That's Fred Wrigley and his family,' Sam said.

The Wrigley family was large. Not in numbers, in size. Mr Wrigley, who was walking around the fire to welcome them, was a giant of a man. He was built like a bullock and looked at least as strong. Everything about him was thick and muscular — shoulders, chest, arms, legs, even his neck. Added to which, he was very tall, well over six feet. The only thing he had been badly shortchanged in was hair, though what he did have — a three-inch band stretching from ear to ear around the back of his head — was a mass of thick black curls. His wife, dark-haired and quite handsome in the face, was also very tall, but not thin in the way that tall women usually are. She had a very comely figure.

Michael, who had run on ahead and halted a short distance in front of the Wrigley's tent, was taking a similar interest in the younger members of the Wrigley household. The older boy, who had the robust build of his father, looked to be about the same age as Michael and the two of them were dubiously appraising each other. Peer, standing beside Michael and also assessing the situation, was swishing his tail back and forth in an uncertain wag. The daughter appeared to be about six or seven, and the younger boy a similar age to Charlotte.

'I was starting to think you weren't coming today, Sam,' commented Fred Wrigley, as Sam drew the wagon to a halt. His moustached lips peeled back to reveal a good set of white teeth unfortunately spoiled by the loss of two or three in the top row on the left hand side. It looked like the sort of damage that a well-aimed fist might do, though it was hard to imagine Fred Wrigley coming off worst in a fight.

Returning his smile, Sam jumped down from the wagon. 'I had a problem with the axle.'

'Broke, did it?'

Sam shook his head. 'No, just a crack in the shaft. It would probably have been all right but I didn't want to take any chances.' He glanced back over his shoulder and moved across to help Alice down from the wagon. Charlotte was fast asleep in her arms.

'Alice — this is Fred Wrigley,' he said by way of introduction. 'Fred, this is my wife, Alice. And my daughter, Charlotte. And my wife's brother, Michael.'

Fred smiled genially. 'I'm very pleased to make your acquaintance, Mrs Kenyon. Pleased to be having you as neighbours too.' Turning, he flapped a massive hand in the direction of his wife. 'And you'll no doubt be making the acquaintance of my wife, Bella, soon enough. And my three children here. There's Robert, the oldest, and Jane, and Sidney, the youngest.' Alice nodded in acknowledgement and smiled.

The introductions finished, Fred's eyes swivelled across to the wagon. 'You'll be needing a hand with unloading, and pitching your tent, Sam.'

'I'll not say no, if you're offering,' Sam said.

'Have your meal first, Fred,' Bella said quietly from behind him. 'A man can't work on an empty stomach. You'll have a bite to eat with us?' Her eyes flicked from

Sam to Alice. 'Sit yourselves down beside the fire. I've a big pot of broth in the tent.'

Sam hesitated, cast a quick glance at the wagon looking as if he would sooner have started unloading it at once, then said warmly, 'That's very kind of you, Mrs Wrigley. It smells too good to refuse.'

Bella gave a soft, musical laugh. 'Well, the proof of a good meal is in the eating, not the smelling. The food that the Chinamen eat smells all right while it's cooking.' She dipped her head towards the two smaller tents. 'One of them gave me a taste of it a day or two ago and it took me all my time to swallow it. Rice. They eat it by the panful. It looks like boiled maggots and I couldn't even begin to describe what it tastes like. Anyway, make yourselves comfortable beside the fire,' she said, waving a hand in invitation. 'I'll not be long with the broth. It's all ready for spooning out.'

Leaving Sam to talk with Fred, Alice tentatively followed Bella to the tent. She glanced around the interior, wondering if there was somewhere that she could lay Charlotte down. Reading her mind, Bella pointed a long finger to the far corner of the tent. 'Lay your daughter on the blankets over there, Mrs Kenyon. Might I ask how old she is? She looks to be of a similar age to Sidney.'

'She'll be two in September,' Alice said, not bothering to correct her mistaken assumption about her relationship to Charlotte. She bent over to lay Charlotte on a pile of neatly folded blankets. The whole tent was extremely neat and orderly and the furniture had been arranged as fastidiously as if it was inside four solid walls, giving the impression that the makeshift arrangement had been in operation for some time.

'I thought they were much of an age,' Bella said. 'Sidney will be two in July.'

'Have you been at Black's Point long, Mrs Wrigley?' Alice enquired.

'Eight weeks,' she said, reaching for a bowl. 'We shall be moving into a cottage in Lucas Street in a month's time though, and I must say I shall be glad to have a proper roof over my head again.' She glanced up from her ladling and added quietly, 'You lost your home in a fire, I believe.'

'Yes, we did, a week ago,' Alice said. She was about to volunteer a brief account when the tent fell into sudden darkness as Fred stepped inside, effectively blocking out most of the light from the fire.

Stooping, he took the steaming bowl of broth from Bella's hands. 'Here,' he said, grinning as he passed it back to Sam. 'Eat that, then maybe my wife will let you unload your wagon.'

Two hours later they were installed, albeit very chaotically, inside the tent. There was barely room to lay a foot, let alone a mattress. On Bella's advice they had brought inside every last thing they possessed, right down to the horse's harness and bridle. The only things not inside were the horse and wagon. Even Peer, who was still being treated as something of a hero, had wheedled his way in.

'Keep a close watch on your belongings. If it can be carried it's likely to disappear,' Bella had warned. Bella's kettle apparently had, on their second day there. On her way to the river for water, stopping to heed an urgent call of nature, she had left it outside the privies which had been erected for common use on the edge of the township. When she had emerged a few minutes later it was to find that her kettle had vanished into thin air.

'Sam,' Alice said, keeping her voice low so as not to

wake the children. 'Do you know where the other mattress is?' She leaned over a tea chest in order to rummage through the pile of bedding behind it. Blankets, sheets, pillows, but no mattress.

'No,' he said, yawning. 'Find it tomorrow, Alice. We can manage for one night without it. The ground's not too stony. Come on, let's get to bed.'

An hour later she was dearly wishing she'd searched for longer. Sam was wrong. The ground was very stony, at least her thinly fleshed hips thought so. With a sigh she rolled onto her back again and stared into the darkness. She turned her head towards Sam, wondering if he was asleep. His breathing was deep and slow, which suggested that he was. Fred Wrigley was definitely asleep. She could not only hear his snores, she was quite sure she could feel the ground vibrating with them. God knows how Bella and her children slept through it all. Presumably they had grown accustomed to it and slept regardless. With another sigh she rolled onto her side again and closed her eyes. She liked the Wrigleys very much, but if this was a sample of how nights were going to be from now on, she was very glad it was only a month till they decamped.

Chapter 15

Fred and Bella Wrigley were of Cornish stock, as were a number of families in Black's Point. They had left England eight years ago, travelling as steerage passengers; the journey had not been without its heartache.

'We set off from Portsmouth with two children — Robert and Sarah,' Bella said quietly. 'But we lost Sarah on the voyage out. She took ill with a fever and died within a week. There was a doctor aboard but he could do nothing for her.' She lowered her eyes, frowning, as she proceeded to fold the blanket she was holding into a neat square. 'Life hasn't been easy at times.'

Bella Wrigley's life had certainly not been easy. Far from it. She'd been raised on a small farm, very happily by the sound of it, until her father had died and she'd been sent to live with an aunt, who had promptly found her a position at the local tin mine. She had been ten at the time. She had worked on the surface as a balmaiden, laboriously breaking up the ore with a spalling hammer before it went on to be crushed at the stamping mill. It was at the mine she had met Fred.

Bella shook her head, smiling. 'I can still remember the first time Fred spoke to me — I'd just turned eighteen. He'd just finished his shift and he came to stand beside me. "I was wondering if I might call on you, Sunday morning, and walk you to the chapel," he said. Six months later I was walking down the chapel aisle beside him.

'Then in seventy-four the mine closed and Fred was without work,' she said matter-of-factly. 'So we decided to take our chances in the colonies and booked a passage for New Zealand. We lived in Brunnerton till a couple of months ago. Fred worked in the coal mine there.' She shook her head ruefully. 'We'd be there still had Fred not involved himself in a fight. All he was trying to do was stop it. When word reached the foreman about what had happened he called Fred and the two men who had started the fight into his office and told them that they needn't trouble to come to work the next day, for he could do without brawlers. Fred tried to explain to him what his part in the fight had been but the foreman wouldn't pay him any heed. He just put the money that was owed Fred on the table and told him there was no more work for him and that was the finish of the matter.'

Alice raised her brows, absently pushing back a loose hairpin. 'That was very unfair of him.'

Bella nodded. 'Well, life is unfair at times and there's not much you can do about it.' She stared for a moment at the folded blanket in her hands then placed it in the tea chest to join the rest of the bedding. 'There's not much more to be done in here now. Would you care for a cup of tea?' she asked. After a combined two-hour effort, the interior of the tent was at last starting to take on some semblance of order.

'I would, thank you,' Alice said, smiling, and followed Bella across the narrow stretch of ground which separated the two tents. Charlotte, who was sitting on the grass beside Sidney, listening with great interest to his animated babble, gave her no more than a passing glance as she walked past her.

'Is there a bakery in Black's Point, Mrs Wrigley?' she enquired.

'There is,' Bella said, spooning tea into a white china teapot. 'In Franklyn Street.' The teaspoon hovered momentarily in midair as she glanced up at the roof of the tent. A few heavy drops of rain had begun to plop onto the canvas, and outside the sky was darkening ominously. 'Oh dear God, rain again.' Bella let out a weary sigh. 'I shall have Sidney under my feet all day.' She stooped to unhook the pot of water from over the fire where it had been simmering since breakfast time and carried it inside the tent. 'This blessed pan!' she complained. 'I nearly scald myself every time I try to pour from it. I wish I had my kettle back.'

'I wonder who stole it,' Alice said. She eyed the nearest houses dubiously. Most of the cottages looked very respectable, running in some cases to a small veranda and fenced garden. The single miners' huts by comparison were very modest affairs — small, single-roomed dwellings with no adornments to speak of at all. All single miners wanted was a dry place to eat and sleep.

Bella shrugged. 'I don't think it was stolen. I think it was taken as a prank. By one of the Molloy youngsters probably. They're an Irish family, with eleven children and another on the way. Those children are always up to mischief of one sort or another.'

'And where do the Molloys live?' Alice asked. Not close by, she hoped.

'They have a cottage on Cross Street. You can't see it from here,' Bella returned, passing her a cup and saucer. 'You'll find most families in the town are decent, hard-working folk, but there are one or two I'd sooner not have as neighbours.' She dipped her head in the direction of a fair-haired young woman who was making her way back from the river, a wicker basket of freshly washed laundry cradled in her arms. She was heavily pregnant and was waddling like a duck under the added weight of the wet washing. 'That's Lydia Donne. She's a nice woman. Oh, and *that*,' she said with a marked change in tone as she turned her head in the direction of another woman, 'is Lily Fielding.'

Lily Fielding looked to be in her late twenties or possibly a little older — it was hard to tell from a distance. She'd just emerged from her cottage and was standing on the veranda combing out a thick black mane of hair.

'She serves ale at an alehouse. One of the less reputable ones.' Bella cleared her throat expressively. Alice didn't need to ask what she meant — it was common knowledge that certain public houses in the district rented rooms to certain ladies who, for a price, would entertain gentlemen in them. 'And that's Zac, her husband, standing in the doorway,' Bella added. 'He works the night shift at the Wealth of Nations mine. He's not well liked in the town.' She gave a disapproving cluck with her tongue. 'Allowing his wife to do what she does . . . No decent man would think of letting his wife stand behind a public bar serving strong liquor, mixing with all manner of drunken riffraff. It's quite shameful!' Bella and Fred Wrigley, staunch Wesleyans, drank nothing stronger than tea.

Alice lifted her cup and took a few sips, but as she lowered it again her eyes drifted back to the Fieldings' cottage. Lily Fielding had gone indoors, but her husband was still there. He was leaning on the wooden rail of the veranda, blatantly staring across the street at them. Bella had noted the fact too and pointedly turned her back on him.

Zac Fielding made several trips onto his veranda during the course of the morning. By the fourth trip Alice was in no doubt as to the reason for his frequent excursions into the fresh air. He was watching her. It was a very unsettling feeling. Apart from interfering with her concentration, being watched was having a most unpleasant effect on her bowels. She put off the visit to the privy as long as she possibly could but in the end she could put it off no longer. Her reluctance centred around the fact that the line of privies were located directly behind the Fieldings' cottage.

You're being ridiculous, Alice, she told herself. The man isn't going to accost you in broad daylight. Why would he want to anyway? He was a married man and he must surely know that she was a married woman. Deciding she might as well kill two birds with one stone, she took the kettle with her to fill at the river on her way back.

The combined trip was not without its problems though. Once inside the privy she could see at once why Bella had left her kettle outside; there was simply nowhere to put one inside. There was barely room to turn in the narrow space between the door and the privy seat, let alone set a kettle down. It was also no place to be considering options at length. She leaned out of the doorway, took a quick look round and, satisfied that there were no children lurking nearby, deposited the kettle on the ground and shut the door. When she opened it two minutes later it was to find that her kettle had met the same fate as Bella's.

She glared up and down the street then marched around the back of the privies and glared into the trees, but whoever had taken it was long gone. It was obviously a game to see how many kettles they could collect.

She shook her skirt crossly and glared up the street again. She felt doubly angry because she had actually heard footsteps, but she had also heard the door of the next privy opening and closing and had naturally assumed the obvious. Unless of course . . .

She eyed the closed door of the next privy. And decided to wait.

She felt quite ridiculous hovering outside the privies but she was determined to wait for as long as it took. After two or three minutes though she had reached the end of her patience.

'I know you're in there!' she said, banging loudly on the door. 'Come on, out you come!'

A Molloy lad, I'll wager, she thought as the door swung open.

Her mouth dropped open like a trap door. 'I, I, I beg your pardon,' she stammered. 'Someone has taken my kettle and I, I thought they were hiding . . .' she swallowed and finished stupidly, 'in the privy.'

Zac Fielding's mouth curled into a lazy smile. As he stepped towards her she instinctively stepped back, maintaining the distance between them. He was a leanly built man, not much taller than her, with fine, even features. Quite a good-looking man in fact, and he knew it. He glanced upwards to the corrugated-iron roof of the privy where the kettle was now perched and his smile widened. 'I thought you would see it.'

Alice pursed her lips. Thought you would see it indeed! Whoever would think of looking on the roof of the privy for a kettle!

'Even if I had seen it, I can't reach it!' she said crisply. 'And why, might I ask, did you put it there?'

He tilted his head to one side and the pale blue eyes sparkled playfully. He was flirting with her, in broad daylight. 'I thought it would be safer. Why else would I put it there?'

She could think of several reasons, none of which she felt inclined to discuss.

'Get it down, please,' she said.

He stretched up to retrieve it. Alice held out her hand for it, anxious to be gone, but Zac Fielding was clearly in no hurry to let her go. 'Zac Fielding,' he said, introducing himself.

'Mrs Kenyon,' she returned, trusting he would note her married title.

'Arrived yesterday, did you?'

'Yes,' she said.

'Your husband working at one of the mines?'

She folded her arms impatiently across her chest. She didn't want to be rude but neither did she want to talk to him. Nor, for the sake of her own reputation, did she want to be seen talking to him. 'Yes,' she said shortly. She unfolded her arms and extended her hand again. 'Now, if you'd be good enough to hand me my kettle, Mr Fielding, I'd like to fill it before it starts to rain.'

'Allow me to fill it for you, Mrs Kenyon,' he offered pleasantly. 'It's the least I can do after causing you to think it had been stolen.' And with that he strode down to the river, her black kettle swinging jauntily from his right hand. She was in Bella's tent when he reappeared a few minutes later with the filled kettle. He deposited it on the ground just inside her own tent then turned, inclined in a mocking bow, and nonchalantly walked back towards his cottage. His wife was standing on the veranda, watching him, and looking not at all impressed by her husband's display of chivalry.

Bella, although too polite to enquire, was plainly

wondering what the devil was going on. Deciding it might pay to explain rather than let her draw her own conclusions, Alice told her what had happened.

At the finish Bella shook her head, frowning. 'I did warn you about him,' she said.

'You did,' Alice agreed. She eyed Bella dubiously, wondering how loose her tongue was. She didn't want the tale gossiped all round Black's Point on her first day in the town. 'Mrs Wrigley,' she said, 'you won't mention this to anybody, will you?'

'No, of course I won't,' Bella assured. 'And don't concern yourself too much about Zac Fielding. I doubt he'll trouble you again.' She seemed to hesitate then added softly, 'Watch out for his wife though. She's not a woman I'd recommend you to cross swords with. She broke a young woman's nose about twelve months ago, I've heard — a young Welsh woman. Apparently Zac Fielding took a liking to her and the girl was foolish enough to feel flattered by his attentions. Lily found out and hit her in the face with a log of wood. I don't know what the girl told her husband but they shifted out of the town soon afterwards. Anyway, stay well away from both Fieldings, that's my advice.'

Alice's first day at Black's Point had been a mixed one. Her blossoming friendship with Bella Wrigley had been somewhat blighted by the incident with the kettle. It was only a small incident, but she'd found her mind returning to it all day. A clean white tablecloth you don't notice, her mother had once told her, but a black spot on a clean cloth — that you can't keep your eyes from. It was very true. Deciding that Sam had quite enough black spots to worry about at the moment she resolved not to mention the incident to him and greeted him with a warm welcoming smile when he arrived back from the mine.

'You're soaked,' she said as he handed her his drenched jacket. Having drizzled on and off all day, it had unhelpfully started to pour an hour ago.

'I am,' he agreed from inside his shirt as he dragged it over his head. 'Pass me a towel, will you, Alice? I'm wet to the skin.'

'I've found your oiled cape. You can take that tomorrow,' she said, exchanging a wet shirt for a dry towel.

Shaking the excess water from his jacket she spread it beside the fire to dry.

'You've been busy,' Sam commented, peering out from the folds of the towel as he dried off his hair. 'The tent looks very tidy. You managed to get a fire organised too, I see.'

To be truthful she was quite proud of her efforts with the fire, or to be more precise with the canvas canopy which she had erected to shield it from the weather. Two corners of the canvas sheet were attached to the tent while the other two were secured to two stout metal staves which, with the help of a borrowed mallet, she'd eventually managed to drive into the stony ground. It was a fairly crude arrangement, but it did prevent the fire from being doused by rain. It also provided a very useful place to dry wet clothes. Not having a cooking tripod like Bella's, she'd pondered for quite some time on how she could suspend a pan above the fire. In the end she had lugged six suitably shaped rocks from the river, arranged them in a rough circle and built a fire in the centre. She had then balanced the pan on the stones a few inches above the fire. The cooking pot was far too close to the flames so she had to regularly remove it or risk burning the contents, but it would suffice in the short-term.

'You've done well,' Sam complimented, smiling. 'I'll organise some better cooking arrangements for you when I've eaten.' Taking a dry shirt from her proffered hand his gaze shifted sideways to Charlotte, who had nodded off on a pile of blankets, then to Michael.

'You survived your first day at your new school then?' he asked.

Michael looked up, mumbled 'yes', then lowered his eyes unenthusiastically to his school book again. He too had had something of a mixed day. He'd had an argument with Robert Wrigley as they walked back from school together. It had ended in a scuffle and the two of them had returned home with bloody noses.

'Mutton stew?' Sam asked, wrinkling his nose as he peered into the pot.

'It is,' she said, smiling. Moving him aside, she began to ladle it out.

Even in the short twenty-four hours they had been in the tent, the difficulties which the makeshift accommodation presented were already making themselves felt. The biggest problem was the size of the tent. There was barely room to move and even less once mattresses were laid on the floor. Privacy was the other major difficulty. It was not until late evening therefore, when Michael had finally condescended to fall asleep, that any proper conversation was possible between her and Sam.

'How does it seem here? Have you met any of the other families yet, Alice?' Sam asked quietly, coming up behind her as she cut sandwiches for his food tin for the next day.

'A few,' she said over her shoulder. 'I met Mrs Pringle and Mrs Donne and Mrs Bolitho. They seem very pleasant. Mrs Wrigley says there are one or two families best avoided though.'

'Oh? And which families might they be?' Sam asked with interest.

'The Molloys,' she said, reaching for the cheese. 'Bella Wrigley seems to think it was one of the Molloy children who took her kettle. And the Fieldings.'

Sam chuckled. 'I see. And what have the Fieldings done to be labelled *best avoided*?'

'Mr Fielding's wife serves ale in a public bar, in one of the less reputable hotels, by all accounts.'

'Which one?' he asked.

She shrugged and glanced back at him. 'I don't know. I didn't enquire.'

There was a brief silence then he said in quiet but nonetheless definite tones, 'Well, I don't want you associating with her, Alice. Stay away from her.'

'I fully intend to,' she said.

Her promise to Sam to stay clear of Lily Fielding was in hindsight as naive as promising not to get wet in the rain. You can try to avoid the raindrops as much as you wish, have every intention of staying perfectly dry, but you will nevertheless get wet — the reason being, the rain itself has not been party to the agreement. This unsettling truth was rammed home somewhat forcefully to Alice the very next morning.

With her husband breakfasted and gone to work and Michael and Charlotte still sound asleep, she decided to slip down to the river to fill the empty water ewer and a pail. She'd meant to refill them last night but had forgotten. Moving quietly around the tent she tossed a towel over her shoulder and pushed a cake of soap into her pocket — there was no point in carrying water back to the tent to wash her face with, when she could just as easily wash in the river. It wasn't much past dawn but already she could hear the grind of heavy machinery and the rhythmic thump of the cast-iron stampers crushing and crunching up quartz at the Wealth of Nations and Keep it Dark batteries, a quarter of a mile away. She was kneeling on the riverbank sluicing her face with the icy cold water when another crunching sound, much closer, reached her ears. Footsteps, walking across the pebbles. She didn't even look up. She simply assumed that it was another woman come to wash, like herself. She was partly right. It was a woman. But she hadn't come to wash — not herself at any rate.

Since Alice was already leaning well over the bank, it didn't take much of a shove on her backside to achieve the desired effect. She tumbled headfirst into the water.

Instincts are mostly good, designed to protect and preserve the body from injury, but there are occasions when instincts have precisely the opposite effect. Like her instinctive scream which ended up as an underwater gurgle, and her instinctive reaction to suck some air into her lungs long before air was actually available. Hence she came up not only soaked from head to foot but coughing her lungs out. With hair and water streaming over her face, it took her a few seconds to recognise the owner of the boot that had shoved her in.

Standing high and dry on the bank, Lily Fielding hooked her hands challengingly on her hips. 'Stay away from my husband!' she warned.

'I have no intention of going anywhere near your husband!' Alice retorted, struggling angrily to her feet. Leather-soled boots were not designed for standing on slippery, round wet pebbles though, and she had no sooner straightened than she lost her footing and landed with a splash in the river again.

'D'you think I haven't seen the way he looks at you?' Lily tilted her head to the side and raked her eyes over Alice's dripping face. 'I'm warning you — stay away from him or next time it will be blood running down your face, not water!' The warning issued, she turned on her heel, hitched up her skirts and strode back towards her house.

Alice sat watching her in a state of sheer incredulity. Eventually, though, incredulity gave way to reality, and the reality was she was sitting waist-deep in icy water, freezing to death. Pushing herself to her feet she waded to the bank, dragging her sodden skirts along behind her, then squelched up the slope towards the tent, very thankful that there was no one around to witness her drenched state. God knows what she would have said if she'd met someone — that she'd fallen into the river, she supposed — which would have been almost as humiliating as the truth.

Chapter 16

A dramatic transformation occurred at Black's Point on Sunday. It was suddenly full of men. It was the first time Alice had seen the full male component of the township. The other thing she was seeing for the first time since their arrival a week ago was the sun. They had risen to a damp, murky dawn, but a strong easterly had sprung up, chasing the grey clouds over the tops of the hills and gradually clearing the sky. It was now a bright blue dotted with billowy white clouds. The thickly treed hillsides surrounding the town were glistening like emeralds in the sunlight. Considering the time of year there was still a reasonable amount of heat in the sun, enough to make steam rise from the sodden ground. Ground steam apart, the township was steaming in all manner of places today as the single miners took the opportunity to wash their dirty clothes and spread them out to dry, and mothers aired damp bedding. A number of men were mending roofs, nailing down loose shingles and corrugated iron in preparation for the onset of winter, while others, including Sam, were energetically chopping firewood for the coming week. Quite a few families, the Wrigleys among them, had gone to the chapel to attend Sunday worship. The Kenyon family would not be worshipping today though. Once the firewood supply had been replenished Sam was planning on spending the rest of the day fashioning new shafts for the heads of his salvaged cobbling hammers.

Lydia Donne's husband was also making good use of the fine weather; he'd been up since dawn hammering pegs into the ground and crawling about on his hands and knees with lengths of string, as the preliminaries to building a house — a very necessary procedure, apparently, if a house was to finish up with square true corners. It was to be a modest dwelling, a simple rectangular shape divided into two rooms. Like wasps descending on a pot of jam, it didn't take long for a group of men to gather around to offer the inevitable helpful advice.

'You'll need to dig deeper holes for your supporting timbers, Matt.' The stoutly built adviser shook his head, making the tobacco pipe hanging from the corner of his mouth waggle comically beneath his droopy moustache. 'You'll rue it if you don't. First strong gale and your cottage will tip over onto its side.'

Matt Donne leaned on his spade and wiped his brow. He was sweating profusely in the warm sun. 'If you think they should be deeper, Ben, then you're welcome to go and fetch your spade and dig them deeper. I'm digging them no deeper though.'

'Aye, they are a bit shallow, Matt,' agreed a freckle-faced ginger-haired man. 'But if you pack pebbles around your timbers to halfway then pack earth on top of them they'll probably suffice at that depth.'

'No, no, no. You can't do better than plain soil. Tamp it down with an iron bar. Pebbles will shift but packed earth won't,' contradicted the first man.

A lengthy debate on the merits of pebbles and packed earth ensued. Alice listened, intrigued, as she brushed Charlotte's hair. They were still debating half an hour later when Sam walked into the tent with an armful of kindling. Judging from the wry smile on his face he too had been listening to the continuing conversation about Matt Donne's house foundations.

'Have you been listening to them?' he asked.

'I have,' Alice said, returning his grin. 'And what's your opinion? Earth or pebbles?'

He laughed. 'My opinion is that Matt should tell them all to go home and let him get on with his building. If he doesn't, all he'll have to show for his day's work come nightfall are four holes.'

By nightfall Matt had rather more than four holes to show for his labours, but probably considerably less than he would have liked. Less than Lydia would have liked too. She was due to give birth to their first child in six weeks and was no doubt hoping to be delivered of it in their own cottage rather than in the small hut they were presently renting.

Sam had had quite a productive day though. Four newly shafted hammers lay on the table. Alice picked one up, turning it over in her hand. He had gone to some pains to shape the handle to fit comfortably in his hand, sanding down the wood to a silky smooth finish. She tilted it to examine the top where he had hammered in the wedge of wood to splay the shaft and prevent the hammer head from flying off. It was so neatly finished it was hard to see where the wedge was.

Replacing it quietly on the table, she glanced at the two sleeping children then went outside to join Sam by the fire. He was crouched beside it, his palms spread above the dying embers.

'What else will you need in order to start repairing boots again?' she asked.

He looked up and smiled crookedly. 'Leather.'

She gave a soft laugh. 'I meant in the way of tools.'

'Paring knives, pincers . . .' He shrugged, looking down at the flames again. 'I'll write a note for you to give to the ironmonger next time you're in Reefton. He'll have to send to Christchurch for some of the tools I need. It will be a week or two before I can offer my boot-repairing services again. I intend to make Joel a pair of good stout boots too, to repay him for all his help on the night of the fire.'

Turning his hands palm upwards he rubbed the callouses at the base of each finger with his thumbs, as if assessing them. Unused to wielding a shovel and pick for long periods, his hands were looking considerably worse for wear after eight days down the mine. 'Has Michael finally gone to sleep?' he asked, glancing back into the tent.

She nodded and kneeled down beside him. Used to sleeping in a bedroom behind a closed door, Michael wasn't finding it easy to sleep in a tent where there were people moving about, however quietly.

'Did you happen to notice Mrs Pringle's woollen shawl when she walked past on her way to the chapel this morning?' she asked conversationally. 'She spins her own wool and dyes it with lichen and gets the most beautiful shades — bright yellows and golds. She uses eucalyptus bark too and gets some very fine oranges and browns. I was thinking I might try my hand at dyeing Charlotte's white dress. A gold colour would look very well against her dark hair.'

She tilted her head to the side waiting for a response, a grunt at least, but Sam was staring into the fire, glassy-eyed, lost in thought. She poked his arm. 'Sam, did you hear what I said?'

Starting, he glanced up. 'Sorry,' he mumbled. 'What were you saying?'

'I was telling you about Mrs Pringle and her dyeing,' she repeated.

He stared at her, looking unaccountably shocked. 'But I saw her only this morning. It must have been very sudden.'

She stared back at him. 'Sudden? What was sudden?'

'Her death.'

'Death?' she said, standing up. 'Sam, whatever are you talking about?'

'You said she'd died,' he said impatiently.

She rolled her eyes as the penny suddenly dropped. 'I said she'd been dyeing wool!'

There was a small silence. 'Oh,' he murmured. He rubbed the back of his neck and smiled sheepishly.

'Is something troubling you?' she asked quietly.

He shook his head and reached for her hand as he pushed himself to his feet. 'No. I'm just tired, Alice. Come on, let's get to bed. It's getting late.'

They undressed in silence. With fewer clothes to shed, Sam was as usual first in bed. Shivering in the chilly air, Alice slipped beneath the blankets next to him. Sam might not feel inclined to discuss his own worries, but something was worrying her too and she did want to discuss it.

'Sam . . . the fire . . . do you blame me for it?' she asked quietly.

'Blame you?' he said in surprise. 'Why should I blame you for it?'

'Because I gave that medicine to that baby, and that was the start of all this trouble.'

'No, Alice, I don't blame you,' he said definitely. 'And as I said to you before, there's absolutely no proof that it was Hone's wife who started the fire.'

She sighed, relieved, feeling a load slip from her mind. She wished now that she'd voiced her worry days ago. She wished Sam would voice his worries too, instead of just staring into the fire, tumbling them around in his head. Her father had done the same — kept his problems to himself. Perhaps all men did. Not that she really needed Sam to voice his present worries — she knew very well what was bothering him. Their reduced circumstances. Sam was quite a proud man. A fortnight ago he had owned a good home and a good business, then in a single night years of hard work had suddenly been reduced to char. He didn't find it easy to live in a tent, she could see that, no matter how expedient or short-term it was. He was no doubt worrying whether a cottage would come vacant before the winter set in too. It was enough to make any man stare distractedly into the fire and not hear his wife talking to him.

She leaned her forehead against his, wanting to comfort him, to lift his worry from him somehow, wanting him to make love to her if she was honest. Something she had never expected to *want* from any man. But after the shock of the fire and with the upheaval of moving to a new town, she had needed Sam very badly during the last week and he had needed her, and joining in the act of love had seemed the most natural way of expressing their mutual need of each other, of comforting one another. Not for the first time Reverend Sedgwick's words drifted back into her mind . . . *love and need are not so great a distance apart as you may think* . . . What kind of comfort the act of love offered to Sam it was hard to say and it wasn't the sort of thing that she felt inclined to raise as a point of casual discussion. For her though, it was the comfort of being held in strong arms which she could rely upon to protect her, of feeling the warm solid weight of Sam's body resting on hers, the comfort of, for a few brief moments, joining, being completely one with another human being, being not alone.

'Sam,' she whispered softly, and leaned in to kiss him.

His hand slid around her waist, pulling her closer, the other cupping the back of her head as he returned her kiss, his worries for the moment forgotten.

Chapter 17

'I swear there are few things worse than a child emptying its bowels everywhere in the middle of the night!' Bella wrinkled her nose in disgust as she scooped up the pile of soiled linen and tossed it outside. 'Pray God it doesn't rain today!'

'Do all three of them have loose bowels now?' Alice cast her eye over the three pale faces huddled around Bella's fire.

Bella nodded wearily. 'Robert started during the night. How are your two?'

'Much the same,' she said in resigned tones. She had a similar pile of stained nightwear, napkins and blankets awaiting her attention. Diarrhoea had spread through Black's Point like an ill wind over the last three days, mostly affecting the children, but a number of adults were also laid low with it. The privies had been in heavy demand.

With a sigh Bella reached for her apron. 'Fred was complaining of griping pains in his belly this morning. I hope it's just wind and not more of this.' She shook her head and gave another weary sigh as her gaze settled on an empty bottle on the table. 'I've no more Dalby's Carminative left,' she said ruefully. 'And it's the best remedy I know for diarrhoea. I wish there was a chemist in Black's Point. It's such a nuisance having to walk all the way into Reefton when you're in need of a remedy.'

'If you'll look after Charlotte and Michael I'll be glad to fetch you some,' Alice volunteered. 'I'd better do some washing first though.'

'I've a bit of washing to do myself,' Bella said, unenthusiastically eyeing the waiting pile.

Well before Alice reached Reefton she could smell the coal and wood smoke drifting from the chimneys of its shivering inhabitants. Today was no day for a feeble-flamed fire. It was fine but bitterly cold. Where the road nestled in deep shadow all day the ground was white with frost and frozen pearls dripped from the overhanging branches of the trees. She pulled her woollen shawl more tightly across her chest and lengthened her stride. Soap, candles, meat, bread, baking soda, Dalby's Carminative . . . she mentally ran through her shopping list.

She made for Forsyth & Masters, the ironmongers, first. Edging past the large cast-iron mangle in the doorway, she made her way into the interior of the shop, ducking her head to avoid dangling oil lamps, tin baths, scrubbing boards and numerous other household items for which there was no space on the floor. Mr Fitzgerald, the proprietor, would be sorely disappointed to find that all she required was two bars of soap and a dozen candles. He'd been pleased to take the order for Sam's tools, and each time she set foot in his shop he looked as if he held high expectations of selling her half of his stock of pots and pans.

The soap and candles bought, she continued on to Dick's butchery, where George Withers was employed. Halting outside, she tilted her head back to scan the line of freshly plucked hens strung up by their feet outside the shop. Their heads dangled obscenely from limp necks, pink-rimmed eyes gazing across the street in a blinkless surprised stare. She reached up and gave the white pimply flesh of the nearest one a sound poke. An old bird. It would be all right for boiling though. She ducked beneath it and perused the goods displayed in the window. An impressive display it was too. Beef roasts, legs of lamb, chops, liver, kidneys, hearts, oxtails, long chains of plump pink sausages . . . The beef looked delicious — an opinion which a number of fat black flies appeared to share. They were welcome to it. At eight pence a pound it was well outside Alice's purse. It was a choice today between the mutton flaps, the cheapest thing in the window, or a boiling fowl. She stepped back again and poked a few more birds, decided on the mutton flaps and went into the shop.

'Mrs Kenyon, good morning to you!' George exclaimed, glancing up from his chopping bench. The cleaver landed with a woody thud, narrowly missing his fingers as he chopped up some bacon ribs. He appeared to be managing the shop on his own this morning. 'Well now, Ellen and I were only last night talking about you,' he commented cheerily. Setting down the cleaver, he wiped his hands on his apron. 'We were wondering how you're faring at Black's Point.'

'I'm in very good health, thank you,' Alice replied, smiling. 'But Charlotte and Michael are not very well at present.' She omitted to add the symptoms. From her limited experience of men, they usually preferred not to know about loose bowels and other messy ailments which were wont to afflict children.

George nodded sympathetically. 'And how is Sam faring at the Energetic?'

'Well, he doesn't complain,' she said. 'But I think

he'll be glad to get back to his bootmaking as soon as he can. When his new tools arrive from Christchurch he's planning on mending shoes in the evenings.'

'Still no more clues as to how the fire began?'

She shook her head. Privately she believed Hone's wife was responsible. But as Sam had said, without proof . . .

'Fires don't leave much in the way of clues,' she said.

'No. That's very true,' George agreed. 'The Friars never did find out how the fire in their barn started. Anyway,' he said, smiling cheerfully again, 'how can I be of service to you this morning?'

'Could I have two pounds of those, please.' She pointed to the tray of mutton flaps in the window.

'Indeed you can,' George said. 'Would you like a few bones to boil up for broth as well? I can toss some in for no extra charge if you can use them. We've a surfeit of them at present.'

'I will have some, thank you,' she said gratefully.

A handful of pink mutton flaps landed with a soft thwap on the scales. George waited till the scale had steadied, cut off a small strip to adjust the weight, then tossed them onto a sheet of paper and deftly rolled them up. Disappearing into the back room, he reappeared a minute later with a lumpy parcel of bones.

'Here you are. That will be ten pence, thank you, Mrs Kenyon.'

Alice rummaged in her purse for some small coins and dropped them on the counter.

'Is Ellen keeping well?' she asked as George passed her the two parcels.

'She's in fine fettle!' he said proudly. 'A bit nauseous first thing in the morning, but other than that she's been keeping very well.'

As the shop bell tinkled, George's eyes flicked over her shoulder and his mouth stretched into a bright cheery smile. 'Good morning to you, Mrs Farmer. And how are you this fine day?'

Leaving George to attend to his new customer, Alice made her way along the street to Cavill's bakery, her last port of call. To add to Black's Point's woes, there wasn't a single loaf of bread to be had there today, the town's two bakers being amongst the ranks of those laid low by diarrhoea.

With a cake of soap in each pocket, the mutton, bones, baking soda and Dalby's Carminative in one basket, the candles and two large loaves of bread in a second, and two more loaves slotted under her arms, Alice set off back towards Black's Point. Within half a mile her arms were aching with a vengeance. It wasn't so much the weight in the baskets making them ache, it was the angle she was trying to keep her arms at in order to avoid crushing the loaves she'd wedged under them. She struggled on for a further half mile then stopped to give her arms a rest. Depositing the two baskets on the road, she dropped the two other loaves on top of them then stretched and twisted her arms, listening to the familiar sound of the Inangahua rushing along, hidden from view by dense punga ferns. Somewhere to her left the throaty trill of a pigeon sounded, followed by the noisy flap of wings high in the trees above. As the flapping died away another sound reached her ears. A whistled tune. Moments later, rounding the bend in the road, the whistler stepped into view. The whistling came to an abrupt halt as the pursed mouth stretched into a wide smile and with long cocky strides Zac Fielding approached her.

'Good morning to you, Mrs Kenyon.' Grinning, he

inclined in a low, mocking bow.

'Good morning, Mr Fielding,' she returned coolly.

'You're weighted down, I see.' One eyebrow lifted in amusement as he scanned her purchases. 'Is your husband quite partial to bread?'

'Not particularly. Some is for Mrs Wrigley,' she replied coolly.

'Ah.'

What the 'ah' meant she had no idea and she didn't intend to stay and enquire. She picked up the two loaves, wedged them under her arms again, then stooped to retrieve the baskets.

'Allow me to be of assistance.' His hand brushed lightly against hers as he picked up the nearer basket.

'Thank you, but I can manage quite well on my own,' she said firmly.

'Oh, but your good deed deserves some reward, Mrs Kenyon. Since you've generously undertaken to fetch some provisions for Mrs Wrigley it would be most unneighbourly of me not to offer my help, seeing you laden down so. Allow me to assist you, at least part of the way.' The basket remained firmly in his hand.

'Mr Fielding, you're travelling in the opposite direction from me,' she pointed out with some annoyance. 'And as I said before I really don't need your help, thank you. So if you'd be good enough to hand me my basket . . .' She held out her hand for it. No basket was forthcoming though, just a lazy and very irritating smile. He was playing games again and taking great amusement in it. Zac Fielding wouldn't hurt her or force his attentions on her, she knew that as surely as she'd known the seaman in Akaroa would rape her, and known the man on the banks of the Inangahua intended to do more than just kiss her. It wasn't that she didn't feel safe with him, she just didn't want to walk with him, and she certainly didn't want to be *seen* walking with him. She pressed her lips together crossly and reached out to take the basket from him; it swayed back and forth as she gave it several unsuccessful tugs. She sucked in a deep breath, heaved, and landed with a jarring thud on the ground, surrounded by loaves, candles and everything else that had spilled out of the two baskets.

Zac shook his head, tutting.

Alice glared up at him. The timing with which he had released the basket had been quite deliberate — she had no doubt of that. And now, to add insult to injury, he was reaching for her hands to assist her to her feet. Be damned if he would! She snatched hold of a candle and pointed it threateningly at his left nostril. 'Don't you dare touch me!' she warned loudly.

It was at this point that Meg Pringle rounded the bend in the track.

Only one thing spreads faster than a dry grass fire fanned by a strong nor'wester — gossip. And gossip at Black's Point was by no means restricted to the female component of the tightly knit mining community.

'I hear your wife found herself in worrying circumstances yesterday morning, Sam,' Edwin Bray commented as he reached up to stick a fresh candle on the spider — a metal spike set into the tunnel wall, so named for its spidery shape.

Halting his shovelling, Sam lifted his arm to wipe the sweat from his forehead, watching Bray's huge black shadow leap and quiver as he pressed the candle home on the spike. 'I'm not sure that I know what you're talking about, Edwin,' he said. The 'worrying circumstances' evidently hadn't been sufficiently worrying for Alice to mention them to him. She had obviously mentioned something to somebody though — Edwin's wife, Mary, seemingly, who had in turn mentioned it to Edwin. He glanced across at Fred, who had also stopped shovelling and was waiting, judging by the look on his face, to hear exactly what worrying circumstances Alice had found herself in. Bray might have chosen a more private time to talk to him about it, Sam thought, feeling mildly annoyed. It would have been helpful if Alice had thought to mention it to him too.

Fred lifted his shoulder half-apologetically as Sam's eyes met his. 'We all know what happened. You know how these things get around, Sam.'

Sam's gaze flicked from Fred back to Bray then across to Jack Stone and Archie Meadows, who were also leaning expectantly on their shovels. There had been an odd sort of atmosphere in the mine all morning — muttered conversations, peculiar smiles and looks — now he knew why. So, they all knew what had happened, did they? All save *him*. But what the hell was it they all knew? Scraping his shovel across the rocky floor of the tunnel Sam slowly straightened. Somehow he had to find out the gist of whatever Alice had become involved in, without making it obvious that he didn't know a bloody thing about it. 'What have you heard?' he asked evenly. 'What's the tale that's going round?'

Bray shrugged. 'That Fielding waylaid your wife on her way back from Reefton yesterday morning. The tale we've heard is that she was sprawled on the ground with her groceries spread all around her, trying to fend him off with a candle.'

'It was damned fortunate Meg Pringle happened by when she did,' Fred said, shaking his head.

Sam stared wide-eyed, while his brain tried to do

the impossible — link the distraught, dishevelled woman described in the last three sentences with the woman he had returned home to last night. Alice hadn't looked even remotely distraught or dishevelled — she had served him his dinner as usual, then had her hands full with Charlotte for most of the evening, dealing with the child's loose stools. Something had plainly befallen her though, even allowing for the inevitable exaggerations as the tale had passed from lip to lip. Why had Alice not told him about it!

'Aye, and it's not the first time Fielding has made a play for another man's wife,' Archie Meadows' soft Scottish tones came from the shadows. 'He seduced a young Welsh woman twelve months ago.'

'We're wondering what it was all about,' Jack Stone commented quizzically. An expectant silence settled, broken only by the drip and plop of water.

'I don't know what it was about,' Sam said thickly, and entirely truthfully. 'I've not heard Fielding's version of what happened. I shall be paying him a visit later in the day.' He turned his head to look down the tunnel as the distant hollow rumble and grind of wheels announced the approach of a fresh train of empty wagons.

'What did your wife have to say about it?' Stone probed.

'What she said was between her and me,' Sam returned. He glanced around the miners, meeting their eyes one by one, then gave a curt nod. 'I thank you for your concern about her. She wasn't harmed though. And as for Fielding . . .' He swung up his shovel, catching the shaft deftly in his left hand. 'I shall be having a few words with him.' Turning back towards the blasted rock he resumed shovelling. Thrust, scrape, heave, toss. Thrust, scrape, heave, toss. Thrust, scrape, heave, toss

... Shovelful after shovelful of jagged white quartz rocks landed in the waiting wagons as the miners resumed their work, the air ringing with the scrape and clang of their spades, while Sam's head rang with questions. Why had Alice not told him? She'd been assaulted, or at the very least threatened by Fielding, yet she hadn't said a word to him about it! Was she trying to keep it a secret, hoping that he wouldn't find out? But if so, why? Unless she was trying to protect Fielding, but God knows why she would want to do that. Grunting with effort, he tossed another heavy shovelful of quartz into the wagon. '*He seduced a young Welsh woman twelve months ago . . .*' Archie Meadows' words clamoured in his ears like fire bells. He and Alice hadn't married for love, but things were better between them now. He was growing quite fond of her — he had *thought* she was growing quite fond of him. Fielding was a handsome-looking man though, a charmer too, moreover he worked the night shift at the Wealth of Nations mine — by day he was free to do whatever took his fancy. Had Alice taken his fancy? She was the sort of woman it was hard not to notice with her bright hair. He shook his head, trying to dislodge the thought, but it was firmly stuck there, like a fly caught in a web; it was still stuck there when the call sounded, echoing down the tunnel, announcing that the cage had arrived to take the miners to the surface to enjoy a brief spell in the fresh air while they ate their midday meal.

Leaning his shovel against the wall, Sam followed the other four miners towards the entrance of the tunnel or drive, as the miners called it, listening to the splash of his boots in the shallow puddles which collected on the uneven floor. The drive was purposely constructed on a slight incline to facilitate drainage but it didn't stop the formation of murky little lakes. The roof dripped and water perpetually trickled down cracks and crevices in the walls, writhing like silver worms in the light of the candles, and the air smelled damp and fusty.

Once in the cage, Sam took a firm grasp of the metal safety bar. He counted, as he always counted, the openings to the higher, older drives as the cage made its swaying ascent up the shaft. Drive six, drive five, drive four . . . and finally the topmost drive on level one. Then with a sudden jarring lurch the cage came to a halt and the powerful winding wheel by which it was raised and lowered slowed to a stop. He waited till the other men stepped out of the cage then followed them at a short distance, wondering if he could find some excuse to eat his food alone today. Any thoughts of solitude quickly evaporated, however, as Fred looked back over his shoulder then halted and waited for him.

'Edwin had no call to raise the business of Fielding and your wife the way he did, but you know how he is. Can't resist a bit of gossip,' Fred said in critical tones, his deep voice almost drowned out as they walked past the open door of the engine room.

Thrusting his hands in his pockets, Sam gave a stiff shrug. 'It makes no odds. It seems the business is widely known anyway so he wasn't giving any secrets away.' Except to *him*.

'Nevertheless, there are times and places for saying things and there are times and places for keeping silent,' Fred returned tersely. 'And to my mind, a man's marriage is his own affair and no one else's.'

'Where did the tale start?' Sam glanced across at him, frowning. 'Meg Pringle?'

Fred nodded. 'It was her husband who told Edwin.' He lifted his hand to scratch his bald head, frowning.

'How is it you decided to wait till tonight to have words with Fielding, Sam?'

It was a good question and one to which, for the moment, Sam had no answer. He cleared his throat, then cleared it a second time. 'He was out last night,' he said at length.

Fred made a sharp noise in his throat. 'He'd be out drinking, I expect.' The consumption of strong liquor in Fred Wrigley's eyes, sober Wesleyan that he was, ranked fairly high on the list of deadly sins.

'What I have to say to him will save till tonight,' Sam said thickly.

Fred made another sharp noise, through his nose this time. 'I wonder what sort of an explanation he'll furnish you with. Fielding has a well-oiled tongue. He'll not be short of plausible explanations, I'll wager. Not that I'd be listening to his explanations if it was Bella he'd tried to molest. I'd not be wasting much time on questions either. I'd be letting my fists do the talking.'

Sam drew in a deep breath. He felt much the same himself. He intended, however, to give Fielding the chance to explain himself, and if his explanation didn't satisfy him then he might well take his fists to him. First though, he intended to take his wife somewhere very private and find out why the hell she hadn't told him all this last night!

He ate his sandwiches largely in silence, head bowed over his food tin, trying to force the bread down his throat with mouthfuls of hot tea, while the other miners discussed the likely gold yield for the month, the boiler — which had been overheating a bit of late — and the abysmal weather. It was raining heavily again.

It was a long, trying afternoon; the roof of the tunnel was leaking like a sieve and Sam had a pounding headache. But eventually the call came, signalling the end of the shift. He boarded the cage, counted the drives as it made its swaying ascent past the dark openings in the shaft, then stiffly stepped out on the surface. For once he didn't wait for Fred, merely strode over to the hut where he'd left his jacket and food tin, then set off down the track at a fast stride, too wrapped in his thoughts to notice that it had stopped raining and a weak sun was shining.

'I want to speak to you in private,' Sam said sharply. Taking hold of Alice's arm, he towed her towards the flap of the tent.

'What's the matter?' she asked, staring at him in astonishment as he marched her outside.

'I said I wish to speak to you in private,' he reiterated tersely.

She threw a quick reassuring smile at Michael who, was watching them with wide, curious eyes, then fell into step beside Sam. He looked very cross and she had an uncomfortable suspicion as to what might be at the root of it. Yesterday's incident with Zac Fielding. She had been wondering all day whether she ought to have told Sam about it, but he had arrived home late last night, wet to the skin and exhausted, and it had been such a small incident — a silly tussle with a basket, nothing had really happened — so rather than worry him unnecessarily she'd decided not to mention it. Someone else had mentioned it though, it seemed.

With long strides, he headed towards the river. He continued for some distance along the pebbly banks until they were out of both sight and hearing of the town, careless of the fact that they had left two children in the tent, unattended. Alice braced herself, anticipating loud reproaches. Pulling her round to face him, he took a firm grip on her arms and looked her sternly in the face. 'I've been informed that Zac Fielding tried to molest you yesterday. Is it true?'

'Molest me!' she echoed in astonishment. 'If he'd tried to molest me, do you not think I would have mentioned it?'

Sam's expression remained grim, but the pressure of his fingers eased off slightly. 'Well, he tried something. You were on the ground, I hear, trying to fend him off with a candle!'

She rolled her eyes — how a story could grow in twenty-four hours! — and decided it might be prudent to make a clean breast of everything, including the business of the kettle and her wet encounter with Lily Fielding. So far as she knew no one had witnessed the latter two incidents, but she couldn't be absolutely sure. Better to tell Sam all now, accurately, than risk his being furnished with another distorted account.

'. . . and as I said before, they weren't *large* incidents, Sam. I didn't mention them to you because I thought you had enough to worry about,' she concluded.

Sam stared at her for several seconds in silence then said loudly, 'God Almighty, Alice — you draw trouble like a magnet!'

Her lips parted in shock then snapped shut again. She wrenched free from his grip, glaring at him. 'You do blame me, don't you — for the fire! I knew you did! And what happened to me in Akaroa — do you think that was my fault too? You do, don't you! You think I somehow drew that, that animal to me!'

'I blame you for neither,' he returned sharply. 'But I do know that trouble seems to follow you around. I know also that it is very trying to be informed by fellow miners that Zac Fielding attempted to molest my wife the previous day, when my wife had made no mention of it to me! Nor,' he added in rising tones, 'did I find it very enjoyable having to work alongside them for the rest of the day, wondering why you had kept it from me. Nor,' he added still more loudly, 'did I particularly enjoy hearing the account of how Zac Fielding seduced another young wife twelve months ago!'

'Who told you?' she asked in some irritation.

'Who told me?' he thundered. 'Who told me is of no consequence! What is of consequence is that every damned man in Black's Point appears to know of yesterday's happenings and I did not!'

'All right, I'm sorry!' she said loudly. 'I should have told you and I'm sorry that I didn't, but it wasn't the grave incident it has been made out to be. He didn't try to molest me! He was merely—'

'Trying to seduce you!'

'No! I told you — he offered to carry the basket. I refused. There was a tussle and I fell over. He wasn't trying to seduce me. He was just toying with me . . . trifling, flirting,' she said, vainly trying to find words to bring the nature of the incident into a less damning, less dangerous framework.

'Like he was flirting with you over the business of the kettle! Like he was flirting with that woman twelve months ago. Well, he won't flirt with you again, I can promise you that!'

'Sam! Sam!' She stared after him as he strode away into the darkness. She shouted his name once more, with no response, and ran after him.

By the time she reached the edge of the township he was already hammering on Zac Fielding's door, very loudly, careless of who heard him. She paused to catch her breath, watching curtains pull slyly aside in neighbouring cottages. There was more to this than redeeming *her* honour — Sam Kenyon was out to redeem his own, and he intended to redeem it publicly.

'All right, all right, you don't need to hammer the door down. I'm coming,' came Fielding's voice from within. Eventually he appeared in his stockinged feet, still doing up the buttons of his trousers. Working on the midnight shift, this was the time when he normally slept.

'Step outside, Fielding,' Sam ordered curtly.

Fielding stood staring at him; he looked annoyed and not fully awake. He ran a hand through his hair, scowling. 'Why?'

'Step outside,' Sam repeated.

Judging by the subtle changes occurring in Fielding's face he'd now realised who his visitor was and, perhaps sensing trouble, took a step back.

Not prepared to issue the invitation a third time, Sam leaned into the doorway, grabbed hold of his shirt and hauled him outside. 'We've some business to settle, Fielding,' he gritted, still maintaining a tight hold on the fabric. 'We've not met, so I'll introduce myself. I'm Sam Kenyon. You've already made the acquaintance of my wife, I believe — on one or two occasions, I'm given to understand, and not by invitation.' With a sudden hard thrust, Sam shoved him away.

Fielding glanced up the street as the door of a neighbour's house opened and a curious head appeared, then he turned back to Sam and stepped angrily forward. He was a much lighter build than Sam and shorter by a good two inches, but he didn't seem to be afraid of him. 'No, we've not met,' he said shortly. 'And I can't say that I'm sorry if this is a sample of your manners.

Now, what is it you want? Say what you have to say, then perhaps I can get back to my bed.'

'It's about my wife,' Sam said angrily. 'You've been pressing your attentions on her. Do you deny that you waylaid her yesterday on her way back from Reefton?'

'Waylaid her?' Fielding tossed back his head and gave a rather inopportune laugh. 'I happened across her! I was on my way to Reefton and she was walking back to Black's Point.'

'That's not the way I heard it from my wife,' Sam returned. 'She says you pressed your attentions on her, demanding to accompany her along the road when she had no wish to walk with you, and that you refused to return her basket so that she could continue on her way on her own.'

'Pressed my attentions on her?' Fielding lifted his chin indignantly. 'Your wife tripped and dropped her baskets, and when I tried to help her up she became unaccountably agitated.'

'You caused my wife considerable distress yesterday,' Sam returned in ominously soft tones, 'and you've caused me considerable offence. Nor do I like your implication that my wife is lying. So, put your fists up and we'll settle the matter.'

Fielding went perfectly still, frozen in both expression and stance. Then he did what was probably the worst thing he could have done, given Sam's mood. He laughed again. 'Damned if I will,' he said. He glanced up the street at his neighbour and shouted, 'Can you hear this? This madman wants me to engage in a street brawl with him.' He turned back to Sam, his arms firmly by his sides. 'Damned if I will!' he said again.

'All right,' Sam gritted. 'You had your chance.' His right fist landed with a thud in Zac's belly. Zac doubled over, coughing violently, clutching his stomach with both hands. It hadn't been a hard blow, just hard enough to signal that the fight had officially begun.

Stepping back, Sam waited until Fielding had recovered sufficient wind to straighten, then balled his hands into fists again. 'No. Wait, wait,' Fielding rasped, still struggling to regain his breath. He put up his left hand, palm outstretched, as Sam advanced on him, but as Sam drew back his arm to administer the next blow, Fielding exploded into life. What happened next Alice couldn't quite see. There was a brief noisy scuffle as the two men grappled with each other, moving sideways like locked crabs, then suddenly Sam broke free and swung his fist solidly at Zac's face. Under the impact of the blow Fielding lurched back, his right leg seemed to crumple under him and he keeled over backwards. There was a dull thud as the back of his head hit the wooden corner-post of the cottage. His eyes stared glassily out of their orbs as he slithered slowly down to the ground, rolled upwards in their sockets till only the whites showed, then he slumped sideways, limp as a rag doll. Rubbing the knuckles of his left fist, Sam walked over and crouched down beside him. Blood was oozing out of Fielding's nose, dripping off his cheek onto the grass, and trickling out of the corner of his mouth.

'I'll thank you to stay away from my property in future, Fielding,' Sam said, loudly enough to ensure that his voice carried to the onlookers. His words were purely for their benefit. Fielding was out cold — whether from the blow Sam had landed him or from the blow he'd suffered when he had crashed into the house it was impossible to say. The fight had lasted little more than two minutes but it had not been a quiet altercation and it had brought four or five men from neighbouring homes onto the street, among them Archie Meadows and Fred Wrigley. They had clustered together in a group but had made no move to interfere. A brawl they would have stopped, but this was no brawl, this was justice in their eyes and there wasn't a man among them who would deny Sam his right of redress.

Justice done, honour restored, Sam pushed himself to his feet, turned, and walked across to where Alice was standing in the shadow of the trees. He stood in front of her for a moment, scanning her face, then took her arm. Teeth set hard together, eyes focused firmly on the tent, she walked stiffly along beside him, impervious to the stares and whispers of the onlookers.

Damn you, Sam Kenyon, she breathed silently. She had seen and recognised the look in his eyes as he had briefly examined her face. She knew what he was looking for too — for signs of distress, wretchedness — signs that she had some feeling for Zac Fielding.

Michael was waiting outside the tent, wide-eyed as a fish. He had witnessed the whole episode. A fine example for Sam to show the boy, she thought. A fine example of violence.

The atmosphere inside the tent was brittle and silent. Out on the street, a couple of men had taken it upon themselves to cart Zac indoors. Of Lily there was no sign — she was out, serving ale no doubt.

It wasn't until they were in bed that Sam finally broke the silence. They were both lying on their sides, facing away from each other. 'In future . . .' he said, pronouncing each word very precisely, 'whatever there is to hear, I wish to hear it from your lips and not from the lips of others. Do you understand?'

'Yes,' she said crisply. 'And in future, if you wish to engage in a fist fight, kindly do it where Michael can't see. And if you ever again look at me as you looked at me tonight, Sam Kenyon, I shall slap your face, regardless of how many neighbours are standing by!'

There was a rustle of blankets as he rolled over then Sam's fingers bit into her shoulder, hauling her onto her back. She glared up at him, though in the darkness it was wasted.

'What look?' he demanded.

'The look that said, "Do you care? Do you care that I hurt Zac Fielding?"'

'Can you blame me for wondering?' he hissed. 'I've spent all day wondering why *you* didn't tell me what had happened, and the only reason I could think of was that you hoped to keep it a secret for some reason. Then tonight I learn from you there are other things concerning him that you've held back from me, like the business with the kettle and the business with his wife — she obviously thought something was afoot between the pair of you. I know fine well that you didn't marry me for love — can you blame me for wondering if you had a fancy for him? Yes, I did look at your face to see if you cared about him! And it's as well for both of you that I saw nothing to suggest that you do!'

'I care *nothing* for him!' she whispered fiercely. 'And I don't care much for you tonight either!' She jerked free from his grip and rolled onto her side again.

A cold, damp night under canvas did nothing to thaw the ice between them. Had the tent had a door, it would almost certainly have been slammed as Sam left for the mine next morning. Alice was still seething, too. Nor was her mood helped when Michael rose, still abubble with the excitement of the previous night's events, and began proudly praising Sam's fighting prowess.

'It was his left fist that he hit him in the face with,'

he said in awed tones, scooping large spoonfuls of porridge into his mouth. 'Most people can only use their right fist properly, but Mr Kenyon is as strong in his left as —'

'Michael — eat your breakfast!' she said sharply.

Throwing her one of his glowering, aggrieved looks, Michael reluctantly confined the use of his mouth to chewing his porridge. Not for long though. A minute later he looked up, frowning.

'What was the fight about?' he asked innocently.

'Mr Fielding caused Mr Kenyon some offence,' she said curtly.

'In what way did he offend him?'

She pulled Charlotte's dress over her head, threaded her thin white arms through the sleeves and proceeded to do up the small buttons on her bodice, thankful that she at least was not yet old enough to ask awkward questions. She glanced across at Michael, who was still awaiting an answer. How was she to explain to a ten-year-old boy the incidents that had led up to the reckoning? The incidents in themselves were trivial in their unembellished state, and the last thing she wished to do was give the impression that any trivial incident under the sun justified a fight. She would have to give Michael some explanation though — another reason why she was presently furious with Sam — because the difficult business of explaining had fallen to her.

'Mr Fielding is a married man. I am a married woman. And it isn't appropriate for a married man to do certain things . . . *offer* certain things . . .' she amended. She licked her lips and drew in an impatient breath as a puzzled frown settled on Michael's brow. 'It's to do with *correctness*,' she said, trying a different approach. 'There are certain things which are considered to be inappropriate behaviour between a married man and a married woman — between a married man and a married woman who are not married to each other, that is,' she amplified. The frown on Michael's face deepened.

'It's . . .' She waved an exasperated hand and gave up. 'Oh, when you're grown to a man you'll understand,' she muttered.

As Michael left for school in the company of Robert Wrigley, the diarrhoea epidemic having mercifully relented, she could see their mouths flapping like moths' wings. Robert Wrigley had also witnessed last night's business. By noon the tale would be throughout the school, and would grow with each telling. She dreaded to think what proportions it would have assumed by the end of the day. She had related to Meg Pringle *exactly* what had happened between Zac Fielding and herself on the road between Black's Point and Reefton, but by the time the account reached Sam the following day a small altercation with a basket of bread had grown to attempted molestation.

She had barely finished washing the breakfast dishes when Bella arrived, along with Sidney. Always delighted to see her young playmate, Charlotte scrambled to her feet and ran to greet him, giggling with delight.

'Is your husband a bit calmer this morning?' Bella enquired tentatively.

'I didn't enquire as to his mood,' Alice returned, reaching for a towel.

'Still angry, is he?'

'He seemed so.'

'Well, I want you to know that I didn't tell Fred about what had happened to you, so it wasn't him who told Sam that Zac Fielding tried to molest you,' Bella said.

'Fred didn't know anything about it till yesterday when he overheard Edwin Bray talking to Jack Stone at the mine. I think Meg Pringle must have told somebody about it.'

'I'm sure she did,' Alice agreed with a bitter edge. Only three people had known about the incident — four, counting Zac Fielding. She had confided in Bella, confident that it would go no further, and had assumed that Meg would be as good as her word. 'I don't hold with gossip,' Meg had assured her. 'So you can rest assured that I'll not speak a word of it to anyone. There's nothing worse than being at the centre of tittle-tattle.' So much for assurances.

'Fred said Sam looked quite surprised when Edwin Bray mentioned it,' Bella said hesitantly. 'As if he didn't know anything about it.'

'He didn't. I didn't tell Sam about it,' Alice replied, rubbing the towel briskly round the inside of a teacup. 'I know I should have done, but it was such a trivial incident. Zac Fielding didn't even touch me.' Not strictly true — his hand had brushed hers, quite deliberately.

'Well, it might have saved Zac his front teeth if you'd given your husband your own account of what happened before he heard it from others,' Bella commented bluntly. 'Not that I can say I grieve the loss of Zac Fielding's teeth. He may not be so inclined to smile so freely where he ought not to from now on.'

Alice looked up, frowning. 'Have you heard how he is?'

'Missing his top front teeth, and a broken nose.' She gave a sharp snort through her own finely boned nose. 'I doubt Lily gave him much sympathy when she learned the cause of it.'

Alice turned away and stared at the flap of the tent,

which she had purposely left down this morning, beyond which some thirty yards away was the Fieldings' cottage. 'Do you think Lily will believe that Zac tried to molest me?' she asked quietly. Zac would have given Lily his own account, but Lily would doubtless also have heard the other account that had rapidly travelled around the town.

'I do, I'm afraid,' Bella answered without hesitation. 'He's committed adultery once before. What a man does once he can do twice.'

Frowning, Alice placed the dried teacup on the table. The chances were Lily would believe the story, especially since she knew that Zac had previously shown some interest in her. Lily had warned her to stay away from Zac; God knows how she would react to all this.

Alice had a number of visitors during the course of the morning. Bella hadn't been gone ten minutes when Meg Pringle arrived, in tears, mortified at what had happened. She had told her husband, she said, confided in him, saying he shouldn't tell anyone else. He in turn had told his neighbour, Edwin Bray, saying much the same thing — that Bray should keep it strictly to himself. He hadn't. Meg had genuinely thought to do no harm by confiding in her husband, but as it turned out she might as well have climbed onto the roof and shouted the story out to the whole town. It was pointless to be angry with her though, so she reassured her she bore her no ill feelings and offered her a cup of tea.

Her third visitor arrived about an hour after Meg Pringle left.

'I'd like a word with you, Mrs Kenyon, if I may.' Lily Fielding, arms folded tightly across her middle, ducked her head and stepped into the tent. She was wearing a pale green dress. Her sleeves were rolled up and there were wet patches on her skirt.

Alice cautiously lifted Charlotte from her lap and deposited her on the sofa beside her, then stood. Taking a small step to the side, she positioned herself between the sofa and Lily.

'I did not accuse your husband of trying to molest me, Mrs Fielding,' she said in a firm voice. She assumed that was why Lily was here. 'I encountered your husband when —'

'He told me. I know exactly what happened,' Lily interrupted.

'Then you'll know that *nothing* happened,' Alice said.

To her surprise Lily laughed, though it wasn't a very pleasant laugh. 'Nothing? You call the loss of five teeth, a broken nose, and a face that looks like a plum pudding *nothing*?'

'I meant nothing happened between your husband and me,' Alice clarified, keeping a weather eye on Lily's folded arms. If she didn't keep her wits about her she might shortly find herself missing a few teeth. She wound her arms across her middle, placing them in a better position to cover her face at short notice, should the need arise. She had a good pair of lungs too and if Lily did start to set about her she intended to use them. Bella was out, but there were several other neighbouring women who would come to her aid if she yelled loudly enough.

'What do you want, Mrs Fielding?' she asked bluntly.

Lily tilted her head coquettishly. She'd done her hair up in a loose coil on top of her head and it slipped to the side a little as she scrutinised her. 'I came to warn you,' she said softly.

Alice stiffened, resisting the urge to step back. 'Warn me about what?'

'To watch your husband.'

She narrowed her eyes, not sure what she meant. 'I don't imagine my husband intends to have further dealings with your husband,' she said. 'Not unless your husband tries to have further dealings with me.'

'You mistake my meaning, Mrs Kenyon.' Lily dropped her arms, circling around her before stopping a foot or two from Alice's left elbow. Alice turned, keeping her squarely in front of her. 'I came to warn you to watch your husband of an evening. He's like Zac, you see. Not satisfied with only his wife. He likes a bit of . . . *variety*.'

'My husband,' Alice said icily, 'spends his evenings with me. *All* his evenings!'

'All?' Lily shook her head, smiling crookedly. 'Not quite all. He's spent at least one night that I know of with pretty little Mary Deakin. She works at the same place as I work. Save that Mary works . . . *upstairs*.' Turning away, she walked towards the tent flap. She stooped to pull it aside then glanced back to toss Alice a look of mocking commiseration. 'Ask your husband what he was doing a month or so ago, Mrs Kenyon — the night he wasn't lying in your bed.'

Chapter 18

Lies — every word. Sam wouldn't be unfaithful. He wouldn't bed with a whore. He wasn't that sort of man. Lily Fielding was lying, trying to cause trouble between them in revenge for the damage Sam had done to her husband's face. Resolving not to give it another moment's thought, Alice busied herself with her chores.

Doubt, however, is an integral part of the human make-up. It lurks in the mind, in small, dark corners and recesses, sleeping for the most part — a silent, unseen, slothful companion. But occasionally it rouses, stretches, creeps towards the ear, and whispers, 'Are you sure?'

The truth was — Alice wasn't sure. Not absolutely sure that Sam hadn't been unfaithful to her, and unless certainty is absolute then it is a very uncertain commodity. The thing which was unsettling her was the knowledge that Sam *had* been absent from their bed for one night, the night he had disappeared after she'd told him she wasn't willing to consummate their marriage. Where he'd been she'd never asked and Sam had never volunteered an explanation. He hadn't slept much — that had been plain. He had mentioned that he'd walked — but walked where? To a brothel? He'd been drinking; there were traces of it on his breath when he returned. He'd been sick too — there had been a definite odour about his clothes — which implied he had drunk a lot. Enough to . . . No! Shame on you for even thinking so, Alice Kenyon, she rebuked herself.

'Are you sure? Are you *absolutely* sure?' whispered the small voice in her ear.

The only thing she was sure about was that Sam had had the opportunity to be unfaithful and that in itself was enough to cast doubt, which was exactly what Lily wanted. The question was, had Lily hinted that Sam had fornicated with Mary whatever-her-name was on the offchance that he had been absent from their bed during the last month, or was Lily's claim based on knowledge?

As the day wore on, despite her efforts to put the matter from her mind, her thoughts wandered to any and every small incident which might signify that Sam had been unfaithful. Remarks he had made, looks he had given her, gestures . . . she minutely examined each one. She turned every stone, every pebble, and if enough are turned the chances are eventually a bothersome one will be found. Partway through the afternoon she found one. It was probably nothing at all, but it niggled nonetheless. It was a small conversation they had had regarding Lily Fielding which was bothering her; it had occurred during the evening of their first full day at Black's Point when Sam had enquired what the other families in the town were like. She had mentioned among other things Lily Fielding's profession, namely that she served ale in a public house of dubious repute. Sam had enquired which alehouse Lily was employed in, then sternly ordered her to stay clear of the woman. His stern order hadn't surprised her at all; in fact, she would have been surprised if he hadn't instructed her to stay away from the likes of a woman like Lily Fielding. What had surprised her a bit was his interest in Lily's place of work. It had puzzled her at the time but she hadn't thought any more about it afterwards. Not till now. Now she was wondering if Sam's interest in the alehouse was prompted by a guilty concern that it might be the same alehouse where Mary Deakin offered her services. If Lily Fielding did work there she might possibly remember his visit . . . if indeed he had visited. She bit her lip, frowning. There was also the possibility, of course, that Sam's interest in the alehouse had been nothing more than idle curiosity.

Doubt is a very unsettling companion. It distracts the mind and dominates the thoughts. Worse still, it creates a dilemma. Alice's particular dilemma was that in order to dispel her doubts she would have to ask Sam outright where he had been on the night in question. He would want to know why she was asking, she would have to tell him, which would result in her bluntly asking him whether he had been unfaithful. If she did ask him and he hadn't been unfaithful, Sam would never forgive her for doubting his integrity; on the other hand, if he had been unfaithful she would never forgive him. But if she didn't ask, she would forever have that nagging little question at the back of her mind.

If Sam had returned in a calmer, more conciliatory mood that evening instead of a sullen, cross one, she might have felt more disposed to give him the benefit of the doubt regarding Lily Fielding's nasty, bloody-minded assertions, which was more or less what she had made up her mind to do. Her husband, however, was sulking. Alice had never had much patience with a sulky bottom lip — it irritated her when Michael pouted and it quite riled her to see her husband, a grown man, pouting. He was presently sitting cross-legged by the fire outside the tent with a book spread across his knee, reading, or making a semblance of it.

'Do you want a drink of tea before you go to bed?' she enquired coolly. Since she was making a drink for herself she felt it only common courtesy to offer him one too.

'No,' he returned sourly. His eyes remained firmly glued to the page.

She pursed her lips. Damn your sulks, Samuel Kenyon! Damn your rudeness! Damn you! she thought crossly. What did he want? More apologies from her? She had apologised last night for not telling him about the incident with Zac — an incident in which nothing had happened. It wasn't her fault that the story had been grossly exaggerated and had spread like the plague. Moreover, she had purposely not told him about any of the incidents with the Fieldings because she didn't want to worry him — so much for being a considerate wife!

'I have a question,' she said in the same cool tones. 'Do you by chance know a Mary Deakin?'

He glanced up, frowning. 'No. Is she a Reefton woman?'

She shrugged. 'I don't know exactly where she lives. But I was told that she offered you a bed — the night you stayed away from home, after we quarrelled.'

She didn't need to ask if it was true. She could see very plainly that it was, in the guilt darkening Sam's cheeks like a bloody tide. The vague thought came to her, floating into her mind in a disjointed sort of way as Sam pushed himself slowly to his feet, that she ought to check to make sure that Michael was asleep. A deepseated maternal instinct to protect young impressionable ears from things better not heard.

'Who have you been speaking to?' he demanded softly.

'I asked *you* a question,' she said, matching his tone. 'And you haven't answered me. Do you know a Mary Deakin?' She paused, then added, 'I believe she's a whore.'

Sam flinched visibly.

She stared at him, feeling her stomach suddenly go very hollow and realised that deep down she had believed Sam had been faithful that night, that Lily Fielding was lying.

The bony lump in his throat slid slowly up and down his neck as he swallowed. 'I've met her. I didn't know her name, save that it was Mary. I'd not even recognise her again. I was drunk, too drunk to . . .' he swallowed again and said in a shamed voice, 'to do what I'd paid her for.'

Her hand seemed to move of its own volition to land him a stinging slap across his left cheek. His head shifted slightly with the impact then very deliberately he turned his face so that the right cheek faced her. 'Do it again if it will make you feel better,' he said.

She shook her head, very slowly, her eyes still locked on his face. 'I couldn't slap you enough times to make me feel better,' she said bitterly. 'How could you? How could you defile your marriage bed like that!'

'Defile my marriage bed?' He gave a sharp laugh. 'I didn't have a marriage bed to defile! You'd just informed me that you wouldn't grant me my marital rights, and intended never to grant me them. I was very, very angry, and I'd defy any man not to be angry in those circumstances. I went to an alehouse — one of the less reputable ones — got very drunk, and went upstairs. Crawled, to be precise. I could scarcely stay upright by that stage. Then I . . .' He compressed his lips hard, hard enough to drain the colour from them. 'I made a fool of myself before the woman. I vomited all over her bed and she had me thrown out.' He lifted his hand and rubbed his knuckles across his chin, breathing heavily, then said in a more controlled voice, 'Nothing happened. I swear it.'

'And do you think that exonerates you from blame — because nothing happened? Because you were too drunk to manage anything?'

'I know it was wrong!' he returned sharply. 'And it was wrong of you to deny me what any proper wife ought to willingly give her husband.'

'You know very well why I was unwilling!' she retorted in a gritty whisper. With some difficulty they were both keeping their voices to a suitably low level so as not to rouse the children. 'You know what happened to me! You know I was afraid.'

He jerked his head in angry assent. 'I do know. Now. But I didn't know then — that night. And stop looking at me as if you've been ill-used, damn you. I wasn't unfaithful to you. Nothing happened, I tell you!'

She moved to the other side of the fire and glared at him. 'Nothing happened between me and Zac Fielding but it didn't stop you from taking your fists to him.'

'Zac Fielding was trying to seduce you!' he retorted in scandalised tones. 'What did you expect me to do? Stand by and let him? You're my wife!'

'And you are my husband! And you were unfaithful to me! You didn't fornicate with that woman . . . that whore . . . but you certainly intended to. You may think there's a difference, Sam Kenyon, but the Bible makes no distinction between the two. In God's eyes the one is as sinful as the other. And I agree with Him!'

'But you don't agree with Him when it comes to forgiving one another's sins, it seems!'

'Forgive?' She blinked incredulously. 'You're a fine one to talk about forgiveness. What forgiveness did you show Zac Fielding? What forgiveness have you shown me?' She tossed him an icy look and turned towards the tent.

'Alice!' Sam's voice came sharply from behind her. 'We've not finished this conversation yet.'

'I have!' she said, and disappeared into the tent, leaving Sam to steam beside the fire.

Chapter 19

July brought a number of changes to Black's Point. The Fieldings moved out, the Arbuckles — a new mining family — moved in, the Wrigleys shifted into a leased cottage on Luca's Street, and Lydia Donne gave birth to a fine healthy son.

The Fieldings had left on the morning of 13 July. Zac, his face still mottled with purplish-red bruising, had loaded their belongings onto the wagon then driven off without a word to anyone. Zac had lost more than a few teeth — he had lost his position at the Wealth of Nations mine. Understandably, he had been in no fit state to work his shift on the night of the fight, which on its own might have been excusable. But it was by no means the first time Zac Fielding had failed to report for work, usually with no excuse; the mine foreman had also heard about the cause of the fight. He had consequently stopped by Fielding's house the next evening with the pay he was owed and informed him he was no longer required on the maintenance shift. 'Good riddance to the pair of them, that's what I say,' Bella had muttered as the Fieldings' wagon had disappeared from sight into the fog of a grey, damp morning. It was a sentiment which most people seemed to echo. Zac had got off scot-free when he'd seduced the Welsh girl twelve months earlier and what Sam had meted out most saw as belated justice. Privately Alice felt the penalty Zac had paid was a harsh one, considering the 'crime' he had committed. Regret aside though, she wasn't sorry to see the back of Zac Fielding, or his wife.

One thing which had *not* changed in Black's Point was the cool atmosphere in the Kenyon household. The sleeping arrangements were not helping, which was largely Alice's fault. Following Sam's admission of guilt regarding his dealings with Mary Deakin, or at least his intended dealings with the woman, she had stormed off to bed, rolling herself up like a cocoon in three thick woollen blankets, a silent but very clear statement that she wished to bed alone. After a fortnight of cocooning, having made her point she had started to leave the blankets lying loose on top of her, as a small hint that she would not object to resuming marital relations again. It had soon become obvious, however, that a hint was not going to suffice. Sam was awaiting something more substantial — like a body arriving under the blankets next to him.

He was presently lying with his back to her, a hunched dark shape half an arm's length away. She pursed her lips in annoyance as he gave what she had dubbed 'one of his aggrieved sighs'. Damn his stubbornness, she thought crossly. By rights Sam was the one who ought to make the first placatory move, not her. Neither of them was wholly blameless in the events which had led up to their present estrangement, but if blame were to be apportioned then to her mind the lion's share fell to him, though he no doubt held a different opinion.

She drew up her knees more tightly and slipped her hands between her legs for warmth. On a purely practical level there was another small incentive to mend matters with Sam — two in a bed were twice as warm as one. She eyed his dark shape for another minute or two, yawned, and closed her eyes. It had been a long day. Perhaps tomorrow night.

Alice cast a frowning eye at the brown tin lying on the table beside Sam's empty breakfast bowl. Inside it were six cheese sandwiches — Sam's food provisions for the day. He had gone off to the mine without them.

She walked outside and perused the sky, blinking in the bright sunshine. A heavy frost had covered the ground at dawn, coating the grass with delicate white ice crystals that had crunched softly beneath her boots as she'd gone to the river to fetch water. It had made a chilly start to the day, but a heavy frost was often the crisp forerunner of a clear fine day, such as today promised to be. The winter had so far been a very mild one, which was just as well since there was still no prospect of a leased house coming vacant. The tent had in fact proved much warmer than she expected — by day the interior heated up quite quickly in the sun, weak as it was, and the surrounding trees provided good, solid shelter against the wind. Nights were the worst, the rising damp from the ground as chill as the grave. Charlotte, a restless sleeper with a tendency to fling her arms free of the blankets, could be relied upon to wake at least once each night, crying from cold.

She scanned the sky again and, satisfied that there was no sign of rain, decided to walk up to the mine to deliver the forgotten food tin. An olive branch. And if Sam chose not to respond to it, so be it — but the next gesture would have to come from him. The question was, should she take Charlotte or ask Bella to watch her? It was quite a trek to the mine — it took Sam almost half an hour to walk there, sometimes longer, depending on the condition of the track. She was still debating what to do when she felt a familiar tug at her skirt and a small, heart-shaped face framed by pretty black curls grinned up at her.

Smiling, Alice lifted her into her arms. 'Would you like to see where your papa works, Charlotte?' she asked.

It was a steep climb to the Energetic. For the first half-mile the track followed the course of the Murray Creek, a reasonably easy ascent to begin with. The going quickly became harder though, as the track climbed ever higher along the steep slopes of the wooded hillside till the Murray was no more than a faint gurgle far below. Here and there she occasionally glimpsed bits of it, silvery shimmering little triangles of water that peeped and winked through the dense foliage. The track was for the most part good but there were sections over which water constantly trickled, and here the daily trek of miners' boots had muddied the ground to a quagmire. She took her time, picking her way carefully, keeping close to the bank. As the track climbed still higher Charlotte, who had walked for quite long stretches on the flatter parts, began to tire and demanded to be carried. Whilst carrying her on level ground was not too exacting, it was a different tale on steep inclines and Alice was soon puffing. Not far now, she heartened herself. She could hear the dull, resonating thud of the stampers from the Energetic's battery not too far ahead.

The battery, a substantial wooden building, had been built close to the exit tunnel through which the mined quartz was transported. Close up, the noise from it was deafening; through the soles of her boots Alice could feel the shuddering reverberations as the massive cast-iron stampers relentlessly pounded and crushed the quartz.

'Are you wanting to see Sam?' yelled Jack Stone, popping up from behind one of the wagons.

She nodded and shouted back, 'Yes. How do I get to the mine?'

He pointed a grubby hand to the hill behind the battery. 'Follow the track up the hill. The mine head is just over the summit.'

She waved a thank you and set off up the track.

Alice knew very little about mines but she could see as soon as she reached the summit there was some sort of a problem. The winding wheel was motionless, the two tall chimneys beside the boiler house were disgorging barely any smoke, and there was a considerable amount of head shaking and pointing going on by the door to the engine room. The miners were standing in a group, talking. Fred was there, leaning on his shovel — his big burly figure easily recognisable — but of Sam there was no sign.

Reluctant to interrupt, she waited in the shade of some trees. It was several minutes before anyone noticed her, but eventually Edwin Bray turned round and she waved her hand to attract his attention.

'Well now, what fetches you up to the mine, Mrs Kenyon?' he enquired amiably, walking over to her. He looked down at Charlotte, smiling as she reached out to him, and patted her hand.

Alice glanced down at the food tin in her hand. 'Sam forgot this. Do you happen to know where he is, Mr Bray?'

He shook his head. 'He's about somewhere. Shall I find him for you?'

She hesitated. Having walked all this way to offer

him an olive branch, it would be nice to offer it to him in person. On the other hand, if he was busy he might not welcome being dragged from his work just so his wife could personally hand him a tin of sandwiches. 'No. I don't really need to see him,' she said. 'Would you mind taking them for him, Mr Bray?' She held out the tin and, dipping her head towards the engine room, asked, 'Is there a problem?'

'There is.' He glanced back over his shoulder, frowning. 'We can't raise steam. The boiler failed about an hour ago. There's a bit of controversy as to the cause of it.'

'Is it serious?'

He shrugged and turned back to face her. 'The smithy seems to think not, so let's hope he's right. Anyway, if you'll excuse me, I'd better get back.'

Back to what, she wasn't altogether certain. Back to leaning on his shovel, she supposed, until the steam problem was resolved. She lingered for a minute or two, hoping that Sam might appear, then set off back, feeling disappointed she hadn't seen him.

Somewhat to her surprise the return downhill trek, which she'd expected to be easier, proved a good deal more taxing than the uphill climb. Her spine hurt from leaning backwards, her arms ached from carrying Charlotte, and her knees jarred with every step on the very steep descents. Like it or not Charlotte would have to walk for a while, she decided. Ignoring her protests, Alice set her down on the ground and took hold of her hand. She was beginning to wish she'd left her with Bella.

'Oh look, a bird,' she said, hoping to distract her as she towed her along. Announcing its presence with musical little peeps, a brightly coloured bullfinch was flitting through the trees just ahead of them.

Mimicking her, Charlotte pointed a small finger at the bird. 'Bird! Bird! Bird!' she exclaimed, and continued to utter this excitedly until it eventually flew off. It seemed unnaturally quiet after Charlotte's shrill little exclamations ceased — the only sounds were the soft squish of mud and wet leaves beneath their shoes and the faint flutter of leaves high above as the treetops shifted in the breeze. A few minutes later though a new sound reached Alice's ears. Voices. Women's voices. She slowed, feeling a prickle of unease. They were Maori women, speaking in their own language, two or three of them by the sound of it. She drew Charlotte to a halt, listening as the voices grew steadily louder. They, whoever they were, would soon be in view. To the best of her knowledge there was only one Maori settlement within walking distance of Black's Point and it was there that Hone and his wife lived. She glanced up at the thickly wooded slope edging the path, fleetingly wondering if she should scramble up and conceal Charlotte and herself from view till they'd passed. Hiding was one thing, but keeping Charlotte quiet was quite another. She tightened her hold on her hand and continued walking slowly down the track.

Eventually the women came into view and to her relief Hone's wife wasn't among them. There were three of them, each carrying a woven flax basket; they'd been gathering wild berries. She nodded in acknowledgment as she passed the first two, receiving small nods back, but to her surprise the third woman stopped, spoke a few words in Maori, then scooped a handful of berries from her basket and held them out. Seeing Alice's frown, the woman lifted them to her mouth and made eating gestures then pointed to Charlotte, smiling and nodding. Alice smiled back and held out her hand for the berries. 'Thank you. That's very kind of you,' she said.

She walked on with the berries in one hand and Charlotte's small hand clasped in her other until a turn in the track took them out of sight, then tossed the berries away. She had no idea what they were and had no intention of letting Charlotte eat them, for all the young Maori woman's reassuring smiles and nods. Her feet slowed, and with a frown she turned to glance back at the shiny pea-sized black berries strewn across the track, realising she'd just reacted exactly as Hone's wife had reacted to the cough syrup. She had been able to toss the berries away, but Hone's wife had been forced to allow her child to take medicine about which she felt deeply suspicious. Her frown deepened. And what if she'd had no choice but to let Charlotte eat the berries and then Charlotte had fallen sick . . . 'I would have sworn the berries were the cause of it,' she murmured aloud. And if Charlotte had died . . . how would she have reacted to that? She looked down at the springy black curls bobbing along beside her. She would have reacted exactly as Hone's wife had reacted, a mother like herself; she would have been completely distraught. She wouldn't have resorted to arson, but then there was no proof that Hone's wife had either, just a fleeting glimpse by Jerry Crail of what might just as easily have been shifting shadows. And if it was indeed Hone's wife whom Crail had seen, if it was she who had set fire to the house — and Alice was still inclined to believe that it was — well, it was a wicked act and she couldn't forgive it any more than she could forgive the man who'd raped her, but she could maybe understand how a bereaved mother could do something of that nature. Grief sometimes affected a person's mind, made them quite irrational in their thinking. Moreover the Maori woman had a husband who had seemed more concerned with extracting suitable recompense for his child's loss than with the loss itself; there would be little sympathy and understanding forthcoming from that quarter to ease her grief.

You should count your blessings, Alice Kenyon, she told herself. She had a good husband in Sam. An excellent husband compared with the likes of Hone and Zac Fielding. And when he came home tonight she intended to somehow mend matters between the two of them.

It was halfway through the afternoon that it came, a sound which filled every heart in the town with dread. The wail of a distant siren. From the way it echoed around the hills, it was impossible to tell which mine it was coming from but it meant only one thing — there had been an accident.

Women in the street stopped dead in their tracks and all heads turned, trying to locate the direction of the chilling sound. Even the children fell silent. Picking Charlotte up, Alice hurried along the street to Bella's cottage. Bella was standing in the garden, still holding a freshly washed petticoat in her hands in readiness for pegging it onto her washing line. It was dripping all down her skirt.

'Which mine is it coming from? Can you tell?' Alice asked anxiously.

Bella shook her head, her eyes fixed unblinkingly on the distant hills. 'No. But I pray to God it's not the Energetic.'

It was. Word reached the town a long half-hour later

in the shape of a lad of about thirteen or fourteen who looked as if he had run all the way from the mine. 'Explosion,' he said breathlessly to the twenty or so women gathered together in the middle of the town. 'Pa's trapped. Have to let Ma know.'

'Is anyone else trapped?' Bella grabbed hold of his arm as he made to run off again.

'I don't know,' he said, shaking his head wildly, and raced off.

Alice glanced across at Bella, whose cheeks had gone an ashen colour. She thought her own might well be a similar shade. 'That's Archie Meadows' son,' Bella said in a strained voice.

Alice licked her lips. If Archie Meadows was trapped, other miners could be too. Waves of panic rose in her stomach. Not Sam, oh God, please not Sam, she prayed. 'Will you look after Charlotte for me? I'm going to the mine,' she said, turning to Meg Pringle, who was standing beside her.

Meg stared at her, brows raised in surprise, but after a moment nodded and took Charlotte from her.

'You'll not be welcome there,' Jessie Owens said from behind them. 'A mine foreman doesn't take kindly to wives milling around when there's been an accident.'

Ignoring the comment she turned to Bella. 'Are you coming, Bella?' she asked quickly, anxious to be gone.

Bella's eyes swivelled to the hills and she chewed hard on her lip, her brows gathered in a worried frown. At last she looked back to meet Alice's eyes and nodded. 'We shouldn't go — Jessie's right — but, yes, I'll come.'

Halfway up Franklyn Street they were met by Mary Bray. After two or three minutes' discussion and a brief wait while she arranged for a neighbour to keep an eye on her three daughters when they came home from school, Mary set off for the mine with them. They mostly walked in silence, each wrapped in a private blanket of worry. As the only one of the three who had been to the mine before, Alice took the lead. There was something completely unreal about it, to be walking up the track again, twice in one day, as if it couldn't possibly be happening, as if it was only in her mind, a nightmarish parody of the morning's visit, something she would wake from soon in a cold sweat and find to her relief had been only a dream.

She kept as fast a pace as her legs and lungs would allow, conscious only of the other two women by the rasp of their breath and sound of their boots sucking in and out of the damp earth. Keeping her eyes fixed doggedly ahead, she marked off all the places she recognised — the shiny black berries still strewn across the track where she'd tossed them, a rusty bit of iron poking up through a carpet of deep emerald ferns, a black beech with the initials CM carved crudely into the side — each time trying to estimate how much further it was to the mine, and in between whiles wishing a whole string of things that couldn't be. Wishing she and Sam hadn't quarrelled as they had, wishing she'd reached out to him last night instead of turning over and going to sleep, wishing she'd told him just once that she loved him, wishing she'd realised that she did love him. It was only now, now she was faced with the possibility of losing him that . . . She lifted her chin, alert suddenly. Voices, drifting on the air, men's voices calling to each other, over the rise of the hill. We must be almost at the mine, she thought in surprise. This morning the deafening thud and crunch of the stampers in the battery had loudly announced the mine's proximity long before she reached it; this time as she hurried past the wooden building the stampers stood immobile and silent, the gloomy interior deserted and forbidding.

As she hitched up her skirts and began to climb the last steep stretch of track to the summit, beyond which lay the mine, her legs started to shake. Echoing her own worried thoughts Mary's voice came from a few yards back down the track, hoarse and breathless. 'Well, we'll know the worst soon enough.'

Once at the summit she stood waiting for the other two women, breathing hard and fast through her nose, her heart pounding like a sledgehammer as she surveyed the mine. It was a very different scene from the one she'd stood and watched that morning. No one was standing idle now, miners were rushing about with shovels, picks, hammers, lengths of timber, steam was pouring from the two chimneys in billowing white clouds, and the air was filled with shouting as instructions were yelled back and forth. Her eyes flicked anxiously from miner to miner, then shifted to the cluster of mine buildings, scanning the doorways. She swallowed and turned as Mary and Bella arrived at her side. 'Fred's safe,' she said in a slightly unsteady voice, pointing to the burly figure with a sturdy beam of wood balanced on his shoulder, striding towards the mine shaft.

'Oh thank God!' Bella breathed.

'Have you seen Edwin?' Mary asked, her worried grey eyes darting back and forth.

Alice shook her head. Nor had she seen Sam.

'We'll ask Fred where they are,' Bella said, and hurried off towards her husband.

Four men were trapped, Fred advised them gravely.

Even before he named them Alice knew that Sam was one of them — she could see it in Fred's face. The other three were Archie Meadows, and Charlie and Henry Lloyd — brothers, one seventeen, one nineteen.

'I was in the cage with Edwin Bray and Jack Stone, coming up to the surface when it happened.' Fred shook his head, frowning, his bald brow beaded with grimy sweat. 'We heard the boom of the explosion then dust started to drift up the shaft. We knew straightaway there'd been an accident. We'd left Henry and Charlie Lloyd tapping a hole in the rock face in readiness for blasting again; they'd taken a box of blasting powder into the drive with them and it must have somehow exploded.'

The question floated vaguely into Alice's mind as to why Sam and Archie Meadows hadn't gone in the cage with Fred and the other two miners. It floated quickly out again, replaced by more urgent questions. 'Have you heard them calling? Do you know if they're alive?' The word broke in half as her throat closed in an involuntary swallow.

Fred shook his head again. 'There's too much rock between us and them for us to hear anything at all, Alice.'

'How long before you reach them?' Mary asked, taking hold of Alice's arm in an unconscious gesture of support.

'I don't know.' Fred glanced briefly back at the shaft, frowning. 'There's a lot of rock to clear and it's slow work.'

'You must have some idea of how long, Fred!' Bella said impatiently.

'A while,' he said, in tones which implied a *long* while. Gripping the beam in his hands, he hoisted it onto his shoulder. 'There's one thing in their favour,' he said, turning to Alice. 'There are no poisonous fumes in a gold mine, not like coal mines, so if they survived the blast there's every chance we'll bring them out alive.' And on that dubious note of comfort he strode off.

As Fred reached the shaft, Ben Ogilvie, the foreman, apprehended him, exchanged a few brief words with him, then walked across to the three women. 'You're Mrs Kenyon, I believe,' he said in a slightly breathless voice. He was sweating profusely and raised his arm to wipe his sleeve briskly across his face. 'You know your husband is among the trapped men?' Alice gave a stiff nod and braced herself, anticipating bad news. 'There's nothing I can tell you I'm afraid, save to assure you that we're sparing no effort to reach them.'

She nodded again, her shoulders slackening with relief. No news was better than bad news. 'How long before you expect to reach them?' she asked. She didn't really expect the foreman's answer to be any preciser than Fred's, but she still felt compelled to ask.

He shook his head, frowning, confirming her thoughts. 'It'll be some time — five, six hours at the very least, I'd say. Longer maybe. It's not just a simple matter of clearing the fall of rock — we have to shore up the roof as we go, to ensure there's no danger of it collapsing. As soon as there's any news I shall send word to you, Mrs Kenyon, but in the meantime I suggest you return home to your family.'

'No, I'll stay,' Alice said. She fixed a resolute blue eye on him. 'I'm not leaving till I know how my husband is.'

Ogilvie shook his head apologetically. 'I understand your concern, Mrs Kenyon, but the mine is no place for women, the more so at a time such as this. For your own safety I must ask you all to leave.'

'I mean to stay till I know how my husband is,' Alice repeated firmly.

Ogilvie clamped his mouth shut, his nostrils flared slightly as he drew in a long, low breath. He wasn't accustomed to having his orders dismissed out of hand, particularly by a woman. To her surprise, though, he gave a brief nod, perhaps deciding he hadn't the time to argue, there being more pressing matters to deal with. One of the miners was calling urgently to him from the head of the shaft. Turning, he pointed to the storage sheds beyond the engine room. 'Very well, Mrs Kenyon. Wait over there then, but make sure you don't get in the way of the men.'

The storage sheds, though remote enough to ensure that they didn't interfere with the constant comings and goings of miners, afforded a good view of the shaft. How many times the cage went down and came up again, Alice lost count. Down it went carrying timbers, tools, machinery and grim-faced miners — among them a number of men from the other shifts who had arrived to help. Then after a while — sometimes a few minutes, sometimes considerably longer — the powerful winding wheel would slowly start to turn again, to bring the cage back up. Each time it neared the surface Alice held her breath, hoping it would bring Sam. It never did, and it was foolish to hope that it would at this stage. It was likely to be several hours before the trapped men were reached. Each miner they questioned gave them the same report — still a lot of rock to clear . . . a long while yet. And always it was accompanied by a well-meaning 'You'd be best to go home, Mrs Kenyon, and wait there for news.'

Esther Meadows had chosen to stay at home and

wait for news of her husband. Eight months pregnant with her sixth child, Esther was no doubt worried out of her wits. The boy who'd brought the news of the accident was her oldest son; if she lost Archie, the lad would be the only source of income for the whole family. It wasn't managing in terms of survival which was foremost in Alice's own thoughts, however; it was how she would manage without Sam. She closed her eyes briefly in prayer. Please God, let him come out alive. Alive and unharmed.

Little conversation passed between her and Bella and Mary; they stood for the most part in silence, watching and waiting. Bella and Mary both knew better than to reassure her that all would be well — they were as familiar as Alice was with the miners' graves in the Reefton cemetery. Fatalities were rare, in fact, but they did happen, and it was unplanned explosions such as this that were normally the cause of them.

As the light faded to twilight and the air began to grow heavy with evening dampness the foreman strode over to them again. His face was filthy and his shirt was stained with large dark puddles of sweat. No news yet, she could tell. 'It'll be a few more hours yet before we reach your husband, Mrs Kenyon,' he informed gravely. 'We're making steady progress, but it's a slow business.'

'How much of the tunnel has collapsed?' Alice asked. They'd heard varying estimates — anything from twenty to sixty feet.

'About forty or fifty feet,' he replied. 'I'd say that where we're working now is where the explosion occurred, judging by the damage to the walls and roof. We've cleared about twenty feet, so we shouldn't have much more than another twenty to go. We're about forty feet from the face, by my reckoning, so if your husband was at the face when the explosion occurred there's a good chance he may have escaped serious injury.'

She sucked in a long, low breath. It was the first real ray of hope she'd had. Sam had been at the face when Fred had left him. But had he still been there when the explosion had occurred?

Pausing, Ogilvie folded his arms in the way men did when about to issue a mandate of some kind. When he spoke again his tone was gentle but firm. 'I must insist that you leave now, Mrs Kenyon — you and your companions here. It will be fully dark within a half-hour.' He glanced up at the greying sky then his gaze flicked across to a young miner who was standing a few yards distant holding a lamp in his hand, the flame a feeble, insubstantial glow in the fading twilight. 'John Redpath will see you safely down the track to the town. And you may rest assured that I shall send word to you the moment there's news of your husband.' He gave a small nod. 'You have my word on it.'

Bella's fingers curled around Alice's upper arm, squeezing gently. 'Alice — you'll hear as soon as there's something to hear. You can't stay here all night — you'll catch your death of cold.' Her long fingers quivered suddenly as she gave an involuntary shiver.

Alice glanced across at the other two women, feeling a stab of guilt. None of them were warmly clad, the woollen shawls wrapped around their shoulders no match for the night chill that was settling in a misty blanket, beading Bella's black hair with a fine web of silver droplets. 'Go home, Bella. You too, Mary,' she said quietly. 'I'll be all right on my own.' Bella and Mary exchanged glances while Ogilvie purposefully cleared his throat.

'Mrs Kenyon, you cannot stay here alone at night,'

he stated in tones which defied any further argument on that point.

'Mr Ogilvie,' she returned, matching his tone. She lifted her right hand and pointed to the shaft, now partially hidden in shadow. 'My husband is down there, trapped, and I'm not leaving here until I have some definite news of him!'

Narrowing his eyes, Ogilvie tugged at his moustache several times, looking as if he didn't quite know how to deal with this mutinous situation. Evidently reaching a decision he stepped forward. Gesturing Mary and Bella aside, he placed his hand firmly on Alice's back and steered her towards the waiting John Redpath. 'As mine foreman, Mrs Kenyon, I have a responsibility not only to the miners at the Energetic but to their families also,' he said. 'And I doubt your husband will thank me if I bring him out alive and well, only to find that in a day or two's time his wife is lying in bed suffering from pneumonia because I allowed her to remain at the mine all night with nothing but a thin woollen cloak to keep the cold out of her bones.'

As he stepped aside Bella took hold of her left arm and Mary her right, pulling her on towards the track. 'He's right, Alice,' Bella said quietly. 'You've the children to think of too.'

She glanced back over her shoulder at the receding figure of the foreman and, with little choice, reluctantly set off back for Black's Point. It was fully dark by the time they reached the town. Just as the miners from the other shifts had been quick to lend their help in the emergency, the wives had also rallied. Meg Pringle had put Charlotte to bed and, rather than disturb her sleep, insisted that Alice should leave her be for the night; Matt and Lydia Donne had assumed responsibility for

Michael, and Bella's three children had been taken in by a neighbour.

'Is Mr Kenyon all right?' Michael asked, his coppery brows drawn together in a worried frown as he pushed past Matt Donne.

'Let your sister come in, lad,' Matt reproached him gently, moving him aside so that Alice could get through the doorway.

'Is he all right, Alice?' Michael repeated impatiently.

'I don't know. They haven't reached him yet,' she replied in a strained voice.

'Come and sit down, Alice,' Lydia said, patting the arm of the sofa beside the fire. 'I'll fetch you some hot tea. You look chilled to the bone,' she said in concern.

With a grateful nod Alice walked across to the proffered seat and sank into it. She felt exhausted. Physically and emotionally drained.

'A small drop of brandy wouldn't go amiss in it, Lydia,' Matt said over his shoulder as he shut the door.

'When will we know if he's all right?' Michael demanded, stationing himself in front of the sofa, the anxious frown still creasing his brow.

'It'll be a few more hours yet I think,' she said. She closed her eyes as another wave of exhaustion flooded over her, wishing more than anything in the world she could leave them shut, fall into a deep sleep, and wake up to find that none of this had really happened. 'The foreman will send word as soon as there's some news,' she said, forcing herself to open them again.

'Ogilvie is an experienced foreman. He'll proceed with caution. It's a case of more haste less speed when you're clearing a bad fall of rock from an explosion.' A small popping noise sounded behind her as Matt pulled the cork from the brandy bottle, followed by two little glugs as he poured. Sharp, aromatic fumes wafted beneath Alice's nose as Lydia passed her the fortified tea.

'How is Esther Meadows?' Alice asked, looking up as she took the cup from her.

'Worried,' Lydia said.

Alice nodded and lowered her eyes to stare into the fire. So was she. The Lloyd brothers, the other two men trapped in the mine, haled from Hokitika so their family was presently unaware of the worrying circumstances they were in.

An hour later, having at Lydia's insistence forced down some chicken broth and some bread which had stuck in her throat and almost choked her, Alice made her way back to the tent with Michael. It would probably be some hours yet before news came but she nevertheless felt anxious to be back at the tent, wanting to make sure she was there when news did eventually come.

After the warmth of Lydia's cosy kitchen the tent felt as damp and cold as the grave. Fumbling in the darkness to find the matches and with fingers that shook with more than just cold, she lit the lamp.

'How soon do you think somebody will come with news?' Michael asked, as the wick burst into a fitful circle of flame.

Reaching for the glass chimney Alice slotted it back into the brass base of the lamp. 'I don't know, Michael,' she said for at least the fourth time. 'It will be a while yet.' Her breath drifted down the chimney as she blew out the match, making the flames lick and curl around the sides of the glass before settling into a steady glow. Michael stood in silence watching her as she turned the knob to adjust the flame, then with a sigh he sat down and folded his arms on the table, resting his chin on them as he stared blank-eyed into space.

Unable to sit still, Alice paced back and forth, sometimes inside the tent, sometimes outside, casting hopeful glances up Boundary Street, willing a miner bearing news to appear. The wooden mantel clock which now resided on the table, the mantel having burnt in the fire, had unhelpfully stopped so she had no idea what the time was. Eventually, after one of her pacing sessions outside the tent she came in to find Michael's head had fallen to the side on his elbows on the table and his eyes were shut. She stood for several minutes, listening to the soft, rhythmic sound of his breathing, watching the slight lift and fall of his head and the flutter of his eyelashes as he dreamed, then she turned and went outside again, pacing back and forth in the darkness, listening for another sound — the sound of footsteps, bringing news from the mine.

At last they came. She was sitting inside the tent when she heard them. A man's steps. No, several men's steps. At least two men anyway — it was hard to tell what were footfalls and what were echoes. She stiffened, holding her breath, as the sound of male voices reached her ears, mingled with the footsteps. She was fairly certain she recognised Fred's deep rumble among them. She let out a shaky breath. It was bad news then. The miners were returning to their homes; they had reached the trapped men and Fred had been sent to bring the news to her. She pushed herself slowly to her feet and wrapped her arms tightly around her middle. Her chest felt as tight as a drum and she had started to shake. She took a deep breath and walked outside into the chill night air, peering through the gloom to where four miners were clustered together. It had started to drizzle, a fine grey mist, but even through the mist and gloom she could make out Fred's burly shape.

She stood outside the tent, waiting. All this time she'd been anxiously wanting news and now it was here she wanted more than anything in the world not to hear it. She drew in a sharp breath as the group of men suddenly parted, taking their different ways homewards, to leave one man standing on his own. He was standing quite still, staring at her where she stood silhouetted against the pale light drifting from the tent. 'Sam,' she whispered, hardly daring to speak the word lest she was wrong.

She started to walk, slowly at first, still unsure, then as he began to walk towards her with quick strides she broke into a run. Her legs were as wobbly as a newborn calf's and as she drew close to him she stumbled and almost fell into his arms.

'Alice,' he said hoarsely and clasped her tightly against his chest.

She craned her head back, her cheeks wet with tears, her breath coming in gulping sobs. 'Oh, Sam, I thought you were dead!'

'I'm all right, Alice,' he assured quietly. 'I've taken no harm.'

'And the others?' She knew even before he answered the news was not all good.

'Archie Meadows is dead,' he said softly.

'How did it happen?' she asked.

Sam let out a long breath. They had gone down to the river, wanting to have a few minutes by themselves before going into the tent and waking Michael to let him know Sam was safe.

'I don't know,' he said. 'Nobody knows for certain what happened. I was at the face, talking to Henry Lloyd and his brother Charlie while they tapped a powder hole.

Henry had asked me if I'd make him some new boots so we were discussing what he wanted. The others had all set off back along the drive to go up to the surface, except for Archie, he stayed behind listening to us talking.' He lifted his hand and rubbed his chin with his knuckles, staring out across the dark surface of the water. 'I didn't even notice Archie go. Then I heard him calling to me from down the drive, saying one of the candles was just about spent and asking me to bring a fresh one from the supply box to replace it. I shouted back that I would, then a few seconds later he called out again saying that I needn't bother because he'd found a new candle himself.' He shook his head and swallowed heavily. 'The next I knew there was a deafening explosion, and I flung myself to the ground and covered my head with my arms. I could hear the rocks crashing down further back down the drive and there was a big rush of air and the candles all went out and it was pitch-black. God, it was black,' he whispered.

She tightened her grip on his hand.

'As for what caused the explosion . . .' He shook his head again. 'All we can suppose is that Archie took the spent candle off the spider, tossed it aside without extinguishing it properly, and that it landed in the box containing the blasting powder.'

'But what was the blasting-powder box doing there?' Alice asked, frowning.

'Charlie Lloyd left it there,' he said, turning towards her. 'For safety,' he added with heavy irony. 'A cousin of his was killed when he was tapping a blasting hole and a spark from his hammer ignited his powder box, so Charlie always makes a point of leaving the powder a long way from the face while he's tapping.'

'And the box didn't have a lid on?' Evidently it hadn't

or the candle wouldn't have landed inside it.

'That's the other irony of it all,' he said. 'Normally it did have a lid, but Charlie couldn't find it so he improvised and placed a sheet of tin on top of the box to keep out the drips from the roof. It must have been dislodged.' He paused and gave another deep sigh. 'It was one of those freak accidents that ought never to have happened.'

But happen it had. The only consolation for Archie's widow, if consolation it could be called, was that he wouldn't have felt a thing.

'Poor Esther,' she said, and her eyes filled with tears.

Sam nodded, his mouth set hard as he struggled to hold his own emotions at bay. Wordlessly, he reached for her and she stepped forward into his arms. It was some minutes before either of them moved, but at last Alice lifted her head and stretched up to kiss him, her face wet with tears. 'I love you, Sam,' she whispered.

He stared at her for a long moment, his eyes bright as diamonds with his own unshed tears, then he reached up to gently wipe the wetness from her cheeks with his fingers. 'I love you too, Alice,' he whispered back.

Archie's funeral, held two days later, was well attended. He had been well liked at the mine, a good worker and an open, guileless man who would do no one a bad turn. There wasn't a dry eye among the women, and a good deal of noisy nose-blowing among the miners from the Energetic, who had all come to pay their last respects. Archie's death had brought an unwelcome sobering reminder to the tightly knit mining community. A careless moment and a man had paid the price with his life. It could easily have been four lives lost too. The miners relied as much on each other for their safety as they did upon themselves. As Alice stood watching Archie's coffin being slowly lowered into the grave, her cheeks soaked with rain and tears, she closed her eyes in prayer for her own husband, standing safe and whole beside her. Watch over him, Lord God. Watch over Sam and keep him safe at the mine . . .

A week to the day after Archie's death, Esther Meadows gave birth to a son; he was small, three weeks premature, but seemingly healthy. She named him Archie. A fortnight later she and her family headed north to a brother in Nelson. She had written to him telling him of her circumstances and he had generously offered to take them in.

As was often the way with things, what was misfortune for one was fortune for another. The departure of Esther Meadows and her family had left a rented cottage vacant in the town. Neither Alice nor Sam was keen to take it, reluctant to profit from Archie's death like that, but with the first sprinkling of snow lying on the ground, Charlotte barking like a seal with croup and no prospect of another cottage falling empty, they shifted in.

Chapter 20

Sam leaned closer to the fire as he turned the page of the book. The firelight danced across his cheeks, bathing them in the warm colours of the flames. He was sitting on the sofa with Charlotte on his lap whilst Michael sat cross-legged on the rug in front of the hearth.

'Papa?' Sam glanced down at his daughter, smiling. She was looking up at him, prompting him to continue. The story was far beyond her comprehension, but she'd been listening intently to it. He cleared his throat and carried on.

'The wind roared fiercely through the mizzen mast and the sails shook with a fury. It was as if a devilish fist held them in its grasp, bent on ripping them free and casting them into the surging seas. Rain blasted from the heavens, flaying the seamen's faces, and lightning split open the black sky in crackling forks. The seas were huge. Waves fifty feet high, crested with angry white foam, reared and crashed onto the decks of the *Silver Dawn*, threatening to splinter the timbers. "Hold the wheel steady!" shouted Captain Childs. "Keep her bow pointed into the storm. If she turns we're lost!" An albatross, caught up in the fury of the storm, crashed onto the deck beside him, floundering helplessly with exhausted wings in a futile attempt to gain the skies again. A moment later it was gone, swept into the seething seas. Captain Childs crossed himself. "Lord have mercy on our souls, Lord have mercy on our souls . . ."'

Silence fell as Sam folded over the corner of the page to mark the place.

'Is that the end of the chapter?' Michael asked.

'It is,' Sam confirmed, turning to deposit the book on the sofa beside him.

Michael's mouth wilted in disappointment. 'It was a very short chapter.'

'Complain to the man who wrote it, not to me,' advised Sam. 'Anyway, you should be reading books yourself now. Let it be an incentive for you to try harder with your letters. You'll be able to read whatever you wish once you've mastered them.'

'I can read,' Michael defended. 'It's only the very long words I can't manage.' He glanced down at the closed book, frowning. 'Do they all perish?'

'You'll have to wait till next Sunday to discover that.'

'Will you just tell me if the cabin lad survives the storm then?' he pleaded.

Sam tilted his head to the side, considering, then shook his head. 'No.'

'He dies?' Michael gasped.

Sam rolled his eyes. 'You asked me if I would tell you what befalls him — my "no" was in answer to that question. No, I won't tell you. You must wait to find out.'

Michael's shoulders slumped with relief. 'Oh, I thought you meant he died. I hope he doesn't. He doesn't deserve to die after being so courageous.'

'Courage is no guarantee of a long life,' Sam commented in sobering tones. 'In fact, it's more likely to cut your life short. If you've need of courage it usually means you're in dangerous circumstances.'

'I hope he doesn't die,' Michael repeated. 'It would spoil the story if he died. Was your father ever in any danger when he was at sea, Mr Kenyon?'

'Occasionally he was.' Sam caught Alice's eye and smiled. She was sitting at the table, sewing. 'Before my father became a fisherman,' he continued, looking back at Michael, 'he worked on a whaling boat for a year or two. He was tossed out of the boat once when they were in pursuit of a whale — tossed from the row boat, that is. A wave hit it broadside and swept him into the sea.'

'Did the whale turn on him?' Michael asked, wide-eyed.

Sam laughed. 'A whale with a harpoon in its hide, being pursued by a boat with six men aboard all bent on killing it, tends to be not too concerned about a floundering seaman. No — he was in danger of dying from cold in the water. If the rope to the harpoon hadn't snapped and the boat not gone back for him, he'd probably not have lived to tell the tale at all.'

'Oh,' Michael said, plainly disappointed by the story. 'Did he ever do anything courageous?'

'He did. He got back in the rowboat and took an oar again the next day,' Sam replied drily.

Michael stared at him blankly. The comment had been completely lost on his young mind.

'You'll understand one day, Michael,' Alice said, reaching for a sewing pin.

'Understand what?' he asked, looking blanker still.

'That battling fierce storms and fighting bloody battles are not the only ways a man can prove he's brave,' she said. Michael wasn't old enough yet to appreciate the quiet, unheroic, unsung courage which more often marked life. Sam had never said anything, but she knew he'd not found it easy to go back down the mine after the explosion. He had been entombed for over twelve hours in total blackness, knowing that somewhere in that blackness, beneath all the fallen rock, lay Archie Meadows' mangled body. It was now over two months since the accident, and in terms of their marriage it was the closest she and Sam had ever been. There was nothing like believing you'd lost someone for making you suddenly realise how much you cared for them.

'I'd like to go to sea. Not on a whaleboat though — on a trading vessel,' Michael pronounced, rolling back onto the rug.

'You have a fancy to perish from cold in the sea, do you?' enquired Sam.

'You wanted to be a blacksmith last week, like Mr Tweedie,' Alice commented as she pricked her needle into the white fabric.

'No, I didn't,' he said, glancing back at her. 'I only said that I'd like to forge something out of iron like he does.'

'As we're discussing professions, how is the hunting going? Have you mastered that catapult yet?' Sam asked.

'I'm getting better with it,' Michael replied, sitting up again. 'I can hit things when they're standing still, but I can't hit them when they're moving.'

'You're not meant to hit things when they're moving,' Sam returned. 'You're meant to not disturb your prey, so that you can aim while it's stationary, while it's still unaware of your presence. How long before the dinner is cooked, Alice?' he asked, glancing across at her. 'Have I time to spend an hour in the bush with Michael and his catapult? I think he could do with a lesson or two in stalking.'

She nodded. 'Don't be any longer than an hour

though, unless you like burnt pastry.'

Peer, who was waiting outside the door, gave an excited bark as Michael opened it, and began to bound around in his usual silly fashion.

Michael stooped to pat him. 'All right, Peer. You can come too. We're going hunting again.'

'Do you always take Peer with you when you go hunting with your catapult?' Sam asked.

'Of course I do,' Michael replied, as if that went without saying.

Sam shook his head, chuckling. 'In that case, lad, I'm not surprised you've killed nothing. How do you expect to make a silent approach with Peer barking and bounding around all the while? Tie him up somewhere.'

In a little less than an hour they were back again. The expedition had been fruitful, success written across Michael's face in a beaming ear-to-ear grin. Two fat pigeons dangled from his hands, their lifeless wings hanging limply down, spread out like sails.

Shortly after the midday meal, Sam took out his tools and began to tap away at his last. Over the last two months he'd been spending most evenings and every Sunday mending boots as a means of earning some additional income. He presently had six pairs queued up awaiting his attention. His Sabbath cobbling activities had drawn mixed reactions among the families at Black's Point. Meg Pringle had been very cool in her dealings with them since Sam had started this particular activity. It wasn't that she disapproved of a man working on a Sunday, she had privately told Bella, it was working *for gain* on the Sabbath of which she disapproved. Alice had made no comment, but she had felt quite annoyed with Meg's criticism of Sam — after all, it wasn't as if he was working on a Sunday from greed, he was working in order to put a roof over his family's heads again.

'Can I take Charlotte to see the dead cow in the river, Alice?' Michael asked.

'Dead cow?' Sam looked up with interest.

'Sam — no!' Alice said, reading his mind. Frugality was all very well, but there were limits.

Ignoring her he set down his hammer. 'Where is it?'

Michael shrugged. 'About a quarter of a mile downstream. It's caught between the branches of a tree that's toppled into the river.'

'When did you first notice it?'

'Yesterday afternoon.'

'Yesterday?' Sam stretched across the table for his knife. 'Show me where it is.'

'Sam!' Alice said firmly, positioning herself squarely in front of the door. 'I'm not going to feed my family on beef from a drowned animal. You've no idea how it died — it might have been sick.'

'Alice . . .' Sam patted her arm reassuringly as he moved her aside. 'It's not the meat that interests me. It's the hide.'

Five minutes later he was hanging out over the river, precariously spread-eagled across the branches of a fallen willow, speculatively prodding a very bloated yearling. It had rolled onto its back and all four legs were pointing to the sky, rigid as broomsticks. 'It seems to be in not too bad condition,' he pronounced. 'I don't think it can have been dead for much more than a day.'

'How will you get it ashore?' Michael's voice came from the bank.

'I'll wade out into the river and free it, then push it ashore,' he said, edging his way back.

'I'll help,' Michael volunteered, already dragging his shirt over his head.

'You might regret it,' Sam warned. 'The water is very chilly.'

Undaunted, Michael waded out and began to pull aside branches while Sam manoeuvred the dead animal out of the tree's stranglehold. Ten minutes later he was kneeling in the shallows, shivering uncontrollably, watching intently as Sam cut a clean line around the neck and tail.

'One advantage of an animal which has been dead for a while is that it doesn't bleed,' Sam murmured. It was possibly the only advantage.

'What do you do next?' Michael asked, inching forward on his knees to get a better view.

'Slit open the belly to let out the guts,' Sam said. Frowning in concentration he pressed the animal's belly experimentally. It was as taut as a drum. 'Hold your breath,' he said. Drawing in a deep breath himself, he cut a swift line the length of the dead animal's belly. The effect was instantaneous. There was a sudden whooshing sound as the gases escaped, an indescribable stench filled the air, and the viscera poured out in a mass into the water. Sam swallowed, trying not to breathe in, then glanced across at Michael, who was staring in green-faced fascination at the slithering progress of a fat grey entrail as it slowly slid from the animal's gaping belly.

'Are you all right, lad?' Sam asked. Getting no answer he said more loudly, 'Michael — are you all right?'

Michael swallowed and nodded.

Sam watched him dubiously. The lad didn't look all right — he looked as if he might vomit at any moment. If he watched the rest of the operation, he most certainly would. 'I think I may need a smaller knife,' he said. 'Run back to the cottage and fetch the one I keep on the shelf in the bedroom, Michael.'

By the time Michael returned the guts were disposed of, tossed into the middle of the river, slowly slithering their way to the sea.

In the proper environment, with a handy beam to suspend a dead animal from, skinning is a relatively straightforward task. With a bit of encouragement the hide more or less peels off. Without a beam though, and in the absence of a suitably sturdy tree to serve as one the job proved rather more difficult. Eventually though, the hide lay in a reasonably intact state on the bank.

'Is it a good hide, Mr Kenyon?' Michael asked, prodding it.

'I think it should be all right,' Sam replied, squatting down to examine his handiwork. 'It's thin in places but I should be able to use most of it.'

'What will you make from it?'

'Children's boots and shoes. The leather doesn't need to be so strong for them.'

'How do you get rid of the hairs? Do you shave them off with your razor?'

Sam smiled. It was a reasonable supposition. 'No. You have to soak the hide in a bucket of lye and warm water. The hairs start to loosen after a day or two and you can scrape them off fairly easily then. There's a bit of work to do before we get to that stage though. The hide has to be salted and fleshed first.'

For the next two hours the Kenyon cottage was the scene of the most unSabbathly activity imaginable. It was as well Meg Pringle wasn't around to observe it. While Sam and Michael rubbed copious quantities of salt into the hide, Alice set about plucking and gutting the two pigeons. Typically, once the hide had been dealt with, Michael rapidly became restless again. He was at an age when he needed to be constantly doing something. Normally he would have gone off somewhere with Robert, but unfortunately Robert had earache today.

'Take Charlotte for a walk,' Alice suggested. The suggestion drew a noticeable lack of enthusiasm. She amended it a bit in the hopes of giving it more appeal. 'Take her to the river and show her how you can skim stones on the water.'

The ploy worked. Charlotte, though fairly boring company for a boy eight years her senior, did have one very attractive attribute — she could clap. Moreover she could be relied upon to clap very loudly at the slightest prompting. She was therefore the ideal person to take along if you happened to want to show off your skills in front of a small, enthusiastic audience.

'Come, Charlotte,' Michael said, scrambling to his feet. 'I'll teach you how to bounce pebbles across the water.' Charlotte looked as if she would have preferred to stay playing on the rug with her wooden doll, but she went without complaint as Michael took her hand and towed her off towards the river.

'What are you sewing, Alice?' Sam asked over his shoulder. He held up the shred of white fabric, frowning as he cast his eye over it. It was inside out and the needle which she'd stuck through it was preventing it from falling down fully to show the proper shape of it. It looked more like a rag than the special little garment that it actually was.

She walked across to him and took it from his hands. Slipping free the needle, she turned the fabric right side out, gave it a small shake and held it up for him to see. She had been waiting patiently for over a week now for him to ask about it.

'Oh, that's what it is,' he said, nodding approvingly. 'It's for Ellen's baby, is it? She must be due to have the child quite soon.'

'No, Sam, it's not for Ellen's baby,' she said.

He looked up, took in her spreading smile, and said uncertainly, 'You mean?'

'Yes, I do,' she said, still smiling.

His mouth stretched into an ear-to-ear grin. 'When?'

'Next April.'

He glanced down at her stomach, still flat as a pancake, then with an exultant laugh he pulled her into his arms and kissed her.

'I take it you're pleased,' she said, laughing.

'Of course I am,' he said. 'I'm very pleased!' The pleased grin faded slightly. 'How are you feeling? I've not noticed you looking sick in the mornings.'

'I feel very well,' she said. In fact, she'd never felt better. 'I've not felt sick at all yet.'

'Oh, that's good,' he said with relief. He glanced round the interior of the cottage, looking as if he was already planning for the event.

'Will we still be here at Black's Point in April, do you think?' she asked.

'I hope not,' he said with feeling. 'April — seven months away. I'd like to think we'll be back in our own home when you have the baby.' He bent forward to kiss her again. 'And there's a bit of an incentive for haste now,' he added, grinning.

'Alice.' A peeved voice sounded from behind them.

Sam rolled his eyes, released her from his arms and looked over his shoulder to the doorway where Michael was standing, in a considerably dirtier state than when he had left two minutes ago. His shirt and trousers were splattered with mud.

'Charlotte has fallen over and she's crying,' he announced. 'She won't let me bring her home. She started throwing clods of earth at me when I tried to pick her up.'

Sam gave a weary sigh. 'I'll go and fetch her.' As his eyes briefly met Alice's, his mouth lifted at one corner in a wry smile. 'I daresay she'll be crying even louder in a minute or two.'

As he strode off Alice eyed Michael dubiously. She had a small suspicion that Charlotte might have been throwing clods with good reason. She also suspected that her fall might have been assisted by a little shove. It was equally possible, of course, that Charlotte was simply having a tantrum.

Reading her mind, Michael glared at her. 'I didn't trip her!'

Ah, she thought, so he hadn't shoved her — he'd tripped her up. 'I should hope you didn't,' she said. 'It would be a very mean, cowardly act to trip a child half your size.'

Confirming her suspicions, Michael's cheeks filled with guilty fire. He turned away and a moment or two later asked, 'Will Mr Kenyon smack her?'

'I expect so,' she said.

'He never smacks her very hard,' he mumbled.

'No. But hard enough to make her cry.' Folding the small gown neatly into a square Alice dropped it into her sewing basket then looked up and said casually, 'Anyway, it's of no concern to you if her bottom smarts. She deserves to be smacked — she has to learn that she can't throw mud at you for no reason, especially when you were being so kind to her, trying to help her home.'

The fire in his cheeks turned a shade deeper and as Sam reappeared with his daughter in his arms, advising her that she was going to be punished for her naughtiness, Michael disappeared outside. Alice gave a disappointed sigh as she watched him running off towards the river. Michael still had a lot to learn about the nature of real courage.

Chapter 21

'Hannah Jane,' Ellen pronounced proudly.

Alice leaned over the cradle to admire the new arrival. Ten days ago, on 1 October, Ellen had been delivered of a fine, healthy baby girl. 'She's beautiful, Ellen,' she murmured. It was no lie. Hannah Jane was a very pretty baby, with cherubic pink cheeks, a dainty button nose and wispy fair hair. She promised to be like her mother.

'She weighed seven pounds five ounces,' Ellen said with a sigh. 'I felt like I was pushing out a calf at least!'

'A very pretty calf,' Alice said, laughing. 'Did Dr Martin deliver her?'

Ellen shook her head. 'No. Mrs Bamforth attended me. George wanted Dr Martin to attend the delivery, but I said I wouldn't hear of it. I told him I'd never set foot in church again if Dr Martin delivered my child. How could I ever bring myself to sit in the pew behind the man, knowing what he'd seen of me? I told George I wanted a midwife, a woman like myself.' She patted the sofa, smiling contentedly. 'Come and sit down, Alice. It's weeks since I've seen you.'

Pausing to give Hannah Jane's cheek a parting little stroke, Alice went to join Ellen on the couch. 'Was it a difficult birth then?'

Ellen shrugged. 'Oh, not too bad, I suppose. Twenty

hours from when I first started with my pains so I can't complain too much. Some women are in labour for days.'

'She seems very contented. Does she sleep well during the night?' Alice asked.

A small frown creased Ellen's brow as her gaze drifted back to the cradle. 'Not as well as I'd like. She woke four times last night and she has a good pair of lungs when she's hungry. George was a bit short of patience this morning when he rose. He's very proud of her though — you'd think he was the only man in Reefton ever to have fathered a child. And my mother and father dote on her — I can hardly prise her from my mother's arms when she comes to visit us. She's their first granddaughter though, so I suppose it's understandable.'

'Have you plenty of milk?' Alice asked.

Ellen smiled wryly as she ran a hand over her matronly chest. 'More than plenty. It nearly drowns the poor mite. I wish Mr Hardaker's cows had parted with it so readily.'

Alice laughed, recalling the difficulty they'd had persuading milk to come from one or two reluctant udders. It all seemed a very long time ago now. A lot of water had flowed under the bridge since then.

'Speaking of Mr Hardaker — what do you think about the news about John Barnes?' Ellen asked.

'What news?' she said, frowning.

'You've not heard?' Ellen's eyes widened in surprise. 'He's left the district. Gone to Nelson to marry his cousin, or second cousin or half cousin or something of the sort. I forget which exactly it is. A relative on his mother's side. She's a widow. Anyway, it sounds as if he will do all right from it. She's not without money, I hear. She owns a small farm.'

Alice raised her brows. She wasn't so much surprised at John Barnes' marrying, as his leaving the district. He'd always struck her as a man who would be as hard to shift from Reefton as the hills. 'His mother will miss him,' she commented.

Ellen tossed her head back, laughing. 'Alice — you surely don't think his mother would let him leave her behind! She's gone too. It was his mother who arranged the match. I thought you'd have heard about it. Does news of Reefton happenings not reach Black's Point?'

'Well, we do hear some pieces of news,' she said. She wasn't altogether surprised the news of John Barnes' departure to Nelson hadn't travelled as far as Black's Point though — it was hardly the sort of news which was of widespread interest. News which travelled far and wide was the kind which involved scandal or intrigue — like her sudden marriage to Sam Kenyon, the burning down of their home, and Sam's fight with Zac Fielding. One way or another she and Sam had done quite a bit to spice up an otherwise dull winter for the district.

'There is one piece of news which you don't know,' Alice mentioned casually. 'I'm pregnant.'

'Oh, Alice!' Ellen clapped her hands in delight. 'Oh, I'm so glad for you. It will be so nice for you have a child of your own. I know Charlotte is a sweet child, but ... well, it's not quite the same as having a child you've given birth to yourself. When is your baby due?'

'Next April.' Alice straightened out the corners of her mouth a little, suddenly realising that she was grinning like a village idiot.

'April. Will you still be at Black's Point for the birth?'

She gave a small shrug. 'I'm not sure. Sam's hopeful he'll have enough money to rebuild the house before

I'm delivered of the baby. It won't be as large as the house we lost, but it'll suffice for the time being.'

'I'm sure if it can be managed your husband will manage it, Alice,' Ellen said positively. 'Have you been plagued by sickness in the mornings?'

'No, I haven't,' she said smugly. 'I've felt very well.'

'Oh, that's a mercy — I felt terrible for the first six months. I couldn't eat a thing till midday,' Ellen said, grimacing at the recollection. 'Alice, do have a cup of tea with me,' she said, rising to her feet. 'The midwife said I must drink eight cups a day while I'm nursing.'

Alice turned to glance at the fine black marble clock on the mantelpiece. A recent acquisition by the look of it, which Ellen, bless her, had been diplomatic enough not to mention, knowing there was no spare money in the Kenyon household to buy such luxuries. 'Well, just a quick one,' she said. 'But I mustn't stay too long. I've left Charlotte with Bella Wrigley and I want to stop by the cemetery before I go back to Black's Point.'

Ellen stared at her for a moment then reached out to touch her hand. 'I'd forgotten. It's just over twelve months since your father died, isn't it.' She shook her head, frowning. 'I can hardly think it's a full year ago. It only seems like yesterday that you buried him.'

'It seems a very long time ago to me,' Alice said.

It was months since Alice had visited her parents' grave — she hadn't been since their move to Black's Point. She walked up to it feeling slightly guilty. The patches of lichen on the headstone had grown considerably since her last visit — the largest one was now half obscuring her mother's name. She'd meant to bring a knife to scrape it clean.

Margaret Thorpe . . . died 17th July 1873 . . . aged 42

years. She spoke the words aloud, reading the inscription, her voice small and hollow in the silence of the graveyard. Forty-two years. Eliza Kenyon had had even fewer years — just a brief twenty-four, that was all. Life wasn't always as long as people hoped for. And how long will I have, she wondered. Long enough to raise the child she was carrying? Long enough to see Michael grow to a man? Long enough to hold her grandchildren in her arms? She looked up at the sky, a vast expanse of blue, ribboned with cloud that shone like silver in the spring sun.

'You do indeed move in mysterious, unfathomable ways,' she said softly.

Inside her womb a child was growing — a child whom her mother and father would never see, never hold, never take joy in as Ellen's parents would take joy in little Hannah Jane. Her parents would never know this grandchild. They had known Michael though, at least they had known Michael. She closed her eyes, fighting back tears. She loved Michael with all her heart now, but there was a time when, if she could have turned back the tide and changed the path of her life so that she hadn't conceived him, she would have grasped the chance with both hands. And in grasping it she would have denied her parents the joy of seeing, holding, loving the only grandchild they would ever know. And they really had loved Michael — both of them. Loved him as if he was their own son. Raised him as if he was their own son.

All things work together for good to them that love God — Reverend Murray's pious words drifted back to her. Reverend Murray . . . stout, ruddy-faced Reverend Murray . . . he'd called to visit her a few days after Michael's birth, in her parent's home in Akaroa. His visit had been ill-timed. She'd had a bad night with a demanding, insatiable baby who screamed for food every two hours, she was still weak and sore from a long and gruelling labour, and she'd been in no mood to hear glib godly comments, however well intentioned. Added to which, she wasn't at all sure that she did 'love God' — the biblical prerequisite for all things working together for good. She felt very angry with Him. The rape had occurred on her way home from church and she felt a deep sense of betrayal that God could let such a thing happen to her when she had just been faithfully worshipping Him. 'For good?' she had exclaimed in highly sarcastic tones. 'What possible good can come from being raped, Reverend Murray?' He had blinked at her like a startled owl then intoned gravely, 'The crucifixion of Christ was not a pleasant affair, Miss Thorpe, but great good came out of that.' She'd had no answer to that statement and had subsequently maintained a sullen silence for the remainder of his visit, then been given a sound scolding by her mother for her rudeness after he had left. In hindsight, Reverend Murray's words had been wiser than she had given the man credit for. Things had worked together for good. Eventually.

She lowered her eyes back to the grave, blinking back tears. 'You would be proud of Michael. He's growing into a fine boy, Mother,' she whispered. 'And you would like Sam, Father. He's a good man.'

How good though? Good enough to live with the knowledge that Michael was her son, the product of a vicious rape? Good enough not to hold it against him, to treat him no differently? Good enough to forgive her for not telling him? She bit her lip and shook her head. He would need to be more than good; he would need to be a saint. And to tell him, what would be gained? It would ease her conscience — that's what would be gained. And that was no small thing. But much as she loathed lying, truth wasn't always the best course. As for Michael — he wouldn't thank her for telling him the truth about his parentage, for telling him that his father was not the good man he remembered, but a seaman who had violently raped his sister . . . his mother.

She stood in silence, staring at the grey headstone. A small spider was climbing across it, scaling the chiselled surface as if it were a plain riddled with deep ravines. She watched it as it clambered in and out of the grooved letters of her father's name, but as it reached the *H* it dropped suddenly, drifted in the breeze for a moment, suspended on an invisible thread, then dropped again and was gone. With a sigh her gaze returned to the headstone. She reached out to touch it in silent farewell, then made her way through the long grass towards another grave.

Alice had never visited Eliza's grave before. She'd almost visited it last time she'd come to the cemetery, but something had held her back — an inexplicable feeling she ought not to intrude. Even now she felt awkward as she approached the pale stone that stood in the shadow of a young yew tree. It was here twelve months ago that she'd seen Sam standing with his daughter in his arms, grieving at his wife's graveside, while she had stood grieving beside her father's open grave on the day of his burial. She looked down at the inscription.

In loving memory of Eliza Kenyon who departed this life September 16th 1881 in the 24th year of her life. At the base of the stone, partly obscured by long blades of grass, were inscribed the words *Rest in peace.*

Rest in peace. She swallowed to clear the lump in

her throat and wiped away the tears slipping down her cheeks. It would be very hard to die peacefully knowing you left behind a small daughter like Charlotte, and a husband whom you dearly loved.

'Rest in peace, Eliza,' she whispered hoarsely. 'They're well cared for.'

Chapter 22

'Did you remember to bring some potatoes?' Sam asked.

Alice patted her bulging pockets. 'I did, but the flames are much too high to put them in the fire yet. They cook best if the wood is just glowing.'

He glanced down, smiling. His face was shining like silk in the bright light of the bonfire. The Guy Fawkes celebration, normally just a modest bonfire on the riverbank with a few fireworks, promised to be rather more spectacular this year. Chinese Bill had offered to make some 'special' fireworks. On a perfect evening with hardly a breath of wind, just about the whole town had turned out to enjoy the festivities.

'It's years since I stood beside a bonfire to celebrate November the fifth,' Sam said in a wistful voice as he gazed into the leaping flames. 'The last time was when I was just a lad, in Greymouth. We built an enormous bonfire on the beach — we'd gathered driftwood for weeks beforehand and there was a huge pile of wood. It was still smouldering a week later.' He paused to lift Charlotte into a more comfortable position in his arms — she was wrapped cosily in a woollen blanket, fast asleep. 'Did you have bonfires on the beach in Akaroa?'

Alice shook her head. 'Not on the beach, no, but there were usually some small ones in the town. Mr Butler, who owned the farm where my father worked, organised a bonfire on his property once. It wasn't on November fifth though — it was in February, to mark his son's coming of age.' She tossed back her head, laughing. 'He danced around the bonfire with me and I blushed every time I saw him for weeks afterwards, thinking he had a fancy for me.'

'And did he?' Sam enquired.

She laughed again. 'I shouldn't think so — I was only thirteen, but thirteen-year-old girls have very good imaginations.'

'Thirteen-year-old lads do too,' he said, grinning. 'We used to live next to a family who had six daughters and the oldest one, Clara, was very pretty. She was fifteen and quite a bit taller than me but it didn't stop me from accosting her outside their privy to ask her if she'd walk out with me.'

'Outside the privy?' Alice echoed, raising her brows at him. 'Could you not have found somewhere more tasteful to approach her?'

His mouth crinkled into a wry grin. 'Well, it was the only place I could think of that she visited alone. I'd been trying to find a way to speak to her for weeks but whenever I saw her she was in the company of one of her sisters. Then I had this clever idea about the privy. So one night I hid outside their house and waited.' His grin spread and he gave a soft chuckle. 'I was crouching behind a bush so I wouldn't be seen and when she came out to go to the privy I stood up and stepped out. I was just mustering some courage to ask her if she'd consent to walk out with me the coming Sunday when she grabbed my arm and started cuffing my ear. I was so taken aback I just gaped at her. Then she bent down and shouted in my ear, "Pee behind your own bushes, Samuel Kenyon, you dirty little beggar!"'

'Is that what she thought you were doing there?' she asked, laughing.

'It was,' he said ruefully. 'It ruined my chances with her altogether.'

'I'm not surprised,' she said, her eyes still creased with laughter. 'Do you not think you were a bit young to be approaching her though?'

'Oh, I was far too young,' he said. 'But my brother Dan was walking out with a young woman, you see, and I liked to copy him. Dan is six years older than me but I was as broad in the shoulders and chest as he was, and like most thirteen-year-old lads I had rather an inflated opinion of myself at the time. I thought Clara Bentwick would be very flattered that I was showing an interest in her.'

'Did you think I would be flattered when you approached me?' she asked curiously.

'Lord no!' he said. 'I'd nothing to offer you but a long face, a fractious stepdaughter and a very modest home. You were hardly likely to feel flattered by an offer like that. I was surprised you even heard me out. I was fully expecting you to show me the door as soon as I mentioned the word marriage — assuming I was even invited inside.'

It was thirteen months since that wet Sunday afternoon when Sam had arrived on Alice's doorstep carrying his small daughter in his arms, wrapped in a woollen blanket just as she was now, and she had invited him inside out of the rain. They had been thirteen very chequered months. Their marriage had by no means been all plain sailing.

'Are you glad I didn't show you the door?' she quizzed. Sam seemed to be very content with their marriage nowadays, but he never said much. Still, from what she could gather from conversations with Ellen and Bella, it was quite usual for men not to say much. 'If they're not grumbling then assume they're content,' Bella had advised her.

'Well . . .' Sam said doubtfully. His mouth curled into a wry smile. 'I'm glad most of the time.'

She laughed and turned to smile at Matt and Lydia Donne as they walked over to join them. Lydia was carrying her baby son in her arms, now almost four months old.

'That's a mighty fine bonfire there,' Matt commented approvingly.

'It is,' Sam agreed. 'And a fine night for it too.' He glanced up at the sky, a deep velvet black, blazoned with stars.

'Has the Chinaman arrived yet?' Matt asked, casting his eye about.

'Not yet,' Sam said. 'But I shouldn't think he'll be long now.'

'Do you think his special fireworks will be very noisy?' Lydia asked, throwing an anxious glance at the sleeping child in her arms. 'I've heard they're quite large. I wouldn't want them to frighten Thomas.'

'Lydia, if Thomas can sleep through the din these lads are making he'll not be disturbed by a few crackling fireworks,' Matt assured, patting her hand. The lads in question, about twenty of them, were marching around the fire, swinging their arms like soldiers, loudly and none too tunefully chanting Guy Fawkes rhymes.

'Any sign of the Wrigleys yet?' Sam asked, glancing at Alice as he looked back over his shoulder towards the town. 'Ah, speak of the devil. Here they come now,' he said, smiling.

She turned to see Fred and Bella hurrying down

the slope towards them. Sidney was bouncing about in Bella's arms as she carried him, but he showed no sign of waking. Sidney could sleep through anything. Fireworks would pose no threat to his slumber. Having perforce learned to sleep through his father's thunderous snores, fireworks would seem like bubbles popping by comparison. Fred, looking decidedly disgruntled, was towing a very tearful-faced Jane along beside him.

'Right — stand there and don't move!' he instructed his daughter, positioning her squarely in front of his legs. 'Stupid child,' he muttered, turning to Sam. 'She tripped over as we were leaving the house, tore her good skirt and bloodied both her knees. We'd have been here half an hour ago but for that. You'd think a child of seven would be able to put one foot in front of the other without falling over.'

'She fell over the broom,' Bella whispered, joining Alice. 'It was lying across the doorstep. I think Robert left it there but I daren't tell Fred that.'

'No, best not to,' Alice agreed, smiling. Fred was a very good father but he didn't suffer fools gladly, nor was he blessed with an abundance of patience.

'Ah, here comes Chinese Bill with his firecrackers at last,' Sam announced, pointing to a diminutive figure carrying a sturdy wooden box, weaving his way through the crowd.

Depositing the box on the ground at a safe distance from the bonfire Chinese Bill inclined in a number of low bows. Normally dressed in a ragged old jacket and trousers he looked quite splendid tonight. He had donned a bright red sateen top which hung loosely over black sateen trousers, and a matching black cap with a long tassel. Not sure what sort of response to make to the ceremonial bowing session, several bystanders gave tentative little bows while others gave a few uncertain claps. The bowing finished, Chinese Bill turned his attention to the dozen or so children crowding around the box, jostling and elbowing each other in order to get a better view of the firecrackers. 'Goh! Goh! Goh!' Raising his silken arms he began to flap them wildly about.

'He looks like a goose trying to get airborne,' Bella chuckled.

'Mm, he sounds like one too,' Alice said, as the loud nasal calls of 'goh' continued.

'Michael! Come here!' Sam called. Reluctantly leaving his inspection of the fireworks, Michael ran over with Peer bounding at his heels and Robert following close behind.

'He has a dozen or more fireworks in his box!' Michael exclaimed in great excitement. 'And they're this big!' he said, spanning his hands.

Sam cast a frowning eye at Peer. 'Well, I doubt Peer will appreciate them. They'll frighten the dog out of his wits. You'd better take him back to the cottage. Tether him to the wagon.'

'But I might miss seeing some of the fireworks!' Michael protested.

'You'll miss seeing all of them if you argue,' Sam returned.

Michael pursed his lips, blew out a sharp sigh, then sped off. 'Come, Peer!' he yelled.

Alice turned to watch him run up the slope with Peer bounding after him, then turned back to watch the Chinaman's preparations. He was making quite a show of meticulously straightening the fuses — lengths of waxed string about six inches long.

'I hope these fireworks are more impressive than

they look,' she commented. She had expected them to be brightly decorated; instead they were very drab-looking cylinders fashioned from coarse brown paper.

'They have blasting powder inside and little bits of stone and some of them have scraps of oily rag stuffed inside,' Robert piped up knowledgeably.

Alice, Bella and Lydia exchanged alarmed glances.

'Bits of stone?' Fred echoed dubiously.

Robert nodded, but before he had time to elaborate Michael arrived back, panting and redfaced. 'I've tied him up, Mr Kenyon. I've tied him to the wagon. I couldn't find any rope so I used a piece of string.

Sam grunted, not in the least interested in dogs and string in the light of this recent piece of worrying news.

'Now, about these bits of stone, Robert . . .' Fred started to say again.

'Look! Look!' Michael butted in, pointing. 'He's bowing again. He's ready to start.'

Sam fought to keep a look of concern from his face. 'Thank God we're some distance away,' he muttered. 'I'm beginning to wonder if Chinese Bill knows what he's about.'

Ten uneventful minutes later a number of people were beginning to wonder if the Chinaman knew what he was about. Michael and Robert groaned in disappointment as the fifth firecracker in succession failed to display anything more impressive than a feeble glow on the end of a rapidly diminishing length of waxed string.

'Well, I don't think we need fear injury from the bits of stone he's purportedly put inside the firecrackers,' Sam remarked drily.

The sixth firework, however, did rather better, erupting in a fountain of brilliant white sparks. The display lasted for only four or five seconds, but it drew a loud burst of appreciative claps.

'Oh, that was very pretty,' Alice said, somewhat revising her judgment of the Chinaman's skills.

The next three, though, were as unspectacular as the first five. Disappointed mutters and bored foot shuffling ensued.

Sam stifled a yawn. 'I shall be glad when he's finished then you can put the potatoes into the fire, Alice. The flames are starting to die down now.'

'Peer! What are you doing here?' Michael demanded as a wet nose nudged his hand. 'You should be tied to the wagon! You wicked dog — you've broken the string!'

Sam glanced across at Alice and rolled his eyes. The string in question, the remains of which were still dangling around Peer's neck, looked incapable of tethering a decent-sized rat, much less a large, boisterous dog.

'Must I take him back to the wagon again?' Michael asked dejectedly.

'Oh, I suppose he can stay,' Sam ceded. 'If the last few firecrackers are as disappointing as the rest I don't imagine Peer is going to be unduly terrified.'

Considering the consistent lack of success he was enjoying, to his credit the Chinaman was exhibiting remarkable equanimity. Alice felt quite relieved for him when the final firework crackled suddenly into life and sent out dazzling cascades of shimmering golden stars and soaring red flares. Cheers and hearty clapping broke out from around the fire. The Chinaman, in a curious mixture of shyness and delight, bowed deeply, making the long tassel of his cap sweep gracefully across the ground.

'Why is everybody still clapping?' Michael asked, looking very puzzled as the exuberant applause continued. 'That was the only firework which exploded properly. Most of them failed.'

'Yes, they did,' Alice agreed. 'And that's why people are clapping so loudly — to make him feel less embarrassed about his failures. He spent a long time making the fireworks and it would be a poor thank you if we didn't applaud his effort.'

Michael, plainly not understanding the logic behind this statement, tossed a baffled glance at Robert, who was looking equally mystified by the explanation. 'Can we roast the potatoes now, Alice?' he asked.

She dug her hands into her pockets to retrieve them. 'Watch you don't burn them,' she cautioned.

'I expect they will,' Sam said resignedly as he watched the two boys run off towards the fire.

With the fireworks finished a number of families, many of them with fractious, overtired children, started to make their way homewards. The Wrigleys and the Donnes were among them. Sam fixed a wistful eye on the bonfire. 'How long will the potatoes take to cook, do you think?'

'Not long. Ten minutes. I boiled them for a short while so they really only need heating through.'

'Good, I'm ready for my bed,' Sam said, yawning again. 'I'm glad it's Sunday tomorrow and I won't have to go to the mine.'

'You don't like working in the mine, do you?' she commented quietly.

He shrugged and smiled as he turned towards her. 'Oh, it's not too bad. I suppose what I find difficult is, at the end of the day I've nothing to show for my labours but dirty hands. I'm used to being able to hold up a pair of boots that I've worked on and see something for my day's toil. I don't dislike the work at the mine, but I'll not deny that I shall be very glad to return to Reefton again, to my bootmaking and to my own home.'

'When do you think that will be?' So far Sam had given her only vague indications like 'before the winter sets in' or 'before the baby arrives', but it would be nice to have a definite date to look forward to.

'Well, provided we don't have any unexpected setbacks I think I should have sufficient savings to build a small cottage by the end of March. It won't be as big as the one that burnt down, I'm afraid. Just one bedroom to begin with.' He paused then added, 'I'm thinking of putting a partition and a couple of windows in the shed. I thought I could work in one half of it and make the other half into a small bedroom for Michael. I can't say that I'm altogether in favour of him sleeping in our bedroom.'

'I should think Michael will be delighted to have a room all to himself,' she said. Even if it was only half a shed. And to be honest she would welcome a bit more privacy herself. Michael had been sleeping in the same room as them ever since the fire and the arrangement was not without its drawbacks.

Sam smiled crookedly. 'Let's hope he's delighted enough to stop his complaining for a while. If he complains about his lessons and says he wants to finish his schooling and go to sea one more time, I swear I shall take him to the coast and put him on a vessel myself.'

'Well, you're the one who put the idea into his head,' she said in mildly reproving tones. 'You shouldn't have read that book about the whaling boat to him.'

Sam arched his brows indignantly. 'I read that book to him thinking that it might show him how much pleasure there is to be had from reading, in the hope he might feel inspired to sharpen his skills a bit. God knows they need sharpening. His spelling is abominable.' He lowered his eyes as the sleeping bundle in his arms stirred and gave a grumbling little wail. He watched her for a moment then looked up again and said softly, 'Do you ever find yourself wishing we'd had some time together without the encumbrance of children, Alice?'

She knew what he was saying, but if he was feeling encumbered now with two children how would he feel when the baby arrived? Her thoughts must have been written across her face because Sam's hand settled on hers, squeezing gently. 'I wasn't meaning that I resent having Charlotte and Michael, Alice. I only meant I wish I'd had the chance to . . . well, to have you to myself only for a while, the chance to take you into my arms when the mood takes me and not have to worry whether a ten-year-old lad might catch me kissing you, or whether my daughter might suddenly start wailing or demand to be picked up. Do you ever feel that?'

'Alice — is this cooked?' A smouldering, charred potato impaled on a sooty stick appeared in front of her nose.

'Perfectly,' she said, pushing it aside with her finger. 'Fetch the rest of them.'

As Michael ran back towards the bonfire Sam's eyes met hers humorously.

'Frequently,' she replied.

'It's a warm night,' Sam said, throwing back the blanket. His eyes popped for a second like a surprised bullfrog then he slowly raised his hand and scratched his chin in a slightly bemused fashion as he ran an appreciate eye over something he didn't normally see in bed — his wife's naked breasts.

'As you said, it's a warm night,' Alice said, smiling. Tossing decorum and her nightgown to the wind, she had decided to be bold tonight.

'Mm, it is warm,' Sam agreed, and promptly dragged his nightshirt over his head and dropped it on the floor. The bed springs twanged noisily as he flopped down beside her, but for once noise was not a concern. 'God, this is good. I'd almost forgotten what it feels like to be private at night,' he said.

'Well, make the most of it. It's only for one night,' she said, leaning across to kiss his bare shoulder. To cap off the Guy Fawkes celebrations, Michael and Robert and a few other boys of their age were camping out on the riverbank, sleeping beneath the stars. For the first time in months she and Sam were spending the night in complete privacy. Even Charlotte's cot had been banished into the other room.

'I fully intend to,' he said. Twisting towards her he slipped his hands beneath her arms and pulled her on top of him.

Laughing, she cupped his face in her hands and kissed him. His cheeks and chin felt rough beneath her palms, spiked with dark bristles as they always were at the end of the day. As she pulled away she looked down into his face. His eyes were closed and the corners of his lips were tilted upwards in a relaxed smile.

'Sam,' she whispered.

He stirred slightly. 'Mm?'

'I love you.'

Small creases formed around his eyes as the smile spread to the rest of his face, then he slowly peeled back his eyelids and looked into her eyes. 'I love you too, Alice,' he said quietly. 'More than I ever thought possible.' His hands shifted from her ribs to her arms, sliding along the length of them to her shoulders, then he slipped his fingers through her hair and slowly fanned it out in a silken curtain, a blaze of soft fire in the moonlight. He tilted his head to the side, smiling as he watched it slide free, strand by strand. 'When we first married, this was the only thing I really liked about you — your hair,' he said softly. 'I used to look at it during the night sometimes when you were asleep, curled round like a shrimp with your back to me, and I'd think how lovely it was. Then as the weeks went by I found myself wanting to touch it, to feel it between my fingers like this, and sometimes I'd reach out and touch it while you slept.' He gave a soft laugh and looked up to meet her eyes again. 'Then I found myself wanting to touch other bits of you, and it was damned difficult not to some nights, I can tell you, seeing you lying there all soft and warm beneath the blankets.'

'What made you hold back?' she asked curiously. Eliza's ghost probably.

His right shoulder lifted in a small shrug. 'Well, I'd made up my mind that I'd wait for six months before I had relations with you. I thought it only right and proper to wait for a bit, with being in mourning.'

Yes, it was as she had thought — Eliza's ghost. She didn't believe in ghosts as such, but if she did then she would have sworn that for the first six months of her marriage Eliza Kenyon's had slept each night in the hollow of the blankets which had separated her and Sam.

'I didn't think I'd find waiting much of a problem,' he said honestly. 'And I didn't to start with. But after three or four months of having you sharing my bed, well . . .' He shrugged again, grinning this time. 'I used to stare at the ceiling and try to work out complicated sums in my head to distract my thoughts, and if that didn't work I'd go outside and walk beside the creek for a while.'

She stared at him for a moment then bowed her head, trying not to laugh — it really wasn't the moment to laugh — but it was no use. Her shoulders started to shake and the next she knew she was lying helplessly on her back, laughing so much the bed was rattling.

Eventually Sam's mystified stare gave way to a mildly annoyed frown. 'Alice,' he said. 'What is it that you're finding so amusing?'

'It's, it's just . . .' She sucked in a deep breath, desperately trying to straighten her face. 'I thought . . . when you kept going outside during the night for long periods . . .' She chewed on her cheeks, hard. 'I thought you were constipated. So . . .' Her lips started to twitch and, knowing that she was going to laugh again at any moment, she finished in a rush, 'I took to slipping a teaspoonful of castor oil in your dinner the next day, thinking a laxative might help.'

The bed started to creak again, but this time it was with Sam's laughter. 'There's no justice in this world,' he said, shaking his head. 'There I was pacing up and down beside the creek in the dead of night, manifesting the restraint of a saint, while my wife was lying in bed thinking I was suffering from chronic constipation and laying secret plans to lace my dinner with a bowel purgative!'

'Well, what else was I to think?' she asked, wiping the tears from her eyes with the corner of the bolster slip.

Their eyes met again, still bright with laughter, but as Sam reached out to lay his palm against her cheek the mood changed. 'Come here, my love,' he said softly, and drew her into his arms to kiss her. She slipped her arms around his neck and closed her eyes, running her fingers over his back. The night was warm and humid, his skin damp with sweat, and as she shifted position her breasts peeled slowly away from his bare chest in a pleasantly tickling sensation. There was a time when the very thought of a man's bare body made her feel physically ill and never in her wildest dreams would she have believed that she would lie in bed naked with a man and laugh. She had come a long way from that first night when she had so reluctantly shared Sam's bed.

There was no reluctance in her tonight though. On the contrary, she was eager to make the most of the night. They were alone, enjoying a privacy they hadn't known since the night they had consummated their marriage; the following night the house had burnt to the ground. They had made love quite a number times since then, but making love whilst keeping half an eye and ear on two children sleeping an arm's length away was not altogether conducive to relaxation and physical freedom. Tonight was a rare gift.

She ran her fingers exuberantly through his hair, laughing as he rolled her onto her back and kissed her breasts, enjoying the touch of his lips and hands on her skin, the warmth of his breath drifting across her nipples in a cloudy caress. She let out a deep sigh, feeling completely and utterly relaxed, boneless, fleshless, as insubstantial as moonlight, as fluid as warm oil.

They made love slowly — touching, caressing, kissing, talking, laughing — each knowing that it would be a long time before they could make love with such freedom and leisure again. Even the act itself, the physical joining, was almost dreamlike in its slowness tonight.

Normally Alice lay quite still, but tonight she lifted her hips in welcome and moved like a blade of grass in the wind — rising, falling, rising — as free and weightless as a bird.

In the silent still aftermath, weighted down by an invisible blanket of drowsiness, she stirred unwillingly as Sam's hand sought hers, his fingers twining between her own. His head lay between her breasts, his hair soft and damp, his breath warm and gentle as a summer breeze. When she woke hours later in the pale golden light of dawn, his head still lay pillowed on her breasts in sleep, their hands still loosely intertwined.

Chapter 23

There was a thief in Black's Point.

While the unsuspecting residents of the town had gathered around the bonfire enjoying the Guy Fawkes celebrations, no less than six houses had been robbed, the Wrigley home among them. A thrifty housewife, Bella knew to a farthing how much had gone from the tin in the pantry. Four pounds, two shillings and tuppence ha'penny. Some families had lost more, some less, but all told the thief had pocketed around twenty pounds. He had chosen his time well. Not only had most houses in the town been empty, the miners had also just been paid their week's wages. The question was — who was the thief? At the moment everyone was a potential suspect.

'It's not good for a town, knowing there's a thief in its midst,' Sam said, reaching for his pincers. Being a Sunday and a fine warm one, he had taken a chair and his small workbench outside and was industriously mending boots.

'No, it isn't good,' Alice agreed, watching him wrench off the worn sole. 'There are some wicked rumours going about too.'

He glanced up, smiling lopsidedly. 'That doesn't surprise me. And who are the rumourmongers pointing their fingers at?'

'Mr Pringle thinks it was one of the Chinamen,' Michael piped up. All morning Michael had been running around the town with his ears pricked back gathering gossip, then running back to the cottage to report on who was the latest suspect. 'And Mrs Wrigley thinks it was one of the Molloys,' he added.

'So you said before, and neither of them has a shred of proof,' Sam returned. 'Whoever did it was very clever about it. Nobody seems to have seen anything untoward that might cast some light on who's responsible. You'd think somebody would surely have seen something,' he said, shaking his head.

'I saw Mr Stone near Mr Wrigley's house last night,' Michael piped up again.

Sam sighed and set his pincers down. 'And how, might I ask, did you manage to do that when you were at the bonfire all night?'

'When I took Peer back to tie him up. Mr Stone was walking up the street.'

'There's nothing illegal about walking along a street,' Sam said sternly. 'And I don't want you spreading rumours that Mr Stone is a thief just because you happened to see him near one of the houses that was robbed. Do you hear?'

Michael gave a reluctant nod but continued nonetheless. 'He was in the street for a long while. When I ran back after I'd tied Peer up he was still there, only a bit further up the street.'

Sam stared at him, frowning thoughtfully, then picked up his pincers again and began to methodically pull out the nails which had ripped through the worn sole when he had wrenched it off and remained lodged in the base of the boot. 'I expect he was waiting for somebody. Anyway, make sure you pay heed to what I said — I don't want you spreading groundless rumours about the man — there are more than enough rumours flying about the town at present without adding more.'

Giving a not very convincing grunt of assent, Michael sped off again. Alice turned to watch him as he ran down the street, to gather more gossip probably, then looked back at Sam. His pincers were clamped around a nail in readiness for pulling it out, but he was making no move to do so. He was staring at it glassy-eyed, miles away. Or maybe not quite miles, maybe just a couple of streets. Lucas Street to be exact, where the Wrigleys lived. Sam had dismissed Jack Stone's presence there as being quite legitimate, but the truth was it was very odd. If Michael was to be believed, and there was no reason not to believe him, then Jack Stone had been loitering on Lucas Street for several minutes, which in itself was odd. He'd been at the bonfire during the early part of the evening, Alice could remember seeing him, but if he'd tired of it and decided to return home he would certainly not have gone via Lucas Street — it was well out of his way. No, it really was quite odd.

A few minutes later, with Michael safely out of hearing, Sam was voicing much the same thoughts.

'It's damned odd,' he said, shaking his head. 'Why was Jack Stone on Lucas Street, I wonder? It would have been deserted. Every family in the street was down at the bonfire.'

'Yes, it is odd,' Alice agreed. Neither of them wanted to say what was really in their mind — that four of the six families who had been robbed lived in Lucas Street.

The morning was destined to be a disrupted one from the start. Nor did it improve. Michael continued to rush back and forth, dashing into the cottage to report the latest news to Alice, while interruptions of a different kind beleaguered Sam. Neighbours wandered over to talk to him, Fred arrived, vexedly bemoaning his losses until Bella came to tell him it was time for chapel, then towards the end of the morning just as Sam was settling down to work again Chinese Bill came wandering along the street.

'You heard news plenty people robbed last night, Sam?' he asked.

'I have,' Sam replied, resignedly laying down his hammer again.

'Everybody talk about it this morning.' Chinese Bill shook his head solemnly. His real name was Feng, but several of the miners had apparently decided that Feng sounded uncomfortably like fang and had accordingly dubbed him Chinese Bill. 'You lucky, you not robbed.'

'I am,' Sam agreed. Not that he kept a great deal of money in the house. Most of his savings were lodged safely in the bank.

'You very busy. You work Sunday. You not go to church?' Chuckling, the Chinaman pointed a grimy finger at Sam's chest. 'You bloody heathen like me.'

Sam laughed. The Chinese miners, or 'bloody heathens' as they were called by some, were on the whole not popular among the other miners. They had a tendency to stick together and speak their own language, which didn't help to promote friendships, but it was the sickly smelling incense which one or two of them burned — supposedly to ward off evil spirits — which seemed to generate the most antagonism, particularly among the godly Cornish community of Black's Point. Chinese Bill was the exception. He was well liked, a hard worker, created nothing more offensive than wood and tobacco smoke, was sociable and had a sharp, ready wit. Moreover he was very popular with the town's children.

'You always very busy, Sam.' The grimy finger tapped the sole of the upturned boot on the last. 'Always very busy not good sign. Grandmother, she used say — man who not rest have demon.'

Sam raised an amused brow. He personally didn't believe in demons, but Chinese Bill did and he had no wish to cause him offence in his beliefs, misplaced as they were. He paused, thinking, then said in serious tones, 'We have a saying too — the devil finds work for idle hands.'

Chinese Bill stared at him, looking puzzled, then took a sudden step back and an expression of mild terror spread across his moon-shaped face. 'Devil — he big demon, yes? Big demon — he make you work like this?'

It was Sam's turn to stare. Oh God, he thought wearily. Of all the sayings he could have chosen to quote, why the hell had he chosen one which could be interpreted in two ways? He had simply meant, when he had said it, to imply that idle, bored hands were not a good thing. But the meaning Chinese Bill had drawn from it, judging by the alarmed look on the little man's face, was that Sam was openly admitting that his hands were being made to work by the 'big demon'. Meg Pringle and one or two other rigorously pious honourers of the Sabbath would probably be inclined to agree.

Chinese Bill took a further step back — the only thing stopping him from taking to his heels seemed to be his evident concern for Sam's seriously bedevilled state.

Sam gave a small sigh then endeavoured to smile as undemonically as possible, careful not to bare his teeth. 'No, no, I'm not troubled by demons. The saying . . . what I said . . . it doesn't mean that I have a demon. No.

No. It means . . .' He paused, aware that whatever he said next was absolutely critical to his future relationship with Chinese Bill, and critical also to his future reputation among the Chinese community in general. 'It means that hands which are busy with, er, honourable pursuits . . . honourable *work*,' he amended, lest the word 'pursuits' didn't feature in the Chinaman's limited English vocabulary, 'honourable work like mending boots . . .' *Honourable* — that was a good word to use, he thought. He picked up his honourable hammer and patted it. 'The man whose work is honourable cannot be troubled by demons.'

Sam breathed out a small sigh of relief and lowered the hammer to his lap again. The word 'honourable' seemed to be having the desired effect. Honour rated very highly in Chinese eyes. The particular Chinese eyes in question were looking markedly less terrified, thank God.

'Ah! Honourable work.' Chinese Bill nodded, pointing to the upturned boot again. 'Honour big magic, eh? Drive demons away.'

Sam joined in the vigorous nodding and patted his hammer again. Catching a slight movement out of the corner of his eye, he turned to see Alice standing in the doorway of the cottage. She had plainly been standing there for some time listening to them and was having the greatest difficulty maintaining a straight face. He lifted one eyebrow — the message unmistakable. For pity's sake come and rescue me! Grinning, she walked over to join them, carrying a plate of biscuits wrapped in a clean cloth in her hands.

'Good morning, Mr Feng,' she said pleasantly. 'A fine day, is it not? If you're walking back home, perhaps I could walk along the road with you. I'm on my way to visit Mrs Bray with a gift for her husband. I suppose you heard about his accident?' Edwin Bray had taken a bad fall from his horse two days earlier; he'd broken his ankle and cut his calf muscle badly and was presently in the Reefton hospital. Her eyes flicked briefly to Sam, still twinkling with suppressed laughter. 'I won't be long, Sam,' she said, touching his shoulder as she stepped past him, and in the same breath resumed her conversation with the Chinaman, whilst setting off at a slow stroll down the street. With little alternative but to follow, Chinese Bill inclined before Sam in a low bow then hurried after her.

'It was fortunate that Mrs Bray wasn't robbed last night. She has enough troubles at present with her husband in hospital,' Alice commented. 'You weren't robbed, I hope, Mr Feng?' she asked, turning to smile at him.

'No. Lucky. Like Mrs Bray. You lucky too. You not robbed either.'

'Yes, we were lucky,' she replied.

'Lucky Jack Stone not robbed too.' The wiry little Chinaman patted the pocket of his jacket. 'He owe me money. Pay me back this morning. Lucky he not robbed last night.'

Alice stared at the pocket in question, then blinked and looked back at Chinese Bill. It was insufferably rude but... 'Did Mr Stone owe you much money?' she asked casually.

Chinese Bill shrugged, looking to her relief not in the least offended by the question, and stuck up five fingers. 'Five pounds.'

Alice's eyes widened. Five pounds was no mean amount. It was a fortnight's wages.

'You like fireworks last night?' he asked, grinning.

'Oh, oh yes, very much,' she said, endeavouring to reassemble her reeling thoughts into something vaguely capable of conversation. 'Yes, they were, um, very good.'

'Damp. Big trouble for fireworks.' Chinese Bill shook his head disconsolately. 'Damp make powder not light. Hard to dry. Once damp, stay damp. Only make good again if take powder out . . .' While Chinese Bill continued to explain in his clipped half-sentences the adverse effects which the damp weather had had on his fireworks' performance Alice continued to ponder on the five pounds in his left pocket. Alice, it may signify nothing at all, she told herself reasonably, trying not to think the worst. Just because Jack Stone had been in debt and had repaid his debt this morning didn't necessarily brand him as the thief. There were other explanations. He might, for instance, simply have saved up the money he owed and the fact he'd paid it back this morning could be sheer coincidence. She glanced across at Chinese Bill, who was still prattling on about damp fireworks, wondering if she dared ask him how long he'd been owed the money. No, she decided, that really would look as if she was prying. As they passed the end of Lucas Street her frown deepened. Michael had seen Jack Stone there last night. Another coincidence? And supposing he is the thief, what can you do about it, she asked herself. In the absence of solid proof, nothing at all. All the same, she intended to quietly mention it to Sam when she arrived home.

'You're right. It does seem a bit of a coincidence,' Sam said. He'd given up on his boot-mending and was inside the house, sitting on the couch with Charlotte on his knee. 'Without proof though . . .' He gave a small shrug. 'As you say, there might well be a perfectly innocent explanation for it all.'

'There might,' she agreed. 'And as for proof, well, one pound note looks much like another. To prove that the money a man has in his pocket or in his house isn't rightfully his is practically impossible.'

'True.' Sam looked away, eyes distant, deep in thought. 'That brooch of Lydia Donne's though . . .' he said slowly. In one of Michael's breathless bulletins he had reported that Lydia Donne had had a silver cameo brooch stolen, along with two pound notes and some small coins. It was quite a distinctive brooch by the sound of it; if found in the wrong hands it would be indisputable proof of guilt.

'You're surely not thinking of asking the constable to search Jack Stone's person and premises on the strength of what might only be coincidences?' Alice said, narrowing her eyes at him. She was beginning to wish she'd said nothing at all about Jack Stone's debt.

To her relief Sam shook his head. 'No. I was just thinking aloud, that's all. Anyway, it's too chancy. If the constable searched his premises on my say-so and the brooch wasn't found it would be damned uncomfortable working alongside Stone in the mine afterwards, having as good as accused him of theft. I think it's best we forget about it.'

Forgetting about it was easier said than done though, and not helped by Michael, who for the rest of the morning and throughout the afternoon continued to tirelessly report the latest news like a self-appointed town crier. Then partway through the afternoon Fred arrived again.

'Robert has just told me that Michael saw Jack Stone on Lucas Street last night,' he informed Sam hotly. 'He was loitering outside my cottage, for some considerable time by the sound of it.'

Sam let out a low sigh. So much for telling Michael not to go spreading rumours. He would have some strong words to say to the lad when he next came in.

'I'd like to know exactly what he was doing there,' Fred said in the same heated tones. 'I'm thinking I might go and ask him outright and see what he has to say for himself.'

'Accuse him of theft, you mean,' Sam said.

'No, just ask him what he was doing outside my home last night,' Fred said tersely. His sleeves were rolled up to the elbows and he was clenching his fists so hard that the veins on his forearms stood out in thick pulsing blue lines. 'Some thieving bastard has helped himself to over four pounds of my hard-earned wages, and he might or might not be Jack Stone. All I know is he was loitering on Lucas Street last night, and it may be that he had a legitimate reason for being there — but if he did then I'd like to hear it.'

'And what if he flatly denies being there?' Sam asked. 'What will you do then? Call him a liar?'

'I don't know,' Fred said impatiently. 'All I know is I'd like to ask him to his face and see his reaction. And there's another reason I'm dubious of the man, Sam. He's short of money. He asked me a week ago if I could see my way to lending him a pound or two. I told him I couldn't, that it was all I could do to make my wages stretch to keep my own family fed and clothed — not that I would have lent him anything even if I could have afforded it, knowing how he spends his money. He goes to Craig's Hotel three or four evenings a week, drinking. Then, come the end of the month, he finds he's nothing left to send to his sickly wife in Hokitika.'

Sam exchanged a brief glance with Alice. 'You're not the only person Stone has approached for a loan,' he said, turning back to Fred. 'Chinese Bill told Alice this morning that he loaned five pounds to Jack Stone. What's more, Stone paid him back this morning. In full.'

'That settles it!' Fred said, thumping the table with his fist. 'I'm going to see him. Now.'

'Not so fast, Fred,' Sam cautioned. Already at the door, Fred paused and looked back over his shoulder. 'It might,' Sam said, 'be more profitable to visit him when he's not there. You've no proof that Jack Stone is the thief, only a few things that point that way. As for getting proof . . . Lydia Donne had a silver brooch stolen, and whoever stole it will probably have hidden it in his home somewhere. Now if that were found . . .'

Fred stared at him, eyes narrowed thoughtfully. 'You mean it might be more profitable to visit his house tomorrow evening when he's at Craig's Hotel?'

Sam nodded. 'I'll come with you — you'll need someone to keep watch for you while you're searching.'

'I wish I'd never mentioned to Sam that Chinese Bill had lent Jack Stone that money!' Alice said to Bella for at least the fourth time. She bit on her lip and looked down the street yet again. The two women were standing outside Alice's cottage, anxiously awaiting the return of their husbands.

'Whatever are they doing? They've been gone for over an hour.' Bella tightened her grip on the fence paling as she leaned out to get a better view down the street. 'I told Fred he must have lost his wits to be doing this. If they're caught it will be the two of them who end up behind bars, not Jack Stone.'

'They surely can't be long now,' Alice said, pacing past her.

'I do hope not, Alice. I'm worried to death,' Bella said. 'I only hope it's been worthwhile and that they've found that brooch. Oh — oh, look! Oh, thank God! I think that's them coming now,' she exclaimed with relief. Fred, even at a distance of a hundred yards, wasn't difficult to recognise, given his height and girth.

They waited in silence till the two men reached the cottage but it was clear from the triumphant expressions on their faces that the search hadn't been in vain.

'You found it then?' Bella asked in a low voice.

Fred nodded. 'Underneath his mattress. We've left it there, waiting to be found by the proper authorities. All that remains now is for us to ride to Reefton and tell the constable we've strong reason to believe Stone is the thief and ask him to search his home.'

'And pray God he conducts a thorough search,' Sam chipped in. 'We'll look damned foolish if he doesn't find the brooch.'

'Well, it's a risk we must take,' Fred said. 'If we take the brooch with us we shall have to admit to breaking into Stone's hut, and breaking in is an offence, no matter how laudable the motive might be.'

'Is there no other way of dealing with this?' Alice asked.

Three sets of puzzled eyes settled on her. 'What do you mean, Alice?' Sam enquired.

'I mean, do you have to involve the constable? Can you not just confront Jack Stone with the brooch and demand that he gives the stolen money back, then order him to leave and never come back?' she said.

'And get off scot-free?' Fred exclaimed in loud, scandalised tones.

'Fred — keep your voice down! You'll fetch the neighbours out,' Bella warned in a hushed voice as she glanced anxiously at the surrounding cottages. She turned to Alice and shook her head. 'Alice, I must say I'm surprised at you. Mercy is all very well, but the man has stolen, and from his neighbours, and he must pay for it. If it was your money that had been taken you might feel differently about it.'

'I'm not disputing what he's done is wrong,' she replied in the same hushed tones. 'And I know he deserves to be punished. But Jack Stone has five children and a sick wife in Hokitika.'

Sam made a sharp scoffing noise in the back of his throat. 'There are plenty of men with large families and an ailing wife but they don't steal from the men who work alongside them.'

'I'm not trying to excuse him, Sam,' she said, raising two coppery brows at him. 'I'm merely pointing out he has a wife and several children who are dependent on him. If he's sent to prison his family will find it very hard to manage. I wouldn't like to think that they're forced onto hard times on account of what he's done.' Or more to the point, on account of what *she* had in part done. It was one thing to point a guilty finger at Jack Stone, but Jack Stone was a married man, and she would find it very hard to live with the knowledge that she'd played a part in causing a sick woman and innocent children hardship.

'If Stone's family suffers then I'm sorry for it too, but he should have considered the possible consequences to his family before he took to thieving,' Sam stated in uncompromising tones. 'He stole over twenty pounds on Saturday night, Alice.'

'Sam, I know it's a lot of money and it was wrong of him to take it but I'm worried about what it will mean for his family if he goes to prison,' she persisted. 'Can you not just confront him and demand that he leaves?'

Sam glanced at her with stern eyes. He was starting to look vexed.

'I'll confront him,' Fred gritted through his teeth. 'That bastard has pocketed money from hardworking men, myself included. I'd like nothing better than to confront him!'

Bella laid a restraining hand on her husband's arm. Her fingers, though not particularly small, looked very fragile against Fred's brawny forearm. 'Maybe Alice is right, Fred,' she said. She bit her lip, plainly torn between justice and mercy. 'He does deserve to be punished, but what profit is there in sending him to prison?'

'It will ensure,' Fred said tersely, 'that he doesn't steal again for some years!'

'It might also ensure that his children are forced to turn to theft in order to survive!' Alice returned.

'Well, he should have thought of that before he started stealing,' Fred snapped. 'And —'

'Are you suggesting we should just turn a blind eye to his misdoings, Alice?' Sam cut in.

'I'm suggesting you should consider his family,' she said. 'I'm worried about what it will mean for them if he goes to gaol. I know what it's like to be left in hard circumstances.'

'So you want us to let him go, with no retribution, no punishment?' Fred exclaimed.

Bella's fingers tightened on her husband's arm. 'Hush. Keep your voice down, Fred.'

A pithy silence settled. It was some time before anyone spoke, but eventually, in a more moderate voice Sam said, 'I agree with you, Fred. Jack Stone has been thieving and he deserves to pay for it. However, I can understand Alice's qualms. If you perished, Bella would have had a hard time raising your three children on her own, and if we report Jack Stone his wife will have a hard struggle ahead of her. All things considered, I think I'd rather give him a sound beating, order him to leave, and have done with it. If there's discomfort to be suffered then he's the one who should suffer it, not his sickly wife and family.' He glanced at Alice and the hard line of his mouth softened fractionally. 'And my wife is carrying a child. I don't want her worrying and damaging her health.'

Fred stared at him, stony-faced, considering. 'All right,' he said at length. 'I'll settle for confronting him then.' Removing Bella's hand from his arm, he clasped his hands together and gave them a sharp jerk, making the big knuckles crack like dry twigs.

Bella's eyes rounded in alarm. 'Are you going to confront him now?'

'I can see no reason to delay matters,' Fred returned. His gaze shifted to Sam. 'We'll go and await Jack Stone's return from the hotel, shall we? Are you ready?'

'I'm ready,' Sam said.

'Fred, remember your size. You're a big man. You don't know your own strength. Please be careful not to hurt him more than you mean to,' Bella pleaded.

'Oh, I mean to hurt him quite a bit,' Fred said, rolling up his shirt sleeves more tightly.

As Sam turned to leave, his eyes locked briefly with Alice's. 'Don't wait up for me. I expect we'll be some time. We shall be escorting Stone to the far side of Reefton when we've finished speaking with him.'

Bella and Alice watched in silence as the two men strode off into the darkness. The sky was thickly overcast with cloud, a dark sheet stretching across the heavens, blacking out stars and moon. Within moments they had disappeared from sight.

'Oh dear God . . .' Bella whispered from beside her. 'I shall worry myself to death till they come back. It's going to be a long night!'

Alice stared into the darkness, listening to the assorted sounds that filled the night — the rattle of the tin chimney in the wind, the rustle of leaves from nearby trees, the soft, rhythmic breathing of Michael and Charlotte asleep in their beds. The sound she was listening for was Sam's returning footsteps. Eventually they came. She would have known his long, even strides anywhere. Peer recognised them too and gave a pleased whimper, thumping his tail on the ground. A few murmured words reached her ears as Sam spoke to the dog, quieting him, then a cool draught swept across her face as the door softly opened and closed again. It was so dark she could barely make him out, but she could hear the faint noises as he stripped off his clothes. A minute or so later, he slipped beneath the sheet next to her.

She reached out to touch him, in case he thought she was asleep. 'Sam,' she whispered. 'What happened?'

'He's gone,' he said.

'Did he admit he'd been stealing?'

'Mm,' he said, pulling her into his arms.

She pulled away a little. She wanted a bit more than a two- or three-word explanation. 'What did he say? Did he offer any explanation as to why he'd done it?'

'He said he took the money because his wife was ill and she required the doctor regularly, but since he'd been out all evening drinking at Craig's Hotel his excuses weren't very convincing.'

'Where is he now?'

'We left him lying on the riverbank on the far side of Reefton. That's where Fred dealt with him. I dare say he's still there. I doubt he'll feel like moving far for an hour or two.'

His breath drifted over her cheek in a warm cloud as he let out a deep sigh. 'I hope no one saw us riding with him. The last thing we want is to be linked to his disappearance. In a court of law what we did tonight wouldn't be called mercy, it would be called helping a felon.'

Mercy? Alice raised her brows. She withheld comment, but what had been meted out tonight was not mercy. It was justice of a kind, that she wouldn't deny, but to her mind there was a very fine line between justice and vengeance.

Pushing back his shoulders Sam twisted his neck from side to side, sighing deeply again. 'God, I'm as tense as a bowstring,' he whispered. 'Can you massage my neck, Alice?'

'Lie on your stomach then,' she said.

With a sigh he rolled over and laid his cheek against the pillow, eyes closed. She kneeled up beside him and leaned over his back, pressing her thumbs and fingertips into the bunched taut muscles of his neck and shoulders, pushing and kneading, teasing out the tension until at last they began to relax.

'Mm, that will do,' he whispered at length, and reached up to lay his hand on hers. 'God, I'm tired,' he murmured. His mouth stretched in a cavernous yawn, his hand slipped limply back to the sheet, and within moments his breathing had changed to the slow, even rhythm of sleep.

Alice watched him for a while then with a sigh lay down beside him, not for the first time envying the ease with which Sam could push aside his worries and sleep like a child. She wouldn't rest easy again until she was sure there were going to be no repercussions from tonight's business.

Chapter 24

Worrying news reached Black's Point the following afternoon. It arrived via Mary Bray, returning from visiting her husband in the Reefton hospital. Jack Stone, she announced, had been badly beaten during the night and was lying in the bed next to her husband. The story was fourth-hand by the time it reached Bella, who wasted no time in passing it on to Alice. It was sixth-hand by the time Sam and Fred heard the account when they returned from their shift at the mine.

'You'd better call on Mary Bray, Alice, and find out first-hand what she knows,' Sam advised grimly. He knew only too well how distorted tales could become in the retelling.

Bella glanced across at Fred.

'Go with her,' he said shortly.

'Mary — we've just heard the news about Jack Stone,' Alice said in concerned tones as Mary pulled open the door. 'Is it true that he's been badly beaten?'

Mary nodded her head, frowning. 'Yes, he's in hospital. Isn't it dreadful!'

'It is,' Alice agreed. 'What happened?'

'I don't know,' she said, beckoning them inside. 'The nurse at the hospital told me that three Maori stumbled across him. They'd been fishing and found him on the riverbank lying next to his horse, somewhere on the Grey River I think it was.' She shook her head, grimacing. 'I scarcely recognised him; his face is covered in big purple and black blotches and his eyelids are so swelled up he can hardly see. He's taken a terrible beating, poor man. But when the matron asked him what had happened to him, he said he couldn't remember. I'm quite sure he could though. You can tell when somebody is lying. And he was so offhand; he kept saying that he was all right and wanted to leave and be on his way. Be on his way!' She gave a sharp tch with her tongue. 'I doubt he could find his way to the privy without help. He looked as if it pained him even to breathe. He kept putting his hands to his ribs. Edwin asked him what had happened, thinking he might confide in him, but Jack Stone became quite cross with him, so Edwin . . . well, he's a bit short of patience at present — he has an infection in the cut in his leg, you see, and it's paining him a fair bit — anyway, he became very vexed and swore, then Jack Stone started swearing. Then Edwin bumped his bad leg and, oh dear, did he swear then! So I went for the nurse. Well, it was shocking — there they were, the two of them, ranting at one another with sick patients in the ward. The nurse has moved Jack Stone to a different ward now, I'm thankful to say.'

'How long do you think it will be before Jack can leave the hospital?' Bella enquired casually.

Mary shrugged. 'I don't know, but he seems very anxious to be gone. Edwin said he had two bags with him, as if he'd been intending to travel. Not that he'll be travelling anywhere for a day or two if the matron has her way. Edwin thinks the matron will more than likely advise the constable about his condition. I hope she does — there's been foul play and whoever's responsible should answer for it.' She continued, 'It's not a very Christian thing to say, but to be honest I think the nurses would welcome him leaving, and the sooner the better. He hasn't a civil word to say to anyone. And, oh, he swore so! I was so taken aback — I've never heard Jack Stone swear before. I know Edwin occasionally takes the Lord's name in vain, but it's only when he's in pain that he does it. He never blasphemes in anger.'

'He had some bags with him, you said,' Alice commented. She raised one eyebrow slightly.

'He did.' Mary shrugged a thin shoulder. 'I did wonder if he'd maybe had word that his wife's health had worsened — he sent her to live with her mother in Hokitika two or three years ago, you know, on account of her poor health.'

Half an hour later, satisfied they'd found out what little there was to find, Alice and Bella set off back to report. As they turned into Race Street Alice could see Sam and Fred leaning against the fence, heads bent close together, deep in conversation. A few yards from them, sitting in the middle of the road, Charlotte, Sidney and Jane were issuing loud squeals of delight as Michael and Robert took turns at prodding a large weta with a stick. Not sharing in their amusement, the creature was belligerently waving its long antennae, its big, angular back legs braced ready to leap. An angry weta can jump quite high, and is also inclined to nip — this one was apparently as good at nipping as it was at jumping. Within two seconds what had been a happy little group of playing children became a scene of chaos.

Letting out a shrill yelp as the enraged creature suddenly soared through the air and landed on his bare neck Robert stepped sharply back, colliding with Michael, who tripped and fell and in turn tripped Robert. Instinctively trying to save himself, Robert flung out his arms and in the process unfortunately poked Jane in the ribs with the stick. Wailing loudly, Jane began to scramble to her feet, only to find a very vexed weta land in her lap. Whilst Jane enjoyed wetas from a distance, her attitude to them at close quarters was somewhat less enthusiastic. Shrieking with terror, she flapped her skirt wildly up and down, trying to dislodge the creature's tenacious grip on the fabric. Delighted by the amusing pandemonium all around him, Sidney broke out in loud giggles while Charlotte expressed her approval by vigorously clapping her hands. Robert, who had crashed heads painfully with Michael as he landed, appeared thoroughly unimpressed by this unsympathetic display and promptly clouted the pair of them across the ears. Loud screams followed. Fred, who had witnessed only the latter part of the happenings — namely Robert clouting Sidney and Charlotte for no apparent reason — strode across and launched a hefty boot at Robert's backside, sending him sprawling full length on the road.

'And what's the matter with you?' Fred demanded, fixing a cross eye on his daughter as she continued to yell and flap her skirt.

'A weta! A weta!' she shrieked.

'On her skirt,' advised Bella helpfully as she drew level. Stooping, she deftly plucked it off and tossed it away. Rid of the fearsome insect, Jane's screams subsided to relieved breathless pants, which left only Sidney and Charlotte's noise to deal with.

'Well?' Sam prompted, when peace was finally restored again. 'What did you learn?'

'Not a great deal,' Alice replied. 'The story is right though — Jack Stone is in hospital. He's refusing to say what happened to him and he's keen to be gone, but the matron is insisting that he stays there for at least twenty-four hours.'

'And the matron is considering notifying the constable about his condition,' Bella chipped in, gnawing anxiously at her nail again.

'That's all we need!' Fred gritted. 'If the constable calls on him, Stone may think it's because he knows he's the thief. Then God knows what he's liable to say! If he says the wrong thing the whole damned business will come out, and if it does you can be certain that Stone won't leave anything out. I've no doubt that he'll take the greatest pleasure in telling the whole tale and seeing us punished alongside him for taking the law into our own hands and interfering with the proper course of justice.'

'The constable mustn't see Stone,' Sam said definitely. 'An outbreak of theft and then a beating following close on its heels — only a fool wouldn't wonder if there was a connection between the two, and the constable is no fool.'

'Oh, this is all our fault,' Bella murmured. Her face had completely drained of colour and was a grayish-white.

'I'm glad you realise it,' Fred said shortly. 'If you'd not interfered and let us take him to the authorities as we wished to do, we'd not have this problem.'

'I was only thinking of his wife and family,' Bella defended.

Fred pursed his lips. 'Well, next time think of your own husband and family!'

'It isn't our fault that he's in hospital!' Alice said loudly. 'If you'd just ordered him to leave the district instead of half-killing him, he'd be miles away now.'

'He wouldn't be in hospital if we'd handed him over

to the authorities either. Which is what we intended to do, till you and my wife foolishly interceded for him!' returned Fred, glaring at her.

'Alice!' Sam fixed a silencing eye on her as she opened her mouth to rebut the accusation. 'They were foolish,' he said, shifting his gaze back to Fred. 'But they meant well and neither of them would have asked for clemency for Jack Stone had they realised that it might place us in jeopardy.' He gave a long, low sigh and rubbed his hand across the back of his neck, the way he often did when he was tired or worried. 'I'd better ride into Reefton and pay Jack Stone a visit. If he hasn't already left the hospital, I'll ensure that he does.'

'I'll come with you,' Fred said.

Sam shook his head. 'No, it might be better if Alice accompanies me, Fred. It will look more natural. We'll say we were in Reefton calling on friends and decided to stop by the hospital on our way home. It might look a bit odd if you and I pay Edwin Bray and Jack Stone a special visit.'

Fred pursed his lips, considering, then reluctantly nodded. 'All right. I suppose you're right.'

'Leave Michael and Charlotte with me,' Bella offered quietly.

Alice nodded and went into the cottage to find her shawl.

In the interests of speed they travelled on horseback. Being early evening the hospital grounds were quiet when they arrived, the afternoon visitors long gone. As Sam helped her down from the saddle, she glanced towards at the main door dubiously. She wasn't altogether looking forward to seeing the results of Fred's handiwork. Sam, she'd been pleased to hear, had taken no part in Stone's beating. Not personally affected, having had no money stolen, he had considered it not his place to mete out retribution. Not that Fred would have required any assistance. She did wonder, in fact, whether it was Fred's size that had prompted Sam to accompany him when he had dealt with Stone — to ensure that Fred didn't administer too much 'justice'.

Sam paused to tie the reins to the hitching rail then took her arm. 'The men's ward is at the end of the corridor,' he said as they entered the main door. 'We'll see Edwin first. Hopefully he'll be able to tell us whether Stone has left.'

Her gaze travelled down the length of the whitewalled corridor to the glass-paned door at the end. A faint smell of ammonia drifted into her nostrils from the floorboards, still damp from a recent scrubbing. As they entered the men's ward, a long narrow room with ten metal-framed beds in it, the ammonia fumes gave way to a strong smell of iodine. Only four of the beds were occupied, one of them by Edwin Bray, whose right leg, heavily bandaged, was propped up on two plump white pillows.

Alice glanced at the other patients in the ward as she followed Sam to Bray's bed at the far end of the ward. A very old man lay in one bed and judging by the grey pallor of his face he wasn't far from meeting his maker. The other two patients were younger men. One was sitting up in bed — she could see nothing visibly wrong with him — while the other man had both hands heavily bandaged.

'Sam! Mrs Kenyon!' Edwin exclaimed in surprise as they approached his bed. Alice smiled in greeting and remained at the end of the bed while Sam walked around the side. Normally very ruddy-faced, Edwin Bray looked pale and drawn tonight; judging by the grimace that puckered his forehead as he shifted position he was in some pain.

'We've been visiting friends in Reefton so we decided to call and see how you're faring,' Sam explained. 'How is your leg?'

'Oh, better than it was,' Edwin returned cheerfully. 'It's still paining me, but not so much as it was this morning. I have an infection in the cut. It throbs all the while and if I move it a sharp pain shoots up my leg — it feels like someone is slicing it open with a hot knife. It makes me wince when it does it.'

'We heard that Jack Stone is in the hospital too,' Sam remarked.

Edwin's cheerful smile was promptly replaced by a grim glower. 'He is. He was brought into the hospital by some Maori early this morning. He was lying in the next bed until Mary asked the matron to move him. She told you about the battered state he's in?'

'She did,' Sam affirmed. 'She seemed to think someone took their fists to him.'

'They definitely did. Their boots too, I'd say. He's had a thorough pummelling, but as for who's responsible . . . he won't say a word, says he can't remember. Told me to mind my own business when I asked him about it, and not very politely either. Not that it's very easy to make out what he's saying, with his nose all swollen up. I don't think he wanted to be brought to the hospital at all, but the Maori who fetched him had no English so they brought him willy-nilly.'

'Where is he now?' Sam enquired casually.

Edwin jerked his head towards a green door on the opposite wall. 'Through there. If he hadn't been so damned uncivil to me I might feel a bit more sympathy for his situation.'

Sam folded his arms across his chest and in the same conversational tones asked, 'Have they given you some indication as to how long you'll be in hospital?'

'Nothing definite.' Edwin cast an impatient glance at his leg. 'You'll be short-handed with Stone and myself not there. You'd better tell Ogilvie the doctor says it may be as long as a month before my ankle is fully mended.'

'I'll do that,' Sam said. 'I'll mention it to him tomorrow. Is there anything else I can do for you, Edwin? Alice and I will have to be on our way shortly and we ought to spend a minute or two with Jack Stone before we leave. It would be a bit unchristian to leave without enquiring how he is.'

'I can tell you how he is — damned testy!' stated Edwin, looking visibly ruffled again. 'You'll see that for yourselves if you spend more than a minute or two in his company. Anyway, I thank you for calling to ask after my health and I don't think there's anything else you can do for me.' He frowned, thinking, then glanced up at Alice. 'The biscuits you sent in, Mrs Kenyon, I almost forgot to thank you for them. Mary brought them in. It was very thoughtful of you.'

Alice nodded and mustered a smile, but her thoughts were all on the green door.

'We'd better be on our way. Stone is through there, you said?' Sam said, dipping his head towards the door in question.

'He is,' Edwin confirmed tersely.

The door in fact didn't lead directly into a room but to a short corridor. Alice followed reluctantly in Sam's wake as he strode towards the door at the end. Not bothering to knock, he turned the brass knob and walked straight in. It turned out to be a small single room, ideally suited to a private conversation. Stone, who was sitting on the edge of the bed clad in a grey nightshirt, spun round and rose abruptly to his feet as his eyes alighted on the unexpected sight of Sam standing in the doorway. For a man in his state sudden movements came at a cost, as was evident by the way his hands flew to his ribs and his breathing stalled, becoming suddenly swift and shallow. Alice swallowed, hardly able to look at him. His face was terribly discoloured and swollen; the left side, which had suffered the worst damage, was a deep purple colour and where his eye ought to have been there was only a slit between black puffy eyelids. He had a deep gash on his left temple and his nose was clearly broken. Amazingly his teeth, the ones she had glimpsed at any rate, seemed to be still intact.

'Come to gloat, have you?' Stone asked in a thick nasal voice. 'Want to see Wrigley's handiwork in the daylight, is that it?' His gaze shifted slightly as he caught sight of Alice, a yard or two down the corridor.

'I've come to assist you to leave,' Sam said evenly.

Stone gave an ironic laugh. 'Assist me? Concerned for my welfare now, are you? A bit late for that, I'd have thought.'

'I don't give a damn about your health, Stone,' Sam replied in the same even tones. 'If I'd had my way you'd be festering in the Reefton gaol now.' He glanced down at Stone's bare knees and stockinged feet. 'Where are the rest of your clothes?'

'The matron has them,' Stone said tersely. 'She's refusing to give them back to me. She considers I'm unfit to leave.'

'Go and get them, Alice,' Sam instructed, glancing back over his shoulder to her.

She stared at him in astonishment. 'But . . . I can't just demand that she gives them to me.'

'Then you'll have to persuade her,' he said.

She swallowed and set off along the corridor. Persuade her, Sam had said. That was all very well, but how? By the time she finally found the matron she had come up with a plan of sorts. The matron, a tall, angular woman clad in a dark blue dress and an immaculate white apron and cap, was in the dispensary sorting through a shelf of medicine bottles. Taking a deep breath, Alice tapped on the open door. The matron turned, looking surprised, but smiled pleasantly enough.

'Good afternoon, matron,' she said politely. 'I'm sorry to interrupt you but my husband and I are visiting Mr Stone. Would you be good enough to give me his clothes please. He's very anxious to leave. His wife is extremely sick — she has only a few days to live so it's imperative that he leaves the hospital without delay.'

The pale grey eyes widened in surprise. 'Oh, dear me, why did he not say? He's been insisting that he wished to leave all day but he never said that his wife was very ill.'

'He's a very private man,' Alice said.

The matron pursed her lips, frowning. 'For the sake of his own health it would be far better if he stayed here for at least another day. He has several fractured ribs and he really shouldn't be riding in that condition, but if his wife is dying — well, I can understand he'll be anxious to leave.' She turned to close the doors of the medicine cupboard, turned the key then dropped it into her pocket. 'You've seen him, have you?'

'Yes, I have,' Alice replied.

'He's been beaten very brutally and refuses to say

who's responsible,' she said, turning back to her. 'You're friends of his, I assume — do you have any suggestions as to who might have assaulted him?'

Alice shook her head. 'To the best of my knowledge Mr Stone doesn't have any enemies.' Prior to this business, that had been quite true. Stone hadn't been particularly popular, but he had no enemies to speak of.

'Well, he has at least one enemy you don't know of,' the matron returned, frowning again. 'Anyway, I'm glad to see that he has some friends too. If you'd care to follow me, I shall get Mr Stone's clothes for you.'

A few minutes later Alice was back in Jack Stone's room. Whatever dialogue had passed between the two men it hadn't improved the general mood. 'Here,' she said to Sam, holding out the folded clothes with the boots laid on top of them.

Sam gave a small grunt of acknowledgment as he took them from her then tossed them onto the bed next to Stone. 'Get dressed,' he instructed. 'I shall be waiting for you by the stables. I'll saddle your horse for you.' Turning on his heel, he took hold of Alice's arm then strode down the corridor. As they walked past the end of Edwin Bray's bed, Sam glanced across at him.

'You were right, Edwin. Jack Stone is very testy!' he said.

Edwin gave a self-satisfied nod. 'I did warn you.'

'What do you plan to do now?' Alice asked as they made their way to the main door.

'Saddle his horse, put him on it, and point him in the direction of Hokitika.'

'Do you think he's fit to ride?' she asked dubiously.

'If a man wants to stay in the saddle badly enough he'll stay in it,' he replied. 'And freedom is a big enough incentive to keep a man on his horse, even if he is a bit sore.'

They walked the rest of the way to the stables in silence. While Sam saddled Stone's horse she paced back and forth in front of the stables. Ten minutes later they were both pacing.

'Where the hell is he?' Sam gritted. 'He surely must be dressed by now.'

As if in response Stone appeared, accompanied by the matron and a male attendant carrying his two bags. His shoulders were hunched forward and he was holding his ribs as he walked, but he looked reasonably steady on his feet.

'How very kind of you to saddle Mr Stone's horse for him,' the matron commented, greeting Sam with a warm smile.

'It's no trouble,' Sam replied, and reached for the saddle bags. Slinging them over the saddle he took a few moments to buckle them to the D-rings then turned back towards Stone. 'Can you mount alone or shall I help you?' he asked.

Standing to one side Alice couldn't see Stone's face but she could hear the edge in his voice clearly enough.

'I can manage, thank you.' Taking a firm grip on the pommel he placed his foot in the stirrup then eased himself painfully into the saddle. He took several deep breaths to steady himself then added, 'I shall find a way to repay you one day, Sam. And Fred Wrigley.'

Sam opened his mouth but sensibly said nothing.

'I do hope you find your wife a little improved, Mr Stone.' Stepping forward, the matron held up a small parcel wrapped in brown paper. Some supper by the look of it. 'And may God keep you safe on your journey home.'

As Jack Stone's horse plodded away into the darkening night and the matron headed back to her charges Sam shook his head and said softly, 'The devil looks after his own too. He'll get home safely.'

'He means to be revenged if he has the chance,' Alice said quietly.

Sam nodded. 'He does. But only a fool would return to a town where he's a wanted man.'

Yes, she agreed silently, only a fool would return. But it wouldn't be the first time that vengeance had made a fool of a man.

With Stone safely gone, there still remained a small problem — how to get the stolen goods back to their rightful owners. What was needed was a way of somehow casually discovering the goods in Stone's hut. Numerous flawed suggestions were tabled and dismissed, but eventually a plan which looked as if it would work emerged. It was simple enough. In three days — giving Stone a reasonable length of time to reach his family and move them out of Hokitika — Fred would approach Ben Ogilvie, who held spare keys to all the Energetic's single miners' huts, and tell him that he needed to gain access to Stone's hut in order to retrieve an axe which Stone had borrowed from him. Meanwhile Sam and Alice would make it common knowledge they'd visited Edwin Bray and Jack Stone in the hospital and had helped the latter to leave, saying that Stone had told them he'd received word that his wife was on her deathbed. Having made no secret of their action it wasn't likely to be regarded with suspicion later on. Fred, in the course of searching for his mythical axe in Stone's hut, would then conveniently stumble across the stolen brooch and money.

The plan seemed plausible and fairly foolproof, and in the event it was. The Reefton constable, who was naturally informed of the find of the stolen goods, duly paid Sam and Alice a visit, but he accepted without question their explanation of why they'd helped Stone leave. Sam was fully expecting to be the butt of a few jibes from his fellow miners and neighbours — having 'unwittingly' helped the thief to make good his escape — but as it turned out people were far more interested in speculating on who had given Stone a beating, and why. And why he had left without taking the stolen money with him. For all the speculation though, no one could come up with a satisfactory answer, including the perplexed Reefton constable.

Given the compromising situation in which Alice had placed Sam, she couldn't deny he would have been well within his rights to voice loud, lengthy reproaches — moreover she was expecting him to. He magnanimously made only one comment, however. 'Next time you feel inclined towards compassion, Alice,' he said, fixing a narrow green eye on her, 'I suggest you give it some very careful thought first.'

Chapter 25

By December the events surrounding Jack Stone had largely been forgotten and thoughts were turning to another happening. Christmas. It was shaping up to be a very entertaining one. An enthusiastic band of carollers was practising in the Black's Point school each Thursday evening and the Sunday-school children were keenly rehearsing a nativity play to be performed on Christmas Eve. Then on Christmas Day there was to be a boat race on the river in the afternoon. Who had organised it no one seemed to know; it was all very vague, but it was definitely happening and just about every boy over the age of eight was planning to compete in it.

By Christmas week the town was looking very festive. A number of families had decorated the windows and verandas of their cottages, and a fifteen-foot-high pine tree had been placed in an oak barrel on Franklyn Street, topped by a big silver star. The shopkeepers too had entered into the festive spirit and all the shop windows in the town were gaily decked with bright trimmings and baubles.

When Christmas Eve eventually arrived, unfortunately so did a hot, humid nor'wester, but despite the wilting heat a good crowd had gathered outside the chapel to watch the nativity play. Even the Chinese miners had turned up. The play was going very well too; so far no one had needed to be prompted to say their lines by Mr Green, who in addition to being the schoolmaster was also the Sunday-school superintendent.

'I bring you tidings of great joy!' proclaimed an impressively winged Ellen Lawn, wielding a wooden sword at four fearful, cowering, not to mention perspiring shepherds. It really wasn't the sort of evening to be swathed literally from head to toe in towels, scarves and woollen blankets.

'Why does the angel have a sword?' Sam whispered, leaning over to Alice. 'I don't recall a mention of a sword in the account in the Bible.'

'I expect it's supposed to be the two-edged sword of truth,' Alice whispered back.

Sam frowned dubiously. 'Well, I think she'd look better without it. It looks a bit odd, an angel carrying a sword.' An impatient 'shh' sounded from behind his left shoulder. He turned and threw an apologetic smile at the Bolithos. Their son was playing the part of one of the shepherds and he was about to deliver his lines.

'Come!' Young James Bolitho pointed a dramatic hand due east. 'Let us hasten to Bethlehem to see this King and pay him homage!'

Loud, appreciative clapping broke out as the angel and the four shepherds processed off in an orderly line. It marked the end of the first scene, which to the young actors' credit had been flawless. The next scene though, which featured the arrival of the shepherds and the three kings at the stable in Bethlehem, encountered trouble from the outset. In an attempt to give authenticity to the play Mr Green had gone to some effort to obtain a few animals. The first scene had included two fat sheep, which had nibbled contentedly at a small mound of hay while the shepherds had received the visitation from the angel. The manger scene was to include, as well as the sheep, the blacksmith's donkey and a Jersey cow. All might have been well had not the donkey taken an instant and quite inexplicable dislike to the Jersey cow, which it took to expressing in deafeningly loud brays. Fixing two disdainful brown eyes on the donkey, the cow tossed its horns and proceeded to respond in kind. Whilst the sheep had been quite docile in the first scene when no other animals were present, they began to exhibit distinct signs of nervousness in the face of the combined din issuing from the donkey and the cow. The end result was a discordant cacophony of bleats, brays and bellows, occasionally overridden by Mr Green's shouts as he valiantly tried to restore peace and order in the disgruntled ranks. In the end, after five minutes of unsuccessful attempts to quieten them, he sensibly settled for the line of least resistance and the four-legged members of the cast were led away in disgrace to a less disruptive distance, after which the play resumed.

Apart from a bout of stage fright on the part of the second king which rendered him temporarily tongue-tied, the manger scene was a great success and was loudly applauded at the finish. Over thirty children had participated in it, including Charlotte. Along with all the other young children in the town, she had been invited to be an 'angelic onlooker'. The angelic onlookers had done exactly that — sat in two little groups in white-winged angelic silence and looked on while the three kings kneeled before the crib and offered their gifts of gold, frankincense and myrrh. Young children were by and large quite happy to sit and look on, provided they didn't have to do it for too long and provided they could do it in something they didn't normally wear, like wings. Being an angelic onlooker had clearly pleased Charlotte. The play finished, she scrambled to her feet and ran over to them, giggling excitedly, her paper wings flapping behind her like loose sails.

'Well, you seem to have enjoyed yourself,' Sam said, patting her head. His gaze shifted sideways as Michael suddenly appeared at his left elbow.

'Can I follow the carol singers round the town with Robert, Mr Kenyon?'

Sam gave a nod of assent and Michael ran off again.

'A pity those animals weren't more cooperative,' Fred commented ruefully.

'It was,' Sam agreed. 'Robert Tweedie's donkey is inclined to be a bit temperamental though.'

'It's a pity the privies lie directly due east too,' Alice added, grinning.

Sam gave a soft chuckle. 'You noticed that unfortunate coincidence too, did you?'

'The privies?' Bella echoed in a puzzled voice as she looked up from unpinning two very crumpled paper wings from Sidney's shoulders.

Fred scratched his nose, trying to hide his grin. 'They were in a direct line with young James Bolitho's finger when he was supposedly pointing to Bethlehem. It's a bit irreverent to be smiling about it, but it was amusing.'

'Well, make sure you don't let the Bolithos hear you laughing about it,' Bella said, glancing around.

'They were smiling about it too. I saw them,' Alice said. 'Anyway, they've gone. They left a few minutes ago. I think they've gone to listen to the carollers.'

'Are you going to join in the carol singing around the Christmas tree?' Bella asked.

Alice nodded. 'We'll go for a while. Till Charlotte starts to get fractious.'

'This is shaping up to be a very pleasant Christmas. I'm looking forward to watching the boat race tomorrow afternoon,' Sam commented, glancing towards the river as they walked along the street. 'I don't think there's much chance of Michael and Robert winning though. Have you seen their craft?'

'I have,' she said, laughing. 'It's just as well they can both swim. They'll need to.'

Christmas Day could usually be banked upon to be hot and this year was no exception. Most families in Black's Point, after attending church in the morning, were spending the afternoon picnicking by the river, clustered in whatever patches of leafy shade could be found. Charlotte, attired in her first bathing costume — a pale lemon colour with three pretty frills around each ankle — and a matching frilly bonnet, was delightedly splashing about in the shallows with Sidney, supervised by Jane, while Michael and Robert were endeavouring to paddle a raft of sorts upriver. A supposedly serious competition, the boat race was affording a fair bit of hilarity for the spectators.

Sam shook his head, chuckling. 'Look at John Knight's lad in that wooden tub. He'll be as dizzy as a top. He's done nothing but spin round in it since he started, the idiot. He doesn't seem to have worked out that he must paddle on the one side then the other if he's to get the thing moving in a straight line.'

'He's doing considerably better than Robert and Michael in their craft.' Fred pointed down-river, grinning broadly. Their craft — a few old boards which the two boys had nailed together with more enthusiasm than skill — had from the first suffered from a serious problem of imbalance, the problem being that Robert was considerably heavier than Michael. Robert's side of the raft was consequently very low in the water, so low that Michael, whilst attempting to adjust his position, had suddenly slithered like an eel down the wet incline, collided with Robert, and the two of them had ended with a mighty splash in the river. Freed of its burden, the raft was now floating merrily downstream with its erstwhile crew splashing after it in hot pursuit.

The flotilla was in the main crude rafts, similar to Robert and Michael's, which to give it some credit was floating very well without its crew aboard. A few contestants had constructed more adventurous vessels, vaguely boat-shaped, one of which looked unsettlingly like a coffin. All were suffering from the same problem — lack of watertightness — and without exception were either sunk or in the process of sinking. Only the crews who had had the foresight to take aboard baling pans were managing to stay afloat. A very odd assortment of baling pans there was too — ranging from soup ladles to teacups to chamber pots.

Alice and Bella, sitting on the grass, were doubled up, helpless with laughter.

'Oh, I do hope this is to be an annual event,' Bella said, wiping her eyes. 'It's such — Oh! Oh, look!' she broke off, and burst out laughing again. 'Jonathan Auld's lad is in the river now. His boat has tipped over. And who's that in the water with him?' She lifted her hand to shield her eyes, squinting across the bright surface of the water. 'Is it Alfred Buller?'

'No, it's young Gilbert Ross,' Alice said, managing a few words in between laughs.

'Oh my, he does look cross,' Bella said, and dissolved into loud giggles again.

'Control yourself, woman. You're starting to screech.

People will think you're drunk,' Fred admonished, throwing her a stern look.

Bella clapped her hands across her mouth, dutifully endeavouring to bring her giggles to a more respectable pitch, but her whole body was shaking with the effort.

Half an hour later the amusing interlude had finished, two of the Molloy brothers were declared the winners, and the wet contestants wandered back to rejoin their families. Not all of the contestants were accepting defeat graciously, however.

'It was your fault that we didn't win,' Robert accused, pulling on his left shoe.

Michael's head popped briefly from between the folds of the towel. His hair was sticking up in all directions from its recent vigorous rubbing. 'It was not!' he said loudly.

'It was!' Robert retorted.

'If it was anybody's fault it was yours. Look at you! That's what tipped the raft up!' Michael pointed a water-wrinkled finger at Robert's stomach, which was presently hanging over his trousers in a fat fold as he doubled over to tie his shoelaces.

'Michael, that will be enough of that sort of talk,' Sam warned, as he reached for a cold beef sandwich. 'Now, get yourself dressed then go and congratulate the victors.'

'But they cheated!' Michael said indignantly.

'How? They were further upstream than anybody else by a good twenty yards.'

'They didn't make it though,' Michael protested. 'They didn't make their craft. That was the rule — that we had to make it.'

'You mean . . .' Sam's brows rose in shocked arches.

'It's a *real* coffin?'

Michael nodded. 'It is — isn't it, Robert?' he asked, summoning support. 'It has holes in the sides where the handles were screwed on, the ones that the pall-bearers —'

'Aye, aye, I know very well what the handles on the side of a coffin are for,' Sam cut in. He glanced across at Fred.

'I'd like to know where it came from,' Fred muttered darkly.

'They surely wouldn't have . . .' Bella bit her lip, looking as if she didn't dare voice what she was thinking.

'Do you know how they came by the coffin?' Sam asked.

The two boys shrugged in unison.

'They couldn't have dug it up from the cemetery. They'd have been seen,' Alice said. Added to which, the ground was the consistency of cast iron at this time of year. It was also a three-mile walk from the Reefton cemetery to Black's Point, and a coffin being carried by two young lads would definitely not go unquestioned.

'There was a coffin in that play about Lazarus that the Sunday-school children enacted a month or two ago,' Fred said thoughtfully. 'I'll wager it's the same one.'

'Oh yes, there was,' Bella said, nodding. 'Oh, thank the Lord! I was imagining awful things.' With a relieved sigh she reached for the tin of sweets. 'Another candy or dried fig, anyone?'

'What a lovely evening,' Sam said, gazing up at the sky. It was shafted with wide rays of sunlight fanning out through a veil of rose-coloured cloud. It was that short-lived delicate beauty which fills the sky for the brief few minutes before sunset, changing by the second. He turned to look at Alice and smiled. The sunlight was shining on the small freckles on her nose, turning them to gold. 'I can't remember when I last enjoyed a Christmas so much,' he said quietly.

She slipped her arm through his and smiled back at him. They were standing outside the house together enjoying the welcome coolness of a light easterly breeze that had sprung up. 'No, nor can I,' she said. She had certainly never laughed so much on Christmas Day.

'Another year nearly over.' Sam's smile tilted lopsidedly. 'I'm not complaining, Alice, but I hope the coming year will be less eventful than this one has been.'

'Well, you'd better brace yourself for one small event,' she said. She glanced down at the 'event' to which she was referring, a small bulge beneath the cream fabric of her dress.

'Ah, but there are events and events.' The lopsided smile spread into a grin. 'That one I'm looking forward to. It's the ones that take you by surprise, like the Molloys' dog, that I don't much care for.'

She tossed her head back and laughed. The Molloys' dog had a habit of sheltering inside the privies on wet nights and had been responsible for several near heart seizures in the township.

He leaned across to plant a soft kiss on her cheek. 'I think we'll settle for just the one event we know about this coming year.'

'Agreed,' she said emphatically. But she couldn't help thinking that a statement like that was somewhat tempting providence.

Chapter 26

'I swear this heat will be the death of me!' Bella grumbled, flapping her apron in front of her flushed face.

'It's good weather for drying sheets,' Alice said, pegging the last one onto the washing line.

'About all it's good for,' Bella said, still energetically flapping her apron. 'Have you seen Robert, Alice? I've not seen hide nor hair of him since breakfast.'

She shook her head. 'No, but I expect he's with Michael. He vanished straight after breakfast too. I know where he is though. He left me a note. I found it tumbled among bedding. He's gone to see Michael — I presume he means Michael Lingard in Reefton. They're of a similar age. I can't think of any lads in Black's Point called Michael, except for Michael Brown and he's much younger than our Michael.'

'I'll lay odds Robert is with him,' Bella said.

'When is he not with him?' Alice said, laughing. Michael and Robert, though they argued quite a bit, were always together these days.

Bella gave a short laugh and nodded. 'Dear Lord, it's hot,' she complained again. Pushing out her bottom lip, she puffed a long blast of cooling air up over her face, making wisps of black hair lift from her brow. 'I can't recall a January as warm as this one. I think the heat is affecting my memory too. I could have sworn I had two full loaves of bread in the basket, but when I looked this morning there was only one left.' Her eyes swivelled down to Alice's burgeoning middle. She was almost six months pregnant now. 'How are you weathering the heat, Alice?' she asked.

'Oh, not too badly,' Alice replied. She didn't really mind the heat. It was the winters she found hard.

'Well, I must go,' Bella said. 'If Robert should come here first, Alice, tell him he's to come home at once. I shall have a few words to say to him — wandering off on a Saturday morning without so much as a by-your-leave.'

I shall have a few words to say to Michael too, Alice thought. Admittedly he'd left a note, but he'd still gone off without permission — *not* a habit to be encouraged.

'I wonder when they'll deign to reappear,' Bella muttered as she turned to leave.

'When they get hungry,' Alice said drily.

By six o'clock, though, there was still no sign of either boy, and she and Bella were starting to worry. Michael and Robert had been gone for close on ten hours; moreover they both knew better than to arrive back later than Sam and Fred.

Never tell a man bad news on an empty stomach, Alice's mother had once warned her. It was sound advice, but it wasn't always possible to break bad news to a full stomach.

'What damned mischief are they up to this time?' Fred kicked a stone irritably, sending it bouncing across the hard, parched ground as he paced back and forth in front of the cottage. 'I'll warrant they've got themselves locked up in a cell for the night!'

'The constable wouldn't put lads of eleven in a cell, Fred!' Bella exclaimed in shocked tones. 'No, there's something wrong, I know there is. I can feel it in my bones.'

Fred snorted impatiently. 'Don't talk nonsense, woman. They've been making mischief again!'

'When did they leave?' Sam asked, taking a more practical approach.

'About eight o'clock,' Alice said. 'I went to the river to rinse Charlotte's napkins. I took Charlotte with me and left Michael eating his breakfast. When I came back he'd gone. I thought he'd gone to see Robert, but about an hour later I found a note on his bed. It was covered up by his blankets.'

Sam held out his hand. 'Let me see it.'

She frowned, trying to remember what she'd done with it, then went inside the cottage and rummaged around in the pail of potato peelings until her fingers felt a soggy ball of paper. It tore as she uncrumpled it, but Michael's untidy scrawl was still legible. She hurried back outside and handed it to Sam.

His brow furrowed thoughtfully as he read it. 'Who is this Michael? Do you know?'

'I think it must be Michael Lingard in Reefton. He's about the same age as Michael,' she said.

'Well, they know the way home,' Fred said brusquely. 'I'm not going to look for them.'

'Fred, please, I shall worry myself to death if they aren't home by nightfall,' Bella pleaded, winding her fingers anxiously around her husband's arm.

'Then you'll have to worry,' he said offhandedly. 'I'm not missing my dinner on account of a stupid, thoughtless lad who suddenly takes it into his head to go to Reefton for the day. And when he does return, Bella, I shall make him wish he'd not!'

Straightening, Bella uncurled her fingers. 'I shall

go to look for him myself then.'

'You'll do no such thing, woman! You'll set my dinner on the table,' Fred said, glaring at her.

Bella glanced across at Alice, looking for support.

Alice eyed Sam dubiously out of the corner of her eye. She very much doubted that he would be any keener than Fred to ride into Reefton on an empty stomach, and he certainly wouldn't allow her to go and search, pregnant as she was. 'If they aren't back by the time you've finished eating your dinner, will you go to look for them, Sam?' she asked, hoping that a compromise and the promise of a full belly might get a better response.

Fred made a sharp noise and stamped his foot. Sam grimaced, plainly not enamoured by the suggestion either, but eventually he nodded. 'All right, Alice. I shall get no peace unless I do, I suppose,' he muttered.

Bella threw Fred a cautious glance. 'Fred?'

Turning angrily on his heel he strode away towards their house. 'Come on, woman, give me some food if you want me to find your son!' he shouted back over his shoulder.

Hitching up her skirts, Bella ran after him.

'Thank you,' Alice said quietly.

'I haven't found him yet,' Sam said shortly. 'But when I do, I intend to take my belt to him. The lad sorely tries my patience at times!'

'I'll get your dinner,' she said diplomatically and went into the cottage. Leaving Sam to wash his hands and face, she served out the meal. It was rabbit stew, the rabbit one Michael had killed with his catapult.

They ate in silence. Even Charlotte, who usually prattled constantly at meal times, seemed to sense that something was amiss and was as quiet as a mouse. Eventually Sam laid his knife and fork on his empty plate and rose to his feet. 'Sam,' she said, looking up at him. 'I'm sorry you're —'

'No, Alice!' he cut in. 'I'll not have you making apologies for him. The lad's quite old enough to do his own apologising. He's not a child.'

'He's eleven,' she said. Hardly what she would class as an adult.

'My father,' he returned as he stretched over to lift the horse's bridle from the hook on the wall, 'had been earning his keep for two years when he was eleven. I sometimes think that's what Michael needs — to work. If he worked for eight hours a day he'd have neither the time nor the energy to make mischief.'

She was fleetingly tempted to point out that Sam's father, like many of his generation, her own mother included, had been illiterate, but settled for a less inflammatory comment. 'Things have changed a good bit since your father was a boy. I'd like Michael to have a decent schooling.'

'He's no scholar, Alice, and he never will be!' Sam threw her an irritated look as he tossed the bridle over his shoulder. 'You saw his note — he can't spell even a simple word like "gone" correctly and staying at school for a further two or three years isn't going to significantly improve his ability. He has no interest in his lessons.'

'I don't want him to leave school till he's attained his standard-six certificate,' she said stubbornly.

Sam rolled his eyes. 'He'll be at school when he's fifty then.'

She pursed her lips angrily. Michael wasn't clever but he wasn't an idiot. 'You weren't sent out to work when you were eleven,' she returned.

'No, I wasn't. And *I*,' he said with some emphasis,

'didn't run off and cause my father to have to mount a search for me and my sister to worry for my safety! It's time he learned some responsibility. He's been saying for months that he wants to serve on a trading vessel. I'm of half a mind to take him to the coast and find him a position!' And on that note he strode off into the darkening night.

An hour later, with the children put to bed, Alice and Bella were conducting a whispered worried exchange outside Alice's cottage. They had both quarrelled with their husbands and Bella had been crying.

'Fred is in such a temper. I half hope he doesn't find Robert tonight. He'll hurt the lad if he does.' Bella sniffed into her handkerchief, pacing back and forth in agitation. 'Wherever can those boys be? I'm fearful they may have met with an accident. There are one or two disused mine shafts up in the hills — if they decided to take a different route home, they may have fallen down one. Fred says the shafts have all been fenced off, but fences can topple . . .' She bit her lip and threw Alice a worried look. 'What do you think has happened to them, Alice?'

Alice blew out a long sigh. 'I think they've been up to mischief. I expect someone has caught them and locked them in a shed for the night to teach them a lesson,' she said in resigned tones.

'It may be a blessing if they have,' Bella said. 'Fred might have simmered down a bit by tomorrow.'

'Has Robert ever gone missing before?' Alice asked.

'No', she said. 'Has Michael?'

Alice shook her head. He had, but not for this long.

Bella licked her lips, on the verge of tears again, and closed her eyes. 'Lord God, keep them safe,' she murmured. 'Deliver them from evil and from evildoers.'

An icy finger ran down Alice's spine. 'Oh God,' she whispered. 'Jack Stone.'

Bella's grey eyes flew wide in alarm. 'Jack Stone? What about Jack Stone?'

'He made threats.' She turned to look in the direction of Reefton, visualising Jack Stone seated on his horse outside the stables in the hospital grounds, one hand gripping the reins, the other supporting his damaged ribs. 'When he was leaving, he said he'd find a way to repay Sam and Fred — for the beating he took, he meant.'

Bella stared at her. 'But he's left the district. He's been gone for weeks.'

'Yes, but he could return,' she said.

It was close on midnight when the men arrived back. Alone. Bella had just returned from one of her quarter-hourly trips home to check on Jane and Sidney. As Fred swung down from the saddle she hurried over to him.

'They've not returned, I take it?' he asked tersely.

Bella shook her head. 'When did they leave Michael Lingard's home?'

'Michael Lingard,' he said, brushing her hand off his arm as if it was a nuisance fly, 'has neither seen nor arranged to see them. And there are no other Michaels of their age in the district — we called on Mr Chattock, the schoolmaster, to ask. We also called on the constable to enquire if he'd detained them, but he hasn't seen them either. So where they are I don't know! And I don't much care!'

'Wherever they are, they don't intend to come home tonight, that's plain,' Sam said, dismounting.

'I think Jack Stone might have waylaid them,' Alice said.

Sam went quite still, whilst Fred stared at her in wide-eyed astonishment.

'What makes you say that?' Sam enquired evenly.

'He said he'd find a way to repay you both. They were the last words he spoke before he rode away.'

'Has he been seen in the district recently?' Fred asked, frowning.

'No. I don't know. I don't think so,' she said. 'But that doesn't mean he isn't here.'

Sam folded his arms across his chest, his expression sceptical.

'He said he would pay you and Fred back!' she repeated with more vehemence. 'Michael and Robert are missing and, and . . . Don't look at me like that, as if I'm being foolish!' she snapped.

'You are being foolish,' Sam said. 'Michael left a *note* — he didn't just disappear. And Robert sneaked off without a word. They haven't been kidnapped. The two of them planned this, whatever it is they're up to.'

Fred glanced across at Sam, shaking his head. 'Pay her no heed. It's her condition. Bella was the same when she was carrying a child.'

Bella raised her brows and stared at him blankly. 'What do you mean — I was the same when I was carrying a child?'

'I mean you were thoroughly irrational. You still are on occasions.'

'Well, if you're so rational in your thinking, Fred Wrigley, tell me where my son is!' she said in an uncharacteristic burst of anger.

'If he has any sense — which I doubt — he'll have made himself a bed somewhere and be sleeping,' Fred returned loudly. 'Which is what I'm about to do — go to my bed and sleep. And I don't want to hear that lad's name spoken again till I wake. I've wasted my whole Saturday evening trailing around Reefton, banging on doors asking if people have seen my son, and feeling very foolish too I might add. I'm not going to lie awake all night on account of the damned idiot.' Muttering beneath his breath, Fred snatched hold of the reins and turned to leave. Bella stood for a moment, watching him, then hurried after him.

Alice closed her eyes and sucked in a deep breath, filling her lungs. Ever since Jack Stone had come into her mind, her chest had been so tight she'd scarcely been able to breathe. How she could have jumped to the conclusion that he was involved she couldn't for the life of her imagine now. Maybe pregnancy did make a woman irrational.

'Have you checked to see if he's taken any of his belongings with him, Alice?' Sam asked over his shoulder as he lifted the saddle from the horse's back.

'No, I haven't,' she said in a shocked voice. She was sufficiently rational to grasp what he was thinking.

It didn't take long to discover that quite a number of things were missing. Michael's best shirt, his jacket, a blanket, his catapult . . . Now she knew where Bella's loaf of bread had vanished to.

'Where can they have gone?' she said, pacing back and forth in the kitchen.

'God knows.' Sam ran a hand over his chin, frowning. 'Greymouth. Westport. Nelson. Christchurch. They could be heading anywhere. They — ' He turned suddenly, scanning the sofa and the table. The flame in the lamp flickered as his breath caught it, making his shadow leap and quiver against the wall. 'The note he left — where is it, Alice?'

'Here, in my pocket,' she said, dragging it out.

'Let me see it again,' he said, removing it from her fingers. Leaning over the table he held it close to the lamp so that he could read it better. Being stowed with damp potato peelings hadn't improved its legibility, added to which Michael had a very poor hand.

'God, why did I not think of it before! Damn his poor spelling!' Sam made a sharp noise with his tongue then looked up. 'It doesn't say "Gone to see Michael". It says "Gone to sea — Michael."'

Chapter 27

Dawn broke in a blaze of burnished gold, promising another hot day. Alice had been up and stirring for some time, preparing food; outside Sam was hitching the horse to the wagon in preparation for leaving. Oblivious to all the goings on, Charlotte was still fast asleep in a tumble of blankets. Alice glanced through the open doorway as the slow plod of hooves reached her ears, sharp and hollow on the sun-baked earth. It was Fred, leading his black mare. Bella was walking beside him, carrying a bulging canvas bag of food, her dark hair still hanging loose about her shoulders.

As Fred strode over to Sam, Bella stepped inside the cottage. 'Alice, are you sure it's wise to be travelling when you're pregnant?' she asked in worried tones.

'I shall be all right,' Alice replied definitely. 'Plenty of women travel when they're pregnant and take no harm. A bit of jostling around on a wagon will pose no greater threat to the baby than half a dozen other activities I could name that I do every day.' She had made the same comment to Sam last night when she had been trying to persuade him to let her accompany him when they resumed searching the next morning. He had taken quite a bit of persuading too. Eventually, though, he had ceded. 'All right, you may come then,' he had said. 'But we'll be considerably slower if you do. I'm not having you travelling on horseback, so we shall have to take the wagon. And if you miscarry through accompanying me, Alice,' he had warned, 'I promise you I shall blame you for it.' He had expected her to back down in the face of that last statement, but she hadn't. She had two children, not one — blood children, that was. One, as yet unborn, was lying safe and secure in her womb; the other was out there in the darkness somewhere. In her mind there had been no question as to where her priorities lay.

'I shall be all right,' she repeated.

Bella nodded, looking dubious still, then glanced across at Charlotte, who was starting to stir at the sound of their voices. 'Leave Charlotte with me,' she whispered. 'You'll journey easier without her.'

The offer was too generous to refuse.

Fifteen minutes later they were heading for Reefton, Alice and Sam aboard the wagon, Fred mounted on his mare riding alongside. Peer, delighted to be accompanying them, was bounding along the track ahead of them, barking loudly. Privately Alice questioned the wisdom of bringing the dog along. Moods being what they were though she had kept her reservations to herself. Apart from the one occasion when Peer had inadvertently saved them from burning alive, the dog had no saving graces at all. He had a loud bark and made no attempt to adjust its volume be it night or day, he was riddled with fleas, and he insistently and incorrigibly deposited dead animals on the doorstep for inspection and approval — usually a half-eaten rat or rabbit with bloody entrails spilling from its belly. Sam, however, was of the opinion that his presence might prove profitable, and so the dog had come.

As they rumbled past the partially erected framework

of their new home Sam cast a frowning glance at it. He had been planning to work there today. There was little chance of that now; he might not even be back in time to report for work tomorrow. Both Fred and Sam had informed the foreman as much.

Peer, with typical canine curiosity, wandered across to inspect the new timbers that Sam had recently erected, sniffed them all individually then cocked his leg up against one and peed on it. He turned to nose the steaming wet patch then bounded off down the road again, barking. Alice was half-expecting his barks to bring Joel to his door, but as they passed his house the door remained shut.

Hardly a soul was stirring on the streets of Reefton as they drove through. Even Peer seemed intrigued by the lack of activity in the normally busy town and subsided into a puzzled silence. Sensible families, with sensible sons who didn't run off to sea, were enjoying a leisurely Sunday breakfast. Theirs had been far from leisurely. Alice could still feel her hastily gulped slice of bread lodged uncomfortably beneath her breastbone. What had Michael eaten for breakfast? Probably nothing at all. The loaf of bread which Robert had purloined would be long gone now. It was malicious in its way, but the thought cheered her. If anything would turn a growing lad homewards it was a rumbling, empty belly.

As the wagon continued down the main street, her mind turned to the coming search. There was a major difficulty hampering it — there were two roads to the coast. One veered off northwards to Westport, following the course of the Inangahua and Buller rivers, while the other turned southwards to Greymouth, following the course of the Grey. The question was — which route had Michael and Robert taken? There had been considerable debate over the problem last night, after Sam had tumbled to the meaning of Michael's note. In the end the only thing they had all agreed upon was that they couldn't be certain which road the two boys had taken. The obvious solution was to split forces — she and Sam take one road and Fred the other. But the obvious solution wasn't always the best. In this instance it wasn't, namely because one party would inevitably end up on the wrong road and have a wild-goose chase to the coast, a costly one too since the return trip could take as much as four or five days. In the end it had been decided that the only sensible course of action was to try to ascertain which road the boys were travelling on. Once on the far side of Reefton therefore, Fred set off to station himself on the Westport road half a mile out of town, to question any travellers who happened along, while Alice and Sam stationed themselves on the Greymouth road. Michael's hair was very distinctive — it was the kind people were likely to remember.

'Have you by chance passed two eleven-year-old lads heading for the coast, one with bright hair like my wife's?' Sam enquired of an elderly man in a dray. They had earlier questioned a man on horseback, then two women in a spring cart, but none of them had been able to help.

Fist-shaped clouds of smoke drifted from the corner of the old man's mouth as he puffed on his pipe, perusing the small amount of hair visible beneath Alice's hat. He shook his head with a definiteness that left no room for doubt, sending Alice's hopes plummeting again.

As the dray continued on its way into Reefton, Sam dragged his hat from his head and flapped it in front of his face as he paced restlessly up and down the road. The thin veil of cloud which had earlier covered the sky had now completely dispersed and it was unbearably hot. He glanced up at the sun, frowning as if assessing the time, then looked back along the Greymouth road again.

'I think they'll be heading for Greymouth,' Alice said, following his gaze.

'Why do you think that?' Sam glanced back at her impatiently. The heat, coupled with everything else, was not improving tempers at all.

'Because you were raised there and you've talked about it to Michael. It will feel familiar to him even though he's never been there. And it's the port where your father worked when he was a seaman.'

'You may well be right, but I'd prefer to know for sure,' he said, and resumed his pacing.

In the event her intuition proved correct — the boys were heading for Greymouth. A young couple in a cart had noticed them.

'We passed them . . . oh, how far back would it have been, Martha?' The man glanced across at his wife. 'Fifteen miles?'

'I can't recall exactly, but it was early in the morning. Four hours ago, I'd say.' She raised a hand to shield her eyes, squinting in the bright sunshine, despite the wide brim of her straw hat. 'They were sitting beside the track — a lad with hair the same colour as yours.' She waved a dainty finger at Alice's fiery locks, glinting brightly in the sun. 'And another lad — a stoutly built lad with black curly hair. The stout lad had his boots and socks off. He was inspecting the soles of his feet. I think he maybe had blisters.'

'Thank you. I'm much obliged to you,' Sam said with feeling.

Ten minutes later they were on the Westport road, conveying the news to Fred.

Fred gave a satisfied grunt. 'Fifteen miles, eh? They've made poor progress. Robert is wearing his new boots — the ones you made, Sam. I dare say they're crippling him. There's nothing worse than new leather for blistering your feet. Serves him right, the young fool.'

As Fred mounted his horse Sam turned the wagon though a semicircle and set off in the direction of Greymouth again.

'Well, the road should be in good order,' Alice said positively. There had been no rain for weeks.

'We'll see,' Sam said, glancing dubiously at the sky. A few billowing white clouds were massing in the west. Thunderstorms were not uncommon at this time of year and it took no more than a couple of hours of heavy rain to turn a good road into an impassable bog.

While Sam conversed with Fred, Alice concentrated on scanning the road ahead, hoping at every turn to see two dejected young figures making their way home. The road wound over mainly flat terrain. Where it was bordered by expanses of low-growing grasses and swamp weed, she could see quite some distance, but where the road entered areas of thick bush, she could at times see no more than a few yards. Here the road tended to be worse, the perpetually damp ground soft as a wet sponge. The wheels of the wagon sank deep into the earth, slowing their progress, but never threatened to halt altogether. To her relief Squaretown, notorious for its mud in rainy weather, like the rest of the district, had been sweltering under a scorching sun for the last month and the road was a cracked mosaic of crusted grey earth. They stopped briefly to stretch their legs and let the horses assuage their thirst at the town trough, then enquired at two shops and several houses as to whether two lads answering Michael and Robert's description had been noticed passing through. The fifth house bore fruit — an old woman had noticed them but was at a loss to say exactly when. Yesterday, she said, and that was the most precise she could be. Vague though she was about the time, she could remember the colour of the blanket Michael was carrying. Dark grey, she said, with a white stripe running through. They were definitely on the right road. It was just a case of pressing on now till they overtook them.

Each time they passed through a settlement they made the same enquiries, but apart from the old woman and the couple in the spring cart, no one else had noticed the runaway boys. As they left the small settlement of Ikamatua behind, Alice cast an anxious glance at the sky. It was rapidly taking on that opaque grey colour which heralds dusk, the sun a fast-fading rosy streak over the western hills. It would be dark within a half-hour. Surely they must come across them soon, she thought. Two lads travelling on foot, and one of them with blisters by the sound of it, they couldn't be travelling very fast.

A sudden loud bark drew her thoughts sharply back to earth. She blinked, thinking it was just a trick of the light. But no — it *was* Robert, emerging from a shadowy bend about twenty yards ahead. Issuing several more loud barks, Peer bounded off to greet him, wagging his tail. Thank God, she thought with relief. They'd found them at last.

'Aha!' Fred said in ominous tones and swung deftly down from the saddle.

Pulling on the reins, Sam drew the wagon to a halt.

Alice straightened her back and waited for Michael to appear, keeping her eyes fixed expectantly on the road. Her view was soon blocked by Fred's substantial frame though, as he strode purposefully towards his son. Having simmered visibly for the best part of the day, he wasted no time in administering retribution and promptly landed Robert a stinging slap across the left ear.

'You thoughtless, reckless, stupid young whelp!' he thundered. 'You've worried your mother out of her wits!' Grabbing Robert's shoulders, Fred whirled him round and kicked his backside with the side of his boot then spun him back to face him. The rest of Fred's angry tirade eluded Alice's ears as she leaned to the side, scanning the empty road. There was still no sign of Michael. Gathering up her skirts she clambered down from the wagon. Sam was already striding over to join Fred.

'Where's Michael?' Sam demanded, fixing a steely eye on Robert.

'I, I don't know,' he said in a shaky voice.

Fred glowered at his son. 'Don't know? You most certainly do know!' he roared, and swung his boot at Robert's shin. Letting out a howl of pain, the boy doubled over, clutching his ankle with both hands.

'Where is he?' Sam asked again.

'He's back there,' Robert whimpered. 'Walking to Greymouth. We parted company. My feet are full of blisters so I said I was going no further and turned homewards. He told me it was only twenty miles to the sea. He said we'd be there by dark yesterday.'

'How long ago did you part company?' Fred demanded loudly.

'I, I don't know. About an hour ago, I th-think,' he stammered.

'Is he on foot?' Sam asked.

Robert nodded, snuffling like a small child as he rubbed his shin.

Sam glanced at the road ahead, frowning, then looked back at Fred. 'You may as well set off back, Fred. Alice and I will find Michael. He can't be too far ahead of us. If we don't find him tonight we'll certainly overtake him in the morning.'

Fred seemed to hesitate then nodded. 'All right. As for you,' he said, returning his gaze to his son. 'You think you've bad blisters, do you? Well, I'll tell you something, lad, they're but pimples compared with the ones you'll have by the time you reach home. You're not riding — you can walk alongside the horse, and I don't want to hear so much as a whimper out of you! Do you understand?'

Robert nodded and sniffed, looking as if he might burst into tears at any moment.

Taking Alice's arm, Sam led her back to the wagon. As he helped her up the step his eyes shifted to the small bulge beneath her dress. 'Are you all right, Alice?' he asked quietly. He looked up into her face, frowning.

'Yes. The baby is all right too,' she said, knowing that was what he was really asking about. 'It's kicking,' she said, and smiled reassuringly at him.

Sam wasn't able to feel the vigorous, healthy kicks as she could though, and as he clambered up beside her she could see that he was still concerned about the welfare of his child. Had he known the truth about Michael, he might better have understood why she was so concerned for his welfare.

Chapter 28

A blustery westerly wind was buffeting Greymouth, whipping up the sea into a froth of glinting green foam and tossing the anchored ships like corks. The air rang with the screams of seabirds, while on the ground the wheels of loading wagons squealed and grated along metal rails, coal rumbled down chutes into waiting steamships, and a woman selling fresh fish yelled 'tuppence each' over and over again. To add to the general clamour a clock was announcing midday with loud, raucous dongs. Alice cupped her hands to her eyes to shield them from the stinging lash of salt spray as she gazed along Mawhera Quay. As far as the eye could see were bucking masts and tossing black funnels. Richmond Quay looked equally busy.

Sam's hand settled on her elbow to steady her as a sudden fierce gust caught hold of her skirts and dragged her sideways. 'Come along,' he said, raising his voice to make himself heard above the noise. 'We'd better make a start on enquiring if anyone has seen your brother.' She nodded and fell into step beside him.

They had no firm proof that Michael had reached Greymouth, but if he hadn't they could only assume he wasn't far away. A farm labourer they'd questioned last night, not long after they had parted company with Fred, had seen a red-haired lad sitting on the back of a dray laden with sacks of grain, bound for the coast, and from his description he was almost certainly Michael. They'd continued along the road as far as Totara Flat then, with no sign of the dray, at Sam's insistence had taken a room for the night at the Heatherbell Hotel. After an early breakfast they'd set off again, expecting to overtake the dray and Michael before too long. They had reached Greymouth, however, without seeing either.

'Have you by chance seen a red-headed lad? He's looking for a position as a cabin boy,' Sam asked a young seaman.

The seaman shook his head, as did the next five he asked. The sixth, however, was more helpful. 'Try the *Agnes* — the captain is looking for a cabin lad, I hear. He may have hired him.' He lifted a hand, missing the middle two fingers, and pointed an oily thumb to a steamer further along the wharf.

Alice's skirts billowed and swirled around her ankles in the wind, making walking difficult as they headed down the quay. The *Agnes* was a trading vessel by the look of her. On the quayside crates of oranges were being unloaded from her hull.

'Wait here, Alice,' Sam instructed, releasing her arm. 'I'll go aboard and see if I can find the captain.'

She nodded and went to stand in the lee of a wooden building reeking of fish, grateful to have some shelter from the wind for a short while. There she occupied herself with looking up and down the wharf in the hopes of glimpsing a shock of red hair, but without success. A few minutes later Sam reappeared in the company of the captain — a stocky, stoutly built man with a face as round as a plate, the roundness further emphasised by his baldness. Typical of bald heads, the skin had a smooth, silky look to it. With the sun on it, it was almost outshining the brass buttons on his jacket.

'Captain Andrews, ma'am,' he said, inclining in a small bow as he introduced himself. It was evidently hot below deck because the blue fabric of his shirt was stained across the chest with a dark patch of sweat and his forehead was beaded with perspiration. 'Your husband has informed me you're searching for your brother,' he continued in businesslike fashion. 'I regret to say I'm unable to help you, ma'am, but if he does come aboard my ship looking for work I shall detain him in my cabin and send word to you.'

'Thank you. That's very kind of you, Captain,' Alice said gratefully.

'You'll be staying in Greymouth until you find him, I presume, Mrs Kenyon?' he asked.

'We've not yet made any arrangements for accommodation,' she returned. She threw Sam a questioning glance.

'If you'd be good enough to send word to the Gilmer Hotel, Captain, I'll enquire there later in the day to see if there's a message. We'll take a room there if we haven't found the boy before nightfall,' Sam informed him.

Captain Andrews nodded obligingly. 'You've come from Black's Point, you said. That's quite some distance away. Fifty miles or more. The lad must have a fierce passion to be a seaman.' He paused and raised one eyebrow speculatively. 'You disapprove of his inclinations, I take it.'

'My brother is too young for the sea,' Alice replied tactfully.

The corner of his mouth lifted in an ironic smile. 'But not too young to run off and journey fifty miles to strange parts, alone. What the lad lacks in maturity it would seem he makes up for in courage.'

She returned his smile and made no comment. Courage, was it? She was more inclined to call it foolhardiness, herself.

'How old is the lad?' he enquired.

'He's just turned eleven,' she said.

Captain Andrews nodded circumspectly. 'If you should change your mind about his being too young, I'd be willing to consider him. I don't as a rule hire lads under twelve years of age, but a lad as keen and enterprising as he is would doubtless be a very good worker.'

'There's the small matter of finding him first,' Sam inserted drily.

'Oh, never fear, you'll find him,' the captain said positively. 'A lad with bright hair . . .' His gaze flicked briefly to Alice's fiery locks, glinting like a copper helm in the sun. 'Make it widely known in the port that you're searching for him and he'll not stay missing for long.'

A few minutes later they were walking back along the wharf towards the town centre, leaving Captain Andrews to return to overseeing the unloading of his cargo of oranges.

'He was very helpful,' Sam commented.

'He was,' Alice agreed. All they needed now was another fifty captains to be equally helpful.

They walked on in silence back to the wagon where Peer was patiently waiting, tied to the wheel. He barked loudly in welcome and thrashed his tail against the spokes, straining against the rope. Sam stooped to untie him then slapped the dog's rump. 'Up, Peer,' he ordered quietly. Obediently, Peer leapt onto the back of the wagon.

As Alice gathered up her skirts in readiness for mounting the high step, Sam appeared at her elbow to help her. 'We'll call in to the shipping office,' he said, taking her arm. 'They may be able to tell us if any other captains besides Andrews are wanting to hire a young lad.'

'And if they can't help, then what?'

'Then we continue —'

Alice looked up sharply as Sam broke off in mid-sentence, following the line of his gaze. He had gone quite still, eyes fixed intently ahead. It took her less than half a second to see what had gripped his attention. A boy had stepped out of a narrow alley between two warehouses about fifty yards down the street. A boy with red hair. Michael. She sucked in a sharp breath, then slowly let it out again as her shoulders slumped in disappointment. It wasn't Michael. It wasn't his walk. Walks were as distinctive as features, voices. She would know Michael's loping stride anywhere. And what she and Sam had mistaken for Michael's coppery hair was a light brown cap.

While Sam made enquiries in the shipping office she stayed aboard the wagon, scanning every male figure who was even vaguely Michael's build, and in-between times enquiring from passers-by if they had seen a boy with hair the same colour as hers. It was a shaming business, having to ask strangers if they had seen a runaway child. Sam was no doubt finding his enquiries an equally joyless task. She didn't need to ask if he'd had any success. She could see from his sombre expression when he eventually emerged that his enquiries had been as fruitless as hers. He stood for a minute in the doorway, hands plunged deep in his pockets, looking up and down the wharf as if trying to decide where to go next, then walked over and climbed aboard the wagon.

'They weren't able to help?' she asked.

He shook his head and reached for the reins. 'No. So I suppose all we can do is continue to look and enquire. We'll start at the far end of Mawhera Quay and work our way down to the end of Richmond Quay. Someone must have seen him. Assuming he's here of course. He may not have arrived yet.' He tossed her a sharp look. 'I could strangle the lad for all the trouble he's caused. Does he think we've nothing better to do than run after him?'

Alice folded her hands tightly in her lap and said nothing.

They spent the rest of the afternoon going from one ship to another, buffeted by the wind, asking the same question over and over and each time receiving the same answer. No one could recall seeing a lad with hair the colour of Alice's and none of the captains they spoke to had been approached by a lad seeking a position. By six o'clock Alice had reluctantly reached the same conclusion as Sam — Michael had not yet reached the port. Even so she was loath to quit searching and said so.

Sam, however, was adamant. 'I've done all the walking and enquiring I'm doing for one day, Alice,' he said testily. 'We've been up and down these damned quays twice over and there's nothing to be gained by walking up and down them a third time! There are scores of seamen keeping a lookout for your brother, with the promise of a couple of shillings to keep their eyes sharp,' he added cynically. Aware there was nothing like a small monetary incentive for heightening a man's powers of observation, not to mention his public-spiritedness, Sam had promised a florin to anyone delivering the boy to the Gilmer Hotel, where he had made arrangements with the proprietor to detain Michael in a suitable shed, should he be delivered there in their absence. Alice certainly couldn't accuse him of not doing his utmost to find Michael.

'Moreover, your back is sore,' Sam added. 'Do you think I've not noticed you rubbing it? And,' he said with the kind of emphasis which he used to prologue a statement which was indisputably his last word on a matter, 'I'm hungry.'

An hour later they were seated at a small table in the dining room of the Gilmer Hotel eating a meal of beef, beans and boiled potatoes. Judging by the quantity of the latter the cook was used to catering for famished seamen. There were a number of them dining there tonight.

'Would you like some more food?' Alice asked, nudging a large potato with her fork as she noted Sam's empty plate. 'There are too many for me to eat.'

Sam slid across his plate. It didn't surprise her that he had a good appetite — it was the first food they'd eaten since breakfast. Another reason perhaps why he'd become increasingly tetchy as the afternoon had worn on. She passed his plate back to him with the addition of three large potatoes. She had no appetite at all. Mindful that she was feeding more than herself though, she made an effort and forced a bit more beef down.

'I've been thinking about what Captain Andrews said, Alice.' Sam stared pensively at his plate as he chewed. 'I'm considering taking him up on his offer.' He raised his eyes to meet hers, still chewing. 'Michael could do a lot worse than to serve an apprenticeship under Captain Andrews and the *Agnes* is a good seaworthy vessel.'

She stared at him, taken aback, then shook her head. Vigorously. 'No, Sam, I don't want him to go to sea. If you're set on him working I'll not raise objections to your finding him some gainful employment — in Reefton or Black's Point — but he's far too young to be going off to sea.'

'Well, your brother doesn't seem to think he's too young. And I'm not sure I do either,' Sam added. 'I'm inclined to agree with Captain Andrews. Any lad who is capable of making his way fifty miles to the coast isn't lacking in mettle. To my mind it seems pointless to take the lad back to Black's Point and find work for him there when the work he really wants to do is here. What's more, I can almost guarantee that if we do take him back he'll run off again within six months, and I've no intention of searching for him a second time.'

'So, you'll bow to his whim, will you? Let him have his way?' She made a sharp derogatory noise in her throat. 'I hardly think that's a good lesson for him to learn. He'll think he can make people agree to whatever he likes if he's stubborn enough.'

'If he does think that way, then he's learned it from you, Alice,' Sam returned pointedly. 'If I'd had my way you'd be back at Black's Point. Instead, you're sitting here arguing with me.'

'I'm not arguing with you,' she retorted, realising even as she said it that the statement was something of a paradox. 'I'm simply trying to make you understand that I don't want Michael to go to sea. He's too young — I would worry about him.'

'*Would* worry about him?' He stabbed another potato with his fork. 'Alice, you *do* worry about him. You're forever worrying about him.'

'That's because he's forever getting himself into mischief,' she said.

'All the more reason for him to go to sea,' he said,

forking the potato into his mouth. 'If you can't see what he's doing you'll maybe worry about him less.'

'I don't want him to join the *Agnes*!'

Sam threw her a sharp look as her rising voice drew curious looks from three seamen at a nearby table. He held her eyes for a moment, still chewing on his potato, then reached for his glass of ale. 'Regardless of what you want or don't want, Alice, the fact of the matter is your brother has set his heart on the sea, so much so that he was prepared to run away from home and walk fifty miles to reach a port.' He paused to lift his glass, drained the last of his drink then set it down on the table again. 'He could do a lot worse than the sea. It's a good healthy life, a good deal healthier than down a mine.'

'Maybe it is, but I don't want him to be a seaman,' she said, with an effort at keeping her voice down.

He stared at her for a moment, brows raised, then placed his knife and fork carefully on his plate and leaned back against his chair. 'So it's not only his age. It's the sea in general you're against, is it? Why? Why do you not want him to be a seaman?'

She looked away and didn't answer. Couldn't answer. Why didn't she want Michael to be a seaman? Because his father was a seaman, that was why, and she didn't want Michael to be like *him* in any shape or form. Because she couldn't bear the thought of losing him, of not seeing him for months and months on end.

'Perhaps we should continue this discussion in our room,' Sam suggested, pushing back his chair.

'Yes, I think we should,' she said and rose to her feet. She intended to continue the discussion for as long as was necessary. Even if she had to argue all night to convince Sam, Michael was *not* joining the crew of the

Agnes. It took about two minutes to walk from the dining room to their upstairs room, during which time she hurriedly tried to decide what arguments were likely to fall on fertile ground and which were not. It was pointless to tell Sam she would miss Michael. All Sam would do was reel off the names of a dozen or more other families in Reefton and Black's Point who had one or more children working away from home. Two of Meg Pringle's daughters had left home last year to go into service as kitchen maids in Westport and one of them was only ten years old. No, what was needed in terms of an argument was something that would cause Sam to worry a bit.

'So, why is it you don't care for the idea of Michael becoming a seaman?' The dry timbers of the floorboards creaked as Sam walked across to join her by the window.

She didn't turn to face him, but remained with her hands resting on the sill, gazing down onto the street below. 'The sea might be a healthy life but it's also a very dangerous life, Sam. A fishing vessel capsized on the Hokitika bar only a fortnight ago — George Withers told me about it. Two of its crew drowned and one of them was an uncle of his.' She paused for a second or two to let it sink in, then added, 'And anyway, I don't think Michael is as set on the sea as you seem to think he is. He changes his mind like the wind. All lads of his age do. One week they want to be a farmer, the next a seaman, the next a blacksmith . . . You told me once that you wanted to go to sea when you were young but your father apprenticed you to a bootmaker instead and you've freely admitted that you don't have any regrets about it. If you think it's work Michael needs, all right, find him some. But find him work that's not dangerous. Teach him your trade.'

His hands settled on her shoulders and he turned her round to face him. 'He's tried his hand at working leather, Alice. He doesn't have enough patience to be a good bootmaker. And he doesn't want to be a bootmaker — he wants to be a seaman. I wanted to go to sea when I was young, yes. But after a week of working as an apprentice bootmaker I'd forgotten all about wanting to go to sea. Michael hasn't. He's worked in my workshop countless times and enjoyed doing so, but it's merely a way of passing time for him, doing something different. He's never expressed a wish to learn it seriously as a trade.'

'You've never offered to teach him seriously,' she countered.

'Alice!' he said in exasperation. 'I could shake you at times. The lad doesn't want to be a bootmaker. He wants to be a seaman! It's not a passing whim. He's been saying for months that he wants to be seaman.'

'And I don't want him to be!' she repeated.

'Well, I'm damned if I understand why!' he said. 'The sea is no more dangerous than a score of other professions I could name. A sawmill, a mine, a farm, even a brewery has its hazards . . . things that can kill or maim a man.'

She shrugged his hands from her shoulders and walked past him to the centre of the room. 'You've maybe forgotten, but the man who raped me was a seaman,' she said over her shoulder.

There was a long silence then Sam said in an incredulous voice, 'You cannot seriously think that if Michael becomes a seaman it will make him turn to rape!'

'No, of course I don't think that!' she said, whirling back to face him. She sucked in a deep breath then blew it out again and shook her head in frustration. 'You don't understand!' she said.

'No, I don't understand,' Sam agreed. 'Because you're making no sense.'

Unable to sit still, Alice walked across to the window again and peered down onto the street below. Greymouth was a thriving port, almost as busy and noisy by night as it was by day, the only difference being after dark the bustle and noise centred around the public houses. It wasn't much past eight o'clock, but even now raucous laughter and the sound of well-lubricated singing was coming from somewhere close by. Every street corner in this part of the town seemed to boast a public bar, and if the number of unsteady legged seamen who walked past were anything to go by, they were well patronised. Below their room, the public bar of the Gilmer was doing a brisk trade too, but its patrons were reasonably quiet; there was no riotous singing rattling the windows at any rate, though there were occasional bursts of loud laughter. Her gaze travelled along the street for a few yards, following the limping progress of an old man, his long white beard briefly illuminated by the light from the street lamp. More footsteps sounded and she leaned in so that she could see the lamp further down the street, the glow weakened by distance but strong enough to show at a glance that the footsteps weren't Michael's. Where was he? She pressed her forehead against the cool glass, misting it with her breath. He surely ought to have reached Greymouth by now — unless he'd met with an accident. Alice closed her eyes briefly. She felt sick with worry. A two-edged sword of worry now. The topic of the *Agnes* had been dropped for the time being, but she could tell Sam was still considering it. Still, he hadn't reached a definite decision, and knowing how strongly she opposed the idea of Michael going to sea she thought it unlikely that he would approach Captain Andrews. Unlike some husbands Sam wasn't completely inflexible in his opinions. She glanced over her shoulder at him. He was lying on the bed, hands clasped behind his head, staring at the ceiling.

She turned back to the window, rubbing it with her palm to clear it, then glanced up and down the street from one pool of light to the next. Frowning, she lifted her hand and rubbed the pane again with the edge of her sleeve. There was someone standing across the road in the shadows. He'd been there for some time but she couldn't make out much more than just the shadowy shape of male legs. He looked about the right size for Michael. The right size for a hundred other lads resident in the port too. Foolish as it was she felt half-tempted to ask Sam to slip down and see, despite the fact logic told her that it was most unlikely to be him. Why would Michael be standing opposite the Gilmer? He didn't know they were staying at the Gilmer. And if he did then the last place that he'd be standing was across the street from it.

She tensed suddenly and turned, eyes going to the door as steps sounded on the stairs, each marked by a low creak, coming to a halt on the landing.

'First door to your right, lad,' came a woman's voice from below.

The springs of the bed twanged briefly as Sam curled forward, swinging his legs round, and sat up. He glanced at Alice, his thoughts written in his eyes. *Lad*, the woman had said. A moment later two raps sounded on the door.

Well, it was a lad all right. But not Michael. As Sam

pulled wide the door a boy of about nine or ten, with a jacket badly in need of the attentions of a needle and thread and hair in even more need of a comb and a good wash, stood looking up at him.

'Mr Kenyon?' he asked, frowning.

Sam nodded.

'The lad you're looking for, with the red hair — he's found. I'm to take you to him,' he said. He raised his hand, scratching his scalp as if by habit. Lice. He was probably infested with them.

Sam stared at him for a moment then stepped aside, beckoning him in. 'Where is he?' he asked, closing the door.

'At a house, sir. Down by Richmond Quay.' The boy lowered his hand and thrust it into his trouser pocket, two bony knuckles poking through the frayed hole in it. 'You're to come with me if you please,' he said again.

Sam nodded without enthusiasm and reached for his jacket, looking as if he would far sooner the missing goods had been delivered to his door rather than be obliged to turn out in the dark to collect them.

'I'll come with you,' Alice said from behind him. Seeing him frown she added, 'I don't feel easy about staying here on my own at night, Sam.'

Sam shrugged on his jacket, eyes returning to the lad waiting by the door. Taking his lack of argument to be consent she went to stand beside him.

'He's at a house, you say. Whose house? Yours?' Sam questioned.

The boy shook his head. 'No, sir. I don't know whose house it is. A man told me I was to come and tell you that he's found the lad you're looking for. He said if I fetched you back with me he'd give me a penny for my trouble.'

'A seaman, was he?' Sam asked, pulling open the door again.

The lad nodded and made for the stairs, the scent of the promised penny beckoning him on like a wasp to a pot of jam.

'Down by' Richmond Quay, Alice decided after walking for a good quarter-hour, was their young guide's roundabout way of saying 'the very furthest end of' Richmond Quay. The area seemed to be mainly warehouses.

'Are there any dwelling houses in this part of town?' she asked, casting a dubious eye down one of the numerous narrow alleys they passed. She wasn't afraid, not with Sam, but there was something about the place that made her feel slightly uneasy.

Familiar with the port, having been raised there, Sam nodded. 'A few. Not many.'

She glanced back over her shoulder, peering into the shadows, not for the first time wishing that there were a few more lamps lighting the streets. It was by no means as well lit in this part of town as it was in the centre. There was a very unpleasant mix of smells wafting around too. Rotten fish was the predominant odour, occasionally overridden by the sweet waft of horse excrement, which was liberally strewn around the streets, and to pickle it all there was a very pungent smell of vinegar coming from somewhere. They surely couldn't have far to go now, she thought. They couldn't be far from the outskirts of . . . Her chest tightened suddenly. There it was again, she was sure of it this time. A footfall. 'Sam,' she said, tightening her grip on his arm as she turned to him, 'I think somebody is following us.'

She saw his head tilt to look down at her, his features masked by shadow, then he twisted his head to look back over his shoulder, slowing his stride. 'I can't see anybody,' he said at length.

'I'm sure I heard footsteps,' she said, glancing back. She moved in closer to him, listening as they walked on, but there was nothing now save the sound of their own feet and those of the boy a few yards ahead of them.

Sensing her unease Sam clasped her arm more firmly against his side. 'A dog, I expect. We must be nearly there now anyway.'

They apparently were, for the boy turned suddenly into a narrow alley. Sam halted at it, seeming suddenly wary, then seeing the cheery glow of light coming from a yard going off to the left at the end of it some twenty yards along and the boy's silhouette clearly outlined in it, he turned down it. 'There,' he said, pointing unnecessarily. Their footsteps echoed eerily on the hard earth, the sound bouncing back and forth off the walls of the warehouses which rose up on either side; there was scarcely a six-foot gap between them. A few small clinks sounded — Sam fishing around in his pocket for a florin.

Alice let out a long low breath. A few more yards and she'd see Michael again. Thank God! Over the last three days she had swung from worry to anger and back again so many times . . . She blinked in the unaccustomed light as they turned into the yard, lit by two lanterns at the far end, set on wooden boxes. A man was standing in the middle of the yard, beside him a woman; the boy who had led them there was speaking to the man, palm outstretched awaiting payment. A coin dropped into it, glinting briefly in the light of the lamp before his fingers greedily curled around it. All this Alice took in with her eyes, while her heart rose slowly from her chest up her gorge. Beside her Sam had gone as rigid as an oak. He too had recognised the woman, even partially turned away from them as she was. The woman was Lily Fielding.

Payment received, the boy turned to leave. He had lied for his penny — there was no house, no sign of Michael, just a small warehouse yard with some barrels stacked up at one side. Possibly he didn't realise the peril he had led them into — to him the man and woman who had offered him a penny would seem to pose no great threat to anybody. Which as things stood they didn't. But there was not just the one man, a second man was coming now — his footsteps echoing along the alley. And what, dear God, *what* had they done with Michael?

She swallowed and licked her lips as Sam loosed her arm and withdrew his other hand from his pocket, aware that he was more than likely shortly going to need the use of both his fists. 'Can you still run?' he asked softly.

She could, but not in the dark along rutted streets. Not on legs that were shaking like jellies either. She shook her head and wound her arms protectively around her middle. The baby had lain quiet all day but it was presently kicking vigorously against her belly as if somehow sensing the danger around it. It wasn't the baby who was in danger though — it was the father. She could see from the way Lily's eyes were locked on Sam that it was him she wanted dealt with. Revenge for the beating Sam had given her husband that night.

'You'll remember me, I dare say,' Lily said, breaking the silence. Her pale blue skirt swayed gracefully from side to side as she began to walk towards them. 'And my husband,' she added, with a fine edge in her voice.

Alice glanced sideways, waiting for the husband in question to emerge from the shadows as the footsteps in the alley drew closer. For she had no doubt that was who was approaching.

'No, not Zac,' Lily said, noting Alice's look of surprise as the newcomer, a stranger, stepped into the light. 'Zac's out. Drinking,' she said with a shrug. 'These,' she tilted her head coquettishly to the two men, 'are friends of mine.'

'Where's my wife's brother? What have you done with him?' Sam lifted his chin, eyes fixed darkly on Lily.

She shook her head and gave a small laugh as she stopped a few yards in front of him. 'I don't know where he is. Dead, for all I know. I've not seen him, not since my husband and I were forced to leave Black's Point. Zac lost his position at the mine, you know — on account of you!'

'That's a lie! It was *not* on account of Sam!' Alice burst out. Zac Fielding had lost his position at the Wealth of Nations because the foreman had tired of him repeatedly not turning up for work; the night Sam had had the fight with him had simply added the final straw that had tipped the balance. Turning towards the newly arrived man, she took an impulsive step towards him. Neither of the two men looked rough, quite decent in fact, and while they might not have any qualms about hitting Sam, she felt reasonably confident that they wouldn't do violence to her. Less sure on that count evidently, Sam hauled her back.

Undeterred, she stepped forward again, determined to speak, determined to do something. When she had been raped she hadn't done anything — hadn't screamed, hadn't struggled, she'd been too terrified; during the fire she'd had to look after Charlotte and been forced to stand and watch helplessly while the flames roared and crackled around her husband and son; when Sam had been trapped down the mine, again she'd been able to do nothing. Here though she could do something. And she meant to. She couldn't fight but she could reason, speak out the truth, make these two men understand that Lily Fielding had told them a pack of lies. 'Is that what she told you? That my husband caused her husband to lose his employment?' she demanded. 'Well, it's a lie! It's not true!'

'Alice!' Sam said sharply and pulled her back to his side again.

The newcomer said nothing, just curled his lip, looking mildly amused by her outburst. The other man spoke though, moving casually forward to stand beside Lily. A big man, a seaman by the look of him, his voice was a deep rumble, like the tide tumbling pebbles on the beach. 'You shouldn't have made eyes at Lily's husband, lovey. Been satisfied with your own man.' He shook his head in silent reproach.

Alice's eyes widened. God, what other lies had Lily Fielding spun these two? 'It was the other way round! Her husband,' she retorted, pointing accusingly at Lily, 'made *improper* advances at *me*!'

She felt Sam stiffen beside her. She had never admitted it at the time, had steadfastly claimed there'd been no immoral intention underlying Zac's actions. There had though, or would have been if she'd given him some encouragement.

'Alice.' Sam's fingers tightened on her arm. 'They mean to give me a beating,' he said softly, turning to put his mouth close to her ear. 'If you rile them it will only make them more inclined to make a thorough job of it.'

As he drew away their eyes met briefly, Sam's were narrowed in warning, her own wide and dark with fear.

'Her word against mine.' Lily's voice came again. Turning to the big seaman she slipped her arm through his, her long fingers stroking the coarse hairs on his wrist. 'Who are you going to believe, Henry?' she asked softly.

It was very obvious who Henry was going to believe. And it wasn't Alice.

'My husband used to be a good-looking man,' Lily continued almost conversationally. 'Till he ruined his face.' She pointed a long finger at the he in question then, loosing Henry's arm, walked across to the other man. 'Now, I've a husband with a crooked nose and china teeth that clack when he talks, who lost a good job in a gold mine and has had to settle for labouring on the wharf!' She shook her head, shaking off the last vestiges of pleasantness, her features taut with anger. 'It was a nice piece of luck that I had today when Dan here came into the hotel for a drink and told me that a man and a woman from Black's Point had been enquiring around the quays after a runaway lad — a lad with red hair. He knew as how I used to live at Black's Point, you see. Wondered if I might know you. The couple were wanting to find the lad so badly, Dan told me, that they'd offered to pay a florin to anybody who took him to the Gilmer Hotel.' She laughed again, showing her own good set of teeth in the light of the lamps. 'So I thought to myself that if you were so anxious to get the lad back you could probably be persuaded without too much difficulty to come somewhere nice and private to collect him.'

Heeding Sam's warning, Alice held her tongue, running it along the back of her teeth, right to left along the top row, left to right along the bottom. It was Sam's teeth that were in her thoughts though. Two to one — the odds were not in Sam's favour. Her gaze flicked from the big seaman to the other man. If she fell on her knees and begged... The thought passed as quickly as it came. Pleas for mercy would fall on deaf ears here. These men had come to mete out what they considered justice, just as Sam had meted out what he considered justice to Zac Fielding, and Fred had to Jack Stone. This was the way that men dealt with small personal matters — man to man, fist to fist. Swifter, surer, less cumbersome, yes and perhaps more satisfying too than the official wheels of justice.

'My wife — she's carrying a child. Let her go safely,' Sam said. It was to the two men he addressed the request, his eyes carefully avoiding Lily.

'No. I want her to watch,' Lily's voice came, hard and sharp.

The seamen exchanged a long glance then Henry's head moved in a slow shake. 'She'll be safe enough,' he said.

Nodding his agreement, Dan waggled his fingers. 'Move your wife aside, there's been enough talking. And if you want to father more children then I suggest you advise her not to scream or run for help.'

With little option but to comply Sam escorted Alice to the side of the yard, took off his jacket and handed it to her for safekeeping, perhaps feeling his arms would be freer without it. 'Whatever happens, no matter what, you're to stay here,' he ordered firmly. 'Don't try to summon help, there's none to hand anyway. I don't think he was making idle threats just then. And don't,' he added emphatically, 'try to interfere.'

She stared at him, lips clamped tightly together, then gave a small nod of assent. Sam took a deep breath, filling his lungs, then turned and stepped forward to face his two adversaries.

'An arm each,' Henry instructed casually. Dan nodded and like two crabs agreeing on a kill they fanned out sideways.

'Now!' Henry said, and in a sudden rush they descended on Sam. He managed a single glancing blow to Dan's left ear and a few futile kicks with his feet before his arms were siezed, the left by Henry, the right by Dan. 'I'll hold him,' Henry said, who seemed to be making the decisions.

Alice clasped her arms around her middle and licked her lips, grateful that it was the bigger seaman who was pinioning Sam's arms behind his back. Not that it would make a great deal of difference in the long-term. It would simply take a bit longer for Dan, the lighter of the two, to render Sam senseless. Smaller blows but more of them. She wasn't sure if that was better or worse. She bit hard onto her lip and screwed up her eyes as the first one landed — a mercilessly solid blow to Sam's stomach. He doubled, coughing and retching, gasping for breath, then with a grunt Henry jerked his spine straight again. In the light of the lamps she could see that Sam's face had gone a greyish colour. He was going to be sick. The next blow did it, aimed very precisely at the same spot. He doubled over again, retching violently, and brought his dinner up. He straightened of his own accord this time, maybe so he could breathe better, threads of spittle and vomit dripping from his chin.

To get a better view of the proceedings, Lily took a few steps to her right.

Dan drew back his fist again. It would be the face this time. Alice swallowed as she saw his eyes focus on Sam's teeth, clearly visible as he gasped open-mouthed for breath. She glanced round frantically, looking to see if there was a stick of wood lying about, anything that she could use to stop the blow coming, but there was nothing. The yard was quite empty save for the stacked barrels, the two wooden boxes and — the lamps! Dropping Sam's jacket, she made a dash for the nearest, grabbed it by the handle, took four long strides and swung it at Dan's head. It was hardly a surprise attack though. He ducked aside and, missing its target, the lamp slipped from her fingers and went arcing through the air to land with a crash and a splintering of glass at the far side of the yard. She was vaguely aware of Sam saying her name urgently, but her eyes were still riveted on Dan, who had taken a step or two back and was regarding her with some annoyance. She took a deep breath and did the only thing she could think of — she flung herself at him, vaguely thinking amidst the jumble and turmoil of her thoughts that if she could somehow keep him from hitting Sam for a minute or two Sam could maybe recover sufficiently to deal with the other man. It was a ridiculous thought, given Sam's condition, but a desperate mind is quite prepared to entertain the ridiculous when nothing better presents itself.

As a child she had once cornered a wild kitten and tried to catch it. Having other ideas, it had suddenly seemed to grow a dozen extra legs, each armed with needle-sharp claws which had moved with the speed of light in a vicious ripping blur. It was with the same wild, desperate ferocity that she fought now — she lashed out with her hands, scratching his face and neck with her nails, kicked him, hit him, bit him, completely ignoring in her desperation the danger she was risking to the small life in her womb.

'Christ!' Dan hissed as she sank her teeth into his

wrist. He was trying to prise her fingers from his shirt in order to push her away from him. Hastily withdrawing his hand he gripped hold of her right shoulder. She twisted her head and tried to bite him again, and making the most of the gap which had temporarily opened up between them, swung her foot viciously at his left shin. He gave a sharp grunt of pain, then feeling the edge of her teeth rasp against his knuckles, wisely loosed his grip on her shoulder. A sudden strong whiff of stale, sour sweat reached her as he lifted his arm above his head to safety. 'God save me, she's like a bloody wild ferret!' He glared down at her, looking thoroughly exasperated. He plainly didn't want to hurt her, but at the same time he was becoming rather annoyed. She lashed out at his face again, kicked again, lost her footing, and landed with a whumph against his chest. Above the tangled sounds of grunting, hard breathing and scuffling boots, Sam's voice rang out from behind her, 'For pity's sake, Alice! The child! Alice! Alice!' It wasn't Sam's frantic shouts that finally stopped her though, it was a very hard slap across her face. She reeled backwards three or four steps under the impact and came up abruptly against the stacked barrels, feeling them shift and wobble as her right shoulder jarred painfully against them.

'Alice — stay there!' Sam shouted hoarsely. She glanced across at him. Her left eye was watering and her cheek was stinging and burning, her heart pounding furiously against her ribs. 'Stay there!' Sam ordered again. He was straining forward, looking at her intently, his arms still pinioned firmly behind his back by the big seaman.

'I'd do as he says if I were you,' Lily advised, reaching up to adjust a pin in her hair.

Drawing in a shaky breath, Alice lifted her hand and wiped her fingers across her bottom lip, vaguely aware that it was bleeding. Dan also was assessing his wounds, dabbing his scratched cheek with a handkerchief. Then a queer thing happened. His head suddenly jerked forward as if someone had flicked it with their finger from behind, his eyes flew wide open then rolled slowly upwards, and he crumpled to his knees, finishing up prone on the ground with his left hand lying in the puddle of vomit.

Lily went quite still, eyes round with surprise as she stared at the prostrate man. Alice took a small, shocked step forward, then stopped. What in the name of God had happened to him? Had he fallen down dead, struck down by the hand of God?

Evidently reaching a similar conclusion Henry's voice came from behind Sam, a shaky, urgent whisper. 'Christ have mercy, Christ have mercy, Christ have mercy . . .' Loosing his grip on Sam's arms he dropped to one knee, crossed himself three times with rapid movements of his hand then rose, ashen faced, and ran down the alley to the street. Whatever conclusions Lily had drawn, she seemed not inclined to linger either and ran off after him.

As silence settled on the yard Alice could hear Sam's breath coming in painful wheezy gasps. He was on his knees, his arms wrapped around his middle, head bowed low over his chest.

Hurrying over to him she crouched down beside him and touched his arm. 'Sam — are you all right?'

He nodded, coughed several times, then looked up, his face sheened with sweat. 'What happened to him?' he asked hoarsely.

'I, I don't know,' she said. She glanced at the prone

figure and started to shake. 'He suddenly dropped to the ground.'

'Is he dead?' said a small voice.

She stared mutely at Sam then spun around, lost her balance and landed on her bottom, knees spread wide. 'Michael!' she said in a shocked voice.

'Is he dead?' he repeated anxiously. He was standing a few yards away, half hidden by shadow.

'Michael . . . what . . . how?' she began.

He moved slowly forward from the alley into the light; his feet were bare and something was dangling from his right hand. It took her a moment to realise what it was. A picture of a ten-foot-high giant in full gleaming battle armour and a small goatskin-clad boy with a sling in one hand and a pebble in the other flashed briefly into her mind, then out again, to leave it quite, quite empty.

'No,' Sam answered hoarsely from beside her. 'He's not dead, lad.'

Relief spread like a refreshing dew over Michael's body, washing away the strain from his features, lifting the tension out of his taut shoulders and chest; his hands, which had been clenched into tight fists, slackened suddenly and the catapult slipped from his grip to land with a clatter on the ground. He stooped to pick it up again, tucked it into his belt, and let out a huge sigh. 'Would they have hanged me, Mr Kenyon?' he asked.

Sam stared at him for a long moment, an unreadable expression on his face, then shook his head. 'No,' he said. 'You're too young to hang.'

As if to confirm the recent pronunciation of his aliveness, the inert figure on the ground gave a sudden jerk, making all three of them start; his right hand was trapped beneath his body, but the fingers of his left hand slowly began to uncurl then curl back again, slithering through bile-streaked lumps of half-digested potato. Alice watched transfixed as he continued to blindly gather up handfuls of vomit, then closed her eyes and swallowed back the bile that rose suddenly up her own throat. She took several deep breaths then twisted carefully onto her knees and stood up. Behind her she could hear the pained rasps of breath as Sam gingerly struggled to his feet. Opening her eyes again she turned to him, and seeing him sway reached out to steady him. 'Sam — are you all right?' she asked again.

'Never mind me — are you all right?' he said as his gaze flicked anxiously to her middle.

She didn't answer at once but spread her left hand across the small mound where the baby lay, and pressed down lightly. She let out a relieved breath as she felt the answering prod of a tiny limb; it felt round and hard like a knuckle on an adult hand, pushing with surprising strength against her palm. 'Yes, I'm all right. The baby is too. I think . . . I think he was being careful not to hurt me,' she said, throwing a rueful glance at the unconscious body on the ground.

'Christ, Alice!' Sam murmured. He threw her a sharp reproachful look and shook his head, but with Michael standing only a foot or two away he forebore to say more. Instead he turned to Michael. 'I don't know how you came to be here, lad, and you've a lot of explaining to do, but I'm very glad to see you,' he said, and reached out to lay a hand briefly on his shoulder. 'Where are your boots?' he asked, frowning as he caught sight of Michael's bare feet.

'I left them in a doorway further down the street,' he replied. 'I thought they might hear me in my boots so I took them off.'

Sam gave a small nod but his attention had returned to the man on the ground who was starting to stir. 'It's time we were gone,' he said. 'Get that lamp, will you, Michael.'

Twenty minutes later they were safely back in their room at the Gilmer Hotel where Michael, in between swallowing down mouthfuls of pickled-pork sandwiches, was furnishing them with an account of his activities over the last few days. 'I stopped to take a rest this morning and fell asleep under a tree and I didn't wake till noon so it was late in the afternoon when I reached Greymouth,' he said, briefly pausing to take another hasty bite of bread. It was his first proper meal in three days. 'I walked along the wharf for a bit, looking at all the ships — I hadn't expected there to be so many — then I heard somebody calling "Lad, over here, lad" and when I looked round there was a captain standing on the deck of one of the steamships, beckoning me over to him.'

'Captain Andrews,' Sam inserted. He was standing at the window but turned to speak.

Michael nodded. 'He asked me was I looking for a position on a ship and I said yes, I was, and then he asked me my name and so I told him, and then he said would I care to go below deck with him. So I did. Then he told me how you'd been speaking to him and how you'd been searching the port for me . . .' He paused and had the grace to colour guiltily. 'I didn't think you'd come looking for me,' he said awkwardly.

'You thought I'd just toss your note away and not give you a second thought, did you?' Alice enquired in hurt tones.

The colour in his cheeks took on an even deeper hue as he glanced across the table at her, then he looked away, avoiding her eyes.

'Let him finish, Alice,' Sam instructed quietly from behind her.

Eyes still carefully averted, Michael continued with his account. Captain Andrews, it seemed, had given him something of a stern talking-to, then informed him that he intended to detain him aboard his ship and send word to the Gilmer Hotel that he'd been found. To Michael's surprise though, the captain had gone on to lay an alternative before him, stating that if Michael was prepared to give him his word that he would make his own way to the Gilmer and deliver himself up to his family, then he would allow him to do so. He was offering Michael the chance to redeem himself in his family's eyes in some small measure, trusting Michael to keep his word. There was a risk that he wouldn't of course, but since the captain had also pointed out that every second seaman in Greymouth was presently on the lookout for a red-headed lad seeking work he probably felt there was every likelihood that Michael would steer an honourable course. Michael had kept his word, found the Gilmer, then spent a further two hours skulking in a doorway on the other side of the street with his blanket draped over his head so that no one would see his red hair, plucking up the courage to show his face by the sound of it.

'I was expecting to get a good beating,' he said, with a resigned shrug which suggested that he was still expecting one.

Alice glanced across at Sam, who exchanged a long look with her. The palm of his left hand was splayed wide across his middle just above his belt, gingerly supporting the bruised muscles. He was plainly thinking the same thing as her — it was a bit difficult to take your belt to someone who had just saved your nose and most of your teeth from being smashed to pieces.

'I'd just picked my belongings up and was about to walk across the road to the hotel when I saw you come out of the side door with a boy,' Michael continued. 'I thought he must be known to you, and that you were perhaps going to visit some acquaintances. I didn't know what to do then. I thought you'd maybe not be very pleased if I made myself known when you were on your way to see friends so I thought I'd wait till you came back. But I didn't much like the thought of waiting in a doorway for another few hours so I decided to follow you. I saw you turn into the alley. Then I saw someone approaching from the other end of the street and saw him turn down the alley as well. So I waited for a minute or two then walked on to the entrance.' He lifted a hand to scratch his nose and his brows gathered together in a frown. 'I could hear Mrs Fielding, talking, in the yard down the alley. I knew it was her. I recognised her voice. Then I heard Alice's voice and I knew something was wrong — I could tell by the way Alice's voice was shaking. So I went into a doorway further down the street and took my boots off so I could creep down the passageway unheard. When I realised they were going to give you a beating, Mr Kenyon, I didn't know what to do. I knew there was no time to run for help. I was thinking that I'd maybe just step out and fight alongside you; then I remembered my catapult, so I went back to fetch it and . . .' He gave a small shrug — the rest they knew.

Silence settled on the room. At length Sam spoke. 'In the normal way of things, I would be taking my belt to you and giving you a very sound beating for running off the way you did,' he informed Michael gravely. He dipped his head towards Alice. 'Your sister has been worried out of her wits these last three days.'

Michael lowered his eyes and coloured a little.

'And you'll have cost me the loss of two or three days wages by the time I get back to Black's Point, which I can ill afford at present,' Sam added.

Silence settled again.

'In the normal way of things,' he said again, 'I would beat you. Soundly. For you well deserve it, lad. Your actions were thoughtless and irresponsible. However, I'm mindful that your actions tonight saved *me* from a sound beating. I hardly think I can give you one in the circumstances. Which doesn't mean you're exonerated from blame,' he added as Michael's head jerked up. 'So — stand up and walk round the table to your sister and make your apologies to her for all the distress you've caused her these last few days.'

Another silence settled then Michael's chair scraped back. He walked slowly around the table, halted in front of Alice, bowed his head and said quietly, 'I'm sorry for causing you to worry, Alice.'

She sat very still, eyes fixed on Michael's coppery hair. It was sticking up in untidy tufts, snarled with bits of straw and twigs from sleeping rough; his face was dirty and the hollows above his cheekbones were shadowed with fatigue. Overcome by a sudden overwhelming need to hold him, she reached out and wrapped him in her arms. *In the normal way of things*, Sam had said. In the normal way of things Michael would have made short work of squirming free — considering himself too big now for sisterly displays of affection. This was no normal evening though and to her surprise Michael did something he hadn't done for a long time. He kissed her cheek.

'I'm sorry, Alice,' he said again. Then he did pull away.

She nodded, her throat too tight with emotion to speak.

Turning, Michael walked with slow steps to Sam, who was still stationed by the window. 'I'm sorry for your lost wages, Mr Kenyon,' he apologised quietly.

'So you ought to be,' Sam said. There was no sternness in his voice though — his tone was merely matter of fact. 'That aside though,' he said, his voice suddenly very quiet, 'I owe you my thanks for what you did tonight. You saved me from a bad beating and I must thank you for it.' He reached out to lay a hand on Michael's shoulder in a gesture of gratitude. 'Go and finish your supper now,' he said quietly. 'Your sister and I are going to go outside for a few minutes. I need a bit of air.'

The night was warm and humid, the blustery nor'wester that had buffeted the port for most of the day had dwindled to a gentle breeze, barely enough to lift the damp hair from Alice's temples.

'We'll walk along the wharf for a bit,' Sam said, taking her arm.

She fell into step beside him. His shoulders were hunched forward and he was walking slightly stooped, setting his feet down carefully so as not to jar his bruised stomach muscles.

'Do you feel sick again?' she asked, tilting her head as she assessed his pallor.

He shook his head. 'No. Just sore.' They walked slowly on for a few more yards then he turned to look at her, his lips pressed tight together. 'What in God's name were you thinking, Alice?' He shook his head, looking momentarily lost for words. 'I told you to stay by the wall! Safe by the wall! You could have lost the child, and you're damned lucky not to have done so! What did you hope to do? Did you think you could overcome a man twice your size? And you pregnant?'

Alice looked away, flushing hotly. There was no denying she'd put herself and their child at risk, but having said that, if she were faced with the same situation a second time she had no doubt she'd do exactly the same again. 'I don't know what I thought,' she said, turning back to him. 'There wasn't time to think. All I knew was he was going to knock your teeth down your throat with the next blow.'

'So you risked the child for my teeth?' he said incredulously. He shook his head again and blew out a long breath.

'You don't know what it's like to have to just stand and watch while someone you love is being hurt and in pain!' she defended.

'Oh, do I not?' he said. Halting, he turned to face her. 'You forget, Alice. I watched Eliza for six months before she died, crying out with the pain sometimes, and not a thing I could do to help her. And I watched you tonight too, fearing I might lose both you and the child, and helpless to prevent it!'

She stared at him for a long moment then said softly, 'I thought I could help you. I had to try. I had to.'

A light breeze had sprung up, making the anchored ships thud dully against the wharf on the rising swell. Caught by a sudden gust, Sam's hair lifted from his brow, fluttering like a dark silk ribbon. 'And try you did,' he said. He shook his head yet again, but there was no anger or reproach in it this time. 'You're no coward, Alice, I'll grant you that.'

'Zac Fielding is,' she said, seizing the chance to shift the conversation to fresh ground. 'He was too much of a coward to even show his face!'

To her surprise Sam shook his head. 'No. I've no liking for Zac Fielding, but I'll give the man his due — he's no coward. I'll lay odds he knows nothing about tonight's business. It was his wife who arranged it.'

She screwed her mouth up, unconvinced.

'Well, if he did know,' Sam amended, 'it was pride and not cowardice that kept him away.'

'What do you mean by that?' she asked, raising her brows at him.

'It doesn't do much for a man's standing in his wife's eyes if he has to have the help of two other men to win a fight.'

'Oh,' she said, beginning to understand. Though she doubted she would ever really understand men's reasoning when it came to fights.

'Anyway, enough of the Fieldings. It's Michael I want to talk to you about,' Sam said quietly. He turned his head to look down the wharf to where, some twenty yards away, the *Agnes*' black funnel was dipping up and down on the light swell. 'I know you're against him going to sea, Alice,' he said, turning back to her, 'but it's what he wants to do, and I think his actions tonight have earned him the right to do as he wishes. He's a brave lad. He knew full well the risk he was taking when he let fly that pebble from his catapult. He didn't just act on impulse without taking any thought for the consequences — he knew there was a chance he might murder the man. He thought he might hang for it. Yet he took the risk and let fly hard to ensure that he'd render the man senseless, knowing that if he didn't he'd not get a second chance. I'm in his debt, Alice, and it would be a very poor repayment of that debt if I took him back to Black's Point and settled him in work he hated. The more so when there's a position aboard a good vessel going begging. It's my intention to see Captain Andrews in the morning to see if he'll hire him.'

She gave an involuntary swallow. 'And if I ask you not to see him?'

He gave a deep sigh. 'Alice, I'm in Michael's debt,' he said again. He paused then said softly, 'I mean to see Captain Andrews tomorrow, Alice. With or without your agreement.'

She turned away. Away from Sam, away from the *Agnes*, facing the way they'd come, towards the Gilmer where Michael was finishing off his supper. Her bottom lip was quivering, her eyes welling with tears. She had no idea when the *Agnes* sailed — tomorrow perhaps or the day after — it wouldn't be in port for long. But when it did sail, she knew as certainly as she knew the sun would rise at dawn, that Michael would be aboard. And nothing she could say or do would alter that now. If there was one matter Sam was completely intractable in, it was the matter of debt. When he owed — be it a debt of money, or boots that had burnt to char, or a debt of obligation such as this — there was only one way Sam paid. In full. And he would countenance no half measures.

Chapter 29

'It will be a rough passage today,' commented Captain Andrews, pulling on his jacket. 'Have you been on the open sea before, lad?'

Michael shook his head. 'No, sir.'

'No? Well, in that case you'll probably spend a good part of the day hanging over the ship's rail,' he said matter-of-factly.

Michael glanced over his shoulder at the bucking steamship and the rolling green seas beyond, looking for the first time a bit uncertain. With the naivety of youth, the possibility that he might be seasick seemed not to have occurred to him.

'Your duties will mainly be below deck to start with, helping the cook in the galley,' the captain advised. He glanced across at Sam. 'We'll be leaving port in about a quarter-hour. You and your wife will be wishing to say your farewells to the lad, no doubt.'

'Indeed we shall,' Sam said. 'But may I have a brief word with you before you go back aboard, Captain Andrews?' Stepping past Alice he walked towards the moored ship.

Alice pressed her lips together, watching him. Whatever he wished to say to the captain, he clearly wished to say it out of her hearing. Her lips tightened further as Michael crouched down to cup Peer's head between his palms, scratching him affectionately behind his ears. She wondered sometimes if he cared more for his dog than he did for her. She'd exchanged angry words with both Michael and Sam yesterday and there was a lingering atmosphere still. Ever since Sam had announced to Michael at breakfast yesterday his intention to approach Captain Andrews with a view to securing him an apprenticeship aboard the *Agnes*, Michael had been effervescing like a bottle of ginger beer that had blown its stopper off. He had shown no sign whatever of having any misgivings about leaving her, in fact he would have boarded the *Agnes* yesterday morning, given half a chance. She'd felt very hurt and told him so; not that it had served any useful purpose — Michael had looked completely baffled by her reproaches. She had then made the mistake of expressing her bitterness and hurt to Sam; he had shown a complete lack of understanding, she had told him so, and it had ended with sharp words from both of them. 'Sometimes, Alice,' he had said in exasperation, 'I wish I hadn't married you!' 'So do I!' she had returned. At that particular point in time she had shared his sentiments entirely.

At the sound of Sam's returning footsteps Michael straightened, tucking his shirt back into his trousers. It was an old shirt, tight across his broadening shoulders and short in the sleeves and body. Aside from what he stood up in, all he had to his name, rolled up in the woollen blanket at his feet, was his jacket, a few bits of extra clothing, and his catapult. God knows what use he thought a catapult would be aboard a ship.

'You'd better take your leave of your sister now, Michael,' Sam suggested. He glanced across at Alice, was rewarded with a cold stare, and looked away again.

Michael nodded and stepped forward, somewhat

tentatively. A foot or two in front of her he stopped. 'I'm sorry I worried you, Alice,' he said quietly. Mystified by her black mood, he had evidently drawn the conclusion that this was at the root of it and was endeavouring to put things to rights with a further apology. He didn't understand her reactions any more than Sam did, and for similar reasons. Apology delivered he took another step forward and stuck out his hand. 'Goodbye, Alice,' he said, and grinned at her.

She had made up her mind earlier that morning that she would *not* get upset, that she would go to the wharf and bid Michael a calm, emotionless farewell. But now the moment had arrived, the calm she had resolved to show was nowhere to be found. Her bottom lip started to tremble and the next second she was clasping him tightly to her, sobbing his name against his hair. The embrace was short-lived. Squirming like a tadpole, Michael wriggled free from her hold.

'Don't embarrass the lad, Alice,' Sam admonished quietly. 'There are seaman close by on the decks.'

She swallowed, glanced at the *Agnes*, and hastily wiped her eyes with the back of her hand. Michael, plainly not willing to be party to further unseemly excesses of sisterly affection, had taken the precaution of backing off several yards. She drew in a shaky breath and licked her lips. 'Goodbye, Michael,' she said hoarsely. 'God kee —' Her voice cracked, she swallowed, then finished in a choked whisper, 'God keep you safe.'

'Will you write to me now and again, Alice?'

She nodded, too full of emotion to speak.

Evidently feeling the difficult business of farewelling his sister now done, Michael turned to Sam. 'Thank you for letting me join the *Agnes*, Mr Kenyon. I'll not let you down. I'll work hard,' he assured.

Sam's mouth lifted slightly at one corner in a small smile as he took hold of Michael's extended hand. 'Be sure to remember what I told you yesterday.'

Michael nodded. 'I will, sir.' He glanced down at Peer, then looked back to Sam. 'I wish I could take Peer with me. You'll look after him, won't you?'

Sam nodded. 'I'll see he takes no harm.' Releasing Michael's hand he reached into his pocket and pulled something out. It took Alice a moment to realise what it was. It was the small ivory-handled knife that Sam's grandfather had given to him, the blade safely slotted into its snug leather pouch. He fingered the handle for a moment, running his nail down one of the carved grooves, then held it out. 'Here. Take it. It will be more use to you than your catapult aboard ship.'

Michael stared at it wide-eyed, then his mouth stretched into a delighted smile.

'My grandfather gave it to me when I was a lad,' Sam said.

The grin on Michael's face slowly disappeared and was replaced by something else — a distant stare which seemed to span more years than Michael had. He frowned slightly, then as the frown cleared he lifted his chin and looked Sam full in the eyes. It might have been only a trick of the light, but for a moment it seemed to Alice that the eyes of both man and boy were bright with tears. Or perhaps it was only the tears in her own eyes.

'Here. Take it.' Reaching for Michael's hand, Sam placed it carefully in his palm.

Michael's fingers remained slack and open, the knife balanced on the flat of his palm. 'But your grandfather gave it to you, Mr Kenyon.'

Sam nodded. 'He did. And now I've given it to you.

My grandfather was a seaman, as you are now. I think he would have liked you to have it.'

Alice turned away, unable to watch longer. It was more than just a knife which Sam had given to Michael; and Michael, young though he was, sensed it.

'Go aboard now,' Sam said firmly. 'And be sure to pen your sister a letter when you're next in port.'

'I will, sir,' Michael said, head bowed as he carefully buckled the pouch to his belt. He grinned again as he looked up then turned towards the ship. Sensing Michael was about to move off somewhere, Peer sprang to his feet and bounded back and forth in front of him, wagging his tail and barking loudly.

'Stay!' Michael ordered, fixing a stern eye on the dog. Peer's tail slowed to an uncertain swish, he gave several small whimpers then dropped onto his belly and laid his chin flat on the ground, watching Michael through uptilted pale brown eyes. 'Good dog.' Michael bent to pat his head, smiling. 'Stay. Good dog, Peer.'

At length he straightened, glanced back at Sam and smiled, waved at Alice, then boarded the *Agnes*. He stopped to converse briefly with a seaman then without a backward glance went below.

'Do you want to stay till she sails?' Sam asked, coming to stand beside her. He laid a hand gently on her back.

She shook her head without looking at him and with leaden feet began to walk back along the wharf towards the hotel. They walked in silence, apart.

She went up the narrow stairs to their room alone, leaving Sam to settle the bill. When he entered a few minutes later she was sitting on the edge of the bed, weeping. Ignoring her, Sam began to pack their few belongings together in readiness for leaving.

'You don't care, do you! You don't care how distressed I am!' she accused. The accusation was grossly unfair, but in her present mood she wasn't in the least concerned with what was fair and what wasn't.

His back was to her so that she couldn't see his face, but when he did eventually turn his cheeks were taut, flushed with anger. 'Don't care? Had I not cared I wouldn't have travelled all this distance to Greymouth and forfeited three days wages! I'm beginning to think Fred Wrigley is right — women lose all sense of reason when they're carrying a child! I really don't know what's the matter with you, Alice. You can't keep your brother tied to your apron strings forever. He's not a child any more, and it's high time you stopped thinking of him as one. Now for God's sake stop this . . .' he waved his hand impatiently, ' . . . excessive fretting!'

She threw him a black look and blew her nose.

'What did you say to him when you went out with him yesterday evening?' she demanded. Sam had been out with Michael twice the day before, leaving her alone in their hotel room on each occasion. The first outing during the morning — on which she had absolutely refused to accompany them — had been to the *Agnes* to see Captain Andrews, with a view to persuading him to hire Michael. The second outing, on which she had not been invited, had been in the early evening. All Sam had said was that he wished to speak to Michael in private. They'd been gone for over an hour.

'A number of things,' Sam replied offhandedly.

She rose abruptly to her feet, her hands clenched in tight fists. She could see now how fights broke out. Had she been a man — and at this moment she was heartily wishing she was — she would have been using her fists on Sam, pummelling him as hard as she could, *making* him answer her question. But she wasn't a man, she was a woman, a very angry, frustrated one. 'I have a right to know what passed between you!' she said loftily.

'And I have a right to some respect from you. And I'll not have you speaking to me like that!'

Silence settled, broken only by the muffled sounds drifting from the street below and the creak of floorboards in the next room. It was obvious from Sam's look and stance that he was waiting for an apology. Let him wait, she thought.

'Alice —' he prompted sharply.

She held his gaze for several long, silent seconds then said, 'If you want me to say I'm sorry then I shall. But it will be a lie.'

'Lie then,' he said. 'It won't be the first time you've lied to me.'

'Very well — I'm sorry.'

His eyes narrowed angrily, but he made no comment. Instead he turned back to the table and tossed the remainder of their belongings into the leather travelling bag. Ten minutes later they were rumbling along the Greymouth streets, still ribboned with early morning sea mist, turning now left, now right, heading into the centre of the town. She had a small suspicion where they might be going. Sam had never told her the name of the street where he'd lived, where he'd grown up, but as they turned onto Chapel Street she could see from his face it held special meaning for him. Partway along he pulled on the reins and slowed the wagon to a halt opposite one of the houses. It was a plain, unpretentious cottage with a small verandah at the front, a low wooden fence marking the perimeter of the property. He sat for a minute or two staring at it in silence, then with a sigh flicked the reins.

An hour or so along the road to Reefton the bridge over the Arnold River came into view. Muttering, Sam dug into his pocket for the required half-crown toll. One shilling and sixpence for the wagon and one shilling for the horse. The toll charges on the bridges over the Arnold and Ahaura rivers on the road linking Reefton and Greymouth were the subject of ongoing bitter complaints to the Grey County Council, but to date the council had turned a deaf ear, insisting that the revenue was needed to maintain the road in good order. They had spent little if any of the revenue on the low-lying road through Squaretown though, as a layer of thick, sticky mud six inches deep testified later in the day. It had rained there during the night, a short but heavy thunderstorm, turning the road into a nigh impassable quagmire.

It was almost midnight when they reached Black's Point. Unwilling to forfeit yet another day's pay Sam had kept driving, stopping only once in the late afternoon for a quick bite of food. Alice was so stiff from sitting she could hardly make her knees straighten, her back ached dreadfully, and she felt emotionally exhausted. She tumbled into bed, fully clothed, not even bothering to take her shoes off, and sank into a dead sleep.

A loud clatter woke her. Disoriented, she pushed herself up on one elbow in time to see a metal bowl roll into the bedroom through the open doorway, followed by Sam, the lower half of his face lathered with soap. Rubbing her eyes, she sat up.

'What time is it?' she murmured groggily.

Stooping to retrieve his shaving bowl, now minus water, Sam glanced across at her. 'Just after six,' he said.

She lay back again, watching him as he mopped up

the spilled water, then with a sigh she got out of bed. She needed to go to the privy. Urgently.

Sam was bent over doing up the laces of his boots when she returned. He glanced up but said nothing as she passed him. Barely a word had passed between them since they had left Greymouth yesterday. She looked over to Michael's bed, running her eye over the crumpled blanket, the pillow still indented from when he had last slept there, the canvas satchel in which he kept his school books . . . He'd be at sea somewhere now, and more than likely wishing he wasn't. He'd probably spent the last twenty-four hours retching into a bucket or hanging over the ship's rail, as green as the waves. She raised her brows slightly, realising with a small jolt of surprise that for the first time in her life she really didn't care whether he was sick or not.

Feeling a similar lack of interest in Sam's welfare she was tempted to let him fill his food tin himself. She oscillated for a minute or two while wifely duty battled with less noble emotions, but in the end duty won and she set about finding some food. She stood in silence as he shrugged on his jacket. Their eyes met briefly as he reached over the table for the tin then he left without a word, striding off towards the Wrigleys' cottage.

Lacking the inclination or the energy to do the thousand tasks she ought to be doing, Alice sank onto a chair and stared at the floor. Eventually the sound she had been waiting for came — the clamour of the school bell beckoning the pupils to their lessons for the day, amongst their ranks Robert and Jane Wrigley. With them gone, she would be able to have a proper conversation with Bella.

Two minutes later she was sitting in Bella's kitchen. Bella had already heard the news about Michael from

Sam, who had stopped by on his way to the mine. He had briefly told them about their encounter with Lily Fielding too, painting Michael as something of a hero by the sound of it.

'Michael was so clever to think of using his catapult. You must have felt very proud of him, Alice,' Bella said, leaning across the table to pass her a cup of tea. 'As for Lily Fielding — I can scarcely believe a woman would stoop to that! I mean, violence of that sort!' Bella shook her head, her dark brows raised in appalled arches. She was plainly far more interested in the business with Lily Fielding than she was in the news about Michael going to sea.

'I'm really not interested in discussing Lily Fielding,' Alice returned shortly. 'She can go to the devil for all I care. It's Michael' — her throat tightened on the word and she reached instinctively into her pocket for her handkerchief — 'I'm concerned about.'

'Oh, he'll be fine, Alice,' Bella assured dismissively as Alice buried her face in her handkerchief and gave her nose a loud blow. 'You know where he is, know he's safe, that's the main thing. And the captain sounds to be a good man from what Sam said,' she added, sliding the milk jug across the table. 'And your brother is doing what he wants to do. Some lads end up in work they hate. And the sea is a good healthy life. I'd far sooner Robert went to sea than work down a mine, which is where he'll probably end up. Fred was only last night talking about enquiring at the mines hereabouts to see if he can find work for Robert. He's still very vexed with him.'

'At least you'll see him every day if he's working in one of the local mines,' Alice said impatiently. She paused to dab her eyes and blow her nose again. 'I don't know when I shall see Michael again.'

'Well, it's what lads do, Alice. Leave home,' Bella said matter-of-factly.

Alice reached miserably for the milk jug. She had expected Bella, a woman like herself, to have some understanding, some sympathy for what she was feeling. But Bella was displaying no understanding at all. In fact, she was presently looking quite bewildered. Bella had left home when she was only ten, sent to live with an aunt and put to work in a local tin mine. Small wonder she couldn't understand the fuss Alice was making. Moreover, Michael was one of the fortunate ones who had secured a position he actually wanted. Put like that, Alice really couldn't understand herself why she felt the way she did — all she knew was, she did.

She stayed for half an hour then returned home. The day, never destined to be a good one, grew steadily worse. Charlotte had missed her and was unsettled and tearful, refused to have an afternoon nap and followed her round like a shadow all day, maintaining a leech-like grip on her skirt. By the time Sam arrived home from the mine she was beginning to think she would scream if she ever heard the word 'up' again. Sam glanced briefly at her as he came in, but neither of them spoke. He had plainly had a hard day as well and looked exhausted.

It had been a long day for Charlotte too. Halfway through her dinner she fell asleep over her plate, her cheeks still pouched with food; Alice picked her up, slipped her into her nightgown, put a clean napkin on her, and put her to bed. She stood beside her cot, looking down at the peaceful, limp little body, struggling to see through the watery curtain of tears welling into her eyes. She didn't want to go back to the kitchen at all, back to the silence and the stony atmosphere. Sam was waiting for her to apologise and God knows he was due an apology. She had accused him of not caring. She shook her head, wondering how she could possibly have accused him of that. 'No, you know very well how,' she whispered. 'Because you blame him for letting Michael go to sea.' And that too was unjust. What else could Sam have done? How else could he have repaid Michael for his courage? If she wanted to blame someone then she ought to be blaming Lily Fielding. Prior to the events with her, she had felt reasonably confident that Sam would heed her wishes and bring Michael home with them. Not that blaming Lily Fielding would serve any useful purpose. And anyway blame was not the present issue — the present issue was the apology she owed Sam. She drew in a long breath then turned and walked slowly back to the kitchen. She paused briefly in the doorway then went over to the table, coming to a halt beside Sam's chair. He looked up at her, one brow raised slightly in question.

'I'm sorry, Sam,' she said quietly.

He stared at her for a long moment, then put his knife down on his plate and held out his hand to her. As she placed her hand in his, his fingers curled around hers in a reassuring squeeze. 'Michael will be all right, Alice,' he said. 'Trust me — it's for the best.'

She nodded, sending a roll of tears spilling over her lashes. Best for whom, she wanted to ask, but forebore.

'I'm sorry,' she said again. 'I said a lot of very unfair and unkind things to you, Sam.'

He nodded, evidently agreeing with her, then said quietly, 'I asked Captain Andrews if he would undertake to send Michael back to Black's Point if the lad found the sea not to his taste. I spoke to Michael too. I told him to be honest and not to be too proud to come home if he discovered he'd made a mistake.'

The room went very quiet, so quiet she could hear the sound of her own breath. Winding her arms around Sam's neck she bent to kiss him. 'I do love you, Sam,' she whispered.

Chapter 30

Sam stared at the puddle of water surrounding his wife's feet, then as the significance of it registered he looked sharply up at her. 'Is the baby coming?'

'I don't know,' Alice said uncertainly. 'I think it might be.'

'But you're not due for another ten days yet,' he said in worried tones.

'Yes, I know,' she said. But babies didn't always arrive precisely on cue.

'I'll fetch the midwife,' he said, already halfway to the door.

'Just tell her my waters have broken,' she said, squelching across the room in her sodden shoes in search of a towel. 'It will be hours before I need her.'

Within the five minutes it took him to return from seeing the midwife, Alice was in no doubt at all that she was in labour. The contractions had started, strong from the first. As Sam walked through the door she was leaning on the table, breathing deeply as a fierce spasm took her in its grip. As it eased off she straightened and rubbed the base of her back, digging her fingers deep into the muscles on either side of her spine. 'Oh, that's better,' she said with a grateful sigh of relief. 'It's passing.'

'What can I do?' Sam asked anxiously.

'You can go to work,' she said. She smiled reassuringly at him.

He furrowed his fingers through his hair, making it stand up in untidy tufts. 'I, I feel as if I want to do something though. Something to help,' he said helplessly.

'Take Charlotte to Lydia Donne's then,' she said, stooping to peel off her soaked stockings. 'She offered to look after her when my time came. And ask Bella if she'll come and sit with me. What did Mrs Jackson say?'

'She said she'll come in an hour or two to see how you're progressing. She, she says you'll be a while before she's needed.' He swallowed, no doubt remembering when Eliza had been in labour — it had been long and difficult. In his workshop on the other side of the bedroom wall, Sam would have heard every sound she made. Small wonder he was looking pale.

'Go to work, Sam,' she said again. She held out her hand to him and smiled. 'I shall be all right.'

He nodded, licked his lips, and stepped forward to take her hand, holding it between the two of his as if it were a precious and very fragile flower. 'I don't want to leave you. I shall be worrying about you all day,' he murmured.

'Sam — I shall be all right,' she reassured again. 'Did you call in at Bella's?'

'Yes, she said she'll be here as soon as she's sent Robert and Jane off to school. She's going to take Sidney round to Meg Pringle's and ask her to look after him.'

'Have you time to take Charlotte to Lydia's before you go to work?'

'I'll make time,' he said. Still holding her hand he drew in a deep breath then slowly let it out again, his eyes locked on hers. 'God, I shall be glad when you're safely delivered, Alice.'

'I'll be all right,' she said for the third time. And patted his hand.

He nodded and gave a dry, nervous laugh. 'You're very calm, Alice. I think I'm more worried than you are.' He glanced over to Charlotte who was sitting at the table eating a crust of bread. 'Do I need to take anything for her? Clean napkins?'

'I'll find some,' she said, pulling free her hand. 'Can you put Charlotte's shoes on her please, Sam.'

Leaving Sam to deal with his daughter she set about filling a basket with the bits and pieces that Charlotte would need during the day.

'I think that should do,' she said, handing it to him. She looked round the kitchen, rubbing her back as another contraction came, trying to think if there was anything else that Charlotte might need.

'A strong one?' Sam asked. His hands settled gently on her shoulders and he bent to kiss her forehead as she closed her eyes and breathed in deeply, riding out the pain.

'Yes,' she said at length. 'It was.'

'Alice.' He lifted his hand to touch her cheek. 'You'll send someone up to the mine to fetch me if need be.'

She nodded and smiled, feeling a stab of guilt, knowing that much of Sam's worry stemmed from his belief that this was her first child.

'I will. I promise,' she said.

'Not long now. You're nearly there. Two or three more pushes, that's all,' encouraged Mrs Jackson.

Alice slumped back against the pillow, making the most of the brief respite in between contractions. They were only about a minute apart now — she'd barely recovered from one before the next took her in its grip.

As labours went it had been a relatively short one — a little over six hours — but the contractions had been fierce from the first and for the last half-hour she had been crying out with the pain.

'Here, have a little drink,' Bella said, bolstering her up with her arm as she put a cup of water to Alice's lips.

She took a quick sip then flopped back onto the pillow again. 'Can you see the baby?' she asked hoarsely.

'I can indeed,' Mrs Jackson said. 'The top of the skull. It has a nice crop of dark hair.'

'Has it?' she said hazily. She closed her eyes, trying to picture it, then screwed up her face in anticipation of more pain as the familiar tightening at the base of her spine began again.

'Push. Come along, Mrs Kenyon. Push,' the midwife urged.

She took a deep breath, gritted her teeth and pushed, groaning with the effort. She was lathered in sweat and her fingers slid against the wet skin of her knees as she gripped hold of them, straining forward.

'Push. Push. Push,' came the midwife's voice.

'I am pushing!' she snapped. God, could the woman not see she was pushing! She bowed her head low against her chest and pushed till she went red in the face, but it was still not enough. As the pain subsided she crumpled, exhausted, onto the pillow again.

'Nearly there,' Bella assured, wiping her brow with a cool damp cloth. 'A few more pushes, that's all.'

'How many?' she asked hoarsely. She wanted a definite number — like two. Or better still, one.

'That's up to you,' the midwife said matter-of-factly.

'Oh no, oh God, there's another coming already,' she moaned, leaning forward to grasp her knees again.

'Right — take a deep breath and hold it this time.

Don't push till I tell you to,' the midwife instructed. Alice filled her lungs, eyes screwed up tight in concentration. And waited.

'Now — push!'

She pushed, with every last ounce of her strength, and with a lusty wail James Kenyon slithered into the world.

'Oh, he's a fine big boy!' Mrs Jackson said approvingly as she wiped clean the pink wrinkly little body with a wet cloth. 'Nor far off seven pounds, I should say, Mrs Kenyon.'

'You did very well, Alice,' Bella said, patting her hand. 'Seven hours for a first child! I was in labour for nearly two days giving birth to Robert.'

Alice gave a tired smile. She had been in labour for over two days with Michael. This labour had been very much easier — second labours usually were — but she still felt completely exhausted. Sweet tea was the remedy, according to the midwife. Sweet tea, and plenty of it. It proved a surprisingly effective tonic. Half an hour and half a gallon of sweet tea later, and dressed in a clean nightgown, Alice was sitting up in bed, suckling her new son.

'You're doing fine,' Mrs Jackson encouraged, watching her. 'Most women find that suckling comes quite naturally to them. It will be a day or two before your milk starts to flow properly though and you may find your nipples are a little sore to start with, but that will pass. A little goose fat rubbed into them gently will help if they start to chafe. Or if they're really bad Mr Gissinge, the chemist, has some special ointment — if you can bring yourself to ask him for something so personal.

'You'll probably be a bit sore in your private parts for a few days,' she continued in the same businesslike fashion. 'A bowl of warm water with a tablespoon of salt dissolved in it is the best thing. Night and morning. And if you can manage to soak yourself in a warm salt bath, not too hot, so much the better.'

After a further half-hour of giving helpful advice on essential things like how to wrap, wash, wind, change, suckle, settle and sooth a newborn infant, the midwife left. Seeing Alice's eyelids drooping, Bella left shortly after her, promising to return a little later with a pie for their dinner. For the next two hours she slept like the dead. She would have slept even longer had her son not woken, loudly demanding to be fed. She had just finished suckling him when Sam arrived home from the mine. He had run by the sound of it — she could hear his breathing coming in rapid gasps as he strode across the kitchen to the bedroom.

'Alice!' he said breathlessly, halting in the doorway. He scanned her face anxiously. 'Are you all right?'

'I'm fine,' she said with a tired smile.

'And . . . the baby?'

She tilted her arms to give him a better view. 'You have a son,' she said softly.

'Aye, so I heard. I was expecting you to be still in labour. I could hardly believe my ears when Mary Bray told me you'd been delivered.' He stared at the round little face, blinked several times as if to confirm it wasn't an illusion, then walked slowly towards the bed. Still only a few hours old, his son's eyelids had that bloated look typical of newborn babies, his skin was a blotchy rose pink and he was pouting. 'He's a handsome little fellow,' Sam said proudly. Stooping, he ran the tip of his finger, still grimy from the mine, over his son's cheek. Alice looked up, watching him. He was grinning from ear to ear, with a look of awed wonder in his eyes.

'Oh! He has dark hair like mine.'

He looked so completely surprised she couldn't help but laugh. 'Did you think it would be like mine?'

'I did,' he said. 'They do say though that daughters are often like their mother and sons are like their father.' He gave a soft laugh and shook his head, eyes still glassily incredulous. 'A son. I'd not have minded if you'd given me a daughter, Alice, but I was hoping for a son.'

'James Kenyon,' he pronounced. It was the name they had agreed upon. James, if a boy, after Sam's grandfather. Margaret, if a girl, after Alice's mother.

Still smiling broadly, he sat down on the edge of the bed, but as his eyes shifted to Alice his features took on a more serious expression. 'How was it, Alice?' he said quietly. 'Was it very bad?'

'No. Just exhausting,' she said honestly.

He reached for her hand. 'You look very pale. Can I get your something? A drink? Some food?' Twisting his head he looked speculatively through the door to the kitchen. 'What's that I can smell?'

'Oh, it must be the pie Bella promised to bring,' she said, sniffing the air. She had fallen into such a dead slumber she hadn't even heard her deliver it.

'That was kind of her.' He turned back, frowning. 'Where's Charlotte? Is she still at Lydia Donne's?'

She nodded, gingerly shifting into a more comfortable position. 'She said she can sleep there tonight. She'll bring her home in the morning.'

'Are you sore?' Sam's fingers tightened on her hand in a gentle squeeze.

Was she sore? She felt as if a large and very hard fist had systematically pummelled every muscle in her body. Even her ankles ached. 'Just a little,' she said. 'I'll be all right in a day or two.'

Alice watched as Sam's gaze drifted back to his new son. 'Do you want to hold him?' she asked.

He shook his head. 'No. Don't disturb him.' Smiling, he leaned across the sleeping little body and kissed her softly on the lips. Then like a magnet to metal his eyes returned to his son, and the look of awed wonder settled on his features again. She watched him for a moment, then lowered her eyes to the baby. Ever since he'd been born she had been making a conscious effort not to think of Michael, not to remember the day she'd given birth to him. But it was impossible not to think of it. It had been so poignantly different in every way. There had been no proud father to stare glassy-eyed at Michael, no congratulatory comments from the midwife, no little gifts from neighbours . . . What there had been was a young, distressed mother covering her face with her hands, sobbing, 'Take him away! Take him away! I don't want to see him! I don't want to touch him! I hate him! I hate him!' Those were the words that had greeted Michael's entrance into the world. It had not been a happy day. Even her father, who normally kept his emotions well hidden, had wept at the sight of his new grandson. Eventually she had been forced to touch him, not out of choice but out of necessity. It was impossible to suckle a baby without touching it. It was also impossible to suckle a baby without growing to love it. Her eyes shifted slightly, following the movement of Sam's hand as he stroked his son's cheek again.

'His skin is so soft,' he murmured. 'Sort of velvety. Like the skin of a peach.' He looked up to smile at her. Then frowned. 'What's this?' he asked, gently wiping a teardrop from her cheek.

She shook her head and smiled. 'Nothing. I'm

weeping because I'm happy.' It was true. She was happy. But mingled with that happiness was a sorrow as deep as the ocean that Michael had chosen to make his life.

Chapter 31

Picking up his hammer, Sam edged his way backwards down the sloping roof.

'Have you managed to repair it?' Alice asked, peering up at him from the bottom of the ladder.

'I think I have,' he said, glancing back at her as he made his way down the rungs to terra firma again.

'Let's hope so,' she said. 'I can't say that I'm keen to have the chamber pot perched on the end of the bed whenever it rains.'

To keep expenditure to a minimum Sam had done all the carpentry on the new house himself. He had made quite a creditable job of it too, considering it wasn't his trade. The only notable flaw thus far in his handiwork was the leak in the roof, which had made its presence felt at some ungodly hour last night when it had started to pour down.

'I must have split it when I was nailing it down,' he said, frowning as he examined the damaged shingle which had been responsible for the leak. 'They do say "every man to his trade". I'm definitely a better bootmaker than I am a carpenter.'

'Well, most carpenters wouldn't know where to even start making a pair of boots,' she said.

He turned to smile at her and nodded. 'Mm, I dare say they'd end up with boots that leak in the wet, like my roof,' he commented wryly.

'Have you managed to mend it, Sam?' came Joel's voice from the road.

Sam glanced over his shoulder and smiled at his old neighbour as he ambled over to join them. 'I hope so. I think this was the culprit,' he said, holding out the split shingle to show him. 'I suppose we shall see when it next rains.'

'Well, we could do with some rain. The ground is as dry as a bone and the river is lower than I've seen it for many a year.' A cloud of fine brown dust rose from the ground as Joel scraped the sole of his boot across the earth. The top half-inch was still moist from the overnight rain but beneath that the soil was parched. 'Feel good to be back, does it?' he asked, turning to Alice.

'It does indeed,' she said, smiling. She had a feeling that Joel was quite pleased they were back too. This was his fourth visit today. During the three days they'd been back he'd hardly been off their doorstep.

'The dog's glad to be back by the look of him,' he said, gesturing towards the creek where Peer was nosing around in the long grass, his bushy tail swishing exuberantly back and forth.

'Is all your furniture arranged inside now?' Leaning into the doorway, Joel ran his eye over the interior. You'll find it a bit cramped, I dare say. It's a good bit smaller than your previous house. Still, now the lad's left home you'll not be needing quite as much room,' he added. His perusal completed, he turned back to face them, absently rubbing his knuckles across the sparse white stubble on his chin. 'Still no news from him then?'

Alice shook her head and gently patted James's back as he stirred; he had fallen asleep over her shoulder.

'How long is it since he went to sea? About three months is it now?' Joel asked.

'Yes, about that,' she returned. Eleven weeks and three days to be exact.

'It could be a while yet till you hear from him. Trading vessels are often months at sea.' Joel shook his head dolefully. 'Never fancied the sea, myself. Too much at the whims and mercy of the weather for my liking. Some hold that mines are dangerous, but there are more men lost at sea than die below ground. There —'

'Come away from there, Charlotte!' Sam cut in, calling to his daughter. He waved his hand, beckoning her away from the creek. 'She was looking as if she might fall in,' he explained with a shrug. 'Come and see what I've done to the shed, Joel,' he said, tapping the old man's arm as he walked past him. 'I've put another window in to let in more light. I think it should make quite a serviceable workshop now.'

'It will be damned cold in there in the winter,' Joel commented, following him.

'I'll manage,' Sam said dismissively. As he pushed open the door of the shed and stepped aside to let Joel pass he glanced back over his shoulder at Alice. She was standing where he had left her, absently patting the baby's back, staring at the ground with that distant, despondent look in her eyes again. Damn Joel for his tactless bloody comments! Whatever was he thinking of, making worrying comments about the dangers of the sea like that? Had the old man no brains at all? He had told him only yesterday that Alice was fretting for Michael, worrying because she'd had no letter yet. Damn Michael too, he thought, compressing his lips in annoyance. What was the lad thinking of, not penning a single letter in all these weeks?

'Oh, aye, that's much better, Sam,' Joel said approvingly. 'It's made not a bad workshop.'

Expelling a low sigh Sam dragged his attention back to his neighbour. 'It'll suffice,' he said.

'A letter from Michael!' Sam exclaimed, waving an envelope aloft as he strode into the house. He tossed it onto the table, grinning.

Alice stared at it, still bent low over the washtub, then slowly straightened, leaving James' napkin to slide gracefully down the scrubbing board amid a flurry of tiny rainbow-coloured soap bubbles. Wiping her wet hands on her apron, she walked over to the table, eyes locked on the familiar scrawl. Michael had addressed the letter to both of them — Mr & Mrs S Kenyon — but it was still unopened.

'Well, read it,' Sam prompted, nudging it towards her with his thumb.

She drew in a shaky breath and picked it up, then slit open the envelope with her finger. The letter was brief, a single page.

Dear Alice and Mr Kenyon
I am doing well in my duties, the captin says. I was very sick at the start, but am in good helth now. It is an exiting life at see. I rise erly and work till dark. There is never any shortage of work to do abord a ship. Last week I saw a wale for the first time. You cannot imagin how big a wale is, Alice. Even biger than the ship. I have been to forin parts (so the seemen call other lands) to a land called Tasmania. In two days we are bound for South Africa. I riped my shirt badly a few days ago and have mended it with a needle and thred. Mr Newson, the cook, showed me how it is done.

I hope you are well and in good helth. I will rite when we are next in port.

Your most afectionate brother — Michael.

Alice sniffed, trying to make out the words through tearful eyes. Then the paper fluttered to the floor like a wounded dove and with a choking sob she clasped her hands to her face and burst into tears.

'Alice, what is it? Has he suffered an accident?' Eyes wide with alarm, Sam snatched up the letter from the floor. A moment later he looked up, frowning. 'I don't understand. Why are you weeping? He sounds well and happy.'

'Yes, he does,' she sobbed.

He stared at her in bewilderment. 'Then why are you weeping?'

'Because I was h-hoping that his letter would say that he wasn't happy, that he h-hated the sea, that he wanted . . .' She stopped briefly as the sobs became too much. 'To c-come home.'

Sam rolled his eyes in exasperation. The lad was well and happy — what more could she want? Alice could be bloody frustrating at times! 'Alice,' he said in mildly impatient tones, 'I know you miss him, but you must accept the fact that the sea is the life your brother has chosen. The lad is acquitting himself very well, by the sound of. You ought to feel proud of him.'

'You don't understand, Sam,' she sobbed, shaking her head. 'You don't understand.'

No, he agreed silently, he did *not* understand. Expelling a loud sigh, he drew her into his arms to comfort her.

Alice slipped quietly out of bed and reached into the cot to remove its noisy occupant. Dragging her shawl from the chair, she padded over to the door. She had formed the habit of feeding James in the kitchen during the night. Though a relatively quiet feeder, James raised loud objections to having his nice warm bottom exposed to the cold night air and invariably woke both Sam and Charlotte if she changed his napkin in the bedroom. And while Sam was disposed to suffer intrusions to his sleep in silence, Charlotte was much less forgiving.

'Hush, hush,' she murmured, patting his back as she carried him into the kitchen. The hungry wails continued to rip from his small mouth until the soft fullness of her nipple filled it, bringing the comfort of milk. She closed her eyes and let out a long sigh. It had not been a good day. She had wept for well over an hour after reading Michael's letter, then aware that Sam was losing patience with her, she had pulled herself together and forced herself to get on with the day's chores. Alone now though, in the silence of the kitchen, grief and a bone-deep emptiness were engulfing her again. She had prayed every night without fail that Michael would find the sea a disappointment, that he would decide to return home, but in a few brief lines today's letter had dashed those hopes forever. Her son would not be coming home. Not for a long time.

'No, not my son,' she whispered. 'My brother.' And *that* was the real heart of her pain — the knowledge that Michael didn't and never would love her as a son, only as a 'most affectionate brother'.

She opened her eyes, her hand going automatically to her breast. James's mouth had slipped from the nipple and he was anxiously trying to find it again. With practised ease she took it between two fingers and guided it back again. 'Good boy,' she murmured as the small cheeks contentedly deflated with each suck. She picked up his hand, lying slack on her breast, and gently straightened out the curled little fingers. So tiny, yet so perfectly formed. She had held Michael's hand like this as he had sucked at her breast.

She bit hard on her lip to hold back the tears, determined not to start weeping again. But the memories were too much. She rocked forward, head bowed low over her new son, but it was the name of her first-born that she sobbed in the darkness.

Chapter 32

'Why, Mr Kenyon! Come inside out of the rain.' Waving a lean hand, Reverend Sedgwick beckoned him in. 'Come down into the parlour. There's a fire burning in there.' The door closed with a creak behind him.

'I'll not stay long, Reverend Sedgwick,' Sam said, following him down the narrow passageway. 'I was passing and thought I'd stop by to enquire if you would be willing to baptise my son this coming Sunday during the service.'

'Ah yes — James, I believe you've named him. My housekeeper informed me that your wife had been delivered of fine healthy son.' A blast of warm air rushed into the chilly hall as he pushed open a door on the right. 'Come, sit down beside the fire.' He tapped a long finger on the nearer of a pair of brown leather armchairs arranged around the blazing hearth.

It was the first time Sam had set foot in the manse parlour — he was usually shown into the study. As parlours went it was a very pleasant one. Besides the two leather armchairs, there was also a deep-buttoned leather ottoman, presently littered with sheets of hymn music, and an attractively turned spindle-backed rocking chair. A fine rosewood piano graced the alcove to the left of the fireplace, while the right alcove was occupied by a large bookcase, filled with religious tomes

— commentaries on every book of the Bible by the look of it. He glanced down at the large aspidistra gracing a small round table in the centre of the room. The reverend seemed to have something of a preference for the plant. There were two more in the bay window in enormous brass pots.

'What inclement weather we're having. Winter has come upon us early this year,' Reverend Sedgwick commented as he sat down.

'It has indeed,' Sam agreed, perching on the edge of the other chair.

'Anyway, with regard to your son's baptism — I can see no reason why this Sunday should be inconvenient.' Reverend Sedgwick paused, frowning slightly, then with the look of one who has just made a profound discovery he lifted his hand to his nose and slipped off the wire-framed spectacles. 'Ah, that's better,' he said, smiling. 'Now I can see you much more clearly. So, how does it feel to be back in Reefton, bootmaking again?' he asked, leaning across to deposit them on the nearby table.

Sam gave a soft laugh. 'Well, compared with working a hundred or more feet below ground, standing in filthy water, breathing in rank air, if I can be forgiven the comparison — it feels like paradise, Reverend. I used to take daylight and fresh air and dry boots for granted, expect them by right. I don't any more.'

'Yes, a miner's life is not an unduly pleasant one,' Reverend Sedgwick agreed. 'But there are worse occupations. Tell me, speaking of occupations — have you had word from Michael yet?'

'We had a letter a week ago, as a matter of fact. He seems to be happy with his choice,' Sam replied in flat tones. Would that Alice was as happy with it. She had done nothing but weep since his letter had arrived.

Reverend Sedgwick tilted his head to the side, one brow cocked slightly. 'You seem to have some reservations. Do you think Michael is perhaps not as content as he purports to be?'

'I think Michael is very content with the choice he's made,' Sam answered. 'It's Alice who's not content. She misses the lad badly. She worries about him and nothing I can say seems to assuage her anxiety.'

'Ah.' Reverend Sedgwick smiled sympathetically. 'Well, it is a woman's nature to worry about those in their care. And your wife has been more of a mother than a sister to Michael, has she not?'

'She has,' Sam agreed. And she worried about him a good deal more than most mothers would. With a sigh he rose to his feet. 'Anyway, if you'll excuse me, I must be on my way, Reverend Sedgwick.'

'Can I not persuade you to take a cup of tea with me?'

Sam shook his head. 'No thank you, Reverend. I've too much work to do to tarry, I'm afraid.'

'Well, I shall see you all on Sunday then,' Sedgwick said, preceding Sam down the passageway to the front door.

'You shall indeed,' Sam said. He was looking forward to displaying his new son, decked out in all his christening finery. And pray God he wouldn't spew milk all over himself as Charlotte had when she was baptised. He must remember to mention that to Alice, tell her to make sure she had a cloth handy, just in case.

Leaving Reverend Sedgwick to return to the warmth of his parlour fire Sam pulled up the collar of his coat and set off down the street at a brisk stride. The rain had stopped and had been replaced by a chilly dampness. 'Stewing beef,' he reminded himself as he reached the main street. He had nearly forgotten. Alice had asked him to buy some while he was in the town.

'Good morning, Sam.' John Bell, the barber, nodded at him as he strode past the shop. He was standing in the doorway, smoking his pipe. Business was seemingly slack this morning.

'Good morning,' Sam returned, feeling obliged to halt for a moment or two. John Bell had been amongst the volunteer brigade who had turned out in the middle of the night to douse his burning house.

'I hear you're a father again.'

'I am. I have a fine son,' Sam said proudly.

'So I heard. I'm always glad to hear of a man having a son.' Bell puffed on his pipe sending a cloud of wispy smoke curling from the corner of his mouth. 'A district full of daughters is no good to a barber.'

Sam laughed. 'Well, it will be a year or two yet before my son is sitting in your chair.'

'Maybe so, but it will come.' He puffed on his pipe again, and his gaze swivelled upwards towards the sky. 'Will it rain again, do you think?'

'I do,' Sam said. The sky had that thick, grey sodden look about it.

'You're not wanting a haircut? It's getting a bit long at the back there. Nearly touching your collar,' Bell commented.

'Not today,' Sam said definitely.

Bell nodded and turned back towards the shop. 'Ah well, give my good wishes to your wife. She's well, I hope?'

'She is, thank you,' Sam said. Melancholy, but well.

Stewing beef . . . He headed down the street towards Dick's butchery.

'You're soaked,' Alice said, taking the soggy parcel of beef from him.

'I am. I should have put on my oilskin cape. I didn't think it would do much more than drizzle.' Pushing back a dripping lock of hair Sam walked over to the crib, patting Charlotte's head as he passed her.

Seeing him entering special territory, she ran after him. 'No, Papa,' she whispered, tugging urgently at his hand to draw him away. Sam looked down at her and smiled. 'It's all right, Charlotte. I'll take care not to wake him.' He peered into the crib at the still little form, sleeping peacefully; the fat pink cheeks looked thoroughly replete. 'James looks very content. Have you just fed him, Alice?' he asked, turning back to her.

'About an hour ago,' she said, reaching for the iron. She dipped her finger into the bowl of water on the table and dribbled a few droplets onto the hot surface. Satisfied that it was not going to scorch the fabric, she ran the iron carefully over the white christening gown that she had spent the last fortnight making. It was closely pleated across the bodice, each pleat embroidered with four tiny white roses, and trimmed with a thin edging of fine lace along the neck, cuffs and hem.

'You've made a very fine job of that, Alice,' Sam complimented, walking across to her. 'James will look very handsome in it on Sunday.'

'You spoke with Reverend Sedgwick then?' she asked, glancing up.

'I did. He said this coming Sunday will be convenient. Oh, and I invited George Withers and Ellen to come and have a cup of tea after the service. I thought I might ride up to Black's Point and invite the Wrigleys along as well. And Joel — though I doubt he'll want to come to the service.'

'We'll be very crowded in here if the weather is wet,' she said, eyes focused on her ironing again.

'I know the house is small, but it's not so cramped that I can't invite a few friends inside to celebrate my son's baptism.'

She looked up sharply. There was no mistaking the disgruntled note in Sam's voice, or the look on his face. 'Sam,' she said with a sigh, 'I didn't mean that. I only meant . . .' What had she meant? Certainly not to insult him or imply that she was dissatisfied with the house. She had simply been trying to point out that seven adults, four children and two babes in arms were rather a lot of bodies to cram into a room this size. And hoping, if she was honest, that the comment might make him reconsider and not invite more guests than he already had. It would be hard enough to cope with just the baptism, and all the memories that would evoke, but the thought of having to cope with a gathering afterwards as well, of having to be make jolly conversation . . .

'I thought a small celebration might cheer you up,' Sam said in sour tones. 'Cheer me up as well,' he added.

She lifted the iron quickly as Charlotte's small fingers curled over the edge of the ironing board, coming within a hair's breadth of touching the hot surface. 'I know I'm poor company,' she said. 'I don't want to be and I'm trying not to be but —'

'But you miss Michael. And you blame me for letting him go to sea,' he cut in. 'As for all this weeping, the accusing gloomy silences of an evening . . . if they're meant to make me feel guilty then be assured they do!'

'I don't blame you,' she said. 'And I don't weep on purpose to make you feel guilty — I weep because I can't help it.' She swallowed, hoping that she wasn't going to start weeping now. She lowered her eyes and murmured, 'You have no call to feel guilty. The guilt is all mine.'

He stared blankly at her for a moment, then shook his head and said sharply, 'Alice, you make no sense at all these days! I've tried to be patient with you, but it's over three months now since Michael left; he's well and happy and I'm damned if I can see why you should be fretting for him the way you are.' He gave an impatient click with his tongue. 'It's time you pulled yourself together, and started taking some pleasure in your new son. There will be no danger of him crying when he's baptised on Sunday — he's used to being doused every day with your tears.'

'I do take pleasure in him!' she defended. She glanced down as the iron, still clenched in her hand, gave a soft sizzle. It sizzled again as a second tear landed on it. She turned to set it on the trivet beside the fire and hastily wiped her eyes. But it was too late, Sam had seen.

'Alice!' he said sternly. 'I've had quite enough of all this weeping. It's to stop, do you hear me! I'm heartily sick of seeing you with red eyes, of being greeted with half-hearted smiles, and of watching you stare mournfully into space while you're feeding James. You care more for that brother of yours than you do for your own son!'

She licked her lips and swallowed, trying to muster the courage to tell him what she had balked at telling him so many times before, then blinked, sending more tears spilling down her cheeks. It was hardly a flood, but it was evidently more than Sam was prepared to tolerate. Wrenching open the back door, he slammed it shut behind him, sending a resonating quiver through the floorboards. Startled, Charlotte began to cry; moments later loud screams erupted from the cradle.

Clasping her hands to her face, Alice burst into tears.

'How long? How long is she going to go on like this?' Sam demanded of the stool. Getting no response from it, he thumped it down on the shed floor in front of his workbench and snatched up his hammer. 'She'll be weeping again now, back in the house,' he told the hammer. 'It's a wonder she has any damned tears left — there surely must be a limit to the eyes' reservoirs!' Snatching the box of tacks from the top shelf he banged it on the bench, sending the uppermost tacks leaping into the air like pricked fleas before landing with a clatter in the box again. He sat down, glaring at the last. 'She has a fine son there. A fine, healthy son. But does she take pleasure in him? No, all she does is weep for her brother!' He gave a disgusted click with his tongue, and rammed Ned West's left boot onto the last. 'That letter — that letter is the cause of it all,' he muttered. Before that letter had come, Alice hadn't been too bad. Quiet, but reasonably cheerful — or at least trying to be. Since Michael's damned letter though . . .

'Enough is enough!' he said, prising off the worn heel. He had been patient with her too long. Sterner measures were called for. A week ago — the night after that damned letter had arrived — he'd got up to go to the privy and found her in the kitchen feeding James, weeping, whispering 'Michael' over and over again. Not *James*. Not her son's name. Michael's! She'd jumped like a startled frog when she'd suddenly realised he was there, looking as guilty as if he'd caught her in the arms of a lover.

Sam jumped almost as much himself as the shed door swung abruptly open. It was Alice. Her eyelashes were stuck together with tears, her cheeks were soaked, and there was a large droplet about to drip off the end of her chin. He glanced past her to the house, grimacing. The baby was crying and Charlotte was banging on the back door, yelling 'Mama' at the top of her lungs. He opened his mouth with a view to ordering her in the sternest possible terms to return to the house at once and tend to her children, but Alice was already speaking, or trying to. Her voice was choked with tears and there was so much noise coming from the house he could barely hear her.

'I have something to say to you,' she said hoarsely. Sam set his hammer down on the bench. He had a thing or two to say to her too. 'Something I should . . .' He missed a few words, lost in the general din. '. . . long ago.' He heard the next four words though, each one punctuated by a racking sob. 'Michael is my son.'

How he'd got to the cemetery, Sam had no idea. He had no recollection of walking along the road, no memory of seeing anyone along the way. As for why he was there . . . that also was a mystery. Eliza was dead. She could offer him neither comfort nor counsel. He crouched down in front of her grave and bowed his head, running his fingers through his rain-soaked hair, trying to think.

Michael is my son . . . my son . . . my son . . . The words echoed inside his head, pounding against his skull until he thought it would burst.

Chapter 33

'How could you lie to me all these months!' Water dripped from Sam's chin onto the kitchen floor. He was soaked to the skin, the white shirt clinging transparently to his chest beneath his drenched jacket. 'You had countless opportunities to tell me, yet you deliberately chose to lie to me! That night, when you told me how you'd been raped — why did you not tell me of this then?'

'Because I was afraid. Afraid of how you would react. Afraid that if you knew about Michael's parentage you might treat him differently.' Alice clasped her hands loosely in her lap, feeling oddly calm. It was the same odd sense of calm she'd felt after she'd accepted Sam's proposal of marriage. Not a peaceful calm — no, it was more an empty calm, the calm emptiness which settles on the mind after a great burden has been lifted from it.

Sam looked anything but calm. He ran a hand raggedly through his hair, breathing heavily as he paced past the table where she was sitting. 'You should have told me long ago. When we first married. Before we married. Or at the very least when you told me of the rape,' he said. He was with an effort keeping his voice under control so as not to wake Charlotte and James in the next room. 'For a man to suddenly learn that his wife has given birth to a child he knew nothing of — how could you deceive me like that? You've done nothing but lie to me since I married you! You even lied about how old you were when you were raped so I'd not suspect anything. Is there anything you haven't lied to me about?'

'Would you ever have told me about your visit to Mary Deakin if I hadn't learned of it from Lily Fielding?' His pacing came to an abrupt halt directly in front of her. She lifted her chin, meeting his eyes steadily. 'Would you have confessed that to me? Or would you have deemed it more prudent to say nothing?'

He stared down at her, his fingers still furrowed through his hair, momentarily frozen there, then his hand slowly slid from his head and dropped to his side as if his arm had suddenly lost all strength. He turned away, shaking his head — whether in answer or whether he was simply lost for words it was impossible to tell.

She rose slowly to her feet. 'Why did you not tell me about that? Because you were ashamed? Because you feared how I would react?' She walked around him so that she stood in front of him, forcing him to meet her eyes. 'I too was ashamed, Sam. I too was afraid.'

'Alice.' He swallowed noisily, then, turning his back on her, gripped the edge of the table and bowed his head, swaying slightly. 'The child . . . Michael . . . it wasn't your fault, I know you didn't choose to conceive him. But Christ, Alice, do you think it's easy for a man to suddenly discover that his wife has borne a child he knew nothing of! All this time, all the months I raised Michael under my roof believing him to be your brother, all the while he was your son!'

She reached out to touch his arm but at the last moment lost courage and dropped her hand to her side.

'Sam,' she whispered, 'I know I ought to have told you, but I couldn't.' She wound her arms around her middle and walked over to the fire. She stood for several minutes staring at the glowing logs then said softly, 'If I'd told you about Michael when you offered me marriage, would you still have married me?'

It was a long while before he answered. His back was still to her, his head bowed low as if the weight of it was too heavy for him. 'I don't know,' he said at length. 'I want to say that it would have made no difference, but the truth is — I don't know.'

'I shouldn't have told you,' she said. 'I should have carried the lie to my grave as my mother and father did.'

His shoulders bunched suddenly and he gave a loud sneeze. 'It would have been easier if you had.'

'Do you think it's been easy for me?' she demanded sharply. 'Letting Michael believe me his sister all these years?'

'No, I don't!' he said, matching her tone. Straightening, he turned to face her again. 'Nor is it easy for me! I feel as if my head has been turned inside out and I can no longer tell what's up and what's down.' He raised his hand to rub the back of his neck, then as if realising for the first time that he was soaked and dripping water everywhere, he began to peel off his jacket. As he bent to drape it over the back of the chair to dry he glanced over to her. 'Who else knows of this?'

'No one,' she said.

He frowned, looking as if he'd expected a different answer. 'You've never spoken to Ellen of it?'

'I've never to spoken to anyone of it until today.' And she was deeply ruing that now.

He stared at her, blank-eyed, as if lost in thought,

till a violent shiver shuddered him back to earth again.

'I'll fetch you some dry clothes,' she said. It sounded a ridiculous thing to say, given the tension in the room, but she could think of nothing else to say.

He lifted his hand, staying her. 'No. I'll get them myself.' He licked his lips, seeming on the point of saying something else, but it was only another sneeze which eventuated.

She waited by the hearth, watching the hot embers spark and hiss and blacken as large drops of rain landed on them, while Sam changed into dry clothes in the bedroom. The heat from the flames seared her eyes, raw and dry from weeping. Curiously though, she felt no urge at all to weep now.

She looked up as the bedroom door swung open, their eyes met briefly, then Sam thrust his hands into his pockets and walked across to her. 'I feel as if there are two people inside my head,' he said. 'Two voices talking to me. One of them is talking very quietly and reasonably, telling me that what happened to you was none of your fault, that you were courageous and selfless in allowing Michael to think you his sister all these years, and that you meant only for the best by not telling me the truth. And when I can manage to think dispassionately, I know that all those things are true. But then there's this other voice, a very loud voice that keeps screaming in my head all the while that you should have told me, that you lied, deliberately deceived me! And I cannot, try as I will, shut it out! I want to feel compassion for you — God knows you're due some — but all I feel at present is confusion and anger!'

She stood in silence, watching him as a violent melee of emotions swept across his features. But for the life of her she could think of nothing to say to him.

Nothing that would help. Not that her silence seemed to be helping matters either.

'Do you have any notion at all of how ripped apart I feel?' he demanded vehemently.

'Yes. I do.' She spoke the words very clearly and very precisely. 'That's how I felt — as if two voices were in my head — when I found I was carrying the child of the man who raped me. One voice, as you say, was quiet and reasonable and kept telling me that the baby was innocent of guilt and that I should love it and cherish it, that it was my child, my flesh. But then the other voice would come, screaming that it was *him* inside me, his filthy, vile seed, and that the child would grow to be like him. And when I listened to that voice I hated Michael, hated the feel of him inside me, his writhing little body, and I wished us both dead!' She nodded, her eyes ablaze with emotion. 'Yes, Sam, I know what it is to feel ripped apart.'

She drew in a deep breath and, feeling a sudden need of cool air, stepped past him and walked towards the door. She was feeling slightly faint, whether from the heat of the fire or maybe just from the strain and turmoil of the day.

'Alice — where are you going?' Sam's voice came from behind her, low and tense.

She paused, her hand on the latch, but didn't look back. 'Outside. I need some air,' she said.

The rain had eased to a fine mist, but the sky was still dark and heavy with the promise of further downpours. The waterlogged ground gave softly beneath her feet as she walked along beside the creek. Peer, always delighted to see someone, loped along beside her, wagging his tail. She breathed in deeply, trying to clear her head, pacing back and forth, ten steps each way. She had paced like this when she had been pregnant with Michael, back and forth till her back had felt as if it would break. 'Why? Why did I tell him?' she said aloud. All these years she had kept silence, never told a soul. Why now had she spoken out the truth? Because the situation had changed, that was why. Pretending to friends and acquaintances was considerably easier than pretending to a husband — a husband she had grown to love very deeply these last few months. Her father's death had changed things too — his passing had taken away the only other person who knew about Michael, who understood her feelings. As Sam had once said — it was far easier to face difficulties when you had someone to stand beside you and face them with you. But it was Michael's letter that had tipped the balance. That had been the turning point, the point where her strength had started to crumble. The weight of grief — and it was grief she felt — the grief of eleven years of never once having called Michael *son*, never had him look into her face and call her *Mother*, eleven lost years of being nothing more than a sister to him — worse still, the knowledge of the lost years that stretched ahead — it had overwhelmed her. This morning perhaps the last of her strength had simply run out.

Sam was sitting on the couch when she eventually returned, leaning forward, staring at his clasped hands. As she closed the door he looked up and straightened. He looked a better colour now — his cheeks had lost that grey, pinched look — but his eyes still glittered with accusation and hurt. A familiar wail was filtering through the bedroom wall. James was waking for his mid-afternoon feed.

'I'm sorry,' she said quietly, maintaining her stance by the door.

He sat for a moment without moving then said, 'For what, Alice? For lying to me? Or for telling me the truth?'

'Both,' she said.

He nodded, seeming to understand what she was saying, then turned away to stare sightlessly into the fire. She stood watching him for a long moment, but he made no move to look up or speak, his lips set hard together, his eyes glittering in the dancing light of the fire. With a sigh she went to fetch James.

Icicles fringed the washing line, the puddles were covered in thick crazed sheets of ice, and the grass, white and crisp with frost crystals, crunched beneath Alice's boots as she made her way back from the privy. Even the spiders' webs strung between the eaves of the house were pearled with ice. For three days now the valley had been swathed in a blanket of icy fog and there looked little prospect of change today. The door creaked open on frozen hinges as she stepped into the welcome warmth of the kitchen. Sam was standing by the table with his jacket and hat on, pulling on his leather gloves in readiness to go out.

'I'm going to see Reverend Sedgwick,' he said, smoothing out the leather over his fingers and rather obviously avoiding eye contact with her.

'I thought you'd already made the arrangements for James's baptism on Sunday,' she said, walking over to the fire. She held out her hands to warm them, watching him out of the corner of her eye.

'I'm going to postpone them,' he said. 'I'll make some excuse to Reverend Sedgwick, and to the Withers also. I'm in no mood for celebrating at present and we're neither of us capable of entertaining guests.'

She couldn't argue with either point, but it hurt nonetheless. Sam was making no effort at all to right matters between them. Quite the reverse in fact. She had tried on at least four different occasions to talk to him, said she was sorry more times than she could remember, but always she received the same response — a cool look and a steadfast insistence that he did not wish to discuss it further, that he needed time to come to terms with matters in his own way. The only good thing to come out of the last few days — if good it could be termed — was that the overwhelming feeling of grief and loss which Michael's letter had brought had lifted from her. Her tears for Michael had given way to dry-eyed worry for her marriage. She had hardly thought about Michael at all, in fact — it was Sam who now dominated her thoughts.

An icy blast swept into the room lifting the corner of the hearth rug, then the door closed with a sharp click and he was gone.

Half an hour later Sam was once again sitting in the comfortable leather armchair in the manse parlour warming his knees in front of a cheery fire.

'So in view of that, I think it best we postpone James's baptism.' He cleared his throat and fiddled with his leather gloves, lying in his lap. He loathed telling untruths, added to which he was very poor at it. And to lie to a man of God, and one who had been such a comfort to Eliza when she was dying. 'It's, er, only a snuffle, but Alice is worried that it might turn to something worse if she takes James out in this bitterly cold weather. In a week or two, when James is fully well again . . .' And when relations between Alice and him would hopefully be on a better footing, he added silently.

'A wise decision,' Reverend Sedgwick agreed pleasantly. 'I wholly concur with you. Your wife is quite right — it would be foolish to take a baby out in this inclement weather while he's suffering from a cold.' He lifted one brow slightly. 'Your wife is well, I trust?'

'She's very well, thank you.' Sam nodded his head and smiled. More damned lies. They were breeding like cockroaches in a warm kitchen.

Leaning back in the armchair, Reverend Sedgwick folded his hands loosely in his lap. 'She is beginning to come to terms with Michael going to sea, then? You mentioned when you were here on Monday that she was missing him badly.'

'She's coping,' Sam said. It was one of life's small ironies that ever since Alice had told him the truth about Michael her tearful bouts had completely dried up. Quite a number of things had dried up.

'She must find it hard, with her mother deceased. It's not an easy task for a woman to cope with rearing a first child, with no mother to call on for advice and counsel,' commented Reverend Sedgwick.

'She manages,' Sam said. But then why should she not? James was *not* Alice's first child — he was her second.

'Does she miss her mother, do you think?'

Sam gave a small shrug. 'She doesn't speak of her much — she's been dead a number of years.'

'Yes, indeed she has. It must be, what, ten years now? I never met her, of course; she died some years before I came to the district. I knew Matthew Thorpe, your wife's late father though — he worshipped at St Stephen's from time to time before his death.' He paused then added quietly, 'He came to see me shortly before his death. He'd been suffering chest pains for some time and Doctor Martin had advised him his heart was the cause of them and could fail at any time. He came to me to, well, to put matters aright between himself and his maker, I suppose one might say. I think he sensed, as people do sometimes, that he had little time left on this earth. Being bound by the vows of priesthood, I am naturally not at liberty to divulge precisely what it was he confided in me.' He paused again then said in the same quiet, even tones, 'You may perhaps be able to postulate on the nature of it though.'

Silence settled on the parlour, and stunned realisation slowly settled on Sam's features.

'You know?' he said in a shocked voice. 'You know about . . .'

Reverend Sedgwick nodded. 'And you know also, it seems. Now.'

He blinked, breaking the glassy stare, and said in the same incredulous tones, 'Alice told me a few days ago.'

'And you are finding it hard to come to terms with.' The words were spoken with quiet understanding.

'I am, Reverend,' he said with feeling. 'I am indeed.'

'Alice had already told you some of what happened to her, I presume?' Reverend Sedgwick probed.

Sam looked away and stared at the aspidistra, casting his mind back to the brief account Alice had given him of her rape. She had told him very little, but his imagination had more than filled in the gaps. 'Yes, she told me she'd been violated,' he said hoarsely. He looked up again and said in a clearer voice, 'She didn't tell me about Michael though. Not a word. All these months she's been deceiving me, Reverend! Deliberately deceiving me! I feel . . . I feel . . .' He drew in a shaky breath and shook his head. 'I'm damned if I know what I feel.'

'She was little more than a child. She was only fifteen,' Reverend Sedgwick said gently.

'She was, but she wasn't a child when she married me. She was a grown woman and quite old enough to know that she ought to have been honest with me from the start.' Sam's eyes narrowed slightly and he said in terse tones, 'You also, Reverend, if you'll pardon my saying so, were less than honest. You recommended Alice Thorpe to me. Knowing what you knew, you recommended her to me.'

Reverend Sedgwick regarded him solemnly. 'I commended Miss Thorpe to you on account of the qualities which I believed she possessed — qualities which I deemed would make her a good wife and mother. If she has turned out to be a poor wife to you, or a poor mother to your children, then I offer you my sincere apologies.'

'Reverend Sedgwick,' Sam said impatiently, 'It's not Alice's qualities as a wife and mother that are the issue here.'

'And what is the issue?'

'She deceived me! Lied to me!' Sam drew in a sharp breath to steady himself. His mind was in a complete turmoil again, his chest as tight as a drum. He had only come to postpone James's baptism. And now this!

Reverend Sedgwick pushed himself stiffly to his feet, slipped his spectacles onto his nose, and walked across to the mantel. A small Bible was lying on it. He picked it up, fingered the worn leather cover for a moment as if thinking, then opened it. 'I will not say that I applaud the Thorpe family's decision to lie about Michael's parentage,' he said, flicking over pages. 'But there are some lies which are perhaps more pardonable than others. And what right has any of us to sit in judgement on another? *He that is without sin among you, let him first cast a stone.* It's a verse worth remembering, I believe, when we feel tempted to censure others for their sins or weaknesses. I do not say that it was right of your wife to lie to you all this while — indeed, I am surprised that she did — but I can understand why she was loath to tell you. If a ship is sailing in calm pleasant waters, few would choose to steer it into rough seas and risk calamity.' He looked up, pushing his glasses further up his nose. 'Your wife is a very courageous woman. She sacrificed a great deal in laying aside her rights as a mother in order to allow her son to be raised by his grandparents, that he might not carry a slur on his name. Will you censure her for that? A good parent will instinctively try to protect its young. Your wife's parents, rightly or wrongly, sought to protect their daughter from unkind talk. Your wife likewise was trying to protect her son. If some ill threatened your children, would you not do all in your power to protect them?' His eyes remained on Sam's face for a moment then he lowered them and began to read. 'Who can find a virtuous woman? For her price is far above rubies. The heart of her husband doth safely trust in her, so that he shall have no need of spoil. She will do him good and not evil all the days of her life. Proverbs.' Slipping off his spectacles he placed them and the Bible back on the mantelpiece. 'You have been married to Alice Thorpe for some time now and she has brought much good into your life.' Clasping his hands behind his back he turned slowly to face Sam again. 'Might I suggest that you set the ill days in the balance against the good and weigh her worth accordingly. It is a practice worth employing, I believe, when things go awry in a marriage.'

Sam took the long route home from the manse,

mulling over weights and measures. Seeking solitude, he left the road to walk along the banks of the Inangahua, slithering on slippery frost-coated mud and scratching his good boots on the rocks. His feet were soaked, his toes were numb, and his hands were frozen. He'd left his leather gloves at the manse — he hadn't even missed them till his fingertips had begun to throb with cold. In the distance he could hear the dull, incessant thud of the quartz batteries — the heartbeat of the golden hills. He trudged on until he reached the bend in the river from where he could see the tin chimney of his home rising above the bush. Smoke was curling from it, lifting for a few feet into the chill air then turning abruptly sideways and floating away in a thin white ribbon across the river. He halted on a grassy rise, watching it. Alice would be inside the house, preparing the midday meal, or maybe feeding James. She was forever having to feed the child at all hours of the day and night, though she never complained. 'She never does complain,' he murmured. All those interminable weeks they'd lived in the tent at Black's Point she'd never once complained.

He lowered his eyes, watching the grey waters of the Inangahua swirling past. Stepping off the bank into the shallows he stooped to pick up a chunk of quartz about the size of his fist, and a small oval pebble. He straightened, holding them in the palms of his hands, icy water dripping between his fingers. *Set the ill days in the balance against the good* . . . He studied the pebble. Then the chunk of quartz. His marriage to Alice had without doubt seen some very ill days, but he couldn't deny that the good days far outnumbered the ill. He lifted his hands up and down experimentally, weighing the two stones. Disturbed by the motion the quartz fell over in his palm to show a fine seam of gold running through one side of it. Frowning, Sam ran his finger along it, tracing the thin, dark ochre line standing slightly proud of the white rock.

With a sigh he looked back towards the cottage. He stood for a minute or two watching the smoke twist and drift from his chimney then tossed the pebble back into the river and set off homewards.

Chapter 34

'Papa! Papa!' Charlotte slid down from the sofa, dropping her picture book onto the floor as the back door swung open and her father stepped inside. The corners of Sam's mouth tilted upwards fractionally as she wound her arms around his knees. 'Come on then,' he murmured, and lifted her into his arms.

Alice glanced over to him as she leaned over the fire to stir the pot of broth, trying to assess his mood. It was unlikely that his visit to the manse would have improved his temper. He'd been gone for a long while too and looked half-frozen.

The floorboards creaked as he walked past the table to the crib. 'James looks very replete,' he commented from behind her. 'Have you just fed him?'

She turned, surprised that his voice sounded almost normal. It was the first time it had in four days. 'I fed him about half an hour ago,' she returned. Silence settled again.

'Is the —' She stopped short as Sam's deeper voice rode over the top of hers.

'You were saying?' he said, setting Charlotte down again.

She gave a small shrug. 'Oh, it was nothing important. I was only going to ask if the frost is melting yet.' The weather, Charlotte and James — that was all they'd managed to talk about during the last few days. When conversation around those topics ran dry they lapsed into long silences.

He shook his head. 'No. It's still white and crisp.'

'Oh,' she said. 'What were you going to say?'

He dipped his head towards the pot of broth. 'The broth — it smells good.'

She pushed a stray strand of coppery hair behind her ear, regarding him through the thin cloud of steam. 'It's just a vegetable broth.'

'It smells good,' he said again.

Their eyes held for a moment, awkwardly. Everything was awkward between them at present.

'Alice,' he said hesitantly. He pushed his hands into his pockets and walked towards her. He hadn't touched her at all since she'd told him about Michael and he plainly didn't intend to now, hence his bulging pockets. 'I think we must start again,' he said quietly. 'Put the past behind us.'

'Do you think you can?' she asked bluntly. She had grave doubts that Sam could put the past behind him. It was more than just her dishonesty that he was struggling with. 'Do you think I've not seen the way you look at me sometimes? I can see it in your eyes, Sam,' she said. She looked into the black pupils steadily. 'The revulsion you feel, knowing that I gave birth to his child.'

He had the grace to colour guiltily. 'I can't help myself, Alice,' he said softly. 'Each time I think of it, and I think of it often — God knows, far more than I wish to — I feel sick inside.'

'So did I,' she said. 'When I found I was carrying Michael.'

He nodded, looking for the first time as if he understood something of what she had gone through. 'Alice

. . .' He paused, sighed, then pulled his hands from his pockets and took hold of her hands. 'I know I've shown you little compassion or understanding. I've been too full of my own hurt, my own sense of being wronged, to give any thought to what you've suffered. I'll not deny I still think you should have told me the truth long before you did, but I can maybe understand why you didn't.' He lowered his eyes, rubbing his thumb across the narrow gold band on her wedding finger, then looked up again and drew her into his arms.

Slipping her arms around his back, she pressed her cheek against his and closed her eyes. 'Do you never wish there were just the two of us?' Sam had once asked her. She did now. Oh, she did now. She wished with all her heart that there wasn't a small hand tugging persistently at Sam's trousers and a small voice saying 'Papa' over and over again.

She was evidently not alone in her feelings. 'Charlotte!' Sam said sharply. 'Go away and amuse yourself.' Alice watched out of the corner of her eye as Charlotte obediently let go of her father's trousers, picked up her picture book and clambered up onto the couch. But it was too late, the moment had passed, the fragile link of tenderness was too delicate by far to stand even the smallest intrusion. With a sigh Sam pulled away, their eyes held for a moment, then he let go of her. 'I'd better go back to my workshop,' he said. The corner of his mouth twitched slightly in what looked as if it might possibly have been an attempt at a smile then he turned and went out to the shed, back to his boot repairing.

Partway through the afternoon, with Charlotte and James both asleep, she decided to take a mug of hot tea out to him. It wasn't particularly warm inside the house, even with the fire lit, and in the shed where

Sam worked there was no heat at all. He had taken to wearing a thick woollen scarf and two pairs of socks, but he still looked frozen to the bone whenever he came into the house. The steam swirled from the mug into her face as she walked across the grass, silent and slippery now that the frost had started to thaw in the heat of a weak afternoon sun. The door to the shed was ajar slightly to let in more light and she could see Sam sitting at his bench, bent over his last, tapping away with his hammer. Hearing the door creak open, he looked round.

'I've brought you some hot tea,' she said.

'Thank you,' he said, reaching for it. He clasped the mug in his hands and bowed his head over it, letting the warmth of the steam cloud across his face. His fingernails were a greyish blue, his lips a similar bloodless colour.

'You look cold,' she said, pulling her woollen shawl around her shoulders. It felt warmer outside than inside the shed.

He nodded. 'I am. My feet are the worst. I have to keep standing up and stamping them.'

She hovered in the doorway, trying to think of something else to say. She was determined not to leave just yet. She ran her eye over the shelf of waiting boots and shoes. 'You have a lot of boots waiting to be mended,' she commented.

'Mm, I have,' he agreed. 'I've six orders for new boots too.'

Her gaze drifted to his workbench and the new boot that he was currently working on. A chunk of white quartz was lying to the side of it. 'What's this?' she asked, reaching across for it. She turned it over in her hand to examine it then looked up quizzically.

'There's gold in it,' Sam said.

She turned it over again. There was gold in it, but only a wafer-thin seam. It certainly wouldn't make Sam a rich man. 'It's quite pretty,' she said — it sounded faintly patronising but it was the only comment she could think of — and replaced it on the workbench.

'You're wondering why I brought it home.'

She looked up to find to her surprise he was smiling. It was quite an odd, slightly crooked smile, but since it was the first smile she had seen for days she wasn't inclined to be critical about its symmetry. We must start again, put the past behind us, Sam had said. Well, he was obviously trying to. She smiled back and said, 'Yes, I am.'

The stool creaked as he shifted round to face her, still clasping the mug between his hands for warmth. 'It's to remind me of something that Reverend Sedgwick said to me this morning, lest I should be tempted to forget it in the future.'

She looked at him curiously.

'He reminded me that I should count my blessings.' Putting down the mug he picked up the rock and ran his finger along the thin gold seam. 'You're a good wife, Alice,' he said quietly. 'Who can find a virtuous woman? For her price is far above gold . . .'

She stared at him in surprise for a moment, then her eyes flicked back to the lump of white quartz in his hand. If he was equating her worth to the minute amount of gold in that rock . . . She glanced up again, scanning his features, wondering if he was mocking her, but there was no sign of mockery in his face. He was smiling, and rather less crookedly this time.

She smiled back, a little uncertainly. 'It's rubies, not gold,' she corrected, feeling at a bit of a loss how to respond. 'Her price is far above rubies. It's from the book of Proverbs.'

'I know where it's from, Alice,' he said, having had it quoted to him only that morning. Setting down the quartz on his bench, he rose to his feet and walked over to her. 'There aren't any rubies in these parts though. But there is gold.' Taking her face lightly between his hands he kissed her softly on the lips. And almost to himself he added, 'If you know where to find it.'